MARITIME AFFAIRS–
A WORLD HANDBOOK

MARITIME AFFAIRS–
A WORLD HANDBOOK

A Reference Guide to Maritime Organizations, Conventions and Disputes and to the International Politics of the Sea

Compiled and written by Henry W. Degenhardt
Editorial consultant: Brian Meredith MBE
General editor: Alan J. Day

A KEESING'S REFERENCE PUBLICATION

Longman

MARITIME AFFAIRS—A WORLD HANDBOOK

Published by Longman Group Limited, Longman House,
Burnt Mill, Harlow, Essex CM20 2JE, United Kingdom

Distributed exclusively in the United States and Canada
by Gale Research Company, Book Tower, Detroit,
Michigan 48226, USA

ISBN 0-582-90263-0 (Longman)
0-8103-2051-7 (Gale)

Library of Congress Catalog Card Number: 85-27508

British Library Cataloguing in Publication Data
Degenhardt, Henry W.
Maritime affairs: a world handbook: a
reference guide to maritime organizations,
conventions and disputes and to the international
politics of the sea.
1. Maritime law
I. Title II. Day, Alan J.
341.4'5 JX4411

ISBN 0-582-90263-0

Library of Congress Cataloging-in-Publication Data
Degenhardt, Henry W.
Maritime affairs—a world handbook.
(A Keesing's reference publication)
Bibliography: p. 385.
Includes index.
1. Maritime law. I. Day, Alan J. (Alan John)
II. Title. III. Series.
JX4408.D44 1985 341.4'5 85-27508

ISBN 0-8103-2051-7

Printed in Great Britain by
The Eastern Press Ltd., London and Reading

Contents

Abbreviations used for officers of organizations:

admin.	= administrative	g.s.	= general secretary
ch.	= chairman	gen. man.	= general manager
dep.	= deputy	man. dir.	= managing director
dir.	= director	pres.	= president
dir.-gen.	= director-general	s.g.	= secretary-general
exec.	= executive	sec.	= secretary

Introduction

The world's oceans and seas cover about 71 per cent of the earth's surface, yet it has been only in the last few decades that man has begun to make a major effort to explore and understand the role of the sea in the life of mankind. This book is intended to serve as a guide to the present state of international maritime law, sea transport and communications, the exploitation and conservation of the marine natural resources, scientific research into the various aspects of the marine environment, maritime boundary disputes and military tension areas at sea. The book provides an overview of the activities of international organizations concerned with maritime affairs, and also a comprehensive bibliography which will enable the user to study any particular subject in greater depth than is possible in a one-volume handbook such as this one.

The essential purpose of the book is to provide textual data on the various aspects of present-day maritime affairs. Understanding of some sections will, however, be assisted by the use of a good atlas—by far the best for this purpose being *The Times Atlas of the Oceans* edited by Alastair Couper (Times Books, London 1983).

In addition to the sources indicated in the book, extensive use has been made of the editorial resources of *Keesing's Contemporary Archives*. Every effort has been made to achieve *Keesing's*-style objectivity and balance in the book's coverage. Special thanks for advice and background information are due to Brian Meredith of Canada, whose years of distinguished service to the United Nations and particular interest in the themes of this book combined to make him an invaluable source of ideas for the editor and compiler of the present volume.

September 1985 HWD/AJD

The Keesing's Reference Publications (KRP) series has been developed as an adjunct to *Keesing's Contemporary Archives* (KCA), the international news reference service which over the last half-century has built up an unrivalled reputation for the accuracy and objectivity of its coverage of world events. Other titles available in the KRP series are as follows:

Treaties and Alliances of the World (3rd edition, 1981)

Border and Territorial Disputes (1982)

Political Dissent: An International Guide to Dissident, Extra-Parliamentary, Guerrilla and Illegal Political Movements (1983)

Political Parties of the World (2nd edition, 1984)

State Economic Agencies of the World (1985)

1. The Law of the Sea

This chapter, after tracing the main historical landmarks in the evolution of maritime law, focuses on the activities of the United Nations Conference on the Law of the Sea (UNCLOS), culminating in the adoption in 1982 of a comprehensive UN Convention on the Law of the Sea. Developments subsequent to the adoption of the 1982 Convention and the major continuing obstacles to its full implementation are also described. The chapter concludes with a tabulation of the territorial waters limits and contiguous zones claimed by the world's coastal states as at March 1, 1985.

Historical Development of Maritime Law

Early Claims to Maritime Jurisdiction

An early division of the oceans was agreed upon between Spain and Portugal in 1493. According to a Papal Bull of May 4, 1493, the Portuguese were to be in control of an area between a meridian corresponding approximately to 37°W of Greenwich and a meridian about 143°15′E of Greenwich, but under the Treaty of Tordesillas, signed on June 7, 1494, the Portuguese area was defined as lying between approximately 46°10′W of Greenwich and 134°E of Greenwich. The area outside this zone was to be under Spanish control. (Although this demarcation placed the Philippines in the Portuguese zone, they came, in 1571, under the control of Spain, which had reached them from the east.)

However, this treaty was abrogated by the Treaty of Madrid of Jan. 13, 1750, which in effect established the boundaries of Brazil and Spain's renunciation of all claims to Brazil (as contained in the Treaty of Tordesillas).

Thereafter coastal states made only modest claims to adjacent coastal waters. From the 14th century onwards Venice claimed control of the adjacent sea for the purpose of containing infectious diseases. Only later did it lay claim to the whole Adriatic Sea.

Development of Customary Maritime Law

For several hundred years the customary international law of the sea was dominated by the concept of the freedom of the seas (outside territorial waters), as enunciated by Hugo Grotius, the Dutch jurist (1583-1645). This concept accorded with the needs of the seafaring nations of Western Europe. Under that customary law it was, however, also clearly established that a state was responsible for the effects of its activities on other states, including their environment.

At the end of the 18th century the United States adopted a three-mile limit for its territorial sea, and the United Kingdom did so early in the

19th century. During that century there was a general tendency towards a uniform territorial seas limit of three miles, though different limits were claimed for specific purposes.

The Trinity House Rules (i.e. the rules of the Corporation of Trinity House, the General Lighthouse Authority for England, Wales, the Channel Islands and Gibraltar and also the principal Pilotage Authority in the United Kingdom) published in 1840 were a codification of customary rules of the road applicable also to foreign ships and observed as a matter of common consent though not under any international legal obligation.

Rules contained in a British Order in Council of 1910 were applied by ships of most countries, and they formed the basis of the London Command of 1912. This was followed by the Safety of Life at Sea Conventions of 1928 and 1948 and later by the Conventions of the Inter-Governmental Maritime Consultative Organization (now the International Maritime Organization—see Chapter 2 below).

The 1923 Geneva Convention and Statute on the International Regime of Maritime Ports gives the states parties to this Convention the right of entry to each other's ports (over and above the customary right of foreign vessels to enter ports when in distress). The right provided for in this Convention may also be obtained by bilaterial treaties of commerce and navigation or on the basis of common interest of the parties concerned.

In 1925 all the coastal states of the Baltic Sea concluded the Baltic Liquor Treaty, under which contraband traffic in alcoholic liquor was banned and each party agreed to raise no objection to the enforcement within 12 miles from its coasts (or its outer islands) of its laws against ships "manifestly" engaged in contraband.

In 1930 the League of Nations convened a conference at The Hague on the progressive codification of international law, but the 42 nations represented reached no agreement on a standard limit of the territorial sea and contiguous zone. The conference did not accept the concept (accepted by some nations) of the contiguous zone being a buffer zone of unspecified dimensions between the territorial waters and the high seas, to be used to claim jurisdiction over maritime resources in that zone. (The territorial waters and contiguous zone limit then ranged from three to 12 miles, the latter being claimed by Portugal and the Soviet Union.)

In the years between 1932 and 1942 six-mile territorial sea limits were declared by Uruguay, Colombia, Iran, Cuba, Greece and Italy. A nine-mile limit was declared by Mexico in 1944, and 12-mile limits were proclaimed by Guatemala in 1940 and by Venezuela in 1941.

The Declaration of Panama, adopted on Oct. 3, 1939 (i.e. after the outbreak of World War II), by the Foreign Ministers of the then existing American republics, provided for the establishment of a protective belt encircling the American continent, up to between 300 and 1,500 miles from the coast "to cover the waters adjacent to the American countries which are of fundamental importance and utility ... in respect of any hostile act, whether it be directed from the land, sea or air" (Article 1). However, as neither Germany nor the United Kingdom recognized the legitimacy of such a security zone, its establishment was abandoned in 1940.

Under the Declaration of Antigua (Guatemala) signed in August 1955 (at the first formal meeting of the Organization of Central American States, ODECA) by Costa Rica, El Salvador, Guatemala, Honduras and Nicaragua, it was agreed inter alia that the signatories would defend the "patrimony of Central American States", including the continental shelf and epicontinental sea.

Territorial sea limits were extended to six miles by Yugoslavia in 1948, to 12 miles by Ecuador in 1950, and to 200 miles by El Salvador, also in 1950.

In the Santiago Declaration of 1952 each of the governments of Chile, Ecuador and Peru declared inter alia "sole sovereignty and jurisdiction over the area of sea adjacent to the coast of its own country and extending not less than 200 nautical miles from the said coast". The declaration included the claim to "sole sovereignty over the sea floor and subsoil" but also provided for "the necessary restrictions on the exercise of sovereignty and jurisdiction imposed by international law to permit the innocent and inoffensive passage of vessels of all nations through the zone" (which was described as "the maritime zone"). Under an agreement signed in Lima (Peru) in December 1954 the three countries provided for the common defence of their zones.

Ecuador declared in a decree of Nov. 10, 1966, that the territorial sea under national jurisdiction should comprise the adjacent sea to a maximum distance of 200 nautical miles.

Panama declared, in an Act of Feb. 2, 1967, its sovereignty over "a zone of territorial sea 200 nautical miles in breadth, the bed and subsoil of the said zone and the superjacent airspace".

Brazil extended the limits of its territorial sea from 12 to 200 nautical miles under a decree-law of March 25, 1970, but reaffirmed the right to innocent passage through the zone for ships of all nations.

Under an agreement signed on Dec. 16, 1977, and in force from Jan. 1, 1978, Cuba and the United States agreed on the median line in the Florida Strait as their common maritime boundary.

UN Conferences and Conventions on Law of the Sea

First UN Conference on Law of the Sea

The first UN Conference on the Law of the Sea (UNCLOS) was held in Geneva from Feb. 24 to April 28, 1958, and adopted, after preparation by the International Law Commission, four Conventions and a protocol on compulsory settlement of disputes, but reached no agreement on the maximum width of territorial waters and the maximum limits of exclusive fishing rights.

(1) The *Convention on the Territorial Sea and the Contiguous Zone* defined the "territorial sea" and the "contiguous zone" of the high seas.

Specifically, Articles 1 and 2 of this Convention laid down that the coastal state's sovereignty extended over its territorial sea and to the airspace and sea-bed and subsoil thereof, subject to the provisions of the Convention and of international law. The coastal state might exclude foreign nationals and vessels from fishing and also from coastal trading (cabotage) in its territorial waters.

The Convention emphasized the right of innocent passage for merchant ships (but not warships) through the territorial sea and the coastal state's duty to publicize any dangers to navigation in these waters. A coastal state might, for security reasons, temporarily suspend innocent passage provided the suspension was published and did not cover international straits.

For the latter the Convention provided in Article 16 (4) that "there shall be no suspension of the innocent passage of foreign ships through straits which are used for international navigation". (The question of innocent passage of warships was not dealt with in the Convention.)

Article 3 of the Convention laid down that the width of the territorial sea was to be delimited from the low-water mark around the coasts of the state ("as marked on large-scale charts officially recognized by the coastal state"). Article 4 laid down that in cases of indented coastlines, or a fringe of islands and rocks (*skjaergaard*) running parallel to the coast, the system which could be used was that of a straight baseline linking the outermost parts of land (a system later regarded as a valid principle of international law by the International Court of Justice in an Anglo-Norwegian fisheries case dealt with in 1969).

Article 5(2) of the Convention stated that a right of innocent passage should be deemed to exist in areas enclosed as internal waters as a result of the straight baseline method but previously regarded as part of the territorial or high seas. Article 7 of the Convention declared that "if the distance between the low-water marks of the natural entrance points of a bay does not exceed 24 nautical miles a closing line may be drawn between these two low-water marks, and the waters enclosed thereby shall be considered as internal waters". This provision, however, does not apply to "historic bays", i.e. bays the waters of which are treated by the coastal state as internal (e.g. Canada has thus claimed the Hudson Bay, against opposition by the United States, and the case of Fonseca Bay, disputed by El Salvador and Nicaragua, was decided on that principle by the Central American Court of Justice in 1917—see Chapter 6).[1]

[1] The US Supreme Court took the view (in 1975) that a "historic bay" can be recognized only where there is continuous exercise of authority and acquiescence of foreign states (in the case of Cook Inlet, United States *versus* State of Alaska, where the court ruled that the United States was entitled to the sub-surface lands of Cook Inlet).

Examples of historic bays, where the coastal states have rights approximating to those held in internal waters, are given by Gilbert Gidel in his *Traité de droit international de la mer* of 1934 as being the Rio de la Plata, Chesapeake and Delaware Bays, the Bay of Fundy between Canada and the United States, Cancale or Granville Bay in Normandy, France, the Gulf of Tunis, the Bristol Channel and several Norwegian fjords.

Article 24 of the Convention declared that "in a zone of the high seas contiguous to its territorial sea, the coastal state may exercise the control necessary to (*a*) prevent infringement of its customs, fiscal, immigration or sanitary regulations within its territory or territorial sea, and (*b*) punish infringement of the above regulations within its territory or territorial sea".

Fishing vessels were obliged to observe the laws of the coastal state and submarines to navigate on the surface and show their flag; the coastal state's civil and criminal laws were (to a limited extent) to be applied to merchant vessels but not to non-commercial government ships.

(2) The *Convention on the High Seas* proclaimed the freedom of the high seas (including the freedom to fly over them, to fish and to lay submarine cables and pipelines, as well as other freedoms "recognized by the general principles of international law").

The Convention also proclaimed the right of land-locked states to have free access to the sea; granted each state the right to determine conditions for the grant of its nationality to ships; gave immunity from the jurisdiction of any state other than the flag state to warships and other non-commercial government vessels on the high seas; and enjoined states to ensure safety at sea, to prevent slave trade and piracy and to prevent pollution of the sea.

The Convention also reaffirmed (in Article 23) the customary doctrine of hot pursuit, i.e. the right of a state to pursue, for violations of regulations related to its internal waters, territorial sea or contiguous zone, a foreign vessel on the high seas provided the pursuit is commenced while that vessel is still within those waters; the pursuit can continue on the high seas only if it is not interrupted.

(3) The *Convention on Fishing and Conservation of the Living Resources of the High Seas* provided inter alia for agreement on conservation measures and for arbitration procedure in the event of disputes [see pages 109–10].

(4) The *Convention on the Continental Shelf* gave coastal states exclusive

rights to exploit universal and other non-living resources as well as "sedentary" living organisms (e.g. oysters) of the continental shelf, i.e. "the sea-bed and subsoil of the submarine areas adjacent to the coast, but outside the area of the territorial sea, up to the point where the waters above are 200 metres deep, or beyond that limit if the depth allows exploitation of natural resources". The boundary of the coastal shelf adjacent to any state lying opposite another state on the same shelf was to be determined by mutual agreement or, failing such agreement, would be the median line.

(5) The *Protocol on Settlement of Disputes* provided for compulsory jurisdiction of the International Court of Justice in disputes arising out of the interpretation or application of any Convention on the Law of the Sea (except as covered by the arbitration procedure under (3) above), as well as for arbitration or conciliation where both parties agreed to this procedure instead of resorting to the International Court of Justice.

Second and Third UN Conferences

A second UN Conference on the Law of the Sea, held in Geneva between March 17 and April 26, 1960, and dealing with the width of the territorial sea and the breadth of a "contiguous zone" in which coastal states would exercise exclusive fishing rights, failed to reach agreement on these subjects.

Sessions of a third UN Conference on the Law of the Sea were held in New York on Dec. 3-15, 1973, in Caracas from June 20 to Aug. 29, 1974, and in Geneva from March 17 to May 9, 1975, when provisional agreement was reached (i) on the establishment of an international sea-bed authority which would oversee the exploitation of ocean floor resources beyond national jurisdiction (i.e. in an area described as "the common heritage of mankind" in a "declaration on principles concerning the sea-bed, the ocean floor and the subsoil thereof" adopted by the UN General Assembly in 1970) and (ii) on a territorial limit of 12 nautical miles and a 200-mile economic zone in which coastal states would control both fisheries and mineral resources.

Further sessions of the third conference were held in New York from March 15 to May 7, 1976; from Aug. 2 to Sept. 17, 1976; and from May 23 to July 15, 1977 (whereafter an "informal composite negotiating text" was published, containing provisions for an international regime for the conduct of deep sea-bed mining—which were immediately rejected as "fundamentally unacceptable" by the United States); in Geneva from March 28 to May 19, 1978; in New York from Aug. 21 to Sept. 15, 1978; in Geneva from March 19 to April 27, 1979; in New York from July 19 to Aug. 24, 1979; in New York from March 3 to April 4, 1980; in Geneva from July 28 to Aug. 29, 1980; in New York from March 9 to April 24, 1981; in Geneva from Aug. 3 to Aug. 28, 1981; and again in New York from March 8 to April 30, 1982.

1982 UN Convention on Law of the Sea

A comprehensive UN Convention on the Law of the Sea was eventually approved in New York on April 30, 1982, when 130 delegations at the third UNCLOS voted in favour of the draft Convention and four against it (Israel,

Turkey, the United States and Venezuela); there were 17 abstentions (Belgium, Bulgaria, Byelorussia, Czechoslovakia, the German Democratic Republic, the Federal Republic of Germany, Hungary, Italy, Luxembourg, Mongolia, the Netherlands, Poland, the Soviet Union, Spain, Thailand, the Ukraine and the United Kingdom), 14 other delegations were absent (Antigua and Barbuda, Belize, the Comoros, Dominica, Equatorial Guinea, The Gambia, Kiribati, Liberia, Maldives, Nauru, the Solomon Islands, Tonga, Tuvalu and Vanuatu) and three took no part in the vote (Albania, Ecuador and the Holy See).

The conference also adopted four resolutions: (i) to establish a Preparatory Commission to set up the Sea-Bed Authority and the Law of the Sea Tribunal provided for in the Convention; (ii) to govern preparatory investments in pioneer activities by states and private consortia relating to polymetallic nodules in the deep seabed; (iii) to deal with rights and interests of territories which had not yet attained independence or self-government; and (iv) to grant national liberation movements the right to sign the Final Act of the conference.

In the second of these resolutions four countries (France, India, Japan and the Soviet Union) as well as four multinational consortia—the (US) Kennecott Group (with six mining companies), Ocean Mining Associates (with four companies), Ocean Management Inc. (with four companies) and Ocean Minerals Company (with five companies)—were recognized as "pioneer investors"), each of whom was expected to sign the Convention stating that prior to Jan. 1, 1983, the investor had expended no less than $30,000,000 in pioneer activities of deep-sea mineral extraction and no less than 10 per cent of that amount in the location, survey and evaluation of a specific mining site. It was specified that such a site should be large enough to be later divided into two pioneer areas of equal estimated commercial value; the size of one pioneer area should not exceed 150,000 square kilometres.

At the further session held in New York on Sept. 22-24, 1982, the UN conference approved certain changes made in the Convention by its drafting committee and adopted the Final Act recapitulating the history of the third conference.

At the end of the concluding session of the UNCLOS held in Montego Bay (Jamaica) on Dec. 6-10, 1982, the Convention was signed by representatives of 117 sovereign states as well as the UN Council for Namibia and the Cook Islands (a dependent territory of New Zealand). The Convention was to come into force 12 months after instruments of ratification had been deposited by 60 countries, and it was to become binding for each state which had ratified it.

Also on Dec. 10, 1982, the Final Act of the UNCLOS was signed by 150 delegations (including that of the UN Council for Namibia and nine observer delegations). Of these delegations several industrialized market-economy countries (among them Belgium, the Federal Republic of Germany, Italy, Spain, the United Kingdom and the United States) had not signed the Convention itself (whereas Japan signed it on Feb. 7, 1983).

The delegate of Venezuela had earlier explained that, although he would sign the Final Act, he would not sign the Convention because it might affect his country's disputes with Colombia over the Gulf of Venezuela (where large oil deposits were reported to exist) and with Trinidad and Tobago (see Chapter 6 for these disputes).

Principal Provisions of Convention

The Convention (the full text which is given in Appendix 1) laid down four maritime boundaries as follows:

(1) a boundary of 12 nautical miles (nm) from baselines of a coastal state for that country's territorial sea;

(2) a boundary of up to 24 nm from baselines for a contiguous zone;

(3) a boundary of 200 nm from baselines for an exclusive economic zone (EEZ); and

(4) a continental shelf boundary at 200 nm from the shore baseline, but at up to 350 nm in cases where the true shelf extended further (to be claimed in accordance with a specific formula based on the thickness of the sedimentary rock on the shelf floor) or a further boundary 100 nm outward from a 2,500-metre isobath.

Beyond the continental shelf there would be the "Area", declared to be the "common heritage of mankind", the resources of which would be exploited by the proposed International Sea-Bed Authority headed by a 36-member Council.

In the territorial sea foreign vessels would be allowed "innocent passage" for purposes of peaceful navigation.

In the contiguous zone the coastal state would be able to exercise control of customs, fiscal, immigration and sanitary laws and regulations.

Through straits used for international navigation ships and aircraft would be allowed "transit passage" as long as they proceeded without delay and without threatening the bordering states; states alongside the straits would, however, be able to regulate navigation and other aspects of passage.

Archipelagic states would have sovereignty over a sea enclosed by straight lines drawn between the outermost points of their islands, with ships of all other states having the right of passage through sea lanes designated by the archipelagic state.

In the exclusive economic zone coastal states would have sovereign rights over natural resources and certain economic activities, and jurisdiction over certain types of scientific research and environmental protection. All other states would have freedom of navigation and overflight, as well as freedom to lay submarine cables and pipelines. Landlocked states and "states with special geographical characteristics" would have the right to participate in the exploitation of part of the zone's fisheries when the coastal state could not itself harvest them all. Delimitation of overlapping economic zones was to be effected by agreement. Special protection was to be accorded to highly migratory species of fish and marine mammals.

For the exploration and exploitation of the "Area" (the international sea-bed) a "parallel system" was to be established, with all activities being under the control of the International Sea-Bed Authority which would (i) conduct its own mining operations through its "enterprise" and (ii) contract with private and state ventures by granting them mining rights in the Area. Once mining was authorized, a first generation of sea-bed prospectors, the "pioneer operators", would have guarantees of production. The Convention contained an anti-monopoly clause aimed at ensuring that no single nation obtained too large a share of the sea-bed or a whole or any sizeable area of it.

For the purpose of environmental protection the Convention laid down that states would have to use "the best practical means at their disposal" to prevent and control marine pollution from any source. The Convention determined which category of states (coastal states, port states or flag states) would be responsible for preventing pollution and punishing polluters, and what kind of enforcement actions were allowable. States would be liable for damage caused by violations of their international obligation to combat marine pollution and would be bound to co-operate globally and regionally in formulating rules and standards of environmental protection and to promote technical assistance to developing countries in the area.

All marine scientific research in the exclusive economic zone and on the continental shelf would be subject to the consent of the coastal state, but the latter would be obliged to grant consent to foreign states if the research was to be conducted for peaceful purposes and met certain other criteria laid down in the Convention; a coastal state could deny consent and insist on the cessation of such research only under circumstances defined in the Convention. In the event of a dispute the researching state could require the coastal state to submit to international conciliation.

States would be bound to promote the development and transfer of marine technology "on fair and reasonable conditions", with proper regard to all legitimate interests, including the rights of holders, suppliers and recipients of technology.

States would be obliged to settle by peaceful means their disputes over the interpretation or application of the Convention. When they could not agree on the means of settlement they would have to submit most types of dispute to a compulsory procedure entailing decisions binding on all parties. The dispute could be submitted to (i) an International Tribunal for the Law of the Sea, to be set up under the Convention; (ii) the existing International Court of Justice; (iii) arbitration or (iv) special arbitration procedures. Certain types of dispute would have to be submitted to conciliation, the outcome of which would not be binding on the parties.

International Impact of the Convention

The UNCLOS Convention gave the great naval powers—in particular the United States and the Soviet Union—freedom of navigation (e.g. in straits less than 22 nautical miles wide), enabled them to combat pollution of the sea, and gave each coastal state a vast exclusive fishing area.

France, in particular, benefited greatly from the Convention by obtaining excusive economic zones not only around metropolitan France but also around its Overseas Departments and Territories where it gained sovereignty over the resources of some 11,000,000 square kilometres, which made France the third maritime nation after the United Kingdom and the United States.

The Intergovernmental Oceanographic Commission (IOC) had estimated in a report published on Jan. 1, 1980, that the UNCLOS extension of fishery limits to a maximum of 200 nautical miles by all coastal states would mean that over 35 per cent of the world's oceans would be enclosed within national zones of control which would cover over 90 per cent of the living marine resources currently under exploitation. Moreover, the coastal states would face increased responsibilities for conservation and management measures; for promotion of the optimum utilization of their resources; for determining their own capacity to harvest the available catch and giving other states access to any surplus; and for the conservation and development of any stock shared by two or more coastal states (or any other states) fishing beyond their own zones.

In a report by the UN Secretary-General submitted in compliance with UN General Assembly Resolution 38/59 of Dec. 14, 1983, it was stated that, although not yet in force, the Convention was already having "a stabilizing effect" on the law of the sea through the rationalization of different uses of the oceans and the reconciliation of competing interests of states, and that it was also having an impact on the attitudes of states towards marine affairs at national and international levels. In particular, the report referred to a growing number of states which were bringing their maritime boundaries in line with those set by the Convention; it further stated that the International Court of Justice had, in the settlement of maritime disputes, begun to rely (directly or indirectly) on the Convention.

Three Western Nations' Opposition to the Convention

Opposition to the Convention by the United States and the United Kingdom centred on the provisions relating to the International Sea-Bed Authority.

US Position. President Reagan declared on Jan. 29, 1982, that the United States would seek a treaty which (i) would not deter development of any deep sea-bed mineral resources to meet national and world demand; (ii) would assure national access to these resources by current and future "qualified entities" to enhance American security of supply, to avoid monopolization of the resources by the operating arm of the proposed International Sea-Bed Authority, and to promote the economic development of the resources; (iii) would provide a decision-making role in the deep sea-bed regime which fairly reflected and effectively protected the political and economic interest and financial contributions of participating states; (iv) would not allow for amendments to come into force without approval of the participating states—involving, in the case of the United States, the consent of the Senate; (v) would not set undesirable precedents for other international organizations; and (vi) would be likely to receive the consent of the Senate. President Reagan also expressed the United States' desire to exclude national liberation movements from participation in the treaty.

On March 8, 1982, the US delegation presented the UN conference with a document demanding more than 230 changes to the existing draft Convention. All of these amendments were, however, defeated or withdrawn.

The decisive principle embodied in the US amendments was that the International Sea-Bed Authority awarding contracts for ocean mining should "at all times be guided by the objective of facilitating the development of the resources of the area". Under the US proposals, any change in the treaty would require the approval of all 36 members of the Council of the International Sea-Bed Authority, thus enabling the United States (which was almost certain to become one of the four industrial nations on the Council representing the largest investors in sea-bed mining) to block any proposed changes. This proposal contrasted with the existing draft's specification that the treaty could be revised after 20 years with the agreement of two-thirds of the contracting parties—a provision which the United States feared could allow the developing nations to exclude private mining concerns entirely and thus provide a global cartel with a monopoly.

The US amendment also sought to give the four industrial countries a decisive voice in Council decisions, whereas under the existing draft some decisions could be taken by majorities of two-thirds or three-quarters of the members. In addition, the United States wished to provide four of the seven largest financial contributors (Canada, France, the Federal Republic of Germany, Japan, the United Kingdom, the USA and the USSR) with the power to compel the International Sea-Bed Authority to adopt rules which it might otherwise reject. Among its other proposals, the United States asked for the removal of the requirement that private companies should sell their technical knowledge to a mining enterprise set up by the Authority, and instead suggested that the developed countries should simply be obliged to help the global enterprise to find the technology in the open market.

After the signing of the Convention by representatives of 119 countries on Dec. 10, 1982, Tommy T. B. Koh (Singapore), the president of the UN Conference, issued a strong warning to those states which had not signed not to attempt to undertake sea-bed mining on their own. He proposed that the United States should no longer be invited to periodic meetings of consortia interested in enjoying rights as "pioneer investors".

Koh stated that the Convention was an indivisible whole and that it was "not possible for a state to pick what it likes and to disregard what it does not like"; that it was "factually incorrect and legally insupportable" to argue that apart from the sea-bed mining section the Convention merely codified customary law or reflected existing practice (as had been claimed by Britain and the United States); and that "any attempt by any state to mine the resources of the deep sea-bed outside the Convention" would "earn the universal condemnation of the international community and incur grave political and legal consequences".

On Dec. 30, 1982, President Reagan announced that he had decided that the United States should not pay up to $1,000,000 a year towards the costs of the UNCLOS Preparatory Commission under an assessment approved by the UN General Assembly by 135 votes to two (Turkey and the United States). He said that these funds were "destined to finance the very aspects of the Law of the Sea that are unacceptable to the United States" and that the assessment was "improper" and "not legally binding" because the Commission was "distinct from the United Nations".

The UN Secretary-General, Javier Pérez de Cuéllar, speaking on Jan. 3, 1983, expressed his regret at this decision, which he described as "a matter of the utmost seriousness for the United Nations". (The 1983 budget of the Preparatory Commission amounted to about $4,000,000 and the US share was to have been between $500,000 and $700,000.)

On March 10, 1983, President Reagan proclaimed an exclusive economic zone extending 200 nautical miles from US coasts. Within that zone, he said, the United States would "exercise sovereign rights in living and non-living resources" (i.e. including minerals).

At the same time he declared that "in a manner consistent with those fair and balanced results of the Convention and international law" the United States was "prepared to accept and act in accordance with the balance of interests relating to traditional uses of the oceans, such as navigation and overflight", and would "recognize the rights of other states in the waters off their coasts" as long as those states recognized the rights and freedoms of the United States and others under international law.

He declared further that the United States would "exercise and assert its navigation and overflight rights and freedoms on a worldwide basis in a manner that is consistent with the balance of interests reflected in the Convention" but would "not acquiesce in unilateral acts of other states designed to restrict the rights and freedoms of the international community in navigation and overflight and other related high sea uses".

After the National Oceanic and Atmospheric Administration of the US Department of Commerce had issued licences to various consortia to prospect for manganese nodules in the Pacific Ocean the Soviet Union denounced the issue of these licences on June 5, 1985, as a violation of the UN Convention and reaffirmed its stand on not recognizing "arbitrary" US decisions on matters of the international area of the sea-bed.

UK and West German Positions. In the United Kingdom (which had signed the Final Act of the Convention and was enabled to participate in the work of the Preparatory Commission, though without a vote), Margaret Thatcher (Prime Minister) stated on May 24, 1984, that Britain would like to see a comprehensive regime for the sea acceptable to all, but could not accept the sea-bed mining regime; that she knew of no British body willing to operate in the context established by the Convention, which would involve large costs to states and companies and whose complex and regulatory arrangements would be likely to discourage investment; that the proposed authority would create a bureaucratic and expensive system which would be likely to produce only a small number of deep sea-bed operations, the technology of which was not yet fully understood and still being developed. She also stated that the Convention did not affect existing navigation rights to which Britain was entitled under existing and customary law.

A different attitude was, however, taken by the director of the British Maritime League, who in a letter published in *The Times* on Nov. 12, 1984, called on Britain and the "remaining doubters" in the European Community to sign the Convention "now".

The letter said inter alia: "The United Nations Convention codifies for the first time virtually every facet of maritime law in a period when the world community is extending its use, jurisdiction and authority over the 72 per cent of the earth's surface covered by seawater. Non-contracting parties may seek to rely on current customary law and hope that this will absorb most of those parts of the Convention that they accept. But there is no certainty of that. . . .

"Shipping will always be far more important to the world economy than the resources of the deep sea-bed. In the absence of the old 'Pax Britannica', or any 'Pax Americana' to replace it, an internationally-accepted rule of law will have immense benefits to every maritime state, not least by facilitating the elimination of sub-standard ships and the protection of the environment by improved international standards and better behaviour at sea."

Calls to all states to sign and ratify the UNCLOS Convention without unnecessary delay were made during 1982–83 by Ministers of Commonwealth member countries. At a meeting of Asian and Pacific Commonwealth heads of government in Suva (Fiji) on Oct. 14–18, 1982, and also at a full Commonwealth heads of government meeting held in New Delhi on Nov. 23–29, 1983, it was explicitly acknowledged that "lack of active support from the developed countries could seriously undermine the effectiveness of an instrument designed to establish an international regime for the equitable and orderly management of the resources of the sea for the benefit of developed and developing countries alike".

The Cabinet of the Federal Republic of Germany decided on Nov. 27, 1984, not to sign the Convention but not to oppose the eventual signing of the Convention by the European Communities as a whole (its other members except the United Kingdom having already signed it). This decision was taken by 15 votes to two, the opposing ministers being Hans-Dietrich Genscher (Foreign Affairs) and Hans Engelhardt (Justice), both of the Free Democratic Party, whereas Martin Bangemann, another member of that party and Minister of Economic Affairs, voted with the majority.

The British Government announced on Dec. 6, 1984, that it would not sign the Convention but that (like the Government of the Federal Republic of Germany) it would not oppose signature by the European Communities. British Foreign Office officials stated on Dec. 7 that Britain preferred to work within the existing law-of-the-sea machinery to obtain important revisions of the Convention's section dealing with deep-sea mining, before full accession to the Convention could be considered.

Signatories of the Convention

In the absence of any veto by the United Kingdom or the Federal Republic of Germany, the European Communities subsequently signed the Convention, which by Dec. 9, 1984, had obtained the signatures of 159 states and other entities. However, by Aug. 31, 1985, the Convention had been ratified by only 21 states (mainly in Africa and the Caribbean).

The list of countries whose governments had become signatories of the Convention as of Dec. 9, 1984, was as follows: Afghanistan, Algeria, Angola, Antigua and Barbuda, Argentina, Australia, Austria, the Bahamas, Bahrain, Bangladesh, Barbados, Belgium, Belize, Benin, Bhutan, Bolivia, Botswana, Brazil, Brunei Darussalam, Bulgaria, Burkina Faso, Burma, Burundi, Byelorussia, Cameroon, Canada, Cape Verde, the Central African Republic, Chad, Chile, China, Colombia, the Comoros, the Congo, Costa Rica, Cuba, Cyprus, Czechoslovakia, Denmark, Djibouti, Dominica, the Dominican Republic, Egypt, El Salvador, Equatorial Guinea, Ethiopia, Fiji, Finland, France, Gabon, The Gambia, the German Democratic Republic, Ghana, Greece, Grenada, Guatemala, Guinea, Guinea-Bissau, Guyana, Haiti, Honduras, Hungary, Iceland, India, Indonesia, Iran, Iraq, Ireland, Italy, the Ivory Coast, Jamaica, Japan, "Democratic Kampuchea", Kenya, the Democratic People's Republic of Korea, the Republic of Korea, Kuwait, Laos, Lebanon, Lesotho, Liberia, Libya, Liechtenstein, Luxembourg, Madagascar, Malawi, Malaysia, Maldives, Mali, Malta, Mauritania, Mauritius, Mexico, Monaco, Mongolia, Morocco, Mozambique, Nauru, Nepal, the Netherlands, New Zealand, Nicaragua, Niger, Nigeria, Norway, Oman, Pakistan, Panama, Papua New Guinea, Paraguay, the Philippines, Poland, Portugal, Qatar, Romania, Rwanda, St Christopher and Nevis, St Lucia, St Vincent and the Grenadines, São Tomé and Príncipe, Saudi Arabia, Senegal, Seychelles, Sierra Leone, Singapore, the Solomon Islands, Somalia, South Africa, the Soviet Union, Spain, Sri Lanka, the Sudan, Suriname, Swaziland, Sweden, Switzerland, Tanzania, Thailand, Togo, Trinidad and Tobago, Tunisia, Tuvalu, Uganda, the Ukraine, the United Arab Emirates, Uruguay, Vanuatu, Vietnam, Western Samoa, the Yemen Arab Republic, the People's Democratic Republic of Yemen, Yugoslavia, Zaïre, Zambia and Zimbabwe. Other signatories of the Convention were the Cook Islands, the European Communities, the UN Council for Namibia, and Niue.

Coastal states which, in addition to the Federal Republic of Germany, the United Kingdom and the United States, did not sign the Convention by Dec. 9, 1984, were Albania, Ecuador, Israel, Jordan, Kiribati, Peru, Syria, Tonga, Turkey and Venezuela.

The UN Secretary-General stated on Dec. 10 that "such overwhelming support for a Convention of this universal character" was "unprecedented". According to the UN Law of the Sea Secretariat, the coastlines of the countries which had signed the Convention accounted for 88.67 per cent of the earth's total coastlines.

It was pointed out by the UN Department of Public Information that, although signature of the Convention did not legally bind any government, a signatory was obliged under general international law to refrain from any act which would defeat the object and purpose of a treaty until such time as it had made clear its intention not to become a party, and that any state might accede to the Convention at any time after its entry into force.

Meetings of the Preparatory Commission

The Preparatory Commission designed to set up the institutions of the UNCLOS Convention—notably the International Sea-Bed Authority and the International Tribunal for the Law of the Sea—was established after its creation had been approved by the required 50 delegations and with all states signatories of the Convention becoming members of the Commission.

At its first meeting on March 15-April 8, 1983, in Kingston (Jamaica) the Commission produced a consensus statement of understanding. It constituted its plenum (with a bureau) as its principal organ; special commissions (each also with a bureau) enjoying equal status and reporting to the plenum; and a general committee consisting of the chairman of the Preparatory Commission and the other members of the bureau of the plenum as well as all members of the bureaux of the special commissions (elected on the basis of equitable geographical representation). Non-signatories of the Convention were represented on the Commission by observers, but the United States was not represented. At the end of its first meeting the Commission elected as its president Joseph Warioba (Minister of Justice and Attorney-General of Tanzania).

At this first meeting of the Preparatory Commission the opposition to the Convention by the United States was strongly criticized by the representative of the Soviet Union (speaking for the East European group of states). He said that the United States continued to show a selective approach to the Convention although this had been declared illegal by the majority of states. He emphasized that the United States had not only refused to sign the Convention but had openly stated that it did not recognize Part XI (on the international sea-bed area), and he claimed that the United States intended to use the Convention to gain unilateral advantage, to violate the Convention and to seize those resources which the United Nations had declared to be "the common heritage of mankind".

The Commission held further meetings from Aug. 15 to Sept. 12, 1983, and from March 19 to April 13, 1984, when it set up four special commissions—to deal respectively with problems of the land-based mineral producers, with the Enterprise (designed to exploit the sea-bed mineral resources), with the code required for sea-bed mining of minerals, and with setting up the proposed Disputes Tribunal, to be located in Hamburg (Federal Republic of Germany).

The Preparatory Commission met again (in Kingston) from Aug. 15 to Sept. 1983, and from March 19 to April 13, 1984; in Geneva from Aug. 13 to Sept. 5, 1984; and in Kingston again from March 11 to April 4, 1985.

Feasibility Study for the "Enterprise"

At the request of the Preparatory Commission, the Law of the Sea Secretariat has prepared a detailed project feasibility study (intended merely to facilitate discussion) for the

Enterprise of the proposed International Sea-Bed Authority.

The study analysed the various operational options available to the Enterprise: the leasing of plant and equipment, production sharing, entering into service contracts, joint ventures of various kinds, and independent operation. It assumed the implementation of a 3,000,000-tonne nodule operation which would require a work force of at least 1,600; the setting-up in 1986 of an ad hoc core group consisting of a general, a technical, a financial, and a scientific research and development manager; the entry into force of the Convention by 1989, with the Enterprise being effectively in place by the middle of that year, the mine sites and the available technology reviewed, marketing surveys done and a demonstration plant set up; and a decision to go ahead with a commercial project to be taken in mid-1994, whereafter orders for the plant and equipment would be made and a deep-sea mining system would be set up and debugged, enabling it to function at full capacity in 2001.

The study also stated that between 80 and 90 per cent of the investment would be made between 1996 and 2000 and would be recovered in the next three years of commercial operations. The most capital-intensive option, in which the Enterprise would operate the entire system, would require an investment of US$1,700 million at 1980 prices. Favourable cash flows should make it possible for the Enterprise to obtain 75 to 80 per cent of the amount from financial institutions. In the least capital-intensive case, where the plant and machinery for both mining and processing were leased, equity contributions of states after commercial borrowing would be between $150,000,000 and $200,000,000.

Tasks arising from the UN Convention

Arising from the UNCLOS Convention, new tasks for the surveying and charting of the oceans were outlined in a paper prepared by Capt. J. A. L. Myres RN in connexion with a seminar held in Fiji late in 1984 and with special reference to the South Pacific region. These tasks were directed towards the long-term objective of developing a world geodetic system (WGS) under which boundaries at sea were to be defined in terms readily accepted and understood by all nations, with all nautical charts being eventually based on the WGS.

As specified in Articles 5-16 of the UNCLOS Convention, the delimitation of the various zones of the sea starts from baselines, which require the precise determination of "base points" (with due regard for the need of adjustments in the event of natural changes in the coastline). Once these base points have been co-ordinated (preferably on the WGS but tied to the country's geodetic system if this differs from the WGS); once the low-water line has been accurately defined where this is relevant; and once the rules applying to the use of straight baselines and archipelagic limits have been agreed by lawyers and experts (which for a small country may involve the need for overseas consultancy)—it is then necessary for the baselines to be depicted.

Any disputes between neighbouring countries over their maritime boundaries should be resolved in an amicable fashion, which would be promoted by (i) the general acceptance by nations of a common WGS, (ii) reliable geodetic control along all coastlines; (iii) the existence of reliable hydrographic surveys (for instance during delimitation of continental shelves); and (iv) the spirit of friendship and professional confidence between surveyors of neighbouring countries.

For small island nations with limited resources it would be prudent to carry out modern surveys and the careful delineation of the continental shelf around each island as well as the location of all detached banks or shoals rising from oceanic depths.

In the paper it is suggested that in the case of countries with large sea areas and few available resources an effort should be made to achieve some self-sufficiency in hydrographic surveying. In this connexion "Guidance Notes on Hydrographic Surveying in Small Ports" (published by the British Ports Association in 1981) are recommended to enable an interested person to produce a perfectly satisfactory survey within a port area and its immediate approaches.

It is emphasized that reliable charting is necessary to enable a coastal state to realize the full potential of its offshore national assets and also, as required by the UN Convention, to ensure the safety of shipping in its waters.

Territorial Waters Claims by Coastal States

Territorial Sea Limits

As at March 1, 1985, the territorial sea limits in nautical miles offshore or of baselines were as listed below for the world's different coastal states (whose claims to exclusive economic zones, fisheries areas and continental shelf areas are tabulated on pages 108–09). (*Main source*: "Limits of the Seas, No. 36, National Claims to Maritime Jurisdictions", US Department of State, Bureau of Intelligence and Research, Office of the Geographer, March 6, 1985—where further particulars can be found.)

Three miles: Australia, the Bahamas, Bahrain, Belgium, Belize, Chile, Denmark, the Federal Republic of Germany,[1] Ireland, Jordan, Kiribati, the Netherlands, Qatar, St Lucia, St Vincent and the Grenadines, Singapore, the United Arab Emirates,[2] the United Kingdom, the United States of America.

Four miles: Finland, Norway.

Six miles: Dominican Republic, Greece, Israel, Turkey.[3]

12 miles: Algeria, Antigua and Barbuda, Bangladesh, Barbados, Brunei, Bulgaria, Burma, Canada, Cape Verde, China, Colombia, the Comoros, Costa Rica, Cuba, Cyprus, Djibouti, Dominica, Egypt, Equatorial Guinea, Ethiopia, Fiji, France, the German Democratic Republic, Grenada, Guatemala, Guinea, Guinea-Bissau, Guyana, Haiti, Honduras, Iceland, India, Indonesia, Iran, Iraq, Italy, the Ivory Coast, Jamaica, Japan,[4] Kampuchea, Kenya, the Democratic People's Republic of Korea,[5] the Republic of Korea,[6] Kuwait, Lebanon, Libya, Malaysia, Malta, Mauritius, Mexico, Monaco, Morocco, Mozambique, Namibia, Nauru, New Zealand, Oman, Pakistan, Papua New Guinea, Poland, Portugal, Romania, St Christopher and Nevis, São Tomé and Príncipe, Saudi Arabia, Seychelles, the Solomon Islands, South Africa, the Soviet Union, Spain, Sri Lanka, the Sudan, Suriname, Sweden, Taiwan, Thailand, Tonga, Trinidad and Tobago, Tunisia, Tuvalu, Vanuatu, Venezuela, Vietnam, Western Samoa, the Yemen Arab Republic, the People's Democratic Republic of Yemen, Yugoslavia and Zaïre.

15 miles: Albania.

20 miles: Angola.

30 miles: Nigeria, Togo.

35 miles: Syria.

50 miles: Cameroon, Madagascar, Tanzania.

70 miles: Mauritania.

100 miles: Gabon.

150 miles: Senegal.

[1] The Federal Republic of Germany extended its territorial sea in November 1984 to include a box extending about 16 miles offshore to the island of Heligoland.

[2] Of the United Arab Emirates, Sharjah has claimed a 12-mile territorial sea limit.

[3] Turkey has a 12-mile territorial waters limit in the Black and Mediterranean Seas.

[4] Japan's territorial sea is only three miles wide in five "international straits".

[5] The Democratic People's Republic of Korea has also claimed a 50-mile military zone in which foreign vessels and aircraft are prohibited without permission.

[6] The Republic of Korea's territorial sea limit is three miles in the Korea Strait.

200 miles: Argentina, Benin, Brazil, the Congo, Ecuador,[1] El Salvador, The Gambia, Ghana, Liberia, Nicaragua, Panama, Peru, Sierra Leone, Somalia, Uruguay.

Special claims: Maldives,[2] Philippines.[2]

Contiguous Zones Claims

In addition, and at the same date, claims to contiguous zones (adjacent to the territorial sea) have been made by various states as follows:

Four miles: Denmark.

10 miles: Norway.

12 miles: Australia, the Netherlands, St Lucia, St Vincent and the Grenadines.

15 miles: Venezuela.

18 miles: Bangladesh, Egypt, Saudi Arabia, the Sudan, the Yemen Arab Republic.

24 miles: Antigua and Barbuda, Burma, Djibouti, Dominica, the Dominican Republic, Haiti, Honduras, India, Kampuchea, Malta, Morocco, Pakistan, St Christopher and Nevis, Sri Lanka, Vanuatu, Vietnam, the People's Democratic Republic of Yemen.

---

[1] In 1934 Ecuador declared the Galapagos Islands a national park with a 15-mile territorial sea, and in 1951 it was decreed that the territorial sea was to be measured from the outermost promontories of the farthest islands of the archipelago. The 200-mile maritime zone declared by Ecuador in 1952 was calculated from this polygonal construction, in which certain fishing was prohibited in 1955.

[2] The Maldives and the Philippines both claim territorial waters rights within boundaries defined in relation to their outermost islands and atolls.

2. Major International Organizations, Conventions and Agreements

Described in this chapter is the principal international organization responsible for maritime questions, namely the International Maritime Organization, formerly the Inter-Governmental Maritime Consultative Organization; in addition to data on the origins, structure and purposes of the organization, details of IMO Conventions and other initiatives in the maritime sphere are included. Also treated in this chapter are other major international organizations with maritime responsibilities—although those dealing specifically with shipping, marine resources (including fisheries) and environmental/scientific matters are covered in Chapters 3, 4 and 5 respectively.

International Maritime Organization (IMO)

Address. 4 Albert Embankment, London SE1 7SR, UK.

Officers. W. A. O'Neill (ch.); C. P. Srivastava (s.g.); E. Jansen (ch. of Maritime Safety Committee).

Founded. March 17, 1958.

History of the Organization

The organization was established under the name of Inter-Governmental Maritime Consultative Organization (IMCO) in terms of a Convention which had been approved on March 6, 1948, at an international maritime conference held in Geneva and called by the UN Economic and Social Council (ECOSOC). Following ratification by the required number of 21 governments, the Convention came into force on March 17, 1958, and on Jan. 13, 1959, IMCO became a UN specialized agency.

The 1948 Convention laid down that IMCO was a consultative and advisory body, whose functions were (i) to provide machinery for inter-governmental co-operation on regulations and practices affecting shipping engaged in international trade, and to encourage the adoption of the highest practicable standards of safety and efficient navigation; (ii) to encourage the removal of discriminatory action and unnecessary governmental restrictions on international shipping, though subsidies and other governmental assistance for the development of national shipping and security purposes would not constitute discrimination unless based on measures (e.g., flag discrimination, arbitrary port charges, etc.) designed to restrict the freedom of shipping of all flags to take part in international trade; (iii) to consider unfair procedure by shipping concerns which had proved incapable of settlement through the normal processes of international shipping business; (iv) to consider any matters connected with shipping referred to it by any UN specialized agency; (v) to provide for the exchange of information among governments on matters under consideration by the organization.

Under amendments to the Convention adopted by the IMCO Assembly in November 1975 it was decided to change the name of the organization to International Maritime Organization (IMO), and this decision came into force in May 1982.

IMO Structure, Membership and Publications

The IMO has an Assembly which is composed of representatives of all IMO member states and which meets every two years. The Assembly elects a Council which meets about twice a year and whose 32 members must include six governments of states with the largest interests in providing international seaborne trade and six other governments with special interests in maritime transport or navigation, whose election will ensure an equitable geographical representation. The Council appoints the organization's Secretary-General.

IMO also has a Legal Committee, a Facilitation Committee, a Committee on Technical Co-operation, a Maritime Safety Committee and a Marine Environment Protection Committee (membership of all of which is open to all members of the organization). It also has a Secretariat.

The *Maritime Safety Committee* has a number of sub-committees—on bulk chemicals, cargoes and containers, carriage of dangerous goods, fire protection, life-saving appliances, radio communication, safety of navigation, standards of training and watchkeeping, ship design and equipment, stability and load lines, and fishing vessel safety. (The sub-committee on bulk chemicals is also a sub-committee of the Marine Environment Protection Committee).

The *Secretariat* has divisions for maritime safety, the marine environment, legal affairs and external relations, administration, conferences and technical co-operation, as well as two sub-divisions (for navigation and technology).

The organization has also appointed regional maritime advisers (the first of these having been named in January 1975).

Membership. 126 governments (of all members of the United Nations except those of land-locked states and also Albania, Antigua and Barbuda, Belize, Benin, the Comoros, Grenada, Kiribati, the Democratic People's Republic of Korea, Monaco, Nauru, Nicaragua, St Kitts and Nevis, São Tomé and Príncipe, the Solomon Islands, South Africa, Tonga, Tuvalu, Vanuatu and Western Samoa); Hong Kong is an associate member.

Publications. *IMO News* (in English and French), quarterly; numerous specialized publications, including texts of Conventions, a *Manual on Oil Pollution* and *Technical Co-operation in Maritime Transport*, issued jointly with the UN Conference on Trade and Development (UNCTAD) and the International Labour Organization (ILO).

IMO Conventions

The organization has adopted a substantial number of Conventions relating to all aspects of maritime traffic, including protection of the marine environment, and also codes and regulations. Not all the Conventions adopted have as yet entered into force. [For the 1976 Convention leading to the establishment of the International

Maritime Satellite Organization (INMARSAT), see section on this body on page 29–30.]

OILPOL CONVENTION

An *International Convention for the Prevention of Pollution of the Sea by Oil* (OILPOL), agreed on May 12, 1954, and banning the discharging into the sea of crude oil, fuel oil, diesel oil and lubricating oil within specified zones, came into force for tankers on July 26, 1958, and for dry cargo ships on July 26, 1961. Amendments to this Convention were signed in 1962, 1969, and 1971.

By March 1, 1984, this Convention had been adhered to by 72 contracting states. It was to be superseded by the 1973 MARPOL Convention [see below] when the latter came into force.

SAFETY OF LIFE AT SEA

An *International Convention on the Safety of Life at Sea*, revising the 1948 Convention which had entered into force in 1952, was signed on July 17, 1960, by 34 countries, six more signing during the following month. The Convention dealt with safety of navigation, provisions for nuclear ships and carriage of dangerous goods and came into force in May 1965.

At the seventh meeting of the IMCO Assembly on Oct. 5-15, 1971, amendments were adopted to the Convention, rendering mandatory the observance of traffic-routeing schemes approved by IMCO, including a scheme for traffic separation in the Dover Strait.

This Convention has been superseded by the 1974 SOLAS Convention [see below].

FACILITATION OF MARITIME TRAFFIC

A 1965 *Convention on the Facilitation of Maritime Traffic* relates to the speeding-up of the turn-around of vessels in port by simplifying procedures. Under the Convention ships are required to produce six documents—the General Declaration, the Cargo Declaration, the Ship's Stores Declaration, the Crew's Effects Declaration, the Crew List and the Passenger List. The Convention came into force in 1967, and by March 1, 1984, it had been accepted by 53 contracting states.

LOAD LINES

A 1966 *International Convention on Load Lines* came into force in July 1968 and was amended in October 1971 and November 1975. By March 1, 1984, it was accepted by 101 contracting states. It applied only to cargo ships (and not to fishing vessels).

OIL POLLUTION CASUALTIES

An *International Convention Relating to Intervention on the High Seas in Cases of Oil Pollution Casualties* was adopted at the end of a conference held by IMCO from Nov. 10 to 29, 1969. The Convention dealt with the right of a coastal state to protect its own interests when a casualty occurred on the high seas which might damage those interests. This Convention entered into force on May 6, 1975. By March 1, 1984, it had been accepted by 46 contracting states.

A protocol to the Convention, adopted in 1973, came into force in 1983 and was by March 1, 1984, adhered to by 17 nations.

CIVIL LIABILITIES FOR OIL POLLUTION DAMAGE

At the November 1969 conference, an *International Convention on Civil Liability for Oil Pollution Damage* (CLC) was adopted, providing that the owner of a ship from which polluting oil escaped would be held liable for any pollution damage caused. This Convention entered into force on June 19, 1975. By March 1, 1984, it had been accepted by 54 countries.

A protocol to the Convention, adopted in 1976, entered into force in 1981 and was by March 1, 1984, adhered to by 17 countries.

Under a further protocol, adopted in May 1984, the scope of the Convention was extended into the territorial sea and the exclusive economic zone of contracting states, and a minimal liability was introduced for owners of small vessels, while the liability of owners of larger vessels was increased (by as much as four to six times).

TONNAGE OF SHIPS

A 1969 *International Convention on Tonnage of Ships* came into force in July 1982, and by March 1, 1984, it had been accepted by 63 participating states.

TRADE PASSENGER SHIPS

A *Special Trade Passenger Ships Agreement* was concluded at an IMCO conference in October 1971 to safeguard ships in the "pilgrim trade", and it came into force in 1974. By March 1, 1984, it had been accepted by 13 contracting states.

A protocol to this agreement, adopted by a conference convened by IMO in November 1973, entered into force in January 1974. By March 1, 1984, it was accepted by 13 contracting states.

A protocol on space requirement under the agreement, adopted in 1973, came into force in 1977 and was by March 1, 1984, subscribed to by 11 contracting states.

CARRIAGE OF NUCLEAR MATERIAL

A *Convention relating to Civil Liability in the Field of Maritime Carriage of Nuclear Material*, adopted in December 1971, came into force on July 15, 1975 (90 days after the deposit of the fifth instrument of ratification, countries having ratified it being France, Spain, Denmark, Sweden and Norway). By March 1984, the Convention was in force for 11 countries.

COMPENSATION FOR OIL POLLUTION DAMAGE

At a conference held on Nov. 29-Dec. 18, 1971, another agreement resulted, known as the *Convention on the Establishment of an International Fund for Compensation for Oil Pollution Damage*, which came into force on Oct. 16, 1978. The fund was designed to offer compensation in cases of large-scale pollution where the terms of provisions for civil liability were inadequate to cover the damage incurred. By March 1, 1984, it was adhered to by 29 countries.

A 1976 protocol to the Convention—to cover various substances other than oil and to enable states to take preventive action outside their territorial waters when faced with massive pollution or the threat of it—was by March 1, 1984, agreed to be 12 countries, but this fact did not fulfil all conditions for its entry into force, and the protocol is therefore not yet applicable.

Under a further protocol, adopted in May 1984, the scope of this Convention was extended and the upper limit of compensation payable by oil and shipping companies was raised to £150,000,000. However, implementation of this admendment was expected to take five years, since it was dependent on ratification by the United States, which had refused to sign the Convention.

The International Fund for Compensation for Oil Pollution Damage was established in 1978 and is located at IMO's address. Japan has been the major contributor to the fund. By March 1984 the fund had paid compensation and indemnification amounting to about £29,000,000. It then had a membership of 29 states.

PREVENTING COLLISIONS AT SEA

A 1972 *Convention on International Regulations for Preventing Collisions at Sea* contained a revised text of 1960 Regulations for Preventing Collisions at Sea and came into force on July 15, 1977. In November 1981 these regulations were revised by the IMCO Assembly, and the resulting amendments came into force on June 1, 1983. By March 1, 1984, there were 87 contracting states.

The 1981 amendments meant inter alia that cable-laying vessels and vessels engaged in work connected with the safety of traffic separation schemes were exempt from the special requirements of these schemes; sailing vessels and other vessels under 20 metres long had unrestricted use of inshore traffic zones; and the positioning of lights on certain vessels were modified. (For the full text of the regulations see *Lloyd's Nautical Year Book 1984*, pages 319-65.)

SAFE CONTAINERS

A 1972 *International Convention for Safe Containers* (SCS) came into force in September 1977. It had two main objectives: to maintain the existing high level of safety in the handling and transport of containers by providing generally acceptable test procedures and related strength requirements; and to facilitate international transport of containers by providing uniform regulations to all modes of transport (avoiding the proliferation of divergent national standards).

Amendments to the Convention were adopted by the Maritime Safety Committee in July 1983 and came into force on Jan. 1, 1984. These amendments enabled governments to introduce a continuous examination programme, with examinations to take place at least once every 30 months, and with approved containers to be marked ACEP (Approved Continuous Examination Programme) as from Jan. 1, 1987.

By March 1, 1984, the Convention had 38 contracting states.

PREVENTION OF MARINE POLLUTION BY DUMPING

A *Convention on the Prevention of Marine Pollution by Dumping* was adopted at an intergovernmental conference held in London on Oct. 30-Nov. 13, 1972, and attended by representatives of 81 governments and observers from 12 other countries. The Soviet Union participated, but the People's Republic of China was absent.

The main aim of the Convention is to prevent indiscriminate disposal at sea of waste chemicals and minerals, on the understanding that the sea's capacity to assimilate waste and to regenerate natural resources is not unlimited. The dumping of certain categories of waste will be prohibited or subject to permit.

At the close of the conference the Convention had been initialled by 57 countries. It came into force on Aug. 30, 1975, after ratification by the required seven of the 12 signatories, i.e. by Denmark, France, Iceland, Norway, Portugal, Spain and Sweden.

In December 1975 IMCO (subsequently the IMO) was designated as the organization responsible for handling secretarial duties for the Convention.

MARPOL CONVENTION

A *Convention for the Prevention of Pollution from Ships* (MARPOL) was adopted at a conference held in London from Oct. 8 to Nov. 2, 1973, and attended by delegates from 79 countries and numerous international organizations.

The Convention contained provisions aimed at eliminating pollution of the sea by both oil and other noxious substances which might be discharged operationally, and at minimizing the amount of oil which would be released accidentally in collisions or strandings by ships of any type whatsoever, including also fixed or floating platforms. The Convention did not, however, deal with dumping—which was covered by the Convention listed immediately above—nor with the release of harmful substances directly arising from the exploration, exploitation and associated offshore processing of seabed mineral resources. The Convention incorporated certain amendments made earlier to the OILPOL Convention described above. It also laid down that the Mediterranean, the Black Sea, the Baltic Sea, the Red Sea and the Gulf area (including the Sea of Oman) were designated as special areas in which oil discharge was completely prohibited (except by very small ships). Moreover, the Convention contained special requirements for the control of pollution by over 400 different noxious substances and for sewage and garbage disposal.

Certain forms of pollution were prohibited within specified distances from the coast, these limits being up to three nautical miles (nm) for untreated food wastes, four for untreated sewage, 12 nm for noxious liquids, oil (from non-oil tankers of over 400 gross registered tons), untreated food wastes and untreated sewage, 25 nm for dunnage (light packing material) and 50 nm for oil from oil tankers. The Convention also provided for the establishment of waste reception facilities for oily ballast in ports (this provision coming into force on Oct. 2, 1984).

The MARPOL Convention was modified by a protocol which was adopted in February 1978 by a conference on tanker safety and the prevention of pollution. The amended Convention requires (i) an initial survey before the ship is put into service or before an International Oil Pollution Prevention (IOPP) Certificate is issued; (ii) periodical surveys at intervals not exceeding five years; (iii) a minimum of one intermediate survey to be carried out during the period of validity of the IOPP certificate; and (iv) unscheduled inspection or mandatory annual surveys to be carried out (with most nations favouring the latter).

After the entry into force of the modified Convention any ship which did not conform to its requirements was unable to operate unless modified to meet these requirements.

Both the Convention and the protocol were to come into force one year after ratification by countries representing over 50 per cent of world merchant shipping and by 15 states. These conditions were fulfilled by the ratification by Greece (on Sept. 23, 1982) and Italy (on Oct. 1, 1982), and both the Convention and the protocol thus entered into force on Oct. 2, 1983. The modified Convention was to supersede the OILPOL Convention which had come into force in 1958-61 [see above] and it was to form part of the UN Law of the Sea [see Chapter 1]. By March 1, 1984, it had been adhered to by 25 contracting states.

On Jan. 3, 1984, the IMO stated that it had asked 125 states to provide detailed information on the availability of facilities in ports for the reception of oily wastes from ships.

SOLAS CONVENTION

An *International Convention for the Safety of Life at Sea* (SOLAS), adopted at an IMCO conference which ended on Nov. 1, 1974, incorporated amendments to the 1960 International Convention on the Safety of Life at Sea [see above], repeatedly amended between 1966 and 1973. The revised Convention contained new provisions on fire protection for passenger ships and tankers and on the carriage of grain in bulk. It came into force on May 25, 1980.

The Convention inter alia required ships with 50 or more passengers to be equipped with radio able to transmit messages to at least a radius of 100 miles; ships receiving distress messages to be under obligation to give aid; and ships in distress to be able to demand it; as well as some lifeboats to be radio-equipped. Navigational aids employed under the SOLAS Convention are radio direction finders and radar.

A protocol to SOLAS was adopted in February 1978 by a conference on tanker safety and pollution prevention, and it came into force in May 1981.

A first set of amendments (to the 1974 Convention and the 1978 protocol) was adopted by the IMCO Maritime Safety Committee in November 1981 and came into force on Sept. 1, 1984. By March 1 of that year there had been 79 contracting parties to the Convention and 46 to the protocol.

CARRIAGE OF PASSENGERS AND LUGGAGE

A *Convention relating to the Carriage of Passengers and their Luggage by Sea* (PAL) was adopted in December 1974 by a conference convened by IMCO in Athens. The Convention was amended by a protocol in November 1976. Both the Convention and the protocol were to come into force after ratification by 10 states, but by March 1, 1984, they had been ratified by only nine and six states respectively.

LIMITATION OF LIABILITY FOR MARITIME CLAIMS

A *Convention on Limitation of Liability for Maritime Claims* was adopted in November 1976 by a conference convened by IMCO. It was to come into force after ratification by 12 states, but by March 1, 1984, it had only seven contracting states.

SAFETY OF FISHING VESSELS

An *International Convention on Safety of Fishing Vessels* (SFV) was adopted in Torremolinos (Spain) in 1977 and was by March 1, 1984, adhered to by 11 contracting states. It was to enter into force after ratification by 15 states whose fishing fleets constituted not less than 50 per cent of the number of the world's fishing vessels of a length of 24 metres or more.

The Convention applied only to new fishing vessels exceeding that length. (In 1984 IMO developed guidelines for safety standards applying to fishing vessels of less than 24 metres in length.)

TRAINING, CERTIFICATION AND WATCHKEEPING OF SEAFARERS

An *International Convention on Standards of Training, Certification and Watchkeeping for Seafarers* (STCW), adopted in 1978, came into force on April 28, 1984, and by March 1, 1985, it had been adhered to by 37 contracting states.

MARITIME SEARCH AND RESCUE

An *International Convention on Maritime Search and Rescue* (SAR) was adopted at a conference held in Hamburg under IMCO auspices in 1979. It was by June 22, 1984, acceded to be 15 states (the latest being Denmark) and came into force on June 22, 1985.

This Convention was aimed at facilitating co-operation between the various organizations responsible and neighbouring states by establishing a legal international plan for search and rescue. Parties to the Convention undertook to make the necessary arrangements for coast-watching and for rescuing those in distress and for the provision of the necessary maritime safety facilities. Neighbouring states were encouraged to pool services; to use common procedures, co-operation, training and liaison; and to authorize the entry into their territorial waters of search and rescue units from other states.

The Convention also aimed at the establishment of co-ordination centres and sub-centres, and it outlined procedures to be followed in emergency or distress alerts and during search and rescue operations. It regarded ship reporting systems as necessary to shorten the time involved in initiating action and to alert vessels in the vicinity of the incident, to define the search areas and to speed up the provision of medical aid. It called for continued co-operation between IMCO (later IMO) and the International Civil Aviation Organization (ICAO) in search and rescue operations, and for the allocation of search and rescue frequencies (involving the International Telecommunication Union, ITU), the harmonization of weather forecasts and warnings (involving the World Meteorological Organization, WMO), and the promotion of technical co-operation through IMO itself.

The Convention further provided for the establishment of SAR regions, the delimitation of which would not be related to or prejudice the delimitation of any boundary between states.

Under the Convention the world's oceans have been divided into 14 areas as follows (with the names of countries developing the marine SAR plan for the area concerned shown in parentheses): North Atlantic (United States), North Sea (United Kingdom), Baltic Sea (Sweden), Eastern South Atlantic (not yet determined), Western South Atlantic (Argentina and Brazil), Eastern North Pacific (United States), Western North Pacific (Japan), Eastern South Pacific (Chile), Western South Pacific (New Zealand), Indian Ocean (Australia), Caribbean (not yet determined), Mediterranean (France), Black Sea (not yet determined) and Arctic Ocean (Norway).

The Convention came into force on June 22, 1985, having been ratified by 18 countries (Algeria, Argentina, Australia, Barbados, Belgium, Brazil, Canada, Chile, Denmark, France, the German Democratic Republic, the Federal Republic of Germany, the Netherlands, New Zealand, Norway, Sweden, the United Kingdom and the United States).

CREW STANDARDS

An *International Treaty on Crew Standards* entered into force in April 1984. It covered nearly two-thirds of the world's fleets.

Other IMO Activities

Codes of Practice

IMCO, and later the IMO, has issued codes on specific practices relating to both maritime transport and the exploitation of ocean resources.

An *International Maritime Dangerous Goods Code* (IMDG), adopted by IMCO in 1960 and amended annually since then, had by April 1984 been fully adopted by 37 countries, while among the major seafaring nations Japan had adopted it only in part.

New guidelines (replacing a set issued in 1972) for reporting incidents involving dangerous goods in packaged form were issued in 1984.

A *Code for the Construction and Equipment of Mobile Offshore Drilling Units* (MODU), adopted by the IMO Assembly in 1981, has been applied by Liberia (since Oct. 1, 1980), Japan (since Dec. 25, 1981), China (since Sept. 1, 1982), Yugoslavia (since 1982), Romania (since April 1, 1984) and the United States (since early 1984). Australia, Panama and the United Kingdom were expected to apply it also.

A *Code of Safety for Nuclear Merchant Ships* was adopted by the IMCO Assembly in 1981.

Avoidance of Collisions at Sea

The organization has also issued routeing instructions and designed traffic separation schemes to avoid collisions at sea.

Following the disaster of March 16, 1978, when the Liberian tanker *Amoco Cadiz* went aground, broke up and spilled some 230,000 tons of oil off the coast of Brittany, the IMCO Maritime Safety Committee amended the existing traffic separation schemes off the island of Ushant so as to keep tankers further away from the French coast.

The IMO has also organized a World-Wide Navigational Warning Service in collaboration with the International Hydrographic Organization. [For complementary coastal warning service (NAVTEX), see entry for International Hydrographic Organization on page 36.]

This service issues regular radio warnings on hazards such as the malfunction of navigational aids, the location of wrecks or the completion of new offshore structures. Under this service the oceans are divided into 16 Navareas, on which information is broadcast in a Standard Marine Navigational Vocabulary (in English), The first Navarea, established on July 1, 1983, was the North-East Atlantic (including the North and Baltic Seas).

Paris Memorandum of Understanding on Port State Control

A Memorandum of Understanding (MOU) on Port State Control (adopted in Paris in 1981) has been signed by Belgium, Denmark, Finland, France, the Federal Republic of Germany, Greece, Ireland, Italy, the Netherlands, Norway, Portugal, Spain, Sweden and the United Kingdom. It provides for the inspection of foreign merchant ships entering the respective ports of these countries, on the basis of the provision of six Conventions and protocols of IMCO and of one of the International Labour Organization (ILO).

In the year ending June 30, 1984, a total of 9,847 inspections were carried out on 7,350 ships (corresponding to over 19 per cent of the total number of individual ships visiting the 14 signatory countries), of which 436 were found to have serious deficiencies; 26 per cent of these deficiencies were in life-saving appliances, 19 per cent in fire-fighting equipment and 14 per cent in navigational equipment.

Resolution on Acts of Piracy

At its 13th regular session, held in Londòn in November 1983, the IMO Assembly adopted a resolution on acts of piracy and armed robbery against ships and small craft, urging governments to prevent and suppress such acts in their own and adjacent waters and to inform IMO of any attacks against their ships and of any action taken.

Other International Organizations and their Conventions

International Labour Organization (ILO)

Address. 4 route des Morillons, CH-1211, Geneva 22, Switzerland.

Officer. Francis Blanchard (France, dir.-gen. of International Labour Office).

Founded. 1919.

Objectives. To formulate international policies and programmes for improving working and living conditions, enhancing employment opportunities and promoting human rights; to set international labour standards to be achieved by national authorities; to provide a programme of international technical co-operation towards the implementation of these policies; and to engage in training, education, research and publishing towards these ends.

Structure. The principal organ of the ILO is the International Labour

Conference, meeting annually and attended by delegations from member countries, and with workers' and employers' representatives having an equal voice with those of governments. The ILO's Governing Body is its executive body, consisting of 28 government, 14 employers' and 14 workers' members and meeting three to four times a year. The International Labour Office is the ILO's secretariat, operational headquarters and publishing house.

Membership. 151 states.

ILO Maritime Conventions

The ILO has issued numerous conventions and recommendations, and the substance of those relating to maritime affairs is given in the ILO's publication *Maritime Labour Conventions and Recommendations.* These apply to merchant ships (and not to warships, fishing and whaling vessels, sailing ships and small craft). Those nations which have ratified a convention are bound to implement it once it is in force.

The ILO conventions relating specifically to sea-going personnel or seafarers are listed in chronological order.

No. 7. The 1920 *Minimum Age (Sea) Convention* came into force on Sept. 27, 1921. It lays down that children under the age of 14 years shall not be employed on vessels (except where only members of the same family are employed and except on approved school- or training-ships) and that every shipmaster shall keep a register of all persons under the age of 16 employed on his vessel.

No. 8. The 1920 *Unemployment Indemnity (Shipwreck) Convention* came into force on March 16, 1923. It lays down that, in the event of unemployment arising for seamen from the loss of a vessel, indemnity shall be paid to them by the owner of the vessel or the employer of its seamen.

No. 9. The 1920 *Placing of Seamen Convention* came into force on Nov. 23, 1921. It provides for the abolition of systems of finding employment for seamen as a commercial enterprise conducted for pecuniary gain and for their replacement by public employment offices finding employment for seamen free of charge, and also for freedom of choice of ship to be assured to seamen and freedom of choice of crew to shipowners.

No. 15. The 1921 *Minimum Age (Trimmers and Stokers) Convention* came into force on Nov. 20, 1922. It fixes the minimum age for trimmers and stokers at 18 years, and conditionally at 16 years for those employed (i) in the coastal trade of India and Japan and (ii) in ports.

No. 16. The 1921 *Medical Examination of Young Persons (Sea) Convention* came into force on Nov. 22, 1922. It lays down the requirement that persons under 18 years of age can be employed on any vessel only if their fitness is attested in a medical certificate.

No. 22. The 1926 *Seamen's Articles of Agreement Convention* came into force on April 4, 1928. It lays down exact procedures for drawing up articles of agreement between shipowners and seamen, as well as their scope, in terms of the applicable national laws.

No. 23. The 1926 *Repatriation of Seamen Convention* came into force on April 16, 1928. It defines the seaman's right to repatriation after being landed during the term of his engagement or on its expiry.

No. 53. The 1936 *Certificates of Competency Convention* came into force on March 29, 1939. It lays down the minimum conditions for the granting of certificates of competency to masters and officers on board merchant ships.

No. 55. The 1936 *Shipowners' Liability (Sick and Injured Seamen) Convention* came into force on Oct. 29, 1939. It defines the shipowners' liability in the event of injury, sickness and resultant death of persons employed on board a vessel (within the scope of national laws and regulations).

No. 56. The *Sickness Insurance (Sea) Convention* came into force on Dec. 9, 1949. It provides for compulsory sickness insurance for all persons employed in the service of a ship and lays down the details and scope of such insurance.

No. 58. The 1936 *Minimum Age (Sea) Convention (Revised)* came into force on April 11, 1939. It revises Convention No. 7 of 1920 by fixing the minimum age of children for employment on vessels at 15 years (instead of 14), except when only members of the same family are employed or where children work on approved school- or training-ships). However, children of not less than 14 years of age may be employed if it is officially certified that such employment will benefit them.

No. 68. The 1946 *Food and Catering (Ships' Crews) Convention* came into force on March 24, 1957. It lays down that states parties to the Convention are obliged to promote a proper standard of food supply and services for crews on sea-going vessels under the supervision of a competent authority whose inspectors have wide-ranging powers and which has to submit an annual report to the ILO.

No. 69. The 1946 *Certification of Ships' Cooks Convention* came into force on April 22, 1953. It lays down that a certificate of qualification shall be held by any person engaged as a ship's cook.

No. 70. The 1946 *Social Security (Seafarers) Convention* specifies the entitlement of seafarers and their dependants to medical and death benefits.

No. 71. The 1946 *Seafarers' Pensions Convention* came into force on Oct. 10, 1962. It provides for the establishment of a pensions scheme for retiring seafarers.

No. 73. The 1946 *Medical Examination (Seafarers) Convention* came into force on Aug. 17, 1955. It requires each would-be crew member to produce a medical certificate attesting his fitness for the work for which he wishes to be engaged, such certificates normally remaining in force for two years.

No. 74. The 1946 *Certification of Able Seamen Convention* came into force on July 14, 1951. It provides that no person shall be employed as an able seaman unless deemed competent under national law and regulations and in possession of a certificate of qualification as an able seaman attesting to his previous period of service (normally of three years) and the successful passing of an examination.

No. 91. The 1949 *Paid Vacations (Seafarers) Convention* came into force on Sept. 14, 1967. It lays down minimum periods of paid vacations for each year of service (18 days for masters, officers and radio operators and 12 days for other crew members) subject to specified conditions and under laws, regulations and/or collective agreements.

No. 92. The 1949 *Accommodation of Crews Convention (Revised)* came into force on Jan. 23, 1953. This Convention of 21 articles lays down detailed accommodation requirements with due regard for the safety of the crew.

No. 108. The 1958 *Seafarers' Identity Documents Convention* came into force on Feb. 19, 1958. Under this Convention participant states shall issue an identity document to each seafarer, but when such a document is issued to a foreigner it shall not constitute proof of his nationality.

No. 109. The 1958 *Wages, Hours of Work and Manning (Sea) Convention* has 27 articles and lays down minimum wages and, for different categories of work, maximum hours of work, and it also requires sufficient and efficient manning of vessels.

No. 133. The 1970 *Accommodation of Crews (Supplementary Provisions) Convention* expands the provisions of Convention No. 92.

No. 134. The 1970 *Prevention of Accidents (Seafarers) Convention* came into force on Feb. 17, 1973. It requires all occupational accidents to be adequately reported and investigated, with statistics of such accidents to be kept, and provision to be made for the prevention of accidents.

No. 145. The 1976 *Continuity of Employment (Seafarers) Convention* came into force on June 13, 1979. It lays down that all states with a maritime industry shall as a national policy provide continuous and regular employment to regular seafarers.

No. 146. The 1976 *Seafarers Annual Leave with Pay Convention* came into force also on June 13, 1979. It lays down that seafarers shall be entitled to annual leave with pay of a specified minimum length (of not less than 30 calendar days for one year of service). It revises Convention No. 91.

No. 147. The 1976 *Merchant Shipping (Minimum Standards) Convention* came into force on Nov. 28, 1981. Under this convention a ratifying member state shall have laws and regulations for ships registered in its territory on safety standards, appropriate social security measures, shipboard employment and shipboard living conditions. The convention was open to ratification by member states parties to the International Conventions for the Safety of Life at Sea (SOLAS) of 1960 and 1974 [see pages 19 & 22], the International Convention on Load Lines of 1966 and regulations and conventions on preventing collisions at sea (notably the 1972 convention) or any revisions of such conventions.

Ratifications of ILO Conventions

As at Jan. 1, 1985, the major seafaring nations had ratified the above ILO maritime conventions as shown in the following tabulation:

Brazil 16, 22, 53, 58, 91, 92, 108, 109
China 7, 15, 16, 22, 23
Denmark 7, 8, 9, 15, 16, 53, 58, 73, 92, 108, 134, 147
France 8, 9, 15, 16, 22, 23, 53, 55, 56, 58, 68, 69, 70, 71, 73, 74, 91, 92, 108, 109, 133, 134, 145, 146, 147
West Germany...8, 9, 16, 22, 23, 56, 73, 92, 133, 134, 147
Greece 7, 8, 9, 15, 16, 23, 55, 58, 68, 69, 73, 108, 134, 147
India 15, 16, 22

Italy	7, 8, 9, 15, 16, 22, 23, 53, 55, 58, 68, 69, 71, 73, 74, 91, 92, 108, 109, 133, 134, 145, 146, 147
Japan	7, 8, 9, 15, 16, 22, 58, 70, 73, 134, 147
Liberia	22, 23, 53, 55, 58, 92, 108, 133, 147
Netherlands	8, 9, 16, 22, 23, 68, 69, 70, 71, 73, 74, 91, 92, 133, 145, 146, 147
Norway	7, 8, 9, 15, 16, 22, 53, 56, 58, 68, 69, 71, 73, 91, 92, 108, 109, 133, 134, 145, 147
Panama	8, 9, 15, 16, 22, 23, 53, 55, 56, 58, 68, 69, 71, 73, 74, 92, 108
Singapore	7, 8, 15, 16, 22
Soviet Union	15, 16, 23, 58, 69, 73, 92, 108
Spain	8, 9, 16, 22, 23, 53, 55, 56, 68, 69, 70, 73, 74, 91, 92, 108, 109, 134, 145, 146, 147
Sweden	7, 8, 9, 15, 16, 58, 73, 92, 108, 133, 134, 145, 146, 147
United Kingdom	7, 8, 15, 16, 22, 56, 68, 69, 70, 74, 92, 108, 133, 147
United States	53, 55, 58, 74

Other ILO Activities

The ILO has co-operated with other international organizations in maritime matters. A joint committee of the ILO and the World Health Organization on the health of seafarers, created in 1949, has made numerous recommendations and has been responsible for the publication of an *International Medical Guide for Ships*, which has been amended from time to time. It has also been active in co-ordinating existing forms of medical assistance to ships at sea (the ship's medical guide, its medicine chest and the means of obtaining medical aid by radio). A further *Medical Guide for Use in Accidents involving Dangerous Goods* was published in 1973, to be used in conjunction with the International Maritime Dangerous Goods Code of the IMO [see page 24] and the above *Medical Guide for Ships*.

At an ILO seminar held in Bangkok on Sept. 23–30, 1983, and attended by representatives of 15 Asian governments as well as three each respectively representing shipowners and seafarers, E. M. J. Corten, Economic Affairs Officer of the division of shipping, ports and inland waterways of the (UN) Economic and Social Commission for Asia and the Pacific (ESCAP), pointed out that in the past decade the fleets of developing countries had doubled in capacity and that the average ship size had in gross tonnage increased by 30 per cent (against only 12 per cent in countries outside the ESCAP area). He acknowledged co-operation with ESCAP by the IMO and the South Pacific Bureau for Economic Co-operation in developing uniform maritime standards for the Pacific area and disclosed that ESCAP had developed a unified scheme for the economic statistics of shipping (relating to goods transported to the instrument of transport).

International Maritime Satellite Organization (INMARSAT)

Address. 40 Melton St., London NW1 2EQ, UK.

Officers. E. J. Martin (USA, ch. of council); O. Lundberg (Sweden, dir.-gen.).

Founded. July 1979.

Membership. Ministries and organizations in 37 countries—Algeria, Argentina, Australia, Belgium, Brazil, Bulgaria, Canada, Chile, China, Denmark, Egypt, Finland, France, the Federal Republic of Germany, Greece, India, Iraq, Italy, Japan, Kuwait,

Liberia, the Netherlands, New Zealand, Norway, Oman, the Philippines, Poland, Portugal, Singapore, the Soviet Union, Spain, Sri Lanka, Sweden, Tunisia, the United Arab Emirates, the United Kingdom and the United States.

Objectives. Under a Convention on an International Satellite Organization signed in London by representatives of 42 states on Sept. 3, 1976, and in force since July 16, 1979, the purposes of INMARSAT are "to make provision for the space segment necessary for improving maritime communications, thereby assisting in improving distress and safety-of-life-at-sea communications, efficiency and management of ships, maritime public correspondence services and radio determination capabilities".

Activities. On March 1, 1980, a British maritime communications satellite project known as *Marots* was brought under INMARSAT's programme, and on May 1, 1982, a British-built satellite (*Marces-A*), weighing 1,014 kg and designed for transatlantic communications, was brought into service; it was part of the payload of the European Space Agency's *Ariane* rocket L 04 launched on Dec. 19, 1981. By October 1983 INMARSAT operated via three geostationary satellites (above the Atlantic, Indian and Pacific Oceans) with seven coast earth stations and six others under construction, as well as an NCS network co-ordination station in the United States. It provided services to over 1,600 ships from 47 different countries and was directed by both US and Soviet officials.

The principal shareholders of INMARSAT were then the (US) Communications Satellite Corporation (23.3 per cent), the (Soviet) Morsviazsputnik (14 per cent), British Telecom (9.8 per cent) and Norwegian Telecom (7.87 per cent).

Structure. INMARSAT has an Assembly (which meets every two years and in which each member has one vote), a Council (meeting every three months) and a directorate.

Publications. *Ocean Voice* (quarterly).

United Nations Conference on Trade and Development (UNCTAD)

Address. Palais des Nations, CH-1211 Geneva 10, Switzerland.

Founded. 1964.

Objective. To accelerate the economic development of the developing countries.

Structure. The Conference, which meets every four years, has as its executive organ a Trade and Development Board which has six main committees, among them a committee on shipping. There is also a working group on international shipping legislation (of 98 nations).

UNCTAD Activities relating to Shipping

CODE OF CONDUCT FOR LINER CONFERENCES

Designed to regulate the activities and practices of (mainly Western) shipping companies grouped within "liner conferences", this code was adopted by UNCTAD on April 6, 1974. Its fundamental objectives were (i) to facilitate the orderly expansion of world seaborne trade; (ii) to stimulate the development of regular and efficient liner services adequate to the requirements of the trade concerned;

(iii) to ensure a balance of interests between suppliers and users of liner services.

The code has laid down three basic principles: (i) conference practices should not involve any discrimination against the shipowners, shippers, or foreign trade of any country; (ii) conferences should hold meaningful consultations with shippers' organizations, shippers' representatives and shippers on matters of common interest with (upon request) the participation of appropriate authorities; and (iii) conferences should make available to interested parties pertinent information relevant to those parties and should also publish pertinent information on their activities.

The code also established machinery for a system of settling disputes on the basis of conciliation, and it further provided that (i) the shipping lines of countries at each end of a trading route should have equal rights to participate in the conference traffic between them and (ii) cross-trading countries operating between ports beyond their home base should take a significant part, defined as being around 20 per cent of the traffic in each trade (the major cross-traders being Britain and the Nordic countries). The code has therefore been called the 40-40-20 formula, under which lines of importing countries would theoretically have 40 per cent of the shipping conference business (while non-conference or outsider lines would not be affected); those of exporting countries would have 40 per cent, and cross-traders the rest on each route.

In practice the share-out would never be so precise. The code was not expected to apply to shipping between developed countries (accounting for some 75 per cent of conference line traffic). The member states of the European Community had by 1983 proposed a modification to the code, under which (while 40 per cent of conference trade with a developing country would be reserved for that country's lines) the balance would be open to normal competition among lines of member states of the Organization for Economic Co-operation and Development (OECD), i.e. the developed countries.

The United States has opposed both the original code and the modifications proposed by the European Community on the grounds that the code is protectionist and countries should rely more on free trade, though with some bilateral agreements. (About 10 per cent of US liner trade is categorized as aid shipments reserved to domestic lines under national shipping laws, thus keeping out other countries.) Among developing states only Indonesia and the Republic of Korea had by 1983 been able to obtain 40 per cent of the relevant trade.

To enter into force the code required ratification by a minimum of 24 countries representing 25 per cent of total world tonnage. After being ratified by 58 countries (most of them developing countries with small merchant navies, but including also the Federal Republic of Germany and the Netherlands) accounting for 20,842,921 gross registered tons, or 28.67 per cent of the relevant world tonnage, the code came into force on Oct. 6, 1983, but it has not been ratified or acceded to by a number of developed market-economy states, notably Japan and some members of the European Community. It was to be reviewed five years after entering into force and to be amended where appropriate.

CARGO SHARING AND RESERVATION OF BULK CARGOES

At the fifth UNCTAD session held in Manila in 1979 the majority of delegations adopted Resolution 120 (V) on cargo sharing and the reservation of bulk cargoes for developing countries, incorporating the essence of proposals made by developing countries. The developed countries firmly opposed the resolution on the grounds that its implementation would increase costs and thus work against both shipping and trade interests of all countries. The socialist countries of Eastern Europe abstained from voting on the resolution. (In 1980 about 70 per cent of the world's total shipping tonnage of 406,000,000 gross tons was employed in bulk shipping, but only 7 per cent of this was owned by developing countries.)

FINANCE FOR MERCHANT FLEETS OF DEVELOPING COUNTRIES

At the same Manila session a resolution was passed by 91 votes to none (with 23 abstentions of developed market-economy countries) proposing ways to help developing countries to finance merchant fleets and calling for technical assistance to be extended to them.

INTERNATIONAL MULTIMODAL TRANSPORT OF GOODS

In May 1980 UNCTAD adopted a UN *Convention on International Multimodal Transport of Goods* which established a single liability regime for the carrying of goods involving more than one mode of transport.

FLAGS OF CONVENIENCE SHIPPING

At a special UNCTAD session held in Geneva from May 27 to June 6, 1981, it was resolved by 49 votes to 18 that "flags of convenience" ship registries should "be gradually transformed into normal registries by a process of tightening the conditions under which open registry countries retain or accept vessels on their registers". The resolution was opposed by 16 industrialized market-economy countries and also by Israel and Liberia.

A further conference was held in Geneva under UNCTAD auspices in three parts—on July 16–Aug. 3, 1984, on Jan. 28–Feb. 16, 1985, and on July 8–19, 1985. During the first two parts of the conference some progress was made on the overall framework of an international agreement on ship registration. However, these sessions failed to resolve important differences between developed and developing countries on the extent to which a new international instrument should lay down conditions relating to the ownership, management and manning of vessels.

Developing countries had long been pressing within the UNCTAD framework for action on flags of convenience as part of their efforts to obtain a greater share of world shipping. According to UNCTAD sources on the eve of the Geneva conference, ownership of the world fleet was concentrated in the hands of the traditional maritime countries (all of them developed), which in effect controlled about 80 per cent of world shipping capacity (including tonnage registered in open registry states but beneficially owned by nationals of developed countries). On the other hand, developing countries, despite generating some 60 per cent of world exports and about 40 per cent of world trade, owned only 15 per cent of world shipping tonnage.

Desire for greater profitability motivated shipowners to make use of the small number of countries offering open registration facilities and the right to fly their flag in return for payment of (relatively small) fees but without requiring that their nationals be involved in the ownership or operation of the vessels. Among developing countries (most of which did not permit open registries) this practice was seen as tending to divert investment in shipping away from those countries which insisted on a genuine economic link between themselves and ships of their national registers. In seeking to establish such a link as an internationally endorsed requirement, they cited the 1958 UN Convention on the High Seas and the 1982 UN Law of the Sea Convention, both of which stipulated that "there must be a genuine link" between a ship and the state in which it was registered.

According to UNCTAD sources, flag-of-convenience shipping constituted approximately one-third of the world's merchant fleet by early 1985. The principal open-registry countries were Liberia with 135,200,000 deadweight tons (dwt) in mid-1983, Panama (58,400,000 dwt), Cyprus

(6,100,000 dwt), Bermuda (1,300,000 dwt) and the Bahamas (1,000,000 dwt). (Singapore ceased operating an open registry in 1981.)

In the course of over seven years of preparatory negotiations within the UNCTAD framework, the developed countries had for the most part resisted moves to draw up international regulations relating to ship registration, as had the open registry states themselves. Of the latter, Liberia and Panama had refused to participate in early preparatory meetings on the subject, as had the United States (the main location of beneficial ownership of open-registry tonnage). However, from November 1983 all three countries became actively involved in the negotiations in an attempt to ensure that any international agreement would not be damaging to their interests.

A draft agreement endorsed by consensus at the third session of the conference in July 1985 represented a compromise between the developing countries and the major shipowning nations on the three central and most controversial issues at stake. These were (i) the extent of the registering state's participation in ownership; (ii) the role of flag countries in the management of ship-owning companies and vessels; and (iii) the manning of vessels.

On the ownership question, the draft agreement specified that a flag state should provide in its laws and regulations for the ownership of ships flying its flag and that these should include "appropriate provision for participation by its nationals as owners of the ships flying its flag and for the level of such participation". These provisions "should be sufficient to permit the flag state to exercise effectively its jurisdiction and control over the ships flying its flag".

As regards involvement in management, the principle was enunciated that before entering a ship on its register a state of registration should ensure that the ship-owning company or its subsidiary was established and had its principal place of business within its territory "in accordance with its laws and regulations". Where this was not the case, the flag state should ensure that there was "a representative or management person who shall be a national of the flag state or be domiciled therein" and who "should be available for any legal process and to meet the shipowner's responsibilities". It was further stipulated that the state of registration should ensure that the persons accountable for the management and operation of a ship flying its flag "are in a position to meet the financial obligations that may arise from the operation of such ships".

The key passage of the agreement's section on manning stated that "a satisfactory part of the complement . . . of officers and crew of merchant ships flying the flag of a state of registration [should] be nationals of, or persons domiciled or lawfully in permanent residence in, the state of registration"; at the same time, the flag state could have regard to various factors, including "the availability of qualified seafarers within the state of registration, multilateral or bilateral agreements or other arrangements of any nature valid and enforceable pursuant to the legislation of the state of registration, and sound and economically viable operation of its ships". The agreement also stipulated that the manning of ships should be of such a level and competence as to ensure compliance with international rules and standards, in particular with regard to safety at sea, and that the terms and conditions of employment on board should conform to applicable international conventions.

The Geneva session further agreed that the draft document should be referred to a fourth part of the conference to be held early in 1986, when it would be decided whether it should have the status of an international convention or treaty binding on acceding states, as desired by the developing countries, or whether it should be issued simply as a recommendatory instrument, as desired by the developed countries. [See also section on "Open Registry" or "Flags of Convenience Shipping" on pages 44–45.]

PROPOSALS TO COMBAT FRAUDULENT PRACTICES

A meeting convened by UNCTAD's committee on shipping and held on

Feb. 6-17, 1984, considered a report on fraudulent practices in normal commercial transactions. This report dealt not only with various types of theft and fraud (including fraud concerning hull and cargo insurance by the scuttling or intentional sinking of an over-insured vessel) but also with outright piracy (which had been increasing in recent years). Losses as a result of fraud and piracy were than estimated at US$1,000 million a year (in *Business Week*).

The report's recommendations included proposals for a reform of the banking rules applied to letters of credit, for new methods of transferring title to goods being transported under bills of lading, for improved reporting arrangements which would lead to better identifiability and accountability of shipowners and operators, and for extraditing powers for governmental authorities over perpetrators of maritime fraud and acts of piracy.

International Telecommunication Union (ITU)

Address. Palais des Nations, CH-1211 Geneva 20, Switzerland.

Officer. Richard E. Butler (Australia, s.g.).

Founded. January 1934 (in succession to an International Telegraph Union established in 1865).

Activities. Among the ITU's various bodies is its World Administrative Radio Conference which from 1979 onwards undertook a complete revision of the world's allocations of radio frequencies which was to take effect from Jan. 1, 1982, and to govern the planning and operation of radio communication services, including radio navigation and satellites.

In 1983 the ITU discussed the development of a Future Global Maritime Distress and Safety System (FGMDSS).

On May 17, 1984 (World Communication Day), the ITU noted, on the subject of "expanding horizons", that, although fibre optics provided higher capacity and less expensive channels, satellites would always give better service to ships, aircraft and rural communities. [On satellites see also entry for International Maritime Satellite Organization (INMARSAT) on pages 29–30.]

Status. The ITU is a specialized agency of the United Nations.

United Nations High Commissioner for Refugees (UNHCR)

Address. Palais des Nations, 1211 Geneva 10, Switzerland.

Officer. Poul Hartling (Denmark, high commissioner).

Founded. 1951.

Activities. In October 1979 the Executive Committee of the High Commissioner's Programme endorsed recommendations made by a Sub-Committee of the Whole on International Protection relating to the obligation of coastal states to grant asylum to persons on board vessels in distress. These recommendations contained the following general principles:

(i) States should use their best endeavours to grant asylum to bona fide asylum seekers; (ii) action whereby a refugee is obliged to return or is sent to a country where he has reason to fear persecution constitutes a grave violation of the recognized principle of non-refoulement; (iii) it is the humanitarian obligation of all coastal states to allow vessels in distress to seek haven in their waters and to grant asylum, or at least temporary refuge, to persons on board wishing to seek asylum.

It was also recommended that countries receiving massive influxes of asylum seekers should be given immediate assistance by other states, and that with respect to individual asylum seekers efforts should be made to identify the country responsible for examining an asylum request by the adoption of common criteria (which should be such as to avoid possible disagreement between states), with the asylum seeker's choice of country of asylum being taken into account as far as possible.

UNHCR Guidelines on Disembarkation of Vietnamese Refugees

While it is normal practice (though unwritten law) that refugees picked up at sea are taken to the flag state of the ship which receives them, UNHCR *Guidelines regarding Disembarkation of Vietnamese Refugees rescued at Sea* lay down procedures as follows:

(1) A vessel which picks up refugees at sea will normally proceed to its first scheduled port of call, informing the ship's agent by radio of the number of refugees on board and the circumstances of their rescue.

(2) The agent in turn informs (i) the port and immigration authorities, requesting permission for the ship to enter the harbour, and (ii) the local UNHCR office and the embassy of the country whose flag the ship is flying.

(3) If the embassy is of a country in a position to resettle refugees, it will inform the local authorities of its government's willingness to accept them, normally within 90 days of their disembarkation.

(4) The UNHCR office informs the local authorities of its willingness to cover care and maintenance expenses while the refugees are in port.

(5) If the vessel flies a flag of convenience or of a country which is not normally expected to accept refugees for resettlement, the UNHCR will contact a country which has contributed to a Disembarkation Resettlement Offers (DISERO) pool to provide a resettlement guarantee.

(6) In the case of large numbers of refugees it may be necessary for the UNHCR to contact several countries to provide such guarantees.

(7) Once the guarantees have been conveyed to the local authorities in writing, immigration and UNHCR officials will board the vessel to interview the refugees, who will be allowed to leave the vessel once the interviews are completed.

(8) Thereafter they will be examined by the local health authorities and given medical aid as necessary.

(9) UNHCR officials will then interview each refugee family to obtain all relevant biographical details and to ascertain whether the family has relatives in, or close links with, another country, and where such links exist the UNHCR officials will apply to the embassy of the country concerned for the family's resettlement.

(10) Reimbursement will on request be made to shipowners by the UNHCR for costs related to the care of the refugees rescued at sea (not exceeding $5 per refugee) and also for costs incurred in connection with disembarkation, transport, immigration formalities, inoculation etc. (not to exceed $5,000)—but not where claims are recovered from any insurance carried by the ship or from any Protection and Indemnity (P & I) Club of which the shipowner may be a member.

United Nations Industrial Development Organization (UNIDO)

Address. P.O. Box 300, A-1400, Vienna, Austria.

Officers. Standwell Mapara (Zambia, pres.); George Patterson (USA, sec. of Industrial Development Board); Dr Abderrahman Khane (Algeria, exec. dir.).

Founded. 1967.

Activities. The main contribution of UNIDO to industrial development at sea has been in the field of ship and boat building, repair and maintenance in developing countries wishing to build up national fleets for political, economic and social reasons.

At the second general conference of UNIDO in Lima (Peru) in March 1975, a call was made for the "creation of national, regional and international inter-regional enterprises in the field of maritime transport". The third UNIDO conference, held in New Delhi in 1980, envisaged special measures for the least developed countries and island developing countries for creating and expanding their transportation services. UNIDO has provided advice on development programmes for shipbuilding industries and repair facilities.

Structure. UNIDO has an elected 45-member Industrial Development Board (which meets annually), a permanent Committee (which meets twice a year), a secretariat, numerous national committees and a network of senior field advisers. It is an executive agency of the UN Development Programme (UNDP).

Publications. *UNIDO Newsletter* (monthly); *Guide to Information Sources* (about six times a year); and others.

International Hydrographic Organization (IHO)

Address. Directing Committee, International Hydrographic Bureau (Secretariat of IHO), Ave. Président J. F. Kennedy (B.P.345), Monte Carlo, MC 98000, Monaco.

Directing Committee. Rear Adml. F. L. Fraser (India, pres.); Vice-Adml. O. A. A. Afonso (Brazil) and Capt. J. E. Ayres (USA) (directors).

Founded. June 1921 as the International Hydrographic Bureau, which name it changed to IHO in 1967 (while retaining its former name for its headquarters in Monaco).

Membership. 52 countries (Argentina, Australia, Belgium, Brazil, Canada, Chile, China, Cuba, Denmark, the Dominican Republic, Ecuador, Egypt, Fiji, Finland, France, the Federal Republic of Germany, Greece, Guatemala, Iceland, India, Indonesia, Iran, Italy, Japan, the Republic of Korea, Malaysia, Monaco, the Netherlands, New Zealand, Nigeria, Norway, Pakistan, Peru, the Philippines, Poland, Portugal, Singapore, South Africa, the Soviet Union, Spain, Sri Lanka, Sweden, Syria, Thailand, Trinidad and Tobago, Turkey, the United Kingdom, the United States, Uruguay, Venezuela, Yugoslavia and Zaïre); membership pending for three others (the German Democratic Republic, Papua New Guinea and Suriname).

Objectives. The IHO defines hydrography as the science of measuring and depicting those parameters necessary to describe the precise nature and configuration of the sea-bed, its geographic relation to the landmass, and the characteristics and dynamics of the sea (bathymetry, tides, currents, waves, physical properties of seawater, geology and geophysics).

The IHO's main objects are to bring about (i) the co-ordination of the activities of national hydrographic offices, (ii) the greatest possible uniformity in nautical charts and documents, (iii) the adoption of reliable and efficient methods of carrying out and exploiting hydrographic surveys and (iv) the development of the sciences in the field of hydrography and the techniques employed in descriptive oceanography.

The primary use of the data collected is to complete marine charts and other documents to facilitate and ensure safety of navigation and to assist all concerned with the marine environment, in particular in the planning of exploration and exploitation of marine resources, the determination of seaward limits of national jurisdiction and the delimitation of maritime boundaries. (The establishment of worldwide 200 nautical miles wide exclusive economic zones was expected to necessitate the production of special large-scale charts for these new zones.)

Activities. At the 12th international hydrographic conference held in April 1982 new IHO chart specifications were adopted with a view to producing a worldwide chart series (INT Charts).

The IHO has also published a World Series of Bathymetric Plotting Sheets to collect bathymetric data on a global basis (obtained by 18 member states on a voluntary basis). This has been used to prepare a General Bathymetric Chart of the Oceans (GEBCO) of 18 sheets, with its fifth edition having been completed in 1982.

A worldwide navigational warning service has been established in co-operation with the International Maritime Organization (IMO), and a complementary automated coastal warning service (NAVTEX) using a single frequency worldwide was subsequently developed; it began operations in the North and Baltic Seas in 1983.

On the basis of a joint study by the IHO and the Fédération Internationale des Géomètres (FIG) a comprehensive set of standards of competence has been drawn up for hydrographic surveyors, together with appropriate syllabi.

A computerized Tidal Constituent Data Bank (operated by Canada) supplies data on request for over 4,000 tidal stations.

The IHO has also assisted in the formation of regional hydrographic commissions or groups (for Scandinavia, the North Sea, the Mediterranean and Black Seas, East Asia, the Great Lakes and US-Canadian waters).

Publications. *International Hydrographic Review* (twice a year); *International Hydrographic Bulletin* (monthly); *IHO Yearbook*; *Reports of Proceedings of IH Conferences*; *Chart Specifications of the IHO*; *Standards of Competence for Hydrographic Surveyors*; special publications on technical subjects (in English and French), e.g. *Accuracy Standards for Hydrographic Surveys* (SP 44), *Hydrographic Dictionary* (SP 32); information papers, technical reprints, etc.; *General Bathymetric Chart of the Oceans* (GEBCO) in 18 sheets.

Affiliations. Representatives of the IHB attend meetings of IMO, the Intergovernmental Oceanographic Commission of UNESCO (IOC), the International Association of Lighthouse Authorities (IALA) and the Fédération Internationale des Géomètres (FIG).

World Meteorological Organization (WMO)

Address. Case postale 5, CH-1211, Geneva 20, Switzerland.

Officers. Prof. A. C. Wiin-Nielsen (Denmark, s.g.); K. P. Vasiliev (USSR, pres. of Commission for Marine Meteorology).

Founded. April 1951.

Membership. 157 UN member states.

Objectives. To facilitate worldwide co-operation in establishing networks of stations for meteorological observations; to promote the rapid exchange of weather information; to promote the standardization of meteorological observations and ensure the uniform publication of statistics; to further the application of meteorology to aviation, shipping, agriculture and other activities; and to encourage research and training in meteorology, and to co-ordinate the international aspect of such training.

Activities. The WMO has launched a World Weather Programme involving a global observing system under which information is received from thousands of sources, including some 7,000 ships; a global data processing system; and a global telecommunications system for which services are maintained by member countries on a voluntary basis in areas outside national jurisdiction, including ocean areas and Antarctica.

The WMO's Commission for Marine Meteorology supervises services to ocean activities, i.e. international arrangements for the provision of marine meteorological and related geophysical information (including that on sea ice and waves) to shipping, fishing and other marine activities. Marine climatological information is also prepared internationally for various applications. In these fields there is close co-operation in joint programmes with the Intergovernmental Oceanographic Commission (IOC) of UNESCO.

A Tropical Cyclone Programme has been launched by the WMO in response to a UN General Assembly resolution of 1970 to develop national and regionally co-ordinated systems designed to reduce to a minimum the loss of life and the damage caused by tropical cyclones. There are four regional tropical cyclone bodies [see also entry for ESCAP Division for Shipping Ports and Inland Waterways, page 81].

Status. The WMO is a specialized agency of the United Nations.

International Maritime Committee (IMC)

Address. 17 Borzestraat, B-2000 Antwerp, Belgium.

Officers. Henry Voet-Génicot (admin. s.g.); Prof. Jan Ramberg (Sweden, s.g. of exec.)

Founded. 1897.

Membership. National associations of maritime law in 41 countries (including Argentina, Australia, Belgium, Brazil, Bulgaria, Canada, Chile, Colombia, Denmark, Finland, France, the German Democratic Republic, the Federal Republic of Germany, Greece, India, Ireland, Israel, Italy, Japan, Mexico, the Netherlands, New Zealand, Nigeria, Norway, Peru, Poland, Portugal, the Soviet Union, Spain, Sweden, Switzerland, the United Kingdom, the United States, Venezuela and Yugoslavia).

Objectives. To contribute by all appropriate means and activities to the unification of maritime and commercial law as well as maritime customs usages and practices; to promote the establishment of national associations of maritime law; and to co-operate with other international organizations having the same object.

Structure. The Committee has an assembly as well as executive and administrative councils.

Publications. *CMI Newsletter* (quarterly); *Yearbook/Annuaire.*

Affiliations. Consultative status with IMO, UNCTAD and UNCITRAL (the UN arbitration service).

Conference of the Peripheral Maritime Regions of the European Community

Address. 35 Bd. Liberté, F-35000 Rennes, France.

Founded. 1973.

Membership. Delegates representing member regions (12 in the British Isles, one in Denmark, four in France, two in the Federal Republic of Germany, five in Greece, five in Ireland and eight in Italy) and associate member regions (six in Portugal and four in Spain). Other regions (two in the British Isles, two in the Federal Republic of Germany, three in Greece, one in Italy, one in Portugal and two in Spain) send observers to conference meetings.

Objectives. To give regions "an active part to play in the building of Europe" by bringing together "people who are the most distant and often the most isolated from the continent", by preparing "a strategy of redressing the balance between the industrialized centre of Europe and the generally less developed periphery", by protecting and improving the regional potentialities linked to the sea and the coast; to promote "indigenous renewal" based on common study and the exchange of information, ideas and experience, particularly at youth level; and to co-operate with the European institutions and organizations concerned.

Activities. A European Coastal Charter was decided upon by the Conference in 1978, adopted in 1981 and approved by the European Parliament on June 18, 1982. It provided inter alia for the development of the coastal economy, protection and management of coastal space and the development of coastal research, as well as for a 15-point programme of action for 1982-85, including the promotion of indigenous activities (e.g. in fishing) and actions for island regions carried out by a special commission.

Structure. The Conference meets at least once a year and elects 10 to 15 executive delegates who form an executive council which meets at least twice a year. It has an administrative section and a secretary-general.

Affiliations. The Conference is one of five organizations representing regional and local authorities at the European Community. It has consultative status with the Council of Europe.

South Pacific Bureau for Economic Co-operation (SPEC)

Address. P.O. Box 856, Suva, Fiji.

Officers. Mahe 'Uli'uli Tupouniua (dir.); Trevor H. B. Sofield (dep. dir.).

Founded. September 1972 (by the South Pacific Forum).

Membership. Australia, the Cook Islands, Fiji, Kiribati, the Federated States of Micronesia, Nauru, New Zealand, Niue, Papua New Guinea, the Solomon Islands, Tonga, Tuvalu, Vanuatu and Western Samoa.

Objectives. To promote regional co-operation in the development of the island status of the South Pacific in close partnership with Australia and New Zealand.

Activities. In the field of regional transport a Regional Shipping Council was established in 1974, and the Pacific Forum Line in 1977; in this context the SPEC has been involved in wage rates and working conditions for island seamen and in uniform standards for the region. With the evolution of the Conference on the Law of the Sea and the concept of the 200-mile exclusive economic zone, there was increased realization of the importance of marine resources, and especially fisheries in the South Pacific. [For South Pacific Forum Fisheries Agency, see page 000.] The SPEC has also participated in a South Pacific Regional Environment Programme (with the South Pacific Commission, the UNDP and ESCAP), aimed at a co-ordinated regional approach to the development and proper management of the region's environment and resources.

3. Shipping: International Agreements and Organizations

This chapter covers (i) various general aspects of the prevailing international shipping scene; (ii) world and regional shipping statistics, including total tonnage and number of ships as well as shipbuilding trends; (iii) the main canals and seaways used by ships; and (iv) international organizations and institutions, both world and regional, concerned with shipping and shipbuilding.

The World Shipping Scene: Background

The Shipping Industry

The shipping industry is perhaps more international than any other industry, as any one ship may involve members of different nations—in its ownership, registration, builder, supplier of engines, officers and crew, financing, insurance and chartering.

The industry is still responsible for between 75 and 80 per cent of the transport of world trade, although since 1970 it has been in decline in Western countries. By 1983 its tonnage was about 40 per cent in excess of requirements, and freight rates had fallen to their lowest level for 13 years.

There has always been a tendency towards protectionism in the shipping industry—as illustrated by Cromwell's Navigation Act of 1651 reserving certain English seaborne trades to English ships (as a protection against the Dutch) and the US Jones Act of 1919 reserving US coastwise trades to US-built and US-manned vessels. This trend has in recent years been continued by the "Group of 77" developing countries at UNCTAD [see pages 30–34].

According to H. H. Sparsø, outgoing president of the Committee of Shipowners' Associations of the European Communities (*Comité des Associations d'Armateurs des Communautés Européennes*, CAACE), writing in a foreword to this organization's annual report for 1983, protectionism "inhibits the competitive drive and poses a threat to the development of efficiency with negative effects on world trade"; "artifical restraints are generally counter-productive when the objectives rightly are economies of scale, expansion of trade, price stability and innovation"; "many of the transport systems, as for instance containerization, which have developed over the years, are unlikely to undergo fundamental changes as far as the systems go"; to achieve improved efficiency he sees "a need for the attainment of economies of scale without loss of the practical advantages inherent in the small entity" and "labour's acceptance of new technology and of the use on board ships of labour in a far more flexible manner".

The Question of Jurisdiction over Ships

While there is no clear definition in law what a ship's nationality is, it is generally accepted that ships have the nationality of the state whose flag they fly. It is further accepted that the ship's name and port of registry must be displayed on the ship, and it is common practice to fly the national flag when in foreign waters. For the purposes of conventions, such as those of the International Labour Organization [see pages 26–29], ships are treated as belonging to the country of registration.

The 1952 *International Convention for the Unification of Certain Rules relating to Penal Jurisdiction in Matters of Collisions or Other Incidents of Navigation* lays down that criminal or disciplinary proceedings arising out of collisions or other incidents of navigation may be instituted only in the ship's flag state, which has the sole right to order the arrest or detention of the ship. This, however, does not apply to collisions or other incidents in ports or inland waters, and the parties may reserve the right to institute proceedings in respect of offences committed within their own territorial waters. (This question is also dealt with in Article 11 of the 1958 Geneva Convention on the High Seas and in Article 97 of the 1982 UN Convention on the Law of the Sea—see pages 4 and 269 respectively.)

Types of Merchant Ships and Other Surface Craft

Merchant ships consist mainly of two different categories: (i) liners, which provide a regular service between ports and may be members of a liner conference designed to guarantee reasonable stability and a return on investment and resources to replace tonnage when necessary; and (ii) tramps used for major bulk cargoes (oil, coal, iron ore and grain), the movement of which is less regular than that of cargoes of the liner trades. In addition there are specialist ships, such as are used to carry refrigerated goods, or for passengers.

Nautical Definitions and Measures

dwt	= deadweight tonnage, i.e. the measure of the exact weight (in tons of 2,240 lb) of cargo, bunkers, stores, etc. carried by a ship when floating at its load draught; the normal freight unit for bulk carriers and tankers
grt	= gross registered tonnage, a measure of space (100 cubic feet), including spaces above the deck, used as the normal unit for passenger ships and cargo liners
nm	= nautical mile (= 6,080 feet, or 1·15 miles)
1 knot	= speed of 1 nm per hour
1 fathom	= 6 feet (depth)

Cargo Ships

Cargo ships are used either for solid cargoes, carried in bulk or packaged, or for liquid cargoes, also either in bulk or packaged.

Liquid cargoes include liquefied natural gas, liquefied petroleum gas, crude oil, oil products and chemicals.

Crude-oil carriers are either very large crude-oil carriers (VLCC) of more than

320,000 tons and a speed of 16 knots, or combination carriers which can be used both for carrying crude oil and for bulk solid cargoes. All these tankers are subdivided into a number of separate tanks.

Liquefied natural gas is transported in special insulated tanks at its boiling point (−161°C). Liquefied petroleum gas is carried in tanks which can be pressurized.

Tramp ships can carry different cargoes, generally in bulk.

Solid bulk cargo carriers (with a single deck) can vary greatly in size up to 70,000 dwt (which are able to pass through the Panama Canal).

Ore carriers have no cargo-handling equipment and can have a capacity of up to 122,000 tons.

General cargo liners (of up to 12,500 tons capacity) are progressively being replaced by container ships and small bulk carriers.

Barge carriers are (i) lighter aboard ship (LASH) craft with rectangular barges of 370 dwt each and (ii) SEABEES with 38 barges of 370 dwt each. They can reach a speed of 21 knots.

Container Ships, Surface Skimmers and Icebreakers

Roll-on roll-off (RoRo) container ships carry containers of dimensions laid down by the Technical Committee 104 of the International Organization for Containerization.

Containers generally have a cross-section of 8 × 8 ft. and a length of 10, 20 or 40 ft. (The 20-ft. long container has a maximum payload of about $1\frac{1}{2}$ tonnes.) Container ships are generally used to carry up to 1,450 20-ft. containers at a speed of up to 23 knots. (For details of the dimensions and ratings, i.e. the maximum permitted gross weight of containers and contents, see *Jane's Freight Containers*.)

Containers can also be carried on road vehicles and on trailers on board RoRo ships. Specialized RoRo ships are short-sea ferries (for commercial and passenger vehicles) and car carriers (for export vehicles). Containers have also been used to transport goods across land bridges between oceans, e.g. between Halifax, Nova Scotia (on the Atlantic coast) and Vancouver (on the Pacific coast), between New York and Vancouver, and from or to Europe via the Trans-Siberian Railway (with extensions to and from Hong Kong, Japan and South-East Asia.)

Surface skimmers used at sea include hovercraft (air-cushioned vehicles, ACV) used for ferry services, and hydrofoils (or jetfoils).

Surface skimmers are ships which have their hulls raised clear of the water by means of underwater fins with a flat or curved plane surface attached by struts and retractable, which can reach speeds of up to 60 knots, and which are also used in coastal services. (For details of surface skimmers, see *Jane's Surface Skimmers*, 1982, with an extensive bibliography on ACVs etc. on pages 385–91.)

Icebreakers (some of them nuclear-powered and capable of breaking through ice over one metre thick) have been used in the Arctic Sea and the northern Baltic, sometimes in conjunction with ice-breaking multiduty cargo ships, by the Soviet Union (which has been enabled to maintain navigation all the year round between the west and the mouth of the Yenisei river) and also by the United States in the North-West Passage.

Freight Conferences

Freight conferences were originally set up as liner conferences in the 19th century. They are cartels which have set rates, agreed schedules and decided cargo allotments among members and on routes between particular ports.

Members of freight conferences are listed in *Croner's World Directory of Freight Conferences*,* which is updated every month and contains names and addresses of over 400 conferences and their member lines. It also gives the

* Issued by Croner Publications Ltd., Croner House, 173 Kingston Road, New Malden, Surrey KT3 3SS, UK.

text of a Convention on a Code of Conduct for Liner Conferences adopted by the UN Conference on Trade and Development (UNCTAD) on April 7, 1974, and in force since October 6, 1983 [see page 30].

By that time, however, the trade carried by non-conference lines was estimated at between 30 and 50 per cent of all maritime trade (as against between 5 and 10 per cent when the code had been adopted). The United States had rejected the code and adopted a regulatory reform based on non-discrimination between national and foreign lines.

CODE OF PRACTICE FOR CONFERENCES

This Code was prepared by the Council of European and Japanese National Shipowners' Associations (CENSA) and the European Shippers' Councils (ESC) and was endorsed in November 1971 by the governments which were members of the Consultative Shipping Group (CSG). It was intended to set out general principles to be adopted by all liner conferences and similar associations, and it was prepared with due regard to the relevant UNCTAD resolutions unanimously agreed.

The Code defined the purpose of conferences as "to facilitate the provision of efficient, economic and regular liner services adequate to meet the normal requirements of the trade", for which purpose consultation was regarded as fundamental. The Code provided inter alia that "any existing regional agreements between shipowners and shipper organizations are part of this Code in the trade concerned"; that "shipowners seeking membership of conferences should be able and willing to provide the necessary standard of service on a long-term and commercial basis and shall accept the principles of this Code", and that, "if an application for membership leads to a dispute between the applicant and the conference, either party may refer the matter to a separate panel of shipowner conciliators presided over by a shipowner not directly involved in the trade concerned"; that "conference agreements should include a commitment to adhere to this Code"; that full information regarding member lines of conferences and their agreements should be made available to shipper organizations; and that conferences should publish annually full reports on their activities.

Other general rules contained in the Code were: "Conferences, in undertaking to provide adequate services, are entitled to offer and maintain mutually binding contracts and/or fidelity arrangements with shippers"; conferences are "entitled to maintain a structure of fair and commercially viable freight rates" while "requests for temporary tariff concessions on specific commodities are to be considered within the overall requirements of commercial viability of the conference service". The Code further provided that "where all the relevant procedures under the Code (including conciliation) have been fully implemented and a dispute suitable for conciliation still remains unresolved, that dispute shall, on the initiative of either party, be referred to (a) referee(s)".

"Open Registry" or "Flags of Convenience" Shipping

The "open registry" or "flags of convenience" system of shipping first arose as a device to avoid the prohibition laws of the United States (passed between 1846 and 1920), and later it enabled operators to avoid US neutrality laws and generally any association with politically sensitive states (e.g. when some of the Gulf states imposed embargoes on certain flags in 1967 and 1973).

The 1958 UN Convention on the High Seas [see page 4] laid down (in Article 4) that ships have the nationality of their flag state but allowed registering states alone to fix the conditions for granting their nationality and required only that there should be an undefined genuine link between the state and its flag. This meant that the flags of convenience system was codified, as a state could register ships whose owners were not that state's nationals and might have little connection with that state. [For UNCTAD proposals on flags of convenience shipping, see pages 32–33.]

The Organization for Economic Co-operation and Development (OECD) accused flags of convenience operators in 1979 of enabling "the less scrupulous shipowners to operate substandard ships with inadequate or incompetent crews", but the head of the OECD's Transport and Tourism Division stated later that these substandard practices were being effectively overcome by port state control and inspection regardless of the flag.

Flags of convenience shipping has been consistently opposed by the International Transport Workers' Federation (ITF). Early in 1980 the UK House of Lords ruled (in the case of the *Nawala*, a Hong Kong-registered vessel) that industrial action by the ITF as part of its campaign to improve the terms and conditions of employment of seamen on ships flying flags of convenience was in furtherance of a trade dispute under the 1974 (UK) Trade Union and Labour Relations Act to effect a ruling endorsed by the ITF's policy of "blacking" vessels flying flags of convenience, the use of which facilitated the employment of cheap labour (mainly Asian seamen) whose wages, the ITF demanded, should be raised to ITF-approved levels backdated to the day when each crew member was signed on.

At the end of 1979 some 31.5 per cent of world shipping was under flags of convenience. The principal countries operating the flags of convenience system have been Liberia, Panama, Cyprus, the Bahamas and Bermuda; others have been Hong Kong and Singapore. Flags of convenience ships have also been used by member states of the International Whaling Commission in order to avoid that commission's whaling quotas.

Liberia. In December 1980 73.7 per cent of the tonnage under flags of convenience was under Liberia's flag. In 1982 its merchant fleet was the largest in the world, with 81,500,000 gross registered tons (grt) generating annual revenue of about $12,000,000. The country's open registry system was continued under the military government which came to power in April 1980, but the shipping tonnage tax was increased in June 1980 from 10 cents to 30 cents a ton.

Bermuda. By September 1983 Bermuda had the fifth largest flags of convenience register (after the Bahamas) with more than 860,000 grt. (In 1979 it had 2,100,000 grt and in 1982 435,000 grt.) Bermuda differs from the other open registry countries in that it requires that only British officers should man Bermuda-registered ships (whereas the other countries are free to select their crews).

Bermuda is also the seat of numerous protection and indemnity (P & I) clubs—mutual non-profit organizations which insure shipping interests for secondary risks such as strikes. It has been estimated that 60 per cent of the free world's shipping tonnage was insured through P & I clubs with representation in Bermuda.

Hong Kong. Shipowners in Hong Kong control more than 60,000,000 dwt, and most of this tonnage sails under flags of convenience.

Navigation Aids

Traditional navigation aids on board ship include charts, a compass, tide-tables, a sextant and a chronometer, and external aids have been buoys, lightships and lighthouses, with assistance being given by coastguards or pilots. Minimum standards of navigational aids have been laid down in the 1974 SOLAS convention of the IMO [see page 22]. Modern navigation aids include the following:

(1) Radar (radio detection and ranging), which makes possible the detection of the

bearing and distance of an object when it is within radar range; it is effective within from one to 60 nautical miles off land, and from three to 15 nautical miles off buoys and lightships.

(2) Sonar, an echo-sounding system for measuring depths.

(3) Loran (long-range navigation), a hyperbolic system of radio stations forming chains in the North Atlantic and Pacific Oceans with a range of about 200 nautical miles.

(4) The Decca navigator, which has chains of transmitters with a range of up to 250 nautical miles during the day and 100 at night.

(5) The Omega System has stations spaced at thousands of miles.

(6) The TRANSIT satellite navigation system employs five satellites with polar orbits of 108 minutes, from which the position of a ship can be determined at intervals of between half an hour and three hours.

(7) Ship's Inertial Navigation System (SINS), by which the motion of a ship is constantly monitored, with the result that its position in relation to its starting point is always known.

Various other satellite navigational systems are in use as a result of international co-operation.

They include the US NAVSTAR Global Positioning System (GPS), the Soviet GLONNAS system, and the NAVSAT system of the European Space Agency (for civilian use, whereas the US and Soviet systems have been mainly for military use).

A search and rescue satellite system known as SARSAT/COSPAS has been the result of an understanding signed by Canada, France, the Soviet Union and the United States. The first satellite to be launched under this system was *Cosmos 1383* of the Soviet Union (in June 1982).

Among India's first satellites the *Bhaskara*, which went into orbit on June 7, 1979, supplied information obtained from minor experiments on ocean meteorology. The Indian satellites INSAT-1A and INSAT-1B, launched in the United States in April 1982 and July 1983, were to combine to provide inter alia meteorological information.

Patterns and movements of arctic ice have been charted by satellites using sophisticated microwave equipment in a combined Canadian–US exercise. The US Navy satellites *Nimbus 5* (launched in 1972) and *Nimbus 7* (launched in 1978) have measured ice temperatures in the Beaufort Sea, Hudson Bay and Baffin Bay.

However, the many hundreds of satellites launched in recent years have not generally been related to maritime activities (except by supplying weather forecasts and contributing to oceanographic research). As far as communications are concerned, an expert quoted in 1983 expressed the view (in the journal *Electronics and Power* of the Institute of Electrical Engineers in London) that "submarine cables, together with satellites, will remain the prime media for long-distance communication across the seas, firstly because they are there and secondly because they are proven". [See also entry for International Maritime Satellite Organization (INMARSAT) on pages 29–30].

UN Regional Cartographic Conference

A UN Regional Cartographic Conference for Asia and the Pacific, held in Bangkok in January 1985 and attended by 185 representatives and observers from 38 countries, discussed inter alia hydrographic surveying and nautical charting.

Countries possessing or developing precise geodetic positioning methods (e.g. by the global positioning systems using satellite-orientated equipment and enabling the user to determine his position anywhere on earth) were urged to publicize information about such methods. Other recommendations were for the publicizing of completed navigational and regional maps or atlases; for requests to be addressed to the United Nations for help in technical training in the use of remotely sensed data for the development of natural resources; and for the formation of regional groupings to conduct hydrographic programmes.

Natural Hazards at Sea

Natural hazards at sea are caused by waves, wind and frost. Waves are caused by tides, wind or seismic disturbances (e.g. earthquakes). The last-named type of wave, known as *tsunami*, occurs mainly in the Pacific Ocean, travels at extreme speed (some 400 miles per hour), is particularly destructive as it reaches shallow water and may cause severe flooding of coastal areas. There is a *tsunami* warning system based at Honolulu.

Weather forecasts, issued by radio at least once a day, may contain gale warnings. The forecasts are based on observations made at coastal stations or on lightships, weather ships or offshore platforms. (These warnings are important not only for ships but also for the offshore industry.) For the purpose of forecasts the North-East Atlantic and the North Sea are divided into forecast areas known mainly by topographical names.

The most dangerous weather system is that of tropical cyclones, which involve winds of up to force 12 on the Beaufort scale (i.e. 33 metres per second).

Ice warnings in the Arctic and Antarctic are intended to indicate the possible formation of ice on ships.

The weather plays an important part in determining shipping routes. In the North Atlantic, for instance, modern weather routeing on the basis of available information on weather and sea conditions enables ships to use regions where wave gradients are low and travel is cheaper and safer even if the distance covered is greater.

Ports and their Administration

Of the world's major ports most are owned or controlled by central governments or local authorities, while a number are administered by autonomous bodies.

Traditionally ports have consisted of long and narrow piers between berths and warehouses, and cargo has been handled by ships' derricks, cranes on the pier and/or manual labour. Since the 1960s and the advent of containerization and modern cargo handling equipment, including gantries, more space has been required, and docks have become far more extensive than before to enable them to cope with unitized and bulk cargoes.

Under maritime law deep-water ports, i.e. artificial islands, may be part of the coastal state's internal territory or extra-territorial. Under US law such ports beyond US territorial limits have no status of islands and have no territorial sea of their own.

Under a Commonwealth Merchant Shipping Agreement of 1931 every Commonwealth member country has to grant access to its ports to all Commonwealth ships on equal terms and on a basis that they are accorded treatment equivalent to that given to national vessels.

A number of ports are "freeports", i.e. they are or contain duty-free areas outside national customs jurisdiction. In other ports there may be bonded warehouses where imported goods subject to duty may be stored until they are exported or the duty is paid. By 1984 there were some 400 freeports at enclosed areas near seaports or airports around the world. Six freeports designated in the United Kingdom in that year included Liverpool and Southampton.

World's Largest Commodity Ports

In terms of tonnage handled during 1982 the world's largest commodity ports were as follows:

Port	*Million tonnes (approx.)*
Rotterdam (Europoort)	285
New Orleans (USA)	170
New York (USA)	166
Chiba (Japan)	156
Kobe (Japan)	154
Yokohama (Japan)	124
Houston (USA)	106
Marseilles (France)	103
Mina al Ahmadi (Kuwait)	98
Kawasaki (Japan)	94
Singapore	87
Osaka (Japan)	84
Antwerp (Belgium)	81
Le Havre (France)	78
Ameriport (USA)	72
Tubarão (Brazil)	66
Hampton Roads (USA)	63
Hamburg (West Germany)	61
Tokyo (Japan)	59
Nagoya (Japan)	57

World and Regional Shipping Statistics

World Statistics

According to the annual report of the Maritime Transport Committee of the Organization of Economic Co-operation and Development (OECD) issued in October 1984, Western industrialized nations accounted, in 1983, for only 47 per cent of world tonnage of merchant shipping, compared with 67 per cent in 1970 (with the United Kingdom fleet having been reduced by 40 per cent in eight years); the volume of world shipping had, since its peak in 1979, fallen to 84 per cent of that year's level; the Soviet Union was offering cargo shipping rates from 10 to 40 per cent below those of Western shipowners, and the Soviet Union had failed to respect self-limitation agreements concluded in 1982 (while its fleet was growing at an annual rate of 4 per cent); and among developing countries Indonesia, Malaysia, the Philippines and several African states all had rules reserving cargo to vessels carrying the national flag.

At the end of 1983 the principal flag states of merchant shipping were Liberia with over 67,500,000 grt, Japan with 41,100,000 grt, Greece with 37,500,000 grt, Panama with 35,000,000 grt and the Soviet Union with 25,000,000 grt. The United Kingdom had only 21,000,000 deadweight tons (dwt) (769 ships), against 50,000,000 dwt (1,614 ships) in 1975.

At the end of 1984 total idle merchant shipping tonnage stood at 62,350,000 dwt (1,302 ships or some 9 per cent of the world's total merchant fleet). Greece, Liberia, Norway and Panama had between them about 700 ships laid up, including 182 tankers of nearly 36,000,000 dwt. In particular, Greece had 19 per cent of its fleet idle (461 dry cargo and tanker vessels), the United Kingdom about 15 per cent (59 ships with 3,540,000 dwt), and Japan only 1 per cent of its fleet. Of the world's oil tanker fleet some 17 per cent was laid up (42 per cent of the Netherlands tanker fleet, almost 25 per cent of the United Kingdom's tanker fleet, but only 2 per cent of Japan's).

On March 4, 1985, the International Maritime Industries Forum (IMIF) proposed the accelerated scrapping of surplus shipping at a rate of about 50,000,000 tons a year at a cost of between $100,000,000 and $150,000,000.

Statistics of World Merchant Fleet

Total Tonnage and Number of Ships

July 1	*Million dwt (approx.)*	*Number of ships*
1971	369.7	33,188
1975	544.2	34,934
1976	598.4	35,666
1977	637.2	36,208
1978	658.7	36,888
1979	669.0	37,688
1980	677.3	38,401
1981	683.2	37,959
1982	687.2	38,416
1983	678.6	38,419

Composition as at July 1, 1983

General cargo	114.0	21,924
Cellular container	14.6	786
Ore/bulk carrier	171.9	4,737
Combination carrier	49.9	457
Passenger & ferry	2.3	1,245
Other dry cargo	4.9	707
Total dry cargo	357.1	29,856
Oil tanker	306.1	6,882
Chemical tanker	5.4	794
Liquefied gas carrier	9.5	750
Other tanker	0.5	137
Total tanker	321.5	8,563
Total all ships	678.6	38,419

Percentage Distribution according to Average Age, July 1, 1983

Years	*Oil tankers*	*Bulk carriers*	*Others*
0–4	11.86	20.59	19.15
5–9	48.77	29.20	23.98
10–14	23.24	28.97	21.49
15–19	9.23	15.38	14.59
20–24	4.01	4.07	10.39
25–29	1.70	0.58	5.20
30 and over	1.15	1.17	5.16

Based on grt and including non-trading ships

Average age of total fleet: 11.27 years

Tonnage on Order by Type at January 1, 1984

	Million dwt	*Number of ships*
Tankers	9.9	296
Bulk carriers	27.8	673
Others	10.0	842
Total	47.7	1,811

World Laid-up Shipping (in million dwt)

April 1	*1982*	*1983*	*1984*
Dry cargo	7.0	34.8	32.0
Wet cargo	17.2	88.5	75.5

European Communities

The figures given below cover the total tonnage and number of ships of nine member states of the European Communities (EC)—i.e. all except Luxembourg, which has no merchant navy. The fleets of Denmark, Greece, Ireland and the United Kingdom are included from 1971 onwards although these states joined the EC only later.

Strength of EC Countries' Merchant Fleets

July 1	*Tonnage (in million dwt)*	*Number of ships*	*Percentage of world dwt*
1971	111.9	10,623	30.3
1975	154.9	9,639	28.5
1976	165.5	9,621	27.7
1977	168.5	9,443	26.4
1978	177.6	9,648	27.0
1979	177.2	9,539	26.5
1980	178.2	9,467	26.3
1981	179.2	8,975	26.3
1982	169.7	8,505	24.7
1983	155.5	7,971	22.9

Statistics covering the composition of EC merchant fleets, the age distribution of EC vessels, tonnage on order and the EC's share of world trade by sea are given on the following page.

Composition of EC Merchant Fleets as at July 1, 1983

	Tonnage (in million dwt)	*Number of ships*	*Percentage of world dwt*
General cargo	22.5	4,393	19.7
Cellular container	5.2	205	35.6
Ore/Bulk carrier	42.8	1,182	24.9
Combination carrier	12.2	96	24.7
Passenger & ferry	0.8	403	43.4
Other dry cargo	0.5	77	10.2
Total Dry Cargo	84.0	6,356	23.5
Oil tanker	68.1	1,267	22.3
Chemical tanker	0.9	145	16.7
Liquefied gas carrier	2.2	168	23.2
Other tanker	0.2	35	40.0
Total Tanker	71.5	1,615	22.2
Total All Ships	155.5	7,971	22.9

Percentages of Age Distribution of EC Vessels at July 1, 1983

Years	*Oil tankers*	*Bulk carriers*	*Others*
0–4	7.14	14.27	19.10
5–9	49.48	29.93	26.76
10–14	20.43	29.52	24.26
15–19	14.19	18.96	12.46
20–24	5.58	6.22	9.00
25–29	2.56	0.96	4.98
30 and over	0.58	0.10	3.40

Average age of total EC fleet: 11.53 years
Figures based on grt and including non-trading ships

Tonnage on Order by Type at January 1, 1984

Tankers		*Bulk carriers*		*Others*		*Total*	
number	*million dwt*	*number*	*million dwt*	*number*	*million dwt*	*number*	*million dwt*
37	1.6	101	3.6	145	1.6	283	6.8

Of the total number of 283 ships, 153 (of 3.0 million dwt), were on order in EC yards and 130 (of 3.8 million dwt) in non-EC yards.

EC Trade by Sea compared with World Trade

		EC million tons	*World million tons*	*EC percentage*
Loadings	1980	311	3,650	8.5
	1982	352	3,249	10.9
Unloadings	1980	996	3,650	27.3
	1982	879	3,249	27.1

Shipbuilding Statistics

Set out on page 52 are world shipbuilding statistics covering the number of ships completed in 1980–84, broken down by major country.

In 1984 the prices of Asian shipbuilders were at least 30 per cent below those in Europe. Of the West European countries whose tonnages ordered by the end of the year were most affected were Sweden (with orders falling from 10,700,000 grt in 1973 to 500,000 grt in 1983), the United Kingdom (from 7.500,000 grt in 1973 to 600,000 in 1983), West Germany (from 7,300,000 grt in 1973 to 600,000 in 1983), Spain (from 7,200,000 grt in 1973 to 1,200,000 in 1983) and France (from 5,200,000 grt in 1973 to 500,000 in 1983).

Oil Tanker Fleets

The tables on page 53 show (i) the changes in the tonnage of the world's oil tanker fleets by flag states in the period 1974–84; (ii) the world oil tanker fleet by size in 1984; and (iii) the tonnage of the world oil tanker fleet scrapped in the period 1975–84.[1]

According to figures given in the *World Tanker Fleet Review*[2] for January–June 1985, the approximate tonnage of commercial oil tankers was as follows as at June 30, 1985:

Tanker size	*million dwt*
10–24,999 dwt	11.5
25–44,999 dwt	24.8
45–69,999 dwt	18.5
70–124,999 dwt	40.6
125–199,999 dwt	27.7
200–319,999 dwt	96.5
320,000 and over	25.7
Total	245.3

Of this total tonnage, oil companies owned 1,212 tankers accounting for about 96,600,000 dwt, and private owners held 1,582 tankers totalling over 148,700,000 dwt. The figure given for total tonnage scrapped in the first half of 1985 was 13.59 million dwt.

Also at June 30 1985, the principal flag states controlled tonnage of tankers of over 10,000 dwt as follows (in million dwt):

Liberia	66.69	Spain	5.20
Japan	23.89	Denmark	4.29
Greece	18.38*	Singapore	4.06
Panama	15.58	Brazil	3.33
USA	15.37	India	2.84
Norway	14.66	Turkey	2.71
UK	11.99	Fed. Rep. of Germany	2.52
France	7.87	Saudi Arabia	2.51
USSR	6.10	Kuwait	2.19
Cyprus	6.08	China	2.14
Italy	5.95		
Bahamas	5.81		

* Another 16.5 million dwt were said to be controlled by Greek interests.

Among the numerous details given in the above issue of the *World Tanker Fleet Review,* it was pointed out that existing oil pipelines had continued to reduce the need for tanker transportation and that this trend was expected to be enhanced by the construction of new overland pipelines, in particular in the Middle East. A factor operating against increased oil consumption had been the rise in global coal consumption for the generation of electricity, to be met by increased production of coal, inter alia in North America and Australia.

[1] Source: BP Educational Service, P.O. Box 5, Wetherby, West Yorkshire LS23 7EH, United Kingdom.

[2] Published by John I. Jacobs plc, 5 Devonshire Square, London EC2M 4YD.

Ships completed in 1980–84
(thousand grt)

State	*1980*	*1981*	*1982*	*1983*	*1984*
Belgium	131	96	85	153	81
Denmark	268	363	356	397	503
France	302	302	310	376	339
Federal Republic of Germany	618	922	764	926	704
Ireland	—	17	—	18	0
Italy	320	284	177	143	193
Netherlands	240	255	364	381	295
United Kingdom	514	254	421	349	288
EEC subtotal	2,393	2,493	2,477	2,743	2,403
Finland	324	303	439	268	254
Norway	476	492	473	518	201
Portugal	18	47	54	(273)	(25)
Spain	533	485	549	465	406
Sweden	299	414	248	257	227
Subtotal	1,650	1,741	1,763	(1,785)	1,113
Total Europe OECD	4,043	4,234	4,240	(4,526)	3,516
Australia	(30)	10	(13)	(8)	(8)
Canada	175	146	(72)	(60)	(32)
Japan	4,876	5,620	5,283	4,996	6,949
United States	(325)	387	(179)	(341)	(69)
Grand total OECD	(9,449)	(10,397)	(9,787)	(9,931)	10,574
Rest of world	(2,549)	(3,048)	(3,799)	(4,091)	(3,633)
World total	(11,998)	(13,445)	(13,586)	(14,022)	(14,207)

Figures in parentheses are approximate (source: OECD)

Changes in the Tonnage of the World's Oil Tanker Fleets by Flag States, 1974–84
(million dwt)

States	1974	1977	1978	1979	1980	1981	1982	1983	1984	1984 percentages of total
Liberia	73.9	107.5	103.4	102.5	100.3	91.6	84.4	76.4	71.8	26.6
Japan	29.2	29.4	29.3	30.0	30.0	29.7	28.5	26.3	24.9	9.2
Greece	13.9	18.0	18.0	22.0	22.8	27.0	23.7	21.1	19.1	7.1
Norway	23.9	28.7	26.7	24.4	24.0	24.4	21.2	18.9	15.7	5.8
United States	10.4	13.1	14.4	15.7	16.2	16.4	16.8	16.5	15.6	5.8
Panama	8.4	10.1	9.6	11.7	12.2	14.4	15.9	15.0	14.9	5.5
United Kingdom	32.2	28.9	28.4	24.8	24.8	21.3	17.6	15.3	13.3	4.9
France	11.8	14.9	15.1	15.4	15.0	13.2	11.6	10.4	8.9	3.3
Other Western Europe	31.8	41.1	41.3	39.4	37.1	36.6	35.4	34.9	36.5	13.6
Others	13.7	30.8	31.9	32.1	32.2	35.4	39.0	39.1	38.5	14.3
Total Non-Communist World	249.2	322.5	318.1	318.0	314.6	310.0	294.1	273.9	259.2	96.1
Centrally Planned Economies (Communist)	6.6	10.0	10.4	9.9	10.2	10.2	9.6	9.3	10.5	3.9
Total World	255.8	332.5	328.5	327.9	324.8	320.2	303.7	283.2	269.7	100.0

World Oil Tanker Fleet by Size, 1984
(million dwt)

		Percentage of total
10–25,000 dwt	12.8	4.7
25–45,000 dwt	26.3	9.8
45–65,000 dwt	15.7	5.8
65–125,000 dwt	46.2	17.1
125–200,000 dwt	28.9	10.7
200–320,000 dwt	111.6	41.4
320,000 dwt and over	28.2	10.5
Total World	255.8	100.0

World Oil Tanker Fleet, Tonnage Scrapped, 1975–84
(million dwt)

1975	1976	1977	1978	1979	1980	1981	1982	1983	1984
7.7	10.4	7.6	13.6	6.0	7.7	12.0	21.6	23.5	17.6

International Canals and Seaways

Kiel Canal

The Kiel Canal was built in 1887–97, mainly for the military purposes of the Imperial Government of Germany. It shortened the sea route between the Baltic and North Seas by between 190 and 290 nautical miles (depending on the ships' draught and their possible route through the various straits between Denmark and Sweden).

The canal has a length of 53 nautical miles, and ships using it may be up to 40 metres wide and have a draught of up to 9.4 metres. There is a lock system to make the canal independent of fluctuations in the North Sea tides. The average time for a ship's passage through the canal is seven hours, the official speed limit being eight knots. Most of the ships using it are of not more than 1,000 gross registered tons.

Panama Canal

A canal linking the Atlantic and Pacific Oceans via the isthmus of Panama was first designed in 1879 by Ferdinand de Lesseps (who constructed the Suez Canal—see below), but the company formed to carry out the construction of the canal went into liquidation in 1889 before even one-quarter of the work had been completed. The company's rights were acquired by the United States under the Herrán-Hay Treaty of 1903, but this treaty was strongly opposed by the government of Colombia (of which the present-day Republic of Panama was then still a part). Colombia's rejection of the treaty led to the secession of Panama from Colombia and the conclusion of the Canal Treaty of Nov. 8, 1903, under which Panama granted the United States the use in perpetuity of a strip of land five miles wide on both sides of the centre line of the proposed canal, with the United States having exclusive control in this Canal Zone for police, judicial and sanitary purposes. The United States paid Panama $10,000,000 for the Canal Zone rights and, from 1913 onwards, an annuity of $250,000 (increased to $430,000 in 1936).

The independence of Panama was not recognized by Colombia until a 1914 Treaty of Bogotá, which was ratified by the two countries in 1921. Under a further treaty concluded by Panama and the United States on March 2, 1936 (and ratified by the US Senate on July 25, 1936), the United States was empowered, in the event of war, to defend the canal in any way necessary. From 1939 to 1947 the Canal Zone was under the control of the US Army, while the US Navy controlled the Gulf of Panama and the approaches to the canal from the Atlantic in 1942–47.

The canal itself was built between 1905 and 1914, the first task having been the eradication of the sources of yellow fever and malaria in the area. The work necessitated the excavation of some 262,000,000 cubic yards of earth and rock (but an even larger amount of spoil, some 389,000,000 cubic yards, was dredged from the canal for maintenance and improvement between 1915 and 1981). The cost of the construction has been given as $387,000,000.

On entering the 50-mile long canal from the Atlantic a ship passes through a dredged channel about 300 feet (91.44 metres) wide and 41 feet (12.19 metres) deep, leading to the three successive Gatun locks through which the ship is lifted to 85 feet (25.9 metres) above sea-level; it thereupon passes through a fixed channel in the Gatun Lake (through the former valley of the Chagres River) until it enters the Gaillard Cut, at the Pacific end of which it passes through the Pedro Miguel flight of locks, negotiating a drop of 31 feet (9.45 metres) to the level of Miraflores Lake; it leaves this lake via the two Miraflores flights of locks and thus reaches the shore of the Pacific Ocean. (The Miraflores lock gates are the highest in the system because of the extreme tidal variations in the Pacific Ocean.) The canal was widened between 1930 and 1950 and again in 1957–71.

An average ship takes 9 hours to pass through the canal system, but with time spent at anchorage awaiting transit this time is on average increased to 24 hours.

The number of ships passing through the canal every year was less than 4,000 until 1920, between 7,000 and 8,000 between 1928 and 1940, about 9,000 in 1953 and over 15,000 in 1968–76 (during much of which period the Suez Canal was closed). The volume of commercial cargo has steadily risen from some 40,000,000 long tons in 1953 to about 120,000,000 in 1971; after a drop due to recession it rose to some 150,000,000 long tons in 1973 and to over 180,000,000 in 1982.

Further deepening of the canal is envisaged under a comprehensive modernization programme involving new plant and equipment and aimed at allowing uninterrupted two-way traffic of Panamax-size vessels (i.e. of the largest size which can be accommodated).

Panama Canal Commission
Comisión del Canal de Panamá

Address. Balboa Heights, Republic of Panama (US mailing address: APO Miami 34011, USA)

Officers. Dennis P. McAuliffe (admin.); Fernando Manfredo, Jr. (dep. admin.)

Founded. Oct. 1, 1979

History. The Panama Canal was built by the United States between 1904 and 1914. The Republic of Panama had seceded from Colombia in 1903, and under a treaty between the United States and Panama the former obtained jurisdiction over a Panama Canal Zone (on both sides of the proposed canal), guaranteed Panama's independence, paid it $10,000,000 and agreed to pay it a perpetual annuity from 1903 onwards. The canal was subsequently operated by the Panama Canal Company, which was superseded in 1979 by the Panama Canal Commission in terms of two treaties signed by the United States and Panama on Sept. 7, 1977 (and approved in Panama by a plebiscite on Oct. 23, 1977, and ratified by the US Senate in April 1978). Under the treaties the United States surrendered control of the Panama Canal zone to Panama and transferred the management, operation and defence of the canal to the bi-national Panama Canal Commission (with a nine-member supervisory board) with effect from Oct. 1, 1979, until Dec. 31, 1999, when the canal was to be transferred to Panama.

St Lawrence Seaway

The first canal in the valley of the St Lawrence River (which flows between Canada and the United States from Lake Ontario into the Atlantic Ocean) was built in 1825 to by-pass the Lachine Rapids near Montreal.

The present St Lawrence Seaway was completed by the two countries jointly in 1959 at a cost of $470,000,000. It has enabled sea-going ships with a draught of up to 7.92 metres to proceed from the Atlantic to the western end of Lake Superior (a distance of 2,035 nautical miles). The whole seaway system has 17 locks to overcome the difference between sea level and the level of Lake Superior (at 183.5 metres above sea level). These locks include eight in the Canadian Welland Canal which by-passes the Niagara Falls between Lakes Ontario and Erie.

The seaway is normally open from April 1 to Dec. 15 and closed during the rest of the year because of ice (though traffic up to Montreal is kept open by icebreakers).

St Lawrence Seaway Authority

Address. Place de Ville, Ottawa, Ontario K1R 5A3, Canada.

Officers. William A. O'Neil (pres.); G. Laniel (vice-pres.); V. C. Durant (sec.)

Founded. 1954.

Objective. To allow ocean-going ships to enter the Great Lakes of North America.

Status. A Federal Crown corporation.

Sources of finance. Cargo tolls and Welland Canal lockage fees.

Publications. Annual Report; *Traffic Report* (annual); general information; also *Seaway Review* (quarterly, published by Seaway Review Inc., 8715 Parmater Road, Elmira, MI 49730, USA).

St Lawrence Seaway Development Corporation

Address. 800 Independence Avenue SW, Washington DC 20591, USA.

Officer. James L. Emery (administrator).

Founded. May 1954.

History. The corporation was established by an act of Congress as one of the operating administrations of the (US) Department of Transportation.

Activities. The corporation is responsible for the development, operation and maintenance of that part of the Saint Lawrence Seaway between Montreal and Lake Erie within the territorial limits of the United States.

Sources of finance. Revenue received from tolls charged for the use of the corporation's facilities.

Suez Canal

The Suez Canal was built in 1856–69 by the Compagnie Universelle du Canal Maritime de Suez founded in 1854 by Ferdinand de Lesseps (a French engineer). The company was an Egyptian concern with a capital of 200,000,000 French francs in 400,000 shares of 500 francs each. On completion of the canal it was granted a 99-year concession (due to expire in 1968). In 1875 the British Government acquired a total of 176,602 shares in it for £4,000,000.

On Oct. 29, 1888, Austria–Hungary, France, Germany, Italy, the Netherlands, the Ottoman Empire (Turkey), Spain and the United Kingdom signed a Treaty and Convention (in Constantinople) respecting the Free Navigation of the Suez Maritime Canal. The fundamental provisions of the Convention (in terms of which Egypt is the legal successor to the Ottoman Empire) were contained in Articles 1 and 4 as follows:

"The Suez Maritime Canal shall always be free and open, in time of war as in time of peace, to every vessel of commerce or of war, without distinction of flag. . . . The canal shall never be subjected to the exercise of the right to blockade.

"The maritime canal remaining open in time of war as a free passage, even to ships of war of belligerents . . ., the high contracting parties agree that no right of war, no act of hostilities, nor any act having for its object to obstruct the free navigation of the canal, shall be committed in the canal and its ports of access . . . though the Ottoman Empire should be one of the belligerent powers."

The Convention also confirmed and completed the system of international operation embodied by the Compagnie Universelle.

Under the 1936 Anglo–Egyptian Treaty the defence of the canal was to be maintained by British forces until November 1955; in fact the last British troops were withdrawn from the canal zone on March 31, 1956. In July of that year the Egyptian Government of President Abdul Gamal Nasser seized the canal company's fixed property and nationalized all its assets. France, the United Kingdom and the United States regarded this action as being in breach of the 1888 Constantinople Convention. In October 1956, following the outbreak of hostilities between Egypt and Israel, and brief intervention by Britain and France, the Egyptians blocked the canal in several places, and it was not reopened to traffic until April 30, 1957. The pilots of the canal company had meanwhile resigned; they were replaced by pilots appointed by the Egyptian Government, and such pilots have since then efficiently handled the traffic through the canal.

The canal was again closed by Egyptian action in the June 1967 Arab-Israeli war and was not reopened until June 1975. Under a disengagement agreement concluded by the two warring sides in September 1975 Israel's access to the canal was confined to non-military cargo carried in non-Israeli ships, but under the Egyptian–Israeli peace treaty of 1979 Israeli ships were granted the same right of passage in the Suez Canal and its approaches as the vessels of other countries.

The Suez Canal is currently used by most of the world's seafaring nations, not only for the transit of cargo vessels, including tankers, but also for that of warships.

The canal runs from Port Said southwards through Lake Timsa and the Great and Little Bitter Lakes to Port Tawfik (south of Suez), all at sea level, for a distance of 86.4 nautical miles. Originally its width was 21.9 metres and its depth 7.0 metres. A long-term programme for deepening the canal was not started until the 1950s, and by 1961 its maximum permissible draught was 11.3 metres. The majority of large laden tankers have therefore not used the canal but have travelled via the Cape route (round South Africa).

By October 1980 a further development programme had increased the permissible draught to 16.1 metres, and full development was aimed at enabling fully loaded tankers of 250,000 deadweight tons and a draught of up to 20 metres to pass through the canal. Traffic was likely to depend on how the canal charges compared with the cost of fuel and time needed for the Cape route. The distance comparisons are: London to Bombay—via the canal 6,260 nautical miles, via the Cape 10,700 nautical miles; London to Kuwait—via the canal 6,500 nautical miles, via the Cape 11,500 nautical miles. On average it takes ships 24 hours to pass through the canal.

In July–August 1984 traffic through the canal was adversely affected by a number of mine explosions which damaged some 18 ships of different nations in the Gulf of Suez and other parts of the Red Sea. The Egyptian Government attributed responsibility for these explosions to Libya.

Suez Canal Authority
Hay'at Canal Al-Suess

Address. Irshad Building, Ismailia; 6 Lazokhli St., Garden City, Cairo, Egypt.

Officer. Mashour Ahmed Mashour (ch.)

Founded. 1956.

Status. State-owned.

Publications. Monthly report.

Canals in the Soviet Union

In the Soviet Union extensive waterways have been built to link various seas.

The White Sea-Baltic Canal, built in 1931–33, connects the White Sea with Lakes Onega and Ladoga and through the latter lake with the Baltic Sea. The total length of this waterway is 142 miles, of which 32 miles are canals.

The Volga-Baltic Canal links the Baltic Sea, through Lakes Ladoga and Onega and a number of rivers as well as the Rybinsk reservoir, to the Volga and thus ultimately to the Caspian Sea, and through the Volga-Don Canal to the Sea of Azov and the

Black Sea. This canal is 362 kilometres (195 nautical miles) long and was reconstructed in 1964, replacing an earlier Mariinsky waterway built in 1810.

Traffic Separation Schemes in Straits

Traffic separation schemes have been agreed among riparian states of some of the world's busiest straits with the object of preventing collisions.

Such schemes exist for (i) the Dover Strait linking the English Channel with the North Sea; (ii) the Strait of Gibraltar connecting the Atlantic Ocean and the Mediterranean Sea; (iii) the Bab el Mandeb Strait leading from the Red Sea to the Gulf of Aden (between Ethiopia and Djibouti in the west and North and South Yemen in the east); (iv) the Persian (Arabian) Gulf and in particular the Hormuz Channel linking that gulf with the Gulf of Oman; and (v) the Malacca Strait and the Singapore Roads (since 1950 the main artery for crude oil tankers travelling from the Persian Gulf to Japan and saving a detour of some 1,200 nautical miles via the Lombok Strait, east of the Indonesian island of Bali).

Traffic in the Dover Strait is under the surveillance of a Channel Navigation Information Service, whose broadcasting activities have led to a sharp reduction, though not to complete elimination, of collisions (or the running aground of ships).

International Organizations and Institutions concerned with Shipping and Shipbuilding

Worldwide Bodies

Baltic and International Maritime Conference (BIMCO)

Address. Kristianiagade 19, DK-2100 Copenhagen Ø, Denmark.

Officers. Eduardo Bages (pres.); Atle Jebsen (pres. designate); Torben C. Skaanild (s.g.).

Founded. 1905.

History. The organization was formed as the Baltic and White Sea Conference, and as its membership and activities became worldwide, it assumed its present name in 1927.

Objectives. To further the interests of the shipping industry by uniting shipowners and shipping organizations and to take concerted action on their behalf when appropriate; to prepare, improve, approve and update shipping documents; to inform members of instances of objectionable or unfair working practices; and to represent and assist members in cases of unfair treatment by authorities.

Activities. BIMCO offers members a free information service on port and maritime conditions throughout the world, a free advisory service and a fast-developing educational service providing lecturers and speakers on specialized topics. (BIMCO is a non-political organization.)

Structure. BIMCO's general meeting (its governing body) meets every two years to formulate policy and select the president and officials.

Membership. Open to shipowners, shipbrokers, P & I Clubs, associations of shipowners and shipbrokers, ship agents or chartering agents, freight, demurrage and defence associations, and shipping federations. BIMCO currently has 908 owner members representing nearly half the world's merchant fleet, 1,763 broker members and 51 club members, in total from 101 countries.

Publications. Holiday calendar (annual plus one supplement per year, showing holidays and working hours in over 550 ports); weekly circular (on port and labour conditions, practical news etc.; *Ice Report* (weekly in winter); *Bulletin* (bi-monthly); specimen shipping forms; double-taxation binder; etc.

Affiliations. Consultative status with ECOSOC and IMO; observer status at UNCTAD; relations with International Chambers of Commerce and of Shipping.

The Baltic Exchange

Address. 14–20 St Mary Axe, London EC3A 8BU, UK.

Officer. D. J. Walker (sec.).

Founded. 1900.

Objectives. To negotiate bulk cargo charters on an international scale (and also, through specialized member companies of the Exchange, the charter of aircraft for passengers and freight); to supply information on international trade; to facilitate the sale and purchase of ships and aircraft; and to maintain proper standards of international business conduct under a self-regulatory code.

Activities. It is estimated that about three-quarters of the world's open market bulk cargo movement is handled at some stage by members of the Exchange (the five main commodities being iron ore, grain, coal, bauxite and phosphate rock). The Exchange also conducts two futures markets—(i) in EEC wheat and barley and (ii) in UK potatoes.

Membership. Some 700 corporations and 2,300 persons.

Sources of finance. Members' subscriptions.

Affiliations. Many members are fellows or associates of the Institute of Chartered Stockbrokers. Members involved in the grain trade have a trade association—the Grain and Feed Trade Association (GAFTA), and those engaged in the oilseeds and fats trade have a Federation of Oilseeds and Fats Association (FOSFA).

Council of European and Japanese National Shipowners' Associations (CENSA)

Address. 30–32 St Mary Axe, London EC3A 8ET, UK.

Officers. K. St. Johnston (ch.); I. Ross-Bell (s.g.).

Founded. Jan. 1, 1974.

Objectives. To promote and protect sound shipping policies in all sectors of shipping; to co-ordinate and present the views of its members; and to exchange views with other shipowner groups.

Structure. CENSA has a Council and five sections on (i) the work of the United Nations on shipping policy; (ii) shipping policy developments in the United States; (iii) legislative and policy developments in other areas of the world which may affect its members; (iv) the practice and development of consultation between Liner Conferences in Europe and the European Shippers' Councils; and (v) shipping policy developments in the bulk and tanker trades. CENSA has a chairman and three vice-chairmen chosen from leading shipowners of the member countries, a permanent secretariat based in London and a representative in the United States.

Membership. National shipowners' associations in Belgium, Denmark, Finland, France, the Federal Republic of Germany, Greece, Italy, Japan, the Netherlands, Norway, Portugal, Sweden and the United Kingdom (owning almost half the world's merchant fleet) as well as individual line members (including consortia) trading to or from the United States.

Affiliations. Special adviser and corresponding commercial body to the

Consultative Shipping Group governments; consultative status with UNCTAD; a corporate role with the European Shippers' Councils; and a link with all European-based Liner Conferences.

Federation of National Associations of Ship Brokers and Agents (FONASBA)

Address. c/o Institute of Chartered Shipbrokers, 24 St Mary Axe, London EC3A 8DE, UK.

Officers. Peter Hubble (pres.); John Parker (gen. man.)

Founded. 1969.

Objectives. To promote a fair and equitable practice of the profession of shipbrokers and agents.

Structure. The FONASBA Council meets at least once a year. It elects a president for a two-year term.

Membership. Shipbroking organizations in 22 countries (Austria, Belgium, Brazil, Denmark, Finland, France, the Federal Republic of Germany, Greece, Ireland, Italy, Japan, Malta, Morocco, the Netherlands, Norway, Portugal, Singapore, South Africa, Spain, the United Kingdom, the United States and Uruguay).

Sources of finance. Subscriptions from member organizations.

Affiliations. Consultative status with UNCTAD; relations with the European Free Trade Association (EFTA) and the Organization for Economic Development and Co-operation (OECD).

Institute of International Transport Law Institut du Droit International des Transports (IDIT)

Address. Palais des Consuls, 1 rue Jacques le Lieur, 76000 Rouen, France.

Officers. Fédia Julia (pres.); Pierre Emo (s.g.); Philippe Godin (asst. s.g.); B. Mercadal (scientific dir.).

Founded. June 10, 1969.

Objectives. The study of all juridical, economic or technical questions relating to problems of transport at national as well as international level.

Activities. Every other year the Institute organizes symposiums prepared by committees of transport experts and lawyers, and every year it proposes five study projects for the coming year. It gives guidance to researchers and enables research students to present theses on subjects registered at the Université de Haute Normandie in Rouen. It has correspondents in several European countries and in the United States. Conferences and debates have been held on "The Legal Outlook on the Liability of Carriers of Goods" (Nov. 26, 1980), "Shipowners' Tort: Liability and Insurance" (Nov. 27, 1981), "Seaports and Economic Development in Developing Countries" (March 30, 1981), "The Transportation of Hydrocarbons and the Protections of the Marine Environment within Europe" (June 17, 1981); "Marine Fraud in International Transport" (May 2, 1983).

Membership. Chambers of commerce, forwarders, lawyers, maritime insurance companies, national shipping companies, etc.

Sources of finance. Membership dues and subsidies.

Publications. Les Aspects Juridiques des Problèmes posés par la Pollution des Mers; *Les Problèmes Juridiques du Transport, par Navires, des Gaz Liquéfiés*; M. Mankabady, *Safety Measures for the Carriage of Liquefied Gas*; *Les Problèmes Juridiques posés par l'Exploitation des Conteneurs*; *Le Transport Maritime des Grandes Quantités en Plusieurs Voyages* (two reports in French and one in English); Dr Brian Hoyle, *Ports Maritimes et Aménagement Economique dans les Pays Sous-développés*; *La Faute du Propriétaire de Navires—Responsabilité et Assurances*; *de Rochebouet & Dubosc, Les Conséquences Juridiques du Retard dans la Transmission des Documents Maritimes*; and numerous others.

International Association of Airport and Seaport Police

Address. Maritime House, 1 Linton Road, Barking, Essex IG11 8HG, UK.

Officers. Lt.-Col. F. Mazzone (pres., of the State Maryland Police, USA); G. R. Havens (sec.); E. F. Ellen (exec. sec.)

Founded. March 1970.

Objectives. To prevent and detect criminal activity affecting the international shipment of cargo; to study and recommend methods and uniform practices for establishing safeguards against loss of international cargo; to encourage and develop the exchange of information and material among law enforcement agencies concerned with criminal activities in seaports and airports; and to encourage co-operation between the various sections of the international trade community for the development of improved security measures for international cargo.

Membership. Founder members were: Chicago Seaport Commission; Harbour Police Department, New Orleans, Louisiana; Los Angeles and Long Beach Cargo Security, San Pedro, California; Maryland Port Authority; National Harbours Board (Canada); Oneida (NY) Police Department; Port of San Juan, Puerto Rico; Waterfront Commission of New York Harbour. Membership is open to all and includes representatives in over 35 countries, active members being government law enforcement officers and associate members those involved in other forms of port and cargo security activity.

Publications. Year Book; *Terminal* (magazine).

International Association of Classification Societies (IACS)

Address. Det norske Veritas, P.O. Box 300, 1322 Høvik, Norway.

Officers. Nils Nordenstrøm (ch. of IACS Council, exec. vice-pres. of Det norske Veritas).

Founded. September 1968.

Objectives. To work towards improvement of standards of safety at sea, provide for consultation and co-operation with relevant international and national maritime organizations and co-operate closely with the marine industry of the world.

Structure. The IACS Council consists of one senior executive of each member society. There are working parties on bulk chemicals, containers, drilling units, electricity, engines (with a sub-group on automation), fire protection, gas tankers, inland waterway vessels, marine pollution, materials and welding, mooring and anchoring, pipes and pressure vessels, strength of ships, and subdivision, stability and load lines.

Membership. American Bureau of Shipping; Bureau Veritas; Det norske Veritas; Germanischer Lloyd; Lloyd's Register of Shipping; Nippon Kaiji Kyokai; Polski Rejestr Statkow; Registro Italiano Navale; USSR Register of Shipping.

Associates. DDR Schiffs-Revision und -Klassifikation; Jugoslavenski Registar Brodova; Korean Register of Shipping.

International Association of Dredging Companies (IADC)

Address. P.O. Box 80521, 2508 GM The Hague, Netherlands.

Officers. J.-J. De Cloedt (pres.); G. J. de Wolf (s.g.); J. A. Mulock Houwer (gen. man.); N. Oosterbaan (public relations officer).

Founded. May 21, 1965.

Objective. To promote and defend internationally the interests of the dredging industry.

Activities. The IADC has sought and obtained co-operation with other groups in the dredging industry, interests having ranged from obtaining fairer working conditions, more reasonable dredging contracts and the elimination of non-commercial dredging operators subsidized by the taxpayer. With other international associations the IADC has co-operated in the fields of dredging, shipping, port development, civil engineering and hydraulic engineering.

Membership. Dredging contractors in 17 countries.

Sources of finance. Membership fees.

Publications. *Terra et Aqua* (international journal on public works, ports and waterways development).

Affiliations. Permanent International Association of Navigation Congresses (PIANC); Engineering Committee on Oceanic Resources (ECOR).

International Association of Independent Tanker Owners (INTERTANKO)

Address. Radhusgatan 25, P.O. Box 1452-Vika, N-0016 Oslo 1, Norway.

Officers. J. H. Rand (ch.); O. Høegh (vice-ch.); N. E. Zervudachi (vice-ch.); T. Rafgard (gen. man.)

Founded. 1970.

Objectives. This non-profit-making association provides a forum for exchange of views among its members; promotes free competition, safer tanker operations, cleaner seas; studies chartering documents and conditions; undertakes market research; and supplies an extensive information service on port costs and defaulting charterers.

Membership. Independent tanker owners (not controlled by governments or oil companies) from 33 countries—270 companies representing 170,000,000 deadweight tons.

International Association of Institutes of Navigation (IAIN)

Address. c/o Royal Institute of Navigation, Royal Geographical Society, 1 Kensington Gore, London SW7 2AT, UK.

Founded. 1975.

Affiliations. Consultative status with IMO and ECOSOC.

Membership. Institutes in six countries.

International Association of Lighthouse Authorities (IALA)
Association Internationale de Signalisation Maritime (AISM)

Address. 13, rue Yvon Villarceau, 75116 Paris, France.

Officers. T. Kumaki (Japan, pres.); Capt. Sir Miles Wingate (UK, vice-pres.); J. Prunieras (France, s.g.)

Founded. July 1, 1957.

Objectives. To encourage the continued improvement of aids to navigation, through any appropriate technical means, for the safe and expeditious movement of vessels.

Activities. The IALA has organized conferences held every five years. It has set up committees and working groups on marine marking systems, radio navigation systems, vessel traffic services, visibility and availability of aids to navigation, and the effect of ice on lighthouse structures. It has also organized technical workshops as necessary.

Structure. The IALA has a conference which meets every five years, an executive committee of heads of principal national lighthouse authorities, and technical committees.

Membership. 41 "A" members (mainly lighthouse services), 39 "B" members (mainly among port authorities), 32 associate members (including port administrations and private firms) and 56 independent members (mainly suppliers of navigation aids) in different countries.

The "A" members are: Service de Signalisation Maritime, 6 Boulevard Colonel Amirouche, Algiers, *Algeria*; Servicio de Hidrografia Naval, Avenida Montes de Oca No. 2124, (1271) Capital Federal, Buenos Aires, *Argentina*; Marine Operations Division, Department of Transport and Construction, P.O. Box 111, Dickson, ACT 2602, *Australia*; Administration de la Marine et de la Navigation Intérieure, Ministère des Communications, 104 rue d'Arlon, B-1040 Brussels, *Belgium*; Centro de Sinalização Nautica e Reparos Almirante Morães Rēgo, Diretoria de Hidrografia e Navegação, Ministerio da Marinha, Ilha de Mocangue Grande, Rio de Janeiro 20,000 (Guanabara), *Brazil*; Aids and Waterways, Canadian Coast Guard, Ministry of Transport, Tower A, 6th Floor, Ottawa, Ontario K1A 0N7, *Canada*; Instituto Hidrografico de la Armada, Casilla 324, Valparaiso, *Chile*; Hydrographic Bureau, Beijing, *China*; Instituto Cubano de Hidrográfia, Apartado 606, Mariano 13, Havana, *Cuba*; Farvandsdirektoratet, Overgaden oven Vandet 62 B, P.O. Box 19, DK-1001, Copenhagen K, *Denmark*; Ports and Lighthouses Administration, Arsenal Gate 1, Alexandria, *Egypt*; Trinity House, Tower Hill, London EC3N 4DH, *England*; Pilots and Lighthouse Division, Merenkulkuhallitus, Vuorimiehenkatu 1, 00141 Helsinki 14, *Finland*; Services des Phares et Balises et de la Navigation, 33, rue de Miromesnil, 75008 Paris, *France*; Office des Ports et Rades, B.P. 1051, Owendo, Libreville, *Gabon*; Seehydrographischer Dienst der Deutschen Demokratischen Republik, Dierkower Damm 45, 25 Rostock 1, *German Democratic Republic*; Bundesverkehrsministerium, Postfach 200100, D-5300 Bonn 2, *Federal Republic of Germany*; Lighthouse Service, Hellenic Navy, Palataki, Piraeus, *Greece*; Itastofnun Islands, P.O. Box 1395, Seljaveg 32, 121 Reykjavik, *Iceland*; Department of Lighthouses and Lightships, Ministry of Transport, East Block 10, Level IV, R. K. Puram, New Delhi 110066, *India*; Training and International Relations Office, Ports and Shipping Organization, 751 Enghelab Avenue, Tehran, *Iran*; Irish Lights Office, 16 Lower Pembroke Street (Box 73), Dublin 2, *Ireland*; Stato Maggiore della Marina, Ispettorato dei Fari e del Segnalamento Marittimo, Palazzo Marina Militare, Piazza Della Marina, 00100 Rome, *Italy*; Maritime Safety Agency, 1–3 Kasumigaseki, 2 chome, Chiyoda-ku, Tokyo 100, *Japan*; Korea Maritime and Port Administration, 263 Yeunji-dong, Jongro-ku, Seoul, *Republic of Korea*; Light Dues Board, Peninsular Malaysia, Locked Bag 211, Port Kelang, Selangor, *Malaysia*; Direktoraat Generaal Scheepvaart en Maritieme Zaken, Postbus 5817, 2280 HV Rijswijk, *Netherlands*; Nigerian Ports Authority, Private Mail Bag 12 588, Lagos, *Nigeria*; Kystdirektoratet, Dronningensgt. 6, Postboks 8158 Dep., Oslo 1, *Norway*; Directorate General of Ports and Shipping, Ministry of Communications, Karachi, *Pakistan*; Urzad Morski w Gdyni, ul. Crzanowskiego 10, 81338 Gdynia, *Poland*; Direcção de Farois, Ministerio da Marinha, Paço de Arcos, 2780 Oeiras, *Portugal*; Saudi Ports Authority, P.O. Box 5162, Riyadh 11188, *Saudi Arabia*; Northern Lighthouse Board, 84 George Street, Edinburgh EH2 3DA, *Scotland*; South African Transport Services (P.13/14), Room 1116, Paul Kruger Building, Private Bag X 47, Johannesburg 2000, *South Africa*; Sección de Señales Marítimas, Dirección General de Puertos y Señales Marítimas, Ministerio de Obras Públicas, Paseo de la Castellana, Madrid 3, *Spain*; Sjöfartsverkets Centralförvaltning, S-60178 Norrköping, *Sweden*; Denizcilik Bankasi T.A.O., P.O. Box 1381, Limanlar Müdürlügü, Karaköy, Istanbul, *Turkey*; US Coast Guard, US Coast Guard Headquarters, Washington DC 20593, *USA*; Principal Department of Navigation and Oceanography, 11 Linia, Dom 8, Leningrad 199034, *USSR*; Ustanova za Odrzavanje Pomorskih Plovnih Putova, Obala Lazareta 1, 58 001 Split, *Yugoslavia*.

Sources of finance. Members' subscriptions (95 per cent), sale of IALA documents (5 per cent).

Publications. *AISM/IALA Bulletin* (quarterly); report on conferences; *International Dictionary on Aids to Navigation*; *Radio Aids to Navigation* (manual).

Affiliations. Consultative status with IMO and ECOSOC; contributes to studies undertaken by the International Telecommunication Union and the International Hydrographic Office as well as some non-governmental international organizations. The IALA's president is director general of the Aids to Navigation Department of the Maritime Safety Agency in Tokyo; its vice-president is deputy master of Trinity House, London; and its secretary-general is director of the French Lighthouse Service.

International Association of NVOCCs

Address. 1228 L St., N.W., Suite 410, Washington, D.C. 20005, USA.

Officer. Raymond P. deMember (exec. vice-pres. of general council).

Founded. November 1972.

Objectives. To further the interests of the non-vessel operating common carriers (NVOCCs) industry to ocean transportation and to improve the quality of services to shippers.

Activities. The association holds annual meetings and has been engaged in opposition to and litigation against ILA 50-mile container rules.

Sources of finance. Members' dues.

Publications. Newsletters to members.

International Association of Ports and Harbors (IAPH)

Address. Kotohira Kaikan Bldg., 1-2-8, Toranomon, Minato-ku, Tokyo 105, Japan.

Officers. A. J. Tozzoli (pres., and also dir., Port Department, Port Authority of New York & New Jersey, One World Trade Center, New York N.Y. 10048, USA); Hajime Sato (s.g.).

Founded. Nov. 7, 1955.

Objectives. "To develop and foster good relations and collaboration among all ports and harbors of the world", to promote and increase their efficiency by exchanging information on new techniques and technology relating to port development, organization, administration and management and to protect the legitimate interests and rights of IAPH members within intergovernmental and other organizations, as well as to assist developing ports by providing training opportunities. The 14th IAPH conference was held in Hamburg in May 1985.

Structure. The IAPH's conference meets every two years and elects a president and a vice-president. A board of directors is elected nationally, and there is an executive committee.

Source of finance. Members' dues (fixed according to annual handling of tonnage).

Membership. Regular and associate members in 73 countries.

Affiliations. Consultative status with IMO, ECOSOC and UNCTAD.

Publications. *Ports and Harbors* (monthly); conference proceedings.

International Cargo Handling Co-ordination Association (ICHCA)

Address. International Secretariat, 1 Walcott St., London SW1P 2MY, UK.

Officers. F. Bureau (France, pres.); M. Fernandes Valles (Spain, ch. of council); J. T. Warburton (s.g.).

Founded. 1952.

Objectives. To increase efficiency and economy in the handling and movement of goods by all modes of transport and at all stages of the transport chain by generating contacts and information exchange among members, collecting and disseminating information from all available sources, and by participating in technical and regulatory activities which significantly affect cargo handling in practice.

Activities. ICHCA organizes, and participates in, a wide range of national and international meetings and has consultative status with the major regulatory bodies and training agencies affecting the transport industry. It conducts international study projects and operates a technical enquiry service; it scans all published material on cargo handling and maintains a data base of relevant information for the use of members; and it arranges introductions and technical visits for members visiting other countries.

Structure. ICHCA is administered by a council composed of the chairmen of each national section; it has a biennial general assembly (where members vote on proposals submitted); national and regional sections organize activities of national interest in many countries.

Membership. In some 90 countries (being corporate, private, library, student or sustaining members).

Publications. The Securing of ISO Containers; *The Handling of ISO Containers in Low Throughput Situations*; *An International Survey on Handling Iron and Steel Products.*

International Chamber of Commerce (ICC)

Address. 38 Cours Albert 1er, F-75008, Paris, France.

Officers. Marie C. Psimenos (first dir.); Hans König (s.g.).

Founded. 1920.

Objectives. To represent business interests at international level, to promote freedom of international trade and to harmonize and facilitate business and trade practices.

Activities. These have included the holding of a (fourth) ICC International Shipping Conference in September 1981, which called for an end to political confrontation in maritime affairs and offered ICC co-operation in assisting developing nations to build up their own fleets. The ICC has opposed the UNCTAD decision to phase out "flags of convenience" [see pages 32–33].

Structure. The ICC has a congress held every three years, annual conferences, a council (as governing body) meeting twice a year, a 15-member executive board, an international secretariat and national committees. Its technical commissions and committees include, under its Transport and Trade Facilitation Department, a transport policy board, a transporters consultative committee, an international bureau of transport users, a sea transport commission, an intermodal transport commission and an international maritime arbitration organization.

Membership. Over 5,000 major enterprises and some 1,700 business organizations in over 100 countries.

Sources of finance. Contributions from national committees and other members; revenue from fees for services and from sale of publications.

Publications. ICC Information; *Annual Report*; *Handbook*; general and technical publications.

International Chamber of Shipping (ICS)

Address. 30-32 St Mary Axe, London EC3A 8ET, UK.

Officers. Sir Adrian Swire (ch.); J. C. S. Horrocks (s.g.); M. A. Calder (marine man.).

Founded. 1921 (as International Shipping Conference; present name since 1948).

Objectives. To promote the interests of its members by providing a forum for the discussion of matters of mutual concern, by seeking to co-ordinate members' views and by representing those views nationally and internationally.

Strucutre. The governing body of the ICS is its full membership, which meets annually. There is an elected executive committee, and a secretariat is provided by the General Council of British Shipping. There are specialist committees open to all members and dealing with containers and multimodal transport, facilitation of trade procedures and documents, marine insurance, marine pollution (notably the practical application of international measures for pollution control), marine safety (including navigation, communications, ship construction and equipment, fuel quality and the carriage of dangerous goods), maritime law (in particular shipowners' liabilities), oil tankers, chemical and gas carriers, and international waterways (notably the Panama and Suez Canals).

Membership. National shipowners associations in 33 countries, representing about two-thirds of the free world's merchant tonnage.

Sources of finance. Contributions based on gross registered tonnage entered in member associations, plus a flat fee.

Publications. Annual Report; casualty reports (on navigation, tanker and fire casualties); other publications (mainly on safety, pollution and facilitation), some prepared in conjunction with the Oil Companies International Marine Forum.

Affiliations. Consultative status or close co-operation with IMO, UNCTAD, the ITU, the Economic Commission for Europe, the WMO, ESCAP, the Customs Co-operation Council, the International Hydrographic Office and INMARSAT. At industry level it has close ties with the International Chamber of Commerce, the Baltic and International Maritime Conference, the International Association of Independent Tanker Owners, the International Shipping Federation and the International Association of Ports and Harbors.

International Christian Maritime Association (ICMA)

Address. 81 Orwell Road, Felixstowe, IP11 7PY, UK.

Officers. Rev. W. J. D. Down (ch.); Rev. B. Krug (g.s.).

Founded. 1969.

Objectives. To promote and encourage collaboration and assistance among Christian organizations engaged in work for and amongst seafarers, and to be the collective and respected voice of member organizations within the industry and outside it.

Activities. Promotion of co-operation between members; the organizing of regular plenary conferences (e.g. in the Philippines in April 1985); and the development of regional branches in North America, Northern Europe, the Mediterranean area, East Asia, the United Kingdom and other parts of the world.

Membership. All Seamen's Mission Societies of the Churches (fully international and ecumenical).

Sources of finance. Membership fees.

Publications. ICMA Bulletin; ICMA Directory to Christian Centres, Chaplaincies and other Seamen's Welfare Agencies throughout the maritime world.

International Congress of Maritime Museums (ICMM)

Address. c/o Willem F. J. Mörzer Bruyns, secretary-general, Nederlands Scheepvaart Museum, Kattenburgerplein 1, 1018 KK Amsterdam, the Netherlands.

Officer. J. Revell Carr (pres., also director, Mystic Seaport Museum, Mystic, Connecticut 06355, USA).

Founded. 1972.

Objectives. To facilitate communication among maritime museums throughout the world and to organize triannual conferences of members.

Membership. 73 full, 115 associate, 21 contributing and 2 honorary members (from Africa, Australia, Belgium, Bermuda, Canada, Denmark, Finland, France, the Federal Republic of Germany, Greece, India, Ireland, Israel, Italy, Japan, Monaco, the Netherlands, Norway, Poland, Portugal, Spain, Sweden, the United Kingdom and the United States).

Structure. The congress is governed by an elected executive council.

Sources of finance. Members' dues.

Publications. *ICMM Newsletter* (approx. twice yearly); *Historic Ship Register* (2 vols.); *Sources for Maritime History*; proceedings of conferences.

International Container Bureau
Bureau International de Containers (BIC)

Address. 38 Cours Albert 1er, 75008 Paris, France.

Officers. J. Martial (pres.); M. G. Hartmann (dep. pres.) A. Koenig, H. Wenger, M. Carlier (vice-pres.).

Founded. 1933.

Objectives. To promote door-to-door transport by successive use of several modes of transport; to study and implement administrative, technical and customs advances; and to collect data on behalf of its members.

Membership. 60 organizations and 1,200 associate members in 30 countries.

Publications. *Containers* (quarterly); information sheet.

International Federation of Shipmasters' Associations

Address. 202 Lambeth Road, London SE1 7JY, UK.

Officers. Capt. R. Gronsand (Norway, pres.); Capt. N. W. C. Rutherford (UK, g.s.).

Founded. 1974.

Objectives. To promote and maintain safety at sea and the representation of professional shipmasters at International Maritime Organization (IMO) meetings dealing with safety, marine environment protection and certification standards internationally.

Membership. 19 shipmasters' associations with a total membership of 4,200 sea-going masters, and also 19 individual members (also sea-going shipmasters).

International Ice Patrol

Address. c/o US Coast Guard, 400 7th Street, S.W. Washington DC, 20590, USA.

Founded. 1914 (by 14 nations, following the *Titanic* disaster).

Activities. An iceberg warning system has been established on the Grand Bank of Newfoundland for the period from February to October, known as the International Ice Observation and Ice Patrol Service in the North Atlantic.

International Lifeboat Conference (ILC)

Address. c/o Royal National Lifeboat Institution (RNLI), West Quay Road, Poole, Dorset BH15 1HZ, UK.

Officer. Lieut. Commander B. Miles (sec.).

Founded. March 1924.

History. The ILC was established to mark the centenary of the RNLI by representatives from eight countries meeting in London. Except during the war years the ILC has held meetings in a different country every four years.

Objectives. To exchange information and ideas on boat design, rescue methods, training and administration.

Activities. The next ILC meeting is to take place at La Coruña (Northern Spain) in June 1987.

Membership. National lifeboat societies in 32 countries (Australia, the

Bahamas, Barbados, Belgium, Bermuda, Canada, Chile, China, Denmark, Finland, France, the German Democratic Republic, the Federal Republic of Germany, Guatemala, Iceland, India, Ireland, Italy, Japan, the Netherlands, the Netherlands Antilles, New Zealand, Norway, Poland, Portugal, South Africa, the Soviet Union, Sweden, Switzerland, the United Kingdom, the United States and Uruguay).

Publications. Lifeboat International (annual).

International Maritime Bureau (IMB)

Address. Maritime House, 1 Linton Road, Barking, Essex IG11 8HG, UK.

Officers. Sir John Cuckney (ch.); Eric F. Ellen (dir.); J. Abhyankar (asst. dir.); Peter Lowe (legal adviser).

Founded. January 1981.

History. The IMB was set up by the International Chamber of Commerce (ICC) as a non-profit-making organization and recognized by the International Maritime Organization (then still the Inter-Governmental Maritime Consultative Organization) in October 1981.

Objects. To combat the growing problems of international maritime fraud, to receive information on fraudulent or other suspect practices and to collate it, to suggest avenues of procedure to potential victims of such practices, to give advice on how to set up or improve systems designed to reduce vulnerability to fraud, to design and provide an essential crime prevention service, and to conduct investigations into fraud and assisting injured parties in obtaining financial redress.

Activities. Investigation of maritime fraud, resolution of maritime disputes, collecting information and disseminating it to members, monitoring the passage of vessels, sponsoring academic research into aspects of maritime and international commercial crime, advising the industry on precautions and remedial measures through seminars, special reports and other publications. In 1984 the IMB introduced a Container Intelligence Unit to monitor losses of containers and their cargoes. It was also to set up (i) a port classification system to induce port authorities to improve security and to eliminate "ports of convenience" and (ii) a chartering experience programme to enable charter operators to check on the record of a prospective partner.

Membership. Members include insurance companies and P. & I. Clubs, shipowners and shipping companies, ship brokers, exporters, banks, shipping agents, commodity dealers, surveyors and maritime lawyers.

Sources of finance. Membership fees (£2,500 per annum for large organizations, government agencies and multinational corporations, £600 p.a. for minor organizations); contributions from the ICC.

Affiliations. The members of the IMB's board of directors include the secretary-general of the IMO and that of the ICC, a former deputy chairman of Lloyds, the president of the All-India Shippers' Council and senior officers of the Union of Greek Shipowners. The IMB co-operates with the UN Conference on Trade and development (UNCTAD), and its director is chairman of the Commonwealth Panel of Experts on Maritime Fraud. It is also a sustaining member of the International Association of Airport and Seaport Police (of which its director is the executive secretary).

Publications. Guide to Prevention of Maritime Fraud; Ellen, E. F., and Campbell, *International Maritime Fraud*; *Scuttling: A Special Study*; *Vessel Deviation and Disposal of Cargo*; *Documentary Fraud in International*

Trade: Whose Fault—Whose Responsibility?; *Report into the Incidence of Piracy and Armed Robbery from Merchant Ships*; *Port Security*; *Container Crime & Port Classification*; *Combating International Commercial Crime* (March 1984); *Cargo Theft—An Abuse of the Greek Legal System* (April 1984); *Fire at Sea: Accident or Arson* (May 1984); *Second Report into Piracy and Armed Robbery from Merchant Ships* (June 1984); *International Commercial Crime* (complete set of IMB lecture papers); *Crude Oil Cargoes—Losses through Theft and Fraud.*

International Maritime Industries Forum (IMIF)

Address. c/o Kleinwort Benson Ltd., P.O. Box 560, 20, Fenchurch St., London EC3P 3DP, UK.

Officers. J. G. Davis (ch., also dir., Kleinwort Benson Ltd.); F. Chao (pres., Wah Kwong & Co. Ltd., Hong Kong), H. Cran (chief exec., Fina Marina SA, Brussels), B. A. Nachamkin (senior vice-pres., Bankers Trust Co., London), V. d'Orgeval (dir., Banque de la Société Financière Européenne, Paris), T. J. Parker (ch., Harland & Wolff Ltd., Belfast) (vice-chairmen); B. Molin (asst. sec.).

Founded. 1975.

History. The IMIF was established upon publication of a report on the tanker industries' problems commissioned by tanker owners, banks, shipbuilders and oil companies, all of them concerned at the effect of the surplus tanker capacity on the world's markets. Later the IMIF extended its attention to dry bulk vessels.

Objectives. The re-establishment and subsequent maintenance of a healthy commercial and financial climate for all sectors of shipping through the united efforts of its members, by means of international visits, publications, etc.; the formulation of practicable solutions to mutual problems; the stimulation of changes in traditional thinking on a broad range of subjects; and the promotion of the need for prompt and effective action whenever and wherever it is considered to be most beneficial.

Activities. The IMIF has advocated a "scrap to build" policy (as opposed to purely speculative ordering of new ships without any compensating scrapping). At a 1985 meeting in Hong Kong of European, Japanese and Korean shipbuilders (representing over 80 per cent of world production) it was agreed to establish a fund to stimulate scrapping, including support to new shipbreaking industries in developing countries. The IMIF has also given its attention to the effects of government subsidies on the construction of new tonnage designed to keep surplus shipyards in business; to vessel safety; to an upgrading of standards and their more effective enforcement; to the fact that re-rolled or re-cycled ships' scrap with its high energy content is a most valuable material; to dialogues with classification societies, insurers and salvage associations, etc.; and to the question of port state control.

Structure. In addition to its executive the IMIF has a steering committee, a scrapping committee and study or working groups on different subjects.

Membership. 77 full members and 31 observers from 24 countries (including shipowners, shipbuilders, "users" (e.g. oil companies), bankers, insurers and other interested parties.

Sources of finance. Membership fees (£850 p.a. for members and £425 p.a. for observers).

Publications. IMIF booklet; newsletter; market reports; and papers on various subjects as presented twice a year at full IMIF meetings.

International Maritime Pilots Association (IMPA)

Address. 20 Peel St., London W8 7PD, UK.

Officer. Eric E. Ellen (s.g.).

Founded. May 1971.

Objectives. To provide consultation and exchange of information, to promote the combined interests of member countries, and to enhance the status of pilots.

Structure. An IMPA general meeting is held every two years. There are an executive committee and international technical committees.

Membership. Pilot associations in 27 countries.

Sources of finance. Members' dues.

Affiliations. Consultative status with ECOSOC.

International Maritime Radio Committee
Comité International Radio Maritime (CIRM)

Address. Pier Head House, Narrow Street, London E14 8DQ, UK.

Officers. R. Bryssinck (pres.); G. G. Hill, Ph. J. van Meel (vice-presidents); Cdr. C. C. Wake-Walker (s.g.).

Founded. 1928.

Objectives. To advance the maritime telecommunications service in the most scientific and efficient manner for the benefit of all concerned with marine matters; to foster and make the best use of the most up-to-date scientific and practical knowledge by promoting the exchange between members of information, proposals and opinions on administrative, technical and operational maritime telecommunications matters and navigational aids, by joint consultation and participation in the work of the appropriate committees of the International Telecommunication Union (ITU), such as the International Radio Consultative Committee (CCIR); to present the co-ordinated specialist views of all CIRM members as considered and important international opinions at all international telecommunication conferences and appropriate maritime conferences; to develop an effective voice in the formulation of world marine telecommunications standards and world and regional maritime telecommunications plans by liaison with the ITU, the IMO, the International Civil Aviation Organization (ICAO), the International Chamber of Shipping, the World Meteorological Organization, the International Air Transport Organization and other international organizations with an interest in marine matters or matters of joint concern; to provide suitable and adequate representation at all relevant international conferences and meetings which plan world and regional telecommunications arrangements for the maritime mobile service, and to ensure that the radio maritime needs are adequately considered at any conference whose work impinges on this field; and, through the above arrangements, to enhance safety of life at sea and the speedy and safe voyaging of ships to the benefit of all engaged in maritime affairs.

Membership. 45 organizations and companies dealing with maritime radio and radar matters.

International Shipping Federation (ISF)

Address. 30-32 St Mary Axe, London EC3A 8ET, UK.

Officers. W. N. Menzies-Wilson (UK, pres.); F. J. Whitworth (dir.); C. L. A. Edginton (sec.).

Founded. 1909.

Objectives. To act as a clearing house for its members on developments relating to maritime employment; to propose and co-ordinate the international shipowners' position on these developments; and to represent its members' interests vis-à-vis governments and unions, particularly in the international bodies concerned with these matters.

Activities. The ISF promotes exchange of views and policies on matters affecting the employment of seamen, including pay and conditions of officers and ratings at national level, relations with unions, manning organization on board, the role of management, safe working practices and maritime training. It has set up an International Shipping Information Service (ICIS).

Structure. The ISF has a council which meets annually and a permanent secretariat based in London.

Membership. National shipowners' associations in 28 countries (Australia, Belgium, Brazil, Canada, Denmark, Finland, France, the Federal Republic of Germany, Greece, Hong Kong, India, Ireland, Italy, Japan, the Republic of Korea, Kuwait, Liberia, the Netherlands, New Zealand, Norway, Pakistan, the Philippines, Portugal, Spain, Sweden, the United Kingdom, the United States and Zaïre) representing about 57 per cent of gross registered tons of world merchant shipping and employing more than 500,000 professional seafarers.

Sources of finance. Members' annual subscriptions based on the size of their fleets.

Affiliations. Consultative status with ECOSOC and UNCTAD; close ties with the ILO, IMO, the International Chamber of Shipping, the Oil Companies International Marine Forum, the International Association of Independent Tanker Owners and other international industry associations.

International Union of Marine Insurers

Address. Stadthausquai 5, 8001 Zurich, Switzerland.

Officers. Walter Rostock (Federal Republic of Germany, pres.); Dr Peter Alther (Switzerland, g.s.).

Membership. 50 associations.

Publications. Tables of Practical Equivalence (published in co-operation with the International Chamber of Commerce).

Mariners International Club

Address. 52 Woodville Road, Barnet, Herts, EN5 5NG, UK.

Officer. Erik C. Abranson (hon. ch.).

Founded. 1974.

Objectives. To promote and preserve traditional sailing vessels and related skills; to organize adventure sail training cruises on square- or gaff-rigged vessels; to help members to find crew berths on traditional sailing ships; to help owners of such ships to find officers and crews; and to publish a quarterly newsletter of traditional sail news.

Activities. The club, which does not itself own a vessel, has chartered suitable ships according to demand and has taken part in tall ships races (1976: brigantine *Phoenix*, Plymouth-USA and back; 1978: barque *Marques*, Great Yarmouth-Oslo and back; 1980: topsail schooner *El Pirata* and full-rigged ship *Sørlandet*, Kiel-Karlskrona, Frederikshavn-Amsterdam; 1982: gaff schooner *Stina*, Falmouth-Lisbon-Southampton; 1984: gaff ketch *Irene*, Frederikshavn-Greenock-Liverpool).

Membership. About 500 in some 20 countries.

Sources of finance. Membership fees.

Publications. *Windjammer* (quarterly).

Maritime Transport Committee of the OECD

Address. Organization for Economic Co-operation and Development, 2 rue

André-Pascal, 75775 Paris Cédex 16, France.

Officer. R. A. Humphrey (Head, Maritime Transport and Tourism Division).

Activities. The committee deals with shipping policy problems between OECD member countries; difficulties encountered by member countries in their shipping relations with both developing countries and centrally planned economies; and questions concerning the overall development, changes and commercial viability of world shipping as a whole. Issues discussed in the committee in recent years, with the aim of reaching an overall consensus concerning OECD shipping policy orientations, have been (i) problems between member and non-member countries primarily due to protectionist pressures from developing countries and (ii) problems among OECD member countries caused by different approaches towards the regulation of liner conferences, by restrictions on free access to specific types of cargo, and by different regimes concerning fiscal treatment and financial assistance.

In 1982 the committee expressed the view that the world shipping crisis could find a permanent solution only in the scrapping of surplus tonnage; that the tonnage decline of the OECD fleet was "both absolute and relative"; that open registries were increasing; that there was moderate growth in the fleets of the Soviet Union and the Eastern bloc countries and "substantial" growth in third-world shipping, which was apt to prove protectionist; that steam turbine propulsion was "in inexorable decline"; and that the solution of the freight rates problem was "still far ahead".

Structure. The committee has a special group on international organizations, which serves as a forum for harmonization and co-ordination of positions to be taken by member countries during the shipping negotiations within UNCTAD and certain UN conferences dealing with shipping issues. The committee also has a working group responsible for monitoring shipping policy developments in developing and developed countries, the activity of state trading shipping lines (especially those of the Soviet Union), and developments having a direct or indirect bearing on the economics of world shipping.

Membership. OECD member countries—Australia, Austria, Belgium, Canada, Denmark, Finland, France, the Federal Republic of Germany, Greece, Iceland, Ireland, Italy, Japan, Luxembourg, the Netherlands, New Zealand, Norway, Portugal, Spain, Sweden, Switzerland, Turkey, the United Kingdom and the United States; special status member—Yugoslavia.

Publications. Combating Oil Spills; The Cost of Oil Spills.

The Missions to Seamen

Address. St Michael Paternoster Royal, College Hill, London EC4R 2RL, UK.

Officers. Viscount Leathers of Purfleet (ch. of council); Rev. Canon W. J. D. Down (g.s.); Rev. G. J. Jones (welfare officer).

Founded. 1856.

History. Upon its foundations by an Anglican minister in Bristol, the society soon became involved in campaigning for better conditions for seafarers and meeting their welfare needs. By 1886 it was working in ports around the world, running clubs and hostels for seafarers of all races and creeds.

Activities. Full-time chaplains and staff in 90 ports (in 80 of which there are seafarers' centres) and part-time chaplains in 250 others visit seafarers on their ships and in hospital and offer counselling, practical help and support in emergencies. As ministers of the Anglican Church the chaplains are in liaison with clergy in inland parishes to provide a link between seafarers and their families.

Structure. The society has a council, a central office, a general committee, a finance committee, a pastoral committee and a ways and means committee. It has overseas members (such as the Anglican Church of Canada and the Church of England in Australia), supporting organizations (including the Flying Angel Marketing Enterprises Ltd.) and national, provincial, state and other representatives.

A kindred society is the Mediterranean Mission to Seamen, Diocese of Gibraltar in Europe, 5a Gregory Place, Kensington, London W8 4NG, with representatives in France, Gibraltar, Greece, Italy, Malta, Portugal, Spain and Turkey.

Sources of finance. Voluntary donations.

Publications. The Sea (bi-monthly); *Flying Angel News* (quarterly); Annual Report; Annual Directory of Staff and Centres around the World.

Permanent International Association of Navigation Congresses (PIANC)
Association Internationale Permanente des Congrès de Navigation (AIPCN)

Address. 155, rue de la Loi, B–1040 Brussels, Belgium.

Officers. Ir. R. de Paepe (pres.); Henri Vandervelden (s.g.)

Founded. 1885.

Objectives. To promote design, construction, improvement and operation of inland and maritime waterways and coastal areas, and to disseminate related information.

Structure. The PIANC holds congresses every four years; it has a permanent international commission which meets annually and is composed of delegates appointed by member governments; and it has an executive committee and study commissions on force of waves, reception of large ships, sport and pleasure navigation, locks, ship lifts, drydocks, the environment, effects of dredging and disposal of dredged material.

Membership. 40 governments; 2,587 other members.

Sources of finance. Government subsidies and members' dues, as well as sale of publications.

Publications. Papers and Proceedings of Congresses; *Bulletin* (three times a year); *Illustrated Technical Dictionary* (in six languages); Final Reports of International Study Commission.

Society of International Gas Tanker & Terminal Operators (SIGTTO)

Address. London Liaison Office, Staple Hall, 87-90 Houndsditch, London EC3A 7AX, UK; registered office: P.O. Box 1022, Clarendon House, Church Street West, Hamilton 5-31, Bermuda.

Officers. R. G. Eddy (pres.); Alan Smith (sec.); R. C. Gray (gen. man.).

Founded. October 1979.

Objectives. The society is a non-profit-making organization dedicated to the protection and promotion of the mutual interests of its members in the safe operation of liquefied gas tankers and liquefied gas loading and receiving terminals.

Activities. Safety research concerning liquefied natural gas (LNG) and liquefied petroleum gas (LPG); publication of a textbook on the principles of liquefied gas handling in terminals and on ships; a review of LPG cargo quantity calculations; visual aids for fire fighting training.

Membership. Open primarily to companies owning, directly or indirectly, the whole or a majority interest in, or operating, one or more sea-going liquefied gas tankers of liquefied gas marine loading or receiving terminals. Conditional membership open to companies which have contracted for, or genuinely intend to contract for, the construction of a liquefied gas tanker or a gas terminal.

Affiliations. Consultative status with IMO.

Publications. Guides to Contingency Planning; Safe Havens for Disabled Gas Carriers—A Consultative Document in the Seeking and Granting of a Safe Haven; Hydrates in LPG Cargoes; Recommendation for the Installation of Cargo Strainers on LNG Carriers.

World Maritime University

Address. POB 500, Malmö, Sweden.

Officers. C. P. Strivastava (chancellor).

Founded. July 4, 1983.

History. This university was set up by the IMO with the support of the UN Development Programme (UNDP), the governments of Sweden and several other IMO member states and some shipowners.

Objectives. The university is to provide intensive training, in a two-year course leading to a master of science degree, to students intending to become maritime administrators, teachers at maritime academies, surveyors, casualty investigators, technical managers for shipping companies or other experts, and to fill posts in the shipping industries of developing countries. It has used "seaspeak", a language of standardized terminology for instructions and orders. In 1984 it had 140 students from 59 different countries.

Western Europe

Association of West European Shipbuilders (AWES)

Address. P.O. Box 229, 2990 AE Barendrecht, The Netherlands.

Officer. G. de Vries Lentsch (dir.).

Founded. 1965.

Objectives. To provide means of communication among members, supply information to them and provide facilities for the discussion of questions of mutual interest and concern with a view to enabling members to take common action to maintain and foster the well-being of the West European shipbuilding industry; also to co-operate as desirable with organizations in other countries.

History. The AWES was preceded by an International Shipbuilding Conference set up in 1937 but disbanded after World War II. In 1947 a West European Shipbuilders Informal Contact (WESIC) was established. Consisting originally of Belgium, Denmark, the Netherlands, Norway, the United Kingdom and Sweden, it progressively extended its membership to include France, the Federal Republic of Germany and Italy. After the WESIC had (with the rise of Japanese shipbuilding) become the AWES in 1965, the latter was joined by Spain and Finland in 1967, Portugal in 1973, and Greece in 1981.

Activities. The AWES holds meetings to discuss the situation of the national, European and world shipbuilding industry and mutual problems among members; it established contacts between representatives of member yards, including those active in the same markets; it exchanges information between the national associations; it publishes reports, in particular on future shipbuilding requirements; it cooperates with the OECD; and it keeps in contact with shipbuilders in the rest of the world.

Membership. National associations in Belgium, Denmark, Finland, France, the Federal Republic of Germany, Greece, Italy, the Netherlands, Norway, Portugal, Spain, Sweden and the United Kingdom.

Sources of finance. Contributions by member associations.

Publications. *Review on Global Development in World Shipbuilding to 1995* (for members only).

Committee of Shipowners' Associations of the European Communities
Comité des Associations d'Armateurs des Communautés Européennes (CAACE)

Address. 5, rue Joseph II, B-1040 Brussels, Belgium.

Officers. J. Groenendijk (pres.); Dominique Peugniez (s.g.).

Founded. 1962 (in Paris; in Brussels since 1972).

Objectives. To study and provide a forum for discussions on all matters relating to the maritime industry, including all aspects of the European Communities' shipping policy; to seek a common position among its members and to promote their policies with the authorities of the Communities; and to defend the common interests of the shipping industries of member states and to seek ways of co-operation amongst these interests, with the ultimate objective of preventing the decline of the Communities' fleets and strengthening their viable operation in worldwide trade.

Activities. The CAACE has inter alia supported measures against "unfair competition" by "non-commercial operators" in the Central American, East African and Far Eastern trades, by the use of the Trans-Siberian Railway and by an "increasing incursion by Eastern Bloc ships in the cruising activities of CAACE member states" as well as by "Polish and East German shipowners in certain trades". The CAACE has rejected the view of the "Group of 77" and of trade unions that the use of the "open registry system" (of "flags of convenience") has encouraged substandard ship operations and employment conditions. In regard to promoting the greater involvement of developing countries in ocean shipping, the CAACE has favoured the formation of joint ventures with shipowners of developed countries.

Structure. The CAACE has a board of directors of eight full and 11 alternate members, a social affairs committee, an expert group on non-commercial competition, an expert group on the UN liner conference code and an expert group on competition groups.

Membership. Ten shipping organizations as follows: Union des Armateurs Belges, Lijnwaadmarkt 9, 2000 Antwerp, *Belgium*; Danmarks Rederiforening, Amaliegade 33, 1256 Copenhagen K, *Denmark*; Comité Central des Armateurs de France, Boulevard Haussmann 73, 75008 Paris, *France*; Verband Deutscher Reeder, Esplanade 6, 2000 Hamburg 36, *Federal Republic of Germany*; Union of Greek Shipowners, Akti Miaouli 85, Piraeus, *Greece*; Irish Chamber of Shipping, Bell House, Montague St., Dublin 2, *Ireland*; Confederazione Italiana degli Armatori Liberi, Via dei Sabini 7, 00187 Rome, *Italy*; Federazione Italiana dell'Armamento di Linea, Via Barberini 20, 00187 Rome, *Italy*; Koninklijke Nederlandse Redersvereniging, P.O. Box 16638, 2500 BP 's-Gravenhage, *Netherlands*; General Council of British Shipping, 30-32 St Mary Axe, London EC3A 8ET, *United Kingdom*.

Sources of finance. Contributions from member associations based on gross registered tonnage.

Publications. *Annual Report; EEC Shipping Statistics 1983/1984.*

EEC Shipbuilders' Linking Committee

Address. c/o Fabrimetal, rue des Drapiers 21, B-1050 Brussels, Belgium.

Officers. T. Dilling (ch.); Ing. M. A. P. de Lange (sec.).

Founded. 1968.

Objectives. To maintain liaison with EEC departments with regard to EEC shipbuilding industrial policy.

Activities. Current exchange of information with EEC departments.

Membership. All national shipbuilders' associations in EEC member countries.

Sources of finance. Contributions of national associations.

European Association of Shipping Informatics (EASI)

Address. Jozef II Straat 5, B-1040 Brussels, Belgium.

Founded. March 18, 1980.

Objectives. To develop data handling systems appropriate to various aspects of the information network set up by shipping companies of the European Communities (EC).

Membership. Representatives of shipping companies in EC member countries.

European Shippers' Councils (ESC)

Address. P.O. Box 350, 2700 AJ Zoetermeer, Netherlands.

Officers. J. Draaijer (ch. of standing committee/exec.); G. J. M. Verhaar (s.g.).

Founded. June 19, 1963.

Objectives. To develop and support the common interests of shippers (exporters or importers) in member countries in all matters concerning the maritime and related intermodal transportation of goods.

Activities. The emphasis of the ESC's work has, during the organization's lifetime, shifted from improving the conference system and the position of individual shippers to influencing governments and several international organizations such as the UN Conference on Trade and Development (UNCTAD) and the European Communities. Negotiations and consultation with shipping conferences have taken place on a great variety of matters of mutual interest.

Membership. Shippers' Councils of Austria, Belgium, Denmark, Finland, France, the Federal Republic of Germany, Greece, Israel, Italy, the Netherlands, Norway, Spain, Sweden, Switzerland and the United Kingdom.

Sources of finance. Membership dues.

European Tugowners Association

Address. Tamesis House, 9 Wapping Lane, London E1 9DA, UK.

Officers. A. N. Vernicos (ch.); D. C. Randell (sec.).

Membership. 137 companies engaged in the salvage and towage industry, operating almost 1,000 vessels in ports of 17 European countries (Belgium, Denmark, Finland, France, the Federal Republic of Germany, Greece, Iceland, Ireland, Italy, Malta, the Netherlands, Norway, Portugal, Spain, Sweden, the United Kingdom and Yugoslavia).

Nordic Institute for Maritime Law
Nordiska Institutet för Sjörätt

Address. Karl Johansgt. 47, Oslo 1, Norway.

Officer. Prof. Erling Selvig (ch.).

Founded. 1970.

Nordic Shipowners' Defence Club
Nordisk Skibsrederforening

Address. Kristinelundv. 22, P.O. Box 3000 El., Oslo, Norway.

Officers. Ole Lund (man. dir.); Halfdan Ditlev-Simonsen Jr. (ch.).

Founded. 1889.

Membership. Mainly Finnish, Norwegian and Swedish shipowners representing about 1,500 ships and drilling rigs with gross tonnage of about 32,000,000.

Publications. A Law Report of Maritime Cases (annually); quarterly members' periodical.

Nordic Ships Officers Congress

Address. c/o Norsk Styrmandsforening, Arbiensgate 11, N-Oslo 2, Norway.

Founded. Feb. 24, 1910.

Membership. National associations comprising some 20,000 members in Denmark, Finland, Norway and Sweden.

Eastern Europe

Conference of Chartering and Shipowning Organizations (CCSO) of the Council for Mutual Economic Assistance (CMEA) Member Countries

Address. Prospekt Kalinina 54, 121 205 Moscow, USSR.

Founded. 1963.

Objectives. To co-ordinate the activities of its members to counteract "the co-ordinated actions of the capitalist market (including the Baltic Exchange, numerous conferences and shipowners' pools operating major routes of seaborne transportation of foreign trade cargo of socialist countries, boycott of Cuban cargo shipments, etc.)" by "the united and agreed policy of socialist chartering organizations leaving no room for competition and ensuring their co-ordination on the world freight market".

History. The first meeting of representatives of CMEA member countries' chartering organizations was held in Moscow in 1952. Initial co-operation was centred on analysis of the freight market, joint forecasting of its development, and mutual information exchange. With the growth of the CMEA member countries' merchant fleets co-operation was expanded to the fields of material production and commercial operation of sea-going transport. Following its formation in 1963 by chartering and shipowning organizations of Bulgaria, Czechoslovakia, the German Democratic Republic, Hungary, Poland, Romania and the Soviet Union, the CCSO was joined by organizations of Cuba in 1973 and of Vietnam in 1979.

Activities. As at Dec. 31, 1981, the merchant fleets of the CMEA member countries participating in the CCSO—excluding cargo vessels of 100 grt or less and passenger, technical and subsidiary vessels as well as transport vessels supporting fishing fleets—were as follows:

	Number of ships	*Tonnage grt*	*dwt*
Bulgaria	96	1,053,491	1,598,061
Cuba	99	720,917	1,049,131
Czechoslovakia	19	184,193	275,252
German Dem. Republic	177	1,290,265	1,856,093
Hungary	21	79,815	112,362
Poland	305	2,773,673	4,338,929
Romania	179	1,671,442	2,606,429
Soviet Union	1,704	13,497,639	19,221,065
Vietnam	25	174,914	270,914
Total	2,625	21,446,349	31,328,236

Structure. The Conference, which meets at least once a year, deals inter alia with the "co-ordination of member countries' activities in chartering tramp tonnage and in booking liner tonnage, specialization of individual chartering organizations to carry out certain chartering operations on behalf of other countries' organizations, the unification and drafting of new forms of freight documentation, and the arrangement of joint actions by the CMEA member countries to protect their interests from discriminatory moves of capitalist countries in the sphere of shipping". It has, as its executive body, a ship-chartering co-ordination bureau, and also a documentary council which, in addition to drafting maritime transport documentation, deals with matters concerning legal defence of CMEA member countries' organizations engaged in the carriage of goods by sea. Regional meetings are held to consider problems respectively of the north-western basin (the Baltic and North Seas) and the southern basin (the Black and Mediterranean Seas).

Membership. 27 shipowning organizations and nine chartering organizations (figures in parenthesis showing the year of their foundation):

Shipowners

Bulgaria: Navigation Maritime Bulgare/Navibulgar (1892).
Cuba: Empresa de Navegación Mambisa/Cuban Steamship Company (1959).
Ceskoslovenska Namorni Plavba/Czechoslovak Ocean Shipping Company (1959).
Ceskoslovenska Plavba Dunajska/Czechoslovak Danube Navigation (1922).
German Democratic Republic: Deutfracht Seereederei/DSR Lines (1952).
Mahart Hungarian Shipping Company (1895).
Polska Zegluga Baltycka/Polish Baltic Shipping Company (1976).
Polska Zegluga Morska/Polish Steamship Company (1950).
Polskie Linie Oceaniczne/Polish Ocean Lines (1950).
Romania: Navrom/Shipowning Enterprise.
Soviet Union: the Azov, Baltic, Black Sea, Caspian, Estonian, Far Eastern, Georgian, Kamchatka, Latvian, Lithuanian, Murmansk, Northern, Novorossisk, Primorsk, Sakhalin and Soviet Danube Shipping Companies.
Vietnam: Ocean Shipping Company.

Chartering Organizations

Bulgaria: Bulfracht (1965).
Cuba: Cuflet Chartering Agency (1961).
Czechofracht–Czechoslovak Shipping and International Forwarding Corporation (1949).*
German Democratic Republic: Deutfracht.
Mafracht/Hungarian Shipping Agency.
Poland: Polfracht (1950).
Romania: Navlomar.
Soviet Union: Sovfracht (All-Union Corporation) (1928).
Vietnam: Vietfracht (1958).

"Interlighter" International Shipping Company

Address. H-1367, Budapest, P.O. Box 65, Hungary.

Founded. May 19, 1978.

Activities. This organization has operated 200 lighters (which carry 20-ft and 40-ft containers) and two lighter carriers under contract from the Soviet Danube Shipping Company. These carriers have served the Danube–India/Pakistan line and the Danube–Mekong line, calling in Saigon, Penang and river ports of Kampuchea and Vietnam on the Mekong River.

Membership. The governments of Bulgaria, Czechoslovakia, Hungary and the Soviet Union.

International Organization for Seaports (INTERPORT)

Address. 70-464 Szczecin, Ul. Armii Czerwonej 37, Poland.

Founded. 1973.

Objectives. Co-ordination and rationalization of seaport capacities.

Membership. German Democratic Republic, Poland.

Status. An organization of the Council for Mutual Economic Assistance (CMEA).

International Shipowners' Association (INSA)

Address. Sieroszewskiego 7, 81-376 Gdynia, Poland.

* Member of the Baltic and International Maritime Conference (BIMCO) and other international organizations.

Officer. A. M. Ionkov (pres.); G. N. Fedtchenko (s.g.).
Founded. 1970.
Objectives. Organization of joint maritime traffic services.
Membership. Nine companies and three associations representing another 75 companies in member countries of the Council for Mutual Economic Assistance (CMEA).
Status. An organization of the CMEA.

Middle East

Arab Maritime Petroleum Transport Company (AMPTC)

Address. POB 22525, Safat, Kuwait.
Officers. Abdul Aziz al-Turki (ch.); Abdul Rahman Sultan (man. dir.).
Founded. 1973.
Objectives. To undertake transport of crude oil, gas, refined products and petrochemicals, and thus to increase Arab participation in the tanker transport industry (ultimately to 40 per cent of this trade).
France. Authorized and subscribed capital: $500,000,000.
Membership. Algeria, Bahrain, Iraq, Kuwait, Libya, Qatar, Saudi Arabia, United Arab Emirates.
Status. Sponsored by the Organization of Arab Petroleum Exporting Countries (OAPEC).

Arab Maritime Transport Academy

Address. P.O. Box 1552, Sharjah, United Arab Emirates.
Officers. Capt. Abdulwahab al Diwani (dir.-gen.); Dr Samir Odeh (dir. of education and planning).
Founded. 1972.
Affiliations. An Arab League institution.
Publications. *The Nautical Magazine.*

Arab Shipbuilding and Repair Yard (ASRY)

Address. P.O. Box 50110, Hidd, Bahrain.
Officer. A. J. Machado Lopes (gen. man.).
Founded. Nov. 30, 1974.
Activities. The ASRY opened its drydock in December 1977. (It is managed by the LISNAVE shipbuilding and repair yard of Portugal.)
Publications. *ASRY News*; *Al-Mersa*; *Annual Review*.
Affiliations. Organization of Arab Petroleum Exporting Countries (OAPEC).

Middle East Navigation Aids Service (MENAS)

Address. P.O. Box 66, Manama, Bahrain.
Officer. Capt. M. J. F. Rawlinson, RN (retd.) (gen. man.).
Founded. 1949.
Activities. MENAS is a company registered in London and Bahrain and responsible for the installation and maintenance of maritime aids to navigation in the Arabian Gulf and the approaches thereto.
Affiliations. Associate member of the International Association of Lighthouse Authorities (IALA).

United Arab Shipping Company (UASC)

Address. P.O. Box 3636, Jamal Abdul Nasser St., Salat, Kuwait.
Officers. Abdul Sattar Farman Al-Rrawi (ch. of board); Abdulaziz H. Salatt (chief exec.).
Founded. July 1, 1976.
Objectives. To perform on its own account or on the account of other parties all shipping and maritime transport operations as well as all operations connected therewith in any manner whatsoever; to purchase, sell, charter,

utilize, equip and own all types of vessels, boats, water craft and other maritime conveyances; and to perform all operations related to its objectives and to conclude all such agreements and contracts which promote its various functions.

History. The nucleus of the UASC on its establishment was the Kuwait Shipping Company, whose assets and commitments were devolved to the new company. The UASC started operations as a breakbulk carrier with 25 vessels and launched an ambitious containerization programme soon afterwards.

Activities. The UASC currently has a modern fleet of 43 breakbulk vessels (i.e. general cargo liners, combination carriers or tramp ships) with 1,000,000 tons capacity and 16 container vessels, connecting ports of the Arab Gulf and the Red Sea with ports of the Far East, Europe, North and South America, and the Mediterranean, and also active in cross trades. It is also an active member of various liner conferences, including the (US) 8900 Rate Agreement.

Structure. The UASC has three subsidiary companies: (i) Kuwait Shipping Agencies; (ii) Arab Transport Company (Aratrans), active also in Iraq, Jordan, Saudi Arabia and the United Arab Emirates (UAE); and (iii) United Arab Chartering (London), a joint venture with Wallace Chartering of London. It also has three joint ventures: (i) Container Repair Company in Dubai with a UAE private sector; (ii) Shipping Agencies Services Company in Saudi Arabia with a private sector in that country; and (iii) a petro-chemical carrier under construction in Saudi Arabia.

Membership. Bahrain, Iraq, Kuwait, Qatar, Saudi Arabia, United Arab Emirates.

Sources of finance. Nominal capital 500,000,000 Kuwaiti dinars; issued capital 280,000,000 Kuwaiti dinars.

Publications. *Arab Anchor*; *Commercial Bulletin*; *Link* (employees' newsletter); *Annual Report*; various brochures.

Asia–Pacific Region

ESCAP Division for Shipping, Ports and Inland Waterways

Address. UN Building, Rajadamnern Avenue, Bangkok 10200, Thailand.

Officers. Haroon Ebni-Ali (chief); P. K. Lim (senior economic affairs officer); four other economic affairs officers; (Mrs) Lusnee Pringpuangkeo (associate admin. officer).

Founded. 1975 (within the UN Economic and Social Commission for Asia and the Pacific).

Objectives. To review and analyse developments in shipping, ports, inland waterways and dredging; to recommend shipping policy measures aimed at the development of maritime industries in the area; to promote regional, subregional and national co-operation on specific aspects of shipping and port expansion; to study the special problems of the developing member countries; and to assist in elaborating measures to improve the efficiency of maritime transport as the main carrier of international trade.

Activities. These have been carried out in the following fields of maritime affairs: (i) policy and institutions (guidelines on maritime legislation, a uniform system for the collection of shipping statistics, and freight study units function); (ii) merchant marine and shipping services (continuous review of developments, fleet development, regional co-operation and joint ventures, energy saving and fuel efficiency, shipping and cargo handling technology, fleet maintenance, ship/shipping documents and clearance facilitation, and shipping services); (iii) ports (development policy and strategy, management seminars, impact of containerization and new technologies, port efficiency and productivity, planning and rationalization of investment, port management information systems (PORTMIS), port pricing, and chief executive meetings); (iv) dredging (policy, management, projects, low cost technology, inventory of equipment, hydrographic surveys, and agitation dredging); (v) shippers' organizations (strengthening of shippers' national and regional organizations and co-operation, data information service and national information networks, ship-users' co-operation project, cargo consolidation scheme and chartering techniques, joint planning of shipping services, analytical and negotiating techniques with shipowners' conferences, and chief executives' regular meetings); and (vi) manpower development (establishment of regional, sub-regional and national centres for maritime personnel at all levels, organization of training programmes study tours, seminars and workshops on shippers' co-operation, port management, fleet development, policy, etc., and the upgrading of training institutes for seafaring and managerial personnel). Advisory services have been supplied in all these fields. (The division evolved in 1979 from a Staff Service for Shipping and Ports established in 1975.)

ESCAP also participates with the World Meterological Organization (WMO) in regional bodies concerned with the prediction of typhoons and cyclones and the mitigation of their effects. These bodies include a panel in Colombo (Sri Lanka) with Bangladesh, Burma, India, Maldives, Pakistan and Sri Lanka as members, and a committee (c/o UNDP, P.O.B. 7285 ADC, Manila, Philippines) with China, Hong Kong, Japan, Kampuchea, the Republic of Korea, Laos, Malaysia, the Philippines, Thailand and Vietnam as members. [See also entry for the WMO, page 38.]

Membership. Afghanistan, Australia, Bangladesh, Bhutan, Brunei, Burma, China, Fiji, France, India, Indonesia, Iran, Japan, Kampuchea, the Republic of Korea, Laos, Malaysia, Maldives, Mongolia, Nauru, Nepal, the Netherlands, New Zealand, Pakistan, Papua New Guinea, the Philippines, Samoa, Singapore, the Solomon Islands, the Soviet Union, Sri Lanka, Thailand, Tonga, the United Kingdom, the United States, Vanuatu and Vietnam.

Associate membership. The Cook Islands, Guam, Hong Kong, Kiribati, Niue, Tuvalu and the US Trust Territory of the Pacific Islands.

Sources of finance. United Nations resources, the UN Development Programme, a number of advanced maritime countries and ESCAP member countries.

Publications. Numerous reports on activities of training courses, seminars, workshops, study tours etc., and also bulletins.

Federation of ASEAN Shipowners' Associations (FASA)

Address. c/o Wisma MISC, 2 Jalan Conlay, P.O. Box 371, Kuala Lumpur 04–09, Malaysia.

Officer. Tan Sri Dato Ngah Mohamed (ch.).

Membership. Shipowners' associations of the member countries of the Association of South East Asian Nations (ASEAN), i.e. Brunei, Indonesia, Malaysia, the Philippines, Singapore and Thailand.

South Pacific Bureau for Economic Co-operation in Developing Uniform Maritime Standards for the Pacific Area

Address. P.O. Box 856, Suva, Fiji.

Officer. Mahe U Tupounina (dir.).

Founded. September 1972 (by the South Pacific Forum).

Membership. Australia, the Cook Islands, Fiji, Kiribati, Nauru, New Zealand, Niue, Papua New Guinea, the Solomon Islands, Tonga, Tuvalu, Vanuatu and Western Samoa.

Affiliations. Co-operation with the ILO and ESCAP.

The Americas

Association of Maritime Transport Users in the Central American Isthmus (USUARIOI)

Address. c/o Secretaría de Integración Económica Centroamericana (SIECA), Apartado Postal 1237, Guatemala City, Guatemala.

Founded. May 27, 1969.

History. This association was established under the aegis of the Secretariat for the General Treaty of Central American Economic Integration, concluded on Dec. 15, 1960, and ratified by September 1963 by Costa Rica, Guatemala, El Salvador, Honduras and Nicaragua, i.e. the member states of the Organization of Central American States (ODECA).

Affiliations. The association has close relations with Central American port and shipping organizations.

Caribbean Multinational Shipping Company
Naviera Multinacional del Caribe (NAMUCAR)

Address. Apartado 10095, San José, Costa Rica.

Founded. May 28, 1975.

Membership. Six states.

Central American Association of Shipowners
Asociación Centroamericana de Armadores (ACAMAR)

Address. c/o Secretaría de Integración Económica Centroamericana (SIECA), Apartado Postal 1237, Guatemala City, Guatemala.

Founded. Feb. 17, 1970.

Status. An organization under the auspices of the Organization of Central American States (ODECA).

Membership. Shipowners in the ODECA member states: Costa Rica, Guatemala, El Salvador, Honduras and Nicaragua.

Central American Commission of Maritime Transport
Comisión Centroamericana de Transporte Marítimo (COCATRAM)

Address. c/o Proyecto Transmar, Torre Roble Norte, Boulevard de los Heroes, San Salvador, El Salvador.

Officer. Manuel E. Calvo Vego (sec.).

Status. Established under the auspices of the Organization of Central American States.

Latin American Shipowners Association (LASA)
Asociación Latinoamericana de Armadores (ALAMAR)

Address. Rio Negro 1394, Of. 502, Casilla 767, Montevideo, Uruguay.

Officer. Enrique Oslen-Provist (exec. vice-pres.).

Founded. July 13, 1967.

Objectives. To promote the development of the merchant marine in the member countries of the Latin American Free Trade Association (LAFTA), replaced under a Treaty of Montevideo signed on Aug. 12, 1980, by the Latin American Integration

Association (Asociación Latinoamericana de Integración, Aladi), and to work for zonal integration.

Structure. The association has a general assembly, a governing board and a secretariat-general.

Membership. National associations in 10 countries (Argentina, Brazil, Chile, Colombia, Ecuador, Mexico, Paraguay, Peru, Uruguay and Venezuela).

Affiliations. Consultative status at UNCTAD, ECOSOC and IMO.

Publications. ALAMAR documents.

South Atlantic and Caribbean Ports Association

Address. c/o International Paper Co., Georgetown, S.C., USA.

Officer. C. E. Rhodes (pres.).

Membership. Mainly ports in the United States serving the South Atlantic and Caribbean area.

Standing Committee of Ministers Responsible for Transportation (SCMT) of the Caribbean Community

Address. c/o Caribbean Community Secretariat, P.O. Box 10827, Georgetown, Guyana.

Founded. April 30, 1976.

Objectives. To formulate policies and perform functions as necessary for the achievement of the maritime transportation objectives of the Caribbean Community, including measures to rationalize fares and rates to be charged by providers of transport services to and within the region; to promote and arrange for the financing of joint Community investments in intra- and extra-regional maritime freight and passenger carriers in which some or all Community members would jointly have a controlling interest; to coordinate seaport development; to recommend the updating of member states' merchant shipping legislation: to establish and maintain suitable training institutions; and to encourage the growth of the Region's shipbuilding and ship repair industry.

Structure. Each member state of the Caribbean Community has one representative on the SCMT, which meets at least once a year, with two-thirds of its members, including at least two from the more developed countries (MDCs), constituting a quorum.

Membership. The member states of the Caribbean Community (Antigua and Barbuda, the Bahamas, Barbados, Belize, Dominica, Grenada, Guyana, Jamaica, Montserrat, St Christopher and Nevis, Saint Lucia, Saint Vincent and the Grenadines, and Trinidad and Tobago.

West Indies Shipping Corporation (WISCO)

Address. 48-50 Sackville St., P.O. Box 448, Port of Spain, Trinidad, Trinidad and Tobago.

Officer. Sherman Thomas (gen. man.).

Founded. 1961.

Activities. WISCO is the shipping corporation of the 12 member states of the Caribbean Community (Antigua and Barbuda, the Bahamas, Barbados, Belize, Dominica, Grenada, Guyana, Jamaica, Montserrat, St Christopher and Nevis, St Lucia, St Vincent and the Grenadines and Trinidad and Tobago). It has agencies in all these countries and also in Miami (Florida, USA), the Dominican Republic and Puerto Rico—but it operates only six vessels.

Structure. WISCO has a board of governors constituted by the Standing Committee of Ministers Responsible for Transportation (SCMT) of the Caribbean Community [see separate entry above].

Publications. Annual Reports.

Africa

Ministerial Conference of West and Central African States on Maritime Transport (MCWCS)
Conférence Ministérielle des Etats d'Afrique de l'Ouest et du Centre sur les Transports Maritimes (CMEAOC)

Address. c/o IDREM, B.P. V 196, Abidjan, Ivory Coast.

Officer. J. S. Walla (s.g.).

Regional Academy of Maritime Sciences and Technology
Académie Régionale des Sciences et Techniques de la Mer

Address. B.P. V 158, Abidjan, Ivory Coast.

Officer. Souleimane Sogodogo (dir.-gen.).

Founded. 1957.

Activities. The academy trains deck and engine cadets from 17 countries.

4. The Resources of the Ocean

This chapter is concerned principally with the living resources of the sea, i.e. mainly with fisheries. An introductory survey is followed by (i) tabulations of detailed statistics on exploitation and consumption of the sea's living resources by country and type, (ii) a survey of coastal states' claims to maritime areas for economic reasons (i.e. as distinct from territorial waters claims, which are dealt with in Chapter 1), (iii) descriptions of major conventions, agreements and national legislation on fisheries and (iv) a directory of international organizations concerned with marine resources. The chapter concludes with a section on the non-living resources of the sea, notably hydrocarbons.

Living Resources of the Sea—Background

Introduction

The oceans occupy 70.8 per cent of the earth's surface and have an average depth of 3,370 metres. However, the zone of maximum importance to mankind for the exploitation of the oceans' natural living resources is the uppermost layer of 100 metres, where most of the photosynthetic production of organic matter occurs. This zone forms only about 1.8 per cent of the world's oceans, and from this zone more than 50 per cent of the world's fish catch is obtained.

The regions of this zone are either fairly close to the coast or in very fertile areas of coastal or offshore upwelling regions called "oases" in the sea, which constitute only 25 per cent of the total oceanic area.

The preservation of fish stocks requires an understanding of the position of fish in the food chain of the living resources of the oceans. The distribution of phytoplankton (microscopic algae) in the surface waters of the oceans determines the concentration of zooplankton (small invertebrate animals) which graze on phytoplankton and which, directly or indirectly, form the food for numerous species of fish. The distribution of phytoplankton and zooplankton is shown on maps on pages 70 and 71 of *The Times Atlas of the Oceans* (1983).

Their concentration occurs mainly in three different groups of ocean waters, namely: (i) upwelling and divergencies off the subtropical western coasts of the continents, in particular of Peru, California, north-west and south-west Africa, and in cold nutrient-rich waters rising to the surface along the equator; (ii) in temperate and sub-arctic waters (in the North Atlantic and the North Pacific); and (iii) in shallow continental shelf waters. Fish which are low in the food chain (e.g. the anchoveta off Peru) will occur mainly in these areas, whereas migratory fish (e.g. tuna) are not closely tied to the plankton areas.

Space research carried out by the Soviet Union and the United States has contributed to scientific knowledge relating to the oceans and their resources.

The activities of the crew of the Soviet spacecraft *Soyuz 37*, launched on July 23, 1980, included photographing the surface of the Earth for oceanologists and fisheries experts.

The programme of the US space shuttle *Columbia* for its flight launched on Nov. 12, 1981, included an Ocean Colour Experiment (OCE) to map the distribution of algae and so to locate fish schools or ecological disturbances caused by pollutants.

Brandt Commission's Recommendations

The Independent Commission on International Development Issues (the "Brandt Commission") stated among its recommendations made in its *North-South: A Programme for Survival*, published in 1980, that "ocean resources outside the 'exclusive economic zones' of 200 miles should be developed under international rules in the balanced interests of the whole world community".

With regard to the need for international regimes for the "global commons", including the oceans, the Brandt report stated that the creation of an International Sea-Bed Authority as proposed by the UN Conference on the Law of the Sea [see pages 7–8] would represent a breakthrough, but that there was a real risk that only the least valuable and most remote portions of the seas would be under its jurisdiction. It pointed out that responsibility for research and pollution control in the "exclusive economic zones" of 200 miles or more would not be subject to internationally agreed codes of practice, although "halting the destruction of the oceans" was "of vital concern to all mankind".

The report referred to the importance of fish in the following terms: "Increased consumption of fish could . . . help to reduce hunger and malnutrition. This requires increased supplies and often promotion of new food habits. Most developing countries remain considerably below the average world intake of fish protein per capita. However, many smaller developing countries have technical and managerial difficulties which prevent the adequate exploitation of this resource. . . . At present ocean fishing is largely in the hands of developed countries. To obtain a fair place in ocean fishing, developing countries would have to organize co-operation among themselves, especially among the smaller island states which are potential managers of some of the larger exclusive economic zones but which individually are not capable of developing an efficient fishing industry. Such efforts deserve the support of multilateral institutions and of advanced countries."

World Bank's Policy

The World Bank's policy on fisheries was set out in a *Sector Policy Paper—Fisheries* issued in December 1982. In the paper it was stated that in many developing countries fishery contributed over 5 per cent of the gross national product; that there were at least 12,000,000 fishermen in these countries and that a greater number than that were employed in related activities; and that in Asia over 1,000 million people relied on fish as their primary source of protein (the average per capita consumption of fish exceeding 13 kilograms a year). Of the total world fish catches of some 70,000,000 tonnes a year, some 50,000,000 tonnes were said to be consumed by human beings, with the remainder being reduced to fishmeal and other by-products.

By 1979 five developing countries—Chile, China, India, the Republic of Korea and Peru—accounted for 25 per cent of the world's catch and were among the 10 largest fishing nations [see pages 93–94]. The bulk of under-exploited fish stocks was in tropical inshore areas of developing countries and offered potential to smallscale domestic fisheries.

Between 1964 and 1981 the World Bank and the International Development

Association (IDA) provided loans worth US$259,000,000 for 27 fishery projects (costing altogether $470,000,000)—funds being allotted to boat-building (32 per cent), ports (27 per cent), technical assistance (13 per cent), fish ponds (15 per cent), onshore infrastructure (5 per cent), processing and marketing (4 per cent), and working capital, project preparation, repairs and maintenance (3 per cent). Almost 60 per cent of the loans were used for large-scale fishing development for the export of fish. The rates of return on investment were repeatedly less than expected. In recent years the emphasis has shifted to financing inshore coastal fisheries with the aim of increasing benefits to the rural population and raising the fishermen's standard of living. For 1982–86 the Bank was to provide about $540,000,000 in loans for 20 fishery projects with emphasis on smallscale fisheries.

UN World Fisheries Conference

A World Fisheries Conference was held in Rome from June 27 to July 6, 1984, by the Food and Agriculture Organization (FAO) of the United Nations. It attracted participation from 147 governments (including that of the Soviet Union, invited although not a member of FAO) and some 70 organizations and institutions. The aim of the conference was to approve a global strategy for the fishing industry and its development (on the basis of the 200-mile exclusive economic zones of coastal states as laid down in the UN Convention on the Law of the Sea—see pages 7–8 and 258–65), as well as five action programmes related to the strategy.

The world demand for fish and fish products was, until the year 2000, estimated at the conference at about 100,000,000 tonnes a year, whereas the total catch was 76,000,000 tonnes in 1983, rising to 84,000,000 in 1984, of which about two-thirds were for human consumption and the remainder used for fishmeal (to feed pigs and poultry) or lost through wastage. Since the 1970s catches had risen by about 1 per cent per annum on average, and FAO experts therefore considered it necessary not only to double catches in the next two decades but also to ensure that a reasonable part of the increase should be made available to the neediest developing countries.

FAO reports said the nutritional value of fish had been found comparable to that of meat and dairy products, as fish contained from 18 to 22 per cent of easily digestible protein and also amino-acids not produced by the human body. Fish had accounted for almost one-quarter of world consumption of animal protein. It was noted by the conference that the export of fish and fish products from certain developing countries had increased significantly since 1970. Ecuador exported fish to the value of $6,000,000 in 1970, but in 1982 the value of its fish exports was $221,000,000 (exceeded only by the value of oil exports but surpassing that of bananas). Senegal trebled the value of its fish exports between 1976 and 1982, and the value of fish exports from the Philippines rose from $28,000,000 to $108,000,000 over the same period. More than 20,000,000 tonnes of fish converted into fishmeal were exported to developed countries, especially from Chile, Peru and Thailand, in 1982.

FAO work undertaken in India, Mexico, Morocco, Senegal, Tanzania and Thailand had shown that the period during which fish catches could be preserved could be prolonged by up to six days if the catch was immediately placed in refrigerated seawater.

The universal application of the 200-mile exclusive economic zone had had far-reaching effects on the fishing fleets of many countries, notably Cuba, Ghana, Japan, the Republic of Korea, the Soviet Union, Spain and Thailand, all of them losing many of their traditional fishing grounds and having to redeploy their fleets. The fisheries conference was therefore seen as a logical sequel to the UN Convention on the Law of the Sea.

The 1984 conference unanimously approved a proposal by Norway that emphasis should be placed on the role of fish in FAO programmes to combat hunger. A proposal by Sri Lanka to hold an international Year of the

Fisherman was recommended to FAO's Director-General for consideration. The conference also adopted a report on a global strategy for the management and development of world fisheries, placing the fisheries problem within the context of a world food policy designed to achieve self-sufficiency of nations. It emphasized the need to provide training, the transfer of technology and the conservation of resources in order to prevent the eventual transition from abundance to penury.

The five action programmes—to be implemented on a bilateral or multilateral basis at national, regional and international level and to be financed on a voluntary basis—covered the following tasks:

(1) The planning, management and development of fisheries by improving statistical information, technical co-operation and training over a five-year period, for which an annual budget of $5,500,000 would be necessary.

(2) A special programme for smallscale (artisanal) fishing (important in developing countries, notably in Africa), for which $3,550,000 would be needed per annum ($900,000 of this sum for inland waters in Africa in addition to activities currently financed in West Africa by Denmark and Norway, and in the Gulf of Bengal by Sweden). It was envisaged that this programme should be considered as part of an integrated rural development, with an expansion of the role of women in smallscale fishing communities together with improvements in storage, processing and transport of fish (wastage being put at 40 per cent of catches in Africa). Special technical aid to smallscale fishing was offered by France, Israel and the Soviet Union.

(3) The development of aquaculture (in inland waters), which was growing at the rate of between 4 and 6 per cent per annum, and for which $3,500,000 per annum would be necessary.

(4) The reorientation of international trade in fish and fish products in favour of developing countries (at a cost of $2,000,000 a year). In this context the conference decided (against opposition by the Soviet Union) that it was possible to develop international trade in sea products by offering increased commercialization in exchange for fishing facilities, seeing that many countries were unable to exploit the resources to which they had access, whereas other countries possessed the necessary technology and expertise. (In a conference document it was shown that about 60 per cent of the catches along the coasts of West Africa were made by foreign fleets along the 200-mile limit, and that there were unexploited fishing zones, e.g. off the 450-kilometre long coast of Kenya, where only 7,000 tonnes of fish were caught.)

(5) The promotion of the use of sea products in combating malnutrition, in particular by reducing wastage and increasing aid to poor countries to enable them to reach self-sufficiency (at a cost of $1,100,000 per annum).

Edouard Saouma (Lebanon), the Director-General of FAO, declared in his closing speech on July 6, 1984, that the conference had for the first time reached a worldwide consensus on one of the world's essential food resources. He described the approved documents as a "world fisheries charter" which had given a new orientation to the philosophy of fishery development and provided an integrated framework for aid to the fishing sector in developing countries.

Smallscale (Artisanal) Fishing

Research carried out at the Centre de Recherches Océanographiques at Dakar-Thiaroya (ISRA) has shown that in Senegal the traditional (smallscale) fishing sector has proved that it is possible to reconcile high return on capital with low investments, labour-intensiveness and high added valued.

In particular, return on capital was found to be around 50-70 per cent in traditional fishing concerns and only 3-7 per cent in industrial fishing. Traditional fishing employed 27,000 persons, and industrial fishing 2,700. For the price of one large sardine boat employing 12 persons, 50 small boats employing 1,500 men and producing 30 times more fish could be equipped with seine nets. The cost of creating one job in the industrial sector was over 20 times that in the artisanal sector. Industrial fishermen threw at least 45 per cent of their catches back into the ocean, but traditional fishermen less than 5 per cent, as they sent species impossible to sell fresh (among others) to processing plants, thus obtaining added value. Of catches landed in Senegal, 65 per cent came from small fishermen and 35 per cent from industrial concerns, but of the finance involved only 23 per cent went to the small concerns, against 77 per cent to the industrial sector (according to 1981 figures of the Ministry of Planning and Co-operation).

The researchers have also pointed out that some pirogues (as used by artisanal fishermen) are bigger than some trawlers, and that the size of the vessel is therefore not relevant of an absolute criterion; that industrial units are entirely imported while small fishing concerns only import outboard motors and synthetic nets; and that fuel represents 12–16 per cent of the turnover of small concerns but 25–30 per cent of the industrial ones.

Variability of Fish Stocks

The problem of the variability of fish stocks was discussed in an article in the May-June 1984 issue of *The Courier* (a European Communities journal for relations with the African, Caribbean and Pacific states) as follows;

"The past decades have seen dramatic changes in catches from individual fish stocks. Some of these have involved collapses, of which the most striking was the decline in Peruvian anchoveta catches from well over 10,000,000 tonnes annually, in terms of weight, by far the biggest single species fishery in the world, to under 1,000,000 tonnes in several recent years. Other collapses, including those of many herring stocks in the North Atlantic, have been equally dramatic. Catches from other stocks have, in contrast, expanded. Production of sardines off Japan, and off Chile/Peru have each increased from a few tens of thousands of tonnes in the 1960s to some 3,000,000 tonnes annually. These, and similar changes and their implications for the development and management of the fisheries concerned, were discussed at an FAO Expert Consultation to Examine Changes in Abundance and Species Composition of Neritic Resources, held in Costa Rica in April 1983.

"Historic records covering periods in which there has been little or no fishing show that considerable fluctuation can take place in the absence of fishing. Shoaling pelagic fish in upwelling areas seem particularly liable to long-term natural changes. The causes of these natural changes are seldom clearly determined. The recurrent large-scale oceanographic changes off Peru ('El Niño') do seem to affect the distribution, feeding, and recruitment of anchoveta, but the effects are not consistent. Some El Niños (e.g., 1965) seem to have little or no impact on the fish stocks or the fishery. It is quite possible that the intensity and duration of the impact is modified by the intensity of exploitation. Prior to 1965 the anchoveta was unexploited or relatively lightly exploited, and might have been able to withstand natural events with only short-term changes in abundance and general distribution. In the 1970s the stock had become so heavily fished that it collapsed under the additional stresses of environmental changes.

"Very often the collapse of one species has been associated with the rise of another. Anchovy increased off the Californias at about the same time as the sardine stock collapsed. Off Peru/Chile there has been a big increase in sardine since the anchoveta collapsed. However, the relation is not necessarily simple, such that there is a neat, mechanical balance between the decline of one species and the rise of another. Off Namibia there are few signs of the rise of the anchovy stock there in response to the near-disappearance of the sardine. . . .

"The interactions between fish stocks of different species are becoming of increasing importance. They may contribute significantly to the variation of fish stocks and to the uncertainty in scientific advice. They can be of various types, among which the direct competition between two species with similar ecological requirements (e.g., sardine/anchovy) and the feeding of one species on another, e.g., cod/sprat, are the most obvious.

"Important special cases of the latter are those when marine mammals feed on species of actual or potential economic value. If the fishery of krill in the Southern Ocean expands much beyond its present level it is likely to affect the recovery of the baleen whales. The Convention on the Conservation of Antarctic Marine Living Resources, which has now come into force, requires that these interactions should be taken into account in setting management measures. The scientific problem is that even in the relatively simple system of the Antarctic it is not clear how much krill can be taken without affecting whale stocks, or beyond this level, what are the quantitative impacts on the whale stocks of different levels of krill harvest. . . .

"As it becomes generally recognized that any fishery will sooner or later (and usually sooner rather than later) need managing, it is also recognized that there is more to management than introducing some simple recommendation based on a biological assessment of the stock, for example 'the Total Allowable Catch should be 25,000 tonnes'."

Fishing Vessels and Gear

Specialization of vessels used for fishing has taken place according to the principal species of fish to be caught.

Small craft (below 100 grt) are used in their millions by traditional (artisanal) fishermen.

The length of industrial fishing craft ranges from about 16 metres to over 100 metres. They are usually classified according to the gear they use.

In coastal areas (up to 200 or 300 miles from the shore) fishing is carried out for pelagic fish (living close to the surface, such as sardine, anchovy, herring or mackerel) caught mainly by the use of purse-seines and trawls, while fish traps and surface gill nets are used in shallow waters. In deeper waters demersal fish (which include cod, hake, whiting and plaice) are fished by means of gill nets, purse-seine nets, bottom otter trawls or longlines. Harpoons are used to catch species of high value such as tuna (also caught by longline) or whales.

For long-range fishing, especially by Soviet-bloc countries, use is made of self-contained fleets comprising catching, processing, supply and transport vessels, while Japan and the Republic of Korea have used large individual freezer stern-trawlers which can take thousands of tonnes of fish.

Fisheries research vessels are used by numerous countries, notably by Australia, Canada, China, France, Iceland, Italy, Japan, Kenya, Norway, Poland, South Africa, the Soviet Union, the United Kingdom, the United States, Vietnam and Yugoslavia.

Aquaculture (Fish Farming)

In 1980 the (UN) Food and Agriculture Organization (FAO) estimated the total production of aquaculture at 8,700,000 tonnes per annum, of which 37.1 per cent were finfish (mainly species of high value, such as salmon, trout, plaice and turbot), 36.7 per cent molluscs, 25.4 per cent algae and 0.8 per cent crustaceans. Of the total harvest 75 per cent came from farming of the seas (mariculture), especially in coastal areas, with over 7,350,000 tonnes coming from Asia and Oceania, and over 1,135,000 tonnes from Europe. Aquaculture then accounted for about 12 per cent of capture fishery production and was expected to expand. It has also been a factor in providing employment in areas of unemployment or underemployment.

At an international conference convened by the World Resources Institute in May 1984 and attended by 75 prominent persons, a call was made, inter alia, on all nations with substantial coastal areas to amend their coastal zone regulations and encourage substantially higher rates of investment to expand aquaculture production with the object of achieving a five-fold increase in the aquaculture harvest by the year 2000.

Fish farming has been a commercial success in Norway, and in a report released by the Science Council of Canada in March 1985 it was concluded that jobs lost in traditional fisheries could be replaced by new jobs in profitable fish farming along Canada's coasts, in particular for export purposes.

Specialized Exploitation of Marine Resources

Shrimp. On the fishing of shrimp *The Courier* (published by the European Commission) had this to say in its May/June 1984 edition:

"Shrimp fishing, . . . only calls for small freezer-ships of 20-22 metres in length, which are deliberately simple and have local or regional crews. Although the size and fittings of the vessels are on a small scale, the fishing itself is industrial, being literally solid along the coasts of the developing countries on the continental shelf. A handful of managerial staff is all that is required to run several hundred shrimp boats—which catch and decapitate the shrimp prior to delivery to processing plants all along the coast. Everything is designed to handle just shrimp tails—which are then exported on one of a continuous chain of small freezer-cargo boats. . . .

"Shrimp only represents 10 per cent of the total catch sorted on the deck each time the net is pulled in. So for an annual 20,000 tonnes of shrimps caught on the Guyano-Brazilian continental shelf, 180,000 tonnes of fish are thrown back, although there is a shortfall on the Caribbean market in general."

Krill. Krill (*Euphasia superba*), a shrimp of up to 6 centimetres in size, is found in abundance in the seas around Antarctica, in particular in the Weddell sector (between 30°E and 60°W), including South Georgia and the South Shetlands.

Krill has a high protein content of up to 50 or 60 per cent of dry weight, and it also contains vitamins A, D and B. It has been the principal food of whales (a whale being able to take two or three tonnes of krill in a single feeding, especially as krill occurs in swarms of very high density). The reduction in the number of whales by the whaling industry has reduced the pressure on the krill population, but as krill is also eaten by various seals, penguins, fish and squids, it may be premature to speak of an "excess" population of krill.

Under a Biological Investigations of Marine Antarctic Systems and Stocks (BIOMASS) project launched in 1977 by the signatories of the 1959 Antarctic Treaty, the Scientific Committee on Antarctic Research (SCAR) and the Scientific Committee on Oceanic Research (SCOR) a better understanding has been obtained of the krill phenomenon. Krill has since been caught for human consumption in various forms and inter alia for the production of meal used as animal feed; it has also been used in the pharmaceutical and other industries.

Seaweed. Seaweed is used for its vitamins, iodides, calcium and vegetable gum, and in various industries—in particular in the manufacture of pharmaceutical, dairy, confectionery and textile products. It is harvested for human consumption in the North-West and West Central Pacific, between Indonesia and Japan, where both red and brown algae have been harvested most intensively.

Seabirds. There are about 300 species of birds for which the oceans are their normal habitat and their main source of food—although they all nest on land. They are therefore most numerous where their food supply is abundant and the oceans' nutrients feed quantities of fish and invertebrates. Most seabirds feed on resources of the upper layer of the ocean—on fish of many species and all sizes, on flying fish, on squids and on crustaceans.

The principal families of seabirds are penguins, albatrosses, petrels and shearwaters, pelicans, gannets, cormorants, frigate birds, skuas, gulls (including kittiwakes, which feed on plankton), terns, skimmers and auks (including guillemots, puffins and razorbills).

Migration of some of these birds takes place from the arctic to the southern hemisphere and vice versa (e.g. by the arctic skua and the shearwater) and from the arctic to the antarctic and vice versa (by the arctic tern), and also across the antarctic (giant petrel and wandering albatross).

Some species of seabirds are scavengers, among which the herring gull and the lesser black-backed gull have caused harm to the human environment (inter alia by spreading disease). Seabirds which catch their prey by diving are the auk, the cormorant, the diving petrel and the penguin, while the gannet and the shearwater catch it by plunging.

The impact of seabirds on the world's fish population is difficult to assess.

The guano of some species (including penguins and gannets) is industrially exploited as fertilizer in some regions.

Seal-Hunting. The continued hunting of the harp seal in Canadian waters has been opposed by various conservation groups and also by the European Parliament.

The conservation groups involved have included (i) the (international) Sea Shepherd Conservation Society, headed by Paul Watson, whom the Canadian authorities fined and placed on three years' probation in 1982 for spraying dye on seals to make their pelts useless, and (ii) the International Fund for Animal Welfare, which annually monitored seal culls around Newfoundland and persuaded British store chains to boycott Canadian fish products while seal hunts continued.

The European Parliament called, on March 11, 1982, by 160 votes to 10, with 20 abstentions, for a total ban on the import to EEC member countries of products derived from baby harp and hooded seals. On Nov. 19, 1982, the European Parliament again voted for such a ban (by 52 votes to 10 with four abstentions). Opponents to the ban had pointed out that under existing agreements Britain had the right to fish 15,000 tonnes of cod in Canadian waters; that the Federal Republic of Germany relied on fish from these waters; and that, if the agreements were cancelled, European fishermen would want to find an equivalent catch in the already overfished North Sea. After Britain had been reported to be blocking the proposed ban, the European Council of Ministers decided on Dec. 16. 1982, that the problem should be solved by a voluntary agreement on trade in products derived from young seals. The Canadian government pointed out a few days later that the International Council for the Exploration of the Sea (ICES) had concluded that the stock of harp seals had increased significantly during the past decade and now numbered at least 1,500,000.

The Environment Ministers of the European Communities imposed, on March 1, 1983, a ban on the importation of all baby seal products into the Communities for two years as from October 1983 (unless the Council of Ministers were to decide differently and Canada and Norway agreed to stop the clubbing of young seals off Newfoundland). (Norway had decided in January 1983 to cease killing baby seals and to reduce the hunting of adult seals, whereas Canada continued to hunt seals and decided to seek alternative markets for seal skins, e.g. in Japan.) The British government ceased in September 1983 to issue licences for the commercial taking of seal pelts.

Seal-hunting in the North-West Atlantic is regulated by the Sealing Commission for the North-West Atlantic (SCNWA).

Statistics of the Living Resources of the Sea

The statistics in the following section are taken from the *Yearbook of Fisheries Statistics* (Vol. 56) of the Food and Agriculture Organization of the United Nations, published in Rome in 1984.

1983 Total Catches

In 1983 total catches of marine fish, crustaceans, molluscs, etc. were 67,611,300 metric tons (on a live-weight basis). These were distributed over ocean regions as follows:

Northern Atlantic	13,839,300
Central Atlantic	7,339,000
Southern Atlantic	4,308,100
Indian Ocean	4,070,000
Northern Pacific	23,629,000
Central Pacific	7,793,100
Southern Pacific	6,632,900

Between 1960 and 1984 the annual increase in the world catch declined from about 5 to less than 1 per cent. About half the world's catch has regularly been by developed countries, but in 1981 the value of their catches accounted for more than 86 per cent of that of the world total. About one-quarter of the total catch has been derived from smallscale (i.e. non-industrial) fishing.

Glossary of Terms relating to Fish Species

anadromous	spawning in fresh water, travelling out to sea and returning to fresh water (e.g. salmon)
catadromous	spawning at sea but living mainly in fresh water (e.g. mullet, eel)
clupeoids	members of the herring family
demersal	living near the bottom
pelagic	living near the surface
percoids	members of the perch family
percomorphs	members of the order of spiny-finned fishes
saithe (pollock)	also known as coley (in Britain)

1983 Catches of Fish, Crustaceans, Molluscs etc.

The principal fishing countries' nominal catches of fish, crustaceans, molluscs etc. in marine fishing areas during the year 1983 were as follows (E=estimate).

Country	*tonnes*
Japan	11,020,000 (E)
Soviet Union	8,960,273
United States	4,066,793
Chile	3,977,825
China (excl. Taiwan)	3,372,486
Norway	2,799,303
Republic of Korea	2,353,487
Thailand	2,100,000
Denmark	1,837,500
Indonesia	1,591,930
India	1,558,300 (E)
People's Democratic Republic of Korea	1,510,000 (E)
Peru	1,462,205
Canada	1,287,296
Philippines	1,271,431

Spain	1,226,980 (E)
Mexico	1,049,351 (E)
United Kingdom	839,615
Iceland	838,796
France	784,004
Malaysia	725,898
Poland	704,703
Brazil	646,000 (E)
South Africa	599,097
Turkey	526,873
Vietnam	505,000 (E)
Netherlands	499,325 (E)
Burma	442,930
Morocco	438,544
Italy	437,040
Nigeria	390,306 (E)
Namibia	340,931
Pakistan	283,043
Federal Rep. of Germany	282,820
Sweden	255,486
Portugal	246,270
German Democratic Rep.	217,547
Senegal	212,895
Venezuela	206,860
Ireland	203,400
World total	67,611,300

The world total of catches from inland fishing for the year 1983 was given as 8,859,300 metric tons.

1983 Catches by Species

The total marine fish catches during 1983 for the principal groups of species were as follows:

	tonnes
Flounders, halibuts, soles, plaices, etc.	1,182,701
Cods, hakes, haddocks, etc.	11,350,717
Redfishes, basses, congers, etc.	5,151,433
Jacks, mullets, sauries, etc.	7,899,839
Herrings, sardines, anchovies, etc.	17,144,810
Tunas, bonitos, billfishes, etc.	2,765,448
Mackerels, snoeks, cutlassfishes, etc.	3,663,945
Sharks, rays, chimaeras, etc.	656,752
Miscellaneous marine fishes	8,072,820

The figures relating to 1983 catches of marine molluscs (for their principal groups of species) were as follows:

	tonnes
Abalones, winkles, conches, etc.	92,219
Oysters	1,019,150
Mussels	745,710
Scallops, pectens, etc.	525,161
Clams, cockles, arkshells, etc.	1,305,026
Squids, cuttlefishes, octopuses, etc.	1,629,852
Miscellaneous marine molluscs	134,018

1983 Catches by Country and Species

Major marine fish-catching countries or territories and their catches of over 10,000 metric tons per species of fish during 1983 (E = estimate) were as follows:

Country or Territory	*Species*	*Tonnage*
Algeria (E)	European sardine (pilchard)	38,875
Angola	Cunene horse mackerel	49,135
	Sardinella	27,661
Argentina	Anchoveta (Argentine anchovy)	10,577
	Argentine hake	257,100
	Argentine seabass	10,891
	Atlantic croaker	18,160
Australia (E)	Sharks, rays, skates, etc.	10,661
	Southern bluefin tuna	18,551
Belgium	European plaice	10,591
Brazil (E)	Atlantic croaker	39,670
	Chub mackerel	38,170
	Jack, crevalle	16,190
	Mullet	25,300
	Sardinella	240,150
	Sea catfish	31,700
	Sharks, rays, skates, etc.	16,690
	Skipjack tuna	12,570
	Weakfish	51,160
Bulgaria	Cape horse mackerel	51,177
	Chilean jack mackerel	24,324
	Sprat	12,023
Canada	American plaice	54,000
	Atlantic cod	506,701
	Atlantic herring	142,428
	Atlantic mackerel	19,325
	Atlantic redfish	58,290
	Capelin	31,040
	Greenland halibut	20,037
	Haddock	39,777
	Pacific herring	38,000
	Pacific Ocean perch	11,150

Country or Territory	*Species*	*Tonnage*
Canada (*cont.*)	Pink (humpback) salmon	37,743
	Saithe (pollock)	33,849
	Sockeye salmon	13,720
	White hake	13,117
	Yellowtail flounder	11,665
Chile	Chilean hake	25,249
	Chilean jack mackerel	865,272
	Chilean pilchard (sardine)	2,823,424
	Chilean sprat	18,557
	Patagonian grenadier	22,436
	Patagonian hake	30,894
China	Chub mackerel	153,932
	Elongate ilisha	13,584
	Filefish	137,923
	Greater yellow croaker	33,554
	Japanese Spanish mackerel	62,102
	Largehead hairtail	451,772
	Lesser yellow croaker	28,462
	Pacific herring	21,267
Congo	Sardinella	12,617
Cuba	Cape hake	15,318
	Cape horse mackerel	15,440
	Chilean jack mackerel	54,875
Denmark	Atlantic cod	185,553
	Atlantic herring	173,861
	Atlantic mackerel	35,815
	Blue whiting	82,783
	European plaice	30,549
	Haddock	34,323
	Norway pout	317,881
	Saithe (pollock)	10,530
	Sandeel (sandlancer)	526,821
	Sprat	239,929
	Whiting	32,622
Ecuador	Central Pacific anchoveta	31,593
	Chilean jack mackerel	24,937
	Chub mackerel	96,527
	Clupeoids	69,966
	Pacific thread herring	28,706
	Yellowfin tuna	11,057
Faroes	Atlantic cod	69,537
	Atlantic mackerel	10,047
	Blue whiting	72,634
	Capelin	36,466
	Haddock	15,130
Faroes (*cont.*)	Norway pout	33,878
	Saithe (pollock)	42,446
Finland	Atlantic herring	59,890
France	Atlantic cod	46,650
	Atlantic herring	16,755
	Atlantic mackerel	12,442
	European hake	22,359
	European sardine (pilchard)	25,982
	Haddock	19,367
	Ling	16,151
	Monk (anglerfish)	23,001
	Picked (spiny) dogfish	14,901
	Saithe (pollock)	63,668
	Sharks, rays, skates	10,006
	Skates and rays	13,335
	Skipjack tuna	39,861
	Whiting	39,464
	Yellowfin tuna	35,018
German Democratic Republic	Atlantic cod	11,122
	Atlantic herring	51,990
	Cunene horse mackerel	22,304
	Jack and horse mackerel	64,461
	Sardinella	13,096
Federal Republic of Germany	Alaska pollack	23,740
	Atlantic cod	68,832
	Atlantic herring	17,083
	Atlantic mackerel	22,924
	Atlantic redfish	45,942
	Saithe (pollock)	18,811
Ghana (E)	Bigeye grunt	11,636
	European anchovy	30,700
	Sardinella	36,217
	Skipjack tuna	22,404
	West African seabream	10,661
Greece (E)	European anchovy	10,523
	European sardine (pilchard)	13,113
Greenland	Atlantic cod	51,292
Guinea	Sardinella	12,750
Hong Kong	Bigeyes	13,266
	Threadfin bream	12,371
Iceland	Atlantic cod	293,890
	Atlantic herring	58,867
	Atlantic redfish	122,749
	Atlantic wolffish (catfish)	12,138
	Capelin	133,478
	Greenland halibut	28,360
	Haddock	63,889
	Saithe (pollock)	55,904
India (E)	Anchovy	75,740
	Bombay duck	83,230

Country or Territory	Species	Tonnage
India (E) (*cont.*)	Butterfish, harvestfish	42,650
	Carangids	25,070
	Clupeoids	31,610
	Croaker, drum, etc.	122,610
	False trevally	12,510
	Flatfishes	18,580
	Goatfish	10,850
	Hairtail, cutlassfish	75,830
	Indian mackerel	36,420
	Indian oil sardine	290,280
	Jack, crevalle	11,250
	Jack, mullet, saury	11,820
	Kelee shad	24,160
	Lizardfish	10,810
	Percoids	34,130
	Ponyfish (slipmouth)	56,540
	Sea catfish	58,160
	Seerfish	32,230
	Sharks, rays, skates, etc.	56,710
	Tuna-like fish	18,230
	Wolf-herring	14,410
Indonesia	Carangids	58,290
	Croaker, drum, etc.	16,860
	Emperors (scavengers)	15,050
	Flying fishes	12,540
	Fringescale sardinella	105,850
	Hairtail, cutlassfish	16,810
	Indian halibut	14,270
	Indian mackerel	104,735
	Indian oil sardine	59,980
	Jack, crevalle	11,900
	Mullet	21,720
	Narrow-barred king mackerel	51,080
	Needlefish	21,610
	Ponyfish (slipmouth)	39,750
	Rainbow sardine	13,440
	Scad	80,850
	Sea catfish	34,960
	Sharks, rays, skates, etc.	34,280
	Skate and ray, etc.	15,960
	Skipjack tuna	71,045
	Snapper	42,240
	Stolephorus anchovy	105,570
	Threadfin	14,490
	Tuna-like fish	124,260
	Wolf-herring	12,570
Indonesia (*cont.*)	Yellowfin tuna	34,460
Ireland	Atlantic herring	32,025
	Atlantic horse mackerel	15,085
	Atlantic mackerel	90,375
Italy	European anchovy	54,418
	European hake	22,525
	European sardine (pilchard)	60,193
	Surmullet (red mullet)	10,046
Ivory Coast	Bonga shad	14,618
	Sardinella	19,420
Japan (E)	Alaska pollack	1,623,662
	Albacore	69,936
	Amberjack	39,748
	Atka mackerel	106,465
	Bigeye tuna	143,855
	Blue marlin	17,055
	Cape horse mackerel	17,407
	Chub mackerel	741,962
	Chum (keta, dog) salmon	115,737
	Clupeoids	75,422
	Common dolphin fish (dorado)	14,112
	Croaker, drum, etc.	29,974
	Daggertooth pipe-conger	14,765
	Deepsea smelt	12,335
	Demersal percomorphs	71,486
	Flatfishes	181,126
	Frigate and bullet tuna	17,075
	Greater lizardfish	19,017
	Japanese amberjack	151,269
	Japanese anchovy	204,153
	Japanese jack mackerel	112,444
	Japanese pilchard (sardine)	3,500,000
	Japanese sandfish	12,580
	Japanese scad	71,432
	Kamchatka flounder	13,630
	Largehead hairtail	37,168
	Northern bluefin tuna	26,814
	Pacific cod	99,203
	Pacific herring	25,018
	Pacific Ocean perch	16,592
	Pacific sandlance	130,956
	Pacific saury	213,981

Country or Territory	*Species*	*Tonnage*
Japan (E) (*cont.*)	Pink (humpback) salmon	21,506
	Porgy, seabream	15,191
	Red-eye round herring	35,916
	Scorpion fish	13,007
	Sharks, rays, skates, etc.	10,329
	Silver seabream	36,394
	Skipjack tuna	313,277
	Southern bluefin tuna	14,858
	Striped marlin	14,075
	Striped mullet	11,541
	Swordfish	16,605
	Tuna-like fishes	12,307
	Whip stingray	10,329
	Yellowfin sole	66,794
	Yellowfin tuna	121,433
Republic of Korea	Alaska pollack	367,422
	Atka mackerel	18,733
	Bigeye tuna	33,740
	Chub mackerel	122,883
	Croaker, drum	39,013
	Double-armoured gizzard shad	14,119
	Flatfishes	26,946
	Japanese anchovy	131,859
	Japanese jack mackerel	11,539
	Japanese pilchard (sardine)	139,763
	Japanese scaled sardine	10,606
	Japanese Spanish mackerel	16,224
	Korean sandeel	24,048
	Large yellow croaker	19,294
	Largehead hairtail	152,633
	Pacific cod	11,357
	Porgy, seabream	15,616
	Skate and ray	16,989
	Skipjack tuna	17,722
	Threadsail filefish	172,732
	Yellow croaker	10,153
	Yellow striped flounder	23,912
	Yellowfin tuna	28,348
Malaysia	Clupeoids	24,782
	Croaker, drum, etc.	11,999
	Hardtail scad	11,287
	Indian mackerel	91,624
	Jack, crevalle	19,454
	Kawakawa	20,249
	Russell's scad	20,914
	Seerfish	12,646
	Stolephorus anchovy	35,426
	Threadfin bream	10,711

Country or Territory	*Species*	*Tonnage*
Malaysia (*cont.*)	Yellow-striped trevally	18,564
Maldives	Skipjack tuna	19,700
Mexico (E)	Californian pilchard	316,010
	Groupers	10,130
	Mullet	13,762
	North Pacific anchovy	232,355
	Ponyfish (slipmouth)	66,461
	Requien shark	10,344
	Sharks, rays, skates	18,135
	Yellowfin tuna	20,170
Morocco	Chub mackerel	55,125
	European anchovy	12,938
	European sardine (pilchard)	217,857
	Jack and horse mackerel	18,652
Namibia	Cape anchovy	183,391
	Cape horse mackerel	105,273
	South African pilchard	44,014
Netherlands	Atlantic cod	29,127
	Atlantic herring	49,181
	Atlantic horse mackerel	48,207
	Atlantic mackerel	115,000
	Blue whiting	11,497
	Common sole	17,041
	European hake	10,628
	European plaice	56,251
	Whiting	10,628
New Zealand	Orange roughy	17,656
	Snoek (barracouta)	12,620
Nigeria (E)	Barracuda	16,898
	Bonga shad	31,622
	Carangids	39,755
	Grunt	12,793
	Largehead hairtail	15,635
	Mullet	15,584
	Sea catfish	17,019
	Sharks, rays, skates	33,163
	Snapper	12,404
	Threadfin	30,520
	West African croaker	63,735
Norway	Argentines	13,723
	Atlantic cod	281,143
	Atlantic herring	68,301
	Atlantic mackerel	79,899
	Atlantic redfish	11,268
	Atlantic salmon	18,874
	Blue whiting	190,229
	Capelin	1,492,342

Country or Territory	*Species*	*Tonnage*
Norway (*cont.*)	Haddock	26,285
	Ling	28,575
	Norway pout	190,558
	Saithe (pollock)	225,448
	Sandeel (sandlance)	12,264
	Sprat	22,728
	Tusk (cusk)	26,823
Oman	Demersal percomorphs	10,877
	Pelagic percomorphs	97,889
Pakistan (E)	Croaker, drum	17,840
	Dorab wolf-herring	10,500
	Indian oil sardine	45,660
	Requien shark	15,470
	Sea catfish	11,180
	Skate and ray	52,830
Panama	Central Pacific anchoveta	127,172
	Pacific thread herring	11,775
Peru	Anchoveta (Peruvian anchovy)	118,160
	Chilean jack mackerel	67,904
	Chilean pilchard (sardine)	1,064,448
	Chub mackerel	21,015
	Eastern Pacific bonito	17,058
	Mullet	30,358
Philippines	Bigeye scad	23,658
	Carangids	44,288
	Flying fish	21,886
	Frigate and bullet tunas	61,968
	Fusilier	18,002
	Grouper, seabass	20,178
	Hairtail, cutlassfish	10,232
	Indian mackerel	34,762
	Kawakawa	44,972
	Milkfish	246,788
	Narrow-barred king mackerel	19,268
	Percoids	32,850
	Ponyfish (slipmouth)	54,331
	Rainbow sardine	21,609
	Sardinella	152,868
	Scad	165,547
	Short mackerel	21,949
	Skipjack tuna	59,489
	Snapper	17,890
	Spinefeet (rabbitfish)	19,652
	Stolephorus anchovy	73,844
Philippines (*cont.*)	Surmullet (red mullet)	17,371
	Threadfin bream	30,803
	Yellowfin tuna	53,074
Poland	Atlantic cod	77,401
	Atlantic herring	82,329
	Cape hake	13,346
	Cape horse mackerel	108,297
	Chilean jack mackerel	39,943
	North Pacific hake	13,346
	Southern blue whiting	233,029
Portugal	Atlantic cod	11,860
	Atlantic horse mackerel	36,520
	Cape hake	17,581
	European sardine (pilchard)	86,040
Romania	Cape horse mackerel	116,245
	Jack and horse mackerel	12,029
	Round sardinella	15,789
Senegal	Jack and horse mackerel	17,797
	Porgy, seabream	10,676
	Sardinella	63,920
	West African croaker	10,480
Sierra Leone	Bonga shad	21,127
Solomon Islands	Skipjack tuna	30,904
South Africa	Cape anchovy	240,555
	Cape hake	137,619
	Cape horse mackerel	21,644
	Chub mackerel	13,271
	Red-eye round herring	63,009
	South African pilchard	61,814
Soviet Union	Alaska pollack	2,747,044
	Antarctic icefish	161,020
	Atlantic cod	120,085
	Atlantic herring	112,914
	Atlantic redfish	200,119
	Blackmouth cardinal fish	11,187
	Blue grenadier	12,108
	Blue whiting	109,831
	Cape hake	135,023
	Cape horse mackerel	117,240
	Capelin	860,530
	Chilean jack mackerel	591,005
	Chub mackerel	278,976
	Chum (keta, dog) salmon	18,980

Country or Territory	*Species*	*Tonnage*
Soviet Union (*cont.*)	Cunene horse mackerel	60,850
	European anchovy	230,852
	European sardine (pilchard)	198,898
	Greenback horse mackerel	10,651
	Greenland halibut	16,146
	Grenadier	27,687
	Indian mackerel	12,386
	Jack and horse mackerel	280,340
	Japanese pilchard (sardine)	579,914
	Kamchatka flounder	15,940
	Large-eye dentex	18,367
	Largehead hairtail	54,494
	Longspine snipefish	10,909
	Morid cod	16,548
	Oreo dory	13,072
	Pacific cod	88,600
	Pacific herring	132,892
	Pink (humpback) salmon	96,270
	Polar cod	37,316
	Porgy, seabream	14,879
	Round sardinella	57,616
	Roundnose grenadier	11,279
	Salmonoids	13,333
	Sardinella	126,057
	Senegalese hake	12,871
	Silver hake	27,377
	Snoek (barracouta)	60,907
	Southern blue whiting	44,484
	Sprat	39,209
	Triggerfish	71,141
	Tuna-like fish	12,443
	Wachna cod	30,620
	West African croaker	15,195
	Whitefishes	21,528
	(Also Clupeonella, cultivated, partly in freshwater	396,649)
Spain	Albacore	27,281
	Atlantic cod	36,140
	Atlantic horse mackerel	43,504
	Atlantic mackerel	15,036
	Blue whiting	34,510
	Cape hake	130,354

Country or Territory	*Species*	*Tonnage*
Spain (*cont.*)	Cape horse mackerel	18,364
	European anchovy	48,176
	European hake (E)	40,483
	European sardine (pilchard) (E)	211,911
	Megrim (E)	17,725
	Monk (anglerfish) (E)	29,165
	Skipjack tuna	33,279
	Yellowfin tuna	58,810
Sri Lanka (E)	Clupeoids	68,320
	Demersal percomorphs	22,496
	Mackerel-like fishes	11,565
	Sharks, rays, skates	20,059
	Skipjack tuna	13,775
	Tuna-like fishes	13,075
Sweden	Atlantic cod	60,983
	Atlantic herring	152,511
	Sprat	13,242
Thailand	Anchovy	25,883
	Bigeye	10,109
	Carangids	13,520
	Croaker, drum	11,571
	Indian mackerel	112,752
	Russell's scad	37,697
	Sardinella	122,896
	Seerfish	10,779
	Threadfin bream	18,209
	Tuna-like fishes	51,826
Tunisia	European sardine (pilchard)	10,004
Turkey	Atlantic bonito	33,993
	Bluefish	12,212
	European anchovy	323,161
	European sardine (pilchard)	10,732
	Mediterranean horse mackerel	64,657
	Mullet	19,043
	Whiting	11,564
United Kingdom	Atlantic cod	135,654
	Atlantic herring	56,767
	Atlantic mackerel	189,217
	European plaice	22,343
	Haddock	139,496
	Picked (spiny) dogfish	10,558
	Saithe (pollock)	20,998
	Sandeel (sandlancer)	50,052
	Whiting	64,251
United States	Alaska pollack	284,486
	Albacore	10,513

Country or Territory	*Species*	*Tonnage*
United States (*cont.*)	American plaice (long rough dab)	12,485
	Atka mackerel	11,302
	Atlantic cod	51,018
	Atlantic herring	23,253
	Atlantic menhaden	420,337
	Chinook salmon	11,079
	Chub mackerel	33,075
	Chum (keta, dog) salmon	36,251
	Coho (silver) salmon	13,909
	Finfishes	46,460
	Flatfishes	44,031
	Gulf menhaden	923,585
	Haddock	14,770
	Mullet	11,587
	North Pacific hake	79,973
	Pacific cod	66,186
	Pacific halibut	20,440
	Pacific herring	38,621
	Pacific jack mackerel	17,962
	Pink (humpback) salmon	88,061
	Polar cod	37,316
	Sable fish	18,575
	Saithe (pollock)	13,980
	Scorpionfish	45,367
	Silver hake	17,022
	Skipjack tuna	62,750
	Sockeye (red) salmon	140,681
	Summer flounder	11,757
	Yellowfin sole	22,529
	Yellowfin tuna	73,096
	Yellowtail flounder	33,069
	Winter flounder	15,473
Uruguay	Anchoite (Argentine anchovy)	17,234
Venezuela	Round sardinella	41,078
	Skipjack tuna	15,799
	Tuna-like fishes	15,577
	Weakfish	10,179
	Yellowfin Tuna	20,531
Democratic People's Republic of Yemen	Demersal percomorphs	34,876
	Pelagic percomorphs	36,240
Yugoslavia	European sardine (pilchard)	40,372

Other Marine Living Resources

Catches of countries accounting for more than 10,000 metric tons per species in 1983 were as follows (E=estimate):

Country or Territory	*Species*	*Tonnage*
	Crustaceans	
Malaysia	Marine crustaceans	10,700
Sri Lanka (E)	Marine crustaceans	10,222
Marine Crabs		
Brazil	Marine crabs	12,260
Canada	Queen crab	41,421
Chile	Marine crabs	10,095
China (E)	Marine crabs	307,700
Japan (E)	Marine crabs	78,269
	Pacific snow crab	10,119
Republic of Korea	Gazami crab	17,854
Mexico (E)	Blue crab	11,265
Philippines	Marine crabs	12,308
Soviet Union	King crab	24,637
Thailand	Swimcrab	20,938
United Kingdom	Edible crab	13,272
United States	Blue crab	87,033
	King crab	11,603
	Pacific snow crab	27,705
Lobsters		
Australia	Australian spiny lobster	12,600
Canada	American lobster	27,613
Chile	Squat lobster	14,808
Cuba	Caribbean spiny lobster	10,929
France	Norway lobster	10,303
United Kingdom	Norway lobster	24,224
United States	American lobster	20,052
Marine Shrimps, Prawns, etc.		
Argentina	Argentine red shrimp	18,975
Australia	Natantian decapod	20,814
Brazil (E)	Natantian decapod	50,660
Canada	Pink (pandalid) shrimp	11,604
China	Akiami paste shrimp	167,890
	Fleshy prawn	(E)17,900

Country or Territory	*Species*	*Tonnage*
Ecuador	Natantian decapod	36,600
Federal Republic of Germany	Common shrimp	13,362
Greenland	Northern prawn	41,243
Iceland	Northern prawn	13,091
India (E)	Natantian decapod	214,980
Indonesia	Banana prawn	41,180
	Giant tiger prawn	20,410
	Metapenaeus shrimp	29,920
	Natantian decapod	38,100
Italy	Caramote prawn	10,511
Japan (E)	Natantian decapod	56,703
Republic of Korea	Akiami paste shrimp	16,994
Malaysia	Natantian decapod	16,262
	Penaeus shrimp	64,254
	Sergestid shrimps	12,221
Mexico	Natantian decapod	65,586
Norway	Northern prawn	75,035
Pakistan	Penaeus shrimp	27,502
Peru	Penaeus shrimp	10,849
Philippines	Penaeus shrimp	27,936
	Sergestid shrimps	26,217
Soviet Union	Common shrimp	29,114
United States	Northern brown shrimp	64,034
	Northern pink shrimp	10,853
	Northern white shrimp	30,064
Krill		
Japan	Antarctic krill	42,529
Soviet Union	Antarctic krill	180,290
	Marine Molluscs	
Australia (E)	Cupped oysters	10,100
	Scallops	34,600
Canada	Sea scallop	51,253
Chile	Sea snail	15,990
	Taca clam	23,699
China	Clams	367,416
	Sea mussels	(E)90,100
Denmark	Blue mussel	66,493
France	Blue mussel	51,307
	Cupped oysters	105,000
	European flat oyster	12,819
Federal Republic of Germany	Blue mussel	31,634

Country or Territory	*Species*	*Tonnage*
Iceland	Great scallop	15,181
Indonesia	Blood cockles	27,560
Italy	Marine molluscs	19,575
	Striped Venus	34,899
Japan (E)	Clams	93,437
	Japanese clam	39,750
	Japanese (Manila) clam	144,110
	Japanese scallop	182,356
	Pacific cupped oyster	258,781
Republic of Korea	Ark clams	11,955
	Clams	25,262
	Hen clam	12,453
	Japanese clam	10,474
	Japanese (Manila) clam	40,375
	Korean mussel	47,112
	Pacific cupped oyster	218,463
Malaysia	Blood cockles	38,565
Mexico	American cupped oyster	32,723
	Cupped oyster	11,320
	Venus clam	(E)10,166
Netherlands	Blue mussel	119,643
Peru	Cholga (choro) mussel	14,763
	Scallops	10,422
Philippines	Cupped oysters	11,324
	Sea mussels	18,675
Soviet Union	Mediterranean mussel	14,802
Spain	Blue mussel	124,388
Thailand	Green mussel	61,686
	Horse mussel	30,991
	Short-necked clam	36,586
United Kingdom	Queen scallop	14,280
United States	American cupped oyster	286,511
	Blue mussel	14,472
	Calico scallop	96,509
	Hard clam	44,724
	Ocean quahog	132,674
	Pacific cupped oyster	20,522
	Sea scallop	74,376
	Soft clam	17,840
	Surf clam	137,918
Squids, Cuttlefishes, Octopuses, etc.		
Argentina	Argentine shortfin squid	28,687
China	Inshore squids, flying squids	53,394

Country or Territory	*Species*	*Tonnage*
Italy	Common cuttlefish	12,795
Japan (E)	Inshore squids, flying squids	367,742
	Japanese flying squid	187,886
	Octopuses	43,927
Republic of Korea	Cuttlefishes, bobtail squid	71,154
	Inshore squids, flying squids	38,842
	Japanese flying squid	38,816
	Octopuses	19,583
Malaysia	Inshore squids	10,167
Morocco	Cuttlefishes, bobtail squid	10,071
	Octopuses	32,203
Norway	European flying squid	17,912
Philippines	Common squid	22,374
Poland	Inshore squids, flying squids	110,342
Soviet Union	Inshore squids, flying squids	53,440
Spain (E)	Cuttlefishes, bobtail squids	18,623
	Octopuses	68,513
Thailand	Common squid	77,478
	Cuttlefishes, bobtail squid	42,816
United States	Longfin squid	13,867

Other Aquatic Animals

Canada	Sea urchins	11,826
China (E)	Jellyfish	19,000
Japan (E)	Sea urchins	26,856
Malaysia	Jellyfish	17,196
Thailand	Jellyfish	173,756

Other Living Resources

*Seaweeds**

Argentina	Red seaweed	10,740
Canada	Red seaweed	18,430
Chile	Red seaweed	136,762
China	Brown seaweed	1,387,776
	Red seaweed	99,870
France	Brown seaweed	44,281
Iceland	Brown seaweed	15,781
Japan (E)	Brown seaweed	329,000
	Red seaweed	280,000

Country or Territory	*Species*	*Tonnage*
Republic of Korea	Brown seaweed	272,008
	Green seaweed and other algae	13,150
	Red seaweed	95,399
Mexico (E)	Brown seaweed	25,000
Norway	Brown seaweed	136,665
Philippines	Red seaweed	132,607
Portugal	Red seaweed	11,077
South Africa	Brown seaweed	12,267
United Kingdom (Scotland)	Brown seaweed	10,400

Aquatic Bird Guano, Eggs, etc.

Peru	Guano	10,378
South Africa	Guano	5,515

* The world total of seaweeds and other marine plants harvested was 3,205,000 metric tons in 1983. The quantities of brown seaweeds (kelp) and red seaweeds (laver), expressed nationally on a dry-weight basis, have been converted by FAO to the wet-weight equivalents.

1983–84 Whaling Quotas

For the 1983–84 pelagic season and the 1984 coastal season the International Whaling Commission [see pages 126–27] set quotas at 6,655 minke whales (3,027 for Japan, 3,028 for the Soviet Union and 600 for Brazil) and 165 Bryde's whales (Peruvian stock). According to industry statistics, these numbers were actually caught.

1983 Seal Catches

Important catches of seal per species were made in 1983 by the countries listed below as follows (in number of seals):

Country	*Species*	*Number*
Canada	Harp seal	57,889
Greenland	Harp seal	19,153
	Hooded seal	5,485
	Ringed seal	67,182
Norway	Harp seal	21,407
South Africa	Cape fur seal	46,739
Soviet union	Northern fur seal	7,799
United States	Northern fur seal	25,815

Seals have traditionally been hunted for their furs. In addition their numbers have been reduced by regular culls in order to protect the fishing industries of Canada and Greenland by reducing fish consumption by seals.

Farming of Oysters and Mussels

Various species of oysters and mussels are farmed on coasts in many parts of the world, and the production of the principal producer countries in metric tons during 1983 was as follows (E=estimate):

Country	*Oysters*	*Mussels*
Argentina		730
Australia (E)	1,190	1,100
Brazil	440	
Canada	3,087	244
Chile	582	13,555
China (E)		90,100
Cuba	2,370	
Denmark		66,493
France	182,218	51,707
Federal Republic of Germany		69,767
Indonesia	1,580	
Ireland	316	5,739
Italy		9,008
Japan (E)	258,781	
Republic of Korea	218,463	51,254
Malaysia		2,005
Mexico (E)	36,017	
Netherlands	681	119,643
New Zealand	11,791	5,560
Peru		14,763
Philippines	11,324	18,675
Sierra Leone	900	
South Africa	349	
Soviet Union		14,880
Spain	549	124,388
Thailand	5,343	88,177
Turkey		1,180
United Kingdom	318	5,860
United States	287,950	14,517
Venezuela	755	
Yugoslavia		635
Grand total of all producers	1,019,050	745,704

Disposition of World Catch

Of the total world catch (fish and other aquatic animal resources) of 76,470,600 tonnes during 1983, 56,836,200 tonnes (or 74.3 per cent) were used for human consumption. This included:

Fresh fish marketed .... 23.8 per cent
Frozen fish .... 22.9 per cent
Cured fish .... 14.6 per cent
Canned fish .... 13 per cent

19,634,000 tonnes were used for other purposes, with 18,834,400 tonnes of this amount being whole fish destined for the manufacture of oils and meals.

Consumption, Exports and Imports

The principal fish-consuming countries (per head of population) are Iceland, Norway, Portugal, Japan, Korea (both North and South), Hong Kong, Thailand, Vietnam, the Philippines, Malaysia, Indonesia, Sri Lanka, Singapore, the island states of the Pacific, the People's Democratic Republic of Yemen, Spain, Senegal, Cape Verde, São Tomé and Príncipe, Sierra Leone, Liberia, the Ivory Coast, Ghana, Togo, the Congo, Angola, the Indian Ocean island states except Madagascar, and most of the East Caribbean states.

The value of fishery commodities exports during 1983 by the 24 largest exporters was as follows (E=estimate):

Country	*US$000*
Canada	1,279,165
United States	996,651
Norway	977,932
Denmark	928,363
Japan	787,634
Republic of Korea	734,602
Thailand	544,941
Iceland	527,165
Netherlands	511,402
Chile	419,049
Mexico	393,661
India	349,901
Soviet Union	324,037
Australia	319,166
France	315,621
United Kingdom	311,881
Federal Republic of Germany	304,444
China	281,790 (E)
Spain	280,978
Indonesia	267,250 (E)
Ecuador	239,400 (E)
Hong Kong	210,273
New Zealand	198,929
Morocco	172,489

The largest importers of fishery commodities during 1983 were the following 20 countries (E=estimate):

Country	*US$000*
Japan	3,946,568
United States	3,621,380
France	1,049,656

Country	*US$000*
United Kingdom	908,608
Federal Republic of Germany	831,422
Italy	735,373
Hong Kong	439,506
Spain	395,673
Canada	335,853
Belgium	318,804
Denmark	309,211
Netherlands	272,858
Sweden	261,840
Nigeria	234,842 (E)
Australia	197,779
Singapore	196,963
Switzerland	194,265
Soviet Union	133,389
Finland	94,613
Malaysia	88,126

Coastal States' Claims to Maritime Areas*

Early Claims to Maritime Areas

Few claims to maritime areas were made before 1900. Under the British Cornwall Submarine Mines Act (1858) mines below the sea (even beyond the three-mile territorial sea limit) were claimed as crown territory. In 1907 Russia extended its jurisdiction to 12 miles from the shore for fisheries and customs purposes. In 1910 Portugal claimed jurisdiction over fishing up to the 100-fathom depth line on the grounds that the continental shelf was a natural extension of the land mass. In 1916 Russia claimed arctic islands as being linked to the mainland by the continental shelf of Siberia.

1945 Truman Proclamation

A claim to the natural resources of the continental shelf was first put forward in a proclamation issued by President Truman of the United States on Sept. 28, 1945.

According to this proclamation coastal states were entitled to jurisdiction over the continental shelf on the grounds that utilization and conservation of the subsoil and sea-bed of the shelf depended on co-operation from the shore; that the continental shelf itself could be regarded as an extension of the land mass of the coastal state, and its resources were often merely the extension into the sea of deposits lying within the coastal state's territory; and that for reasons of security the coastal state had a vital interest in activities off its shores.

The proclamation therefore declared that the United States regarded the natural resources of the subsoil and sea-bed of the continental shelf beneath the high seas but contiguous to the coasts of the United States as appertaining to the United States, subject to its jurisdiction and control (while the waters above the continental shelf would retain their status as high seas).

In a Fisheries Conservation Proclamation (issued simultaneously with the Truman Proclamation of Sept. 23, 1945), the United States expressed its intention to conserve fisheries off its coasts, stating in particular that in areas where fishermen of other states were also engaged in fishing "zones may be established by agreement between the United States and such other states, and joint regulations and control will be put into effect".

Continental Shelf Claims to 1951

The Truman Proclamation was followed in the period to 1951 by numerous unilateral claims made to the continental shelf. Such claims were made by Mexico* (on Oct. 29, 1945), Argentina (on Oct. 11, 1946), Panama, Chile, Peru, Costa Rica (on Sept. 28, 1949), Guatemala, Brazil*, Nicaragua*, Honduras (on March 7, 1950), and Ecuador*, as well as the United Kingdom for Trinidad, Jamaica, nine Persian Gulf sheikhdoms, and various other colonies (the Bahamas, British Honduras and the Falklands), and also by Iceland, Saudi Arabia, Iran, the Philippines and Pakistan*. Most of the Latin American countries claimed the shelf as part of their sovereign territory.

When Argentina declared its sovereignty over its continental shelf in 1946 it explicitly linked this claim to jurisdiction over coastal fisheries. This example was later followed by Chile, Costa Rica, Ecuador, El Salvador, Honduras, Panama and Peru.

Chile proclaimed (on July 23, 1947) its "national sovereignty over all the continental shelf adjacent to the continental and island coasts of its national territory,

* For claims to territorial waters limits and contiguous zones, see pages 15–16.

whatever may be their depth below the sea . . . [and] over the seas adjacent to its coasts whatever may be their depths, and within those limits necessary in order to reserve, protect and exploit the natural resources of whatever nature found on, within and below the said seas". It also declared "protection and control . . . over all the seas contained within the perimeter formed by the coast and the mathematical parallel projected into the sea at a distance of 200 nautical miles from the coasts of Chilean territory".

(The motive for this decision was the wish to protect Chile's whaling industry; the choice of the limit of 200 miles, rather than the 50 miles asked for by the whaling industry, was somewhat arbitrary.)

Similar proclamations were issued by Peru in August 1947 and by Ecuador in February 1951, in both cases reference being made to the continental shelf and the waters above it.

Panama, in its constitution of March 1, 1946, listed the submarine continental shelf as belonging to the state.

El Salvador stated in its constitution of Sept. 17, 1950, that the territory of the Republic included "the adjacent seas to a distance of 200 sea miles from the low-water line and the corresponding airspace, subsoil and continental shelf".

*These countries set the limit of the continental shelf at a depth of 600 feet (or 200 metres).

Declarations and Claims, 1952–80

1952 Santiago Declaration. Representatives of the governments of Chile, Ecuador and Peru, meeting in Santiago de Chile in 1952, signed a joint declaration enunciating the following principles: Governments are bound to ensure for their peoples access to the necessary food supplies and to furnish them with the means of developing their economy. It is therefore the duty of each government to ensure the conservation and protection of its natural resources and to regulate the use thereof to the greatest possible advantage of their country. Costa Rica subscribed to this declaration in 1955.

1970 Montevideo Declaration. A Montevideo Declaration on the Law of the Sea, unanimously adopted on May 8, 1970, by the nine Latin American states which had claimed a 200-mile jurisdictional zone (Argentina, Brazil, Chile, Ecuador, El Salvador, Nicaragua, Panama, Peru and Uruguay) contained six basic principles on the law of the sea as follows:

"(1) The right of coastal states to avail themselves of the natural resources of the seas adjacent to their coasts and of the soil and subsoil thereof in order to promote the maximum development of their economies and to raise the levels of living of their peoples.

"(2) The right to establish the limits of their maritime sovereignty and jurisdiction in accordance with their geographical and geological characteristics and with the factors governing the existence of marine resources and the need for their rational utilisation.

"(3) The right to explore and conserve the living resources of the sea adjacent to their territories and to establish regulations for fishing and aquatic hunting.

"(4) The right to explore, conserve and exploit the natural resources of the soil and subsoil of the sea-bed and ocean floor up to the limits within which the nature of superjacent waters admits of the exploitation of such resources.

"(5) The right to explore, conserve and exploit the natural resources of the soil and subsoil of the sea-bed and ocean floor up to the limit within which the state exercises its jurisdiction over the sea.

"(6) The right to adopt, for the aforementioned purposes, regulating measures applicable in areas under their maritime sovereignty and jurisdiction, without prejudice to freedom of navigation by ships and overflying by aircraft of any flag."

1970 Lima Declaration. The Lima Declaration of the Latin American States on the Law of the Sea was adopted on Aug. 8, 1970, by 14 of the 20 participating states at a special meeting (i.e. by the nine which signed the Montevideo Declaration [see above] and also Colombia, Guatemala, Honduras, the Dominican Republic and Mexico) against the votes of three states (Bolivia, Paraguay and Venezuela), with three others abstaining or being absent. It contained a further principle (additional to those of the Montevideo Declaration) "on the right of the coastal states to authorize, supervise and participate in all scientific research activities . . . in the maritime zones subject to its sovereignty and jurisdiction".

1972 Santo Domingo Declaration. The Declaration of Santo Domingo was adopted on June 9, 1972, by 10 votes (Colombia, Costa Rica, the Dominican Republic, Guatemala, Haiti, Honduras, Mexico, Nicaragua, Trinidad and Tobago and Venezuela) to none with five abstentions (Barbados, El Salvador, Guyana, Jamaica and Panama). It contained a section on the patrimonial sea, an area (adjacent to the territorial sea defined as having a limit of 12 miles from the shore), in which the coastal state claimed (i) "sovereign rights over the renewable and non-renewable natural resources . . . in the waters, in the sea-bed and in the subsoil"; and (ii) "the duty to promote and the right to regulate the conduct of scientific research". The breadth of this zone was not to exceed 200 nautical miles. In the zone all states were to enjoy the right of freedom of navigation and overflight and for the laying of submarine cables and pipelines.

1973 OAU Declaration. In a declaration adopted by the Council of Ministers of the Organization of African Unity on May 24, 1973, the rights of coastal states were affirmed as covering permanent sovereignty over all mineral and biological resources in the exclusive economic zone; exclusive jurisdiction of the coastal states for the purposes of pollution prevention and control; safeguards against undue interference with the freedoms of navigation, overflight and the laying of submarine cables and pipelines; and the right of landlocked and other disadvantaged states to participate on an equal footing with the coastal state in the exploitation of the living resources of the zone.

1978 Action by Baltic States. In the Baltic Sea all seven coastal states extended their fisheries limits in 1978 on the principle of the median line between their respective baselines. However, the determination of the boundaries presented difficulties (i) between Denmark and Poland, as the former wished to calculate the median line from the island of Bornholm and Poland from the Danish mainland, (ii) between the two Germanies in the Bay of Lübeck, where a special arrangement had to be agreed, and (iii) between the Soviet Union and Sweden over a disputed area east of the island of Gotland [see page 191].

Exclusive Economic Zones

The concept of an exclusive economic zone (EEZ) resulted from a proposal made on Sept. 21, 1967, by Dr Arvid Pardo (Malta) to the effect that the UN General Assembly should examine "the question of the reservation exclusively for peaceful purposes of the sea-bed and ocean floor, and the subsoil thereof, underlying the high seas beyond the limits of present national jurisdiction, and the use of their resources in the interest of mankind". This proposal led to the adoption, on Dec. 17, 1970, by 120 votes to none (with 14 abstentions) of the UN General Assembly resolution declaring the sea-bed and ocean floor, and the subsoil thereof, beyond the limits of national jurisdiction, as well as the resources of the sea, to be "the common heritage of mankind".[1]

The exclusive economic zone as specified in the UN Convention is part of neither the territorial sea nor the high seas, i.e. the freedoms of navigation and overflight as well as the laying of submarine cables and pipelines are maintained in this zone, and states do not have to comply with the restrictive regime of "innocent passage" (see Article 86 of the Convention). It was generally agreed, however, that in practice there would be a tendency of coastal states to transform their economic rights in the zone to territorial rights.

A recent survey published by the Geographer of the US State Department showed that as at March 1, 1985, exclusive economic zones, exclusive fisheries areas and continental shelf claims had been declared by states as follows (offshore or from baselines and in nautical miles except where otherwise indicated):

Exclusive Economic Zones

200 miles. Antigua and Barbuda, Bangladesh, Barbados, Burma, Cape Verde, Colombia, the Comoros, Costa Rica, Cuba, Djibouti, Dominica, the Dominican Republic, Egypt, Fiji, France, Grenada, Guatemala, Guinea, Guinea-Bissau, Haiti, Honduras, Iceland, India, Indonesia, the Ivory Coast, Kampuchea, Kenya, the Democratic People's Republic of Korea, Mauritania, Mauritius, Mexico, Morocco, Mozambique, Nauru, New Zealand, Nigeria, Norway, Oman, Pakistan, Papua New Guinea, the Philippines, Portugal, St Christopher and Nevis, São Tomé and Príncipe, Seychelles, the Solomon Islands, the Soviet Union, Spain, Sri Lanka, Suriname, Thailand, Togo, Tonga, Tuvalu, the United States, Vanuatu, Venezuela, Vietnam, Western Samoa, the People's Democratic Republic of Yemen.

[1] For a detailed history of the EEZ concept within the framework of the UN Conference on the Law of the Sea until 1977, see Winston C. Extavour, *The Exclusive Economic Zone—A Study of the Evolution and Progressive Development of the International Law of the Sea* (Thesis No. 279, Institut de hautes études internationales, University of Geneva, 1978).

50 miles. Madagascar.

Special claim. Maldives has claimed an exclusive economic zone varying in breadth from 35 to more than 300 nautical miles and adjacent to the maritime boundary with India.

Exclusive Fisheries Areas

12 miles. Finland, St Lucia, St Vincent and the Grenadines, United States.

25 miles. Malta.

50 miles. Iran (in the Sea of Oman, but up to the median line boundary in the Persian Gulf).

150 miles. Gabon, Madagascar.

200 miles. Angola, Australia, the Bahamas, Belgium,* Brunei,* Canada, Chile, Denmark,† the German Democratic Republic,* the Federal Republic of Germany, Guyana, Ireland, Japan, Kiribati, Malaysia, the Netherlands, Poland, Senegal, South Africa, the Soviet Union, Sweden, Trinidad and Tobago, the United Kingdom, Zaïre.

Special claims. Qatar and Singapore claim fishery zones defined by bilateral maritime boundaries or an equidistant line.

* Defined by the country's bilateral maritime boundaries or by an equidistant line.

† For further details of the Danish claim, see page 118.

The Soviet Union's 200-mile continental shelf and fishery zone claim is, in regard to its delimitation against Japan's zone, an equidistance line based on the Soviet-held islands (but claimed by Japan) immediately to the north of the northern main Japanese island of Hokkaido [see also pages 241–43].

Continental Shelf Claims

200 metres' depth. Argentina, Australia, the Bahamas, Brazil, Canada, Colombia, Cuba, Cyprus, Denmark, Ecuador, Egypt, Fiji, Finland, France, the German Democratic Republic, the Federal Republic of Germany, Greece, Honduras, Italy, the Ivory Coast, Liberia, Malaysia, Malta, Morocco, Nicaragua, Nigeria, Norway, Oman, Papua New Guinea, Portugal, Romania, South Africa, the Soviet Union, the Sudan, Sweden, Syria, Thailand, Tonga, Trinidad and Tobago, the United Kingdom, the United States, Uruguay, Venezuela, the Yemen Arab Republic, the People's Democratic Republic of Yemen, Yugoslavia.

150 miles. Madagascar.

200 miles. Cape Verde, Chile, Costa Rica, Kampuchea, Peru.

Other claims. Claims to the continental

shelf down to an unspecified depth of exploitation have been made by Haiti, Indonesia, Israel and the Philippines. Ghana has claimed a continental shelf to a depth of 100 fathoms.

Unspecified claims to the continental shelf have been made by Bahrain, Belgium, Cameroon, The Gambia, Guatemala, Iran, Iraq, Kuwait and Saudi Arabia.

Claims to a continental margin up to 200 nautical miles from their shores have been made by Burma, the Dominican Republic, Guyana, Mauritania, Mauritius, New Zealand, Pakistan, Senegal, Seychelles, Sri Lanka, Vietnam and the People's Democratic Republic of Yemen. An unspecified claim to the continental margin has been made by Bangladesh.

[The continental margin consists of three parts—(i) the continental shelf proper, varying usually from 130 to 200 metres in depth; (ii) the continental slope, extending from the outer edge of the continental shelf to a depth of 1.5 to 3.5 kilometres, with an inclination of from three to 50 degrees; and (iii) the continental rise, a deposit of sediments at the base of the continental slope, and found between 1,500 and 5,000 metres of water, partly overlying the oceanic crust and potentially mineral-bearing. Beyond the continental margin there lies the abyssal sea-bed.]

In an interview published in *The Courier* (an organ of the European Communities for their relations with African, Caribbean and Pacific, or ACP, states) of May/June 1984, Dr J. Carroz, secretary-general of the World Conference on Fisheries Management and Development, pointed out that, regardless of the delay in ratifications of the UN Convention on the Law of the Sea, the regime of the 200-mile exclusive economic zones had become a reality and had entered into customary international law.

Other assessments pointed out that the 200-mile exclusive economic zone limit had been adopted unilaterally by most coastal states to counteract the over-exploitation of their coastal fish stocks. Previously some 12,000,000 tonnes of fish, mostly for human consumption, were taken annually by the distant-water fleets of all nations in waters which have since 1977 been under coastal state management (the total world catch for human consumption being then 46,000,000 tonnes). While many countries lost access to traditional fishing grounds, some have gained grounds, among them Australia, Canada, Greenland, Iceland, New Zealand and the United States.

Some fishing grounds have been retained through bilateral agreements (e.g. by Spain) with other countries. However, joint stock management of fish resources has not always been successful. In the Baltic Sea, for instance, the total allowable catch has often been exceeded because there has been no effective enforcement system.

The Intergovernmental Oceanographic Commission (IOC) [see pages 175–77] estimated in a report published on Jan. 1, 1980, that the extension of fishery limits to a maximum of 200 nautical miles by all coastal states would mean that over 35 per cent of the world's oceans would be enclosed within national zones of control, covering over 90 per cent of the living marine resources currently under exploitation. Moreover, the coastal states would face increased responsibilities for conservation and management measures; for promotion of the optimum utilization of their resources; for determining their own capacity to harvest the available catch and giving other states access to any surplus; and for the conservation and development of any stocks shared by two or more coastal states (or any other states) fishing beyond their own zones.

Fishery Conventions, Agreements and Legislation

Fishery Conventions

1958 UN CONVENTION ON FISHING

The 1958 UN Convention on Fishing and Conservation of the Living Resources of the High Seas [see page 4] defined "the principal objective of conservation of the living resources of the sea" as being "to obtain the optimum sustainable yield so as to secure a maximum supply of food and other marine products". (The optimum sustainable yield was later defined as the "maximum sustainable yield", or

MSY.) The convention has not been widely ratified, however.

It was stated in the convention that a coastal state had "a special interest in the maintenance of the productivity of the living resources in any area of the high seas adjacent to its territorial sea" (Article 6), but no fishing limit was laid down. The convention also required states to adopt, or co-operate with other states in adopting, conservation measures for their nationals as necessary.

EUROPEAN FISHERIES CONVENTION

Under a convention signed on March 9, 1964, the governments of Austria, Belgium, Denmark, France, the Federal Republic of Germany, Ireland, Italy, Luxembourg, the Netherlands, Portugal, Spain, Sweden and the United Kingdom defined their rights to fisheries in their coastal waters. The convention was eventually largely subsumed into the common fisheries policy of the European Communities [see pages 111–13].

They agreed that (i) "the coastal state has the exclusive right to fish and exclusive jurisdiction in matters of fisheries within the belt of six miles measured from the baselines of its territorial sea" (Article 2); (ii) "within the belt between six and 12 miles measured from the baseline of the territorial sea the right to fish shall be exercised only by the coastal state and by such other contracting parties the fishing vessels of which have traditionally fished in that belt between Jan. 1, 1953, and Dec. 3, 1962" (Article 3); (iii) the coastal state may enforce the rule that foreign fishing vessels may not exceed their habitual exploitation of fish stocks or fishing grounds (Article 4); (iv) the coastal state has the power to regulate the fisheries in the six to 12-mile zone (Article 5); and (v) "where the coasts of two contracting parties are opposite or adjacent to each other, neither of these contracting parties is entitled, failing agreement between them to the contrary, to establish a fisheries régime beyond the median line . . ." (Article 6).

The convention also contained provisions on non-discrimination, on non-interference with provisions of existing fishery agreements to which signatory states are parties, and on preferential treatment of local populations overwhelmingly dependent on fisheries. The convention defined for each country the coasts to which its provisions were to apply, as follows: Belgium, Ireland and the United Kingdom and its Crown Dependencies—all coasts; Denmark—coasts of the North Sea, Skagerrak and Kattegat; France—Atlantic, North Sea and Channel coasts; the Federal Republic of Germany—North Sea coast; the Netherlands—North Sea coast; Portugal—Atlantic coast north of the 36th parallel and the coast of Madeira; Spain—Atlantic coast north of the 36th parallel; Sweden—its west coast.

The convention also provided, in an annexe, for arbitration, and, in a draft protocol, for the provisional application of the convention. In two further agreements several of the contracting parties laid down transitional rights for the periods up to Dec. 31, 1965, and up to Dec. 31, 1966.

The convention was to enter into force upon the deposit of instruments of ratification or approval by eight signatory governments. It was to be of unlimited duration, but after 20 years from the date of its entry into force any contracting party was entitled to give two years' notice of withdrawal.

CONVENTION ON FISHING AND CONSERVATION OF LIVING RESOURCES IN THE BALTIC SEA AND THE BELTS

Originally signed in Gdansk (Poland) on Sept. 13, 1977, this convention was amended, with effect from Feb. 10, 1984, in particular to take account of the fact that the states of the Baltic Sea basin had extended their jurisdiction over the living resources to waters beyond and adjacent to their territorial waters.

The convention provided inter alia for close co-operation among the contracting states in preserving and increasing the area's living resources and obtaining the optimum yield. It established an International Baltic Sea Fishery Commission [see separate entry], on which each contracting state would have one vote, provided (under the 1984 amendments) that any recommendation relating to areas under the fisheries jurisdiction of one or more contracting states should enter into force for these states only in case they had given affirmative votes thereto. The amended convention also laid down conditions under which a contracting state might withdraw its acceptance of any recommendation.

The seven original contracting parties to the convention included Denmark and the Federal Republic of Germany (which have been replaced by the European Economic Community)—the five others being Finland, the German Democratic Republic, Poland, the Soviet Union and Sweden. A secretariat for the implementation of the convention has been established in Warsaw.

CONVENTION ON THE CONSERVATION OF ANTARCTIC SEALS

This convention on the protection of seals in the Antarctic, including those on floating ice and in the open sea, was concluded in February 1972 by the original signatories of the 1959 Antarctic Treaty—Argentina, Australia, Belgium, Chile, France, Japan, New Zealand, Norway, South Africa, the Soviet Union, the United Kingdom and the United States. It came into force on March 11, 1978.

INTERNATIONAL CONVENTION FOR THE CONSERVATION OF SALMON IN THE NORTH ATLANTIC OCEAN

This convention was ratified by the European Community, Denmark (for the Faroe Islands), Iceland, Norway and the United States, and also by Canada (in 1983).

In the convention it was recognized that countries in whose rivers salmon originate and spawn have the primary interest in and responsibility for such stocks, and that interception of salmon by fishermen in waters of other countries has to be limited.

Trilateral Fishery Agreements

Denmark, Norway and Sweden. In 1952 the three governments concluded an agreement concerning measures for the protection of the stocks of deep-sea prawns, European lobsters and crabs.

A convention concerning the preservation of plaice and dab (in the Skagerrak, Kattegat and Sound) was concluded by the three parties in 1937.

Iceland, Norway and the Soviet Union. An agreement on the regulation of fishing of the Atlantic Scandinavian herring was concluded by the three parties in 1973.

Norway, the Soviet Union and the UK. An agreement on the regulation of the fishing of North-East Atlantic cod was concluded by the three parties in 1974.

Common Fisheries Policy of the European Communities

A common fisheries policy (CFP) for the European Communities (EC) was agreed on Jan. 25, 1983, its four constituent parts being (i) an EC system for the conservation of resources, including a listing of total allowable catches (TACs), the allocation of quotas to individual states, and agreement on exclusive access zones; (ii) structural measures designed to adjust capacity in the fishing industry and to improve productivity; (iii) a common organization of the market; and (iv) fisheries agreements with non-member countries, together with formal consultations between member countries with a view to concerted action in the context of international agreements.

The TACs were based on scientific analyses of stocks by the independent International Council for the Exploration of the Sea (ICES). The quotas agreed were based on criteria laid down by the EC Council of (Foreign) Ministers in May 1980, viz. traditional fishing activities, specific needs of regions particularly dependent on fish, and the loss of fishing rights in the waters of non-member countries. The quotas for the seven main commercial species (cod, haddock, whiting, plaice, saithe, redfish and mackerel) were allocated in percentages as follows: United Kingdom 37.3, Denmark 25.5, France 11.6, the Federal Republic of Germany 11.4, the Netherlands 7.7, Ireland 4.6, Belgium 1.9, and none for Greece, Italy and Luxembourg. In regard to national fishing zones the existing six-mile limit for Denmark, Ireland and the United Kingdom was extended to 12 nautical miles on a general basis, while taking account of the historic rights of the member countries in the 6-12 mile zone. These arrangements were to apply until Dec. 31, 2002.

For the adjustment of fleet capacity in the light of conservation needs and for the modernization and redeployment of fishing vessels aid totalling 250,000,000 European currency units (ECUs) (about US$235,000,000) would be given for a three-year period.

Measures for the common organization of the market agreed earlier and fully applicable from Jan. 1, 1983, were aimed at helping to prevent third countries from dumping fisheries products on the EC market. The European Commission was empowered to act within six days, either by imposing import duties or by banning imports from a specified third country.

By Jan. 25, 1983, the EC had concluded framework fisheries agreements with Norway, Sweden, the Faroe Islands, Spain, the United States, Canada, Senegal, Guinea-Bissau and Guinea. Agreements with Equatorial Guinea and São Tomé and Príncipe were initialled respectively in June and August 1983. An agreement between the EC and Finland, signed on July 6, 1983, and in force from Jan. 5, 1984, authorized the fishing vessels of either side to fish within the 200-mile zone under the other's jurisdiction up to an agreed TAC to be fixed annually. EC agreements with Seychelles and Madagascar were initialled respectively on Jan. 5, 1984, and in December 1984.

Multilateral agreements had also been concluded on EC participation in international agreements covering the North-West and North-East Atlantic, the Antarctic and salmon fishing in the North Atlantic.

The final form of the CFP constituted a compromise between the widely divergent interests of the EC member countries. Denmark, the Netherlands and the Federal Republic of Germany had strong interests in the fish and processing industries and stood to gain from cheap imports from third countries, but nevertheless accepted greater Community control. Some member countries complained that the expansion of the Danish fertilizer and fishmeal industry had led to the depletion of stocks to the detriment of all concerned. The United Kingdom and the Federal Republic emphasized their claim to quotas sufficient to compensate for lost fishing grounds outside EC waters (especially in the 200-mile zones of Iceland and Norway).

TACs for the year 1984 were fixed on Jan. 31, 1984. At the same time fishing for herring was banned from Jan. 1, 1984, in the northern and central North Sea, while in the southern sector EC vessels were allowed to catch only 17,000 tonnes of herring. The total herring quota was fixed at 34,500 tonnes up to the end of July, with another 20,000 tonnes later if approved in scientific reports.

In September 1983 all EC member countries except Luxembourg were granted 36,400,000 ECUs in structural aid (for fleet modernization and the building of vessels under 24 metres long).

On Dec. 20-24, 1984, the Council of Ministers agreed on TACs for 1985 for the main species of the European Communities and in waters jointly managed with non-member countries as follows (in metric tons): Cod 469,250, haddock 197,950, saithe (pollock) 160,100, whiting 191,450, plaice 208,480, mackerel 350,500, herring 413,350, and redfish 65,320. EC quotas for cod in Greenland waters (following Greenland's withdrawal from the EC) were fixed at 11,500 tonnes (against 12,500 in 1984).

It was disclosed in October 1984 that there had been 18 cases of EC member countries exceeding their TACs. As from April 1, 1985, it was made obligatory for boats of over 10 metres' length to log all catches in log books issued by the EC. In a report by the select committee on European affairs of the UK House of Lords, issued in January 1985, it was found that the EC's TACs were, as a matter of routine, being exceeded in disregard of scientific recommendations and that fish stocks in EC waters were being depleted.

New EC measures to prevent illegal overfishing and to conserve stocks, announced on Jan. 1, 1985, provided that from April 1, 1985, skippers of all vessels of more than 10 metres in length would be required to log their catches and to make statutory landing declarations upon reaching port.

Accession of Spain and Portugal

The accession of Spain (with a fishing fleet larger than that of the whole EC) and Portugal to the EC as from Jan. 1, 1986, meant that the 200-mile exclusive economic zone of the EC was more than doubled (in particular by the inclusion of Atlantic island groups), but the continental shelf area (of fishing grounds and commercial stocks) was increased only marginally. (Spain had, in April 1983, signed an agreement with the EC, regulating catch quotas for 1983 by reducing hake catches from 8,500 tonnes in 1982 to 8,300 tonnes in 1983, and the number of licences for Spanish boats fishing in EC waters from 114 to 111.)

Sundry EC Decisions

Baby Seal Skins. On Feb. 28, 1983, the EC decided to ban imports of all baby seal skins from Canada for two years from October 1983 (unless drastic changes were made in Canadian and also Norwegian seal hunting practices). In retaliation Canada announced on March 3, 1983, a sharp reduction in EC fishing rights in Canadian waters from 16,000 tonnes of cod to 10,600 tonnes.

Norway and Sweden. An agreement between the EC, Norway and Sweden, regulating fishing in the Skagerrak and Kattegat for 1983, was signed in Brussels on March 23, 1983.

United States. A five-year agreement was initialled on June 27, 1984, approved by the EC Council of Ministers on Sept. 10 and formally adopted by it on Sept. 30, 1984; it superseded a 1977 agreement due to expire on July 1, 1984 but extended to Sept. 30 of that year. It was finally signed by both parties in October 1984 and provided for an increase in the EC TAC for herring and a decrease in that for sprat.

Bilateral Fishery Agreements

Bilateral fishery agreements embodying the principle of a 12-mile exclusive fishing zone were signed between 1961 and 1971 by the following countries on the dates shown:

Iceland and the UK .... March 11, 1961
Norway and the Soviet Union .... April 16, 1962
Norway and the UK .... Sept. 28, 1964
Poland and the UK .... Sept. 28, 1964
Soviet Union and the UK .... Sept. 30, 1964
France and Spain .... March 22, 1967
Japan and New Zealand .... July 12, 1967
Mexico and the USA .... Oct. 27, 1967
Denmark and the Federal Republic of Germany .... Nov. 30, 1967
Japan and Mexico .... March 7, 1968

Denmark and the
Netherlands......................May 30, 1968
Australia and Japan............Nov. 27, 1968
Morocco and Spain................Jan. 4, 1969
Finland and the Soviet
Union .... June 13, 1969
Canada and the USA..........April 24, 1970
Japan and the USA .... Dec. 11, 1970
Soviet Union and the USA .... Feb. 2, 1971
Denmark and Poland............June 1, 1971

Further bilateral fisheries agreements are listed below in alphabetical country order:

Angola and the Soviet Union. An agreement allowing Soviet vessels to fish in Angolan waters was signed on April 4, 1977.

Angola and Spain. A fishing agreement signed in Luanda on June 11, 1980, allowed at least 84 Spanish vessels to fish in Angolan waters for three years, whereafter the agreement was renewable automatically for every year. In return Spain was to supply Angola with part of the catch and inter alia establish a refrigeration plant at Porto Alexandre (southern Angola).

Australia and Indonesia. An agreement on regulations controlling fishing on both sides of the median line in the area of the overlap of the two countries' maritime zones [see page 201] was signed in Jakarta in October 1981 and entered into force in February 1982.

Australia and Japan. A provisional fisheries agreement, due to expire on Jan. 31, 1979, was extended before that date to allow Japanese vessels to continue operations in Australian waters. Under an agreement signed on Oct. 17, 1979, the Japanese were to pay A$1,400,000 a year for the right to catch 11,000 tonnes of tuna inside the newly declared Australian 200-mile exclusive economic zone from November 1981 to October 1982.

Australia and Taiwan. Under an agreement signed in February 1982 a total of 60 pairs of Taiwanese trawlers and 30 gill-netting boats were allowed to operate in the Australian fishing zone from November 1981 to October 1982 against payment of more than A$1,000,000 to the Australian Government.

Brazil and the Netherlands. An agreement concerning the catching of shrimp in the South-West Atlantic was signed by the two sides in 1972.

Brazil and Trinidad and Tobago. An agreement concerning the catching of shrimp in the Caribbean was signed by the two governments in 1972.

Brazil and Uruguay. An agreement on fishing and the conservation of living resources was concluded by the two governments in 1968.

Canada and Norway. An agreement on sealing and the conservation of seal stocks in the North-West Atlantic Ocean has been signed by the two parties.

Canada and the Soviet Union. An agreement of Jan. 22, 1971, provided for co-operation in fisheries by the two parties in the North-East Pacific Ocean off the coast of Canada.

Canada and Spain. An agreement signed on May 21, 1982, provided for concessions and quotas for cod and squid to be fished by Spanish vessels off the coast of Newfoundland.

Canada and the USA. A treaty has been concluded on Pacific Coast Albacore Tuna Vessels and Port Privileges. Moreover, an agreement concerning fishing off the west coast of Canada was concluded by the two sides in 1979.

A Canadian–US treaty on salmon fishing, signed in Ottawa on Jan. 28, 1985, regulated fisheries off the coasts of Alaska and British Columbia by reducing chinook catches, limiting the coho salmon fishing off the west coast of Vancouver Island and giving Canada a larger share of the pink and sockeye salmon originating in the Fraser River (British Columbia).

China and Japan. On Jan. 16, 1979, China and Japan agreed to revise a bilateral fishing agreement which had expired on Dec. 21, 1978 (introducing restrictions on Japanese fishing in the Yellow and East China Seas), and to raise from three to four the number of fishery conservation areas, where trawling was prohibited. Under a 1977 convention, the two countries had formed the Japan–China Joint Fisheries Commission.

Colombia and Ecuador. Under a maritime boundary agreement which was signed on Aug. 23, 1975, and which came into force on Dec. 22, 1975, the two sides agreed to delimit the boundary between their respective marine and submarine areas as being the line of the geographical parallel intersecting the point at which the international terrestrial border line between the two countries reaches the sea (Article 1). The two sides also agreed to establish, beyond 12 nautical miles from the coast, a special zone 10 nautical miles in width on either side of the aforesaid parallel for the purpose of ensuring that "the accidental presence of local fishermen of either country in that zone should not be considered a violation of the marine boundary" (Article 2). The agreement also provided for the recognition of the two parties' right to establish "sovereignty, jurisdiction or supervision" in a zone up to 200 miles from the coast (Article 3). In addition it provided for "the most comprehensive co-operation" in protecting the renewable and non-renewable resources of these marine zones and also in facilitating international navigation in the seas under their jurisdiction. (Ecuador had claimed a 200-nautical-mile territorial sea limit in February 1951, whereas Colombia claimed such a limit of 12 nautical miles only.)

Costa Rica and the USA. An agreement concluded by the two parties in 1949 regulated yellow tuna fisheries in the South Pacific.

Denmark and Norway. An agreement was signed in June 1979 by Denmark and Norway on the delimitation of the continental shelf area between Norway and the Faroe Islands and on the boundary between the Faroes' fishery zone and Norway's exclusive economic zone.

Denmark and the USA. An agreement on the conservation of Atlantic salmon was concluded by the two sides in 1972.

Finland and the Soviet Union. An agreement on fishing and sealing in the Gulf of Finland was signed by the two sides in 1969.

Federal Republic of Germany and Mexico. A fisheries agreement signed in Mexico City in August 1974 provided for close co-operation between the two countries in research on fish resources off Mexico's Pacific coast and in the development of Mexican deep-sea fisheries, with an appropriate portion of their products to be exported to the Federal Republic of Germany.

German Democratic Republic and Sweden. A fishery agreement between the two countries was signed late in 1977, and on June 22, 1978, a treaty was concluded between them on the delimitation of their continental shelves and fishing zones on the basis of the median line in the Baltic Sea.

Iceland and Norway. After declaring a 200-mile fisheries zone with effect from Jan. 1, 1977, the Norwegian Government declared a 200-mile exclusive economic zone around the island of Jan Mayen (some 350 miles north-east of Iceland) with effect from May 29, 1980. On the previous day the two countries signed an agreement in which they mutually accepted their above declarations but with the proviso that Iceland would have sovereignty over the 10,000 square miles where the two zones overlapped. Moreover, fishing between Iceland and Jan Mayen would be regulated by a bilateral committee with a view to determining catch quotas for capelin. If no agreement were reached Iceland would decide the catch quota unilaterally, but Norway would not regard itself as bound by a total quota which it considered unreasonable; for 1980–83 Norway's share of the quota would be 15 per cent. This agreement did not cover rights to the area's continental shelf.

Indonesia and Papua New Guinea. In an agreement signed in Jakarta on Dec. 13, 1980, the two sides laid down the boundaries of the continental shelf, the exclusive economic zone and the fishing zone in extension of the border between Irian Jaya and Papua New Guinea. This agreement completed an earlier sea-bed boundary agreement of 1971 and its amendment of 1973.

Japan and the Democratic People's Republic of Korea. Under a provisional agreement reached in August 1977, Japanese fishermen were allowed to operate within North Korea's 200-mile zone but outside the 50-mile military zone proclaimed by North Korea. Following alleged violations of the agreement by Japanese vessels crossing into the 50-mile zone, the agreement was not extended beyond mid-1982. It was, however, succeeded by a new agreement concluded on Oct. 15, 1984, when a joint committee was set up to monitor operations by Japanese fishermen in North Korea's 200-mile economic zone (especially for squid and mackerel) without having to pay fees. (For Japan this agreement was signed by a parliamentary body and not by the Government, which had no diplomatic relations with North Korea.)

Japan and the Republic of Korea. Under a fisheries agreement signed on June 22, 1965, each of the two parties laid down its right to establish a 12-mile fishing zone from which fishing vessels of the other party could be excluded. According to this agreement areas where the two parties' fishery zones overlapped were to be delimited by straight lines joining the ends of the overlapping areas with the midpoints of straight lines drawn across the areas at their widest points. A joint control zone (excluding territorial waters and Korea's fishery zone) was defined around the Korean coast, with joint resources survey zones to be established outside these control zones. The agreement was to be implemented by a Japan–Republic of Korea Joint Fisheries Commission (JKFC).

In an annex to the agreement conditions were agreed on the number, type and size of fishing vessels to be used during different periods of the year, on mesh sizes to be permitted and on the brightness of fish-luring lights.

The two Governments agreed on Oct. 20, 1980, on voluntary regulations on fishing off Hokkaido and the island of Cheju (south of South Korea) with effect from Nov. 1, 1980, thus ending a three-year dispute over operations by South Korean trawlers in the Hokkaido waters.

Japan and the Soviet Union. In April 1978, Japan and the Soviet Union signed an agreement on fishery co-operation and on catching and protecting salmon in the waters of the North-West Pacific outside the Soviet 200-mile exclusive economic zone (EEZ), and also an agreement setting the salmon catch quotas for Japan outside the Soviet EEZ at 42,500 tonnes in the (May 1–July 31) 1978 season, in return for which Japan would supply the Soviet Union with fishing-related equipment. The agreements were to be in force for five years and extended automatically unless abrogation was notified by either side.

Under other bilateral agreements Japan was allowed to catch 850,000 tonnes of fish inside the Soviet 200-mile EEZ in 1978 and 750,000 tonnes (including 300,000 tonnes of Alaska pollock) in 1979, while the Soviet Union was allowed to catch 650,000 tonnes (including 450,000 tonnes of sardine and mackerel) in the Japanese EEZ.

In June 1979 it was announced that under an agreement between Japanese fishing operators and the All-Soviet Fishing Vessel Corporation (SOVRYBFLOT) seven joint operations would be carried out within the Soviet 200-mile limit, with Japan paying 21–25 per cent of the catch revenue as a fishing fee to the Soviet Union, and all Soviet catches being bought by Japan through trading firms.

On Oct. 28, 1980, the two sides signed two agreements on whaling—(i) one (replacing an earlier agreement which expired on Aug. 13, 1980) on a mutual observer scheme for factory ships in whaling operations in the southern hemisphere, and (ii) another fixing a minke whale quota of 3,120 for each side per season from 1981 onwards in the southern hemisphere.

In April 1981 agreement was also reached on the continuation of an existing salmon fishery agreement at the level of 42,500 tonnes to be fished by Japan.

Japan and the USA. Under an agreement signed in July 1980 Japan was allowed to harvest under-utilized species of fish such as pollock in the US 200-mile exclusive economic zone, and in exchange Japan modified its criteria for imports under its quota system to enable US exporters to expand their opportunities in Japan. An earlier agreement concluded in 1974 related to fishing for king and tanner crab.

Mauritania and Spain. An agreement on bilateral co-operation in fisheries, based on a new fisheries policy adopted by the Mauritanian Government, was signed in Madrid in October 1979.

Morocco and Spain. A fisheries agreement of February 1979, which was never ratified by the Moroccan Parliament, was approved by the Spanish Parliament in 1980. A transitional agreement, signed in Rabat on June 30, 1979, for the period from July 1 to Dec. 31, 1979, allowed small Spanish craft to fish in a limited area off Moroccan waters. A new agreement was signed on Dec. 28, 1979; its contents were not made public but it was said to include a secret clause allowing Morocco to transport agricultural produce, notably citrus fruit, through Spain for sale in member countries of the European Communities (a move opposed by Spanish orange and lemon farmers).

The transitional agreement was extended until Jan. 31, 1981, whereafter a new one-year co-operation agreement was signed in Madrid on April 1, 1981. Under this agreement it was provided, inter alia, that the charges payable to Morocco in respect of Spanish fish catches (by some 1,200 vessels with a personnel of 15,000) in Moroccan waters would be increased by 50 per cent (30 per cent payable by the government and 20 per cent by the fishing industry); that vessels between 100 and 150 grt would have a Moroccan crew member and vessels above this tonnage two such members; and that Spanish vessels were prohibited from fishing within one mile off the Moroccan coast. The agreement was approved by the Spanish Congress on Oct. 15, 1981, and by the Senate on Nov. 11. The agreement was later extended to run until Dec. 31, 1982.

After the above agreement had been further extended, a four-year agreement was eventually reached on Aug. 19, 1983. It provided that Spain would pay Morocco the equivalent of £360,000,000 in development aid; that the licence fees payable by Spain would be increased by 70 per cent; that Spanish fishing activities off Morocco's coast would be progressively reduced by 40 per cent; and that Spain would be allowed to fish in coastal waters previously declared a Moroccan security zone (because of the war against the Polisario Front of Western Sahara) but not in waters to the south of this zone (between Capes Bojador and Blanco).

Mozambique and Spain. Under a fishing agreement published in Madrid on May 18, 1982, licences were to be given to Spanish vessels to catch 1,800 tonnes of surface shrimp and 1,000 tonnes of deepwater shrimp in Mozambican waters during 1982.

Norway and Poland. In November 1979 Norway decided to reduce by 50 per cent the annual Polish fishing quota in Norway's exclusive economic zone.

Norway and the Soviet Union. Under an agreement reached in November 1980 on fisheries in the Norwegian and Soviet zones of the Barents Sea [see also pages 189–90], quotas were fixed of 260,000 tonnes of Arctic cod and 40,000 tonnes of coastal cod for Norway and of 40,000 tonnes of Murmansk cod for the Soviet Union. (Of cod quotas fixed for 1978 and 1979 the Soviet Union had not taken up its full share.)

An agreement on measures for regulating the catch and conserving the stocks of seals in the north-eastern part of the Atlantic Ocean was concluded by the two sides in 1957. Under a convention concluded in 1959 the two sides established a Sealing Commission for the North-East Atlantic (SCNEA).

Portugal and Spain. In 1969 Spain obtained "historic rights" to fish in Portugal's coastal waters. An agreement signed on March 14, 1979, gave Spanish fishermen 517 licences to fish (for certain circumscribed species), one-quarter of them for fishing in Portugal's six to 12-mile zone and the rest for the 12 to 200-mile zone, including areas around the Azores and Madeira. This agreement expired on Feb. 28, 1981. Talks intended to renew it broke down, especially as Portugal claimed that the number of licences provided had given Spain a 5 to 1 advantage. Portuguese and Spanish vessels were thereafter banned from fishing in each other's territorial waters.

Under an agreement of April 30, 1985, it was provided that upon becoming members of the European Communities on Jan. 1, 1986, both Spain and Portugal would be banned from fishing in each other's 12-mile coastal waters (except in a few common border areas), and that in the zone between 12 and 200 miles offshore the number of vessels of the two countries would be restricted by licence (as would be that of vessels of other member states of the European Communities in these waters).

Senegal and Spain. Among a number of successive fisheries agreements a four-year agreement signed on May 14, 1975, allowing Spanish vessels to fish in Senegal's waters was extended to Sept. 15, 1979, and under a new agreement signed on Dec. 6, 1979, Spanish vessels were enabled to fish in Senegalese waters under a system of licences.

Soviet Union and Sweden. Under a fisheries agreement signed on Dec. 25, 1977, Soviet fishermen were allowed to catch quotas of herring, sprats and cod in the Swedish zone up to the median line, but with a disputed area around the Swedish island of Gotland remaining subject to further negotiations [see page 191].

United Kingdom and the USA. A reciprocal fisheries treaty has been concluded between the two sides on fishing off the US Virgin Islands and the British Virgin Islands (in the Caribbean).

Fisheries Developments in Individual Countries

Recorded below are details of recent developments in specific countries related to fisheries and associated matters.

Argentina. Under a protocol of Dec. 15, 1983, the Soviet Union was granted fishing rights in Argentine waters. A strong protest against this decision was lodged on March 3, 1983, by the Argentine Chamber of Deep-Sea Fishing Shipowners (Cámara Argentina de Armadores de Buques Pesqueros de Altura).

The Government has imposed draconic fines for illegal fishing in Argentine waters.

Australia. Australian fishing has been regulated under a Fisheries Act of 1952, which was amended in 1978 to extend it to a 200-mile fishing zone around Australia and its external territories. The act required Australians and foreigners engaged in commercial fishing, and boats used for such fishing, to be licensed.

Under a Continental Shelf (Living Resources) Act of 1968 the harvesting of sedentary organisms (e.g. molluscs) was made subject to licensing.

Under a Whale Protection Act of 1980 the killing or capturing of, as well as interference with, whales, dolphins and porpoises within the 200-mile fishing zone was prohibited.

Following the proclamation of Australia's 200-mile exclusive economic zone with effect from Nov. 1, 1979, all foreign fishing vessels had to have permits to fish within that zone (which included waters off the islands controlled by Australia), with responsibility for policing that zone resting with the Federal Government, except for the area up to three miles offshore which was to be policed by the states.

Canada. As from Jan. 1, 1977, foreign vessels other than those of France and the United States were required to have licences to operate within 200 nautical miles from Canada's coasts. More than 200 licences were reported to have been issued, including 20 to Soviet trawlers.

For reasons of stock management and conservation Canada's total allowable cod catch was reduced from 1,400,000 tonnes in 1968 (by both Canadian and foreign vessels) to 400,000 tonnes in 1978, but it was to be brought up to 800,000 tonnes by 1987.

In 1983 Canada's exports of fish products were worth $1,600 million. However, there was over-capacity of its fishing fleet (with the Pacific fleet having a theoretical daily capacity of 300,000 tonnes, against an actual catch of 100,000 tonnes).

On Canada's Atlantic coast alone over 1,400 communities are dependent on fishing for their livelihood.

Canada has agreements with about a dozen nations to allow them access to fishing in its 200-mile exclusive economic zone.

Chile. It was officially stated on Sept. 4, 1979, that only Chilean vessels would be allowed to fish or to operate factory ships within the 200-mile Chilean territorial sea.

By 1980 Chile was the leading fish exporter in South America, having in that year had a total catch of 3,000,000 tonnes and exports valued at $360,000,000. In 1983 a total of some 4,000,000 tonnes of fish were landed in Chile, and some 60,000 persons were working directly or indirectly in fisheries, about 45,000 of them as smallscale fishermen (who, however, caught only 380,000 tonnes a year). Chile has been leading in canned and frozen pelagic species. In addition it has contributed about 50 per cent of the world's marketed production of marine algae (mainly Gracilaria).

China. In September 1980 China banned all fishing within 30 nautical miles off the South China Sea coast (except in the 100-mile stretch of the Pearl River estuary between Hong Kong and Canton), and in December 1980 this ban was extended to up to 40 miles from the coast. The ban affected Chinese fishermen as well as some 1,500 trawlers in Hong Kong and 500 in Macao, and in particular the catching of shrimp in the area.

Denmark. The Fishing Territory of the Kingdom of Denmark Act (announced on Nov. 23, 1976) extended the Danish fishing territory to 200 miles from the baselines.

Falkland Islands. The waters around the Falkland Islands (Las Malvinas) in the South Atlantic were in 1979 identified by the (UN) Food and Agriculture Organization (FAO) as one of the richest fishing grounds in the world. In the absence of any British-declared 200-mile exclusive fishery zone around the Falkland Islands and South Georgia and of the need for any licence, up to 200 fishing vessels, mainly from Eastern Europe, Japan and Taiwan, have been active in the area since 1981, with the total catch for 1983 being worth over £300,000,000. The only benefit to the Falkland Islands has been harbour dues paid by vessels which have entered the three-mile territorial waters to tranship their catches to large ocean-going refrigerated cargo ships (reefers). The total amount thus received by the Port Stanley harbourmaster in 1984 was £356,000, and for 1985 the amount was expected to exceed £500,000.

France. The French fishing fleet consists of (i) deep-sea trawlers operated by private owners who employ masters and crews and (ii) smaller family-owned boats operated by self-employed "craft" fishermen.

In the last few decades the fishing industry has declined as a result of cheap imports of frozen fish, disputes over European Communities' fishing rights and a sharp increase in operating costs, partly caused by rising fuel prices. The number of jobs in the industry was halved between 1955 and 1980, when there were some 25,000 fishermen (including about 12,000 craft fishermen), and it was expected that another 8,000 jobs would be lost by 1985, together with between 40,000 and 50,000 among those indirectly dependent on fishing. Government subsidies to the industry were generally regarded as inadequate by fishermen.

An attempt by trawler owners to reduce both pay and manning levels on trawlers failed after some 30 trawlers had in July–September 1980 intermittently blocked French ports to all traffic (causing considerable losses to the French and the British economies).

On April 14, 1983, the French National Assembly unanimously approved a bill on maritime fishing designed to protect rare resources, in particular herring and sole.

The bill amended a decree of Jan. 9, 1972, which had been the basis for penalties imposed for infringements of fishing regulations. The bill provided inter alia that penalties could include seizure of French or foreign fishing vessels or catches (but not confiscation of vessels), and that fines could be imposed partly or wholly on the shipowner or crew, but that in case of seizure of vessels or confiscation of catch crews might receive compensation.

Greenland. Greenland had, as an autonomous part of Denmark, become a member of the European Communities (EC) in 1973 but it left the EC with effect from Feb. 1, 1985, when the European Commission granted it overseas countries and territories (OCT) status, which meant that Greenland would have duty-free access to EC markets for its fishery products. In addition a fisheries agreement concluded for 10 years (and automatically renewable for six-year periods) provided for quotas for the first five years (up to Dec. 31, 1989) for various species of fish (and for shrimps) to be caught by EC fishing fleets, with the EC paying 26,500,000 ECUs per annum. The agreement also made provision for a reduction of quotas if stocks were found to be depleted, but Greenland was guaranteed a minimum tonnage for its fish catch should overall quotas fall.

Iceland. On April 14 and June 5, 1972, respectively, the United Kingdom and the Federal Republic of Germany instituted proceedings at the International Court of Justice(ICJ) against Iceland in the matter of the latter's declared intention to extend its exclusive fisheries zone from 12 to 50 nautical miles. Iceland maintained that the Court had no jurisdiction on the issue and declined to be represented at the proceedings or to file any pleadings. The Icelandic decision provoked the second "cod war" with Britain (the first such dispute having occurred in the 1950s as a result of Iceland's progressive extension of its fishery limits from three to four miles in 1952 and to 12 miles in 1958).

At the request of the United Kingdom and the Federal Republic of Germany the ICJ indicated later in 1972 and confirmed in 1973 interim measures of protection to the effect that Iceland should refrain from the proposed extension of its fishing zone and limit its annual catch to certain maxima. On Feb. 2, 1973, the ICJ decided that it had jurisdiction in the matter, and on July 25, 1974, it found that the Icelandic regulations extending exclusive fishing rights to 50 miles were not opposable to either the United Kingdom or the Federal Republic of Germany; that Iceland was not entitled unilaterally to exclude their fishing vessels from the disputed area; and that the parties were under a mutual obligation to undertake negotiations in good faith for the equitable solution of their differences.

The ICJ's ruling was rejected by the Icelandic Government, which with effect from Oct. 15, 1975, further extended its fisheries limit from 50 to 200 nautical miles. A further "cod war" with Britain ensued, leading to serious incidents at sea in late 1975 and early 1976 and to the severance of diplomatic relations by Iceland on Feb. 18, 1976. Tensions eased, however, with the signature in Oslo on June 1, 1976, of an interim agreement under which the number of British trawlers fishing within Iceland's 200-mile limit (which was not formally recognised by Britain) was limited to an average of 24 a day.

With an Icelandic-West German agreement having already been concluded in November 1975, the settlement of Iceland's dispute with Britain opened the way for the European Community (EC) to reduce tariffs on Icelandic fish and fish product imports by EC member states (these reductions having been suspended since 1973). Thereafter Iceland's fishery relations with EC member states were negotiated by the Community as a whole within the framework of the latter's evolving common fisheries policy [see pages 111–13].

India. A presidential proclamation of Nov. 29, 1956, empowered the Government to establish conservation zones in areas of the high seas adjacent to the territorial waters, but with an outer limit of 100 nautical miles of these zones, and also to regulate all fishing in these areas.

The Indian Territorial Waters, Continental Shelf, Exclusive Economic Zone and Other Maritime Zones Act, 1976, provided for the establishment of an exclusive economic zone up to 200 nautical miles from the baseline, where India would have (i) "sovereign rights . . . of exploration, exploitation, conservation and management of the natural resources, both living and non-living, as well as [of] producing energy from tides, winds and currents"; (ii) "exclusive rights and jurisdiction for the construction, maintenance or operation of artificial islands, offshore terminals, installations and other structures and devices necessary for the exploration and exploitation of the resources of the zone or for the convenience of shipping or for any other purpose"; (iii) "exclusive jurisdiction to authorize, regulate and control scientific research . . . [and] to preserve and protect the marine environment and to prevent and control marine pollution".

The annual fish production of India has been around 1,000,000 tonnes in recent years. Estimates of the potential yield of the Indian Ocean vary from 7,000,000 to 17,000,000 tonnes per annum. The yield of the Indian exclusive economic zone is expected to be about 3,000,000 tonnes. The projected requirements of India's population by the year 2000 are estimated at 11,400,000 tonnes per annum, of which 60–75 per cent is expected to come from the sea (and the rest from freshwater sources).

India's aquaculture (mainly of prawn and fishes trapped as juveniles) has so far yielded only about 10,000 tonnes per annum. A seaweed industry is under development.

The Government of India has established a Department of Ocean Development which is planning large investments for the exploration and exploitation of ocean resources—food, chemicals, minerals, transportation, recreation and energy—to improve the socio-economic conditions of India's population, of which some 170,000,000 are estimated to be directly dependent on the sea for their living or livelihood.

Indonesia. Indonesia declared its 200-mile exclusive economic zone on March 21, 1980.

Japan. As a result of the declaration of 200-mile exclusive economic zones between 1976 and 1979 Japan lost access to many of its traditional fishing grounds. Its distant-water catch declined from some 4,000,000 tonnes in 1977 to less than 2,200,000 tonnes in 1980. The fisheries sector had provided direct employment to about 450,000 people in Japan, and another 1,000,000 had been engaged in secondary industries and distribution. After being an exporter of fish and fish products Japan became the world's second-largest importer (after the United States). Many Japanese fishing companies have responded to this development by establishing joint ventures with foreign companies operating abroad and switching from catching to buying fish.

Republic of Korea. On Jan. 18, 1952, the Government of South Korea issued a proclamation, which was followed on Dec. 12, 1954, by a Law for the Conservation of Fishery Resources—the effect of these measures being to give Korea control over practically all resources of the sea, at some points up to 200 miles from its coasts, thus excluding Japanese fishing vessels from parts of the high seas. However, under an agreement of June 22, 1965, fishing in the area was placed under a new regime [see page 115].

Malaysia. Large-scale trawling had begun in Malaysia in 1965, and by 1977 this country had 4,720 licensed trawlers which were to confine their activities to the sea outside the 12-mile limit but in fact did not; using a mesh of 25 mm and not one of 37.5 mm which would prevent the depletion of fish resources, they have seriously endangered the livelihood of smallscale fishermen, and catches have been declining.

(In 1980 there were some 6,000,000 smallscale fishermen operating in South-East Asia, constituting 90 per cent of all engaged in fisheries.)

Mauritania. On Nov. 10, 1984, the Government of Mauritania announced that under a decree any foreign vessel engaged in fishing without permission in Mauritania's 200-mile exclusive economic zone would be liable to confiscation, with criminal proceedings being instituted against its captain and crew.

Mexico. The Mexican Law on an Exclusive Economic Zone of 1976 provided for the establishment of an exclusive economic zone up to 200 nautical miles from the baseline of the territorial sea, with the nation holding in that zone (i) "sovereign rights of exploration and exploitation, conservation and management of natural resources, both renewable and non-renewable, of the sea-bed including the subsoil and the superjacent waters"; (ii) "exclusive rights and jurisdictions with regard to the establishment and use of artificial islands, installations and structures"; (iii) "exclusive jurisdiction with regard to other activities relating to the exploration and economical exploitation of the zone"; and (iv) "jurisdiction over preservation of the marine environment, including pollution control and abatement", as well as over scientific research. Foreign states would have freedom of navigation and overflight and the right to lay submarine cables and pipelines.

Morocco. The Moroccan Government declared its 200-mile exclusive economic zone on Dec. 19, 1980, with the effect that only Moroccan vessels were allowed to fish in the zone, although the Government undertook to fulfil all its obligations under bilateral or multilateral agreements. (Morocco's territorial waters had previously been extended to 12 miles and an "exclusive fishing zone" to 70 miles.)

Morocco had earlier detained numerous foreign fishing vessels, most of them Spanish, for alleged infringements of fishing regulations, and imposed heavy penalties. Moreover, the Polisario Front (fighting for the independence of the Western Sahara annexed by Morocco) had attacked Spanish,

Portuguese and South Korean vessels fishing off the Western Sahara coast.

Norway. Norway's fishing fleet, predominantly employed in coastal fishing, consisted in 1981 of some 8,500 decked vessels, of which 6,000 were less than 13 metres long. In 1979–81 about 85 per cent of the total fish catch was taken in Norway's economic zone. Only about 5 per cent of the catch is used as fresh-food fish, the rest being processed in one form or another. Over 90 per cent of the total catch is exported, also in various forms, accounting for about 8 per cent of Norway's total exports.

The fishing industry has gone through a long period of decline. Between 1948 and 1978 the number of fishermen fell from 86,000 to 32,000 (of whom only 17,800 gave fishing as their full-time occupation). Of Norway's then trawler fleet of 78 vessels, 20 were withdrawn by 1982. In addition to the impact on Norway's distant-water fishing of the universal proclamation of 200-mile exclusive economic zones, the growth of petroleum activities on the continental shelf has closed many areas which had previously been important fishing grounds.

On June 11, 1977, Norway declared a 200-mile fisheries protection zone around Svalbard (Spitsbergen), and on May 28, 1980, it proclaimed a 200-mile exclusive economic zone around Jan Mayen [see page 115].

A long-term plan for fisheries, published in September 1981, was aimed at reducing Norway's over-capacity in its fishing industry and at harmonizing the rest of the industry with the strongly reduced fish resources and catch prospects.

Not being a member of the European Communities (EC), Norway banned all fishing vessels of EC member countries on Dec. 2, 1980, from fishing cod and haddock in Norwegian waters, and from Dec. 10, 1980, such vessels were banned altogether from fishing in these waters.

In July 1983 the EC decided to exempt Norway from a general ban on herring fishing in the North Sea (first imposed in 1977 and intended to remain in force) to avoid further retaliation against EC fleets in Norwegian waters.

Norway has, however, concluded agreements to allow fishermen from Finland and Sweden access to Norwegian waters, and also agreements with the German Democratic Republic, Poland, Portugal and Spain allowing them to fish surplus stocks in Norway's economic zone.

By 1985 cod catches in Norway's 200-mile zone were efficiently controlled after being depleted for years through overfishing; capelin stocks were said to be more stable (under joint Norwegian–Soviet management), and herring stocks were being rebuilt to restore an adequate level by 1987–88.

Peru. By the end of the 1960s Peruvian anchoveta catches, at about 10,000,000 tonnes per annum, constituted some 17 per cent of world fish catches. However, as a result of overfishing and a change in the El Niño current off the coast of Peru, the Peruvian anchoveta catch fell to less than 2,000,000 tonnes in 1973 (while the total world catch of fish had increased).

In August 1980 the Government took the advice of its Marine Research Institute (IMARPE) and severely restricted the permitted catch of pilchards (which had replaced the anchoveta as Peru's main source of fish products) and allowed only 28 per cent of the catch to be used by the state-owned fishmeal plants, with most of the rest to go to the canning and freezing industry. Despite these and other measures the pilchard catch in 1983 was only about 60 per cent of that in 1979, while the anchoveta catch had after fluctuations dropped to about 118,000 tonnes in 1983.

The Philippines. In the Philippines, where per capita fish consumption is 32 kilograms per annum, the total annual catch has been about 1,600,000 tonnes. Between 55 and 60 per cent of this has been supplied to coastal areas by some 600,000 municipal fishermen.

Portugal. On April 19, 1978, the Portuguese Government adopted a bill establishing Portugal's 200-mile exclusive economic zone off the coasts of the mainland as well as off Madeira and the Azores.

Senegal. The Senegalese Secretary of State for Marine Fisheries has declared that under Senegalese law the country's territorial waters extend to 150 miles from the coast and that an adjacent exclusive fishing zone extends to a further 50 miles. Within the 200-mile limit fishing is also open to foreign vessels for countries which have signed a fishing agreement with Senegal.

Fish consumption is at about 44 kilograms per capita every year. In 1982 total landings of fish were about 140,000 tonnes; industrial fishing enabled 83,000 tonnes of fish to be processed; and about 30,000 people were employed in smallscale fishing from pirogues.

Solomon Islands. The Prime Minister announced late in June 1985 that his Government had refused a request by the Soviet Union to establish fishing rights in the exclusive economic zone of the Solomon Islands.

Soviet Union. On April 1, 1978, the Soviet Union extended its fisheries zone in the Baltic Sea to 200 nautical miles from its coast, or the median line where applicable.

Spain. The Spanish fishing fleet was in 1981 said to be the largest in the world in number of vessels, giving direct employment to some 125,000 persons. Fish consumption per capita was in 1983 given as 40 kilograms per annum (as against an average 15 kilograms in the European Communities).

Of the total fishing fleet of some 17,000 vessels, about 70 per cent were small coastal fishing boats of less than 20 tonnes; 3,000 of them were vessels of from 20 to 150 tonnes, engaged in coastal fishery; and 1,800 larger vessels concentrated on deep-water and ocean fishing.

Sri Lanka. The Maritime Zones Law of 1976 of the Republic of Sri Lanka provided for the establishment of an exclusive economic zone, in which all natural resources, both living and non-living, on and under the sea-bed and in the subsoil and on the water surface and within the water column were to be vested in the Republic.

United Kingdom. The 1976 Fishery Limits Act extended Britain's fishery limit, to 200 miles from the coast and reaffirmed earlier provisions laying down, inter alia, that foreign sea-fishing vessels should not enter the exclusive fishery zone of the British Isles except for purposes recognized in international law or by treaty. The act also provided that fishing might be made subject to licensing, with the imposition of conditions "necessary or expedient for the regulation of sea-fishing". [For fisheries policy of the European Communities, see pages 111–13.]

Massive overfishing in European and Atlantic waters led, from 1976 onwards, to a decline in the fishing industry, which reached crisis point in 1980. The number of British trawlers fell from 237 in 1976 to 143 in 1979, with up to 30,000 jobs being lost in the deep-sea fleet and its dependent processing industries. Additional causes of the recession were the proclamation of 200-mile exclusive economic zones by other countries (which lost British and other European Communites' fishermen their rights in traditional Atlantic fishing grounds), the rise in fuel prices from 1973 onwards (which greatly increased operating costs), and cheap fish imports from other European Communities countries, which gave financial support to their fishing industries. According to a statement by the British minister in charge of fishery policy on Jan. 18, 1982, the decisive factor in the decline of the British deep-sea fishing fleet had been Iceland's declaration of a 200-mile fishing limit.

By August 1980 aid given by the British Government to fishing vessel owners amounted to more than £37,000,000, and on March 30, 1981, the Government announced another aid package of £25,000,000 (about half of this for fishermen in Scotland).

United States. On March 1, 1977, the US Congress and Senate approved fisheries agreements (to enter into force with the US proclamation of a 200-mile exclusive economic zone) granting preferential treatment to the European Communities, Japan, the Republic of Korea and Spain by allowing them to fish in the 200-mile zone under licence and subject to payment of fees.

International Organizations concerned with Marine Resources

Worldwide Bodies

Commonwealth Secretariat

Address. Marlborough House, Pall Mall, London SW1Y 5HX, UK

Officer. Shridath Ramphal (Guyana, s.g.)

Founded. July 1965

Activities. In a report entitled *An Overview of Fisheries in the Commonwealth*, commissioned by the Secretariat's Food Production and Rural Development Division and published early in 1984, it was claimed that despite the existence of exclusive economic zones foreign fishing fleets were in some regions using large trawlers and purse seiners up to the beaches of small fishing villages and were thus destroying the livelihood of smallscale fishermen. The report stated that of the annual world catch of 72,000,000 tonnes of traditional species of fish 85 per cent constituted marine fish and the remaining 15 per cent freshwater fish; that world demand was, according to the FAO, expected to rise to 110,000,000 tonnes by the year 2000, but that, as world population was increasing faster than fish production, there would be a shortage of fish; that mechanization of fishing boats in some developing countries had created unemployment and decreased the social and economic benefits derived from the existing traditional inshore fishing operations; but that improvements in the catching ability of traditional boats could still be made by supplying simple pieces of fishing gear such as gill net haulers or line-hauling gear; and that the smallscale fishing industry should preferably use only boats which it had built itself. The report also suggested the creation of community fisheries centres (beginning with a fuel supply store, an ice machine, an engine repair shop, a net loft and a marketing section).

The report issued a warning against the catching of krill [see page 91] which, it said, was only within the reach of a few major fishing nations which had to contest with escalating fuel costs, extreme climatic conditions and a short fishing season.

Fisheries Committee of the Organization for Economic Co-operation and Development (OECD)

Address. 2 rue André-Pascal, 75775 Paris Cédex 16, France

Activities. The OECD's Fisheries Committee is responsible for co-ordinating the activities and policies of member states in the broad sphere of exploitation of the living resources of the oceans. It serves in particular as a forum for exchange of views on fishery matters between the European and non-European members of the OECD.

Membership. Australia, Belgium, Canada, Denmark, Finland, France, Federal Republic of Germany, Greece, Iceland, Ireland, Italy, Japan, the Netherlands, New Zealand, Norway, Portugal, Spain, Sweden, Turkey, the United Kingdom and the United States (i.e. all OECD members except Austria, Luxembourg and Switzerland); Yugoslavia (special status).

Food and Agriculture Organization (FAO)

Address. Via delle Terme di Caracalla, 00100 Rome, Italy

Officer. Edouard Saouma (Lebanon, dir.-gen.); K. C. Lucas (asst. dir.-gen., head of fisheries department); A. Labon (dir. of fishery industries division); J. E. Carroz (dir. of fishery policy and planning division); H. Kasahara (dir. of fishery resources and environment division)

Founded. October 1945

Objectives. The FAO was the first United Nations specialized agency to be formed after World War II, its object being to co-ordinate development programmes in the fields of food, agriculture, forestry and fisheries.

Activities. An FAO fisheries department was established in 1963 under an assistant secretary-general and with professional staff and three divisions: (i) on fishery policy and planning, servicing of FAO regional fisheries bodies and liaison with other agencies; (ii) on fisheries resources and the environment; and (iii) on fisheries industries (with technical development services and assistance in fish production marketing). The department is associated with two advisory groups: (i) an advisory committee on marine resources research (ACMRR), linked also to the International Oceanographic Commission (IOC), and (ii) a committee on fisheries (COFI), established in

1966 and advisory to the FAO Council (with its membership being open to all FAO members).

Responsibilities of the department include (i) the collection, analysis and dissemination of information on all aspects of fisheries (science; aquaculture; pollution; processing, storage, transport and marketing of fish and fish products; types of fishing craft and equipment); (ii) an assessment of the world's fishery resources and the state of their exploitation in order to obtain an estimate of their total yield; (iii) assistance to developing countries to enable them to utilize their fishery resources to best advantage (including the collection and dissemination of information on opportunities for industrial development, on advances in technology and marketing, and on changes in the structure of institutions responsible for fisheries throughout the world); (iv) assistance in the establishment, maintenance and expansion of national and regional training institutions, and in accelerated transfer of technology through field operations. FAO's *Yearbook of Fisheries Statistics* distinguishes 27 major areas (including also inland fishery areas).

The FAO has fishery officers at its regional offices at the following addresses: (i) UN Agency Building, North Maxwell Road, P.O.B. 1628, Accra, Ghana, (ii) Maliwan Mansion, Phra Atit Road, Bangkok 2, Thailand; and (iii) Avenida Providencia 871, Casilla 10095, Santiago, Chile.

There are also nine regional fisheries bodies: (i) the Regional Fisheries Advisory Commission for the South-West Atlantic (CARPAS), with Argentina, Brazil and Uruguay as members; (ii) the General Fishery Committee for the Eastern Central Atlantic (CECAF); (iii) the General Fisheries Council for the Mediterranean (GFCM), with 19 member countries; (iv) the Indian Ocean Fishery Commission (IOFC); (v) the Indo-Pacific Fishery Commission (IPFC), (vi) the Western Central Atlantic Fishery Commission (MECAFC), with 26 member countries; (vii) the Committee for Inland Fisheries of Africa (CIFAI); (viii) the European Inland Fisheries Advisory Commission (EIFAC); and (ix) the Commission for Inland Fisheries of Latin America (COPESCAL), with 14 member countries [see also separate entries for these bodies except those for inland fisheries]. These bodies cover less than half the areas of the world's oceans, the rest being served by the independent regional fisheries organizations.

Membership. Practically all UN member states

Publications. Yearbook of Fisheries Statistics, Vol. 56 (*Catches and Landings*), Vol. 57 (*Fishery Commodities*), 1983

International Center for Living Aquatic Resources Management (ICLARM)

Address. MCC P.O. Box 1501, Makati, Metro Manila, Philippines

Officer. Dr Ian R. Smith (dep. dir.-gen.)

Founded. March 1977

Objectives. To conduct, stimulate and catalyse, as an autonomous, non-profit and non-governmental research centre, research on critical problems related to exploitation, management and utilization of living aquatic resources; to work, not as a funding agency but as an active research group, in co-operation with other institutions; and to complement the work of existing national and international organizations which lack the capability of conducting certain essential types of research.

Activities. After working for two years in Hawaii the organization was incorporated in the Philippines as ICLARM in 1977, with the emphasis of its work being in the South Pacific and Asia. Its research has covered areas with broad international significance for tropical fisheries; aquaculture resource development; and traditional fisheries and education and training. Its projects now cover 23 countries around the world.

Sources of finance. Various foundations and government funding agencies

Publications. Five technical series, newsletters and annual report

International Council for the Exploration of the Sea (ICES)

Address. Palaegade 2, DK-1261 Copenhagen K, Denmark

Officers. Prof. Warren S. Wooster (pres.); O. J. Øostvedt (first vice-pres.); Dr. B. B. Parrish (g.s.)

Founded. 1902

Objectives. To promote and co-ordinate international investigations of the marine environment and its living resources in the North Atlantic and adjacent seas, and to publish or otherwise disseminate the results of this research, including the provision of scientific information and advice to national governments and regional fishery management and pollution control commissions.

Activities. The founder members of the ICES were Denmark, Finland, Germany, the Netherlands, Norway, Sweden, Russia and the United Kingdom, whose contract establishing the ICES was renewed every five years but was, as from July 22, 1968, replaced by a 1964 Convention for the International Council for the Exploration of the Sea. Under this convention membership of the ICES was open to any state upon approval by three-quarters of its member states.

The work of the ICES is carried out by (i) its finance committee; (ii) its consultative committee in charge of the general oversight of the Council's scientific interests and work; (iii) an advisory committee on fishery management (ACFM) responsible for liaison with the North-East Atlantic Fisheries Commission (NEAFC) and other fisheries commissions and for giving member governments, groups of governments or commissions scientific advice when requested, and comprising a demersal, a pelagic and a Baltic fish committee; (iv) an advisory committee on marine pollution (ACMP), established in 1972, with sub-committees on hydrography, marine environmental quality and biological oceanography; and (v) a publications committee.

Further work is carried out by standing area and subject committees including the following: a fish capture committee concerned with studies of detection and searching techniques, design and operation of fishing gear, and behaviour of fish in relation to fishing; a statistics committee; a mariculture committee concerned with investigations relating to the culture of marine organisms, including transplantation and introduction of new species; a shellfish committee concerned with molluscs and crustacea; an anadromous and catadromous fish (Anacat) committee; and a marine mammals committee. There are also numerous working groups, meeting usually once a year.

Structure. The ICES Council, which holds statutory meetings every year, has a bureau consisting of a president, a first vice-president and five other vice-presidents. The Council's secretariat is responsible for the administrative, hydrographic and statistical services of the ICES.

Membership. Belgium, Canada, Denmark, Finland, France, the German Democratic Republic, the Federal Republic of Germany, Iceland, Ireland, the Netherlands, Norway, Poland, Portugal, the Soviet Union, Spain, Sweden, the United Kingdom and the United States

Sources of finance. Contributions from member countries, sale of publications and payments by different commissions for advice received

Publications. Journal du Conseil (annual); *Guide to Fish Marks; Rapports et Procès-Verbaux des Réunions; Co-operative Research Reports; Annales*

Biologiques (on principal fish stocks in the area); *Bulletin Statistique des Pêches Maritimes* (annual); *ICES Oceanographic Data Lists and Inventories* (61 issues, 1971–83); *Fiches d'Identification du Zooplancton (Plancton)*

International Whaling Commission (IWC)

Address. The Red House, 135 Station Road, Histon, Cambridge CB4 4NP, UK

Officer. Dr R. Gambell (sec.)

Founded. Dec. 2, 1946

History. An international agreement on the protection of whales was first signed in London on June 8, 1937, by representatives of nine governments (Argentina, Australia, Germany, the Irish Free State, New Zealand, Norway, South Africa, the United Kingdom and the United States). This agreement provided for a nine-month closed season for ships attached to floating factories, for the absolute protection of certain species and classes of whales and a six-month closed season for whaling at land stations; it was amended by a protocol adopted in November 1945, which, inter alia, required contracting governments to supply an International Bureau of Whaling Statistics with weekly data of blue whale units caught by each factory ship.

The IWC was set up under an International Convention for the Regulation of Whaling designed to provide for the proper conservation of whale stocks and the orderly development of the whaling industry.

Objectives. To keep under review and revise as necessary the measures laid down in the schedule to the above convention, which provide for the complete protection of certain species of whales; to designate specific ocean areas as whale sanctuaries; to set the maximum catches of whales which may be taken in any one season; to prescribe open and closed seasons and areas for whaling; to fix size limits above and below which certain species of whales may not be killed; to prohibit the capture of suckling calves and female whales accompanied by calves; and to require the compilation of catch reports and other statistical and biological records. The IWC is also to encourage, co-ordinate and fund research on whales and related matters (such as the humaneness of the killing operations, the ethics of killing cetaceans and the management of aboriginal subsistence whaling).

Activities. The IWC meets at least once a year and is assisted in its work by a scientific, a technical, and a finance and administration committee. Information provided by the scientific committee forms the basis on which the technical committee develops the regulations made by the IWC for the control of whaling. The adoption of regulations requires a three-quarters majority of the commissioners voting. (The changes become effective 90 days later unless a member government has lodged an objection, in which case the new regulation is not binding on that country. This procedure, however, is now only used when a member government considers its national interests or sovereignty to be unduly affected.)

In 1974 the IWC incorporated into its management procedure a strategy recommended by the scientific committee and classifying all whale stocks into three categories: (i) initial management stocks which may be reduced in a controlled manner to achieve "maximum sustainable yield" (MSY) levels or optimum levels as these are determined; (ii) sustained management stocks which will be maintained at or near MSY levels and at optimum levels as these are determined; and (iii) protection stocks which are below the level of sustained management stocks and will be fully protected from commercial whaling. This policy was designed to produce the greatest long-term harvests. However, in 1979 the ICW decided to ban factory-ship whaling for 10 years (except for minke whales) and to impose a complete ban on whaling in the Indian Ocean, as well as to determine quotas for certain species of whales in other seas.

Because of uncertainties about the precise status of the various exploited whale stocks, the IWC decided in 1982 that there should be a pause in commercial whaling from 1985/86 and that a comprehensive assessment of the effects of this decision should be undertaken by 1990. This decision was opposed by Brazil, Iceland, Japan, the Republic of Korea, Norway, Peru and the Soviet Union. Of these, Japan, Norway and the Soviet Union, accounting for about 90 per cent of the world's current whaling catch, maintained their formal objections made in 1982. On April 5, 1985, however, the Japanese Foreign Minister announced that Japan agreed to end commercial whaling from April 1, 1988, and that it would comply with a compromise agreement concluded with the United States (an agreement which had included not only Japan's belated acceptance of the IWC's five-year moratorium on whaling from 1985 but also an interim limit on sperm whale catches).

A minke whale quota of 4,224 set by the IWC for the 1984/85 Southern Hemisphere (Antarctic) catches was not accepted by Brazil, the Soviet Union and Japan; the two last-named countries, however, announced in January 1985 that they would voluntarily limit their minke whale catches to the previous year's level (at 3,027 and 3,028 respectively), while Japan stated that it would consult the United States over its actual catch.

During the IWC's 37th annual meeting held in Bournemouth (UK) on July 15–19, 1985, it was announced that the Soviet Union would temporarily end commercial whaling in the Atlantic from the 1987–88 season "for technical reasons". Decisions taken at the meeting included (i) classification of western North Pacific sperm whales as protection stock from 1988 (agreed unanimously), and (ii) classification of North-East Atlantic minke whales as protection stock from the beginning of the 1985–86 season (Iceland voting against and Norway taking no part in the vote).

All regulations adopted by the IWC are enforced by nationally appointed inspectors and overseen by international observers reporting directly to the IWC. The only whaling for large whales carried on outside IWC control is by Portugal (from the Azores).

Membership. Antigua and Barbuda, Argentina, Australia, Belize, Brazil, Chile, China, Costa Rica, Denmark, Egypt, Finland, France, the Federal Republic of Germany, Iceland, India, Japan, Kenya, the Republic of Korea, Mauritius, Mexico, Monaco, the Netherlands, New Zealand, Norway, Oman, Peru, the Philippines, St Lucia, St Vincent and the Grenadines, Senegal, Seychelles, South Africa, the Soviet Union, Spain, Sweden, Switzerland, the United Kingdom, the United States and Uruguay. (Canada withdrew from the IWC in June 1982.)

Publications. 34 Annual Reports; six Special Issues (containing proceedings of the IWC scientific committee); List of Scientific Committee Documents (1960–84)

International Whaling Statistics
International Hvalfangststatistikk

Address. Postboks 188, N-3201 Sandefjord, Norway

Officer. Einar Vangstein (sec. of bureau)

Founded. 1929

History. The bureau of International Whaling Statistics was established by the Norwegian Government on a recommendation of the whaling committee of the International Council for the Exploration of the Sea (ICES) and charged with compiling statistics from all countries (not only from ICES members). The secretary of the bureau has been the secretary of the International Association of Whaling Companies, which evolved from the Norwegian Whalers' Associations, but whose members (except the Icelandic company Hvalur H.F.) have ceased whaling. In future the statistics are to be published by the International Whaling Commission.

Publications. International Whaling Statistics (annually from 1930 to 1935 and twice a year until 1984); special statistics for the annual meetings of the International Whaling Commission

United Nations Development Programme (UNDP)

Address. One United Nations Plaza, New York, N.Y. 10017, USA

Officer. F. Bradford Morse (USA, administrator)

Founded. 1965

Objective. To aid developing countries to increase the productivity of their natural and human resources.

Activities. As the largest agency for promoting technical co-operation, the UNDP works with over 150 governments and 35 international organizations.

In March 1982 the UNDP approved the allocation of over $1,250,000 for an assessment of the world's renewable marine resources in the light of the extension of the exclusive economic zones to 200 miles from the coasts.

Earlier UNDP research had involved the use of the research vessel *Dr Fridtjof Nansen*, in agreement with the Norwegian Agency for Development (NORAD), to assess fishery resources in coastal waters in several parts of the world. The data gathered were processed at the Institute for Marine Research in Bergen.

A Fisheries Vessels Pool established in 1974 was designed to pool all UNDP-owned fishing vessels provided to aid government programmes under FAO management. By 1982 this pool had been reduced from 25 to 16 vessels, older ships having been eliminated.

Structure. The UNDP has four regional bureaux for Africa, Asia and the Pacific, the Arab States, and Latin America, as well as a unit for Europe. It has offices in most of the countries which receive UNDP assistance.

Sources of finance. Voluntary contributions of UN member states and of participating agencies.

Atlantic Ocean

Atlantic Salmon Trust

Address. 14 Downing St., Farnham, Surrey GU9 7PB, UK

Officer. G. D. FitzGerald Hadoke (dir.)

Activities. The trust has given support to the efficient management of Atlantic salmon and sea trout stocks in the national and international sphere, has sponsored research into all economic and biological factors affecting these issues, and has provided background and detailed information on important matters affecting the development of salmon and sea trout stocks.

Fishery Committee for the Eastern Central Atlantic (CECAF)
Comité des Pêches pour l'Atlantique Centre-Est

Address. c/o UN Development Programme (UNDP), B.P. 154, Dakar, Senegal, West Africa

Officer. M. Ansa-Emmim (sec. and technical co-ordinator)

Founded. Sept. 19, 1967

Objectives. To promote, co-ordinate and assist national and regional programmes of research and development leading to the rational utilization of the marine fishery resources of the area, and to assist in their implementation through sources of international aid; to enable member countries to analyse and monitor the state of their shared stocks and the fisheries fed by these stocks, and to exchange their experiences and points of view on fishery development problems and study programmes for co-management for the resources.

Activities. The CECAF had given special attention to improving the regional statistical system and to stock assessment. In 1972 it recommended the fixing of a minimum mesh size for hake and seabream trawl fishing, and in 1979 it decided in addition to impose the utilization of a single mesh with an opening size of at least 60 mm for the exploitation of all demersal resources, and it also agreed that fish handling, processing and marketing activities should be intensified. The CECAF is assisted by a working party on fishery statistics and resources evaluation, which deals with resource management within the limits of national jurisdiction and is open only to coastal member nations (which can, within this framework, discuss problems specific to their exclusive economic zones, such as management of shared stocks). There is also a sub-committee for fishery development.

Membership. Benin, Cameroon, Cape Verde, the Congo, Gabon, The Gambia, Ghana, Guinea, Guinea-Bissau, Equatorial Guinea, the Ivory Coast, Liberia, Mauritania, Morocco, Nigeria, Sâo Tomé and Príncipe, Senegal, Sierra Leone, Spain, Togo and Zaïre—as well as Cuba, France, Greece, Italy, Japan, the Republic of Korea, Norway, Poland, Romania and the United States

Sources of finance. Regular programme of the (UN) Food and Agriculture Organization (FAO); UNDP; donor countries and agencies

Publications. Statutes and Rules of Procedure; Reports of sessions, subcommittees and working parties; CECAF/ECAF Series; CECAF/TECH Series; CECAF Statistical Bulletin

International Commission for the Conservation of Atlantic Tunas (ICCAT)

Address. Príncipe de Vergara, 17, 28001 Madrid, Spain

Officers. C. J. Blondin (USA, ch.); S. Makiadi (Angola, first vice-ch.); J. G. Boavida (Portugal, second vice-ch.); Olegário Rodríguez Martín (exec. sec.)

Founded. May 14, 1966

History. The ICCAT was founded under an International Convention for the Conservation of Atlantic Tunas approved at a conference of 17 countries in Rio de Janeiro on May 2-14, 1966, and in effect since March 1969 (after ratification by seven countries).

Objectives. To co-operate in maintaining the populations of tunas and tuna-like fishes of the Atlantic Ocean at levels which will permit the maximum sustainable yield for food and other purposes.

Activities. Under the 1966 convention the ICCAT is responsible for research on the abundance, biometry and ecology of the fishes, the oceanography of their environment, and the effects of natural and human factors on their abundance. Activities have included the collecting and analysing of statistical information, the study and appraisal of information concerning measures and methods to ensure maintenance of the populations, the recommendation of studies and investigations to the contracting parties, and the publication and dissemination of reports of findings and other information relating to the tuna fisheries of the convention area. It has carried out an International Skipjack Year Programme (1979–83), culminating in a Skipjack Conference held in Tenerife in 1983 (the skipjack being regarded as the most abundant of the commercial tuna species). It has recently made recommendations concerning the conservation of yellowfin, bigeye and bluefin tunas.

Structure. The ICCAT has a council which normally meets once a year in Spain, and subcommittees and working groups which have held more than 30 meetings at various locations since 1971. Its official languages are English, French and Spanish.

Membership. Angola, Benin, Brazil, Canada, Cape Verde, Cuba, France, Gabon, Ghana, the Ivory Coast, Japan, the Republic of Korea, Morocco, Portugal, São Tomé and Príncipe, Senegal, South Africa, the Soviet Union, Spain, the United States, Uruguay and Venezuela

Sources of finance. Contributions from member countries, calculated on a formula taking into account catches and canned production of tunas and tuna-like fishes

Publications. Biennial Report; Statistical Bulletin; Collective Volume of Scientific Papers; Data Record; Statistical Series

International Commission for the South-East Atlantic Fisheries (ICSEAF)

Address. Paseo de la Habana, 65, 28036 Madrid, Spain

Officers. P. Kruger (South West Africa/Namibia, ch.); Capt. K. N. Gaydarov (Bulgaria, 2nd vice-ch.); Roger Lagarde (France, exec. sec.); Dr Bohdan Draganik (Poland, asst. exec. sec.)

Founded. Oct. 24, 1971

History. The ICSEAF was set up by a conference called by the (UN) Food and Agriculture Organization (FAO) and held in Rome in October 1969 with the participation of Belgium, Cuba, France, the Federal Republic of Germany, Italy, Japan, the Republic of Korea, Panama, Portugal, South Africa, Spain and Togo. The conference adopted a convention which defined the South-East Atlantic area as bordered by the coast of Africa and lying between the latitudes of 6°S and 50°S and the longitudes of 20°W and 40°E, and the objects of the ICSEAF as being to study the living resources in the area and to make recommendations for the regulation of catches which would, under specified conditions, be binding on the contracting parties.

Activities. The ICSEAF has repeatedly imposed quotas for catches, among them one (laid down in December 1976) for an annual quota of 700,000 tonnes of whitefish (hake) in South Africa's 200-mile economic zone (including 149,000 tonnes for South Africa itself).

Membership. Angola, Bulgaria, Cuba, France, the German Democratic Republic, the Federal Republic of Germany, Iraq, Israel, Italy, Japan, the Republic of Korea, Poland, Portugal, Romania, South Africa, the Soviet Union and Spain

North Atlantic Salmon Conservation Organization

Address. Dept. of Agriculture, Fisheries and Food for Scotland, Chesser House, 500 Gorgie Road, Edinburgh EH11 3AW, Scotland

Officer. Dr Malcolm Windsor (sec.)

Founded. 1982

Objectives. The organization was established under an Atlantic Salmon Convention to promote (i) the acquisition, analysis and dissemination of scientific information pertaining to salmon stocks in the North Atlantic Ocean and (ii) the conservation, restoration, enhancement and rational management of the stocks through international co-operation.

Activities. The convention applies to the salmon stocks which migrate beyond areas of fisheries jurisdiction of coastal states of the Atlantic Ocean north of 36°N latitude throughout their migratory range. (Within areas of coastal state fisheries jurisdiction salmon fishing is prohibited beyond 12 nautical miles from baselines used to measure the breadth of the territorial sea except off West Greenland, where salmon fishing may take place up to 40 miles from baselines, and off the Faroe Islands, where it may take place within the Faroes area of fisheries jurisdiction.) The organization held its inaugural meeting on Jan. 17–20, 1984, and its first annual meeting on May 22-25, 1974 (both in Edinburgh).

Structure. The organization has a council, three regional commissions—a North American Commission (NAC), a West Greenland Commission (WGC) and a North-East Atlantic Commission (NEAC)—and a secretary.

Membership. Canada, Denmark (in respect of the Faroe Islands and Greenland), the European Economic Community, Finland, Iceland, Norway, Sweden and the United States

North-East Atlantic Fisheries Commission (NEAFC)

Address. Room 339, Great Westminster House, Horseferry Road, London SW1P 2AE, UK

Officers. J. L. Arnalds (Iceland, pres.); Dr W. Ranke (German Democratic Republic, first vice-pres.); Capt. J. G. Boavida (Portugal, second vice-pres.); (Mrs) E. A. Blackwell (sec.)

Founded. 1959

History. The NEAFC was established under a convention signed on Jan. 24, 1959, by representatives of Belgium, Denmark, France, the Federal Republic of Germany, Iceland, Ireland, the Netherlands, Norway, Poland, Portugal, the Soviet Union, Spain, Sweden and the United Kingdom. This convention came into force on June 27, 1963, and it applied to parts of the Atlantic and Arctic Oceans north of 36°N and between the longitudes of 42°W and 51°E (excluding the Mediterranean and Baltic Seas) and also part of the Atlantic Ocean north of 59°N and between 44°W and 42°W. In 1980 the NEAFC was reconstituted under a new convention which came into force in 1982.

Objectives. To ensure, through consultation and exchange of information, the conservation and the rational exploitation of fish stocks in the North-East Atlantic and adjacent waters of concern to members states; to encourage international co-operation with respect to these resources; and to recommend conservation measures in waters outside national jurisdiction.

Activities. In carrying out its objectives the NEAFC co-operates closely with the International Council for the Exploration of the Sea (ICES), to which it makes a financial contribution, and with the FAO Committee on Fisheries. It holds annual meetings in London, and at its 1983 meeting it decided to set up an ad hoc committee on technical conservation measures (which related inter alia to mesh sizes, fish sizes, attachments to nets and by-catches).

Membership. Bulgaria, Denmark (for the Faroe Islands), the European Economic Community, the German Democratic Republic, Iceland, Norway, Poland, Portugal, the Soviet Union, Spain and Sweden

North-West Atlantic Fisheries Organization (NAFO)

Address. P.O. Box 638, Dartmouth, Nova Scotia, B2Y 3Y9, Canada

Officers. Dr V. K. Zilanov (USSR, ch. of General Council & pres.); V. A. Rikhter (USSR, ch. of Scientific Council); W. M. Murphy (Canada, ch. of Fisheries Commission); Capt. J. C. Esteves Cardoso (perm. exec. sec.)

Founded. 1979

History. The NAFO was preceded by an International Commission for the North-West Atlantic Fisheries (ICNAF), set up in 1949 under a convention signed by 11 nations and responsible for the investigation, protection and conservation of the fishery resources of the North-West Atlantic Ocean. The ICNAF was authorized to recommend measures for the maintenance of a maximum sustained catch from those fisheries which support international fisheries in the area, and (under a 1971 amendment to the convention) to recommend measures to achieve the optimum utilization of those stocks of fish which support such fisheries. In October 1978 Canada and eight other signatories of the ICNAF convention signed a Convention on Future Multilateral Co-operation in the North-West Atlantic Fisheries which replaced the ICNAF by the NAFO with a more developed structure and safeguards for the sovereign jurisdiction of coastal states over the living resources of the sea within their 200-mile limits.

Objectives. The optimum utilization and rational management of the fishery resources of the North-West Atlantic (between the coasts of the United States, Canada and Greenland and the 35°N parallel in the south and the 40°W meridian in the east).

Activities. The collection of basic data relating to the resources, analysis of these data, choice of most suitable conservation measures in light of scientific, economic, social and political factors, and implementation of measures (inspection and enforcement).

Structure. The NAFO's General Council has established a standing committee on finance and administration (STACFAD), and the Scientific Council has set up standing committees on fisheries science (STACFIS), on research co-ordination (STACREC) and on publications (STACPUB). The Fisheries Commission has created a standing committee on international control (STACTIC).

Membership. Bulgaria, Canada, Cuba, Denmark (in respect of the Faroe Islands), the European Economic Community, the German Democratic Republic, Iceland, Japan, Norway, Poland, Portugal, Romania, the Soviet Union and Spain

Publications. Annual Reports; Journal of North-West Atlantic Fishery Science (one or more issues a year); Statistical Bulletin (annual); Scientific Council Studies (one or more volumes a year); Sampling Yearbook; List of Fishing Vessels (triennial)

Regional Fisheries Advisory Commission for the South-West Atlantic Comisión Asesora Regional de Pesca para el Atlántico Sudoccidental (CARPAS)

Address. c/o International Institution and Liaison Unit, Fishery Policy and Planning Division, FAO, Via delle Terme di Caracalla, 00100 Rome, Italy

Officer. Dr Elda Fagetti (sec.)

Founded. 1961

Objectives. To promote fuller use of the marine resources in the western South Atlantic in accordance with sound economic and scientific principles, to co-ordinate studies, research and techniques and to determine common needs.

Activities. The CARPAS is open to all nations with coasts on the Western Atlantic south of the equator. It has a working party on fisheries statistics, an ad hoc working party on fishery economic development in the South-West Atlantic, a working party on biological research and evaluation of fishery resources, a joint working party (with the FAO Advisory Committee on Marine Resources Research, ACMRR) on the scientific evaluation of the state of the stocks in the South-West Atlantic, and a number of experts from its member countries.

Membership. Argentina, Brazil, Uruguay

Sources of finance. FAO budget

Publications. *Boletín Informativo* (irregular); *CARPAS Documentos Técnicos; CARPAS Documentos Ocasionales*

Western Central Atlantic Fisheries Commission (WECAFC)

Address. Via delle Terme di Caracalla, 00100 Rome, Italy

Officer. E. Fagetti (fishery liaison officer, sec.)

Founded. 1973

History. The WECAFC was established, and is administered, by the (UN) Food and Agriculture Organization (FAO)

Objectives. To facilitate the coordination of research leading to the conservation, development and utilization of the living resources including shrimps, of the Western Central Atlantic Ocean; to encourage education and training; to assist member governments in establishing rational policies; and to promote the rational management of resources which are of interest to two or more countries.

Membership. Antigua and Barbuda, the Bahamas, Barbados, Brazil, Colombia, Cuba, Dominica, France, Grenada, Guatemala, Guinea, Guyana, Haiti, Italy, Jamaica, Japan, the Republic of Korea, Mexico, the Netherlands, Nicaragua, Panama, St Christopher and Nevis, St Lucia, Spain, Suriname, Trinidad and Tobago, the United Kingdom, the United States and Venezuela

Pacific Ocean

Commission for Fisheries Research in the Western Pacific

Founded. 1956 (under a convention)

Membership. China, the Democratic People's Republic of Korea, the Soviet Union and Vietnam

Indo-Pacific Fishery Commission (IPFC)

Address. FAO Regional Office for Asia and the Pacific, Maliwan Mansion, Phra Atit Road, Bangkok 10200, Thailand

Officer. V. L. C. Pietersz (regional fisheries officer and sec.)

Founded. Nov. 9, 1948

Objectives. To promote the proper utilization of living aquatic resources by the development and management of fishing and culture operations, and by the development of related processing and marketing activities, and for this purpose to keep under review the state of the resources and of the industries based on them; to formulate and recommend measures and to initiate and carry out projects to create new fisheries and increase the production, efficiency and productivity of existing fisheries, conserve management resources and protect resources from pollution; to keep under review the economic and social aspects of fishing and aquaculture industries and recommend measures aimed at improving the living and working conditions of fishermen and other workers in these industries and at improving the contribution of each fishery to attain social and economic goals; to encourage, co-ordinate and undertake training and extension activities, as well as research and development activities, and to assemble, publish and disseminate information on the living aquatic resources and fisheries based on them.

Activities. The major fields of IPFC activities are training; meetings; publications; fisheries resources assessment, research and development; reduction of post-harvest losses; environmental protection; rural fisheries community development; planning and technical assistance to member governments; investment; co-operation with other regional and international organizations; and promotion of technical co-operation among developing countries.

Structure. The IPFC holds regular sessions every two years. It has nine subsidiary bodies—an executive committee, a special committee on management of Indo-Pacific tuna, a committee for the development and management of fisheries in the South China Sea (SCSC), a standing committee on resources research and development (SCORRAD), a joint working party (with the Indian Ocean Fishery Commission, IOFC) of experts on Indian Ocean and Western Pacifc fishery statistics, working parties of experts on fish technology and marketing, on aquaculture, on inland fisheries and on Central and Western Pacific skipjack. In addition there are three co-operative programmes—on research on aquaculture, on fish product development and on information among fisheries libraries, institutions and scientists in the region.

Membership. 19 governments (i.e. those of Australia, Bangladesh, Burma, France, India, Indonesia, Japan, Democratic Kampuchea, the Republic of Korea, Malaysia, Nepal, New Zealand, Pakistan, the Philippines, Sri Lanka, Thailand, the United Kingdom, the United States and Vietnam)

Status. The IPFC is a regional technical body of the (UN) Food and Agricultural Organization (FAO), which provides the IPFC secretariat in Bangkok.

Sources of finance. The FAO regular budget and other sources, e.g. the UN Development Programme (UNDP)

Publications. IPFC Proceedings (published in three sections, once every two years)

Inter-American Tropical Tuna Commission (IATTC)

Address. c/o Scripps Institution of Oceanography, La Jolla, California 92093, USA

Officers. Dr James Joseph (dir. of investigations); Clifford L. Peterson (asst. dir.)

Founded. 1950

History. The IATTC has operated under a convention originally concluded by Costa Rica and the United States and open to adherence by other governments whose nationals fished for tropical tunas in the eastern Pacific Ocean. It was adhered to by Panama in 1953, Ecuador in 1961, Mexico in 1964, Canada in 1968, Japan in 1970 and France and Nicaragua in 1973. However, Ecuador withdrew from the IATTC in 1968, Mexico in 1978, Costa Rica in 1979 and Canada in 1984.

Objectives. To study the biology of the tunas and related species of the eastern Pacific Ocean with a view to determining the effects of fishing and natural factors on their abundance, and to recommend appropriate conservation measures in order to maintain stocks of fish at levels which would afford maximum sustainable catches if and when the IATTC research showed such measures to be necessary. In 1976 the IATTC defined new objectives as being to maintain a high level of tuna production and also to maintain porpoise stocks at or above levels that assured their survival in perpetuity, with every reasonable effort being made to avoid needless or careless killing of porpoises.

Activities. The IATTC has engaged in monitoring population sizes and mortality incidental to fishing, aerial surveys and dolphin tagging, analyses of indices of abundance of dolphins and computer simulation studies, and gear and behavioural research and education.

Membership. France, Japan, Nicaragua, Panama and the United States.

Publications. 33 annual reports, four special reports and a large number of bulletins and articles in outside journals

International North Pacific Fisheries Commission (INPFC)

Address. 6640 N.W. Marine Drive, Vancouver, Canada V6T 1X2

Officers. C. R. Forrester (exec. dir.); four commissioners from each of Canada, Japan and the United States

Founded. June 12, 1953

History. The INPFC was created by an International Convention for the High Seas Fisheries of the North Pacific Ocean, signed by Canada, Japan and the United States on May 9, 1952, ratified in June 1953 and amended on April 25, 1978, by a protocol which came into force in February 1979 and covered new fishing management rights of Canada and the United States in their respective 200-mile exclusive economic zones.

Objectives. To ensure the maximum sustainable productivity of the fishery resources of the waters of the North Pacific Ocean and adjacent seas (except territorial waters); to promote and co-ordinate the scientific studies necessary to ascertain the conservation measures required; to provide (under the amending protocol) for scientific studies and the co-ordination of collections, exchange and analysis of scientific data regarding anadromous species; and (also under the protocol) to provide, pending the establishment of an international organization with broader membership dealing with species other than anadromous ones, a forum for co-operation in the study, analysis and exchange of information and views on stocks of non-anadromous species of the convention area.

Activities. The INPFC has reported the results of research conducted on its behalf by the three contracting parties in annual reports; a Statistical Yearbook contains catch and effort data for salmon, herring, halibut, groundfish, shrimp, and king and tanner crab fisheries, and in some years data supplied by the Soviet Union for that country's salmon fishery in the Pacific. In the past few years updated joint comprehensive reports have been published on five species of Pacific salmon, on North Pacific oceanography, and on historical salmon and groundfish statistics.

Structure. The INFPC consists of three national sections each of which is assisted by scientific, technical and legal experts and advisers. The Canadian and US sections have formally organized advisory committees of fishing industry representatives. The offices of chairman, vice-chairman and secretary rotate annually among the national sections. The INFPC meets annually in Vancouver, Tokyo or Anchorage (Alaska). It has standing committees on finance and administration, and on biology and research; the latter has sub-committees on salmon and on non-anadromous species; the second of these sub-committees has a Bering Sea panel, a Northeast Pacific panel, groundfish working groups as required, and a king and tanner crab panel; and there is also an ad hoc committee on marine mammals, with a scientific sub-committee.

Membership. Canada, Japan and the United States

Sources of finance. Contributions in equal shares from the three member countries

Publications. Annual Report, Statistical Yearbook; bulletins (all in English and Japanese)

International Pacific Halibut Commission (IPHC)

Address. P.O. Box 95009, Seattle, WA 98145-2009, USA

Officer. Donald A. McCaughran (dir.)

Founded. 1923

History. The IPHC was created as the International Fisheries Commission in 1923 by a convention between Canada and the United States, which came into force on Oct. 23, 1924. It was continued under subsequent conventions of 1930, 1937 and 1953 (when the commission adopted its present name) and amended by a protocol in 1979.

Objectives. To regulate the fishing of halibut (a large-sized flatfish found on the continental shelf of the North Pacific).

Activities. The IPHC meets annually to review all regulatory proposals, including those made by its scientific staff and a conference board representing vessel owners and fishermen. Regulatory alternatives are discussed with an advisory group composed of fishermen, vessel owners and processors. The measures recommended by the IPHC are submitted to the two governments (of Canada and the United States) for approval, and upon approval the measures are enforced by appropriate agencies of both governments.

Structure. The IPHC consists of three commissioners appointed by the Governor General of Canada and three appointed by the President of the United States. The commissioners appoint a director who supervises the scientific and administrative staff. The scientific staff collects and analyses statistical and biological data needed to manage the halibut industry. The IPHC headquarters are located on the campus of the University of Washington in Seattle.

Publications. Numerous general, scientific and technical reports, in particular: *The Pacific Halibut: Biology, Fishery and Management* (Technical Report No. 16, 1976); Annual Reports

North Pacific Fur Seal Commission

Address. c/o Office of International Fisheries Affairs, National Marine Fisheries Service, Washington, DC 20235, USA

Officer. Jack Gehringer (exec. sec.)

Founded. 1958

History. The commission was established under an Interim Convention on the Conservation of North Pacific Fur Seals signed in Washington on Feb. 9, 1957, and in force from Oct. 14, 1957. The convention has repeatedly been extended for four-year periods, most recently in 1984.

Objectives. To achieve the maximum sustainable productivity of the fur seal herds through the co-ordination of research programmes carried out by the member governments, and to implement the desire of the parties to prohibit pelagic sealing because of its past detrimental effect on fur seal populations, and to provide for regulated land harvesting of animals by the Soviet Union and the United States.

Activities. The commission does not conduct programmes of its own but co-ordinates those instituted by party governments. Through the operation of its standing scientific committee the commission may recommend to member governments appropriate measures dealing with the commercial harvest, pelagic or land-based research, collection of data on reproduction, morphology, feeding habits, migration routes and any other topic regarded as important for the conservation, protection and management of the fur seal populations. Through public relations and research the commission seeks to stem the entanglement of fur seals in fishing debris discarded at sea. The commission meets annually to report to the parties on current research activities and to consider the estimates of the yearly harvest by the United States and the Soviet Union.

Membership. Canada, Japan, the Soviet Union and the United States

Sources of finance. Member states' contributions

Pacific Salmon Commission

Founded. 1985

History. This commission, consisting of four members each from Canada and the United States, was established under a treaty signed in Ottawa (Canada) on Jan. 28, 1985, by representatives of the two countries, ending 15 years of negotiations. Previously the two countries had co-operated on the preservation and promotion of salmon fishing within the International Pacific Salmon Fisheries Commission founded in 1937.

A bill designed to implement the new treaty was approved by voice vote in the US House of Representatives on March 5, 1985, and by the US Senate on March 7, when the Senate also approved the treaty by 96 votes to none.

Objectives. To attempt to control over-fishing of salmon in the Pacific Ocean and to manage the fishing rights of the two countries.

Permanent Commission of the Conference on the Use and Conservation of the Marine Resources of the South Pacific (PCSP)

Address. Traslado A, Lima, Peru

Founded. Aug. 18, 1952

Activities. The PCSP has conducted a Regional Study of the El Niño Phenomenon (Estudio Regional del Fenómeno El Niño, ERFEN).

Structure. The PCSP has a general secretariat, a juridical commission and a scientific research co-ordinating commission.

Membership. Chile, Ecuador and Peru (all of whom declared maritime zones of 200 nautical miles at the foundation of the PCSP)

South Pacific Forum Fisheries Agency

Address. P.O. Box 629, Honiara, Solomon Islands

Officers. D. A. P. Müller (dir.); L. G. Clark (dep. dir.)

Founded. August 1977

Objectives. To promote regional co-operation and co-ordination in respect of fisheries policies; to facilitate the collection, analysis, evaluation and dissemination of relevant statistical, scientific and economic information about the living marine resources of the region, and in particular the highly migratory species; to secure the maximum benefits from the marine living resources of the region for the peoples of the region as a whole and in particular of the developing countries; and to police a 200-mile exclusive economic zone of member states.

Membership. Australia, the Cook Islands, Fiji, Kiribati, the Federated States of Micronesia, Nauru, New Zealand, Niue, Papua New Guinea, the Solomon Islands, Tonga, Tuvalu, Vanuatu and Western Samoa

South Pacific Islands Fisheries Development Agency

Address. c/o South Pacific Commission, Post Box D 5, Nouméa Cédex, New Caledonia

Officers. Francis Bugotu (s.g.); Tamarii Pierre (dir. of programmes); F. Vitolio Lui (dep. dir. of programmes); Barney R. Smith (fisheries adviser)

Founded. May 1970

Objectives. To increase fisheries production in line with national planning objectives through a more accurate assessment of the nature and extent of available fisheries resources, the introduction of improved fishing gear and techniques, and an increased understanding of management and conservation measures necessary to sound development; to upgrade the technical expertise of national fisheries administration through the provision of specialized training opportunities, intercountry study visits etc., and the promotion of interchange of experts, information and experience between countries of the region.

Activities. In the technical assistance given by the South Pacific Commission on request to the countries of its region particular emphasis is laid on the assessment and development of marine resources, and training and provision of expert advice on a wide range of problems associated with subsistence, artisanal, commercial and international fisheries. The Commission also carries out investigation projects, assists applied research, acts as a centre for collection and dissemination of information and produces technical publications.

The Commission's fisheries programme covers assessments of (i) deep bottom fishery resources and the development and practical demonstration of fishing techniques suitable for Pacific Islands situations, (ii) the skipjack and baitfish resources of the region, and (iii) the resources of all highly migratory species and the impact of extended fisheries jurisdiction on the harvesting of these resources. It also covers (i) the provision of short-term specialist advice in areas of specific interest or concern to individual countries (including selection of the appropriate experts, supervision and the presentation of reports) and of training opportunities for Pacific Islanders at courses both within and outside the region; (ii) the collection and dissemination of information on fish and fisheries; (iii) the promotion of interchange of information and experience; and (iv) awards for applied research. A regional technical meeting on fisheries is held every year.

Membership. American Samoa, the Republic of Belau, the Cook Islands, Fiji, French Polynesia, Guam, Kiribati, the Marshall Islands, the Federated States of Micronesia, Nauru, New Caledonia, Niue, the Northern Mariana Islands, Papua New Guinea, Pitcairn Island, the Solomon Islands, Tokelau, Tonga, Tuvalu, Vanuatu, Wallis and Futuna, and Western Samoa

Publications. SPC Newsletter (quarterly, in French and English); reports; handbooks (for fishermen on a wide range of subjects); technical papers

Other Regions

ANTARCTIC

Commission for the Conservation of Antarctic Marine Living Resources

Address. 25 Old Wharf, Hobart, Tasmania 7000, Australia

Officer. Dr Darry L. Powell (exec. sec.)

Founded. 1982

Objectives. The Commission was founded under a 1982 convention based on an ecosystem-wide approach to the conservation of marine living resources in the waters surrounding Antarctica, and incorporating standards designed to ensure the conservation of not only individual populations and species but also the maintenance of the breadth of the Antarctic marine ecosystem as a whole.

Activities. The Commission has planned a management programme for which baseline information is supplied by international scientific programmes under the Scientific Committee for Antarctic Research (SCAR).

Membership. Argentina, Australia, Chile, the German Democratic Republic, the Federal Republic of Germany, France, Japan, New Zealand, South Africa, the Soviet Union, the United Kingdom and the United States, as well as the European Economic Community

BALTIC SEA

International Baltic Sea Fishery Commission

Address. ul. Hoza 20, 00–950 Warzawa, Poland

Officers. Stefan de Maré (Sweden, ch.); Z. M. Eventov (USSR, ch. of working group on regulatory measures); Pekka Niskanen (Finland, ch. of working group on finance and administration); Jan Piotr Jaremczuk (Poland, sec.)

Founded. Sept. 13, 1973

Objectives. To co-ordinate the management of the living resources in the Baltic Sea and the Belts by collecting, aggregating, analysing and disseminating statistical data (concerning catch, fishing effort, etc.) and other information; to promote co-ordination of scientific research and joint programmes and, in particular, to prepare and submit recommendations regarding total allowable catches, the type of fishing gear used, establishing closed seasons or areas, the amount of fishing effort and other measures related to the conservation and rational exploitation of the living resources.

Activities. The Commission has sought to implement a Convention on Fishing and Conservation of the Living Resources in the Baltic Sea and the Belts, signed in Gdansk (Poland) on Sept. 13, 1973, and amended with effect from Feb. 10, 1984. It has issued fishery rules (last revised with effect from Jan. 1, 1984), for the application of which the Baltic Sea and the Belts are divided into 11 areas, each of which is broken down into statistical rectangles as laid down by the International Council for the Exploration of the Sea (ICES).

Membership. Six contracting parties (the European Economic Community, Finland, the German Democratic Republic, Poland, the Soviet Union and Sweden)

Shellfish Commission for Skagerrak and Kattegat

Founded. 1962

Membership. Denmark, Norway and Sweden

BLACK SEA

Mixed Commission for Black Sea Fisheries (MCBSF)

Founded. 1959 (under a convention)

Membership. Bulgaria, Romania and the Soviet Union

CARIBBEAN SEA

Fisheries Unit, Organization of Eastern Caribbean States (OECS)

Address. Castries, St Lucia, West Indies

Officer. Dr Vaughan Lewis (dir.-gen. of OECS)

Founded. 1984

Activities. Fisheries legislation passed by the OECS member states is based on the extension of the states' fisheries jurisdiction to 200 miles off their coasts and on the need for regional co-operation in the management of fisheries. Three FAO-OECS workshops were established by 1984 to implement administrative and management measures under the new laws and regulations. These measures included the creation of local management areas, fishing priority areas and marine reserves; the prosecution of offences; monitoring and control; licence conditions for foreign fishing vessels; and the prevention of marine pollution.

Membership. Antigua and Barbuda, Dominica, Grenada, Montserrat, St Christopher and Nevis, St Lucia and St Vincent and the Grenadines

INDIAN OCEAN

Indian Ocean Fishery Commission (IOFC)

Founded. 1948

History. The IOFC was established under a resolution of the Council of the (UN) Food and Agriculture Organization (FAO).

Objectives. To promote national programmes as well as research and development activities, and to examine management problems.

Membership. 40 states

MEDITERRANEAN SEA

General Fisheries Council for the Mediterranean (GFCM)

Address. F-122 Fisheries Department, Via delle Terme di Caracalla, 00100 Rome, Italy

Officer. Dr D. Charbonnier (sec.)

Founded. 1952

Objectives. To promote in the Mediterranean and Black Seas the development, conservation, rational management and best utilization of living marine resources; to keep under review the economic and social aspects of the fishing industry and recommend any measures aimed at its development; to encourage, recommend and, as appropriate, undertake training, extension, research and development activities in all aspects of fisheries, including the protection of living marine resources.

Activities. At its 15th conference, held in Palma de Mallorca in September 1980 and attended by representatives of 19 coastal states (but not of Albania and the Soviet Union), the Council agreed on a regional management programme for the Mediterranean area. A pilot project, conducted jointly with the UN Development Programme (UNEP) at 49 research centres, to combat pollution and to detect metals and hydrocarbons, was to be followed, from February 1981, by a new five-year plan for the surveillance of certain substances, especially nitrates and phosphates, in the sea. To preserve fish stocks the Council called, inter alia, for the adoption of a 30 mm net within three years.

Structure. The Council, which meets at least once every two years and on which each member has one vote, takes decisions by a simple majority of the votes cast, but the adoption and amendment of the Council's rules of procedure, as well as recommendations on management, require a two thirds majority. Members may object to a recommendation within 120 days, and if they do they are not obliged to effect that recommendation. The Council establishes committees and working parties, including an executive committee which meets at least once between regular Council meetings.

Membership. Bodies in 19 countries (Algeria, Bulgaria, Cyprus, Egypt, France, Greece, Israel, Italy, Lebanon, Libya, Malta, Monaco, Morocco, Romania, Spain, Syria, Tunisia, Turkey and Yugoslavia)

Sources of finance. Budget of the (UN) Food and Agriculture Organization (FAO)

Publications. Report of the 17th Session of the GFCM (September 1984)

SOUTH-EAST ASIA

South East Asian Fisheries Development Centre (SEAFDEC)

Address. P.O. Box 4, Phrapradeng, Samutprakarn, Thailand

Founded. Dec. 28, 1967

Membership. Japan, the Philippines, Singapore and Thailand

Non-Living Resources of the Sea

Oil and Gas Resources

Most oil and gas obtained from below the sea has been found at depths of up to 200 metres, and none has yet been extracted from depths below 350 metres. Oil production from below the sea started as an expansion of onshore fields—in Venezuela, Mexico, Texas/Louisiana, Indonesia and the Persian (Arabian) Gulf. In more recent years exclusively offshore deposits have been discovered and developed, most notably in the UK and Norwegian sectors of the North Sea.

Offshore oil and gas production requires exploration drilling, well-logging and the installation of production rigs. Exploration is often carried out from drill ships or mobile submersibles. According to the depth of the water, rigs can be steel or concrete platforms standing on the sea-bed, or they may, in water up to 100 feet deep, stand on legs on the continental shelf. Above greater depths rigs may be semisubmersibles held in position by the use of anchors. Rigs are built on land and towed to their final position.

Technical developments have led to the construction of ever larger rigs, such as the Magnus complex in the northern sector of the British North Sea field, which produces both oil and gas (taken by pipelines to Sullom Voe or St Fergus respectively). The oil is brought up from a sea-bed 700 feet below the surface and from a reservoir of oil 4,000 feet down at the rate of 120,000 barrels a day. The whole complex has nine storeys of modules and weighs more than 65,000 tonnes. Like other platforms it has a helicopter pad and its crew of 200 enjoys high-standard amenities.

The hazards of offshore oil exploitation have been illustrated by a number of disasters. Between 1978 and 1981 there was a total loss of 18 rigs, and another 10 suffered blowouts which caused pollution in their environment. Severe loss of life was caused (i) in the case of the semi-submersible platform *Alexander Kjelland* in the Norwegian Edda Field, which capsized on March 27, 1980, when 123 persons were killed, and (ii) in that of the semi-submersible drilling ship *Ocean Ranger*, which capsized in a storm on Feb. 15, 1982, in the Hibernian Field off Newfoundland, with 84 persons losing their lives. Both these incidents led to numerous improvements in offshore safety measures.

The principal offshore oil areas are to be found off the shores of the following countries (in order of importance and grouped by region):

Europe:	United Kingdom, Norway, Denmark, Spain, Italy
America:	Venezuela, United States, Trinidad and Tobago, Mexico, Brazil, Peru, Canada

Africa:	Nigeria, Gabon, Angola (including Cabinda), Tunisia, the Congo, Zaïre, the Ivory Coast, Ghana
Asia:	Indonesia, Malaysia, the Soviet Union, Brunei, India, the Philippines, Japan, China
Middle East:	Saudi Arabia, Abu Dhabi, Egypt, Dubai, Qatar, Iran, Sharjah, Iraq
Oceania:	Australia, New Zealand

The principal offshore natural gas resources are found off the coasts of the following countries (again in order of importance and grouped by region):

Europe:	United Kingdom, Norway, the Netherlands, Ireland, Italy
Middle East:	Abu Dhabi, Egypt
America:	United States, Trinidad and Tobago, Brazil, Colombia, Mexico, Canada
Africa:	Nigeria, Ghana
Asia:	Soviet Union, Brunei, Indonesia, Japan, India
Oceania:	Australia, New Zealand

Hydrocarbons Production Figures

Offshore Oil Production in 1984

Separate figures for offshore oil production only are not available. However, for the countries with major offshore oil resources total oil production in 1984 was, in barrels per day (1 barrel—0.136 metric tons or 35 imperial gallons or 42 US gallons), as follows:

Country	*bp/d*
Saudi Arabia	4,690,000
Mexico	3,010,000
United Kingdom	2,580,000
Venezuela	1,875,000
Canada	1,555,000
Indonesia	1,440,000
Nigeria	1,405,000
Kuwait	985,000
Abu Dhabi	840,000
Norway	710,000
Malaysia	525,000

(The total production of the United States was 10,385,000 barrels per day, most of it from onshore fields.)

Natural Gas Production in 1984

While separate figures for offshore gas production are likewise not available, the principal countries producing natural gas in 1984 were as follows, with production given in tonnes of oil equivalent (toe):

Country	*toe*
Soviet Union	526,500,000
United States	439,900,000
Canada	65,200,000
The Netherlands	61,500,000
Mexico	32,100,000
United Kingdom	31,500,000
Norway	26,300,000
Algeria	18,300,000
Indonesia	16,400,000
Venezuela	14,900,000
Federal Republic of Germany	13,100,000
Italy	11,700,000
China	11,500,000
Saudi Arabia	10,600,000

North Sea Hydrocarbons

In the North Sea the hydrocarbons province is delimited by the occurrence of basement (i.e. non-productive) rocks at or near the surface around the periphery of the North Sea. It includes parts of eastern and southern England, of the Federal Republic of Germany and of the Netherlands. In the delimitation of their respective continental shelf zones Britain and Norway have agreed to extend their median line boundary north of 62°N. The median line agreed in 1963 has been to Norway's advantage.

The continental shelf boundaries in the North Sea were delimited under agreements concluded between 1964 and 1972 as listed below (the second column showing the date of signature and the third the date of entry into force).

Agreement	*Signed*	*In force*
1. Norway-UK	10.3.1965	29.6.1965
2. Denmark-Norway	8.12.1965	22.6.1966
3. Denmark-UK	25.11.1971	7.12.1972
4. Netherlands-UK	6.10.1965	26.12.1966
amending protocol	25.11.1971	7.12.1972

Agreement		Signed	In force
5. Denmark-W.Germany		28.1.1971	7.12.1972
6. W.Germany-Netherlands	(a)	1.12.1964	18.9.1965
	(b)	28.1.1971	7.12.1972
7. W.Germany-UK		25.11.1971	7.12.1972

The first four of the above agreements were cases where the agreed boundary line was based on the equidistance principle (with minor divergencies in the case of the Norway-UK agreement). Agreement 5 laid down a boundary determined by nine specified turning points (and was not based on the equidistance principle). The boundary established under agreement 6 was partly negotiated and partly based on the equidistance principle. The boundaries under agreements 3 and 7 related only to short stretches between the UK-Norway and UK-Netherlands boundaries.

United Kingdom

In a Brown Book published by the British government in 1984 it was estimated that there were under the British continental shelf between 1,408 million and 5,278 million tonnes of oil deposits (including between 480,000,000 and 3,275 million tonnes which had still to be discovered). Moreover, the Brown Book also referred to undiscovered recoverable reserves between the parallels of 56°N and 62°N in the North Sea.

In 1985 it was believed that there were oil resources not only in the northern part of the North Sea (i.e. the Brent and Forties deposits already being exploited) but also in the more southerly areas of the North Sea, in the English Channel approaches, in the Irish Sea and off the south-western coasts of England and Wales. According to an estimate made by the chief executive of Shell UK on April 17, 1984, Britain would remain self-sufficient in oil until the year 2000.

Oil from the northernmost British wells is piped to the Sullom Voe (Shetland) terminal completed in 1982 and operated by British Petroleum on behalf of a consortium of some 30 companies. From the Piper and Claymore wells (in the Forties field) oil is piped to Flotta (Orkney). A pipeline for oil from the Norwegian Ekofisk field to Teesside has been in operation since October 1975.

At the end of 1983 there were 25 wells in production. In 1984 a total of 106 new wells were drilled, and finds were made in 23 of them.

The 1984 Brown Book gave the estimated British natural gas reserves at between 897,000 million and 2,259 million cubic metres (of which only 185,000 million to 570,000 million were listed as undiscovered but likely).

Under a Far North Liquids and Associated Gas System (FLAGS) "wet" gas from a group of fields north-east of Shetland is supplied through pipelines to an extraction plant of the British Gas Corporation at St Fergus (near Peterhead, north of Aberdeen), where methane and some ethane are removed and piped into the British natural gas grid, while the remaining gas fluids are passed through a land pipeline to fractionation and ethylane plants at Mossmorran (Fife).

According to a survey published on July 2, 1985, the profitability of British North Sea oil would be severely affected by any downward movement of the world oil price and of the pound–dollar exchange rate.

The survey covered five offshore oil fields—Auk, Balmoral, Clyde, Ninian and Tern (and one inland field). It found that all the offshore fields would remain profitable only provided that the world oil price was $27 per barrel in 1985–87 and increased by 5 per cent per annum thereafter, while the dollar–pound exchange rate was $1.35. At a dollar price of $24 per barrel and an exchange rate of $1.25, only the Clyde and Ninian fields would remain profitable. If the dollar price of oil were

$20 per barrel and the exchange rate $1.10, all five offshore fields would make losses ranging from $9,000,000 to $206,000,000.

The UK Department of the Environment has commissioned an important Hydrocarbons (Offshore) Research Programme carried out by the British Geological Survey. All commercial exploration data concerning hydrocarbon prospectivity in the UK designated areas of the sea are held in confidential files of the British Geological Survey.

In 1973 the British Government set up an Offshore Supply Office (OSO) which was to ensure the interests of the Government in North Sea oil development. The OSO has been responsible for an oil platform programme and has helped to place 70 per cent of North Sea oil installations contracts with British firms.

Norway

The Norwegian Petroleum Directorate estimated on Jan. 24, 1985, that production from Norway's continental shelf in 1984 had been 35,000,000 tonnes of oil and 26,000,000 tonnes oil equivalent (toe) of gas. Discoveries made north of the 62°N parallel were, however, expected to be extremely expensive to exploit.

Norwegian oil has been partly delivered to Britain (through the pipeline from the Ekofisk field to Teesside, in operation since October 1975). Of Norway's gas output, that from the Frigg field has been connected by pipeline to the British network via St Fergus (north of Aberdeen). The Norwegian Government however, decided that gas from the Statfjord field, including Gullfaks and Oseberg (north of Frigg), and the Heimdal deposits (south of Frigg) were to be connected with Norway by direct pipelines in order to be cleared of gas liquids, ethane, propane and buthane and then piped to the Heimdal, Sleipner and Ekofisk fields, to be transmitted via an existing pipeline to Emden (Federal Republic of Germany).

Under agreements signed on Sept. 1, 1982, a group of seven foreign gas companies (the Belgian, Dutch and French state gas companies and four German corporations) would import 3,500 million cubic metres of natural gas via Emden, mainly from the Statfjord field, from 1968. These agreements were expanded in March 1984 to increase the gas supply to 7,000 million cubic metres per annum.

In the Ekofisk oil and gas field, where there are seven platforms and production has proceeded since 1974, the underground rock structure has been weakened and one of the platforms had by 1985 sunk by up to seven and a half feet. Moreover, platforms were liable to be damaged by high waves originating to the north-east of the field. It was thought that the power of the largest waves could be reduced by the building of a concrete wall (500 yards long, 50 yards high and 120 yards thick) on the seabed, or by the sinking of four supertankers in the area.

Regional and National Offshore Hydrocarbons Developments

Angola. Offshore oil has been prospected for, with varying success, in 10 different blocks along the coast of Angola by the Sociedade Nacional de Combustives de Angola (Sonangol, the Angolan national company) in co-operation with foreign groups—most successfully with the (US) Gulf Oil Corporation in Cabinda, and elsewhere with the (French) Elf Aquitaine and Compagnie Française des Pétroles (CFP–Total), British Petroleum, Texaco, Petróbras (the Brazilian state oil company), Mobil, Agip (of Italy), Petroleos de Portugal and two Yugoslav companies. More than $1,000 million was to be invested in Angola's offshore hydrocarbon industry between mid-1983 and 1985.

Antarctica. Offshore oil in the continental shelf of the Antarctic was first reported to exist in 1969. The *Glomar*

Challenger found traces of gaseous hydrocarbons in the Ross Sea floor in 1972. A confidential US Geological Survey document, disclosed in February 1974, claimed that there were 45 million barrels of petroleum and 115,000,000 million cubic feet of natural gas under the Ross, Weddell and Bellingshausen Seas. However, the exploitation of such resources would depend on the resolution of unresolved sovereignty disputes among the parties to the Antarctic Treaty [see also pages 216–17 and 225].

The signatories of the 1959 Antarctic Treaty agreed at a meeting held in Washington from Sept. 17 to Oct. 5, 1979, inter alia to maintain voluntary restraint in the exploration and exploitation of Antarctic minerals, and notably oil and gas.

Asia. In 1966 the (UN) Economic Commission for Asia and the Far East (ECAFE, which in 1974 changed its name to Economic and Social Commission for Asia and the Pacific, ESCAP) set up a Committee for Co-ordination of Joint Prospecting for Mineral Resources in Asian Offshore Areas (CCOP/East Asia). At a meeting held in Tokyo on Aug. 22, 1975, the committee reached agreement between Indonesia, Japan, the Republic of Korea, Malaysia, the Philippines, Singapore and Thailand on extending their offshore oil and mineral survey activities beyond the continental shelf. By mid-1985 membership of the Committee also included China, Kampuchea, the Federated States of Micronesia, Papua New Guinea and Vietnam.

In the South China Sea [see also section on China below] US companies now hold concessions to carry out oil exploration and exploitation in all areas in which maritime boundaries are in dispute except around the Spratly Islands [see pages 201–03].

On Nov. 29, 1981, Vietnam issued a warning to foreign companies not to conduct survey and exploration operations in disputed areas without Vietnam's consent. Vietnam has also condemned the granting, by China, of contracts enabling US companies to conduct oil exploration in areas of the Gulf of Tonkin bordering on disputed areas. As the Soviet Union has been prospecting for oil in the area on behalf of Vietnam, its ally, and the United States is bound to protect the activities of US companies, the South China Sea is liable to become an area of open conflict.

In March 1982 Kampuchea protested against the granting of concessions by Thailand to the (US) Amoco company on part of the continental shelf claimed by Kampuchea.

Malaysia and Thailand, on the other hand, having set aside the question of the demarcation of their common maritime boundary, have reached agreement on the joint exploration and exploitation of hydrocarbons in the overlap area of their respective continental shelves claimed—this agreement being the first such arrangement in the South China Sea—conforming to the recommendation of "provisional arrangements of a practical nature" made in Article 83(3) of the 1982 UN Law of the Sea Convention.

Canada. The offshore oil resources of Canada are largely in the Arctic (in the Beaufort Sea and off Melville Island) and their exploitation is possible only with the help of massive icebreakers.

An Atlantic Accord signed on Feb. 14, 1985, by the federal Government of Canada and the provincial government of Newfoundland provided for the sharing, between the two governments, of revenue from resources of the continental shelf off Newfoundland. The accord, however, contained no reference to the provisions of Article 82 of the 1982 UN Convention on the Law of the Sea under which Canada would have to contribute to the international community from 1 to 7 per cent per annum of the value or volume of production of any given site beyond the 200-mile limit.

China. In the People's Republic of China the exploitation of offshore oil reserves is managed by the China National Offshore Oil Corporation and the Joint General Petroleum Service Corporation of the South China Sea. These state organizations have entered into joint ventures with foreign companies.

In 1983 concessions were awarded by the Chinese organizations to (i) a consortium led by British Petroleum (to operate in the China Sea and Yellow Sea areas), (ii) the (US) Occidental Corporation and (iii) an Exxon–Shell consortium. Earlier concessions had been granted in 1982 to Japanese, French and US oil groups.

Guinea-Bissau. In February 1984 Guinea-Bissau signed an agreement with a group of French, British, Canadian, West German and United States oil companies for the first offshore oil prospecting along its shores. On March 7, 1985, the Presidents of Guinea-Bissau and Guinea agreed on joint offshore oil prospecting in the area of their common maritime boundary, which had been delimited on Feb. 14 by an arbitral tribunal of the International Court of Justice [see pages 217–18].

Mineral Resources of the Sea

Between 1872 and 1876 the research vessel *Challenger* carried out, under the direction of Sir C. Wyville Thomson, the first systematic overall study of the world's oceans. Among more than 12,000 geological samples collected from the sea-bed were nodules of manganese (restricted mostly to the deepest parts of the oceans).

After World War II a start was made in exploring the sea floor sediments or basalts, and within the past 15 years drilling techniques applied by the *Glomar Challenger* expedition have achieved the penetration of the ocean floor to a depth of more than 1,000 metres. This has led to the discovery of numerous other resources, but not in sufficiently high concentrations to present economic conditions for exploitation.

Of these resources of the sea those found in the exclusive economic zones (EEZ—up to 200 nautical miles from coasts) include placer deposits of iron, gold, platinum, tin, diamonds, rare earth elements, zirconium, titanium, and others. Those found mainly in the EEZ are petroleum, gas, and phosphorites (phosphorus, uranium, rare earth elements and others). Those from the "Area" (lying outside the EEZ and to be placed under the Sea-Bed Authority envisaged in the 1982 UN Convention on the Law of the Sea—see pages 7–8) are hydrothermal ore deposits (of iron, manganese, copper, zinc, lead, silver and others) and manganese nodules (containing also iron, cobalt, copper, nickel, titanium, molybdenum and others).*

Economically exploitable deposits of mineral placers (chemically stable concentrates) are known from the beaches and the shelves of Australia, Brazil, Canada, India, Japan, Malaysia, Norway, South Africa, the Soviet Union and the United States (including Alaska).

Mining from the sea is carried out by pumping, tunnelling or dredging. Since the 1960s it has been possible to mine polymetallic nodules from a depth of between 4,000 and 5,000 metres and to extract the economically important metals from them. The nodules range in size from 0.5 to 10 centimetres, but mostly between 3 and 4 centimetres. Their chemical composition also varies greatly—their content of manganese (by weight) between 42.3 and 9.5 per cent; that of iron between 19.64 and 2.47 per cent; and those of cobalt, nickel and copper between lesser percentages.

The most promising area where such nodules are found has been the Clarion-Clipperton Zone (between 7°N and 15°N and 115°W and 160°W) in the North Pacific

* For details see Peter Rothe, "Marine Geology: Mineral Resources of the Sea", in the UNESCO journal *Impact of Science on Society*, No. 3 of 1983.

Ocean. Total reserves have been estimated at 60,000,000 tonnes.

A Red Sea Commission has been set up jointly by Egypt and the Sudan to administer the exploitation of metalliferous mud in the Atlantic II Deep in the north and central Red Sea.

Extraction of Fresh Water by Desalination

As a result of population growth the world supply of drinking water is dwindling and drinking water has to be obtained from all possible sources. Desalination of sea water technologies in use include the following:

Solar stills. These are ideal for small coastal villages where they can be run on a non-expendable energy source, are simple to construct and to operate, and incur minimal maintenance costs. (A still of 5,000 litres per day capacity has provided drinking water for 500 families in a village in Gujarat, India.)

Flash distillation. In this process saline water is made to flow through a series of chambers maintained at different pressures below atmospheric and decreasing progressively towards the end of the series, so that saline water evaporates in each section, the vapour is released and condensed over a bundle of tubes cooled by circulating seawater inside them. Distillate of fresh water produced at each stage is gathered either separately or collectively to be used as fresh water.

Electrodialysis. In this technique ion-selective membranes are employed for the desalination of brackish water. The cost of the process is directly proportional to the salinity, and for salinities beyond 5,000 ppm (parts per million) it is no longer economical.

Reverse osmosis. In this (most widely used) technique suitable osmotic membranes are used which reject salts and allow the water to pass through. Plants with daily capacities of from 10,000 to 15,000 litres have been set up in some Indian villages.

The costs of desalination plants have been reduced where they have been combined with electric-power-generating plants or with nuclear generating plants.

Sea Salt

The extraction of salt from the sea is mainly carried out in shallow pans along the coasts, especially of the Mediterranean Sea and East Asia, where the water is evaporated by insolation and the salt is left behind. In modern production sodium chloride is separated from other salts contained in the seawater. The total annual world production of sea salt is more than 6,000,000 tonnes.

Permanent Sources of Energy in the Oceans*

Tidal energy. Of major plants exploiting the energy created by alternating tidal flows, two are in operation—one in the estuary of La Rance in Brittany (France), completed in 1967, and the other at the Kislaya inlet on the Barents Sea (Soviet Union). Others are under consideration, notably one based on a barrage to be built across the Severn estuary near Bristol (England).

Wave energy. This has been used primarily for smallscale power plants for offshore operations (e.g. in the *Kaimei* project in Japan).

Ocean thermal energy conversion (OTEC). This technique exploits the temperature differences between the surface and the bottom waters of the ocean. A first commercial plant was under construction in Nauru in 1983. This process is viable only where the difference between surface water and water at a depth of 500–1,000 metres is more than 20°C (i.e. in the tropics).

* For details of the schemes described in this section, see *The Times Atlas of the Oceans*, pp. 120–21.

5. Environmental and Scientific Interest in the Sea

This chapter presents data on (i) dimensions of the marine pollution problem; (ii) conventions, agreements and legislation on marine pollution; (iii) international organizations concerned with the protection of the marine environment, notably the UN Environment Programme (UNEP); (iv) aspects of scientific research related to the sea; and (v) international bodies involved in ocean research.

Dimensions of the Marine Pollution Problem

Principles of Environmental Protection

A Declaration on the Human Environment adopted by the Stockholm Conference on the Human Environment held on June 5–16, 1972, enumerated 25 principles, including the following relating to the marine environment:

"(2) The natural resources of the earth, including the air, water, land, flora and fauna, and especially representative samples of natural ecosystems, must be safeguarded for the benefit of present and future generations through careful planning or management as appropriate.

"(6) The discharge of toxic substances or of other substances and the release of heat, in such quantities or concentrations as to exceed the capacity of the environment to render them harmless, must be halted in order to ensure that serious or irreversible damage is not inflicted upon ecosystems. The just struggle of the peoples of all countries against pollution should be supported.

"(7) States shall take all possible steps to prevent pollution of the seas by substances that are liable to create hazards to human health, to harm living resources and marine life, to damage amenities or to interfere with other legitimate uses of the sea.

"(21) States have, in accordance with the Charter of the United Nations and the principles of international law, the sovereign right to exploit their own resources pursuant to their own environmental policies, and the responsibility to ensure that activities within their jurisdiction or control do not cause damage to the environment of other states or of areas beyond the limits of national jurisdiction.

"(22) States shall co-operate to develop further the international law regarding liability and compensation for the victims of pollution and other environmental damage caused by activities within the jurisdiction or control of such states to areas beyond their jurisdiction."

At a United Nations environment conference held in London in mid-1982 conflicting views were expressed (on June 16) on the existing threats to the marine environment.

Michael Heseltine, then UK Secretary of State for the Environment, said that there was "no evidence that the pollution of the sea" had "significantly affected fisheries", and that the control of pollution by industrialized nations had produced "a rate of progress faster than the rate of deterioration".

Jacques-Yves Cousteau, the French marine explorer and Secretary-General of the International Commission for the Scientific Exploration of the Mediterranean

Sea (ICSEM), stated on the other hand that the state of the ocean was "very alarming" as the seas suffered not only from pollution but from "mechanical aggression" in which fish were dynamited, rivers were diverted and marine temperatures were raised artificially by coastal industry, and that he had come to the conclusion that these threats to the oceans were "even more important than pollution".

Impact of Tourism and Recreational Uses of the Sea

As 70 per cent of the world's population live within 50 miles of a coast, the influence of human activities on the ecology of the sea has been considerable. In recent decades this influence has been greatly increased by the phenomenal growth of tourism and of recreational activities on the world's seas and oceans.

The largely seasonal influx of millions of tourists in certain areas has aggravated the problem of sewage disposal at sea and has profoundly changed the nature of the coastal economy by urbanization (involving the erection of high-rise buildings, the creation of marinas, shipbuilding and repair yards for pleasure craft, and the displacement of traditional fishing industries).

The recreational activities have included swimming and diving, yacht and powerboat cruising and racing, water-skiing, sailing, windsurfing, and ocean cruises, all of which have led to the development of related industries.

An example of negative effects of these developments is the case of coral reefs, which provide an important stimulus to the tourist industry but are expected to shrink and die as a result of pollution and industrial development along the coastline (unless they are preserved in coastal marine parks).

Additional developments have been in the field of archaeology (i) of shipping, with hundreds of museums having been created showing original or reconstructed vessels of all ages, or models of them, (ii) of historical treasures retrieved from the sea-bed and (iii) of fisheries.

Threat of Rise in Coastal Waters

The US Federal Environmental Agency published, on Oct. 19, 1983, a report forecasting that a potentially catastrophic warming of the earth would start in the 1990s, disrupting food production and raising coastal waters as a result of melting polar icecaps. The report claimed that the continued burning of coal and other fossil fuels would produce so much carbon dioxide that it would have a "greenhouse effect" (allowing the sun's rays to reach the earth but not allowing the escape of the heat created).

A research team led by Dr Hal Rosen of the Lawrence Berkeley Laboratory of the University of California had on May 24, 1982, been reported to have found evidence of soot pollution in the Arctic both on the surface and in the air which would contribute significantly to the heating of the air—to an extent equivalent to doubling the carbon dioxide concentration, which would cause a greenhouse effect.

Marine Pollution by Oil

The 10 largest oil spills of those which occurred between 1967 and 1979, according to *Oil Spill Intelligence Report* published by the Center for Short-Lived Phenomena in Cambridge (Mass., USA), were as follows (listed by the tanker's name unless otherwise specified):

Torrey Canyon, grounded on March 18, 1967, off Land's End, United Kingdom; 119,000 tonnes spilled.

Othello, collided on March 20, 1970, in Tralhavet Bay, Sweden; from 60,000 to 100,000 tonnes spilled.

Wafra, grounded on Feb. 27, 1971, at Cape Agulhas, South Africa; 63,000 tonnes spilled.

Sea Star, collided on Dec. 19, 1972, in the Gulf of Oman; 115,000 tonnes spilled.

Jakob Maersk, grounded on Jan. 29, 1975, at Porto de Leixões, Portugal; 84,000 tonnes spilled.

Epic Colacotroni, stranded in May 1975 in the Caribbean; 57,000 tonnes spilled.

Urquiola, grounded on May 12, 1976, at La Coruña, Spain; 100,000 tonnes spilled.

Hawaiian Patriot, caught fire on Feb. 25, 1977, in the North Pacific west of Honolulu; 99,000 tonnes spilled.

Venoil and *Venpet* (Liberian supertankers), collided and caught fire on Dec. 16, 1977, less than 25 miles off the South African coast near Port Elizabeth; 30,000 tonnes spilled.

Amoco Cadiz, grounded on March 16, 1978, at Portsall, France; 223,000 tonnes spilled, much of it polluting holiday beaches on the Brittany coast.

The well *Ixtoc I*, a blow-out on June 3, 1979, off Bahia de Campeche, Mexico; some 210,000 tonnes spilled.

A blowout not listed in the above report occurred on April 22, 1977, on the Bravo production platform in the Norwegian Ekosfisk field (in the North Sea); it was brought under control by April 30 after crude oil had gushed into sea at a rate of up to 2,000 tonnes a day.

Other major oil spillages occurred from the following tankers:

Betelgeuse, exploded at the Bantry Bay oil terminal in Ireland in January 1979; about 13,000 tonnes spilled and over 50 persons killed.

Atlantic Express and *Aegean Captain*, collided on July 19, 1979, off the coast of Trinidad and Tobago; about 90,000 tonnes spilled.

Alvenus, grounded on July 31, 1984, about 10 miles off the Louisiana coast; the oil spill of some 270,000 tonnes affected about 25 miles of the coastline.

During the Iran-Iraq war severe oil spillages occurred in the northern part of the Gulf in March 1982 when Iraqi missiles struck wells in the Norwuz field (40 miles west of the Iranian island of Kharg). Plans to cap the leaking wells were delayed by continued disagreement between the warring parties on a possible ceasefire. The leaks were feared to have caused permanent damage to the Gulf's ecosystem. In recent years periodic attacks by Iraqi planes on tankers in the Gulf have not resulted in major oil spills into the sea.

Liability for "Amoco Cadiz" disaster

The complex question of liability for the pollution damage caused on the French coast by the *Amoco Cadiz* disaster of March 1978 was dealt with in an opinion issued on April 19, 1984, by Judge Frank J. McGarr of the Eastern Division of the Northern District Court of Illinois.

The conclusion drawn in this opinion was that the French claimants and the cargo insurers were "entitled to the full extent of their incurred damages" against Standard Oil of Indiana, Amoco International Oil Company (the operator of the *Amoco Cadiz*) and Amoco Transport (the vessel's owner); that Amoco was entitled to damages against the Spanish shipyard which had built the *Amoco Cadiz*; that the operator had "negligently performed its duty to ensure that the *Amoco Cadiz* in general and its steering-gear in particular were seaworthy, adequately maintained and in proper repair . . . [and] that the crew of the *Amoco Cadiz* was properly trained"; and that the operator had failed to make the vessel seaworthy before its last voyage.

Damages arising from the *Amoco Cadiz* disaster were, also in April 1984, assessed at about $148,000,000.

The disaster was followed by a complete revision of British anti-pollution measures in March 1979, including the fields of command, control and communication; spraying gear; the acquisition of a new oil recovery system known as Springsweep; the availability of aircraft equipped for aerial dispersant spraying, commercial tugs, salvage vessels and lightening tankers; and liability and compensation for oil pollution damage.

Agreements on Tanker Liability for Pollution

The *Tanker Owners' Voluntary Agreement concerning Liability for Oil Pollution* (TOVALOP), a voluntary agreement, is administered by the International Tanker Owners Pollution Federation [see page 168] and came into force on Oct. 6, 1969. It has repeatedly been amended and renewed.

The agreement provides a means by which tanker owners furnish compensation for pollution damage and clean-up costs arising from oil spills from their tankers. The Federation checks the eligibility of tankers for membership and issues TOVALOP certificates. Tanker owners who become a party to TOVALOP are obliged to insure their obligation and normally arrange cover with their Protection and Indemnity (P & I) Clubs. The principle of TOVALOP is that when a tanker under the agreement spills oil the owner will either remove the oil himself or accept responsibility for reimbursing any public or local authority, or any individual, who suffers pollution damage or incurs reasonable clean-up costs. Compensation may be up to US$160 per ship ton with an upper limit of US$16,000,000 per incident. TOVALOP incurs no liability for incidents to which the International Convention on Civil Liability for Oil Pollution Damage (CLC) of 1969 applies.

The *Contract regarding an Interim Supplement to Tanker Liability for Oil Pollution* (CRISTAL), concluded in 1971 and funded by oil companies, provides for additional compensation to TOVALOP [see above] and other existing sources and ensures the availability of US$36,000,000 per incident (or more if advisable). CRISTAL can be invoked only when all other compensation sources are exhausted.

The *Offshore Pollution Liability Agreement* (OPOL) concluded by a number of oil companies in 1974 has been in force since 1975.

Threat of Radioactive Pollution of the Oceans

Dumping of Nuclear Waste

The practice of dumping radioactive waste from nuclear installations into the sea has given rise to serious concern among scientists and others in view of its unpredictable longer-term consequences on marine life and thus on man's food chain.

United Kingdom Dumping. Under the 1974 Sea Dumping Act the United Kingdom is bound to observe the international dumping rules. The UK Ministry of Agriculture, Fisheries and Food disclosed on June 14, 1984, that radioactive waste had been dumped in the sea by Britain as follows:

(1) 16,000 tonnes of packaged low-level radioactive waste (laboratory equipment and material from civil and military nuclear programmes) were dumped between 1950 and 1963 at a depth of about 170 metres in the Hurd Deep (20 miles north of Guernsey, about 20 miles from Cap de la Hague—the site of a French nuclear reprocessing plant—and less than 10 miles from Alderney and the dumping site of World War II explosives).

(2) About 25,400 tonnes of radioactive waste were dumped between 1949 and 1976 at two sites some 250 miles west of the Outer Hebrides, three sites in the Bay of Biscay and three sites within 200 miles of Madeira.

(3) 75,000 tonnes of nuclear waste (about 90 per cent of it packaged) were dumped from 1964 to 1983 some 300 miles south-west of Land's End. (It was reported that in September 1983 the USS *Sam Reyburn*, a Poseidon-class nuclear submarine, had hit a nuclear-waste dump 175 miles south-west of Land's End and contaminated its hull.)

In 1982 it was said that Britain was responsible for the dumping of 90 per cent of all man-made radioactivity known to enter the world's oceans. The United States had ceased dumping radioactive waste at sea in 1970.

Under the 1972 London Dumping Convention [see page 21], it was decided in February 1983 to observe a two-year moratorium on the dumping of nuclear waste, in particular by Britain, Belgium and the Netherlands.

The Belgian authorities were on Aug. 28, 1983, reported to have ceased the dumping of radioactive waste in the Gulf of Gascony (the south-eastern Bay of Biscay) for an indefinite period. On April 11, 1984, the British Government announced that it had suspended all nuclear waste dumping in the Atlantic while a review of its effect was being carried out.

At a conference held in London in February 1984, and attended by representatives of 32 governments which were parties to the London Dumping Convention, it was decided to extend the 1983 moratorium by another six months. However, no agreement was reached on a proposal for burying radioactive waste in holes drilled in the sea-bed.

In October 1984 it was reported that proposals for British dumping of radioactive waste in deposits beneath the sea-bed should be submitted to the Nuclear Industry Radioactive Waste Executive (at Harwell, Oxfordshire), which considered it possible to dump low- and intermediate-level waste offshore on the continental shelf.

The British Government decided in December 1984 to continue the moratorium until it could be shown that disposal at sea of nuclear waste was the best environmental option.

1983 Sellafield Discharge. In November 1983 a 25-mile stretch of beach in Cumbria (north-west England) was contaminated by a discharge of radioactive solvent from the government-owned British Nuclear Fuels reprocessing plant at Sellafield (formerly Windscale). The discharge had been discovered by members of the environmentalist Greenpeace movement and was followed by widespread protests and allegations that the discharge might be linked to an abnormal level of cases of leukaemia and of Down's syndrome in the area as well as in Ireland.

On June 22, 1984, it was reported that the Government had agreed in principle to end discharges of radioactive material from Sellafield into the sea and to produce a plan on how this could be achieved by the end of 1984. At a meeting of the Paris Commission, held in Oslo on June 21, the British Government did not oppose a proposal by Denmark, Iceland, Norway and Sweden that contracting parties to the 1974 Paris Convention [see page 155] should minimize radioactive discharges into the marine environment and take account of the best available technology at existing nuclear reprocessing plants and whenever new such plants were constructed.

After cleaning of the beaches and continued monitoring the Government claimed on July 31 that the Sellafield beaches were safe again.

It was disclosed in February 1984 that high-level radioactive wastes were kept in bunkers at Sellafield for later conversion into vitrified blocks, on the ultimate disposal of which no decision had yet been made.

The chairman of the Nuclear Industry Radioactive Waste Executive stated on May 16, 1985, that the result of extensive experimental studies had indicated "zero spread" of radioactivity from the disposal site for solid wastes used in the North Atlantic, and that measurements of the low levels of radioactivity in the English Channel (regularly made and recorded by the Ministry of Agriculture, Fisheries and Food) had detected no radioactivity which could be ascribed to the previous disposal of solid wastes in the Hurd Deep.

In the opinion of British scientists the method of placing containers of highly radioactive waste beneath the sea-bed (i.e. "sea-bed emplacement") was not within the scope of the 1972 London Dumping Convention.

Carriage of Nuclear Waste Cargoes at Sea

In August 1984 the *Mont Louis*, a French freighter which sank in the Channel off Ostend after colliding with the *Olau Britannia*, a German-registered passenger ferry, was found to have carried 30 containers of uranium hexafluoride (which were subsequently salvaged). It was pointed out at the time that, although up to 9,000,000 separate nuclear cargoes were notified annually to the International Atomic Energy Agency, under that Agency's safety regulations there was no legal requirement for ships to identify themselves as carrying dangerous cargoes while on the high seas and even of specifying the types of ships suitable for such work.

Arising out of this incident Greenpeace and the (UK) National Union of Seamen were in September 1984 joined by seamen's unions in Belgium, Denmark and Sweden in a campaign for the use of special markings for ships carrying dangerous cargoes and for advance warnings to coastguards.

French Nuclear Tests in the Pacific

Between 1966 and 1985 the French nuclear research agency, the Centre d'Expérimentation du Pacifique, conducted over 100 nuclear tests above and below ground at the atolls of Mururoa and Fangataufa (in French Polynesia). In a case brought by Australia and New Zealand against the continued nuclear tests by France, on the grounds that the complainant governments had a legal interest in the protection of the seas from the hazards of nuclear fallout, and also in the freedom of the seas, the International Court of Justice declared in 1973 that it had no jurisdiction because the dispute had ended with a French announcement that all future testing would take place underground.

A joint scientific mission from Australia, New Zealand and Papua New Guinea, which visited the test site on Mururoa in 1983 at the invitation of the French Government, reported to the South Pacific Forum in August 1984, that it had no reason to believe that any pollution by radioactive material had taken place on Mururoa.

The continued tests were nevertheless strongly opposed by most governments of the region, notably by the member states of the South Pacific Forum, and on June 9, 1983, the Australian (Labor) Government announced the suspension of further shipments of uranium from Australia to France. [For the related question of the proposal for a nuclear-free zone in the Pacific, see pages 224–25.]

Threats of Pollution by Toxic Substances

The Finnish tanker *Enskeri*, carrying several tons of arsenic trioxide to be dumped in the South Atlantic (an area not covered by the London and Oslo conventions on dumping) without the knowledge of the Finnish Government (although it belonged to the Finnish state oil company, Neste) suffered a leak while en route in March 1975. It was refused landing rights in Gibraltar and the Canaries but was eventually allowed to enter Lisbon harbour, where the waste cargo was containerized in the hold, whereafter the *Enskeri* returned to Finland with it.

In June 1984 it was reported that 15 containers holding 2,700 barrels of cyanide of potassium had been sunk when a ship capsized in the Gulf of Papua near the mouth of the Fly River.

Conventions, Agreements and Legislation on Marine Pollution

Described below are the conventions administered by the Oslo Commission as well as regional anti-pollution agreements and certain national legislation in this field. Other major conventions and agreements concerned with the marine environment are covered under the United Nations Environment Programme [see pages 158–63].

Conventions administered by the Oslo Commission

Conventions and an agreement administered by the Oslo Commission, set up in London under the first convention listed below, are as follows:

(1) A *Convention against Marine Pollution*, designed to prevent sea pollution by the dumping of waste from ships and aircraft, was signed in Oslo on Feb. 15, 1972, by Belgium, Denmark, Finland, France, the Federal Republic of Germany, Iceland, the Netherlands, Norway, Portugal, Spain, Sweden and the United Kingdom.

The area covered by the convention comprised the high seas and territorial waters of the north-east Atlantic and part of the Arctic area, its western boundary being the longitude of Greenland and its southern boundary the latitude of the Straits of Gibraltar.

The convention laid down that all dumping was subject to the approval of the national authorities; it prohibited all dumping of highly hazardous substances (enumerated in a black list); and it laid down special requirements for dumping "greylist substances".

This convention came into effect on April 7, 1974, after the required ratification by seven of its 12 signatories, i.e. by Denmark, France, Iceland, Norway, Portugal, Spain and Sweden.

(2) A *Convention for the Prevention of Marine Pollution from Land-based Sources* was signed in Paris on June 4, 1974, by Belgium, Denmark, France, the Federal Republic of Germany, Iceland, Ireland, Luxembourg, the Netherlands, Norway, Portugal, Spain, Sweden and the United Kingdom, as well as by the European Communities. It entered into force on May 6, 1978.

(3) An *Agreement for Co-operation in Dealing with Pollution of the North Sea by Oil* was concluded in Bonn on June 9, 1969, by representatives of Belgium, Denmark, France, the Federal Republic of Germany, Norway, Sweden and the United Kingdom on June 9, 1969. It required the signatory governments to request ships and aircraft to report major oil slicks; to circulate reports on the presence, extent and movements of slicks; and on request to use their best endeavours to assist other countries in disposing of oil threatening their coasts. The agreement also established zones of responsibility for each country in the North Sea area.

The agreement entered into force on Aug. 9, 1969, in all signatory states except Norway, where it came into force on Nov. 28, 1970, and it was acceded to by the Netherlands on March 8, 1974.

Regional Anti-Pollution Agreements

Europe. The Council of Ministers of the European Economic Community issued, in 1979, a directive on pollution caused by certain dangerous substances discharged into the aquatic environment of the European Communities (EC), setting down detailed rules and standards of emission by reference to limit values of toxicity, persistence and bio-accumulation in respect of listed substances.

A ministerial conference of the Council of Europe, held at Vouliagmeni near Athens on April 21–23, 1984, adopted a "policy guide" (prepared by Greece) introducing the concept that protection of the environment could actually enhance economic development, e.g. by the control of pollution leading to economies in fuel consumption.

The delegates called on the 21 member governments of the Council of Europe to draw up a list of water and coastal zones to be protected by law for their flora and fauna, and also to sign a European convention for the protection of inland waterways against pollution.

North Sea. At a conference held in Bremen (Federal Republic of Germany) on Oct. 30–31, 1984, by ministers concerned with the environment from eight states (Belgium, Denmark, France, the Federal Republic of Germany, the Netherlands, Norway, Sweden and the United Kingdom) it was agreed to reinforce anti-pollution measures in the North Sea, in particular by strengthening existing surveillance measures on ships and their discharges, reducing the sewage discharge from rivers, attempting to reduce the dumping of radioactive waste and intensifying research on the impact of air pollution on the sea.

The conference failed to endorse a proposal by the Federal Republic of Germany to declare the North Sea a "special area" (under the MARPOL convention—see pages 21–22) in which the disposal of chemicals and the dumping of all dangerous waste would be prohibited. (It was estimated that some 22,000 tons of poisonous heavy metals were dumped into the North Sea every year, in addition to oil spills and sewage disposal. On the other hand the water of the North Sea was said to be replaced on average at the rate of once every twelve months—but not in the German Bight, where this process was three times slower, largely as a result of the pollution of continental rivers.)

On Sept. 14, 1983, Norway and the United Kingdom signed an agreement relating to oil spills.

The Baltic Sea. Agreements relating to the protection of the whole or parts of the Baltic Sea area were the result of bilateral or multilateral negotiations between riparian states.

(1) Denmark, Finland, Norway and Sweden concluded, on Sept. 16, 1971, an agreement (which came into force on Oct. 16, 1971) on co-operation in taking measures against pollution of the sea by oil.

(2) Denmark and Sweden signed a convention, in April 1974, on the protection of the Öresund (linking the Baltic Sea proper with the Kattegat). It involved the construction, by 1979, of a purification plant to reduce oil pollution by industrial and organic waste.

(3) Finland and the Soviet Union formed, in 1968, a Working Group on the Protection of the Gulf of Finland (in association with a Finnish-USSR Committee for Scientific and Technical Co-operation).

(4) Finland and Sweden have formed a Committee for the Gulf of Bothnia.

(5) The German Democratic Republic and Poland have formed an Odra Haff Committee.

Adriatic Sea. Italy and Yugoslavia signed, in 1974, an agreement on co-operation for the protection of the waters of the Adriatic Sea.

English Channel. The United Kingdom Government announced on Aug. 9, 1972, that it had concluded agreements with Belgium and France on co-operation in the surveillance of oil slicks in the Channel area.

Asia and the Pacific. In a memorandum of understanding signed in Jakarta on Feb. 11, 1981 by representatives of Indonesia, Japan, Malaysia and Singapore it was agreed to set up a fund of 400,000,000 yen for the prevention of pollution in the Malacca Strait, with Japan contributing three-quarters of the amount required and the management of the fund rotating every five years between Indonesia, Malaysia and Singapore.

A conference on the protection of the environment in Asia and the Pacific was held in Tokyo on June 5–11, 1984, with the participation of some 60 experts from 15 countries (Australia, China, Fiji, India, Indonesia, Japan, the Republic of Korea, Malaysia, Nepal, New Zealand, Papua New Guinea, the Philippines, Sri Lanka, Thailand and the United States). The conference agreed on a regional action programme intended to harmonize development and environmental protection, in particular to create a system of monitoring residual agricultural chemicals harmful to nature and health.

Wetlands Convention

A Convention on Wetlands of International Importance, especially as Wildfowl Habitat, was adopted at a conference held at Ransar (Iran) on Feb. 2, 1971. By 1981 it was adhered to by 27 countries, and its protection applied to sites at 216 localities totalling 6,000,000 hectares. Under this convention Denmark and the Netherlands co-operated in the conservation of the Wadden Zee off their coasts.

National Legislation against Pollution

Canada. Under a Canadian Arctic Waters Pollution Prevention Act of 1970 Canada claimed jurisdiction over an extensive area of the sea for anti-pollution measures which it regarded as essential for the protection of the environment and the prevention of the destruction of whole species. The act was criticized by the US government.

United States. A Marine Protection, Research and Sanctuaries Act (MPRSA), also known as the Ocean Dumping Act, was passed in 1972. Under a further law of 1979 the use of the ocean as a dumping ground for municipal sewage sludge was to be gradually ended by Dec. 31, 1981. In 1982 this law was extended for another year, while the dumping of low-level nuclear waste in the oceans was banned for two years.

Notwithstanding this act the dumping of sewage sludge had almost doubled by 1984, as cities turned to the oceans as the most economical and least sensitive repository for sludge which contained, in addition to nutrients, a number of toxic substances as well as viruses and bacteria. Moreover, radioactive waste was said to have been dumped off the coast of California.

Canada and the United States signed, in 1974, an agreement relating to the establishment of joint pollution contingency plans for spills of oil and other noxious substances.

United Kingdom. The Food and Environmental Protection Bill, introduced by the UK Ministry of Agriculture, Fisheries and Food in December 1984, contained a clause under which the Government would authorize dumping operations at sea by order rather than by licence (as hitherto, with all such licences being notified to other nations parties to international agreements).

In a report of Aug. 30, 1984, by the (UK) Water Authorities Association it was stated that 15 per cent of Britain's 1,210,000 dry tonnes of sewage sludge was discharged into the North Sea and the Atlantic Ocean (this being cheaper than its use as fertilizer) and was rapidly dispersed over a wide area. However, it was admitted that improvements were still needed as 16 per cent of Britain's estuary water was still poor or grossly polluted.

International Organizations concerned with Protection of the Marine Environment

United Nations Environment Programme (UNEP)

Address. P.O. Box 30552, Nairobi, Kenya

Officer. Mostafa K. Tolba (Egypt, exec. dir.)

Founded. 1972

Structure. UNEP has a Governing Council of 58 members (representing 16 African, 13 Asian, 10 Latin American, six Eastern European and 13 Western European and other states) and a Secretariat.

It also has a Liaison Office in New York (at ALCOA Bldg., Room A-3630, 866 United Nations Plaza, New York NY 10163, USA) and four regional offices—for Europe (at the Palais des Nations, 1211 Geneva 10, Switzerland), for Asia and the Pacific (at UN Bldg., 10th floor, Rajadamnern Ave., Bangkok, Thailand), for Latin America (at Presidente Mazaryk 29, Ap. Postal 6-718, México 5, DF, Mexico) and for West Asia (at P.O. Box 4656, Ouiedat Bldg., Bir Hassan, Beirut, Lebanon).

Regional Seas Programme

UNEP's activities include a Regional Seas Programme covering 10 different areas as described below. This programme has had some success over the past decade in helping to reduce marine pollution both in coastal waters and in the open seas.

A study entitled *The Health of the Oceans*, conducted by the Regional Seas Programme of UNEP with the help of several other international bodies and nearly 100 scientists from 36 countries, mandated by the 1972 UN Conference on the Human Environment and released in October 1982, came to the conclusion that the levels of most toxic substances in coastal waters and also in the less-polluted open-sea areas had decreased in the past decade. The study indicated that this decline was the result of environmental laws in the most industrialized countries which had restricted the production and distribution of many toxic substances such as DDT, polychlorinated biphenyls (PCBs) as well as other chlorinated hydrocarbons and harmful metals.

The contributors to the study found that in coastal areas of the Atlantic and Pacific Oceans the effects of sewage, food and beverage processing wastes, pulp and paper mill effluents, mine tailings and dredge spoils were mainly local. They pointed out that sewage discharges threatened bathers with infection and could contaminate seabeds filled with shellfish but found that in open areas of the Mediterranean, Baltic and North Seas and the Gulf of Mexico the toxic substances had been assimilated or degraded sufficiently to make them harmless. Although the problem of oil pollution of the seas was admitted to be a major one, the study found that oil-spill effects on animal and plant life in the open sea were "rarely drastic" and that recovery was "usually a question of weeks or months", but that in intertidal and subtidal areas recovery could take years or decades. The study also noted several general trends of increasing contamination, e.g. through sewage micro-organisms and radioactive wastes, which should serve as warning signals on the oceans' health.

Dr George Harvey, of the National Oceanic and Atmospheric Administration in Miami (a contributor to the study), was quoted as saying that the ocean was healthier in 1982 than it had been in 1972, that the ocean was more resilient and able to protect itself than had been thought, and that one reason for the improvement was that many industrial nations had ceased using certain poisonous chemicals (which were, however, now being used in underdeveloped countries, which had caused increasing concern in the southern hemisphere).

MEDITERRANEAN SEA

An Action Plan for the protection of the Mediterranean Sea (from the entrance to the Straits of Gibraltar to the southern end of the Dardanelles Straits) was agreed upon at a conference of representatives of 16 Mediterranean coastal states (i.e. all except Albania and Cyprus), of three observer countries (Britain, the Soviet Union and the United States) and of several international organizations, held in Barcelona from Jan. 28 to Feb. 4, 1975, under the auspices of UNEP.

The plan provided for "integrated planning of the development and management of the resources of the Mediterranean basin"; "co-ordinated pollution monitoring and research" in the Mediterranean; the drafting of a "framework convention and related protocols with their technical annexes for the protection of the Mediterranean environment"; and "institutional and financial procedures" to be followed in respect of the plan.

At a further conference of the 16 coastal states, held in Barcelona on Feb. 2–16, 1976, under UNEP auspices, a convention and two protocols were signed by 12 of these states. They entered into force on Feb. 12, 1978, after being ratified by 16 states (but not by Albania or Turkey).

The Barcelona convention laid down that its signatories should take all necessary measures to prevent pollution of the sea by dumping from ships and aircraft, by exploitation of the continental shelf and the seabed, or by sources of pollution on land such as rivers or sewage effluent. The first protocol banned the dumping at sea of toxic substances from ships and aircraft and contained a "black list" of prohibited substances and a restricted list of substances for which a special permit was required. The second protocol provided for co-ordinated action in the event of oil spills and for the establishment of regional headquarters (opened in Malta on Dec. 11, 1976) to direct such operations [see entry for Regional Oil-Combating Centre for the Mediterranean Sea on pages 166–67].

A "blue plan", designed to cover the period up to the end of the century and to harmonize activities in order to ensure continuous economic and social development of the ecological environment of the whole Mediterranean region was unanimously adopted at a meeting in Split (Yugoslavia) from Jan. 31 to Feb. 4, 1977, by representatives of 15 nations (i.e. all coastal countries except Albania, Lebanon and Syria). The plan is carried out by a Group Co-ordination and Synthesis (GCS) multi-disciplinary unit co-ordinating all study activities.

A protocol on the protection of the Mediterranean against pollution from land-based sources was signed at a conference organized by UNEP and held in Athens on May 12–17, 1980. An annex to the convention listed prohibited substances (as laid down in the first protocol to the Barcelona treaty—see above) to be eliminated progressively from wastes and also specified common guidelines, criteria or standards for implementing the protocol.

All Mediterranean coastal states except Albania had in February 1979 agreed to take over the burden of financing the Mediterranean action plan, with UNEP aid to cease by 1981. In May 1980 it was announced that the headquarters of the secretariat for the Mediterranean action plan would be transferred from Geneva to Barcelona.

At a conference held in Cannes (France) on March 2–7, 1981, by representatives of 16 Mediterranean states it was decided to move the headquarters of the action plan co-ordinating group from Barcelona to Athens and to set up in Tunis a regional centre to monitor a network of specially protected reserves to help preserve plants and animals threatened with extinction throughout the Mediterranean region, including the monk seal and the marine turtle. The conference also found that the rapid depletion of stocks of some 500 species of Mediterranean fish was due to the pollution of the posidonic grass beds providing shelter, food and spawning and nursery grounds for these fish.

For 1982 the annual figures relating to pollution of the Mediterranean were: oil from ships 350,000 tonnes, oil from industries around the coasts 115,000 tonnes (this oil pollution being four times that of the North Atlantic and 40 times that of the North-East Pacific). Weak coastal currents were said to keep sewage and industrial waste close to the shore and to spin floating oil and tar towards the beaches. Sewage treatment plants were not able to cope with the 100,000,000 residents and a further 100,000,000 tourists a year (expected to double in the next 20 years).

At a meeting held in Geneva representatives of the European Community and 16 Mediterranean states approved, on April 2, 1982, a fourth protocol to the Barcelona convention, calling for the establishment of up to 100 protected marine areas in the Mediterranean Sea to conserve endangered species, halt the spread of pollution and enhance tourism. Albania and Syria were not represented at the conference, and Turkey registered a strong protest, objecting to possible Greek establishment of marine parks in the eastern Aegean Sea, which would prejudice the two countries' dispute over maritime boundaries [see pages 191–95].

Representatives of 11 European cities agreed at a meeting in La Coruña (Spain) on April 2–3, 1982, on a Charter for the Protection of the Environment, in particular against marine pollution. (According to UNEP sources about 500,000 tonnes of hydrocarbons were dumped in the Mediterranean every year, against 4,000,000 tonnes in the remaining seas of the world.)

Turkey signed the Barcelona convention and its first two protocols in November 1980. The convention as amended in Athens in 1980 came into force in August 1983 after it had been ratified by six states (Algeria, Egypt, France, Monaco, Tunisia and Turkey).

At a further meeting held in Athens on April 10–13, 1984, the Mediterranean states failed to reach agreement on a single standard for measuring water pollution at all beaches of the Mediterranean. By that time the pollution monitoring and research programme was being carried out at 84 laboratories in 17 countries (which did not include Albania).

In January 1984 UNEP experts were reported to have found that the concentration of lead in the Mediterranean Sea was 10 times higher than that in the open ocean. This was said to be due to lead, mainly from car exhausts, being brought down by rain at the rate of between 5,000 and 10,000 tonnes a year, with rivers bringing in another 2,200 to 3,100 tonnes. The lead pollution was feared to cause brain damage to persons eating fish or shellfish from the Mediterranean.

PERSIAN (ARABIAN) GULF

A Regional Convention for Co-operation on the Protection of the Marine Environment was approved at a conference held under UNEP auspices in Kuwait on April 15–25, 1978, by representatives of eight states bordering the Persian Gulf—Bahrain, Iran, Iraq, Kuwait, Qatar, Saudi Arabia and the United Arab Emirates. The convention, together with a protocol and an action plan also adopted at the conference, came into force on June 30, 1979.

In the convention the signatory states undertook to "prevent, abate and combat pollution . . . caused by intentional or accidental discharge from ships . . ., by dumping of waste and other matter from ships and aircraft, . . . by discharges from land reaching the sea, whether water-borne or directly from the coast, including outfalls and pipelines" or "resulting from land reclamation and associated suction dredging and coastal dredging".

The protocol called upon the signatories to "co-operate in protection of the coastline" from "the threats and effects of pollution due to the presence of oil or other harmful substances . . . resulting from marine emergencies".

The action plan stressed the need for applied research and development, for contingency planning for accidents and for the establishment of a permanent pollution monitoring system.

A Regional Organization for the Protection of the Marine Environment (ROPME) [see page 167] was subsequently formed by Bahrain, Iran, Iraq, Kuwait, Oman, Qatar, Saudi Arabia and the United Arab Emirates.

The Iran-Iraq war was reported to have resulted in large-scale oil pollution from the offshore oil wells of the Nowruz field, leading almost to the extinction of the rare dugong (seacow) and to the closure of several desalination plants in Saudi Arabia.

WEST AND CENTRAL AFRICA

The Abidjan Convention for Co-operation in the Protection and Development of the Marine and Coastal Environment of the West and Central African Region (covering the coastal states from Mauritania to Namibia) was signed on March 23, 1981, together with a Protocol on Co-operation in Combating Pollution in Cases of Emergency. They were to enter into force 60 days after the sixth ratification or accession. The signatories were Angola, Benin, Cameroon, Congo, Equatorial Guinea, Gabon, The Gambia, Ghana, Guinea, Ivory Coast, Liberia, Mauritania, Nigeria, Senegal, Togo and Zaïre. The four absent countries of the region were Cape Verde, Guinea-Bissau, São Tomé and Príncipe, and Sierra Leone.

The major problems of the region had been identified as oil pollution from ships, landbased pollution from industry, sewage, pesticides and fertilizers, and coastal erosion. The action plan therefore provided for assessment of oil pollution, suspended and dissolved matter in rivers, chemical residues and domestic wastes; training in coastal management and waste control; and the establishment of facilities for the inspection of tankers before they deballasted.

The 16 states also (i) agreed on a protocol committing them to co-operating in pollution emergencies; (ii) pledged $2,500,000 over the period 1982–83 for a special regional trust fund to which Nigeria would contribute $550,000 and UNEP (during 1981–83) $1,400,000; and (iii) approved a resolution giving their naval vessels the "right of hot pursuit" of oil tankers which cleaned their tanks in West African coastal waters. Both the convention and the protocol had earlier been approved at a meeting of legal experts from 13 of the countries in Togo in 1980.

SOUTH-EAST PACIFIC

The Lima Convention for the Protection of the Marine Environment and Coastal Areas of the South Pacific was adopted under UNEP auspices in November 1981, together with an Agreement on Regional Co-operation in Combating Pollution of the South-East Pacific by Hydrocarbons and Other Harmful Substances in Cases of Emergency.

RED SEA AND GULF OF ADEN

The Jeddah Convention for the Conservation of the Red Sea and Gulf of Aden Environment was adopted under UNEP auspices in February 1982, together with a Protocol concerning Regional Co-operation in Combating Marine Pollution by Oil and Other Harmful Substances in Cases of Emergency.

CARIBBEAN SEA

The Cartagena Convention for the Protection and Development of the Marine Environment of the Wider Caribbean was signed in Cartagena (Colombia) on March 24, 1983, by representatives of Colombia, Grenada, Honduras, Jamaica, Mexico, Nicaragua, Panama, St Lucia, the United States and Venezuela, as well as of France, the Netherlands and the United Kingdom on behalf of their respective dependent territories in the region. It was supported also by delegates from Costa Rica, Cuba, Guatemala and Trinidad and Tobago.

The convention arose out of an action plan drafted in Managua (Nicaragua) in February 1981 and approved by experts from 23 countries at a conference held on April 6–8, 1981, and sponsored by UNEP and the UN Economic Commission for Latin America (ECLA).

The countries participating were Barbados, Colombia, Costa Rica, Cuba, Dominica, Dominican Republic, Grenada, Guyana, Haiti, Honduras, Jamaica, Mexico, Nicaragua, Panama, St Lucia, Suriname, Trinidad and Tobago, Venezuela and the West Indies Associated States, as well as Britain, France, Netherlands and the USA; a proposal of the Commission of the European Community to participate actively was also accepted. Those countries which did not attend the conference were Bahamas, Guatemala and St Vincent and the Grenadines, although the latter expressed support in a telegram.

The action plan contained 66 specific environmental projects for the combating of oil spills, the protection of coral reefs, mangroves, tropical forests and endangered species such as turtles and parrots, the management of watersheds, and the monitoring of coastal water pollution, as well as for studies on the impact of tourism and on ways of mitigating natural disasters. To finance the plan, a sum of $8,200,000 was initially to be raised over the period 1981–83, including $1,500,000 for a Caribbean trust fund. A nine-country monitoring committee (Colombia, Costa Rica, Cuba, Dominican Republic, France, Grenada, Mexico, St Lucia and Venezuela) was named to carry out the plan in conjunction with UNEP, and Jamaica was chosen as the headquarters of the action plan co-ordinating unit.

Of the waters of the wider Caribbean some 80 per cent are more than 1,800 metres deep, and half more than 3,600 metres. Contamination of the deepest levels is not easily eliminated. Less than 10 per cent of wastewater entering the Caribbean passes through treatment installations, and the waste generated by some 30,000,000 people has been dumped into the sea direct. This has caused serious destruction of tropical forests and disruption of the fragile ecosystem of the islands, coral reefs, swamps, mangrove forests, seagrass meadows and spawning grounds of fish and shrimp. In many parts there has been a shortage of drinking water and of energy. The greatest danger has been caused by oil, of which more than 76,500,000 barrels were discharged into the sea in 1978 alone.

The Caribbean had become the crossroads for oil traffic destined for the United States. Oil from Mexico, the Netherlands Antilles (Aruba and Curaçao), Trinidad and Tobago, and Venezuela, was exported to all parts of the United States; supertankers (at the average rate of 25 a day) were transporting crude oil from Africa and the Middle East to Aruba, the Bahamas, Curaçao, Puerto Rico, Trinidad and the Virgin Islands for refinement and re-export to the United States; and crude oil from Alaska reached the Caribbean via the Panama Canal to be refined or sent to refineries in Louisiana or Texas or on the US Atlantic coast.

EAST AFRICA

In June 1985 an agreement reached in Nairobi was signed by representatives of the governments of the Comoros, France (for the French overseas department of Réunion), Kenya, Madagascar, Mauritius, Mozambique, Seychelles, Somalia and Tanzania. The agreement provided for joint action to reduce and prevent pollution in the Indian Ocean and to protect the area from the effects of encroaching urbanization along the African coast. The European Communities were to assist in the financing of a joint organization designed to monitor any threat to the sea in the area, especially that presented by the heavy traffic of oil tankers from the Persian (Arabian) Gulf to Europe.

SOUTH-EAST ASIA

At a meeting held in Manila in April 1981 five South-East Asian nations (Indonesia, Malaysia, the Philippines, Singapore and Thailand) adopted an action plan on the protection and development of the marine environment and coastal areas in the South-East Asian region.

SOUTH-WEST PACIFIC

An action plan for this region was adopted at a regional conference held under UNEP auspices in February 1982.

SOUTH-WEST ATLANTIC

Similar arrangements were to be made under UNEP auspices for this region also.

Other UNEP Activities

UNEP further took part in a South Pacific Regional Environment Programme (SPREP), together with the South Pacific Bureau for Economic Co-operation (SPEC), the South Pacific Commission (SPC) and the (UN) Economic and Social Commission for Asia and the Pacific (ESCAP), in drafting, in June 1981, an action plan which led to the adoption, at a conference on the human environment in the South Pacific held in March 1982, to a South Pacific Declaration on Natural Resources and the Environment (the Rarotonga Declaration).

The documents contained guidelines for the sustainable management of land, sea and air resources of the region. In the declaration it was also stated that "the storage and release of nuclear wastes in the Pacific regional environment shall be prevented" and that "the testing of nuclear devices against the wishes of the people shall not be permitted".

In July 1984 UNEP launched a global action plan for the conservation of whales and other marine mammals, including the creation of whale sanctuaries [see also pages 126–27].

Other Governmental Organizations

Baltic Marine Environment Protection Commission (Helsinki Commission)

Address. Etaläesplanadi 22 C 43, 00130 Helsinki 13, Finland

Officers. Dr Peter Ehlers (ch.); Dr Hans Moebs (vice-ch.); Prof. Harald Velner (exec. sec.); Cdr Fleming Otzen (maritime sec.); Ms Terttu Melvasalo (scientific sec.)

Founded. May 3, 1980

History. Following the UN Conference of the Human Environment held in Stockholm in 1972, experts from the Baltic Sea states held a preparatory meeting in Helsinki early in 1973, which led to a conference at which a Convention on the Protection of the Marine Environment of the Baltic Sea Area was signed on March 22, 1974. This Helsinki convention was the first international convention on the protection of the marine environment against pollution form all sources. The Commission was established to implement the convention.

Objectives. The Commission's contracting parties are to take all appropriate legislative, administrative or other relevant measures to prevent and abate pollution and to protect and enhance the marine environment of the Baltic Sea area, and to use their best endeavours to ensure that the implementation of the Helsinki convention shall not cause an increase in the pollution of sea areas outside the Baltic Sea area. The Commission is to prepare proposals and recommendations to the contracting parties for measures to prevent and reduce pollution and to protect and improve the marine environment of the Baltic Sea area.

Activities. The Helsinki convention covers the Baltic Sea area consisting of the Baltic Sea proper, the Gulf of Bothnia, the Gulf of Finland and the entrance to the Baltic Sea bounded by the parallel of the Skaw in the Skagerrak at 57°44.8′N; it does not include the contracting parties' internal waters (on the landward side of the baseline from which the breadth of the territorial sea is measured).

In the convention the contracting parties undertake to counteract the introduction, whether airborne, waterborne or otherwise, into the Baltic Sea area of certain hazardous substances (Article 5), as specified in an annex and including PCBs and DDT. Land-based pollution, caused by direct discharges via sewers or by substances carried in river water discharge or so-called diffuse load originating from agricultural and less densely populated areas—including the pollution load carried by air, is to be controlled and minimized in respect of 16 specified substance groups listed in another annex (Article 6).

The provisions concerning the prevention of pollution from ships (Article 7) follow closely those of the MARPOL 73/78 convention of the International Maritime Organization (IMO) [see pages 21–22], where the Baltic Sea is defined as a "special area" requiring severe discharge restrictions. The provisions of the convention are binding only on the contracting parties, while IMO recommendations apply to ships of other nations. The convention also applies to pleasure craft (Article 8). Dumping in the Baltic Sea area is prohibited, except where human life is at risk or a craft is threatened by complete destruction or loss, or in the case of dredged spoils without substances listed in the annexes, for the dumping of which special permission is required (Article 9).

The convention came into force on May 3, 1980, all Baltic Sea states having ratified it. The Commission has issued 32 recommendations concerning the detailed implementation of the convention.

Structure. The offices of chairman and vice-chairman of the commission rotate between the member states every two years. The commission has a scientific-technological committee, a maritime committee, an expert group on co-operation in combating matters and ad hoc subsidiary bodies.

Membership. Denmark, Finland, German Democratic Republic, Federal Republic of Germany, Poland, the Soviet Union and Sweden—*contracting parties*; the Oslo and Paris Commissions, the UN Environment Programme (UNEP), the UN Economic Commission for Europe, the IMO, the World Health Organization, the International Council for the Exploration of the Sea (ICES), the International Baltic Sea Fishery Commission and the International Atomic Energy Agency (IAEA)—*observers*.

Sources of finance. Annual contributions of the contracting parties, with extra contribution by the Government of Finland

Publications. Baltic Sea Environment Proceedings 1–14; *Manual on Co-operation in Combating Matters*; other informative publications

Co-ordinating Unit for the Mediterranean Action Plan, UNEP

Address. 48, Leoforos Vassileos Konstantinou, GR-11635, Athens, Greece

Officer. Aldo G. Manos (co-ordinator)

Founded. January 1980 (in Athens since July 1982)

Objectives. To function, on behalf of the UN Environment Programme (UNEP) [see pages 158–63] as the secretariat of the Barcelona convention of 1976 [see page 159] for the protection of the Mediterranean Sea against pollution; to serve as the co-ordinating mechanism dealing with national authorities, national institutions and international organizations to carry out a pollution monitoring and research programme (MEDPOL) and integrated planning and development of legal measures.

Activities. The UNEP-sponsored Action Plan for the Mediterranean was adopted by an intergovernmental meeting in Barcelona in 1975; the Convention for the Protection of the Mediterranean Sea against Pollution and two related protocols—on dumping and on co-operation in cases of emergency—were adopted in 1976; protocols on land-based sources and on specially protected areas were adopted in Athens in 1980 and in Geneva in 1982; a pilot phase of monitoring and research involving 16 states has been carried out. The unit operates through four regional centres (in France, Malta, Tunisia and Yugoslavia).

The unit convenes regular meetings of the contracting parties to review the state of pollution of the Mediterranean and to adopt remedial measures; it co-ordinates the long-term monitoring and research programme (MEDPOL Phase 2) of the coastal states; it co-operates in the programme with the WHO, FAO, UNESCO (IOC), WMO, IAEA and IMO; and it develops scenarios for the sustainable development of the basin and promotes networks of co-operative projects.

Membership. Contracting parties to the Barcelona convention (Algeria, Cyprus, Egypt, France, Greece, Israel, Italy, Lebanon, Libya, Malta, Monaco, Morocco, Spain, Syria, Tunisia, Turkey, Yugoslavia and the European Communities)

Sources of Finance. Mediterranean Trust Fund, administered by UNEP and financed by contributions from all coastal states and the European Communities

Publications. Reports submitted to governments

International Oil Pollution Compensation Fund (IOPC Fund)

Address. 4 Albert Embankment, London SE1 7SR, UK

Officers. M. Jacobsson (dir.); M. Dobashi (legal officer); S. O. Nte (finance officer)

Founded. Oct. 16, 1978

History. The Fund was established as a result of the adoption, in Brussels on Dec. 18, 1971, of an International Convention on the Establishment of an International Fund for Compensation for Oil Pollution Damage, this convention having come into force on Oct. 16, 1978. It was supplementary to a 1969 International Convention on Civil Liability for Oil Pollution Damage (CLC), which established the strict liability for pollution damage of the owner of a sea-going vessel carrying oil in bulk as cargo. On April 20, 1979, the compensation limit was increased from $29,000,000 to $44,000,000. Two protocols (of Nov. 19, 1976, and May 25, 1984, respectively) intended to amend the convention have not yet come into force.

Activities. The IOPC Fund has dealt with more than 20 incidents which have occurred in its member states. It has paid compensation and indemnification totalling $41,000,000, including the cases of the *Antonio Gramsci* (which spilled 35,000 barrels off Sweden in February 1979, for which the fund paid $11,000,000) and that of the *Tania* (off France in March 1980, for which $22,000,000 has been paid so far). The Fund adds to the compensation available to victims under the CLC and also indemnification to shipowners who are liable for an incident under the CLC, always provided that the ship has complied with the requirements of international conventions enumerated in the convention.

Membership. Algeria, the Bahamas, Cameroon, Denmark, Fiji, Finland, France, Gabon, Federal Republic of Germany, Ghana, Iceland, Indonesia, Italy, Japan, Kuwait, Liberia, Maldives, Monaco, the Netherlands, Norway, Papua New Guinea, Spain, Sri Lanka, Sweden, Syria, Tunisia, Tuvalu, the United Arab Emirates, the United Kingdom and Yugoslavia

Sources of finance. Contributions payable by those who receive crude or heavy fuel oil in excess of 150,000 tonnes per annum in member states

Publications. Annual Reports, 1979–83; *Claims Manual*

Oslo Commission
Paris Commission

Address. New Court, 48 Carey Street, London WC2A 2JE, UK

Officers. P. A. Hayward (sec.); F. Bjerre and (Mrs) C. Nihoul (dep. secs.)

Founded. April 6, 1974 (Oslo Commission); May 6, 1978 (Paris Commission)

History. The Oslo Commission was established by the Convention for the Prevention of Marine Pollution by Dumping from Ships and Aircraft (the Oslo convention), opened for signature in Oslo on Feb. 15, 1972, and in force since April 7, 1974 [see page 155]; it has been ratified by Belgium, Denmark, Finland, France, the Federal Republic of Germany, Iceland, Ireland, the Netherlands, Norway, Portugal, Spain, Sweden and the United Kingdom.

The Paris Commission was established by the Convention for the Prevention of Marine Pollution from Land-Based Sources (the Paris convention), opened for signature in Paris on June 4, 1974, and in force since May 6, 1978 [see ibid.].

Activities. The Commissions administer the above two conventions and an Agreement for Co-operation in Dealing with Pollution of the North Sea by Oil concluded in Bonn on June 9, 1969 [see ibid.].

Sources of finance. Contributions from contracting parties

Publications. Annual Reports (of which the ninth of the Oslo Commission and the sixth of the Paris Commission contain an assessment of the results of a joint monitoring programme of 1982); *Report on Mercury in the Paris Convention Area*; *Oslo and Paris Commissions: The First Decade*

Regional Oil-Combating Centre for the Mediterranean Sea

Address. Manoel Island, Malta

Officers. M. Voirin (dir.); J. Camilleri (dep. dir., administration); D. Domovic (technical expert); R. Laiviera (information officer)

Founded. Dec. 11, 1976

Objectives. To strengthen the capacity of the coastal states in the Mediterranean region, and to facilitate co-operation among them, in order to combat massive oil pollution, especially in emergencies when there is grave and imminent danger to the marine environment; also, upon request, to assist coastal states in the development of their own national capabilities to combat oil pollution, and to facilitate information exchange, technical co-operation and training.

Activities. The action plan drawn up under the Barcelona convention of 1975 [see page 159] involved the preparation of an Anti-Pollution Guide for the Mediterranean; the drawing-up and revision of directories and inventories on equipment stockpiles, experts, commercialized products and equipment, societies offering services in cases of emergency, etc.; the organization of regional and national training courses and seminars in the region on marine anti-pollution measures; and assistance, upon request, by the centre to coastal states to set up their own national contingency plans.

Publications. *ROCC-INFO* (four-monthly newsletter)

Sources of finance. Mediterranean coastal states

Regional Organization for the Protection of the Marine Environment (ROPME)

Address. P.O. Box 26388, Safat, Kuwait

Officers. Dr Abdul Rahman Al-Awadi (acting exec. sec.); Dr Badrya Al-Awadi (dep. exec. sec.); Talib K. Al-Zubaidi (dir. of admin. & finance); Dr Badr Al-Bassam (dir. of programmes); Abdul Latif Al-Zaidan (dir. of public awareness, regional & international co-ordinator)

Founded. Jan. 1, 1982

Objectives. Protection of marine environment, implementation of regional actions plans, application of the Kuwait Regional Convention, co-ordination and co-operation in case of pollution by oil or other harmful substances in the marine environment resulting from marine emergencies.

Activities. The Kuwait Regional Convention provided for a Kuwait Action Plan (KAP) for the protection of the marine environment and came into force on June 30, 1979, financed by contributions from the eight contracting states and the UN Environment Programme (UNEP). The KAP interim secretariat co-operated with the Regional Seas Programme Activity Centre of UNEP, and in November 1979 a total of 17 specific projects were approved. A Marine Emergency Mutual Aid Centre (MEMAC) was set up between December 1979 and April 1981. A Task Team on Oceanography and a Task Team on Baseline Studies of Oil and Non-Oil Pollutants held their first meetings in Kuwait on Sept. 5–10, 1981, and decided on the formulation of their programmes.

Membership. Bahrain, Iran, Iraq, Kuwait, Oman, Qatar, Saudi Arabia and the United Arab Emirates

Structure. The ROPME has a council which has established an executive committee (consisting of the ministers of health of Bahrain, Iraq and Kuwait and the Iranian ambassador in Kuwait) and a scientific advisory committee.

Sources of finance. Contributions from member states

Publications. Documents, reports, technical reports, results of seminars, and a newsletter

Oil Industry Organizations

International Petroleum Industry Environmental Conservation Association (IPIECA)

Address. 1 College Hill, London EC4R 2RA, UK

Officer. S. Hope (exec. sec.)

Founded. March 1974

Objectives. To represent the views of its members before the UN Environment Programme (UNEP), the World Health Organization (WHO) and other agencies concerned with environmental and health issues, and to facilitate communications between the petroleum industry and relevant international organizations on environmental and health matters of international concern.

Activities. Joint IPIECA/UNEP activities have included an ad hoc workshop on the application and environmental effects of oil spill chemicals (Brest, November 1979).

Membership. 24 international and national petroleum enterprises and six international and national petroleum industry associations

Sources of finance. As a non-profit-making association IPIECA receives from its members a basic annual subscription and a further amount related to the member's operations.

Publications. Non-commercial reports and booklets, including *Application and Environmental Effects of Oil Spill Chemicals* (1981); *Oil Spill Chemicals—a Bibliography on the Nature, Effects and Testing of Chemicals used against Oil spilled in the Marine Environment* (1981); and *Environmental Management of Refineries and Terminals* (1984)

Affiliations. Co-operation with the Commission of the European Communities, the (UN) Economic Commission for Europe, the EEC, the International Chamber of Commerce Commission on the Environment, etc.

International Tanker Owners Pollution Federation Ltd. (ITOPFL)

Address. Staple Hall, Stonehouse Court, 87–90 Houndsditch, London EC3A 7AX, UK

Officers. C. J. Goulandris (ch.); J. N. Archer (man. dir.)

Founded. 1968

Objectives. To administer the Tanker Owners' Voluntary Agreement concerning Liability for Oil Pollution (TOVALOP) [see page 151] and to provide response to oil spills, consultancy and information.

Sources of Finance. Membership dues

Publications. Measures to Combat Oil Pollution (written and researched by the ITOPFL on behalf of the Consumer Protection Service of the Commission of the European Community and published by Graham & Trotman); Wardley-Smith, J. (ed.), *The Control of Oil Pollution on the Sea and Inland Waters* (Graham & Trotman); Wardley-Smith, J. (ed.), *The Prevention of Oil Pollution* (Graham & Trotman); *Newsletter*; a series of technical information papers on different aspects of oil spills

Oil Companies' European Organization for Environmental and Health Protection (CONCAWE)

Address. Babylon-kantoren A, Koningin Julianaplein 30-9, 2595 AA Den Haag, Netherlands

Officers. Dr H.-W. Wittmeier (gen. man.); J. B. Berkley (ch. of council); Dr G. F. Goethel (ch. of exec. committee)

Founded. 1963

Objectives. The collection and dissemination of information on all aspects of environmental and health protection topics relating to the oil-refining industry, including causes and effects of environmental pollution; prevention, abatement and clean-up measures; and technical and economic consequences of legislative proposals.

Activities. Current work areas have included industrial atmospheric emissions, water protection, oil spill clean-up technology, and pipeline safety performance.

Membership. 28 companies producing and/or refining oil.

Sources of finance. Participating companies

Publications. Annual Report; Current Reports, including *A Field Guide to Coastal Oil Spill Control and Clean-up Techniques* (9/81) and *Characteristics of Petroleum and its Behaviour at Sea* (8/83).

Oil Companies International Marine Forum (OCIMF)

Address. 6th Floor, Portland House, Stag Place, London SW1E 5BH, UK

Officer. I. B. Blackwood (dir.)

Founded. April 8, 1970.

Objectives. The promotion of safety and prevention of pollution from tankers and at terminals. Co-operation with IMO and the International Chamber of Shipping (ICS) (in various fields, including the planned passage of the Malacca/Singapore Straits), as well as with the International Association of Ports and Harbors, and with other international industry organizations concerned with marine pollution and safety.

Structure. The OCIMF has a chairman and three vice-chairmen elected at the annual general meeting, an executive committee, a secretariat and committees (on general purposes, ports and terminals, legal affairs and gas) as well as sub-committees and inter-industry groups.

Members. 35 oil companies in various countries and 13 Japanese companies represented by the Petroleum Industry Marine Association of Japan (all these companies controlling about 80 per cent of crude and fuel oil moved by sea).

Status. The OCIMF is incorporated under the Oil Companies International Marine Forum Act 1977 of Bermuda. It has consultative status with IMO and ECOSOC.

Publications. Numerous technical studies and monographs, including *Action Against Oil Pollution* (1981); *Oil Spills: Their Fate and Impact on the Marine Environment* (1980); *Oil Spill Contingency Planning—A Brief Guide* (1979); *Clean Seas Guide for Oil Tankers* (1978); *International Safety Guide for Oil Tankers and Terminals* (1984).

Research and Pressure Groups

European Centre for Marine Environment Problems
Centre d'Études Européen pour les Problèmes de l'Environnement Marine (CEPEM)

Address. 141 Boulevard Saint Germain, F-75006, Paris, France.

Officer. Thierry Martin (pres.).

Publications. Miscellaneous studies.

Greenpeace International

Address. Temple House, High Street, Lewes, Sussex, UK

Officer. Daniel McTaggart (founder & ch.)

Founded. 1971 (in Vancouver, British Columbia)

Objectives. To engage in protest actions—on principles of non-violence and non-involvement in political parties or movements—against pollution or other acts harmful to the natural environment, including the extermination of endangered species, and to campaign for nuclear disarmament.

Activities. Greenpeace has actively campaigned, partly by intervention with its own vessels, against the killing of whales, dolphins, seals and other marine animals, the dumping of radioactive wastes in the Atlantic and the discharge of poisonous chemical wastes in the coastal waters of Europe and North America. It has been active in Britain, the rest of Europe, North America and Australasia.

It claims to have been instrumental in achieving that commercial sealing in Norway and Canada was "drastically curbed"; that Iceland, Peru and Spain committed themselves to stop commercial whaling; that the International Whaling Commission voted to end all commercial whaling in 1986; that atmospheric testing of nuclear weapons by the French in the Pacific was stopped in 1974; that in 1983, for the first time in 30 years, no barrels of nuclear waste were dumped in the Atlantic; and that tougher pollution control laws were implemented in many countries.

In June 1983 Greenpeace campaigners protested against proposed mineral exploitation in the Antarctic which—Greenpeace argued—should be designated as a "world park" to protect its wildlife and in particular its whale population.

In July 1983 the Greenpeace vessel *Rainbow Warrior* was used to obtain photographs of a Soviet whaling station in eastern Siberia where grey whales were allegedly being caught in violation of International Whaling Commission decisions.

On July 10, 1985, the *Rainbow Warrior* was sunk (and one crew member killed) by a bomb explosion while anchored in Auckland harbour, New Zealand; it had been scheduled to make a protest voyage into an area of the South Pacific banned to shipping because of the imminence of a further French nuclear test [see page 154]. The French Government subsequently admitted that those responsible were members of the French security service.

Structure. Greenpeace International has an international council and is a confederation of national chapters in 15 countries. It has a Greenpeace Environment Trust (registered as an educational charity) and a company, Greenpeace Rainbow, running its four vessels, on which it employs its own crews and scientists.

Membership. 1,100,000

Sources of finance. Public support through donations. In 1984 it had a budget of about £12,000,000.

International Institute for Environment and Development (IIED)

Address. 3 Endsleigh St., London WC1H 0DD, UK

Officer. Brian Walker (pres.)

Founded. January 1971 (as International Institute for Environmental Affairs, present name since 1973)

Objects. To study and analyse environment policies, to serve as a clearing house for ideas, and to provide information.

Structure. The IIED has an international board of directors, a council and an advisory board for its *Earthscan* news and publications service. Its US office is at: 1717 Massachusetts Ave., Suite 302, Washington DC 320036, USA

Sources of finance. Private sources, UN agencies and governments

Publications. Study reports, books and proceedings

Aspects of Marine Scientific Research

Marine Research and Survey Vessels

Research and survey vessels owned by international or national research organizations or institutes are mainly purpose-built and of varying designs and sizes. They are engaged in hydrographic survey, oceanography, fisheries research, geophysical research, weather and oceanographic research or general marine research.

The distribution of their numbers by country in 1981 was as follows:

Soviet Union	147
United States	93
United Kingdom	85
France	39
Canada	31
Federal Republic of Germany	15
Japan	13
Poland	11
South Africa	11
Italy	10
Norway	10
Brazil	9
Australia	8
Sweden	8
Argentina	7
Cuba	7
Denmark	7
Spain	6
China	5
India	5
Republic of Korea	5
Netherlands	5
Belgium	4
New Zealand	4
Philippines	4
Portugal	4

Three each: Colombia, Finland, Greece, Yugoslavia

Two each: Burma, the Dominican Republic, Ecuador, Iran, Malaysia, Mexico, Taiwan, Thailand, Turkey, Venezuela

One each: Brunei, Cameroon, Chile, Hong Kong, Iceland, Israel, Kenya, Nigeria, Pakistan, Puerto Rico, Singapore, Uruguay, Vietnam

Diving and Underwater Technology

Diving and the rapidly developing underwater technology have been used for recreational purposes, in fisheries (including spear-fishing), for general marine research, in marine archaeology (including the location of wrecks and the recovery of artefacts), in the retrieval of parts of wrecked ships and aircraft, and in the exploration and exploitation of offshore and sea-bed resources (including the related engineering activities).

Diving in which the diver's body is exposed to the pressure of the surrounding water has been described as ambient diving. This may be free diving, in which the diver has to return to the surface for breathing after less than two minutes and can reach depths of only up to 30 metres. He may wear a wetsuit and/or use a snorkel which enables him to swim longer near the surface. He may also wear fins for better propulsion. In SCUBA diving the diver breathes from a self-contained underwater breathing apparatus (giving the initials by which the activity is generally known) which consists of a metal container holding compressed air or a mixture of breathing gases; in an open circuit the diver breathes air and the exhaled air is released into the water; in a closed circuit the gas used is pure oxygen and the diver may breathe the same gas again and again.

As pressure increases by about half a pound per square inch (0.04 kilogram per square centimetre) for every foot of depth, a diver 33 feet (10 metres) below the surface is exposed to pressure twice as great as that at the surface. Excessive pressure can cause air embolism. An ambient diver breathing compressed air absorbs large amounts of nitrogen in his blood, and if a diver rises too quickly bubbles of nitrogen form in his blood; this condition, known as the bends or decompression, may cripple or kill him. This can be avoided by rising slowly and by the use of a decompression table which shows how long the diver can stay at a certain depth without absorbing too much nitrogen and how slowly he must rise to avoid the bends. A diver who has air embolism should immediately be placed in a decompression chamber where the pressure is reduced in stages.

The first independent breathing devices for ambient divers included the aqualung invented in 1943 by Jacques-Yves Cousteau and Emile Gagnan.

Diving is also carried out in equipment which protects the diver's body from water pressure. Such surface-supplied equipment consists of a waterproof suit and a helmet designed to resist water pressure, or of a metal suit (articulated armour). Air or breathing gas is supplied to the diver through a hose connected to an air pump on a surface vessel. The diver may also be supplied with hot water to warm the diving suit, with electricity or high-pressure air to operate power tools and with gases for welding torches. Divers may also use underwater cameras.

Diving bells, which may be attached to a force pump, have been used since the 18th century in depths of up to 35 feet. Modern developments since the 1930s are ball-shaped chambers built to resist high pressures. Among these the bathysphere, connected to the surface with a cable, was first used in 1930 by William Beebe. The first bathyscape, a thick-walled sphere attached to a hull filled with petrol, was designed in 1948 by Prof. Auguste Piccard, who in 1953 descended, with his son Jacques, to a depth of 10,300 feet (3,140 metres) in the Mediterranean Sea; in 1960 the bathyscaphe *Trieste*, manned by Jacques Piccard and Don Walsh, descended to 35,800 feet (10,910 metres) in the Pacific Ocean. Another such ball-shaped chamber, with windows for underwater observation, is known as the benthoscope.

Manned experimental underwater saturation habitats (the first of them designed by J.-Y. Cousteau) have been placed on the ocean floor at depths of from 130 to 600 feet, where divers can live for weeks, as compartments inside the building are filled with compressed breathing gas, and they can leave the station daily to carry out work of exploration.

A further step has been the development of manned of unmanned submersibles, lowered form surface ships and electronically guided from them. These submersibles have their own motors and can manoeuvre independently; they also have their own supply of breathing gas; they may carry cameras and have mechanical claws or grappling arms to pick up objects from the ocean floor. One such *Scarab* submersible reached a depth of over 6,000 feet on July 10–11, 1985, south of Ireland, after diving for 89.5 hours to pick up a voice recorder and a flight recorder from an Air India airliner which had crashed into the sea.

Scientific Ocean Drilling

A deep-sea drilling project carried out by the United States in 1968–75 was in the latter year succeeded by an International Phase of Ocean Drilling (IPOD) with the participation of France, the Federal Republic of Germany, Japan, and for a time also the Soviet Union and the United Kingdom (through the Natural Environment Research Council, NERC).

The IPOD used the drillship *Glomar Challenger* and had its office at the Cripps Institute of Oceanography (La Jolla, CA 92093, USA). The drillship undertook over 92 legs and drilled at numerous sites, 16 of them in areas close to Britain—on the Hatton-Rockall Bank, the Goban Spur (of the Celtic Shelf south of Ireland), the northern edge of the Bay of Biscay and further north towards the Norwegian Sea, and these drills have furthered the understanding of the formation of passive continental margins, which is of value for future petroleum exploration.

Altogether the results obtained from the IPOD have radically altered our knowledge of the evolution of the oceans in all its aspects—tectonics, geochemistry, sedimentation and palaeoceanography. The IPOD was ended in 1983.

However, the United States has agreed to sponsor a new Ocean Drilling Program (OPD) for which a new vessel, the *SEDCO/BP 471* (half-owned by British Petroleum), has been chosen.

This ship is superior to the *Glomar Challenger* as it has greater sea-going stability allowing drilling in more adverse weather conditions and higher latitudes, as well as a larger complement of scientists. The operator of the OPD is the Texas A & M University (College Station, TX 77843, USA).

An international consortium known as the Joint Oceanographic Institutions for Deep Earth Sampling (JOIDES) has operated a research drilling ship, the *JOIDES Resolution*, which has taken samples of the crustal rocks below the sea south-west of Ireland in the northern part of the Bay of Biscay. In 1977 the vessel took a core from about 5 kilometres deep on the southern edge of the Bermuda Rise in the Atlantic Ocean, and in 1985 it returned to the borehole made in 1977 in order to take geophysical measurements with new miniature electronic instruments.

Submarine Communications

Communications by means of cables laid on the sea-bed began in 1851, when the first submarine cable was laid in the Channel between Britain and France. The first transatlantic cable was laid in 1866, and from 1874 onwards cables have increasingly been laid by specially constructed cable vessels.

In 1894 a Convention for the Protection of Submarine Cables was signed in Paris, and it provided inter alia that warships of contracting parties should have the right to stop and ascertain the nationality of merchant ships suspected of infringing the terms of the convention.

The first submarine cables were telegraph cables, and the first transatlantic telephone cable was not laid until 1956. There now exists a vast network of submarine cables, and with advancing technology their capabilities have been greatly extended. By 1980 a single cable could carry up to 5,000 telephone conversations, and a large number of cables provide facsimile, sound programme and data transmission. Cables cannot, however, compete with satellite communications except in so far as they are less expensive and more confidential.

International Organizations and Institutions concerned with Ocean Research

Worldwide Bodies

Commission for Marine Biology (of the IUGS)

Address. Maison de la Géologie, 77 rue Claude Bernard, 75005 Paris, France

Founded. March 1961

History. This Commission was founded within the framework of the International Union of Geological Sciences (IUGS).

Objective. To promote investigations on the study of the earth.

Committee on Climatic Changes and the Ocean (CCCO)

Address. UNESCO, 7 Place de Fontenoy, 75000 Paris, France

Officers. R. Stewart (ch.); V. Varadachari and A. McEwan (vice-chairmen); B. Thompson (sec.)

Founded. 1978

History. The CCCO was established by the Scientific Committee on Oceanic Research (SCOR) and is co-sponsored by the Intergovernmental Oceanographic Commission (IOC). It began its work in 1979 and has co-ordinated its activities through annual meetings and technical sub-groups.

Objectives. To identify ocean-climate problems requiring increased international attention, to stimulate research activities thereon and to recommend to the IOC and the SCOR how these recommendations should be implemented.

Activities. Studies and projects of the CCCO have related to a world ocean circulation experiment (WOCE), the international variability of the tropical oceans and global atmosphere (TOGA), non-anthropogenic changes in atmospheric carbon dioxide, early detection of climate change, ocean observational systems, ocean observational systems data management, national and multi-national ocean research and monitoring programmes contributing to the world climate research programme (WCRP), and ocean climate-related polar research. It has also held meetings of a CCCO Tropical Pacific Panel.

Membership. 14 committee members

Publications. Session Reports, in particular *Summary Report of Fifth Session*, December 1983

Engineering Committee on Oceanic Resources (ECOR)

Address. c/o Institute for Marine and Coastal Studies, University of Southern California, University Park, Los Angeles CA 90007, USA

Officer. Donald L. Keach (sec.)

Founded. March 1971

Objectives. To provide an international centre for professional engineering interests in marine affairs, to collect and disseminate relevant information and to give advice in order to encourage the development of the engineering profession's capability in the uses of the ocean and the enhancement of the quality of the marine environment.

Membership. Five international organizations, including the International Association of Dredging Companies and the International Ship Structures Congress; national committees or academics in 14 countries (Argentina, Canada, Colombia, France, Japan, Mexico, the Netherlands, Norway, Poland, Portugal, South Africa, Tahiti, the United Kingdom and the United States).

Affiliations. A subsidiary body to the Intergovernmental Oceanographic Commission (IOC) of UNESCO, with consultative status at the IMO and ECOSOC.

Group of Experts on the Scientific Aspects of Marine Pollution (GESAMP)

Address. c/o IMO, 4 Albert Embankment, London SE1 7SR, UK

Founded. 1968

Activities. This group is sponsored jointly by the International Atomic Energy Agency (IAEA), the UN Environment Programme (UNEP), the (UN) Food and Agriculture Organization (FAO), the World Health Organization (WHO), the World Meteorological Organization (WMO) and the International Maritime Organization (IMO). It produced material for a report on "transmarine cycling behaviour in the marine environment" which was published jointly by the IAEA, IMO and UNEP in June 1983. This report (IAEA-TECDIC 265), dealing with environmental assessment methodologies for the sea-dumping of radioactive waste, covered a review of the present knowledge of pathways by which substances might be transferred from a deep ocean dumping area to man; methods for calculating the concentration of substances arising from containers dumped on the deep ocean floor and in the water column throughout an ocean basin; and assessment of the reliability of the calculated concentration (and possible improvements).

The report followed the completion of work by the GESAMP on (i) hydrodynamic modelling of littoral zones; (ii) control of global behaviour of radionucleides released into the terrestrial environment; and (iii) chemical durability of solidified high-level waste forms.

The GESAMP had also done preparatory work on the behaviour of radium in aquifers and waterways, on a revision of the IAEA's definition and recommendations under the 1972 London Dumping Convention [see under International Maritime Organization, page 21], and an oceanographic model for the dispersal of radionucleides from the storage of radioactive waste in the terrestrial environment.

The GESAMP has also reported on a review of potentially harmful substances, on the evaluation of the hazards of harmful substances carried by ships, on the interchange of pollutants between the atmosphere and the ocean, on the biological effects of thermal discharges in the marine environment, and on the marine pollution implications of ocean energy developments (in which the risks should be reduced to acceptable levels through proper planning and design).

Intergovernmental Oceanographic Commission (IOC)

Address. c/o UNESCO, 7, Place de Fontenoy, 75700 Paris, France

Officers. Dr A. Ayala-Castañares (Mexico, ch.); Dr Mario Ruivo (Portugal, sec.)

Founded. 1960

Object. To promote scientific investigation into the nature and resources of the oceans through concerted action of IOC members.

Activities. The IOC has a Long-Term and Expanded Programme of Ocean Exploration and Research (LEPOR) involving an International Decade of Ocean Exploration (IDOE, 1971–80). LEPOR comprises sections on ocean science, ocean services, and training, education and mutual assistance (TEMA).

The ocean science section embraces a Comprehensive Plan for Global Investigation of Pollution in the Marine Environment (GIPME) and a first regional association for the Caribbean and adjacent regions (IOCARIBE). The latter has a small secretariat in Trinidad and Tobago; it has 18 member states, including Brazil and the Soviet Union; its activities are co-ordinated with those of FAO, the (UN) Ocean Economics and Technology Office (UN-OETO) and UNEP in the region; it has conducted scientific studies on the improvement of trap fisheries management in the Lesser Antilles and on the support of the management of lobster fisheries in Central America; and it has explored the environmental geology of the Caribbean coastal areas (in particular of Costa Rica and the Gulf of Paria between Venezuela and Trinidad).

Ocean services include (i) an Integrated Global Ocean Station System (IGOSS), which has planned regional components of a Marine Pollution (Petroleum) Monitoring Pilot Project (MAPMOPP) to monitor tanker routes; (ii) an International Oceanographic Data Exchange (IODE), which has working groups concerned with (*a*) studies on East Asian Tectonics and Resources (SEATAR) (jointly with the Committee for Co-ordination of Joint Prospecting for Mineral Resources in Asian Offshore Areas, CCOP); and (*b*) investigations into the El Niño current, jointly with the World Meteorological Organization and the Committee on Climatic Changes and the Oceans (CCCO) [see separate entry], the Western Pacific (WESTPAC), including its equatorial undercurrent, and the North and Central Western Indian Ocean

(CINCWIO), including research on a monsoon experiment (MONEX).

A Marine Environmental Data Information Referral System (MEDI) provides an internationally accepted means of cataloguing data on a multi-disciplinary basis; it offers a catalogue or index of details of marine data holdings of all participant countries, a computerized retrieval system, specialized indexes for broad subject areas, and geographic plots of worldwide data distribution.

IOC projects have included co-operative studies of (i) the Kuro-Shio current system (in the North-West Pacific); (ii) the northern part of the East Central Atlantic (CINECA), jointly with the International Council for the Exploration of the Seas; (iii) the Mediterranean (CIM); (iv) the Caribbean and adjacent regions (CICAR); (v) an International Ocean Expedition (completed in 1965); and (vi) the tropical Atlantic (ended in 1973).

The IOC has also been involved in the production of the General Bathymetric Chart of the Oceans (GEBCO) of the International Hydrographic Organization, the formation of an Aquatic Sciences and Fisheries Information System (jointly with FAO and UN-OETO) and the oceanic aspects of a Global Atmospheric Research Programme of the World Meteorological Organization and the International Council of Scientific Unions.

At the 12th session of its Assembly in November 1982 the IOC adopted inter alia (i) an action plan for an ocean-observing system to be developed jointly by the Scientific Committee of Ocean Research (SCOR), the IOC Committee on Climatic Changes and the Oceans, and a joint IOC-IMO working committee for IGOSS [see above], with the object of intensifying and expanding bathythermographic observations of the oceans and routine measurements of the surface salinity, mean sea level, surface wind and radiation (using ships, satellites and drifting buoys); (ii) a plan for the implementation of GIPME [see above] and the development of a marine pollution monitoring system (MARPOLMON); and (iii) two programmes on ocean science in relation to living resources (OSIN) and non-living resources (OSNIR).

The IOC also approved a comprehensive plan for a major assistance programme to enhance the marine science capabilities of developing member states (with TEMA activities). The framework of the Inter-Secretariat Committee on Scientific Programmes (ICSPRO) was also to be expanded. (ICSPRO was set up in 1969 to organize co-operation among UN organizations concerned with oceanic programmes.)

A summary report on the fifth session of the CCCO (held in December 1983) refers inter alia to a planned World Ocean Circulation Experiment (WOCE), a study of the Interannual Variability of the Tropical Oceans and Global Atmosphere (TOGA) and the activities of a Tropical Pacific Panel.

Structure. The IOC is assisted by a Scientific Advisory Board (SAB) of 15 members and by three non-governmental advisory bodies—the Scientific Committee on Oceanic Research, the Advisory Committee of Experts on Marine Resources Research (ACMRR) and the Engineering Committee on Oceanic Resources (ECOR). International groups of the IOC deal with the co-ordination of multinational scientific activities (either regional or disciplinary). These include one for the Southern Oceans (SOC) and one for a Tsunami Warning System. [For *tsunamis*, see page 47.]

Membership. 103 governments

Publications. Summary Reports of Assembly Sessions (every two years), *Biennial Reports of Activities*; *Future Ocean Research* (FORE); *IOC Technical Series* (irregular); IOC Guides and Manuals (irregular); *Regional Co-operation in Marine Sciences* (a survey of marine research establishments, with maps, tables and a list of acronyms, published on behalf of ICSPRO in 1980)

International Association for Biological Oceanography (IABO)

Address. c/o Institut für Meereskunde an der Universität Kiel, Düsternbrookerweg 20, 2300 Kiel, Federal Republic of Germany

Officers. Timothy R. Parsons (Canada, pres.); John Costlow (USA, sec.)

Founded. 1966

Affiliations. Relations with the Division of Environmental Biology of the International Union of Biological Sciences (IUBS)

International Association for the Physical Sciences of the Ocean (IAPSO)
Association Internationale des Sciences Physiques de l'Océan

Address. LaFond Oceanic Consultants, P.O.B. 7325, San Diego, California 92107, USA

Officers. Prof. Wolfgang Krauss (Federal Republic of Germany, pres.); Dr Eugene C. LaFond (USA, s.g.)

Founded. 1919

Objectives. To promote the study of scientific problems relating to the ocean and interactions taking place at its boundaries, chiefly in so far as such studies may be carried out by the aid of mathematics, physics and chemistry; to initiate, facilitate and co-ordinate research into and investigations of those problems of the ocean which require international co-operation; and to provide for discussion, comparison and publications.

Activities. Holding of symposia; participation, with the International Association of Meteorology and Atmospheric Physics (IAMAP), in a Scientific Assembly held in Honolulu, Hawaii, on Aug. 5–16, 1985; General Assembly to be held in Vancouver, Canada, in August 1987.

Membership. 78 countries and territories

Publications. Procès-Verbaux Nos. 1–16; *Publications Scientifiques* Nos. 1–33

Affiliations. International Council of Scientific Unions (ICSU); International Union of Geodesy and Geophysics (IUGG); consultative status at ECOSOC

International Council of Scientific Unions (ICSU)

Address. 51 blvd. de Montmorency, 75016 Paris, France

Officers. Prof. D. E. Bekoe (Ghana, pres.); L. Ernster (Sweden, s.g.); F. W. J. Baker (UK, exec. sec.)

Founded. 1919 (as International Research Council; present name since 1931)

Activities. The numerous committees and commissions of the ICSU include an Inter-Union Commission on the Application of Science to Agriculture, Fisheries and Aquaculture.

Structure. The ICSU's policy is formulated by a General Assembly of representatives of national and scientific members, meeting every two years. A finance committee prepares an annual budget and determines contributions from members.

Membership. Academic or research councils in 70 countries; 20 international unions; 17 associates; scientific members and associations

International Laboratory of Marine Radioactivity

Address. Musée Océanographique, Monaco-ville, Monaco

Officer. Dr Alan Walton (dir.)

Activities. Research on the chemical, biological and geochemical behaviour of radioactive and non-radioactive substances in the oceans, including sea water, suspended matter, biota and sediments; inter-calibration and quality control studies for transuranic elements and some non-radioactive pollutants.

Publications. Series on radioactivity in the sea (RITS), research reports and congress papers.

Affiliations. International Atomic Energy Agency; Government of Monaco; Oceanographic Institute (Institut Océanographique, Paris)

International Ocean Institute (IOI)

Address. Old University Bldg., Merchants' St., Valletta, Malta

Officers. C. F. Vanderbilt (asst. dir.); Mrs Elisabeth Mann Borgese (ch. of programme committee), P.O. Box 4716, Santa Barbara, CA 93103, USA

Founded. 1972

Objectives. Also known as Pacem in Maribus (PIM), the IOI seeks to promote research on peaceful uses of ocean space and resources.

Activities. The IOI holds conferences and summer schools and it keeps an information system on Mediterranean marine affairs.

Structure. A Board of Trustees of 12–15 members meets annually, and a Planning Council of up to 24 members elected for three years meets four times a year.

Membership. Algeria, Australia, Bulgaria, Canada, Chile, El Salvador, France, India, Italy, Jamaica, Japan, Malta, Mexico, the Netherlands, Portugal, Romania, the Soviet Union, Sri Lanka, Sweden, Switzerland, Tanzania, Tunisia, the United Kingdom, the United States, Yugoslavia

Sources of finance. Private subscriptions, grants from foundations and support from governments on a project basis.

Publications. Proceedings of PIM Convocations (annual); *Friends of the Mediterranean* (newsletter, irregular)

Affiliations. Consultative status at ECOSOC and the UN Environment Secretariat.

International Oceanographic Foundation

Address. 3979 Rickenbacher Causeway, Virginia Key, Miami, FL 33149, USA

Officer. F. May Smith (exec. sec.)

Founded. 1952

Publications. Sea Frontiers; *Sea Secrets* (both six times a year)

Marine and Coastal Technology Information Service (MACTIS)

Address. UN Department of International and Social Affairs, Ocean Economics and Technology Branch, New York, NY 10017, USA

Founded. November 1977

Ocean Economics and Technology Office of the UN Department of Economic and Social Affairs

Address. United Nations Plaza, New York, NY 10017, USA

Activities. As the only UN organizational unit with a separate programme in the field of marine science and its applications, this office has published a number of reports, including *Sea-Bed Mineral Development* (1976), *Coastal Area Management* and *Marine and Coastal Technology* (1977)

Scientific Committee on Oceanic Research (SCOR)

Address. Secretariat, Department of Oceanography, Dalhousie University, Halifax, Nova Scotia B3H 4J1, Canada

Officers. Dr A. Longhurst (sec.); Mrs E. Tidmarsh (exec. sec.)

Founded. 1957

Activities. As a scientific committee of the International Council of Scientific Unions (ICSU), SCOR promotes international scientific activity in all branches of oceanic research.

It has set up working groups and commissions to consider scientific problems arising from international oceanic research programmes including, among others, the development of new methods and the standardization and inter-calibration of existing ones, on: oceanic tables and standards; internal dynamics of the ocean; Baltic pollution; ocean-atmosphere materials exchanges; river inputs to ocean systems; oceanographic programmes; living resources in the southern ocean; prediction of El Niño (off Peru); equatorial upwelling processes; coastal and estuarine regimes; arctic heat budget; mathematical models in biological oceanography; mangrove ecosystems; sedimentation processes on continental margins; carbon budget of the ocean; marine geochronological methods; oceanic atoll drilling; coastal-offshore ecosystems relationships; and climatic changes and the ocean.

SCOR has also studied the long-range problem of the use of the deep sea as a receptacle for waste products and that of the ocean as an important source of proteins. It organized an international Indian Ocean expedition which was in 1962 placed under the control of the Intergovernmental Oceanographic Commission (IOC).

Membership. Representatives of 16 ocean research organizations or groups, and of 34 national committees (from Argentina, Australia, Belgium, Brazil, Canada, Chile, Colombia, Denmark, Finland, France, the German Democratic Republic, the Federal Republic of Germany, India, Indonesia, Israel, Italy, Japan, Mexico, Monaco, the Netherlands, New Zealand, Norway, the Philippines, Poland, Portugal, South Africa, the Soviet Union, Spain, Sweden, Switzerland, Taiwan, Thailand, the United Kingdom and the United States).

Affiliations. Adviser to UNESCO and the IOC

Technical Commission for Marine Meteorology (CMM)

Address. c/o World Meteorological Organization (WMO), Case postale 5, 1211 Geneva 20, Switzerland

Officer. K. P. Vasiliev (Soviet Union, pres.)

Activities. The CMM holds sessions at least once every four years. It supervises international arrangements for providing marine meteorological and related geophysical information (including sea ice and wave information) to shipping, fishing operations and other marine activities. It also prepares marine climatological information. It co-operates closely with the Intergovernmental Oceanographic Commission (IOC).

Membership. Experts appointed by WMO member governments

Publications. Reports on Marine Science Affairs

United Nations Educational, Scientific and Cultural Organization (UNESCO)

Address. 7 Place de Fontenoy, 75700 Paris, France

Officers. Amadou Mahtar M'Bow (Senegal, dir.-gen.); Abdul Razzak Kaddoura (Syria, asst. dir.-gen. for science)

Founded. 1946

Activities. Among its numerous departments UNESCO has a Division of Marine Sciences, the object of which is to assist member states to attain higher quality marine science programmes and scientific infrastructures, to enable them to take part in programmes organized by the Intergovernmental Oceanographic Commission (IOC) and to meet their own science needs. The Division's activities have included studies on mangrove swamps, coastal lagoons, coral reefs and estuaries (but most of its programmes have been on a modest scale).

UNESCO has inter alia set up a major interregional project on research and training which has led to an Integrated Management of Coastal Systems (COMAR), in which UNESCO collaborates with non-governmental organizations under the umbrella of the International Council of Scientific Unions (ICSU) and including the Scientific Committee on Oceanic Research (SCOR) and the International Association for Biological Oceanography (IABO). This project is to deal with problems of the increasing population of coastal zones, inhabited by two-thirds of the world's population (which has almost doubled since 1950).

Another UNESCO programme has resulted in the production of a World Register of Rivers Discharging into the Ocean.

European Bodies

Baltic Marine Biologists (BMB)

Address. c/o General Secretary, Institute of Marine Research, Box 4, S-453 00 Lysekil, Sweden

Officers. Prof. Dr E. A. Arndt (pres. to June 1985); Dr Bernt I. Dybern (g.s.); Dr Julius Lassig (vice-sec.)

Founded. 1968

Objectives. To further contacts between marine scientists, to work out common methods in marine biological research, to make joint investigations and to arrange Baltic marine biological symposia (every second year).

Activities. Exchange of scientists between, and joint investigations and surveys with, institutes of the Baltic countries on the methodology of research on plankton, benthos, meiofauna, small algae, microbiology, etc., as a basis for a manual used by the Helsinki Commission [see page 163]; co-operation with that Commission, the International Council for the Exploration of the Sea (ICES) and other organizations working on Baltic problems; and the holding of Baltic marine biological symposia and of meetings of working groups, with one on coastal fish ecology being planned.

Structure. The BMB has a committee as its steering body, which issues special reports on its meetings.

Membership. Individual members from Denmark, Finland, the German Democratic Republic, the Federal Republic of Germany, Poland, the Soviet Union, Sweden.

Publications. Irregular reports

Baltic Oceanographers Group

Address. P.O. Box 4031, S-40040, Göteborg, Sweden

Officer. Dr S. Fonselius (pres.)

European Oceanic Association
Association Européenne Océanique (Eurocean)

Address. Villa Richard, rue de l'Abbaye, Monaco-ville, Monaco

Officers. Dr H. Kippenberger (pres.); B. Lachmann (dir.-gen.)

Activities. This group of major industries from many European countries is organized to co-ordinate research, evaluation, development and promotion of projects in the marine field, in particular projects of large magnitude requiring international co-operation and co-ordination with (inter)national and (inter-)governmental organizations. It also provides services of experts attached to the association and an up-to-date information and documentation service.

Publications. European technical reports; *Amer-Seamarks*; and information bulletins (for members only)

International Commission for the Scientific Exploration of the Mediterranean Sea (ICSEM)
Commission Internationale pour l'Exploration Scientifique de la Mer Méditerranée (CIESM)

Address. Secrétariat Général, 16 blvd. de la Suisse, MC-98030, Monaco

Officers. Prince Rainier III of Monaco (pres.); Commandant Jacques-Yves Cousteau (France, s.g.)

Founded. 1919

Membership. 17 countries, 1,200 scientists and 12 scientific committees

Publications. Rapports et Procès-Verbaux des Réunions de la CIESM; Bulletin de Liaison des Laboratoires (annual)

International Organization for Marine Geology (INTERMORGEO)

Address. c/o Vniimorgeo, 13 Lachplesha Street, Riga 50, USSR

Founded. 1973

Objectives. To co-operate in sea-bed mineral exploration by preparing joint geological expeditions and supplying equipment for exploration and exploitation.

Membership. Seven member states of the Council for Mutual Economic Assistance (Bulgaria, Czechoslovakia, the German Democratic Republic, Hungary, Poland, Romania and the Soviet Union) and Yugoslavia

Mediterranean Association for Marine Biology and Oceanology (MAMBO)

Address. c/o Fondazione A. Dohrn, presso Stazione Zoologica, Villa Comunale, I-80121 Naples, Italy

Founded. 1964 (in accordance with Maltese law)

Objectives. To hold symposia and courses and to organize working parties and the exchange of students and research workers.

Sources of finance. UNESCO, the Dohrn Foundation, the University of Malta and the Italian Research Council, as well as local support.

Nordic Council for Marine Biology
Nordisk Kollegium for Marinbiologi

Address. Institute for Water Research, Box 333, Blindern, Oslo 3, Norway

Officer. Torgeir Bakke (g.s.)

Founded. 1956

Objective. To co-ordinate the work of biological institutions in Denmark, Finland, Iceland, Norway and Sweden

Membership. 23 institutions

Publications. Nordmar (annual)

Other Organizations

Arab League Educational, Cultural and Scientific Organization (ALESCO)

Address. P.O.B. 1120, Al Qabadha, Al-Asleya, Tunis, Tunisia

Founded. 1964

Activities. In October 1974 the ALESCO set up a Workshop on a Marine Sciences Programme for the Red Sea in Bremerhaven (Federal Republic of Germany), and it later prepared an action plan which was adopted at an ALESCO conference in Jeddah in 1976.

Association of Latin American Marine Scientists
Asociación de Especialistas Latinoamericanos en Ciencias del Mar (ASELACMAR)

Address. c/o UNESCO/ROSTLAC, 1320 Bulevar Artigas, Apart. de Correos 859, Montevideo, Uruguay

Founded. 1977

Activities. The association has held symposia since 1974.

Caribbean Meteorological Council

Address. c/o Caribbean Community

Secretariat, P.O. Box 10827, Bank of Guyana Building, Georgetown, Guyana

Activities. This Council has as its training and research arm a Caribbean Meteorological Institute which has been engaged in various projects involving inter alia (i) a Caribbean Operational Hydrology Institute (COHI), funded mainly by the UN Development Programme, for the training of personnel for hydrological units to carry out data collection and analysis, (ii) a wind assessment project and (iii) hurricane detection systems. There are meteorological stations in Antigua, Barbados, Belize, Guyana, Jamaica, Saint Lucia and Trinidad and Tobago.

Foresta Institute for Ocean and Mountain Studies

Address. c/o Dr Richard Gordon Miller, 6205 Franktown Rd., Carson City, Nevada 89701, USA

Founded. 1960

Activities. The institute has created a Latin American Natural Areas Program (LANAP) for conservation in Latin America.

Affiliations. Consultative status at ECOSOC

Scientific Committee on Antarctic Research (SCAR)

Address. c/o Scott Polar Research Institute, Lensfield Rd., Cambridge CB2 1ER, UK

Officer. G. E. Hemmen (exec. sec.)

Founded. March 1958

Activities. The study of all aspects of marine science in the southern oceans; promotion of international co-operation in scientific research in the Antarctic through the work of specialist groups on: biology; geodesy and cartography; geology; glaciology; human biology and medicine; logistics; meteorology; oceanography; living resources of the southern ocean; seals; etc.

Structure. An executive committee (comprising a president, vice-president and secretary) is approved for four years by the bureau of the International Council of Scientific Unions (ICSU).

Membership. Representatives of seven ICSU member unions and national delegations from Argentina, Australia, Belgium, Chile, France, Japan, New Zealand, Norway, South Africa, the Soviet Union, the United Kingdom and the United States

Affiliations. A scientific committee of the ICSU

6. Maritime Boundary Disputes

Described in this chapter are current or recent maritime boundary disputes between governments, including a number between state or provincial authorities and the relevant federal government. The accounts are grouped in regional sections covering (i) North European and North Atlantic waters; (ii) the Mediterranean Sea and peripheral waters; (iii) the Persian (Arabian) Gulf; (iv) Asian and Far Eastern waters; (v) the Pacific Ocean; (vi) Caribbean, South American and Antarctic waters; (vii) African waters; and (viii) Arctic waters. A number of the maritime disputes dealt with below relate to unresolved land boundary issues.*

North European and North Atlantic Waters

Canada–Denmark

A dispute has existed since 1971 over the uninhabited island of Hans, situated north of the Arctic Circle between the Canadian island of Ellesmere and the coast of Greenland, at a point more than 300 kilometres (186 miles) from any other land.

The island was discovered by a Danish expedition in 1873, and it was first shown on an official (Danish) map in 1932. In 1971 Canada entered into negotiations with Denmark over the continental shelf between Canada and Greenland, but in the agreements reached in 1973 the fate of Hans Island remained undecided.

In 1980 a Canadian professor (Kenn Harters) claimed that the island had become Canadian in accordance with international law, as the Danes had failed to show any presence on it for years. The Danish Government, however, rejected this contention, especially as it had in 1983 sent fighter aircraft to overfly the island with the sole purpose of reaffirming Danish sovereignty over it.

In August 1984 it was reported that the Danish Minister for Greenland (Tom Hoeyem) had personally raised the Danish flag on the island and would ask the Minister of Transport to set up an automatic weather station on it.

Canada–France

In the area of the French overseas department of Saint Pierre and Miquelon (off the coast of Newfoundland) there exists an unresolved dispute over dividing the sea-bed and involving also Canada's fisheries management. In April 1982 the department's representative in the French National Assembly urged the French Prime Minister to show greater firmness in negotiations with the Canadian Government to

* For such disputes, see Alan J. Day (ed.), *Border and Territorial Disputes* (Longman, Harlow 1982).

secure acceptance from the latter of the historic rights of French fishermen in the area, and he also called for a French naval presence. In response the Prime Minister expressed his conviction that the Canadians would "show an imaginative approach" to a solution of the problem, possibly on the basis of a Franco-Canadian association to exploit the resources of the area jointly.

On March 27, 1972, Canada and France had signed an agreement (which entered into force immediately) regulating their mutual fishing relations off the Atlantic coast of Canada. Annexed to the agreement was a declaration delimiting the territorial sea between Newfoundland and Saint Pierre and Miquelon. However, Article 9 of the agreement stated that "no provision of the present agreement shall be interpreted as prejudicing the views and future claims of either party concerning internal waters, territorial waters or jurisdiction with respect to fisheries or the resources of the continental shelf, or the bilateral or multilateral agreements to which either government is a party".

Under the 1972 agreement, about 10 large trawlers from metropolitan France and Saint Pierre and Miquelon were allowed to fish in the Gulf of St Lawrence. However, early in 1985 the Canadian Government refused a licence for a trawler registered in the French overseas department on the grounds that it was a refrigerator vessel capable of preparing fish fillets (a right not enjoyed by Canadian trawlers, for the sake of protecting Canadian fish processors on land).

Canada–Newfoundland

On March 8, 1984, the Supreme Court of Canada rejected a claim by the Province of Newfoundland to ownership of the continental shelf (which includes the Hibernia ridge oil field discovered in 1979) and confirmed that the Federal Government of Canada had the right to explore and exploit the continental shelf.

The province's claim had been based on the fact that it had held the right to the continental shelf until 1949 when Newfoundland had joined the Canadian Confederation. However, the court held that the right had until then been held by Britain and not by Newfoundland (until 1949 a British colony) and had, with other British rights, devolved upon the Government of Canada. (A similar Supreme Court judgment of 1967 related to the offshore area of British Columbia.)

Canada–United States

Disputes between Canada and the United States over maritime boundaries on the Atlantic seaboard are described below. West coast disputes between the two countries are dealt with on pages 208–09.

Gulf of Maine

A dispute over the delimitation of the maritime boundary in the Gulf of Maine (on the two countries' Atlantic coasts) was finally settled by a chamber of the International Court of Justice (ICJ) on Oct. 12, 1984.

The dispute first materialized in the 1960s in relation to the continental shelf, as soon as petroleum exploration began on both sides, in particular on Georges Bank. In 1976–77 both states proceeded to set up an exclusive 200-mile fishery zone off their coasts and specified the limits of the zone and the continental shelf which they claimed.

In a treaty between Canada and the United States (approved by the US Senate on April 29, 1981, ratified by the two governments on Nov. 20, 1981, and in force from that day), it was provided that the final determination of the maritime boundary in the Gulf of Maine should be decided by a five-member chamber of the ICJ.

Both sides subsequently submitted to the chamber proposals of which the Canadian one was described as calling for an equidistance line, primarily with the continental shelf in mind, whereas the US proposal was for a line adjusted to avoid the splitting of fishing banks.

The chamber examined the 1958 Geneva Convention on the Continental Shelf, which both parties recognized as being in force between them. From this it deduced a principle in international law to the effect that any delimitation of a continental shelf effected unilaterally by one state regardless of the view of the other state or states is not opposable to those states; at the same time, it added that there should be a latent rule that any agreement or other equivalent solution should involve the application of equitable criteria. The chamber also noted that certain provisions concerning the continental shelf and the exclusive economic zone were, in the 1982 UN Convention on the Law of the Sea, adopted without objection and might be regarded as consonant with general international law on the question.

The chamber therefore reformulated a fundamental norm, acknowledged by the parties as follows: "No maritime delimitation between states with opposite or adjacent coasts may be effected unilaterally by one of those states. Such delimitation must be sought and effected by means of an agreement, following negotiations conducted in good faith and with the genuine intention of achieving a positive result. Where, however, such agreement cannot be achieved, delimitation should be effected by recourse to a third party possessing the necessary competence. In either case, delimitation is to be effected by the application of equitable criteria and by the use of practical methods capable of ensuring, with regard to the geographic configuration of the area and other relevant circumstances, an equitable result."

The chamber eventually rejected both the US proposal, inter alia as being "too biased" towards the fisheries aspect to be considered as equitable overall, and the Canadian proposal, largely because it appeared to neglect the distinction made in the 1958 convention between adjacent and opposite coasts.

With regard to that segment of the disputed area which lies outside the Gulf of Maine and was of the "greatest concern of the parties on account of the presence in the area it traverses of Georges Bank, the principal stake in the proceedings on account of the potential resources of its subsoil and the economic importance of its fisheries", the chamber rejected both the US and the Canadian positions. The former was based on the claim that US nationals had, over the greater part of the period since independence, been practically alone in being engaged in fishing, navigational assistance, rescue, research and defence; the latter was based on socio-economic aspects, especially during the last 15 years, and the wish to maintain the existing structures of fishing. For the Georges Bank the United States claimed fisheries rights over the whole, and Canada over about one-half.

The chamber finally laid down the course of a "single maritime boundary" dividing both the continental shelf and the exclusive fisheries zones of Canada and the United States by fixing co-ordinates for this line between four specified points. Under this award Canada retained fishing rights in only about one-sixth of the Georges Bank while the maritime area outside the Gulf of Maine was divided by a line perpendicular to the closing line of the Gulf. The decision was taken by four votes to one, the dissenting vote being cast by Judge André Gros (France), who formulated a dissenting opinion.

The French judge expressed doubt whether the line drawn by the chamber was really more equitable than any of the other lines considered in the course of the proceedings. In his view, the ICJ's judgment of Feb. 24, 1982, concerning the continental shelf between Libya and Tunisia [see page 196] had brought to an end the situation resulting from the 1958 Convention on the Continental Shelf as previously interpreted by the ICJ in its 1969 judgment on the North Sea continental shelf and in a 1977 decision by an Anglo-French Court of Arbitration. He also felt that the chamber's judgment amounted to exclusive reliance on the work of the Third UN Conference on the Law of the Sea, whose solution of maritime delimitation disputes based on agreement plus equity he considered to be "very feeble". He concluded that it would henceforth be open to each judge to decide what was equitable.

On Dec. 7, 1984, the US Government formally requested Canada to suspend the implementation of the court's decision for a year (to allow fishermen of both sides to continue their fishing pattern as before).

Machias Seal Island

Machias Seal Island, covering only 15 acres (six hectares) and situated 12 miles (19 kilometres) off Cutler, Maine, is claimed by the United States under the 1788 Treaty of Paris and the 1816 Treaty of Ghent (defining the north-eastern boundary between Canada and the United States). It is also claimed under the latter treaty by Canada, which in 1832 constructed a lighthouse on it and has declared it a national bird sanctuary.

On June 28, 1984, the United States protested against the landing on the island, on June 18, of two Canadian law enforcement officers. In reply Canada claimed that the island—inhabited by two Canadian lighthouse keepers and their families and a Canadian wildlife official—was Canadian territory and that the police officers had been enforcing bird protection laws endorsed by both countries.

Bay of Fundy

In the Bay of Fundy (bordered by the US state of Maine and the Canadian province of New Brunswick in the north-west and Nova Scotia to the east) a dispute arose in 1983 over the proposed siting of an oil refinery at Eastport (Maine) which would involve the transit of oil-bearing supertankers through the (Canadian) Head Harbour Passage, constituting a potential pollution threat to the coastal ecosystem and to the commercial fisheries in the Bay of Fundy. The United States has claimed the right of innocent passage through the Canadian waters but Canada has claimed that the high risk involved does not constitute innocent passage.

Denmark–Iceland–Ireland–United Kingdom

The uninhabited island of Rockall (in the Western Approaches of the

North Atlantic about 250 miles west of the Outer Hebrides) with the sea and sea-bed around it has been the subject of a dispute which has involved the United Kingdom, Denmark (representing the Faroe Islands), Iceland and Ireland.

The British Government annexed the island to the Crown in 1955 and incorporated it in Scotland in 1972. In the British view Rockall is part of the continental shelf and should therefore be taken into account in the determination of the UK section of the shelf.

The Government of Ireland, however, has rejected the British contention that the area of Rockall is part of the UK continental shelf. In 1977 Britain and Ireland reached an agreement in principle to establish an international arbitration court to settle various differences over the delimitation of the median line in the waters between Britain and Ireland, in particular in the Western Approaches and in the waters north of Ireland.

The Danish Government had meanwhile claimed that Rockall was a natural extension of the Faroe Islands and that it should not be used as a base point for the determination of the UK economic and fishery zones.

In July 1984 the Government of Iceland presented Britain, Denmark and Ireland with a statement outlining Iceland's case for extensive jurisdiction over mineral resources south of its 200-mile exclusive economic zone.

In 1978 a public debate had been launched in Iceland on the country's claim to the sea-bed rights in the Rockall area; the subject was also broached at the United Nations, and a formal request was made for talks with the other countries involved. Three relevant resolutions were subsequently passed in Iceland's Parliament; and talks were held with Britain and Denmark (and also directly with the Faroese), whereas the Government of Ireland refused to enter into such talks.

Iceland's claim was based on a number of arguments: (i) that the Rockall-Hatton plateau (out of which Rockall arises) is part of Iceland on the basis of geological considerations and "the spirit of fair-minded pragmatism" on the question of sea-bed rights embodied in the UN Convention on the Law of the Sea; (ii) that the area could be thought of as a natural prolongation of the Iceland-Faroes ridge and a product of the same geophysical action which had formed Iceland; (iii) that the Hatton-Rockall area was cut off from Britain and Ireland by a deep trough; and (iv) that, if a median line were drawn between Iceland and its rival claimants, virtually all of the Hatton Bank would fall under Icelandic jurisdiction.

It was also reported (in August 1984) that Iceland's parliamentary committee for foreign affairs had advised the Government to adopt the recommendations of its special adviser on the subject and inform the UN Commission on the Limits of the Continental Shelf of its intention to claim sea-bed rights up to the 200-mile limits of its rival claimants, i.e. thus incorporating the Hatton-Rockall plateau in Iceland's exclusive economic zone.

The British Government has continued to reaffirm its sovereignty over the island of Rockall, and a plaque proclaiming this sovereignty on the island was found intact by a Royal Navy landing party in the summer of 1984.

On May 7, 1985, the Danish Foreign Ministry formally laid claim to sea-bed rights on the "Faroe-Rockall plateau" and declared that no attempt should be made to explore and exploit the natural resources of the area (of about

116,000 square miles) without a licence from the Danish Government. The Danish Foreign Minister made it clear that his Government did not contest Britain's sovereignty over Rockall, but stated that the rock was not an island (as claimed by Britain) but only a "cliff" with few, if any rights, other than a 12-mile territorial waters limit. The minister added that Denmark was ready to negotiate with Britain, Iceland and Ireland to resolve the existing dispute over territorial rights in the area.

The 1982 UN Convention on the Law of the Sea lays down, in Article 121 paragraph 3, that "rocks which cannot sustain human habitation or economic life of their own shall have no exclusive economic zone or continental shelf".

Denmark–Sweden

In 1983 the Danish Government allowed a Danish shipowner (the A. P. Moeller group) to begin oil exploration east of the islet of Hesseloe in the Kattegat. The Swedish Government complained in August 1983 that the Danish Government had failed to give notice of its intention.

Under a temporary settlement reached on Oct. 29, 1983, the two governments agreed on the drawing of an equidistant boundary line in the sea between their countries and on the establishment of fishing, gas and oil rights.

France–United Kingdom

A longstanding dispute between France and the United Kingdom over the delimitation of the continental shelf in the English Channel and the Western Approaches was partially resolved in March 1978 by a five-member international arbitration court sitting in Geneva which had been set up by the two governments concerned in July 1975. In response to a British submission, the court made certain adjustments to an original decision of July 1977 concerning the boundary north and west of the (UK) Channel Islands but confirmed its original delimitation of the Atlantic median line, to which the UK Government had also objected.

In objecting to the court's original award (which was published on July 25, 1977), the United Kingdom claimed in particular (i) that the court's cartographer had failed to take account of the curvature of the earth's surface when drawing the Atlantic boundary on the basis of the court's written decision and had thus increased the French sector by some 300 square miles of potentially hydrocarbon-bearing waters, and (ii) that the boundary drawn around the Channel Islands did not take account of a 12-mile fishing limit accepted in the court's written judgment.

After further oral hearings the court finally decided on March 22, 1978, that the UK submission concerning the Channel Islands was admissible and made appropriate adjustments to the boundary in that area. These effectively established a 12-mile zone around the islands, with France obtaining shelf rights beyond the islands to mid-Channel. At the same time, the court found that it had no power to correct the median line in the Western Approaches, with the result that an area of some 40,000 square miles (to a distance of 70 nautical miles into the Atlantic) was divided almost equally between France and the United Kingdom. The reaction of the French Government was to assert that it had "clearly gained more by arbitration than Britain had offered in negotiations".

The French-UK median line beyond the 70-mile mark and to the edge of the continental shelf remained to be delimited, together with the relationship of the British and French sectors with that applicable to Ireland.

Iceland–Norway

In a dispute over the delimitation of the continental shelf between Iceland and Norway (including the Norwegian island of Jan Mayen, north-east of Iceland and between the coasts of Greenland and northern Norway), Norway's position was that the median-line principle should be applied, notwithstanding the fact that Norway had accepted the full extent of Iceland's 200-mile exclusive economic zone originally applied unilaterally from Oct. 15, 1975.

The question of fishing rights was settled in an agreement signed on May 28, 1980, when Norway declared a 200-mile exclusive economic zone around Jan Mayen with effect from the following day, with both sides agreeing to respect their respective 200-mile zones, but with Iceland retaining sovereignty over the 10,000 square miles where the two zones overlapped.

Under a further agreement signed on Oct. 23, 1981, the continental shelf boundary was fixed in line with Iceland's 200-mile exclusive economic zone, but special conditions were laid down for the exploitation of possible mineral resources on both sides of the boundary (covering the greater part of the "Jan Mayen ridge"). In the Norwegian part of this area Iceland was to have a right to 25 per cent of any oil finds, while Norway would have the right to 25 per cent of finds in the Icelandic part.

Ireland—United Kingdom

The Irish Republic lays claim to the waters off Northern Ireland (part of the United Kingdom) on the grounds that the 1921 treaty establishing the Free State and subsequent boundary commission findings refer only to land areas. Article 2 of the Irish constitution claims all seas pertaining to Ireland in line with its claim to the whole land area of Ireland. Diplomatic exchanges between the two Governments have resulted from British vessels patrolling Northern Ireland waters (especially Strangford Lough and Lough Foyle in the border area). However, the Dublin Government has not actively pursued its maritime claims, seeing them as essentially dependent on the eventual achievement of Irish reunification.

Norway–Soviet Union

Negotiations conducted intermittently between Norway and the Soviet Union on the delimitation of the continental shelf in the Barents Sea have remained inconclusive and no agreement has been reached on the boundary between the two countries' sectors.

The Norwegian position has been that the boundary line should be based on the median-line principle (as applied in the North Sea sector of the continental shelf), i.e. it should be equidistant from the islands of Spitsbergen and Novaya Zemlya. The Soviet Union wants the boundary to be defined by a sector line running from the Norwegian–Soviet land border along the meridian of the point at which that land border reaches the sea and towards the North Pole.

Both countries had declared 200-mile exclusive economic zones in 1976. In regard to the disputed "grey zone" of some 155,000 square kilometres between the above-mentioned two proposed demarcation lines, an interim fisheries agreement was concluded in January 1978; this agreement, laying down fishing quotas for both sides, has been extended annually for 12-month periods from July 1 of each year. Attempts to solve the dispute were made in inconclusive negotiations until December 1981, and new negotiations were begun on Dec. 3, 1984.

In 1982–83 Soviet vessels began drilling for oil in the Soviet part of the Barents Sea near the disputed "grey zone". The Soviet Union has indicated its desire to enter into a bilateral Norwegian–Soviet arrangement for exploring the area (allegedly because this would keep foreign, notably US, companies away from the vicinity of Soviet naval bases on the Kola peninsula) but Norway has refused to be drawn into such a scheme.

A further disputed area of the Barents Sea, claimed by both Norway and the Soviet Union, lies to the east of Spitsbergen (the main island of the Svalbard archipelago). Norway has claimed that Svalbard lies on the Norwegian continental shelf and is not entitled to a continental shelf of its own beyond its territorial waters. The Soviet Union, on the other hand, has claimed that Svalbard has continental shelf entitlements under the Svalbard Treaty of 1920, to which both Norway and the Soviet Union are parties. Under that treaty, Norway had "full and absolute sovereignty" over the archipelago, but economic activities such as fishing, hunting and mining were open to nationals of all the contracting states on a footing of absolute equality.

Norway–United Kingdom

In a fisheries limits dispute, dealt with by the International Court of Justice in 1951, the United Kingdom, in its arguments against the Norwegian method of measuring the breadth of the territorial sea, referred to an alleged rule of custom whereby a straight line may be drawn across bays of less than 10 miles from one projection to the other, which could then be regarded as the starting point of the territorial sea. In a judgment of historical importance, the Court dismissed this argument by pointing out that the actual practice of states did not justify the creation of any such custom.[1]

In a decree delimiting Norway's territorial sea along some 1,000 miles of its coastline the Norwegians, instead of measuring the territorial sea from the low-water line, constructed a series of straight baselines linking the outermost parts of land running along the *skjaergaard* (or fringe of islands and rocks) which run parallel to the Norwegian coastline. This had the effect of enclosing within its territorial limits parts of what would normally have been the high seas if the traditional method had been utilized. As a result certain disputes involving British fishing boats arose, and the United Kingdom challenged the legality of the Norwegian baselines at international law.

The Court held that it was the outer line of the *skjaergaard* that was relevant in baseline principles here, and not the low-water line of the mainland. This, noted the Court, was dictated by geographical realities. Having decided that, the Court went on to say that the normal method of drawing baselines that are mostly parallel to the coast (the *trace parallèle*) was not applicable in this case because it would necessitate

---

[1] For details of this case, see Malcolm N. Shaw, *International Law* (Hodder & Stoughton, London 1977), pp. 66, 241–43.

complex geometrical constructions to cover the extreme indentation of the coastline and the series of islands fringing the coasts.

Since the usual method did not apply, and taking into account the principle that the territorial sea must follow the general direction of the coast, the concept of straight baselines drawn from the outer rocks could be considered. The Court also made the point that the Norwegian system had been applied consistently over many years and had met no objections from other states, and that the United Kingdom had not protested until many years after if had first been introduced. In other words, the method of straight baselines operated by Norway "had been consolidated by a constant and sufficiently long practice, in the face of which the attitude of governments bears witness to the fact that they did not consider it to be contrary to international law".

Nevertheless, although noting that Norwegian rights had been established through actual practice coupled with acquiescence, the Court regarded the straight baseline system itself as a valid principle of international law in view of the special geographic conditions of the area.

Another vital factor brought out by the International Court was the importance of local economic interests, as evidenced by long usage in the precise drawing of the baselines. For example, traditional fishing rights in a certain area, "founded on the vital needs of the population and attested by very ancient and peaceful usage", would be taken into account in the determination of the relevant territorial limits.

The principles emerging from this case were readily accepted by states within a comparatively short period as part of international law, and they were followed in Article 4 of the 1958 Geneva Convention on the Territorial Sea.

Soviet Union–Sweden

Inconclusive talks were held on Dec. 11-15, 1981, in an attempt to find a solution to a dispute concerning the delimitation of the sea-bed between the two countries in the region of the Baltic island of Gotland (part of Sweden). Sweden has insisted on a 12-mile territorial sea around the island, whereas the Soviet Union has maintained that the delimitation of the continental shelf should follow a line equidistant from the mainland shores of the two countries.

Incidents in the area included the temporary impounding of a Swedish trawler and the fining of its captain for fishing in what were claimed to be Soviet waters (in March 1982).

Mediterranean Sea and Peripheral Waters

Greece–Turkey

An unresolved dispute exists between Greece and Turkey over the two countries' respective rights to the continental shelf between them and also on the question of sovereignty over some of the islands in the Aegean Sea. The historical enmity between the two countries was exacerbated by the Turkish invasion of Cyprus in 1974.

The political boundary between Greece and Turkey was laid down in the 1923 Treaty of Lausanne, concluded after the Greek–Turkish war of 1921–22 in which Greek forces and civilians were driven out of Anatolia. Under the treaty Greece retained sovereignty over all major islands in the Aegean Sea except Imbroz (Gökçeada) and Tenedos (Bozcaada), which were left to Turkey, and the Dodecanese (ceded to Italy but incorporated in Greece in 1948).

The Turkish Government stated on Nov. 18, 1975, that it wished to find a solution to the dispute through bilateral negotiations, and that any unresolved differences should be referred to the International Court of Justice for arbitration. On Dec. 5 of that year it proposed periodic meetings between the two countries' Foreign Ministers to resolve all outstanding bilateral problems, but the Greek Government rejected this proposal as unacceptable on Dec. 11.

On March 21, 1976, it was disclosed in Ankara that Turkey had proposed the formation of a joint company with Greece to exploit and share the resources of the Aegean Sea. However, a week later the then Turkish Deputy Prime Minister declared that all Greek islands within 50 kilometres (about 31 miles) from the Anatolian coast, including the Dodecanese and Lesbos, should belong to Turkey.

On April 21, 1976, it was announced in Ankara that the Turkish Government had granted the (state-owned) Turkish Petroleum Corporation (TPAO) licences covering 2,000,000 hectares for oil exploration within the continental shelves and beyond Turkish territorial waters, including areas contested by Greece. On May 19, 1976, a Greek official statement listed the matters in dispute as follows:

(1) Rights to the continental shelf in terms of the 1958 Geneva Convention on the Continental Shelf (ratified by Greece but not by Turkey), whereby, in the Greek view, the Greek islands off the Turkish coast had their own rights to the sea-bed and subsoil "to a depth of 200 metres or, beyond that limit, to where the depth of the superadjacent waters admits of the exploitation of the natural resources of the said areas".

[The 1958 convention also provided that, in cases where a continental shelf bordered on two or more countries (as, for example, the Aegean borders on Greece and Turkey), the boundary of the shelf was to be determined by mutual agreement; failing that, and unless unusual circumstances justified a different solution, it would, according to Article 6, follow the median line "every part of which is equidistant from the nearest points of the baselines from which the breadth of the territorial sea of each state is measured" (i.e. a line half-way between what could reasonably be described as the broad coastal outlines of the two countries). Failing bilateral agreement, disputes were to be settled by the compulsory jurisdiction of the International Court of Justice (a principle rejected by Turkey as a non-signatory of the convention), or by an independent arbitral tribunal.]

(2) The extension by Turkey of its control of flights to and from Turkey "to the middle of the Aegean" in connection with Turkey's invasion of Cyprus, with the result that Greek islands were overflown by Turkish aircraft and that aircraft flying from Athens to Ankara had to fly via Bulgaria.

(3) Turkish threats to annex some of the Greek islands off the Turkish coast.

Greece also asserted that the 1958 Convention on the Continental Shelf had passed into international customary law and pointed out that in its judgment of February 1969 on the North Sea continental shelf dispute between Denmark, the Federal Republic of Germany and the Netherlands the International Court had observed that Articles 1–3 of the convention were regarded at least as "reflecting or crystallizing received or emergent rules of customary international law relative to the continental shelf".

The Turkish Prime Minister (as reported on May 20, 1976) gave a list of areas of dispute with Greece which included the following:

(1) The conflict over Cyprus.

(2) The militarization by Greece of Aegean islands in contravention (he claimed) of the 1923 Treaty of Lausanne and the 1947 (Italian Peace) Treaty of Paris.

(3) Greece's intention of extending its territorial waters limit from six to 12 miles which would, in Turkey's view, make the Aegean Sea "a Greek lake".

(4) The continental shelf claim under which oil, minerals and other resources of the shelf would belong to Greece, and which Turkey would not accept.

(5) The "ban on flights over maritime areas which separate us and which the Greeks see as frontiers".

In the Turkish view the Aegean Sea is a special case. Although Turkey has not seriously disputed Greek sovereignty over the islands, it has claimed that geologically they are an extension of the Anatolian peninsula and therefore fall within the scope of a statement made by the International Court during the 1969 North Sea continental shelf case to the effect that the rights of the coastal state extend "over the areas of the continental shelf which constitute a natural prolongation of its land territory". On this basis, Turkey has claimed practically half the Aegean Sea, defining the rightful delineation of the continental shelf as that which follows the north-south median line between the Greek and Turkish mainlands. [On an official Turkish map published on Nov. 1, 1973, the boundary line was shown as starting from the mouth of the river Evros (Meric) on the Greek–Turkish mainland border and passing to the west of Samothrace, Lemnos, Aghios Efstratios, Lesbos, Psara and Chios, with each island being allowed a six-mile territorial waters limit (i.e. not a 12-mile limit as demanded by Greece).]

In response to this claim, Greece has pointed out that Turkish shipping would enjoy the right of innocent passage both through Greek territorial waters and over the Greek continental shelf—although military shipping would be subject to certain restrictions, including a ban on manoeuvres.

Despite Greek objections, the Turkish seismic research vessel *MTA Sismik I* began in July 1976 to carry out oil prospecting between Lemnos and Lesbos, after Turkey had, on July 15, threatened that any Greek interference with the ship's mission would be met by force. There followed a serious military confrontation between the two sides. Greece protested to Turkey on Aug. 7 at the alleged violation of its continental shelf, but Turkey replied that there was neither a Greek nor a Turkish continental shelf while the issue was in dispute.

At the request of Greece (made on Aug. 9, 1976) the UN Security Council met in emergency session on Aug. 12, and on Aug. 25 it passed, by consensus, a resolution recommending that the two countries should seek a negotiated settlement and consider submitting the dispute to the International Court.

The Greek Government had, on Aug. 10, 1976, filed an application to the International Court for proceedings against Turkey in the matter of the continental shelf in the Aegean Sea, and also a request for an interim injunction directing both governments to refrain from all exploration activity in the disputed area and from all military actions which might endanger their peaceful relations. The Turkish Government, however, rejected the Court's jurisdiction in the matter on Aug. 26.

Greece asked the International Court in particular to declare that the Greek islands in the Aegean Sea were entitled to their "lawful" portion of the continental shelf, to delimit the respective parts of that shelf to Greece and Turkey and to take interim measures of protection so that neither state should, without the consent of the other, engage in exploration or research.

On Sept. 12, 1976, the International Court rejected the Greek request for an interim injunction, with the result that Turkish research in the Aegean Sea continued. On the previous day the Court had decided that interim measures of protection were not required and that, seeing that Turkey had denied that the Court was competent to deal with the issue, the proceedings should first concern the question of the Court's jurisdiction. On Dec. 11, 1978, the Court found that such jurisdiction was not conferred upon it by either of the two instruments relied upon by Greece, namely (i) the application of a 1928 General Act of Geneva (whether or not that act was in force), as this act was excluded by the effect of a reservation made by Greece upon accession to it, and (ii) a Greek–Turkish press communiqué of May 31, 1975, as it did not contain an agreement binding upon either side to accept the unilateral referral to the International Court of the dispute, which it described as one of domestic jurisdiction.

Direct negotiations between Greece and Turkey had begun in September 1976, when the Turkish Government abandoned its previous insistence on the demilitarization of the Greek islands in the Aegean. On Nov. 11, 1976, an agreement was signed on the establishment of a joint standing committee of experts to study "interstate practice and international rules for the determination of sea-bed boundaries" and also on an undertaking by both sides to refrain from any initiative or action which might have an adverse effect on the negotiations. However, on March 15, 1977, the Turkish Minister of Energy and Natural Resources announced that Turkey intended to drill for oil in three disputed areas selected by the *MTM Sismik I.*

During Turkish manoeuvres held in the Aegean Sea on March 20-28, 1977, the Greek Government proclaimed a 10-mile aerial territorial limit. Late in 1978 both countries made allegations of violations of their territorial waters limits. Greek oil exploration on the continental shelf was started in March 1982, but later that month the Greek Government gave an assurance that such operations would cease.

Intermittent bilateral talks on the issue since 1980 have remained inconclusive. Attempts to achieve a reconciliation of the two countries, made by the North Atlantic Treaty Organization (NATO), of which both are members, have also been unsuccessful. After the Turkish invasion of Cyprus in 1974 Greece withdrew from NATO's integrated military structure and rejoined only temporarily in 1980–81.

At a meeting of the NATO defence planning committee held on Dec. 8-9, 1981, the Greek Prime Minister listed a number of conditions for Greece's continued membership of the NATO military structure, as follows: (i) the abandonment of plans to establish two national command centres (one at Larissa, Greece, and the other in Izmir, Turkey), which would undermine the status quo in the Aegean and erode the almost complete control of the airspace of the Aegean previously held by Greece; (ii) safeguards for a genuine balance of forces in the Aegean between Greece and Turkey; (iii) confirmation that the protection and defence of the entire air, land and sub-sea area of Greece in peacetime should be the exclusive responsibility of the Greeks; (iv) guarantees of Greece's eastern frontiers (i.e. with Turkey) against any threat; and (v) withdrawal of all foreign occupation forces from Cyprus. The Turkish Minister of Defence protested immediately, in particular against the proposed Greek 12-mile territorial waters limit which, he claimed, would deny Turkey access to its own ports.

In October 1982 Greece again insisted that there was no dispute with Turkey, that it had no claims against that country and that it was not prepared to cede an inch of what it possessed and controlled.

At a NATO defence planning committee meeting held on Dec. 1-2, 1982, the Greek Prime Minister (and Minister of Defence) complained that Turkey had "massively" invaded Turkish airspace in defiance of an agreed moratorium.

In October 1983 and January 1984 Greece refused to take part in NATO manoeuvres in the Aegean Sea on the grounds that they did not include the island of Lemnos, which Turkey insisted should remain demilitarized under the 1923 Treaty of Lausanne. In March 1984 the Greek Government claimed that five Turkish destroyers had fired at a Greek destroyer, but the Turkish Government declared that this was untrue and that the Turkish vessels had been 10 miles from Greek waters on a routine exercise of which Greece had been notified in advance.

Libya–Malta

In the absence of any mutual delimitation of their respective offshore waters, a crisis developed between Libya and Malta in 1980 over the issue of oil prospecting in those waters. Malta claimed jurisdiction over waters to a distance of 98 miles to the south of its shores. This area contained oil resources in the Medina Bank at 68 nautical miles to the south-east of Malta, which hoped that these resources might enable it to attain economic self-sufficiency. Libya, on the other hand, claimed two-thirds of the whole maritime area up to a point only 65.5 nautical miles to the south of Malta.

On May 23, 1976, the two sides signed an agreement in which they requested the International Court of Justice to decide on the following question: "What principles and rules of international law are applicable to the delimitation of the area of the continental shelf which appertains to the Republic of Malta and the area of continental shelf which appertains to the Libyan Arab Republic and how in practice such rules can be applied by the two parties in this particular case in order that they may without difficulty delimit such areas by agreement. . . ." This agreement, however, did not enter into force until March 20, 1982, when instruments of its ratification were exchanged (the Libyan General People's Congress having until January 1981 delayed its decision to ratify the agreement).

Malta had meanwhile refrained from prospecting in the region, whereas Libya had given no undertaking to refrain likewise. In 1981 the Libyan Government laid down new conditions, viz. that no drilling should take place in the disputed area until the International Court had decided the issue. However, Malta rejected this condition as "unacceptable".

An application filed by the Government of Italy on Oct. 24, 1983, for permission to intervene, on the grounds that it wished to participate in the proceedings to the full extent necessary to defend its rights over certain areas claimed by the parties, was rejected by the International Court by 11 votes to five on March 21, 1984.

The International Court heard the case for Malta between Nov. 26 and Dec. 3, 1984, and the case for Libya from Dec. 6, 1984, onwards. On June 3, 1985, the Court decided—in response to Libya's request to state the general principles on which maritime boundaries should be drawn—that the median line between the two countries should be adjusted northwards (i.e. a median line drawn between the meridians of 13°50′E and 15°10′E should be transposed northwards by 18 minutes so as to intersect the 15°10′ meridian at a latitude of approximately 34°30′N) in favour of Libya. It took this decision by 14 votes to three.

The two parties had agreed that their dispute should be governed by customary international law, but they disagreed on the legal basis of continental shelf rights. Libya insisted on the natural prolongation of the state's territory as being the fundamental basis of legal title. Malta held that the continental shelf rights were controlled by the concept of distance from the coast.

The Court took the view that the principles underlying the regime of the exclusive economic zone (EEZ) could not be left out of consideration; that, although there could be a continental shelf where there was no EEZ, there could not be an EEZ without a corresponding continental shelf; that the distance criterion must apply to both; and that geological and geophysical factors did not play any role. It therefore rejected the Libyan argument (of "natural prolongation").

The Court also stated that the equidistance method must not necessarily be used to determine the boundary, but that, as both parties agreed on the application of equitable principles, the equidistance method would have to be demonstrated to lead to an equitable result.

The Court rejected various other arguments (by both Libya and Malta) and inter alia took no account of the uninhabited Maltese island of Filfla in the construction of the proposed median line. However, the fact that Libya's coastline was 192 miles long and that of Malta only 24 miles was considered a relevant factor in the Court's decision to adjust the median line in favour of Libya.

Libya–Tunisia

A ruling by the International Court of Justice, delivered on Feb. 24, 1982, divided a disputed area of the continental shelf of the two countries largely along the lines of demarcation observed by France and Italy during their period of colonial rule over Tunisia and Libya respectively.

The ruling confirmed (i) that oil exploration concessions granted by the Libyan Government in recent years were in the Libyan sector and (ii) that

Libya had fishing rights in certain areas where Tunisia had traditionally enjoyed such rights. The substantive passages of the court's ruling were as follows:

"(1) The principles and rules of international law applicable for the delimitation, to be effected by agreement in implementation of the present judgment, of the areas of continental shelf appertaining to the Republic of Tunisia and the Socialist People's Libyan Arab Jamahiriya respectively, in the area of the pelagian block in dispute between them as defined in Paragraph 2 (i) below, are as follows: (i) the delimitation is to be effected in accordance with equitable principles, and taking account of all relevant circumstances; (ii) the area relevant for the delimitation constitutes a single continental shelf as the natural prolongation of the land territory of both parties, so that in the present case no criterion for delimitation of shelf areas can be derived from the principle of natural prolongation as such; (iii) in the particular geographical circumstances of the present case, the physical structure of the continental shelf area is not such as to determine an equitable delimitation.

"(2) The relevant circumstances referred to in Paragraph 1 (i) above, to be taken into account in achieving an equitable delimitation, include the following: (i) the fact that the area relevant to the delimitation in the present case is bounded by the Tunisian coast from Ras Ajdir [Ras Agedir] to Ras Kaboudia and the Libyan coast from Ras Ajdir to Ras Tajoura and by the parallel of latitude passing through Ras Kaboudia and the meridian passing through Ras Tajoura, the rights of third states being reserved; (ii) the general configuration of the coasts of the parties, and in particular the marked change in direction of the Tunisian coastline between Ras Ajdir and Ras Kaboudia; (iii) the existence and position of the Kerkenna Islands; (iv) the land frontier between the parties, and their conduct prior to 1974 in the grant of petroleum concessions, resulting in the employment of a line seawards from Ras Ajdir at an angle of approximately 26° east of the meridian, which line corresponds to the line perpendicular to the coast at the frontier point which had in the past been observed as a de facto maritime limit; (v) the element of a reasonable degree of proportionality, which a delimitation carried out in accordance with equitable principles ought to bring about between the extent of the continental shelf areas appertaining to the coastal state and the length of the relevant part of its coast, measured in the general direction of the coastlines, account being taken for this purpose of the effects, actual or prospective, of any other continental shelf delimitation between states in the same region.

"(3) The practical method for the application of the aforesaid principles and rules of international law in the particular situation of the present case is the following: (i) the taking into account of the relevant circumstances which characterize the area defined in Paragraph 2 (i) above, including its extent, calls for it to be treated, for the purpose of its delimitation between the parties to the present case, as made up of two sectors, each requiring the application of a specific method of delimitation in order to achieve an overall equitable solution; (ii) in the first sector, namely in the sector closer to the coast of the parties, the starting point for the line of delimitation is the point where the outer limit of the territorial sea of the parties is intersected by a straight line drawn from the land frontier point of Ras Ajdir through the point 33°55′N/12°E, which line runs at a bearing of approximately 26° east of north, corresponding to the angle followed by the north-western boundary of Libyan petroleum concessions numbers NC 76, 137, NC 41 and NC 53, which [angle] was aligned on the south-eastern boundary of Tunisian petroleum concession *Permis complémentaire offshore du Golfe de Gabès* (Oct. 21, 1966); from the intersection point so determined, the line of delimitation between the two continental shelves is to run north-east through the point 33°55′N/12°E, thus on that same bearing, to the point of intersection with the parallel passing through the most westerly point of the Tunisian coastline between Ras Kaboudia and Ras Ajdir, that is to say, the most westerly point on the shoreline (low-water mark) of the Gulf of Gabès; (iii) in the second sector, namely in the area which extends seawards beyond the parallel of the most westerly point of the Gulf of Gabès, the line of delimitation of the two continental shelves is to veer to the east in such a way as to take account of the

Kerkenna Islands; that is to say, the delimitation line is to run parallel to a line drawn from the most westerly point of the Gulf of Gabès bisecting the angle formed by a line from that point to Ras Kaboudia and a line drawn from that same point along the seaward coast of the Kerkenna Islands, the bearing of the delimitation line parallel to such bisector being 52° to the meridian; the extension of this line north-eastwards is a matter falling outside the jurisdiction of the Court in the present case, as it will depend on the delimitation to be agreed with third states."

During the proceedings a request was made by Malta to be allowed to intervene on the ground of an interest of a legal nature under Article 62 of the Court's statute, but this request was rejected by the court.

On July 27, 1984, the Tunisian Government filed an application requesting the International Court to revise and interpret the above judgment. Tunisia based its application on the "discovery of a new fact" (this being, in terms of Article 61 paragraph 1 of the Court's statute, the only admissible ground for making such an application). In particular Tunisia requested the Court to declare that it was for the experts of the two parties to establish the exact co-ordinates of the most westerly point of the Gulf of Gabès.

Public hearings were held on the Tunisian application on June 13–18, 1985—this being the first instance of a state requesting revision of a previously-rendered judgment of the Court.

Spain–United Kingdom

In addition to the unresolved dispute concerning sovereignty over Gibraltar (acquired from Spain by Britain under the 1713 Treaty of Utrecht), there is a special dispute over jurisidiction over the waters surrounding Gibraltar. The Treaty of Utrecht contains no reference to these waters, but the United Kingdom has consistently held that all coastal land territory has a territorial sea.

The question of rights over these waters first arose early in the 19th century, when the British and Spanish authorities disagreed over the question of smuggling jurisdiction. From 1811 onwards the British law officers expressed doubts on whether Britain had authority over shipping in these waters, but they held that the anchorage might be regarded as part of the port of Gibraltar because of usage. In 1875 the law officers suggested that a median line boundary in Algeciras Bay might be agreed (even though Spain would oppose this). After the question of designating the limits of the port of Gibraltar (for customs purposes) had arisen in 1876, the law officers expressed doubt over the wisdom of giving the Governor of Gibraltar power to declare limits of the port.

On April 27, 1967, when the Spanish Government proclaimed a prohibited zone for overflight (which would make it difficult to use the Gibraltar airport), it defined, for this zone, a boundary which was not the median line but a straight line extending from the frontier line at La Linea across the Bay of Algeciras to a point halfway between the Spanish coast at the projection of that line and the outermost harbour works of Gibraltar, and from that point in a straight line down the Bay.

Persian (Arabian) Gulf Continental Shelf

The Persian (Arabian) Gulf, covering approximately 90,000 square miles, is underlain in its entirety by a continental shelf, having an average water depth of only some 240 feet. The Gulf is virtually an enclosed sea (with the only access being through the Strait of Hormuz at the eastern end) and is bordered by eight states, namely Bahrain, Iran, Iraq, Kuwait, Oman, Qatar, Saudi Arabia and the United Arab Emirates. Of at least 16 continental shelf boundaries required for the complete delimitation of the Gulf, only seven have been agreed: between Bahrain and Iran, Bahrain and Saudi Arabia, Iran and Oman, Iran and Saudi Arabia, Iran and the United Arab Emirates (in respect of Dubai), and Qatar and the United Arab Emirates (in respect of Abu Dhabi). At least nine boundaries remain to be negotiated: between Bahrain and Qatar, Iran and Iraq, Iran and Kuwait, Iran and the United Arab Emirates (two boundaries), Iraq and Kuwait, Kuwait and Saudi Arabia, Oman and the United Arab Emirates, and Qatar and Saudi Arabia. As described below, a number of these prospective boundaries are the subject of dispute between the states concerned. (For an assessment of military tensions in the Gulf, see pages 234–36.)

Bahrain–Qatar

An unresolved dispute exists between Bahrain and Qatar relating to sovereignty over the Hawar (or Huwar) Islands, situated about 1½ miles (2.4 km) off the east coast of Qatar, and their surrounding waters. Both countries are members of the Gulf Co-operative Council of Arab States, comprising also Kuwait, Oman, Saudi Arabia and the United Arab Emirates.

The islands have been under the sovereignty of Bahrain on the basis of a British decision made in 1939. In 1965 (i.e. before the two countries achieved independence in 1971) Bahrain granted a concession to the Continental Oil Company (Bahrain) including the islands and their surrounding waters in the area where oil exploration was to take place. In March 1967 the Ruler of Qatar raised the question of the sovereignty over the islands, and the subject was thereafter discussed within the framework of a proposed offshore boundary settlement between the two countries, with Qatar insisting on ownership of the islands before agreeing to a settlement favourable to Bahrain, but the latter did not agree to this demand.

On March 1, 1980, Bahrain's Minister of Industry and Development stated that the islands were governed by a concession agreed between the Government of Bahrain and a group of US companies planning to drill a new experimental well in search of oil (following the failure of two earlier drilling attempts). The Qatar Minister of Finance and Petroleum thereupon replied on March 4 that "all geographical, historical, legal and logical indications" categorically proved that "these islands constitute an indivisible part of Qatar, since they are situated within its territorial waters".

The Qatar minister added that Qatar considered the British decision of 1939 to be "null and void" since it contradicted "the basic norms of international law governing such matters" and also "established geographical, material and historic facts"; he furthermore accused the Bahrain minister of disregarding the fact that there was "an agreed mediation being conducted by a big sister state [i.e. Saudi Arabia] for solving the dispute"; and he declared that Qatar was "keen" to safeguard its close fraternal relations with Bahrain and that he hoped that the two countries would settle their dispute "in a manner that would restore right in accordance with the principles of justice and law".

Saudi Arabia was later reported to be continuing its mediation efforts, but there is as yet no written agreement on the frontier between the two states.

Iran–United Arab Emirates

Delimitation of the Persian (Arabian) Gulf maritime boundary between Iran and the United Arab Emirates (UAE) has been rendered additionally complex by a continuing dispute between the two states over the sovereignty of the islands of Abu Musa, Greater Tunb and Lesser Tunb, which are strategically situated at the entrance to the Gulf opposite the Strait of Hormuz. The islands were occupied by Iranian forces on Nov. 30, 1971—two days before the proclamation of the UAE as a new state—having previously been under the jurisdiction of UAE constituents.

Iran's occupation of Abu Musa was carried out under an agreement with the Ruler of Sharjah (the UAE state which held sovereignty over the island), which provided inter alia that the two sides would recognize a 12-mile territorial waters limit around the island. The other two islands were occupied by force after negotiations on their peaceful cession by the Ruler of Ras al-Khaimah had failed.

Since the late 1970s, and particularly since the outbreak of the Iran–Iraq war in September 1980, the UAE and other Arab states have repeatedly called for the restoration of UAE sovereignty over all three islands.

Kuwait–Saudi Arabia

Under an agreement signed in 1965 and ratified by both Kuwait and Saudi Arabia in 1966, a new land boundary between the two countries was defined as a result of the partition of a neutral zone between them created under the Uqair Convention of 1922. The 1965 agreement, followed by a demarcation accord signed in 1967 and ratified in 1969, applied only to the land boundary between the two countries and not to their offshore boundaries or the two Gulf islands of Qaru and Umm el-Maradim, situated respectively some 23 miles (37 km) and 16 miles (26 km) off the coast of the northern part of the partitioned zone.

The 1965 agreement laid down inter alia that "for the purpose of exploiting natural resources" in territorial waters of the partitioned zone "not more than six marine miles shall be annexed to the principal land of that partitioned zone" and that both sides would "exercise their equal rights" in the submerged zone beyond the six-mile limit by means of observance of "shared exploitation".

On the basis of an exchange of letters between Iraq and Kuwait in 1923 and 1932 the two Gulf islands belonged to Kuwait, but Saudi Arabia contested that sovereignty. In 1961 Kuwait offered to share with Saudi Arabia any oil proceeds which might accrue from the islands in return for Saudi Arabia's acknowledgment of Kuwait's sovereignty over them. Saudi Arabia, however, declined this offer, preferring to delay a decision on the islands until the boundaries of the neutral zone had been settled. The islands have remained under Kuwaiti control but Saudi Arabia has never formally abandoned its claim to sovereignty over them.

Asian and Far Eastern Waters

Australia–Indonesia

In 1971–72 Australia and Indonesia concluded agreements on their mutual maritime boundary, but these agreements did not cover a stretch of about 250 kilometres south of the island of Timor, the eastern part of which was then still under Portuguese control. Nor was agreement reached on the western end of the agreed boundary and on a separate boundary between (the Australian) Christmas Island and (Indonesian) Java.

The line then agreed was roughly that of the Timor Trough, a canyon more than 3,000 metres deep in the sea-bed between 30 and 50 nautical miles from the south coast of Timor, but much closer to Indonesia than to Australia.

Four rounds of "technical" talks on how to solve the problem of the "Timor gap" ended in October 1981 without success. The question subsequently became acute again with the discovery in 1983 of the Jabiru oil field (in the Bonaparte Basin, off north-western Australia), which led to speculation about the existence of oil in a jurassic rock structure, known as Kelp, in the Timor gap.

The Indonesian position is that the continental shelf between East Timor and Australia is continuous and that the maritime boundary should be drawn along a median line equidistant from both shores. The Indonesian Foreign Minister said on March 29, 1984 (after new negotiations on the subject had begun in Canberra on Feb. 2), that the median line would be a fair settlement because the UN Convention on the Law of the Sea (signed by both Australia and Indonesia) had abandoned the definition of the continental shelf of the 1958 convention (on which previous negotiations had been based). The Australian side, however, insisted that a line should be agreed connecting the boundary lines agreed in 1971–72.

A provisional fisheries arrangement had been reached in 1981 to overcome the practical problems of overlapping fisheries jurisdiction. This arrangement roughly followed the median line, except in the west, where it came close to the (Australian) Ashmore and Cartier islands. It was declared to be without prejudice to the final position to either government or to sea-bed delimitation negotiations.

Brunei–China–Malaysia–Philippines–Taiwan–Vietnam

An unresolved dispute exists over the area of the South China Sea around the Spratly Islands (called Nansha Islands by China, Truong Sa by Vietnam and Kalayaan by the Philippines). The islands are a group of islets, coral reefs and sandbars dispersed over 600 miles (965 km) and lying nearly 300 miles west of the Philippine island of Palawan, slightly over 300 miles east of Vietnam and about 650 miles south of Hainan (the nearest Chinese territory). The largest of these islands, Itu Aba (called Taiping by the Chinese), has an area of only 90 acres (36 hectares) but their position is of strategic importance as they command the sea passage from Japan to Singapore. Oil discovered in 1976 at Reed Bank (midway between Palawan and the Spratlys) has been exploited by the Philippines since 1979.

The claims of China and Taiwan to the area are based on the fact that the islands were discovered by Chinese navigators, used by Chinese fishermen and administered by China from the 15th century onwards (Chinese sovereignty over them being undisputed until the 1930s). The French Government, then in control of Indo-China, occupied nine of the Spratly Islands in 1933, but in 1939 the Japanese occupied all the islands. After the Japanese surrender at the end of World War II the Kuomintang Government of China took possession of them in 1946 and subsequently maintained a garrison on Itu Aba.

In a document issued by the Foreign Ministry of the People's Republic of China on Jan. 30, 1980, China's claim to the islands was reasserted on the grounds that since 1949 its Government had continued to administer and develop the islands; that at the 1945 San Francisco conference (at which the United Nations Organization was founded) it had been decided that Japan should renounce the islands (which it did in the 1951 peace treaty) and the leader of the Soviet delegation (Andrei Gromyko) had stated that the islands were China's "inalienable territory"; that China's sovereignty over them was "widely acknowledged internationally" and in many encyclopedias and atlases; and that they had also been recognized as Chinese territories by North Vietnam until 1974.

A claim to part of the area by the Sultanate of Brunei does not appear to have been actively pursued. However, a claim by Malaysia to an area south of the Spratly Islands was shown on an official map of the Malaysian continental shelf published in December 1979. On Sept. 4, 1983, a Malaysian naval commando was reported to have landed on an atoll (named as Terumbu Layang Layang) of the Spratly Islands, and in response to protests by both China and Vietnam the Malaysian Foreign Ministry asserted on Sept. 14, 1983, that the atoll (and also the Vietnamese-occupied atoll of Pulau Kecil Amboyna Cay, some 64 km to the south-east) lay within Malaysia's 200-mile exclusive economic zone and had "always been marked as Malaysian territory on maps of the area". However, on Oct. 3 of that year it was announced that the Foreign Ministers of Malaysia and Vietnam had agreed to conduct "friendly negotiations" on their respective claims.

The Philippine Government first laid claim to the islands in May 1956 after a private Philippine expedition had surveyed and occupied a number of the islands. The claim was disputed by China, Taiwan and South Vietnam, with the last-named sending a garrison to one of the islands in August 1956. After the Taiwan garrison on Itu Aba had fired on a Philippine fishing boat, the Philippine Government sent a note in July 1971 demanding their withdrawal. At a press conference on July 10, 1971, President Marcos of the Philippines maintained that after Japan renounced its sovereignty over the islands they had become a de facto trusteeship of the allied powers, and that this trusteeship precluded the setting up of garrisons on any of them without the allies' consent. He stated that the Philippines were in effective control of three of the larger islands, however, and according to news agency reports Philippine troops were landed on these islands. In May 1976 the Philippine Government announced that a consortium of Swedish and Philippine companies had contracted to explore for oil in the area; there followed renewed protests by China, Taiwan and South Vietnam. (The reunification of Vietnam in July 1976 brought about a direct confrontation between China and Vietnam on the issue.)

The Philippine Government set up a military command on Palawan in March 1976 and by March 1978 had established garrisons on seven of the islands. It reached an agreement with Vietnam in January 1978 to solve the dispute "in a spirit of conciliation and friendship", however, and concluded a similar agreement with China in the following March. At a press conference on Sept. 14, 1979, President Marcos made it clear that the Philippines confined its claim to the seven islands under its occupation. These islands, he declared, were "unoccupied, unowned and unpossessed islands" which had not even been shown on maps before World War II, and the Philippines had therefore occuped them as "new territory or *res nullius*".

The Government of South Vietnam had in September 1973 incorporated the Spratly Islands in one of its provinces in order to make it possible to grant contracts to foreign companies for oil exploration and exploitation in the area off the Spratlys. The Chinese Government condemned this step and occupied three of the islands in January 1974. In April 1975 Vietnamese communist troops took over the islands previously occupied by South Vietnamese garrisons. An official Vietnamese map issued in 1976 showed the Spratlys as Vietnamese territory. Early in 1979 the Government of unified Vietnam rejected all Chinese claims to the islands but added that all international disputes should be settled by peaceful means. On Sept. 28, 1979, the Vietnamese Government reaffirmed its claim in a White Book, and in August 1980 it protested to the Philippines over what it called the latter's "occupation" of the Comodor Reef in "the Vietnamese archipelago of Truong Sa".

Burma-India

Under a draft agreement initialled in New Delhi in April 1984 the maritime boundary between Burma and India in the Andaman Sea, the Coco Channel and the Bay of Bengal was delimited and to be confirmed in a formal agreement to be signed shortly.

Under this agreement the Andaman Islands, which had been part of British Burma before World War II but had been ceded to India when the two countries became independent in 1947–48, remained part of India, and the Coco Islands, some 40 miles north of the Andamans, remained part of Burma.

The agreement also settled a dispute over the channel between the two island groups, where there was an overlap of the 200-mile exclusive economic zones claimed by the two countries in the Bay of Bengal.

China–Taiwan

A dispute exists between the governments of the People's Republic of China and the Republic of China (Taiwan) concerning sovereignty over the waters and sea-bed of the Macclesfield Bank in the South China Sea, south-east of the Paracel Islands and some 200 miles off the east coast of the island of Luzon (Philippines), involving both fish and offshore hydrocarbon resources.

China–Vietnam

Gulf of Tonkin

No agreement has been reached over the maritime boundary between China and Vietnam in the Gulf of Tonkin, which contains good fishing grounds as well as potentially extensive hydrocarbons.

The Gulf of Tonkin (known to the Vietnamese as the Bac Bo Gulf and to the Chinese as Beibu Wan) lies between Vietnam to the west, the Chinese mainland to the north, and the Luichow Peninsula and the island of Hainan (both Chinese) to the east, and at its greatest extent is 170 nautical miles wide. It has two outlets to the South China Sea, that to the south, which is 125 nautical miles wide at its narrowest point, and another to the east through the Hainan Strait.

A Franco–Chinese convention of 1887 stated that islands in the Gulf lying to the east of longitude 105°43′ east of the Paris meridian (or 108°03′13″ east of the Greenwich meridian) belonged to China, and islands to the west of this meridian belonged to Vietnam. The Vietnamese maintain that this meridian marks the boundary between the two countries' territorial waters across the entire Gulf. The Chinese, however, contend that both the wording of the convention and the attached map make plain that this article refers only to the offshore islands and does not lay down a sea boundary line.

The North Vietnamese Foreign Ministry informed the Chinese Government on Dec. 26, 1973, of North Vietnam's intention to prospect for oil in the Gulf of Tonkin, and proposed that, as the sea boundary had not been delimited, negotiations should be held on the subject. The Chinese Foreign Ministry accepted this proposal on Jan. 18, 1974, but stipulated that prospecting should not take place in the area between the 18th and 20th parallels and the 107th and 108th meridians, and that third countries should not be involved in the exploration and exploitation of the Gulf. When negotiations opened in Peking on Aug. 15, 1974, the Vietnamese delegation maintained that the boundary had already been delineated in the 1887 convention, and proposed that it should be officially delineated. As the Chinese refused to accept this contention, the talks were suspended at the end of November without agreement being reached.

At negotiations on the land and sea boundaries which began on Oct. 7, 1977, the Chinese refused to discuss the land border unless the Vietnamese gave up their claim that a sea boundary already existed. As a compromise, the Vietnamese suggested that the land border should first be discussed and that each side should maintain its own views on the Gulf of Tonkin, which would be discussed later. As no agreement was reached on the land border, the question of the sea boundary also remained unsettled. A Vietnamese Foreign Ministry statement of Dec. 13, 1979, protested against reports that China had signed contracts with foreign firms to explore for oil in the Gulf of Tonkin as a breach of the convention of 1887. (During 1979 two survey vessels working in the Gulf for US oil companies were fired on by Vietnamese gunboats.)

An official statement of the Chinese case published on Dec. 2, 1980, put forward the following additional arguments: (i) If the line were extended southward to take in the entire Gulf it would be more than 130 nautical miles east of the Vietnamese coast and only about 30 miles west of Hainan, and would give Vietnam two-thirds of the area of the Gulf. (ii) No expert on international law had ever mentioned that the Gulf belonged to Vietnam and China. (iii) Under international law the sea area within a territorial bay was regarded as inland waters (through which ships could pass only with a special permit), but since 1887 neither France nor Vietnam had ever treated foreign ships sailing across the Gulf as ships passing through inland waters. (iv) A French decree on the fishery area in Indo-China laid down that territorial waters extended 20 kilometres from the shore, and made no special provision for the Gulf of Tonkin. (v) Vietnam announced in 1964 that its territorial waters extended 12 nautical miles from the shore, and this was accepted in the latest fishery agreement between China and Vietnam.

Paracel Islands

A further unresolved dispute exists between China and Vietnam in respect of sovereignty over the Paracel Islands and rights in the adjoining seas. The Paracel Islands, known to the Chinese as the Xisha (Western Sands) Islands and to the Vietnamese as Hoang Sa, consist of about 130 barren and waterless islands, none larger than a square mile (1.6 sq km) in area, lying about 165 miles (265 km) south-east of the Chinese island of Hainan and 225 miles (360 km) east of the Vietnamese coast. They are divided into two main groups, the Crescent group to the west and the Amphitrite group to the east. The Western name "Paracels" is derived from the Portuguese word for reef.

The French Government, which then exercised sovereignty over Cochin China and a protectorate over Annam and Tonkin, claimed in a note to China in 1931 that the Empire of Annam had a prior title to the islands, and in 1938 the Emperor Bao Dai annexed them to the territory of Thua Thien province. In the following year, however, they were occupied by the Japanese. Japan renounced her claim to them by the peace treaty signed in San Francisco in 1951, but the treaty did not state to whom they belonged. A Chinese official statement commenting on the draft treaty claimed that they had "always been China's territory". At the San Francisco conference, the Vietnamese delegate formally affirmed Vietnam's claim to the islands, whilst in the absence of China, which was not represented, the Soviet delegate described them as China's "inalienable territory".

After Vietnam was divided in 1954 into two states, the South Vietnamese Government continued to assert its claim to the Paracels, whereas the North Vietnamese Government temporarily accepted China's claim to them. According to the Chinese Foreign Ministry document cited above, North Vietnamese official statements in 1958 and 1965 referred to the islands as Chinese territory, and they were shown and referred to as such in maps and textbooks issued by the North Vietnamese Government down to 1974. Both China and South Vietnam exercised control over some of the islands during the period from 1954 to 1974; Woody Island, the main island in the Amphitrite group, was occupied by the Chinese, whilst South Vietnam maintained a small garrison on Pattle Island, the largest of the Crescent group, to man a radio and meteorological station.

After the South Vietnamese Government had announced its intention of carrying out surveys for oil off its coast opposite the Paracels, the Chinese Foreign Ministry issued a statement on Jan. 11, 1974, affirming its claim to the islands, this claim being rejected by South Vietnam on the following day. South Vietnamese warships which were sent to the islands withdrew after an engagement with Chinese warships on Jan. 19, and on the following day Chinese troops occupied the three islands still under South Vietnamese control. A North Vietnamese spokesman commented in a non-committal statement on Jan. 21 that "disputes handed down by history, often very complex ones", should be settled through negotiations. Both the United States and the Soviet Union adopted a strictly neutral attitude towards the dispute, and a request by the South Vietnamese Government for a meeting of the UN Security Council failed to secure the necessary support for placing the question on the Council's agenda.

An official Vietnamese map issued in 1976 showed the Paracel Islands as Vietnamese territory. A Vietnamese Government statement of May 20, 1977, said that Vietnam's territorial waters were 12 nautical miles wide and that its exclusive economic zone extended to 200 nautical miles from the coast; it referred to "islands and archipelagos belonging to Vietnamese territory and situated outside the territorial waters mentioned" without specifying these islands.

In a memorandum handed to the Vietnamese Prime Minister on June 10, 1977, China accused Vietnam of making the Paracels, "over which there was never any issue", a subject of dispute. However, in a White Book of Sept. 28, 1979, Vietnam based its claim on the islands' history, maintaining that according to Vietnamese geographical works of the 17th and 18th centuries "the Vietnamese feudal state was the first in history to occupy, claim ownership of, exercise sovereignty over and exploit" the islands; that the Emperor of Annam had ordered their occupation in 1816; and that his successor had in 1836 commanded a survey of them to be carried out and markers to be erected.

After it had been reported that China had signed contracts with foreign companies for oil prospecting around the Paracels, the Vietnamese Foreign Ministry issued a warning, on Dec. 13, 1979, that such companies conducting exploration in this area without Vietnam's consent "must bear all consequences of their wrongdoings".

A Chinese Foreign Ministry document of Jan. 30, 1980, claimed that the islands were discovered by Chinese mariners and were described in Chinese geographical works of the third century AD; that the Chinese Emperor exercised jurisdiction over them in the 11th century; and that they were shown as Chinese territory in official maps of the 18th and early 19th centuries. A Chinese fleet which visited the islands in 1909 set up stone tablets and hoisted the Chinese flag, and two years later they were placed under the administration of Hainan island. The document therefore claimed that "consecutive jurisdiction was exercised over them by successive Chinese governments for more than a thousand years".

On July 24, 1981, the Vietnamese Foreign Ministry reaffirmed Vietnam's claim to the islands and rebutted Chinese warnings issued to Vietnam and the Soviet Union not to prospect for oil off the islands.

Vietnam's claim to both the Paracel and the Spratly Islands was strongly reiterated in a further detailed White Paper published by the Foreign Ministry in January 1982 and describing this claim as part of Vietnam's "just struggle" against "imperialism and Beijing's expansionism and hegemonism".

An armed clash involving Chinese and Vietnamese fishing boats and armed vessels took place early in March 1982 in an area off the Paracels which both parties claimed to be their territorial waters.

Indonesia–Malaysia

Under a treaty on maritime boundaries, signed on Feb. 25, 1982, Malaysia formally recognized (as the first country to do so) Indonesia's "archipelagic principle" whereby the 13,000 scattered islands of Indonesia were enclosed within territorial seas delineated by straight baselines drawn from the outermost points of the outer islands. In the treaty Malaysia recognized Indonesia's sovereignty and exclusive economic rights in this zone, and Indonesia undertook to respect Malaysia's traditional fishing rights, rights of free sea and air passage between Peninsular Malaysia and the Borneo states, and rights to lay submarine cables and pipelines.

The treaty thus settled earlier disputes which had arisen out of a map published by Malaysia in 1979 showing as Malaysian certain islands south of Sabah, in the Sulawesi Sea, which Indonesia had claimed.

Japan–North Korea

A military zone declared by the Government of the Democratic People's Republic of (North) Korea off a baseline drawn between the extreme ends of North Korean territory bordering the Sea of Japan, and some 50 miles wide, is disputed by Japan.

Japan–South Korea

Disputes exist over the sovereignty over certain islands situated between Japan and the Republic of (South) Korea.

The Take-shima (or Liancourt) Rocks, known as Tokdo Islands in Korea, lie about 150 kilometres north-west of the Japanese island of Oki (off Honshu) in the Sea of Japan. They are marked as Japanese in most current atlases but are claimed by both countries. They were occupied by South Korea in 1954, and on Aug. 17, 1983, the Japanese Foreign Minister made a formal protest against the presence of South Korean fishermen on the islands. The Government of South Korea rebuffed Japanese claims of "illegal occupation" and reaffirmed that the islands were an inseparable part of the Republic of Korea.

The Danjo Islands, west of Kyushu, are held by Japan but the Republic of Korea contends that they lie on its continental shelf. (In fact, the continental shelf extends from coast to coast between the two countries.)

Japan–Soviet Union

Peter the Great Bay (Zaliv Petra Velikogo)—near the north-eastern end of which Vladivostok is situated—was closed by the Soviet Union in 1956 by a line based on "historic bays" rights and security considerations. The closure has, however, been disputed by Japan.

On July 21, 1957, the Soviet Union defined its territorial sea in the bay by a line from the Korean frontier to Cape Povorotny and prohibited all international navigation within the closing line of 110 miles. Protests by France, the Federal Republic of Germany, Japan, Sweden, the United Kingdom and the United States were rejected by the Soviet Government on Jan. 7, 1958, when that Government insisted that the waters of the bay "historically belong to the Soviet internal waters owing to the special geographic conditions of the bay and to its significance in economy and national defence".

Kampuchea–Thailand–Vietnam

On March 29, 1982, the Foreign Ministry of the People's Republic of Kampuchea (PRK) issued a statement protesting against Thai oil exploration in areas of the Gulf of Thailand which the PRK claimed as lying on its continental shelf.

Under an agreement signed on July 7, 1982, the PRK and Vietnam defined their respective territorial waters. On July 31 of that year the Government of the PRK decreed that Kampuchea's territorial waters extended to 12 nautical miles (with their limit in the west being determined by a Franco–Siamese treaty of 1907); that a contiguous zone under Kampuchean control extended to a further 72 nautical miles; and that the exclusive economic zone and the continental shelf (in which Kampuchea would exercise sovereign rights for fishing and the exploitation of natural and mineral resources) extended to 200 nautical miles from the coast.

Disputes in the Pacific Ocean

Alaska–United States

In a dispute between the state of Alaska and the Federal US Government over the waters of Cook Inlet (a bay in southern Alaska with considerable oil deposits), Alaska claimed rights to the subsurface lands of the inlet on the grounds that it had been regarded as a historic bay since Russian times (i.e. before 1867, when Alaska was purchased from Russia by the United States). The US Supreme Court, however, decided in 1975 that the inlet had not been so regarded under Russian, US or Alaskan sovereignty, and that it was the United States rather than the state of Alaska which was entitled to the subsurface lands of Cook Inlet.

Canada–United States

Canadian–US disputes over maritime boundaries on the Pacific seaboard are described below. East coast disputes are dealt with on pages 184–86.

Hecate Strait and Dixon Entrance

An unresolved dispute exists between Canada and the United States concerning jurisdiction over the waters of the Hecate Strait (between the Canadian Queen Charlotte Islands and the mainland of British Columbia) and Dixon Entrance (between the northern end of Queen Charlotte Island and the Alaskan Prince of Wales Island).

The boundary between Alaska and British Columbia was first defined in a treaty of 1825 between Russia and the United Kingdom, and it was finally delimited, with respect to the entrance to the Portland Channel from Dixon Entrance, in an award by a special commission in 1903. In 1908 the Canadian Government expressed its opinion to the effect that it claimed jurisdiction over the whole extent of the Hecate Strait, but the US Government stated that it did not wish to admit that the Hecate Strait and Dixon Entrance were British.

In 1909 the Canadian Privy Council adopted the view that the 1903 Alaska boundary award had been intended to divide waters as well as land, and this view was reaffirmed by the British Privy Council in 1914. The law officers of the British Crown, however, had previously advised that an international tribunal would certainly decide that the great extent of water north and east of Queen Charlotte Islands was part of the high seas. In 1954 the British Minister of Fisheries stated that the Canadian Government had always claimed that the Hecate Strait was part of Canada, as it had asserted in 1908. This claim has not been formally accepted by the United States, which in 1976 continued to assert that the 1903 award referred only to land boundaries.

Other Disputes

Other unresolved maritime boundary disputes between Canada and the United States relating to the western seaboard are as follows:

(1) Over the continental shelf in the Beaufort Sea north of Alaska and the Canadian territory of Yukon.

(2) Over the Straits of Juan de Fuca, between the US state of Washington and Vancouver Island (British Columbia), where the equidistance principle has not yet been agreed to. (In this area an agreement has, however, been reached on a mandatory vessel traffic management system.)

France–Vanuatu

A dispute arose in 1982 over two uninhabited islands, known as Matthew and Hunter, situated about 350 kilometres south-east of the island of Anatom (at the southern end of the islands constituting the state of Vanuatu, formerly the Anglo–French Condominium of the New Hebrides) and about 450 kilometres due east of the mainland of New Caledonia (a French overseas territory).

The Government of Vanuatu declared in May 1982 that it regarded the islands as part of its territory and renamed them Umaenupnae and Umaeneag respectively, whereas France claimed them as part of New Caledonia. Both islands are barren volcanic rocks, but their owner would, under the 200-mile exclusive economic zone system, be entitled to about 150,000 square miles of the surrounding ocean and its fishery, mineral and other rights.

The islands were said not to have been formally claimed by any state until the 1960s. Maps, including official French ones, had generally shown them to be part of the New Hebrides. In 1975 France officially laid claim to them, with a landing party setting up a plaque on Matthew Island, and in December 1976 a French law declared them to be part of New Caledonia. This was also stated in a memorandum issued by Britain and France to the Vanuatu authorities which succeeded those of the New Hebrides.

The Government of Vanuatu, however, did not recognize the French claim. When it appeared that a maritime boundary agreement between France and Fiji recognized the French claim, Vanuatu protested and the Government of Fiji thereupon stated that the agreement was without prejudice to Vanuatu's claim. In March 1983 a Vanuatu landing party removed the French plaque from Matthew Island and erected one claiming the island for Vanuatu. France has since insisted that its claim is "incontestable".

Soviet Union–United States

The precise maritime boundary between the United States and the

Soviet Union in the Bering Strait (separating Alaska from the Chukhotski peninsula and only about 20 miles wide at its narrowest point) and adjacent areas has never been properly demarcated. The boundary was set in an 1867 convention after the United States purchased Alaska from the Tsarist Government of Russia.

Inconclusive boundary negotiations were held by the two sides in 1981–83. In 1982 the Soviet Union passed a law allowing Soviet organizations to exploit mineral resources on the ocean floor outside Soviet territorial waters—in response to attempts by the Reagan Administration to change the draft UN Convention on the Law of the Sea and in order to protect Soviet interests, seeing that other countries had already begun unilaterally to exploit the seabed. In March 1983 the United States proclaimed its 200-mile exclusive economic zone which, in the Bering Strait region, overlapped to a considerable extent with that of the Soviet Union.

On Jan. 23, 1984, it was announced that the Soviet Union had notified the United States that it was prepared to resume demarcation negotiations, which were expected to define zones of each nation's continental shelf to be reserved exclusively for their exploitation of mineral resources. Two rounds of talks were subsequently held during 1984.

Caribbean, South American and Antarctic Waters

Argentina–Chile

Since the 19th century the small islands of Picton, Lennox and Nueva, situated at the eastern end of the Beagle Channel (off Tierra del Fuego and north of Cape Horn), have been at the centre of a dispute between Argentina and Chile. The islands have de facto been under Chilean sovereignty and were in 1977 awarded to Chile by a court of arbitration. This decision was rejected by Argentina, which feared that its access to the Atlantic from its naval base at Ushuaia (on the north bank of the Beagle Channel) as well as access to its Antarctic bases and to potential resources of oil, minerals, fish and krill in the South Atlantic and Antarctic region might be impeded if Chile was allowed formal access to the Atlantic under the 1977 award.

However, following mediation by the Holy See, initiated in January 1979, a draft treaty of peace and friendship was signed at the Holy See on Jan. 23, 1984, by the two countries' Foreign Ministers.

This draft treaty, seen as a compromise, provided inter alia that Picton, Lennox and Nueva should be confirmed as Chilean territory and that in Atlantic waters Chilean sovereignty should extend only to a zone of 12 nautical miles from the islands, while beyond this limit Argentina should have jurisdiction up to 200 nautical miles. (Argentina had earlier asked for the implementation of the "bi-oceanic principle" whereby Argentina should have sovereignty up to 200 miles over Atlantic waters and Chile over offshore Pacific waters only, whereas Chile had wanted to establish rights in the Atlantic partly in order to improve its claim to jurisdiction in Antarctica, which conflicted with Argentina's claims.)

The final treaty of peace and friendship between Argentina and Chile was initialled in Buenos Aires on Oct. 19, 1984.

The treaty contained detailed provisions on maritime demarcation, whereby the dividing line between the two countries' sovereignties over the sea-bed and under the sea-bed in the southern sea was fixed as running from a point at 55°7′0″S and 66°25′0″W to a point at 55°11′0″S and 66°4′7″W (between the coasts of Nueva Island and the large island of Tierra del Fuego); from there to a point at 55°22′0″S and 65°43′6″W, continuing from their along this meridian to parallel 56°22′8″S; from there along that parallel 24 nautical miles south of the outermost point of Hornos Island towards the west until it meets the meridian of that southernmost point at 56°22′8″S and 67°16′0″W; and from this point continuing to the south to a point at 58°21′1″S and 67°16′0″W. The exclusive economic zones (EEZ) of Argentina and Chile were to be located respectively east and west of the above boundary line, with the Chilean EEZ extending south of the final point of the boundary line "as far as international law allows", west of meridian 67°16′0″W and to the east up to the high seas (Article 7).

In the area between Cape Horn and the easternmost point of Staten Island (Isla de los Estados) the jurisdiction of each of the two states in its territorial sea was to be limited to a three-nautical-mile line measured from its base line. Within that area each party might claim before third countries the maximum width of the territorial sea allowed by international law (Article 8).

In the eastern mouth of the Straits of Magellan (between Punta Dungeness in the north and Cape Espiritu Santo in the south) the boundary between the two sovereignties was to be established by a straight line between the "boundary marker at the former Punta Dungeness lighthouse" and "boundary marker I Cape Espiritu Santo". The boundary line was by no means to alter the provisions of an 1881 border treaty which established the Straits of Magellan as neutral in perpetuity with free passage of vessels of all nations (Article 10).

The two parties also agreed to create a permanent binational commission which inter alia would promote the establishment of duty-free ports and zones (Article 12). The treaty further laid down, in an annex, conciliation and arbitration procedures for the solution of any controversy.

In a second annex rules were laid down for navigation between the Straits of Magellan and Argentine ports in the Beagle Channel, requiring Argentine ships to follow a specified route under the guidance of a Chilean pilot, and also to refrain from any activity not directly related to the passage. Generally Argentine ships were to conform to the rules of international law; in particular submarines must sail on the surface, and all ships must navigate with the lights turned on and ensign hoisted.

Rules were also laid down for (i) navigation by Argentine vessels between Argentine ports in the Beagle Channel and Antarctica, and vice versa, or between Argentine ports in the Beagle Channel and the Argentine EEZ adjacent to the maritime boundary between the two countries, and (ii) navigation of Chilean vessels through the Strait of Le Maire (between the eastern end of Tierra del Fuego and Staten Island). Moreover, in the Beagle Channel on both sides of the limit set by meridian 68°36′38.5″W and meridian 66°25′0″W Argentine and Chilean vessels were to have free navigation but third-nation merchant vessels were to exercise the right of passage subject to the rules established in this annex, while third-nation warships headed towards a port of either party in that segment must have previous authorization from the party concerned, which would have to inform the other party of arrivals and departures of such warships.

Argentina–Uruguay

In a joint declaration of Jan. 30, 1961, Argentina and Uruguay defined the exterior limit of the Plate River (Rio de la Plata) as a line joining Punta del Este with Punta Rosa and affirmed this limit as the baseline of the territorial sea, with the regime of the river remaining (as agreed in 1909–10) that of free navigation and use of the waters (with any differences to be removed in a spirit of harmony). The 1961 declaration was reaffirmed in a protocol of Jan. 14, 1964.

Colombia–Nicaragua

There is a dispute concerning sovereignty over the archipelago of San Andrés and Providencia and three cays (Quitasueño, Roncador and Serrano), all situated on the Nicaraguan Rise (an undersea bank between Nicaragua and Jamaica, thought to contain hydrocarbon deposits). All are administered by Colombia as part of its national territory.

The Colombian claim to the islands dates back to a Spanish royal order of 1803 under which the defence of San Andrés and Providencia was delegated to the Vice-royalty of Santa Fé de Bogotá (of which present-day Colombia and Panama were then a part). (Colombia is farther from the islands than Panama, which was part of Colombia until 1903.)

Colombia's sovereignty over San Andrés and Providencia (but not over the three cays) was recognized by Nicaragua in a treaty signed with Colombia on March 24, 1928, and ratified by Nicaragua on March 6, 1930. Under an agreement of April 10, 1928, between Colombia and the United States, which had taken over the cays in 1919, the status quo in respect of the cays was reaffirmed, with Colombia retaining the right to fish around the cays and the United States maintaining navigational aids. In a treaty signed in Bogotá on Sept. 8, 1972, and ratified by the US Senate on July 31, 1981, the United States recognized Colombia's sovereignty over the three cays.

However, the Sandinista Government of Nicaragua decided on Feb. 4, 1980, unilaterally to declare the 1928 treaty to be null and void, claiming that the islands were part of Nicaragua's 200-mile continental shelf over which it had asserted jurisdiction in December 1979. Nicaragua based the delimitation of its territory on a "natural boundaries" principle enshrined in the 1826 Declaration of Independence of the United Provinces of Central America and endorsed in 19th-century Nicaraguan constitutions.

With regard to Colombia's claims, Nicaragua described the 1803 Spanish royal order as purely military and added that a further royal order of 1806 had restored responsibility for the defence of the areas to the Captaincy-General of Guatemala (under which Nicaragua had been administered at the time). Nicaragua also disputed Colombia's assertion that the cays had always been considered, geographically and juridically, to be part of the San Andrés archipelago, and it rejected the 1972 treaty between Colombia and the United States.

In support of its claim Nicaragua has also referred to a number of other treaties, among them a Nicaraguan–Spanish treaty of 1850 in which Spain recognized the independence of Nicaragua and the adjacent islands. It has further pointed out that the Nicaraguan constitution of 1911 stated that the territory of Nicaragua included "the adjacent islands" and that the 1948 constitution also included Nicaragua's continental shelf as being under Nicaraguan jurisdiction.

After Nicaragua's abrogation of the 1928 treaty, the Colombian Government reinforced its military presence in and around San Andrés. The two governments agreed to hold talks (pending which they maintained their original positions), and Colombia referred its case to the UN Conference on the Law of the Sea. In February 1982 Colombia reaffirmed its sovereignty over the disputed islands by "implementing" its 1972 treaty with the United States.

Colombia–Venezuela

The boundary between Colombia and Venezuela—originally based on that between the (1810) Spanish captaincies-general of Venezuela and Granada—was not properly determined until 1932, when the final implementation was achieved of an arbitration award made on March 24, 1922, by the Swiss Federal Council, to which the two countries had in 1916 decided to submit their long-standing dispute for arbitration. Notwithstanding this land border settlement the two countries have in recent years been at issue over the delimitation of their respective sovereignties in the Gulf of Venezuela and the area around the Los Monjes Islands to the north-east of the Goajirá Peninsula.

In connexion with the discovery of oil resources in the area of the Gulf of Venezuela and Lake Maracaibo, a dispute arose in the 1920s on the question of sovereignty over the waters and resources of the Gulf of Venezuela and the area around the islands of Los Monjes. The latter are situated to the north-east of the Goajirá Peninsula and were occupied by Venezuela under the dictatorship of President Pérez Jiménez in 1953–58.

In December 1965 it was alleged in Venezuela that Colombia had granted certain US oil companies concessions for prospecting for oil in Venezuelan territory. The two Governments nevertheless agreed in that year to engage in talks on the "delimitation of marine and submarine areas" between their two countries. In 1968 the Venezuelan Foreign Minister defined his Government's position as follows: "The submarine areas of the Gulf of Venezuela south of the parallel through Castilletes and Punta Salinas [i.e. roughly 12°N] in their entirety form part of Venezuelan territory [and] are in no case the object of negotiations, and therefore we recognize no kind of concessions in this area." In Bogotá it was claimed in April 1973 that the islands of Los Monjes did not have their own continental shelf, and in the same month the talks were broken off by Colombia.

On July 20, 1975, President López Michelsen of Colombia declared that the Gulf of Venezuela was "a historic bay, a condominium of the two riparian states—Colombia and Venezuela". He also quoted a statement which he had made in August 1974, as follows: "Our right to the continental shelf and the waters which cover it is derived from the geographical fact that this bay is not exclusively surrounded by Venezuelan territory." His thesis was, however, utterly rejected in Venezuela.

On Jan. 28, 1976, it was reported that the Colombian Government would not submit its claim regarding the Los Monjes Islands area to the International Court of Justice but was ready to discuss it in direct talks with Venezuela on the delimitation of marine and submarine areas in the Caribbean Sea. At the same time, the Venezuelan Foreign Minister was reported to have stated that Venezuela's sovereignty over the Los Monjes Islands was unquestionable.

The Colombian Foreign Minister disclosed on Nov. 17, 1978, that talks were being held with Venezuela "in a spirit of cordiality and understanding" on the dispute over marine and submarine areas in what he called the Gulf of Maracaibo [i.e. of Venezuela] and added that Colombia rejected the appointment of a tribunal to arbitrate in the dispute. This idea was also rejected by the Venezuelan Foreign Minister during talks held in Bogotá on Dec. 11-13, 1978.

On March 14, 1979, President Luis Herrera Campíns of Venezuela was reported to have appointed a commission to travel to Colombia to resume negotiations on the demarcation in the Gulf of Venezuela. In response to a statement by the Colombian Council of State recognizing Venezuelan sovereignty over the Los Monjes Islands, the Venezuelan Foreign Ministry issued, on March 30, a statement welcoming this announcement as "a positive factor" in the talks but noting that the status of the islands had never been the subject of debate during marine and submarine demarcation talks between the two countries.

The talks were continued until it was announced in a broadcast in Bogotá on Oct. 21, 1980, that agreement had been reached on a draft treaty on the delimitation of marine areas, including "internal waters" and "exclusive economic zones". The draft treaty provided inter alia for the "innocent passage" of all merchant vessels using ports of the two countries and that of their warships and non-commercial state-owned vessels. It reaffirmed that the Los Monjes Islands were part of Venezuela but recognized limited Colombian rights in the Gulf. The delimitation would be "half the median line and half the equidistant line"; the Los Monjes Islands would have a four-mile (and not a 12-mile) territorial waters limit; Colombia would have a four-mile limit along the La Goajirá coast in the Gulf; and the Gulf would be closed to other nations. On the question of oil production the draft treaty laid down (in Article 4) that "if a hydrocarbons field extends to both sides of the boundary line established in this treaty each party will explore and exploit the deposit within its own marine areas and will receive one-half of the hydrocarbons extracted but will also be responsible for one-half of the corresponding cost" and that "those deposits that do not cross the boundary line will be developed unilaterally by the country in which they are found".

The draft treaty was strongly opposed by certain circles in both countries, but particularly in Venezuela (where there was widespread hostility towards Colombians, of whom several hundred thousand had entered Venezuela in search of work in recent years). Those opposing what they called "the ceding of Venezuelan waters to Colombia" included some members of the ruling Christian Social Party (COPEI), leading members of the opposition *Acción Democrática* (but not ex-President Carlos Andrés Pérez, who publicly supported the draft treaty), all left-wing parties and, above all, the armed forces.

President Herrera Campíns had stated after its publication that the treaty would not be signed unless a clear consensus existed on its terms. At the same time the Venezuelan Minister of Energy assured Colombia that Venezuela would not drill for oil in the disputed area until the issue was settled. Further talks between representatives of the two Governments on the boundary issue were suspended in November 1980, and it was only at a meeting of the two countries' Presidents in Venezuela on Oct. 2, 1981, that the possibility of renewed talks on the sea boundary dispute was mentioned, but there was no indication of the terms on which it might eventually be settled.

El Salvador–Honduras–Nicaragua

The Central American Court of Justice ruled in 1917 (in the case of El Salvador versus Nicaragua) that the Gulf of Fonseca belonged to the three states which bordered it (i.e. including Honduras) because the riparian states had "for its political organization and for police purposes" performed acts and enacted laws having to do with the national security, the observance of health and fiscal regulations, and that the Gulf's geographical position and the intense development along its shores made it an "area of vital interest" to the littoral states. The question which remained to be settled was that of the boundary delimitation between the three states.

Puerto Rico–United States

The use of Vieques Island, nine miles east of the (US) Commonwealth of Puerto Rico (of which it is part), as a target practice area by the US Navy has been opposed by the Puerto Rican administration which in 1978 sued the US Navy for a number of violations of environmental regulations. However, the US Supreme Court ruled finally on April 27, 1982, that the navy could not be barred from using the island (most of which was owned by the Federal Government).

Trinidad and Tobago–Venezuela

In a Treaty relating to the Submarine Areas of the Gulf of Paria (between Trinidad and Venezuela) concluded on Feb. 26, 1942, by the United Kingdom (as the colonial power in Trinidad and Tobago) and Venezuela, the two sides agreed to refrain from asserting "any claim to sovereignty or control over the submarine area of the Gulf of Paria" on either side of the agreed demarcation line and adjacent to the territory of the other, and to "recognize any rights to sovereignty or control which have been, or may hereafter be, lawfully acquired (by either party) over the said parts of the submarine areas of the Gulf of Paria". The effect of this treaty was to confer on the coastal states exclusive jurisdiction over the resources of the continental shelf which had previously been part of the sea-bed and subsoil of the high seas.

The treaty came into force on Sept. 22, 1942, and upon achieving its independence in August 1962 Trinidad and Tobago acceeded to the treaty's provisions. However, it was found that the demarcation of the continental shelf boundary as agreed in the text of the treaty did not entirely tally with that shown on an accompanying map. A revised boundary, said to be in accordance with the treaty's text, was based on a 1966 US Navy hydrographic chart. The original line was based on the Venezuelan three-mile territorial sea limit, and it was thought that the difference, which was generally slight, might result from geomorphic changes in Venezuela's coast line. The revision, however, left unresolved the problem of a narrow (2.75 nautical miles long) overlap of claims by the two parties in the Western Channel leading from the gulf of Paria to the Serpent's Mouth (south of the south-eastern end of Trinidad).

Antarctic Ocean

In the seas surrounding the continent of Antarctica large sections (some of them overlapping with each other) have been claimed by various states. However, the question of territorial claims in the Antarctic south of 60° latitude was frozen for 30 years—until 1991—under a treaty which was signed by 12 countries in 1959 and which entered into force in 1961. Seven of the signatories have claims to territory in the Antarctic (Argentina, Australia, Britain, Chile, France, New Zealand, Norway) and the claims of three of these—Argentina, Britain and Chile—overlap. Argentina and Chile have both proclaimed 200-mile limits off their sections of Antarctica.

The Antarctica mainland covers 5,350,000 square miles (13,900,000 sq km) and its ice mass represents about three-quarters of the world's store of fresh water. The area is believed to contain oil, gas, hydrocarbons, iron, coal and other minerals (in quantities not yet ascertained), as well as substantial resources of fish and krill (a protein-rich crustacean which is most dense around the Antarctic Convergence, where the cold waters of the Antarctic meet the warm waters of the southern oceans). The main harvesters of krill in the area are the USSR, Japan, Chile, Norway, Poland, South Korea, East and West Germany and Taiwan.

A number of islands within the Antarctic Convergence are claimed by more than one country. The South Shetlands are claimed by Argentina, Britain and Chile, while the South Sandwich Islands, the South Orkneys, South Georgia Island and Shag Rocks are disputed by Argentina and Britain. The South Shetlands and South Orkneys form part of the British Antarctic Territory, established on March 3, 1962; this territory includes that part of Antarctica lying between 20°W and 80°W longitude stretching south of 60°S to the South Pole, plus the islands, and covers a total land and sea area of about 3,000,000 square miles (7,750,000 sq km) including the Weddell Sea.

Chile claims the same right of sovereignty over its sector and has incorporated the sector into its own regional administration. Part of the Chilean sector is claimed by Ecuador because of the position of the Galapagos Islands (over 500 miles east of the South American continent). The United States and the Soviet Union both emphasized in 1959 that, although they had no specific territorial claims to parts of the Antarctic, they did not relinquish the right to make such claims nor did they necessarily recognize the claims of other powers.

Under the 1959 treaty the region was set aside for peaceful scientific research, all military activities were banned and the region was proclaimed nuclear-free. On territorial claims the treaty laid down (in Article 4) that (i) nothing contained in the treaty shall be interpreted as (*a*) a renunciation by any contracting party of previously asserted rights or of claims to territorial sovereignty in Antarctica, (*b*) a renunciation or diminution by any contracting party of any basis of claim to territorial sovereignty in Antarctica which it may have, whether as a result of its activities or those of its nationals in Antarctica, or otherwise, (*c*) prejudicing the position of any contracting party as regards its recognition or non-recognition of any other state's right of, or claim or basis of claim to, territorial sovereignty in Antarctica; (ii) no acts or activities taking place while the treaty is in force shall constitute a basis for asserting, supporting or denying a claim to territorial sovereignty in Antarctica, or create any rights of sovereignty in Antarctica, and no new claim, or enlargement of any existing claim, to territorial sovereignty in Antarctica shall be asserted while the treaty is in force. [For summary of treaty provisions, see page 225.]

Argentina and Chile stated at the time that, while agreeing to the freezing of territorial claims for 30 years, they did not thereby relinquish claims to the territory included within British Antarctica.

Disputes in African Waters

Guinea–Guinea-Bissau

On Feb. 14, 1985, a three-member arbitral tribunal of the International Court of Justice, consisting of three judges, unanimously made an award delimiting the maritime boundary between Guinea and Guinea-Bissau.

A dispute had arisen between the two countries in January 1978 concerning an overlap of their territorial waters as defined in a convention of May 12, 1886, in which France and Portugal delimited their respective colonies in West Africa. In this convention it was laid down that Portugal would possess all the islands, notably the Bijagos Archipelago, included between the meridian of Cape Roxo (on the boundary between Guinea-Bissau and Senegal), the coast and a southern limit following the line of the thalweg of the Cajet River and subsequently turning south-west to a point at 10°40′N latitude which it followed as far as the meridian of Cape Roxo.

In 1958 Portugal granted an oil concession in the area, and the Portuguese Government thereafter proceeded to define its territorial waters, with the result that an overlap was created with the French territorial waters. On Feb. 18, 1983, Guinea and Guinea-Bissau, as the successor states to France and Portugal respectively, decided to seek arbitration through an arbitral tribunal, and this was established by the International Court of Justice on Oct. 14, 1983.

Guinea-Bissau took the view that the "southern limit" mentioned in the 1886 convention was merely to designate the islands belonging to Portugal, whereas Guinea held that this limit also represented a general maritime boundary. Both parties agreed that the boundary provisions of the convention were to be interpreted in accordance with the 1969 Vienna Convention on the Law of Treaties.

The tribunal found that until 1978 none of the parties to the 1886 convention had interpreted it as having established a maritime boundary, and that neither France nor Portugal had intended to establish a general maritime boundary.

Guinea asked the tribunal to determine the boundary on the principle of an equidistant line, whereas Guinea-Bissau argued in favour of applying the "southern limit" of the 1886 convention, extending it as far as necessary.

On the basis of Article 74 paragraph 1 and Article 83 paragraph 1 of the 1982 UN Convention on the Law of the Sea (although not yet in force), the tribunal sought an equitable solution which would enable each state to control the maritime areas situated in front of its coasts and in proximity to them. It found that the equidistance line would cut off Guinea's maritime area and that, if it were applied seaward of the Guinean island of Alcatraz, it would operate to the detriment of Guinea-Bissau. The tribunal also noted that there were no agreed maritime boundaries (i) between Guinea-Bissau and Senegal (where there was an "ongoing dispute"—see below) and (ii) between Guinea and Sierra Leone (where there was only a unilateral delimitation by Guinea).

The award by the tribunal was therefore based on the overall convex shape of the West African coastline, and it accordingly defined the boundary as following successively (i) Pilots Passage, starting from the mouth of the Cajet River, (ii) the parallel of 10°40′N as far as 12 miles west of Alcatraz, and (iii) the bearing of 236° as far as the outer limit of the maritime territories recognized under general international law.

The tribunal further emphasized that the two parties' economic concerns should motivate them to practise mutually beneficial co-operation with a view to attaining their right to development.

Guinea-Bissau–Senegal

Under a treaty signed in 1960 France and Portugal, then the colonial powers for Senegal and Guinea-Bissau respectively, had delineated their offshore zones in the area. Senegal has accepted the terms of this treaty but Guinea-Bissau has not, on the grounds that the Portuguese Parliament never ratified it.

A dispute arose over the question of whether the land frontier between the two states should be extended seawards from Cape Roxo along the parallel of that cape, or whether the maritime boundary should run along a line perpendicular to the coast (which would give Senegal a greater share of the ocean and its resources).

An oil drilling programme, carried out by the Petro-Canada Assistance Corporation (a subsidiary of Canada's state-controlled Petro-Canada) in an area which Senegal had described as not being in dispute, was suspended in January 1984 after Guinea-Bissau had strongly protested against it. It was later pointed out that, if the disputed area were divided equally between the two states, the site of the Canadian exploration would be in Guinea-Bissau's part of the Atlantic, while another site, successfuly explored between 1958 and 1971 (and known as the Dôme Flore), would be in Senegalese waters.

In early 1984 the dispute reached an acute stage when, as part of a Canadian assistance programme, the Petro-Canada International Assistance Corporation (PCIAC) began to drill for oil in the disputed waters. This drilling was, however, stopped on an order by the Government of Guinea-Bissau issued on Jan. 14, 1984. On March 12, 1985, the Presidents of Guinea-Bissau and Senegal agreed to submit the dispute to an international arbitration panel to sit in Geneva and to reach agreement within a year. They also agreed to "accept the verdict of the tribunal, which will be definite and obligatory for the two states, which will be held to taking all steps necessary to ensure its execution".

Morocco–Saharan Democratic Arab Republic

In 1978–80 the armed conflict between Morocco and the forces of the Saharan Arab Democratic Republic (SADR) spread to the sea off the shore of the Western Sahara.

Control of the Western Sahara had been relinquished by Spain in November 1975 when the territory was partitioned between Morocco and Mauritania (but the latter renounced all claims to Western Saharan territory in August 1979). The Polisario Front, founded in May 1983 as a national liberation movement, took up armed struggle against both Morocco and Mauritania upon Spain's withdrawal.

Spain, on the other hand, agreed under a fisheries treaty signed with Morocco in Rabat on Feb. 17, 1977, that the fishing grounds off the Western Sahara were "under the territorial jurisdiction of Morocco". This treaty was ratified by the Spanish Parliament on Feb. 15 and 23, 1978, but it was not ratified by the Moroccan Parliament. On Feb. 15, 1978, it was denounced by the Polisario Front, which had proclaimed the SADR in February 1976, and which claimed that the fishing grounds off the Western Sahara were a war zone. The SADR also threatened to take military action against Spanish vessels in the area, and its motor boats subsequently harassed fishing vessels in these waters.

After the SADR had seized the crew of a Portuguese fishing boat on June 4, 1980, the Portuguese Government obtained the crew's release by signing, on July 21, an agreement recognizing the Polisario Front as "the sole legitimate representative of the Sahrawi people". A number of Spanish fishermen, seized by the SADR in 1979–80, were also released after Spain had, on Dec. 17, 1980, agreed in effect to recognize the Polisario Front.

The 1977 fisheries treaty between Morocco and Spain was later superseded by new fisheries agreements between the two countries (see page 116).

Arctic Waters

Canada—Soviet Union—United States

In 1970 Canada enacted an Arctic Water Pollution Prevention Act by which it was enabled to control shipping in an ecologically delicate region.

Under an Order-in-Council of Sept. 10, 1985, the Canadian Government established the baselines, effective from Jan. 1, 1986, for a 12-mile territorial sea in the area of the Canadian Arctic archipelago between longitude 60° W in the east and the Beaufort Sea in the west, with all waters enclosed in the baselines being declared Canadian internal waters. (Baselines were also drawn for the limits of Canada's 200-mile fishing zone ond its 100-mile pollution prevention zone.)

This order followed the transit through the North-West Passage, in July 1985, of the US Coastguard's icebreaker *Polar Sea* without a prior US request for Canadian permission—although both governments had agreed that the voyage was "without prejudice to Canadian claims".

Canada had repeatedly claimed the North-West Passage as its internal waters, whereas the United States had regarded it as international waters. On the Canadian side it was argued that the North-West Passage was not an international strait because it had never been used for international navigation, but that, based on the assumption that the waters of the passage were not "internal", it was a legal or territorial strait in which the right of transit or of innocent passage obtained but might be suspended by Canada on security grounds, while Canada might also impose conditions concerning the design, manning and equipment of foreign ships. [See Articles 36, 37, 38(1) and (2) and 45(1)(b) of the 1982 UN Convention on the Law of the Sea, in Appendix 1.]

It was also announced that the Canadian Government had decided to build a 37,000-ton icebreaker (the largest in the world) to operate in the Canadian Arctic.

When announcing the Order-in-Council in the Canadian House of Commons the Minister of External Affairs said inter alia "Soviet submarines are being deployed under the Arctic ice pack, and the United States Navy in turn has identified a need to gain operational experience to counter new Soviet deployments." It was pointed out (in *The Times* of London on Sept. 14, 1985) that Canada had no nuclear submarines and, as far as was known, no underwater sonar devices and no military ground forces to speak of in the north.

The Canadian Minister of External Affairs also said (on Sept. 14) that Canada had to lay claim to the Arctic "now", as the United States and the Federal Republic of Germany were both preparing for commercial navigation in the north, while the Japanese, "with a keen eye to the development of oil and gas flows from polar regions", were working on specialized tankers.

Soviet Union—United States

A controversy arose in 1967 between the two states over a proposal that two US Coastguard icebreakers would circumnavigate the Arctic Ocean to conduct scientific research. Although the US interpretation was that the planned course of the icebreakers was in the high seas, the Soviet Government was officially informed in advance of the project as a matter of courtesy, and on Aug. 24, 1967, the USA notified the USSR Foreign Ministry that it would be necessary for the two vessels to pass through the Volkitsky Straits (between the coast of Siberia and the islands of Severnaya Zemlya or Northland). The Soviet ministry stated in reply that the straits constituted Soviet territorial waters and that passage of the ships through the straits would be a violation of Soviet frontiers. The United States thereupon cancelled the proposed circumnavigation and at the same time propested strongly that there was a right of innocent passage for all ships through straits used for international navigation between two parts of the high seas, whether or not they were overlapped by territorial waters.

7. The Military Dimension of the Sea

This chapter deals generally with the military dimension of man's use of the seaways of the world, focusing in particular on (i) agreements and initiatives on this theme; and (ii) the nature of military tensions currently manifesting themselves in certain maritime areas.

Agreements and Initiatives on Military Use of the Sea

Maritime Laws affecting Warships and the Production, Testing, Deployment and Use of Nuclear Weapons

Under customary law (i.e. for states not parties to the UN Convention on the Law of the Sea), the right of innocent passage through the territorial sea of a coastal state is limited by the provision that states may limit the passage of warships by making it conditional upon prior authorization or notification.

Under international law of warfare a belligerent state is entitled to establish a blockade of the enemy coast but such a blockade must be totally effective, limited to enemy ports, applied against ships of all states and notified in advance to neutral states.

On the other hand the United Nations Charter forbids, in Article 2(4), "the threat or use of force against the territorial integrity or political independence" of any state. However, Article 51 of the UN Charter provides that "nothing in the present Charter shall impair the inherent right of individual or collective self-defence if an armed attack occurs against a member of the United Nations".

Under Chapter VII of the UN Charter the UN Security Council may authorize blockades as Article 41 provides for "measures not involving the use of armed force", including "complete or partial interruption of economic relations and of rail, sea, air, postal, telegraphic, radio and other means of communication, and the severance of diplomatic relations". Under Article 42 the Security Council may "take such action by air, sea or land forces as may be necessary to maintain or restore international peace and security [including] demonstrations, blockades and other operations by air, sea or land forces of members of the United Nations".

Nuclear Test Ban Treaty

The Nuclear Test Ban Treaty concluded between the Soviet Union, the United Kingdom and the United States on Aug. 5, 1963, and banning all nuclear tests except those held underground, specifically lays down, in Article 1(1)(a), that the parties to the treaty undertake "to prohibit, to prevent and not to carry out any nuclear weapon test explosion, or any other nuclear explosion, at any place under its jurisdiction or control: in the atmosphere; beyond its limits, including outer space; or under water, including territorial waters or high seas".

Treaty of Tlatelolco

The Treaty for the Prohibition of Nuclear Weapons in Latin America (Treaty of Tlatelolco), signed on Feb. 14, 1967, by representatives of 21 Latin American states, contains, in Article 1, an undertaking by the contracting parties "to prohibit and prevent in their respective territories (*a*) the testing, use, manufacture, production or acquisition . . . of any nuclear weapons . . . directly or indirectly . . . and (*b*) the receipt, storage, installation and any form of possession of any nuclear weapon . . .". This absolute ban accordingly also applies to the territorial waters of the contracting states.

Treaty on Control of Arms on the Seabed

A Treaty on the Prohibition of the Emplacement of Nuclear Weapons and Other Weapons of Mass Destruction on the Seabed and the Ocean Floor and in the Subsoil Thereof, which had been submitted to the UN General Assembly by the Conference of the Committee on Disarmament, was signed on Feb. 11, 1971, by the Soviet Union, the United Kingdom and the United States. By the time of its entry into force on May 18, 1972, a total of 34 countries had deposited instruments of ratification, while another five had signed the treaty but not yet ratified it. By mid-1985 the treaty had secured 74 ratifications and a further 14 countries had signed but not ratified it.

The parties to the treaty undertook not to place on the sea-bed "any nuclear weapons or any other types of weapons of mass destruction as well as structures, launching installations, or any other facilities specifically designed for storing, testing, or using such weapons".

The treaty implicitly forbids the emplacement of chemical, biological and nuclear weapons and of vehicles carrying or intended to carry weapons of mass destruction—but not of conventional mines—on the sea-bed.

In the coastal zone up to 12 nautical miles the treaty's prohibition applies to all states other than the coastal one, which also retains the right to invite allied states to place weapons of mass destruction on the sea-bed of its territorial sea. (However, this does not apply when a coastal state claims a territorial waters limit of less than three miles from the baselines.) Outside the 12-mile coastal zone the prohibition applies to all states parties to the treaty.

The treaty thus does not prohibit the placing on the sea-bed of submarines, of anti-submarine warfare (ASW) devices and of conventional weapons. Neither does it provide for an adequate method of verification.

ABM and SALT Treaties

In the US-Soviet Treaty on the Limitation of Anti-Ballistic Missile Systems (the ABM Treaty) and the Interim Agreement on Certain Measures with Respect to the Limitation of Strategic Offensive Arms, concluded as a result of the Strategic Arms Limitation Talks (SALT) and in force since Oct. 3, 1972, the two sides have undertaken "not to develop, test or deploy ABM systems which are sea-based, air-based or mobile land-based" (Article V (1) of the ABM Treaty) and "to limit submarine-launched ballistic missile (SLBM) launchers and modern ballistic missile submarines" (Article III of the Interim Agreement).

Under a Protocol to the Interim Agreement, the United States might have up to 44 modern ballistic missile submarines and the Soviet Union up to 62, while the United States would have not more than 710 SLBMs on nuclear-powered submarines and the Soviet Union up to 950.

The Interim Agreement remained in force until Oct. 3, 1977, but both sides formally declared in September 1977 that they would continue to refrain from any action incompatible with the provisions of the Agreement.

Convention on the Prohibition of Military or Any Other Hostile Use of Environmental Modification Techniques

This convention was adopted by the UN General Assembly on Dec. 10, 1976, by 96 votes to eight with 30 abstentions (being approved by all nuclear powers except France, which abstained, and China, which took no part in the vote). Provisions contained in this convention included the following:

"**Art. I.** (1) Each state party to this Convention undertakes not to engage in military or any other hostile use of environmental modification techniques having widespread, long-lasting or severe effects as the means of destruction, damage or injury to any other state party.

"(2) Each state party to this Convention undertakes not to assist, encourage or induce any other state, group of states or international organization to engage in activities contrary to the provisions of paragraph 1 of this article.

"**Art. II.** As used in Article I, the term 'environmental modification techniques' refers to any technique for changing—through the deliberate manipulation of natural processes—the dynamics, composition or structure of the earth, including its biota, lithosphere, hydrosphere and atmosphere, or of outer space.

"**Art. III.** (1) The provisions of this Convention shall not hinder the use of environmental modification techniques for peaceful purposes and shall be without prejudice to generally recognized principles and applicable rules of international law concerning such use. . . ."

The convention was to be of unlimited duration, but its operation was to be reviewed by a conference of the states parties to the convention to be convened five years after its entry into force—which would take place upon the deposit of instruments of ratification by 20 governments.

The convention came into force on Oct. 5, 1978, the 20 countries which had ratified it by then comprising mainly communist states but also Cyprus, Denmark, Sri Lanka, Tunisia, Finland, Britain, Ghana and Spain.

Treaty of Rarotonga

The Treaty of Rarotonga, proposed by Australia in 1984 and signed on Aug. 6, 1985, by Australia, the Cook Islands, Fiji, Kiribati, New Zealand, Niue, Tuvalu and Western Samoa, declared a nuclear-free zone covering most of the Pacific Ocean south of the equator, where ownership, use, the stationing or testing of nuclear devices and the dumping of nuclear waste were prohibited. However, it was left to individual governments to set their own policy on calls by nuclear-capable ships and aircraft. The treaty had earlier on the same day been endorsed by all 13 member governments of the South Pacific Forum.

Calls for Nuclear-Free Oceans

Calls for the establishment of nuclear-weapons-free oceans have been made by the UN General Assembly and other bodies as described below.

Indian Ocean

Under a declaration adopted by the UN General Assembly on Dec. 16, 1971, by 61 votes to none with 55 abstentions, the Indian Ocean, together with the airspace above it and the ocean floor below it, was "designated for all time as a zone of peace", from which the great powers were asked to eliminate "all bases, military installations, logistical supply facilities, disposition of nuclear weapons and weapons of mass destruction". A further resolution, urging all states to accept the above resolution, was adopted by the Assembly on Dec. 6, 1973, by 95 votes to none with 35 abstentions (including France, the Soviet Union, the United Kingdom and the United States—i.e. four of the five permanent members of the UN Security Council).

In another resolution, adopted by the Assembly without a vote on Dec. 20, 1983, it was proposed that a conference on the question should be held in Colombo in 1985.

Pacific Ocean

The idea of a nuclear-free zone in the Pacific Ocean was first endorsed by the UN General Assembly under a resolution adopted on Dec. 11, 1975, by 110 votes to none with 20 abstentions.

The call for a nuclear-free zone in the South Pacific was also taken up by the South Pacific Forum (SPF), founded in 1971 and embracing Australia, the Cook Islands, Fiji, Kiribati, Nauru, New Zealand, Niue, Papua New Guinea, the Solomon Islands, Tonga, Tuvalu, Vanuatu and Western Samoa (with the Federated States of Melanesia as observer).

In 1976 the SPF called for the banning of land-based nuclear weapons from the region. An SPF conference held on Aug. 27-28, 1984, decided to work for the establishment of a nuclear-weapon-free zone in the South Pacific by a treaty which would give individual states the option of allowing access to their waters or ports by nuclear-powered or nuclear-armed vessels. (Australia favoured free passage for such vessels on the high seas and in the territorial waters of countries which so wished.)

The SPF has also consistently opposed the continued French underground testing of nuclear weapons at the atolls of Mururoa and Fangataufa (French Polynesia), where the French nuclear research agency (Centre d'Expérimentation du Pacifique, CEP) has conducted more than 100 such test explosions since 1966.

At its conference held on Aug. 28-29, 1983, the SPF reaffirmed its total opposition to the French nuclear test but it did not support an Australian proposal to declare the South Pacific region a nuclear-free zone. (The Australian Labor Government had announced on June 9, 1983, that it would suspend Australian uranium shipments to France in an effort to exert pressure on the French Government to call off the tests.)

The authorities of several Pacific islands have taken anti-nuclear measures, notably (i) the Republic of Belau, which declared in its constitution of July 1980 that its territory was a nuclear-free zone (although an agreement of July 1, 1983, between Belau and the United States referred only to a ban on the entry of nuclear substances "intended for use in warfare"), (ii) Fiji, which temporarily banned nuclear vessels from its waters in 1982–83, (iii) Pohnpei (Ponape, one of the four Federated States of Melanesia), which banned the entry of nuclear material under its 1984 constitution; and (iv) the Solomon Islands, which early in 1984 prohibited the entry of nuclear vessels and nuclear-armed aircraft into its waters or airspace.

The Labour Party Government which came to power in New Zealand in July

1984 reaffirmed the country's commitment to the 1951 Pacific Security Treaty between Australia, New Zealand and the United States (the ANZUS Pact), the scope of which had been expanded in 1982 (by setting out procedures for providing New Zealand with logistic support in the case of an emergency), although the Labour Party's election manifesto had contained the proposal to ban the entry of nuclear-powered or nuclear-armed ships into New Zealand waters. (The US Secretary of State said on July 17, 1984, that no presence of such vessels in New Zealand waters was envisaged in that year.)

Demilitarized Zones

The Aaland Islands

The Aaland Islands, situated at the entrance to the Gulf of Bothnia (between Finland and Sweden) and an autonomous part of Finland, enjoyed a status of demilitarization and neutralization under a London Convention of Oct. 20, 1921, until they were temporarily fortified by the Finnish Government from December 1939 until October 1940. The peace treaty concluded with the Allied powers (including the Soviet Union) on Feb. 10, 1947, and in force from Sept. 16, 1947, laid down that the Aaland Islands would remain demilitarized as part of Finland.

Antarctica

Antarctica has remained demilitarized under the 30-year Antarctic Treaty signed on Dec. 1, 1959, in Washington at the end of a 12-nation conference on peaceful international scientific co-operation in Antarctica. The 12 original signatories were Argentina, Australia, Belgium, Britain, Chile, France, Japan, New Zealand, Norway, South Africa, the Soviet Union and the United States, who have subsequently been joined by Brazil, Czechoslovakia, Denmark, the German Democratic Republic, the Federal Republic of Germany, the Netherlands, Poland (as a consultative member) and Romania. The treaty came into force on June 23, 1961. [See also the section on Antarctica under Maritime Boundary Disputes on pages 216–17.] Its main provisions were as follows:

Art. 1. Antarctica shall be used for peaceful purposes only. The contracting parties are forbidden to establish military bases in the area, to carry out military manoeuvres, or to test any kind of weapons.

Art. 2. Freedom of scientific investigation and co-operation towards that end should be maintained.

Art. 3. Scientific information and personnel should be exchanged by the contracting parties.

Art. 4. Nothing contained in the treaty may be interpreted as a renunciation, denial or support of a claim to territorial sovereignty in Antarctica. No new claim to territorial sovereignty may be asserted while the treaty is in force.

Art. 5. Any nuclear explosions in Antarctica and the disposal there of radioactive waste shall be prohibited.

Art. 6. The provisions of the treaty apply to the land area south of 60 degrees South latitude.

Art. 7. Each contracting party has the right to send observers to carry out inspections in Antarctica. Notification must be given of all expeditions and stations in Antarctica.

Art. 8. Observers and scientific personnel in Antarctica are subject to the jurisdiction of their own country.

Art. 9. The contracting parties shall meet at suitable intervals to consult together on measures for the furtherance of the principles and objectives of the treaty.

Maritime Areas of Military Tension

Introduction

There are over 60 states with navies of sea-going ships with modern weapons systems equipment, and 12 or more others with patrol craft with defensive powers.

In the 1890s the basic elements of sea power were analysed as consisting of a fighting fleet, a trading fleet and bases. These elements were later expanded by adding geographical circumstances, financial and economic elements, political will and "elements of a moral nature" such as aptitude, character and courage.

Maritime forces can perform different functions, notably (i) strategic deterrence; (ii) formal combat at sea; (iii) the projection of power ashore (e.g. amphibious landings, bombardment by sea or seaborne aircraft, and missile strikes); (iv) control of the use of the sea (e.g. convoy protection and anti-submarine patrols); (v) support of diplomatic objectives; and (vi) surveillance and intelligence gathering. It has been recognized that, to produce a decisive outcome to a major conflict, seapower has to be joined to land-power.[1]

The military use of the oceans took on a new dimension from about 1900 when efficient submarines were first built. Mines moored to the sea-bed were used in the Russo-Japanese War of 1904–05 and in World War I. Work on the use of sound to locate submarines led to the eventual development of sonar (sound navigation and ranging, i.e. detecting sound under water).

The possibility of conducting warfare from the sea-bed has been investigated by the US Navy. In 1964 it started Sealab I experiments with four men living at a depth of 58.8 metres for nine days. This was followed by Sealab II stationed off the coast of California at a depth of 62.5 metres, with 28 divers taking part in three 15-day tours, one of them for 30 consecutive days, in a cylindrical tank 17.4 metres long and 3.6 metres in diameter, and with free access to the sea.

[1] See Peter Nailor, *The Contemporary Use of Maritime Power*, quoted in Barston, R.P., & Birnie, Patricia, *The Maritime Dimension* (George Allen & Unwin, London 1980).

North Atlantic Ocean

The maritime area of tension of overriding importance since 1949 has been the North Atlantic Ocean, where the naval and air forces of the North Atlantic Treaty Organization (NATO) and those of the Warsaw Treaty Organization have been in mutual confrontation. While there have been varying views on the relative military strength of the two sides and of the two super-powers (the United States and the Soviet Union), there has in fact been a state of mutual deterrence under which an outbreak of open hostilities has been avoided.

North Atlantic Treaty Organization

The North Atlantic Treaty, setting up the North Atlantic Treaty Organization (NATO), was signed on April 4, 1949. By 1959 it had 15 members—Belgium, Canada, Denmark, France, the Federal Republic of Germany, Greece, Iceland, Italy, Luxembourg, the Netherlands, Norway, Portugal, Turkey, the United Kingdom and the United States, and it was joined by Spain in 1982. France withdrew from NATO's integrated military structure in 1966–67, and Greek participation in that structure, interrupted in 1974–80 because of the Turkish invasion of Cyprus, has again been frozen since late 1981.

NATO's highest military authority is its Military Committee, which has among its military agencies several of special relevance to naval warfare, such as the Allied Naval Communications Agency (ANCA) located in London, the Allied Radio Frequency Agency (ARFA) located in Brussels, the Allied Technical Communications Agency (ATCA), inter alia for liaison with ANCA, and located in Brussels, the NATO Electronic Warfare Advisory Committee (NEWAC) located also in Brussels, and the SACLANT Anti-Submarine Warfare Research Centre at La Spezia (Italy). In 1950 the NATO Council decided to create a North Atlantic Planning Board for Ocean Shipping. [For NATO's military structure, see table on page 170 of *Treaties and Alliances of the World*, 3rd edition, published in this series in 1981.]

NATO Naval Bases. Naval bases in the NATO area (the Atlantic north of the Tropic of Cancer, the North Sea and the Mediterranean Sea) include the following:

In Greenland: Grönnedal, Thule
In Iceland: Keflavik
In the Faroes: Thorshavn
In Norway: Tromsö, Harstad, Bergen, Horten
In Denmark: Frederikshavn, Copenhagen
In West Germany: Kiel
In Scotland: Faslane, Holy Loch, Rosyth
In England: Chatham, Portsmouth, Portland, Devonport
In Portugal: Lisbon, Lajes (Terceira, Azores)
In Spain: Rota
In Italy: Venice, La Spezia, Ancona, Naples, Messina, Cagliari, Augusta, Brindisi and Taranto
In Cyprus: Akrotiri and Dhekelia (British Sovereign Base Area)
In Turkey: Istanbul and Gölcük
In Greece: Salamis
In Canada: Argentia (Newfoundland) and Halifax (Nova Scotia)
In the United States: Brunswick (Maine), Boston (Mass.), Newport (New Hampshire), New London (Conn.), New York, Philadelphia, Norfolk (Virginia), Charleston (South Carolina), Brunswick (Georgia), Mayport/Jacksonville (Florida)
Gibraltar and *Bermuda* also accommodate NATO naval bases.

US Caribbean Bases. Guantãnamo Bay (Cuba), Roosevelt Roads (US Virgin Islands)

US Pacific Bases. Whidley Island and Bangor (Washington State), Treasure Island, Long Beach, San Diego, Colorado (California), Hawaii, Apra (Guam), Subic Bay (Philippines)

Other Bases. Canada has a Pacific Ocean base at Esquimalt (British Columbia), the United Kingdom a base on Ascension Island in the South Atlantic and France a base in Djibouti (Horn of Africa). (Bases in metropolitan France are outside the NATO military structure.)

Warsaw Treaty Organization

In response to the creation of NATO, the Warsaw Treaty Organization was set up under a Treaty of Friendship, Co-operation and Mutual Assistance signed in Warsaw on May 14, 1955, by Albania, Bulgaria, Czechoslovakia, the German Democratic Republic, Hungary, Poland, Romania and the Soviet Union. After 1961 Albania took no part in the organization's activities, and it withdrew from the organization on Sept. 11, 1968.

According to the (US) Soviet Military Powers Survey of the US Defence Department (second edition, 1983), the Soviet Navy has two missions, namely (i) to protect the seaward approaches to the USSR and its allies, and (ii) to destroy NATO naval forces which could threaten Soviet military operations. (The Soviet Navy operates in four fleets—the Baltic Fleet, the Black

Sea Fleet, the Northern Fleet and the Pacific Fleet.)

According to *The Military Balance, 1982–83*, published by the International Institute of Strategic Studies in London in 1982, the Soviet Union then had naval airpower consisting of 750 combat aircraft and 300 helicopters; 480 minor surface ships (corvettes, fast attack-craft, minelayers, minesweepers and amphibious vessels); submersibles embracing 168 diesel-powered attack submarines, 105 nuclear-powered attack submarines, 62 strategic nuclear submarines; three V/STOL aircraft carriers; two helicopter carriers; 33 cruisers (one of them nuclear-powered and 27 armed with missiles); 70 destroyers (42 of them armed with missiles); and 183 frigates (77 of them armed with missiles).

The most modern aircraft under construction for the Soviet Naval Air Force was the supersonic variable-geometry-wing *Backfire* capable of carrying air-to-surface anti-ship cruise missiles with speeds of about three times the speed of sound. The biggest Soviet warship was the aircraft carrier *Kiev*. The Typhoon strategic nuclear submarine displaced about 25,000 tons when submerged.

In the area off the Norwegian coast both NATO and Warsaw Pact naval forces have repeatedly carried out exercises involving the simulation of a situation of armed conflict. In response to "Exercise Teamwork" held by NATO forces in March 1984, the Warsaw Pact naval forces (in the main the Soviet northern, Baltic and Black Sea fleets) held an exercise in July 1985 involving the aircraft carrier *Kiev* (of some 43,000 tons), a Kirov-class nuclear-powered battle cruiser and eight or nine escort ships, all from the Soviet Northern fleet, meeting up with forces from the Baltic and Black Sea fleets, including submarines and 11 Badger bombers, simulating a NATO attack (said to have led to the "sinking" of the *Kiev* and the battle cruiser).

A Soviet-US Agreement on Prevention of Incidents at Sea, signed on May 26, 1982, was designed to reduce the danger arising from the practice of shadowing each other's vessels.

A declaration issued at a Warsaw Treaty Organization summit meeting held in Prague on Jan. 4-5, 1983, contained inter alia the suggestion that the Mediterranean Sea should be barred to all ships carrying nuclear weapons (and that the north of Europe, the Balkans and the Indian Ocean would be declared "zones of peace and co-operation").

The declaration also contained a proposal for the conclusion of a treaty on the mutual non-use of force by the member states of both NATO and the Warsaw Pact, including "the commitment of the member states of both alliances not to jeopardize the safety of the international sea, air and space communications passing through areas outside any national jurisdiction".

Soviet Naval Bases. The Soviet Navy has the use of the following bases:

In the Arctic: Motovskiy Goliy, Severomorsk, Murmansk, Polyarnyy, Arkhangelsk, Severodvinsk

On the Baltic Sea: Kronstadt, Tallinn, Riga, Liepala, Korsor Baltiysk

On the Black Sea: Poti, Tuapse, Balaclava, Sebastopol, Odessa

In the Middle East: Aden, Dahlak (Ethiopia), Socotra

In the Far East: Vladivostok, Sovetskaya Gavan, Magadan, Petropavlovsk and Adak (Kuriles)

In Vietnam: Da Nang, Cam Ranh Bay

Comparative Naval Strengths of NATO and Warsaw Pact

In a booklet entitled *Whence the Threat to Peace?* and issued by the USSR Ministry of Defence in January 1981 it was claimed that the United States had 1,500 military bases in 32 countries around the world, with more than 500,000 US servicemen stationed on them. It was also asserted in the booklet that the United States had never lagged behind the Soviet Union in armaments and that its rearmament on the pretext of achieving parity with the Soviet Union was in fact "a drive for military superiority".

It was stated in particular that while the Soviet Navy had improved its technical and combat capability the Western countries had 25 aircraft carriers and "air-capable ships", whereas the Soviet Union had only two, designed principally for anti-submarine warfare; that while the Warsaw Pact nations had more small surface ships with a limited cruising range NATO countries had "almost three times as many battleships, cruisers, destroyers and missile frigates"; that the Warsaw Pact nations had an advantage in the number of submarines (385 compared to NATO's 279) and a substantial advantage in the number of minesweepers; and that NATO had 3,173 sea-based combat planes and helicopters (compared with the Warsaw Pact's 1,126).

In a second edition of *Whence the Threat to Peace?* published in 1983 it was maintained that the US naval forces not only had a special role in war but were also an "instrument for demonstrating force and direct military intervention", for which they had fleets operating in the Pacific Ocean, the Atlantic Ocea, the Mediterranean and the Indian Ocean.

These forces were said to consist of about 1,350 combat aircraft (with 12 attack carrier wings), 220 helicopters, surface vessels comprising 79 frigates (24 of them armed with missiles), 27 cruisers (all of them armed with missiles and nine of them nuclear-powered) and 14 aircraft carriers (all armed with missiles and four of them nuclear-powered); submersibles including 33 strategic nuclear submarines, 85 nuclear-powered attack submarines and five diesel-powered attack submarines (armed with missiles); as well as an unspecified number of missile-carrying hydrofoils and minesweepers. The biggest US warships were said to be the 94,100-ton Nimitz-class aircraft carriers, while the US Trident submarine displaced about 18,700 tons when submerged.

The regional distribution around Europe of the two sides' naval forces in 1985 (excluding NATO countries outside the organizations military structure) was as follows:

	NATO	Warsaw Pact
	North America	North Sea
Surface ships	106	80
Submarines	50	147
Aircraft	500	400
	Northern Europe	Baltic Sea
Surface ships	120	60
Submarines	80	30
Aircraft	600	300
	Southern Europe	Black Sea
Surface ships	70	80
Submarines	30	40
Aircraft	450	400

The NATO naval forces have a numerical advantage in all categories of major surface combatant vessels, this superiority being greatest in the category of aircraft and helicopter carriers and also in frigates. The Warsaw Pact navies are numerically superior in light vessels (corvettes and fast patrol boats) and in mine-warfare forces, and they have about 100 more submarines than NATO. Of modern submarines carrying ballistic missiles NATO has 42 (against 62 of the Warsaw Pact, of which only about 15 per cent are out of port, compared with 50 per cent of the NATO submarines). The technological trend is in favour of the development of fast patrol boats and hydrofoils becoming heavily-armed multi-purpose warships at a cost greatly below that of larger ships.

Significance of Submarines

The development of nuclear-powered strategic ballistic submarines (SSBNs) has enabled submarine warfare to be carried out over a wide area as SSBNs have a range of up to 6,000 nautical miles, can stay below the surface for long periods and can traverse the Arctic area below the ice. Most importantly, they can deliver nuclear missiles with great accuracy from below the surface. They have been regarded as an effective nuclear deterrent—a role which they may not retain for ever.

To counter the threat of the SSBNs both NATO and the Warsaw Pact countries have developed anti-submarine warfare (ASW) and detection forces, including hunter-killer submarines and recording devices. The latter may include intelligence-gathering surface ships, submarines, aircraft and helicopters, and the use of sound surveillance systems (SOSUS), for which sonar buoys may be placed on the sea-bed or moored to it; monitoring may also be carried out by means of satellites.

The principal area monitored by NATO is the North East Atlantic between the coasts of Norway, Svalbard, Greenland, Iceland and the United Kingdom—i.e. the ocean area forming the access to the Atlantic for naval forces of the Soviet Union's northern fleet based on Murmansk. This area is monitored continuously, and the information gained by NATO is co-ordinated at Northwood (United Kingdom) and the US Navy Anti-Submarine Warfare Centre Command and Control System (ASWCCCS) at Norfolk, Virginia.

The Warsaw Pact side was said to have established three anti-submarine barriers—(i) between Iceland, the United Kingdom and Norway, (ii) between Norway and the waters north of Iceland and (iii) off the North Cape towards Svalbard.

Baltic Sea

Sweden's foreign policy is founded on the principle of "non-adherence to alliances in peacetime, aiming at neutrality in case of war". Against this background, the Swedish authorities have made great efforts to protect the country's territorial waters from intrusions of potentially hostile ships, and since 1980 Sweden has greatly expanded and modernized its defence forces.

By 1980 the Swedish Navy was reported to have recorded an annual average of about 10 infringements of Sweden's territorial waters limit by submarines of different nationalities. On Sept. 29, 1980, the Swedish Minister of Defence referred to "the most serious violation of Swedish territorial waters since the end of World War II" caused by the presence of an unidentified foreign submarine in a high-security area of the Stockholm archipelago. A search for this submarine was, however, abandoned by Oct. 8.

On Oct. 27-28, 1981, a Soviet submarine ran aground inside a Swedish restricted military area near the naval base at Karlskrona (southern Sweden). The Swedish Government alleged that the submarine had been engaged in illegal reconnaissance or minelaying work and that there was good reason to believe that the submarine had been carrying nuclear weapons; on Oct. 29 the Swedes towed away a Soviet tug and an unidentified submarine, both of them apparently trying to contact the stranded submarine.

After making strong protests to the Soviet Union and claiming that the latter had not denied that the submarine had been nuclear-armed, Sweden released it on Nov. 6. On the same day the Swedish Government also expressed the view that previously-made Soviet proposals to turn the Baltic into a "sea of peace" through the prohibition of nuclear weapons in the area were "no longer credible". (On May 6, 1982, the Soviet Union was reported to have agreed to reimburse Sweden's costs arising out of the incident to the value of some $212,000.)

Unidentified submarines were again detected in Swedish territorial waters between Nov. 12, 1981, and March 22, 1982. Sightings and suspected detections of further unidentified submarines involved eight such cases in the three months from July to September 1982. Under a law adopted on June 17, 1982, and in force since July 1, 1983, the Swedish armed forces are authorized to use all necessary force to bring to the surface for identification purposes and for detention any unknown submarines in Swedish territorial waters; the Navy is empowered to escort such submarines to a safe anchorage and to board them if they are believed to be carrying nuclear arms.

On Oct. 1, 1982, the Swedish Navy and Air Force launched a major search operation for an unidentified submarine sighted in Swedish territorial waters near the Muskö naval base (about 40 miles south of Stockholm), but the search was called off on Oct. 26.

In an official report published on April 26, 1983, it was stated that 40 incidents had been recorded in 1982 (against only four in 1981), and that in the October 1982 incident six alien submarines had probably been involved, including three Soviet midget submarines of a previously unknown type which could crawl along the seabed by means of caterpillar tracks.

On April 28, 1983, the Swedish Navy began a search for two suspected Soviet midget submarines off the Swedish coast near Sundsvall (250 miles north of Stockholm) but the search was called off on May 10. (Unsuccessful searches for suspected submarines were also made in Norway—on April 27, 1983, in the Hardangerfjord and on May 2 in the Selbjoernsfjord, some 30 miles south of Bergen.)

The Soviet Union has repeatedly denied any involvement in such incidents and has rejected the Swedish allegations as unfounded.

Bosphorus and Dardanelles

The use by naval warships of the Bosphorus and Dardanelles straits linking the Black Sea with the Mediterranean has been a delicate international issue for well over a century.

A conference held in Montreux (Switzerland) from June 22 to July 20, 1936, by delegates from Bulgaria, France, Greece, Italy, Japan, Romania, the Soviet Union, Turkey, the United Kingdom and Yugoslavia agreed to replace the 1923 Straits Convention (part of the peace treaty signed with Turkey at Lausanne on July 24, 1923) by a new convention.

The 1923 convention had provided for freedom of transit and navigation by sea and air in the Bosphorus and the Dardanelles; for the demilitarization of both shores of the straits, the Sea of Marmara and certain islands in the Aegean Sea; and for the establishment in Constantinople (now Istanbul) of an international commission to supervise the implementation of the convention. The 1936 convention essentially restored Turkish sovereignty over the straits area by ending their demilitarization and transferring the duties of the international commission to the Turkish Government. Its principal provisions are as follows:

If Turkey considers itself menaced by a danger of war the straits shall remain open to merchant vessels except that entry must be made by day and the route indicated by the Turkish authorities must be followed (Art. 2). (Traffic schemes have been in force since May 1, 1982.) In time of peace light surface craft (whether those of a Black Sea power or not) have complete freedom of passage through the straits (Art. 10).

Black Sea powers may send their vessels through the straits even if their tonnage is in excess of 15,000 tons, provided the vessels make the passage singly and are escorted by no more than two torpedo boats (Art. 11). The Black Sea powers have the right to send through the straits submarines constructed or purchased at some port not on the Black Sea provided satisfactory notice is given to the Turkish Government. Submarines must pass by day and on the surface.

At least eight days' notice, and for non-Black Sea powers preferably 15 days' notice, must be given to the Turkish Government prior to the passage of warships through the straits. The maximum tonnage for all non-Turkish naval forces in transit must not exceed 15,000 tons (except under the conditions laid down in Art. 11—see above). Courtesy visits of non-Turkish warships made by invitation of the Turkish Government are exempt from the provisions of the convention. Limitations on the tonnage of warships of non-Black Sea powers within the Black Sea in times of peace are: (1) a total of 30,000 tons and (ii) 45,000 tons if the strongest Black Sea fleet should at any time exceed by at least 10,000 tons the strength of the strongest fleet present in the Black Sea on the date of signature of the convention.

If, however, "for humanitarian reasons", several non-Black Sea powers should desire to despatch naval forces, they may be admitted to the Black Sea, but their tonnage is in no case to exceed 8,000. The permission will be extended by the Turkish Government as expeditiously as possible after consultation with the other Black Sea powers. If the authority is granted the maximum delay incurred shall be 48 hours.

In time of war, Turkey not being a belligerent, warships will have complete liberty of passage and of navigation in the straits under the limitations above mentioned (limit of 30,000 tons, prior authority and passage by day).

Nevertheless, warships of any belligerent power shall be accorded passage through the straits only if acting under obligations devolving from the League of Nations Covenant or "in the event of assistance being given to a state which is the victim of aggression in virtue of a mutual assistance pact to which Turkey is a party and concluded within the framework of the League of Nations Covenant." (For the purposes of the convention, the League of Nations Covenant has been superseded by the UN Charter.)

Belligerent warships may not have rights of search or capture or perform hostile acts within the straits.

In time of war, Turkey being a belligerent, the passage of warships through the straits is left entirely to the discretion of the Turkish Government.

If Turkey considers herself menaced by "an imminent danger of war" she may use her discretion regarding permitting the passage of warships, that is to say, she may close the straits as in time of war.

Civil aircraft have the right of passage from the Mediterranean to the Black Sea along a route outside the prohibited zones and prescribed by the Turkish Government. Warning, but no prior authority, is necessary. Unmolested passage of civil aircraft from Europe to Asia is, notwithstanding remilitarization of the straits, accorded by Turkey. This air passage is effected through a prescribed corridor, but prior authority is necessary from the Turkish Government.

Although the convention provided, in paragraph 3 of Article 28, that it would remain in force for 20 years, it was also laid down in that article that it would continue to be in force only until two years after a contracting party had given notice of denunciation of the convention "two years prior to the expiry of the said period of 20 years". No such notice has been given, and the convention is therefore still in force, the parties to it being Australia, Belgium, France, Greece, Japan, Romania, the Soviet Union, Turkey, the United Kingdom and Yugoslavia.

In 1976 the passage through the straits of the Soviet vessel *Kiev*—described by the Soviets as a "large anti-submarine cruiser" and in the West as an "aircraft carrier"—raised some doubts as to the legality of the vessel's passage in terms of the convention. A Soviet commentator took the view (in *Morski Sbornik* of July 1976) that "a thorough analysis of the convention shows . . . from a legal point of view that passage through the straits by any ships of states of the Black Sea does not contradict the letter and the spirit of the convention". A British expert (Professor Col. G. I. A. D. Draper) pointed out in a letter to *The Times* dated Sept. 22, 1984, that the intention of the framers of the convention with regard to the passage of aircraft carriers was not clear; that advances in naval design and armament made "a nonsense of the categories of warships afforded by the Montreux Convention"; and that Turkey, in spite of her NATO membership, was "in no position to respond to NATO requests to decline permission to Soviet requests for passage of aircraft carriers through the straits".

Eastern Mediterranean Sea

In the Arab–Israeli conflict both the Soviet Union and the United States have repeatedly displayed their sea power in the Eastern Mediterranean—the Soviet Union to cover its supply of equipment and personnel to Arab states, notably to Syria, and the United States to defend Israel and its own interests in the Middle East.

The most serious confrontation between Soviet and US naval forces took place in October 1973, when a US fleet, including three aircraft carriers, was arrayed along an air route used by the Soviet Union to send supplies to Syria and Lebanon; at the same time, units of the US Sixth Fleet had been assembled in the north-eastern Indian Ocean, while the Soviet Union displayed anti-carrier and other surface vessels against the US ships in the Mediterranean as well as patrol boats along the coasts of Syria and Egypt. The situation was eventually defused by a ceasefire which became operative on Oct. 25, but intelligence-gathering ships remained in the area.

Under a strategic co-operation agreement concluded on Nov. 29, 1983, the United States and Israel agreed to give "priority attention to the threat to mutual interests by increased Soviet involvement in the Middle East" and to set up a "joint political-military group" to establish "ways to enhance US–Israeli co-operation". Under this agreement a joint Israeli–US naval exercise involving the transfer of simulated casualties from US ships to Israeli hospitals was held on June 20, 1984.

After the Government of Lebanon had, on Aug. 16, 1983, defined Lebanon's territorial waters limit as 12 nautical miles from the coast, it decided on Oct. 21, 1984, that as from Nov. 3 of that year ships within Lebanese territory would be prohibited from proceeding to illegal ports and forced to proceed to any of three legal ports—Beirut, Tripoli and Juniyah; that ships anchored near illegal ports or outside the area of legal ports would be impounded; and that those which did not comply with instructions given by government patrols would be destroyed.

Gulf of Sirte

Since 1973 Libya has regarded the whole of the Gulf of Sirte (Sidra), covering about 3,000 square miles, as Libya's territorial waters. In addition, it later declared a 12-mile territorial waters limit along the rest of Libya's coast and also north of a straight line (at 32°30'N) drawn across the mouth of the Gulf.

The United States has refused to recognize Libya's claim to the Gulf, and in 1979 the Carter Administration reaffirmed during the Third UN Conference on the Law of the Sea that the United States would not recognize any country's claim to jurisdiction over territorial waters and airspace beyond a three-mile limit. However, it was disclosed on Aug. 19, 1981, that in 1980 President Carter had given orders to the US armed forces not to penetrate beyond three miles north of the 32°30'N line in order not to exacerbate a crisis which had arisen between the United States and Iran (over the taking of US hostages by the latter).

On that day (Aug. 19, 1981) it was announced in the United States that there had been an incident in a "previously announced routine exercise in international airspace over international waters in the south-central Mediterranean", where two (Soviet-built) Libyan Su-21 jet fighters had been shot down by US F-14 jet fighters. A US protest against an alleged "unprovoked attack" by Libyan aircraft was rejected by Libya's authorities, and a Libyan military spokesman claimed on the same day inter alia that the US Air Force had been carrying out "intensive, continuous and provocative violations of our airspace and territorial waters in the Gulf of Sirte". A Libyan protest (rejected by the United States) described the incident as "part of an international terrorist campaign orchestrated by Washington against Libya" and "a flagrant and overt violation of all international laws".

President Ronald Reagan said on Aug. 20, 1981, that he had personally ordered the US Navy to challenge Libya's claim to the Gulf of Sirte and to conduct manoeuvres in the disputed waters in order to show that "America has the muscle to back up its words". However, he insisted that the US military action was not provocative but defensive. He added that the United States had "some time ago" been "faced with the knowledge that we could not go on recognizing this violation of international waters and that we were going to plan our manoeuvres as we would have planned them without that rule, without [the Libyan] artificial line".

It was also reported at the time that during manoeuvres held in the region in September 1980 two previous incidents had taken place (though without any aircraft being hit).

Persian (Arabian) Gulf

In the Iran–Iraq war, which broke out in September 1980, one of Iraq's war aims was to achieve the withdrawal of Iran from the islands of Abu Musa, Greater Tunb and Lesser Tunb (at the western end of the Strait of Hormuz) which Iranian forces had occupied on Nov. 30, 1971, and over which the Government of the United Arab Emirates has claimed full sovereignty [see also page 200].

On Sept. 19, 1980, it was reported that President Anwar Sadat of Egypt (i) had suggested that a joint Egyptian–Saudi Arabian naval force should police the Gulf, and (ii) had granted the United States permission to set up a base at Ras Bana (on the Red Sea, opposite the Saudi Arabian coast) as a third US base (in addition to those west of Cairo and at Qena, 400 miles south of the capital). A request by President Sadat to provide the United States with military facilities at Egyptian airfields and harbours was approved by a congress of the ruling National Democratic Party on Oct. 1, 1980.

The United States had, in 1979, decided to expand its naval forces in the Indian Ocean, the Arabian Sea and the Mediterranean. Since its withdrawal from Indo-China in 1975 the United States had had no major permanent bases west of the Philippines (where it retained Clark Field and Subic Bay) except the facilities which it had developed from 1970 onwards on the British island of Diego Garcia.

President Jimmy Carter declared on Jan. 23, 1980, that an attempt by any outside force to gain control of the Gulf region would be regarded as an assault on the vital interests of the United States and would be repelled by the use of any means, including military force. On Sept. 18, 1980, the United States made it clear that it would undertake what was necessary, including naval action, to keep open the Strait of Hormuz for tankers shipping crude oil from the Gulf to the Western world and Japan. By Oct. 15, 1980, there were at least 60 warships of the United States and its allies (Britain, France and Australia) in the Indian Ocean area to protect the Strait of Hormuz (as against 29 Soviet warships monitored as being in the area). This Western fleet included the US aircraft carriers *Midway* and *Eisenhower*, six destroyers and several guided-missile frigates. Late in October this fleet was joined by three US ships from the Mediterranean fleet, among them the helicopter carrier *Saipan* (with some 30 helicopters and 50 landing craft).

In addition a US rapid deployment force of 100,000 men (not committed to NATO and capable of being sent at short notice anywhere in the world) had become operative on March 1, 1980. Its preparation had first been disclosed on June 21, 1979. In the Soviet Union the assembly of large US forces near the Gulf was described as an attempt to test the newly-formed rapid deployment force.

Some 70 foreign ships were trapped in the Shatt-al-Arab waterway (between Iran and Iraq) from Sept. 23, 1980, when Iraq had prohibited navigation in the area.

On Sept. 30, 1980, Iraqi aircraft bombed a pumping station on Kharg Island, Iran's main oil export terminal, and on Oct. 9-20 Iraqi aircraft attacked the Iranian port of Bandar Khomeini. Iran, on the other hand, seized foreign ships on suspicion of carrying military equipment to Iraq.

On Jan. 14, 1982, Iraq warned international shipping to keep clear of the western part of the Gulf after it had claimed to have sunk three vessels which had left the Iranian port of Bandar Khomeini. Iraq was also said to have mined the channel between that port and Bandar Mashshahr (west of Bandar Khomeini).

From May 1982 onwards Iraq made further attacks on Kharg Island and also on Iraqi and foreign ships, a number of which were sunk. On Aug. 12, 1982, Iraq declared an exclusive zone extending up to 65 kilometres from Kharg Island in which ships were liable to attack. Iran, on the other hand, pledged itself to safeguard foreign tankers and to provide armed protection; nevertheless a Turkish ship was sunk early in September while travelling in a convoy of some 10 ships escorted by Iranian naval vessels at 240 kilometres from the exclusive zone.

On Nov. 22, 1982, Iraq again raided Kharg Island, and on March 3, 1983, the Iraqi news agency claimed that five Iranian ships had been sunk by Iraqi naval units in an attack on oil installations at Norwuz (some 50 miles north-west of Kharg Island), where a serious oil spill was caused.

On Oct. 15, 1983, the (Iranian) Islamic High Council of Defence declared that any aggression by Iraq (which had received French *Super Etendard* aircraft equipped with Exocet missiles) would result in an Iranian response consisting of (i) the closure of the Gulf to all shipping; (ii) the destruction of Western oil interests in the region; and (iii) an attack on the Kirkuk oilfield in northern Iraq.

On Nov. 25, 1983, the Iraqi Government renewed its warning that all shipping in the north of the Gulf was subject to attack. Various foreign ships were hit between Nov. 3 and Dec. 22, 1983, among them a Greek merchant ship reported sunk on Nov. 3 after being hit by an Exocet missile while travelling in convoy to the Iranian port of Bushire.

On Jan. 2, 1984, Iraq announced that its aircraft had destroyed "five enemy naval vessels" south of Bandar Khomeini; on Jan. 31 it reported "five enemy naval targets" sunk; and on Feb. 3 it claimed to have sunk an Iranian gunboat and captured another. Early in February three Cyprus-registered merchant ships were reported sunk by Exocet missiles, and on Feb. 15 seven "naval targets" were said to have been destroyed. On the previous day Iraq had announced that it would sink any ship approaching Bandar Khomeini or Bushire. The US Navy thereupon issued a warning that no aircraft should approach within five miles of US ships in the area.

Further Iraqi attacks on Kharg Island and on ships took place in March-May 1984, a Panamanian merchant vessel being sunk off the island on May 19. On the other hand, a Saudi Arabian tanker had been set ablaze on May 16, apparently by an Iranian fighter aircraft, within Saudi Arabian territorial waters. On May 24 a Liberian-registered tanker was sunk in the western Gulf by Iranian aircraft which were pursued by US-supplied F-4 fighters of the Saudi Arabian Air Force, and on May 29 it was reported that in addition to US airborne warning and control systems (AWACS) aircraft supplied to Saudi Arabia the United States would provide Saudi Arabia with further equipment, including 400 shoulder-launched Stinger anti-aircraft missiles.

In subsequent weeks a number of ships were damaged, some by mines, others by missiles from Iraqi, Iranian or unidentified aircraft.

The UN Security Council, in a resolution adopted on June 1, 1984, called on all states to respect freedom of navigation in the Gulf and condemned attacks on Kuwaiti and Saudi Arabian shipping (without mentioning Iran specifically). The Iranian permanent representative at the United Nations said afterwards: "We strongly support freedom of navigation; the Gulf should remain a zone of peace and security for all. But we cannot permit anyone to use the Gulf against us; it will either remain free and open to all of us, or nobody will be allowed to use it."

Iraq, however, continued its warfare against Iranian targets in the Gulf, and on July 21, 1985, it claimed that its navy had attacked the offshore Cyrus oilfield in the northern Gulf and had set fire to four oil wells, a pumping station and a storage tank.

Red Sea

Between July 9 and Aug. 20, 1984, about 18 ships of varying nationalities were damaged by explosions of small mines in the Gulf of Suez and the Bab el Mandab Strait. On Aug. 1 a telephone caller to several London news agencies claimed that the militant Shi'ite organization *Al Jihad al-Islam* was responsible for planting 190 mines in the area.

Minesweeping operations were begun in August not only by Egypt but also, at Egypt's request, by vessels of other riparian states of the Red Sea, by Soviet vessels from South Yemen and by British, French, Italian and United States ships, and these operations were completed by the end of September 1984. During August the incidents reduced traffic through the Suez Canal by about 10 per cent.

In an interview published on Oct. 13, 1984, President Hosni Mubarak of Egypt absolved Iran from any blame for the mining and stated that "all indications" pointed to Libyan responsibility (Egyptian intelligence sources having claimed that a Libyan officer in charge of mine-laying had been on board the Libyan cargo ship *Ghat* which had been present in the Red Sea during July).

Cape Sea Route

From the late 1960s onwards the Government of South Africa, faced with growing isolation from the international community which condemned its racial policies, made a number of attempts to convince the Western powers that it would be in their interest to co-operate with South Africa in the field of defence, in particular of the Cape sea route, important as a lifeline between the Atlantic and Indian Oceans. In this context the South African Government pointed out that supertankers carrying oil from the Gulf oilfields were unable to use the Suez Canal and had to travel to the West around the Cape of Good Hope, and that the importance of this route as an international waterway was enhanced whenever the Suez Canal was closed to traffic.

The naval base at Simonstown, near Cape Town, designed to serve naval forces providing protection for this sea route, was under the control of the British Admiralty from 1814 onwards. A naval agreement concluded between the United Kingdom and South Africa in 1955 provided for co-operation between the two parties both in peace and in war, even when South Africa was not a belligerent, but it did not contain any guarantee by either party to the other as would have been the case under a defensive alliance.

In response to a United Nations General Assembly call for an arms embargo against South Africa, the United States imposed such an embargo in 1963. The British Labour Government ceased supplying South Africa with arms in November 1964; this embargo was rescinded by the British Conservative government in July 1970, but it was reimposed by the subsequent Labour Government in September 1974. On Nov. 4, 1977, the UN Security Council decided by 15 votes to none to impose a mandatory arms embargo on South Africa.

The British Government had earlier, on April 12, 1967, withdrawn from the control of the Simonstown base, and the South African Government had begun to expand its own naval forces. On Sept. 2, 1969, it announced that it would establish a third naval base at Saldanha Bay (about 80 miles north of Cape Town) in addition to those existing at Simonstown and Salisbury Island, Durban.

Also in April 1967 the South African Foreign Minister visited South America and discussed with his counterparts in Argentina and Brazil possible measures against "communist penetration" in the South Atlantic. The then South African Prime Minister (J. B. Vorster) disclosed in the House of Assembly in Cape Town on April 23, 1969, that his government was discussing with other nations plans to fill the power vacuum in the Indian Ocean after Britain's proposed withdrawal from the area in 1970, and he declared that if the Cape route were barred to international sea traffic Europe and the United States would suffer more than South Africa. The South American states, however, did not respond to South African suggestions to create a South Atlantic Treaty Organization which would be complementary to NATO.

On Sept. 10, 1974, P. W. Botha, then South African Minister of Defence, said that South Africa would provide bases and communication facilities to the Western nations interested in the defence of the Cape route and would also expand its own naval units, but that the West should contribute by supplying the long-range maritime patrol aircraft and more powerful ships required.

The 1955 Anglo-South African naval agreement was terminated on June 16, 1975, when a new agreement was concluded under which the South African Government was to contribute to the "defence of southern Africa, Africa and the Middle East gateways to Africa". For this purpose the South African Navy was to be expanded with British support. In a memorandum to the agreement it was agreed that southern Africa must be defended against aggression from outside.

After pro-Soviet governments had been established in both Mozambique and Angola in 1975, South African forces invaded the latter country in the same year. However, these troops were withdrawn when it became clear that the action was not supported by the Western nations.

Following this rebuff by the West, P. W. Botha said on Jan. 27, 1977, that in the event of an East-West conflict Western nations should no longer take South African support for granted and that his country might decide to "remain neutral". On April 6, 1978, he stated that the international arms boycott had forced South Africa to change its strategy on naval defence. "From now on," he said, "South Africa's Navy will be specially geared and designed to coastal defence for protecting the sovereignty of home waters. The West will have to conduct its own patrols of the shipping lane to, from and around the Cape, and will have to look after its own interests."

A Marine Traffic Bill (which passed its third reading in the South African House of Assembly on Feb. 2, 1981, with the support of all parties) provided for the right of "innocent passage" through South Africa's territorial waters up to the 12-mile limit but also empowered the Minister of Transport Affairs to order ships to be stopped and searched if they were believed to be carrying drugs or cargo or persons which might constitute "a threat to the sovereignty, integrity or political independence of South Africa", of if he considered the stopping of any vessel as "essential for the security of the republic".

Indian Ocean

As a result of the abrogation by Iran of the 1959 US-Iran defence agreement and the seizure of hostages at the US embassy in Iran in November 1979, as well as of the Soviet intervention in Afghanistan at the end of that year, the United States decided in January 1980 to maintain a permanent military presence in the Indian Ocean and to seek the regular use of facilities in Oman, Kenya and Somalia.

Under a co-operation agreement with Oman concluded on June 4, 1980, the United States was to obtain land and naval facilities in Oman "similar to those enjoyed by other friendly countries" (but it was not intended to seek permission to station any military units in Oman). Of an agreement reached with Kenya on June 26 no details were made public, but the US State Department explained that there would be an expanded relationship between the two countries in the development of security assistance and economic co-operation. An agreement with Somalia, announced on Aug. 22, was understood to allow the United States the use of the Berbera naval base and of the port of Mogadishu, together with associated airfields.

At the same time the US Government expanded the facilities which it enjoyed on the island of Diego Garcia, in the British Indian Ocean Territory, where it established a permanent US military force.

Straits of Malacca

A 1969 declaration of a 12-mile territorial waters limit by both Indonesia and Malaysia was followed by the signing of an agreement between the two countries establishing a boundary through the Straits of Malacca and thus ending disputes which had arisen out of the overlap of the two countries' respective territorial waters zones. (The 600-mile long straits are for more than 200 miles of their length less than 24 miles wide and at their narrowest point only 21 miles, while at certain points they have a depth of only some 20 metres.)

On Nov. 16, 1971, the two governments jointly announced that they did not recognize the Straits of Malacca as an international waterway and that these straits would in future be open only for shipping on innocent passage. In March 1972 both governments made it clear that they claimed the right of prior consultation from foreign governments wishing to use the straits for the passage of naval vessels, and that for reasons of maritime safety and anti-pollution measures they would impose a ban on foreign tankers of over 200,000 deadweight tons using the straits.

It was clear that implementation of this decision would be of major significance for Japanese shipping and oil interests, since more than 90 per cent of Japan's oil imports passed through that route, generally in tankers exceeding 200,000 tons; a detour via the Lombok Straits east of Bali or the Macassar Straits between Borneo and Celebes (Sulawesi), as suggested by Indonesia, would greatly increase Japan's costs.

The claims by Indonesia and Malaysia were strongly opposed by both Japan and the Soviet Union. The Soviet ambassador to Japan stated on March 4, 1972, that the straits must be kept open for free passage of foreign ships, and he called for their internationalization. Later in March 1972 the Soviet Government stated that it regarded the straits as an international waterway "for economic and many other purposes". The Japanese Government declined to recognize the 12-mile territorial waters limit in the straits and stated that it would seek a settlement of the legal status of the straits through the Third UN Conference on the Law of the Sea.

In Singapore, which had refused to sign the Indonesian-Malaysian declaration of Nov. 16, 1971, the Foreign Minister called, on March 17, 1982, for free access for all to the straits. No official opposition to the declaration was expressed by Australia, the United Kingdom or the United States. China, however, had supported the Indonesian and Malaysian stand on March 12, 1972.

Nicaraguan Waters

The US-backed Nicaraguan Democratic Front (FDN)—formed in Honduras in August 1981 as an armed organization opposed to the Sandinista regime in Nicaragua—announced that on Oct. 7, 1983, it had mined the entrance to the Nicaraguan Pacific port of Corinto in an effort to prevent Mexican tankers from supplying oil to Nicaragua.

On Feb. 25, 1984, a trawler was sunk by a mine at the entrance to the Nicaraguan Atlantic port of El Bluff, which had been attacked by members of the Democratic Revolutionary Alliance (ARDE), another anti-Sandinista organization, founded in Costa Rica in September 1981.

In March 1984 the port of Corinto was again mined, and two other Pacific ports (Montelimar and San Juan del Sur) were attacked from motor launches and helicopters. Four foreign vessels were hit by mines at Corinto, and a Soviet oil tanker was hit at Puerto Sandino. The Nicaraguan Government alleged that the mining had been organized from US warships currently patrolling off the Honduran coast, and the ARDE claimed in mid-March that the mining of Corinto, El Bluff and Puerto Sandino had been carried out by a "special commando unit directed by an American". The Nicaraguan Government thereupon announced that it would seek to purchase minesweepers and other military equipment from abroad.

Early in April 1984 it was disclosed in a letter to the US Senate Select Committee on Intelligence that agents of the (US) Central Intelligence Agency (CIA) had directed the mining operations from a "mother ship" stationed outside Nicaragua's 12-mile territorial waters limit. President Reagan stated on April 4 that the US administration would not take any steps to stop guerrillas from mining Nicaraguan ports.

At the UN Security Council, meeting at Nicaragua's request, a draft resolution presented on April 4, 1984, condemned the mining and called on other countries "to refrain from carrying out, supporting or promoting any type of military action against any state of the region, as well as any action which hinders the peace objectives of the Contadora group" (established in January 1983 by the governments of Mexico, Venezuela, Panama and Colombia). The draft resolution was supported by 13 Council members but was vetoed by the United States, while the United Kingdom abstained from voting.

On April 9, 1984, the Nicaraguan Government filed with the International Court of Justice (ICJ) at The Hague a suit against the United States, calling for "a declaration in depth on the violations and aggressions of the United States" through its "military and paramilitary activities in and against Nicaragua". The United States, however, had on April 6 informed the UN Secretary-General that it was imposing "a temporary and limited modification" of its acceptance of the ICJ's jurisdiction in any dispute associated with events in Central America for a period of two years. (According to the rules of the ICJ a nation could refuse its jurisdiction only before a specific case was brought against it.)

A unanimous interim judgment of the ICJ, urging the United States to cease preventing access to Nicaraguan ports through mine-laying was accepted by the United States on May 10, 1984. After considering the Nicaraguan suit on Oct. 8-18, 1984, the ICJ announced on Nov. 26 that the case fell within its jurisdiction.

The US Administration, however, did not officially admit that it had ordered the mining operations. On April 10, 1984, the US Senate passed by 84 votes to 12 a non-binding resolution sponsored by Senator Edward Kennedy (Democrat), stating "that no funds heretofore appropriated in any act of Congress shall be obligated or expended for the purpose of planning, executing or supporting the mining of the ports or territorial waters of Nicaragua". A similar resolution was passed by the US House of Representatives by 281 votes to 111 on April 12.

The US Deputy Secretary of State said on April 11, 1984, that if the United States were involved in such an operation it would be justified in this act of "collective self-defence" under the provisions of the charters of the United Nations and the Organization of American States. Moreover, the US permanent representative at the United Nations (Mrs Jeane Kirkpatrick) said on April 15 that the mining operation was "legal because Nicaragua is engaged in a process of armed aggression against her neighbours". The FDN leader, however, stated on April 10 that the United States was not involved and that the FDN was acting on its own initiative "in order to stop the massive flow of Soviet arms . . . intended for use in a genocidal campaign against Miskito Indians and Nicaraguan peasants".

However, on April 16 1984, it was reported that the FDN had suspended its mining operations because it feared that the opposition to the operations in the US Congress might jeopardize future US aid (but that the ARDE had announced its intention to continue mining the ports).

Manuals issued by CIA officers in July and October 1984 and calling for the "selective use of violence" and for acts of sabotage to be carried out by the anti-Sandinista guerrillas were found to be in conflict with an executive order signed by President Reagan on Dec. 4, 1981, forbidding US government employees from engaging in, or conspiring to engage in, assassinations or other activities forbidden by the order.

On the other hand President Reagan gave support to the anti-Sandinista forces by declaring, on May 1, 1985, a US trade embargo and other economic sanctions against Nicaragua. A draft UN Security Council resolution critical of this step was vetoed by the United States on May 10, 1985.

Southern Kurile Islands Area

The Japanese claim to the islands of Shikotan, Kunashiri, Etorofu and the Habomai group (the southernmost of the Kurile Islands), occupied by the Soviet Union at the end of World War II, has been consistently rejected by the Soviet Union.

The islands occupy an important strategic position in that the seas around them provide the Soviet Navy with ice-free deep-water access from the Sea of Okhotsk to the Pacific Ocean, and the islands themselves contain several deep-water ice-free natural harbours as well as large tracts of open land suitable for bases.

The islands were surrendered to the Soviet Union in terms of the agreements reached by the war-time allies at Yalta in February 1945 and at Potsdam in July-August of that year. Marshal Stalin explicitly stated on Sept. 2, 1945, when he announced Japan's surrender and the Soviet occupation of Sakhalin and the Kurile Islands: "From now on [these territories] will not serve as a means for isolating the Soviet Union from the ocean and as a base for Japanese attacks on our Far East, but as a means of direct communication for the USSR with the ocean and a base for the defence of our country against Japanese aggression."

Japan, however, has consistently maintained that the Habomais, Shikotan, Kunashiri and Etorofu "are distinct from the Kurile Islands and are inherent territories of Japan".

The United States Government stated on Sept. 7, 1956, that Japan was not a party to the Yalta agreement, and that there was no mention of the Yalta agreement in the Potsdam declaration which Japan accepted; that Japan was therefore not legally bound by it; and that likewise the Soviet Union could not claim any rights against Japan on the basis of that agreement, which was not binding on Japan. In a further statement issued by the US Government on Sept. 7, 1956, it was declared inter alia: "The USA has reached the conclusion, after careful examination of the historical facts, that the islands of Etorofu and Kunashiri (along with the Habomai Islands and Shikotan, which are part of Hokkaido) have always been part of Japan proper, and should in justice be acknowledged as under Japanese sovereignty. The USA would regard Soviet agreement to this effect as a positive contribution to the reduction of tension in the Far East."

The conclusion of a new Japan-US mutual co-operation and security treaty in January 1960 brought about a hardening of the Soviet stance on the islands. In a memorandum of Jan. 27, 1960, the Soviet Union protested against the treaty and stated: "It perpetuates the actual occupation of Japan, places her territory at the disposal of a foreign power . . . and its provisions inevitably lead to the military, economic and political subordination of Japan." The memorandum continued that in this "new situation" and in view of the fact that the treaty was "directed against the Soviet Union and also against the Chinese People's Republic" the Soviet Union could not "allow itself to contribute to an extension of the territory used by foreign armed forces" by handing over the Habomai Islands and Shikotan, which would be transferred to Japan "only on condition that all foreign troops are withdrawn from the territory of Japan and a peace treaty is concluded between the USSR and Japan".

On Dec. 10, 1976, the Soviet Union proclaimed a 200-mile fishing zone around its coasts. The Japanese Government thereupon extended, on Jan. 26, 1977, Japan's territorial waters limit from three to 12 nautical miles (with the exclusion of the three international straits of the region), specifying that the new 12-mile limit would encompass the disputed northern islands. The Soviet Government announced on Feb. 24 that it would enforce the 200-mile fishing zone from March 1 and made it clear that the zone would incorporate the waters around the northern islands—this being described by the Japanese Government on Feb. 25 as "an unfriendly and regrettable act" and as unacceptable to Japan.

During 1979–80 the Japanese Government repeatedly drew attention to what it claimed was a significant build-up of Soviet forces in the northern islands, including the stationing of some 2,000 troops on Shikotan (which had not been militarized since 1960). By May 1980 Soviet military strength in the northern islands was estimated by Japan at some 13,000 troops, compared with about 1,000 in 1976, and Japan also claimed that direct command communications had been established between Kunashiri, Etorofu and Vladivostok (the base of the Soviet Pacific fleet). On Oct. 6, 1979, the Japanese Government announced its intention to begin aerial reconnaissance over Shikotan as part of its periodic inspections of the northern islands—this step being condemned as "wild interference" by the Soviet Union.

On May 7, 1980, the Soviet ambassador to Japan defended the Soviet military build-up in the region on the grounds that "it should not be considered in isolation from the military and political situation in that area" and that the Soviet Union could not neglect such factors as the anti-Soviet co-operation of Japan and the United States, the strengthening of US-Chinese relations and the instability of the Korean peninsula and Indo-China.

Further deterioration of Japanese-Soviet relations occurred late in 1980 when a Japanese salvage company began operations to lift the contents of a former Tsarist naval vessel (the *Admiral Nakhimov*) which had sunk off the Japanese coast in 1905 with a cargo of gold, platinum and other precious metals whose current value was variously estimated at between $3,800 million and $40,000 million. The vessel had been seized by the Japanese during the Russo-Japanese war and had subsequently been sunk outside the former three-mile territorial waters limit of Japan but inside the 12-mile limit introduced in 1977. On Oct. 3, 1980, the Soviet Union claimed proprietary rights over the ship, to which the Japanese Government responded (on Oct. 10) that no precedent existed for the return of a ship submerged for so long and (on Oct. 20) that the vessel was rightfully the property of the Japanese Government. The salvage company, however, claimed the ship as its own property and directly offered it to the Soviet Union in exchange for the return to Japan of the northern Islands (whereas the Japanese Government insisted that only governments could negotiate on the "territorial issue").

The Japanese Goverment has since then repeatedly reiterated that a peace treaty with the Soviet Union could be concluded only on the basis of the return of the islands to Japan—a condition which has continued to be rejected by the Soviet Union.

Falkland Islands/Las Malvinas

On April 2, 1982, Argentinian armed forces occupied the Falkland Islands (British sovereignty over which since 1833 was disputed by Argentina, which called the islands Las Malvinas). On April 3 other Argentine forces took South Georgia, a dependency of the Falklands, after a first Argentine party had landed there on March 18, 1982.

Britain's campaign to regain the Falklands, involving a major naval operation, began on April 5, 1982.

On April 7 the British Government declared a 200-nautical-mile "maritime exclusion zone" around the Falklands with effect from April 12, in which all Argentine warships and naval auxiliaries would be treated as hostile. Also on April 7 Argentina declared a 200-nautical-mile "defence zone" off its coasts and also around the Falklands and South Georgia. A British task force, assembled near Ascension Island, moved south, and units of it recaptured South Georgia on April 25.

On April 28, 1982, the British Ministry of Defence announced that a "total exclusion zone" of 200 nautical miles would be established around the islands from April 30 and would apply to all ships, naval or merchant vessels operating in support of the Argentine occupation of the Falklands. On May 2 the Argentine cruiser *General Belgrano* was sunk (with heavy loss of life) outside the total exclusion zone by a British nuclear-powered hunter-killer submarine, and on May 4 the UK destroyer HMS *Sheffield* was destroyed by an Exocet missile from an Argentine aircraft. On May 7 the British "total exclusion zone" was extended up to 12 nautical miles off the Argentine coast, and a warning was given that any ship or aircraft crossing this limit would be attacked. On May 11 Argentina declared the entire South Atlantic a war zone and threatened to attack any British warship, merchant vessel or aircraft deemed to constitute a threat to Argentine security. British troops first landed on Falklands soil on May 15, and by June 15 Port Stanley, the islands' capital, was taken and fighting was ended.

The total exclusion zone established by Britain on April 30 and the blockade of the Argentine coast imposed on May 7 were lifted on July 22, 1982. However, Argentina was requested to keep its warships and military aircraft outside a 150-mile "naval protection zone" around the Falklands, while Argentine civil aircraft and shipping were asked not to enter the zone except by prior agreement with Britain.

In an annex to a British White Paper (Cmnd. 8758) of Dec. 14, 1982, on the lessons of the Falklands campaign it was stated that the British forces had inflicted on Argentina 72 confirmed aircraft kills and a further 14 probables; that an estimated 117 Argentine aircraft had been destroyed (including probables and those destroyed on the ground); that 22 British aircraft or helicopters had been lost to enemy fire and 12 through other causes; and that six British ships had been lost (two Type 42 destroyers, two Type 21 frigates, the Royal Fleet Auxiliary *Sir Galahad* and the merchantman *Atlantic Conveyor*). In the White Paper itself it was confirmed that a sizeable garrison would be retained on the islands for the foreseeable future.

The lessons of the campaign included the confirmation of the effectiveness of nuclear-powered submarines the presence of which could not easily be detected, whereas Argentine diesel-electric-powered submarines could be detected by anti-submarine warfare ships and by sonar buoys used by *Nimrod* aircraft. The successful use of Exocet missiles by Argentina illustrated the vulnerability of large surface warships, and this would point to the need for improved interceptor missiles or for the deployment of smaller and more numerous surface warships.

In the view of the Argentinian Government a state of hostilities has persisted between Argentina and the United Kingdom. In February 1984 the Argentine Government stated (in reply to British proposals for a normalization of relations between the two countries) inter alia that the "naval exclusion zone" should be lifted before there could be any Argentine declaration of an end to hostilities. Attempts during 1984 and 1985 to bring about a resumption of talks between the two sides have foundered on Argentina's insistence that negotiations should include the sovereignty question, whereas the UK Government has ruled out any discussion of sovereignty for the foreseeable future and has continued to maintain substantial military forces on the islands.

Appendix 1

United Nations Convention on the Law of the Sea

The full text of the UN Convention on the Law of the Sea (see Chapter 1 for adoption), consisting of a preamble, 17 parts (running to 320 articles) and nine annexes, is published below.

The States Parties to this Convention,

Prompted by the desire to settle, in a spirit of mutual understanding and co-operation, all issues relating to the law of the sea and aware of the historic significance of this Convention as an important contribution to the maintenance of peace, justice and progress for all peoples of the world,

Noting that developments since the United Nations Conferences on the Law of the Sea held at Geneva in 1958 and 1960 have accentuated the need for a new and generally acceptable Convention on the law of the sea,

Conscious that the problems of ocean space are closely interrelated and need to be considered as a whole,

Recognizing the desirability of establishing through this Convention, with due regard for the sovereignty of all States, a legal order for the seas and oceans which will facilitate international communication, and will promote the peaceful uses of the seas and oceans, the equitable and efficient utilization of their resources, the conservation of their living resources, and the study, protection and preservation of the marine environment,

Bearing in mind that the achievement of these goals will contribute to the realization of a just and equitable international economic order which takes into account the interests and needs of mankind as a whole and, in particular, the special interests and needs of developing countries, whether coastal or land-locked,

Desiring by this Convention to develop the principles embodied in resolution 2749 (XXV) of 17 December 1970 in which the General Assembly of the United Nations solemnly declared *inter alia* that the area of the sea-bed and ocean floor and the subsoil thereof, beyond the limits of national jurisdiction, as well as its resources, are the common heritage of mankind, the exploration and exploitation of which shall be carried out for the benefit of mankind as a whole, irrespective of the geographical location of States,

Believing that the codification and progressive development of the law of the sea achieved in this Convention will contribute to the strengthening of peace, security, co-operation and friendly relations among all nations in conformity with the principles of justice and equal rights and will promote the economic and social advancement of all peoples of the world, in accordance with the Purposes and Principles of the United Nations as set forth in the Charter,

Affirming that matters not regulated by this Convention continue to be governed by the rules and principles of general international law,

Have agreed as follows:

PART I

Introduction

Article 1

Use of terms and scope

1. For the purposes of this Convention:

(1) "Area" means the sea-bed and ocean floor and subsoil thereof, beyond the limits of national jurisdiction;

(2) "Authority" means the International Sea-Bed Authority;

(3) "activities in the Area" means all activities of exploration for, and exploitation of, the resources of the Area;

(4) "pollution of the marine environment" means the introduction by man, directly or indirectly, of substances or energy into the marine environment, including estuaries, which results or is likely to result in such deleterious effects as harm to living resources and marine life, hazards to human health, hindrance to marine activities, including fishing and other legitimate uses of the sea, impairment of quality for use of sea water and reduction of amenities;

(5) (a) "dumping" means:

(i) any deliberate disposal of wastes or other matter from vessels, aircraft, platforms or other man-made structures at sea;

(ii) any deliberate disposal of vessels, aircraft, platforms or other man-made structures at sea;

(b) "dumping" does not include:

(i) the disposal of wastes or other matter incidental to, or derived from the normal operations of vessels, aircraft, platforms or other man-made structures at sea and their equipment, other than wastes or other matter transported by or to vessels, aircraft, platforms or other man-made structures at sea, operating for the purpose of disposal of such matter or derived from the treatment of such wastes or other matter on such vessels, aircraft, platforms or structures;

(ii) placement of matter for a purpose other than the mere disposal thereof, provided that such placement is not contrary to the aims of this Convention.

2. (1) "States Parties" means States which have consented to be bound by this Convention and for which this Convention is in force.

(2) This Convention applies *mutatis mutandis* to the entities referred to in article 305, paragraph 1(b), (c), (d), (e) and (f), which become Parties to this Convention in accordance with the conditions relevant to each, and to that extent "States Parties" refers to those entities.

PART II

Territorial Sea and Contiguous Zone

Section 1. General Provisions

Article 2
Legal status of the territorial sea, of the air space over the territorial sea and of its bed and subsoil

1. The sovereignty of a coastal State extends, beyond its land territory and internal waters and, in the case of an archipelagic State, its archipelagic waters, to an adjacent belt of sea, described as the territorial sea.

2. This sovereignty extends to the air space over the territorial sea as well as to its bed and subsoil.

3. The sovereignty over the territorial sea is exercised subject to this Convention and to other rules of international law.

Section 2. Limits of the Territorial Sea

Article 3
Breadth of the territorial sea

Every State has the right to establish the breadth of its territorial sea up to a limit not exceeding 12 nautical miles, measured from baselines determined in accordance with this Convention.

Article 4
Outer limit of the territorial sea

The outer limit of the territorial sea is the line every point of which is at a distance from the nearest point of the baseline equal to the breadth of the territorial sea.

Article 5
Normal baseline

Except where otherwise provided in this Convention, the normal baseline for measuring the breadth of the territorial sea is the low-water line along the coast as marked on large-scale charts officially recognized by the coastal State.

Article 6
Reefs

In the case of islands situated on atolls or of islands having fringing reefs, the baseline for measuring the breadth of the territorial sea is the seaward low-water line of the reef, as shown by the appropriate symbol on charts officially recognized by the coastal State.

Article 7
Straight baselines

1. In localities where the coastline is deeply indented and cut into, or if there is a fringe of islands along the coast in its immediate vicinity, the method of straight baselines joining appropriate points may be employed in drawing the baseline from which the breadth of the territorial sea is measured.

2. Where because of the presence of a delta and other natural conditions the coastline is highly unstable, the appropriate points may be selected along the furthest seaward extent of the low-water line and, notwithstanding subsequent regression of the low-water line, the straight baselines shall remain effective until changed by the coastal State in accordance with this convention.

3. The drawing of straight baselines must not depart to any appreciable extent from the general direction of the coast, and the sea areas lying within the lines must be sufficiently closely linked to the land domain to be subject to the régime of internal waters.

4. Straight baselines shall not be drawn to and from low-tide elevations, unless lighthouses or similar installations which are permanently above sea level have been built on them or except in instances where the drawing of baselines to and from such elevations has received general international recognition.

5. Where the method of straight baselines is applicable under paragraph 1, account may be taken, in determining particular baselines, of economic interests peculiar to the region concerned, the reality and the importance of which are clearly evidenced by long usage.

6. The system of straight baselines may not be applied by a State in such a manner as to cut off the territorial sea of another State from the high seas or an exclusive economic zone.

Article 8
Internal waters

1. Except as provided in Part IV, waters on the landward side of the baseline of the territorial sea form part of the internal waters of the State.

2. Where the establishment of a straight baseline in accordance with the method set forth in article 7 has the effect of enclosing as internal waters areas which had not previously been considered as such, a right of innocent passage as provided in this Convention shall exist in those waters.

Article 9
Mouths of rivers

If a river flows directly into the sea, the baseline shall be a straight line across the mouth of the river between points on the low-water line of its banks.

Article 10
Bays

1. This article relates only to bays the coasts of which belong to a single State.

2. For the purposes of this convention, a bay is a well-marked indentation whose penetration is in such proportion to the width of its mouth as to contain land-locked waters and constitute more than a mere curvature of the coast. An indentation shall not, however, be regarded as a bay unless its area is as large as, or larger than, that of the semi-circle whose diameter is a line drawn across the mouth of that indentation.

3. For the purpose of measurement, the area of an indentation is that lying between the low-water mark around the shore of the indentation and a line joining the low-water mark of its natural entrance points. Where, because of the presence of islands, an indentation has more than one mouth, the semi-circle shall be drawn on a line as long as the sum total of the lengths of the lines across the different mouths. Islands within an indentation shall be included as if they were part of the water area of the indentation.

4. If the distance between the low-water marks of the natural entrance points of a bay does not exceed 24 nautical miles, a closing line may be drawn between these two low-water marks, and the waters enclosed thereby shall be considered as internal waters.

5. Where the distance between the low-water marks of the natural entrance points of a bay exceeds 24 nautical miles, a straight baseline of 24 nautical miles shall be drawn within the bay in such a manner as to enclose the maximum area of water that is possible with a line of that length.

6. The foregoing provisions do not apply to so-called "historic" bays, or in any case where the system of straight baselines provided for in article 7 is applied.

Article 11
Ports

For the purpose of delimiting the territorial sea, the outermost permanent harbour works which form an integral part of the harbour system are regarded as forming part of the coast. Off-shore installations and artificial islands shall not be considered as permanent harbour works.

Article 12
Roadsteads

Roadsteads which are normally used for the loading, unloading and anchoring of ships, and which would otherwise be situated wholly or partly outside the outer limit of the territorial sea, are included in the territorial sea.

Article 13
Low-tide elevations

1. A low-tide elevation is a naturally formed area of land which is surrounded by and above water at low tide but submerged at high tide. Where a low-tide elevation is situated wholly or partly at a distance not exceeding the breadth of the territorial sea from the mainland or an island, the low-water line on that elevation may be used as the baseline for measuring the breadth of the territorial sea.

2. Where a low-tide elevation is wholly situated at a distance exceeding the breadth of the territorial sea from the mainland or an island, it has no territorial sea of its own.

Article 14
Combination of methods for determining baselines

The coastal State may determine baselines in turn by any of the methods provided for in the foregoing articles to suit different conditions.

Article 15
Delimitation of the territorial sea between States with opposite or adjacent coasts

Where the coasts of two States are opposite or adjacent to each other, neither of the two States is entitled, failing agreement between them to the contrary, to extend its territorial sea beyond the median line every point of which is equidistant from the nearest points on the baselines from which the breadth of the territorial seas of each of the two States is measured. The above provision does not apply, however, where it is necessary by reason of historic title or other special circumstances to delimit the territorial seas of the two States in a way which is at variance therewith.

Article 16
Charts and lists of geographical co-ordinates

1. The baselines for measuring the breadth of the territorial sea determined in accordance with articles 7, 9 and 10, or the limits derived therefrom, and the lines of delimitation drawn in accordance with articles 12 and 15 shall be shown on charts of a scale or scales adequate for ascertaining their position. Alternatively, a list of geographical co-ordinates of points, specifying the geodetic datum, may be substituted.

2. The coastal State shall give due publicity to such charts or lists of geographical co-ordinates and shall deposit a copy of each such chart or list with the Secretary-General of the United Nations.

Section 3. Innocent Passage in the Territorial Sea

Subsection A. Rules Applicable to All Ships

Article 17
Right of innocent passage

Subject to this Convention, ships of all States, whether coastal or land-locked, enjoy the right of innocent passage through the territorial sea.

Article 18
Meaning of passage

1. Passage means navigation through the territorial sea for the purpose of:

(a) traversing that sea without entering internal waters or calling at a roadstead or port facility outside internal waters; or

(b) proceeding to or from internal waters or a call at such roadstead or port facility.

2. Passage shall be continuous and expeditious. However, passage includes stopping and anchoring, but only in so far as the same are incidental to ordinary navigation or are rendered necessary by *force majeure* or distress or for the purpose of rendering assistance to persons, ships or aircraft in danger or distress.

Article 19
Meaning of innocent passage

1. Passage is innocent so long as it is not prejudicial to the peace, good order or security of the coastal State. Such passage shall take place in conformity with this Convention and with other rules of international law.

2. Passage of a foreign ship shall be considered to be prejudicial to the peace, good order or security of the coastal State

ıgages in any of

orce against the
grity or political
al State, or in
olation of the
ıw embodied in
lations;
e with weapons

ting information
ence or security

anda aimed at
security of the

g or taking on

g or taking on
;
oading of any
son contrary to
tion or sanitary
coastal State;
erious pollution

earch or survey

fering with any
or any other
ie coastal State;
having a direct

rwater vehicles
ubmarines and
are required to
l to show their

e coastal State
passage
ay adopt laws
mity with the
ion and other
v, relating to
e territorial sea,
e following:
ation and the
c;
ational aids and
or installations;
s and pipelines;
of the living

(e) the prevention of infringement of the fisheries laws and regulations of the coastal State;

(f) the preservation of the environment of the coastal State and the prevention, reduction and control of pollution thereof;

(g) marine scientific research and hydrographic surveys;

(h) the prevention of infringement of the customs, fiscal, immigration or sanitary laws and regulations of the coastal State.

2. Such laws and regulations shall not apply to the design, construction, manning or equipment of foreign ships unless they are giving effect to generally accepted international rules or standards.

3. The coastal State shall give due publicity to all such laws and regulations.

4. Foreign ships exercising the right of innocent passage through the territorial sea shall comply with all such laws and regulations and all generally accepted international regulations relating to the prevention of collisions at sea.

Article 22

Sea lanes and traffic separation schemes in the territorial sea

1. The coastal State may, where necessary having regard to the safety of navigation, require foreign ships exercising the right of innocent passage through its territorial sea to use such sea lanes and traffic separation schemes as it may designate or prescribe for the regulation of the passage of ships.

2. In particular, tankers, nuclear-powered ships and ships carrying nuclear or other inherently dangerous or noxious substances or materials may be required to confine their passage to such sea lanes.

3. In the designation of sea lanes and the prescription of traffic separation schemes under this article, the coastal State shall take into account:

(a) the recommendations of the competent international organization;

(b) any channels customarily used for international navigation;

(c) the special characteristics of particular ships and channels; and

(d) the density of traffic.

4. The coastal State shall clearly indicate such sea lanes and traffic separation schemes on charts to which due publicity shall be given.

Article 23
Foreign nuclear-powered ships and ships carrying nuclear or other inherently dangerous or noxious substances

Foreign nuclear-powered ships and ships carrying nuclear or other inherently dangerous or noxious substances shall, when exercising the right of innocent passage through the territorial sea, carry documents and observe special precautionary measures established for such ships by international agreements.

Article 24
Duties of the coastal State

1. The coastal State shall not hamper the innocent passage of foreign ships through the territorial sea except in accordance with this Convention. In particular, in the application of this Convention or of any laws or regulations adopted in conformity with this Convention, the coastal State shall not:

(a) impose requirements on foreign ships which have the practical effect of denying or impairing the right of innocent passage; or

(b) discriminate in form or in fact against the ships of any State or against ships carrying cargoes to, from or on behalf of any State.

2. The coastal State shall give appropriate publicity to any danger to navigation, of which it has knowledge, within its territorial sea.

Article 25
Rights of protection of the coastal State

1. The coastal State may take the necessary steps in its territorial sea to prevent passage which is not innocent.

2. In the case of ships proceeding to internal waters or a call at a port facility outside internal waters, the coastal State also has the right to take the necessary steps to prevent any breach of the conditions to which admission of those ships to internal waters or such a call is subject.

3. The coastal State may, without discrimination in form or in fact among foreign ships, suspend temporarily in specified areas of its territorial sea the innocent passage of foreign ships if such suspension is essential for the protection of its security, including weapons exercises. Such suspension shall take effect only after having been duly published.

Article 26
Charges which may be levied upon foreign ships

1. No charge may be levied upon foreign ships by reason only of their passage through the territorial sea.

2. Charges may be levied upon a foreign ship passing through the territorial sea as payment only for specific services rendered to the ship. These charges shall be levied without discrimination.

Subsection B. Rules Applicable to Merchant Ships and Government Ships Operated for Commercial Purposes

Article 27
Criminal jurisdiction on board a foreign ship

1. The criminal jurisdiction of the coastal State should not be exercised on board a foreign ship passing through the territorial sea to arrest any person or to conduct any investigation in connection with any crime committed on board the ship during its passage, save only in the following cases:

(a) if the consequences of the crime extend to the coastal State;

(b) if the crime is of a kind to disturb the peace of the country or the good order of the territorial sea;

(c) if the assistance of the local authorities has been requested by the master of the ship or by a diplomatic agent or consular officer of the flag State; or

(d) if such measures are necessary for the suppression of illicit traffic in narcotic drugs or psychotropic substances.

2. The above provisions do not affect the right of the coastal State to take any steps authorized by its laws for the purpose of an arrest or investigation on board a foreign ship passing through the territorial sea after leaving internal waters.

3. In the cases provided for in paragraphs 1 and 2, the coastal State shall, if the master so requests, notify a diplomatic agent or consular officer of the flag State before taking any steps, and shall facilitate contact between such agent or officer and the ship's crew. In cases of emergency this notification may be communicated while the measures are being taken.

4. In considering whether or in what manner an arrest should be made, the local authorities shall have due regard to the interests of navigation.

5. Except as provided in Part XII or with respect to violations of laws and regulations adopted in accordance with Part V, the coastal State may not take any steps on board a foreign ship passing through the territorial sea to arrest any person or to conduct any investigation in connection with any crime committed before the ship entered the territorial sea, if the ship, proceeding from a foreign port, is only passing through the territorial sea without entering internal waters.

Article 28
Civil jurisdiction in relation to foreign ships

1. The coastal State should not stop or divert a foreign ship passing through the territorial sea for the purpose of exercising civil jurisdiction in relation to a person on board the ship.

2. The coastal State may not levy execution against or arrest the ship for the purpose of any civil proceedings, save only in respect of obligations or liabilities assumed or incurred by the ship itself in the course or for the purpose of its voyage through the waters of the coastal State.

3. Paragraph 2 is without prejudice to the right of the coastal State, in accordance with its laws, to levy execution against or to arrest, for the purpose of any civil proceedings, a foreign ship lying in the territorial sea, or passing through the territorial sea after leaving internal waters.

Subsection C. Rules Applicable to Warships and Other Government Ships Operated for Non-Commercial Purposes

Article 29
Definition of warships

For the purposes of this Convention, "warship" means a ship belonging to the armed forces of a State bearing the external marks distinguishing such ships of its nationality, under the command of an officer duly commissioned by the government of the State and whose name appears in the appropriate service list or its equivalent, and manned by a crew which is under regular armed forces discipline.

Article 30
Non-compliance by warships with the laws and regulations of the coastal State

If any warship does not comply with the laws and regulations of the coastal State concerning passage through the territorial sea and disregards any request for compliance therewith which is made to it, the coastal State may require it to leave the territorial sea immediately.

Article 31
Responsibility of the flag State for damage caused by a warship or other government ship operated for non-commercial purposes

The flag State shall bear international responsibility for any loss or damage to the coastal State resulting from the non-compliance by a warship or other government ship operated for non-commercial purposes with the laws and regulations of the coastal State concerning passage through the territorial sea or with the provisions of this Convention or other rules of international law.

Article 32
Immunities of warships and other government ships operated for non-commercial purposes

With such exceptions as are contained in subsection A and in articles 30 and 31, nothing in this Convention affects the immunities of warships and other government ships operated for non-commercial purposes.

Section 4. Contiguous Zone

Article 33
Contiguous zone

1. In a zone contiguous to its territorial sea, described as the contiguous zone, the coastal State may exercise the control necessary to:

(a) prevent infringement of its customs, fiscal, immigration or sanitary laws and regulations within its territory or territorial sea;

(b) punish infringement of the above laws and regulations committed within its territory or territorial sea.

2. The contiguous zone may not extend beyond 24 nautical miles from the baselines from which the breadth of the territorial sea is measured.

PART III

Straits Used for International Navigation

Section 1. General Provisions

Article 34
Legal status of waters forming straits used for international navigation

1. The régime of passage through straits used for international navigation established

in this Part shall not in other respects affect the legal status of the waters forming such straits or the exercise by the States bordering the straits of their sovereignty or jurisdiction over such waters and their air space, bed and subsoil.

2. The sovereignty or jurisdiction of the States bordering the straits is exercised subject to this Part and to other rules of international law.

Article 35
Scope of this Part

Nothing in this Part affects:

(a) any areas of internal waters within a strait, except where the establishment of a straight baseline in accordance with the method set forth in article 7 has the effect of enclosing as internal waters areas which had not previously been considered as such;

(b) the legal status of the waters beyond the territorial seas of States bordering straits as exclusive economic zones or high seas; or

(c) the legal régime in straits in which passage is regulated in whole or in part by long-standing international Conventions in force specifically relating to such straits.

Article 36
High seas routes or routes through exclusive economic zones through straits used for international navigation

This Part does not apply to a strait used for international navigation if there exists through the strait a route through the high seas or through an exclusive economic zone of similar convenience with respect to navigational and hydrographical characteristics; in such routes, the other relevant Parts of this Convention, including the provisions regarding the freedoms of navigation and overflight, apply.

Section 2. Transit Passage

Article 37
Scope of this section

This section applies to straits which are used for international navigation between one part of the high seas or an exclusive economic zone and another part of the high seas or an exclusive economic zone.

Article 38
Right of transit passage

1. In straits referred to in article 37, all ships and aircraft enjoy the right of transit passage, which shall not be impeded; except that, if the strait is formed by an island of a State bordering the strait and its mainland, transit passage shall not apply if there exists seaward of the island a route through the high seas or through an exclusive economic zone of similar convenience with respect to navigational and hydrographical characteristics.

2. Transit passage means the exercise in accordance with this Part of the freedom of navigation and overflight solely for the purpose of continuous and expeditious transit of the strait between one part of the high seas or an exclusive economic zone and another part of the high seas or an exclusive economic zone. However, the requirement of continuous and expeditious transit does not preclude passage through the strait for the purpose of entering, leaving or returning from a State bordering the strait, subject to the conditions of entry to that State.

3. Any activity which is not an exercise of the right of transit passage through a strait remains subject to the other applicable provisions of this Convention.

Article 39
Duties of ships and aircraft during transit passage

1. Ships and aircraft, while exercising the right of transit passage, shall:

(a) proceed without delay through or over the strait;

(b) refrain from any threat or use of force against the sovereignty, territorial integrity or political independence of States bordering the strait, or in any other manner in violation of the principles of international law embodied in the Charter of the United Nations;

(c) refrain from any activities other than those incident to their normal modes of continuous and expeditious transit unless rendered necessary by *force majeure* or by distress;

(d) comply with other relevant provisions of this Part.

2. Ships in transit passage shall:

(a) comply with generally accepted international regulations, procedures and practices for safety at sea, including the International Regulations for Preventing Collisions at Sea;

y accepted inter-
edures and prac-
, reduction and
hips.
sage shall:
es of the Air
ational Civil Avi-
ey apply to civil
normally comply
s and will at all
gard for the safety
onitor the radio
competent inter-
ir traffic control
riate international

40
ey activities

ge, foreign ships,
ific research and
ps, may not carry
y activities without
f the States border-

41
aration schemes in
tional navigation

h this Part, States
designate sea lanes
aration schemes for
where necessary to
e of ships.
when circumstances
ving due publicity
r sea lanes or traffic
or any sea lanes
schemes previously
d by them.
nd traffic separation
to generally accepted
ns.
g or substituting sea
r substituting traffic
ates bordering straits
to the competent
tion with a view to
ganization may adopt
nd traffic separation
greed with the States
after which the States
be or substitute them.
strait where sea lanes
schemes through the
e States bordering the

strait are being proposed, the States concerned shall co-operate in formulating proposals in consultation with the competent international organization.

6. States bordering straits shall clearly indicate all sea lanes and traffic separation schemes designated or prescribed by them on charts to which due publicity shall be given.

7. Ships in transit passage shall respect applicable sea lanes and traffic separation schemes established in accordance with this article.

Article 42

Laws and regulations of States bordering straits relating to transit passage

1. Subject to the provisions of this section, States bordering straits may adopt laws and regulations relating to transit passage through straits, in respect of all or any of the following:

(a) the safety of navigation and the regulation of maritime traffic, as provided in article 41;

(b) the prevention, reduction and control of pollution, by giving effect to applicable international regulations regarding the discharge of oil, oily wastes and other noxious substances in the strait;

(c) with respect to fishing vessels, the prevention of fishing, including the stowage of fishing gear;

(d) the loading or unloading of any commodity, currency or person in contravention of the customs, fiscal, immigration or sanitary laws and regulations of States bordering straits.

2. Such laws and regulations shall not discriminate in form or in fact among foreign ships or in their application have the practical effect of denying, hampering or impairing the right of transit passage as defined in this section.

3. States bordering straits shall give due publicity to all such laws and regulations.

4. Foreign ships exercising the right of transit passage shall comply with such laws and regulations.

5. The flag State of a ship or the State of registry of an aircraft entitled to sovereign immunity which acts in a manner contrary to such laws and regulations or other provisions of this Part shall bear international responsibility for any loss or damage which results to States bordering straits.

Article 43
Navigational and safety aids and other improvements and the prevention, reduction and control of pollution

User States and States bordering a strait should by agreement co-operate:

(a) in the establishment and maintenance in a strait of necessary navigational and safety aids or other improvements in aid of international navigation; and

(b) for the prevention, reduction and control of pollution from ships.

Article 44
Duties of States bordering straits

States bordering straits shall not hamper transit passage and shall give appropriate publicity to any danger to navigation or overflight within or over the strait of which they have knowledge. There shall be no suspension of transit passage.

Section 3. Innocent Passage

Article 45
Innocent passage

1. The régime of innocent passage, in accordance with Part II, section 3, shall apply in straits used for international navigation:

(a) excluded from the application of the régime of transit passage under article 38, paragraph 1; or

(b) between a part of the high seas or an exclusive economic zone and the territorial sea of a foreign State.

2. There shall be no suspension of innocent passage through such straits.

PART IV

Archipelagic States

Article 46
Use of terms

For the purposes of this Convention:

(a) "archipelagic State" means a State constituted wholly by one or more archipelagos and may include other islands;

(b) "archipelago" means a group of islands, including parts of islands, interconnecting waters and other natural features which are so closely interrelated that such islands, waters and other natural features form an intrinsic geographical, economic and political entity, or which historically have been regarded as such.

Article 47
Archipelagic baselines

1. An archipelagic State may draw straight archipelagic baselines joining the outermost points of the outermost islands and drying reefs of the archipelago provided that within such baselines are included the main islands and an area in which the ratio of the area of the water to the area of the land, including atolls, is between 1 to 1 and 9 to 1.

2. The length of such baselines shall not exceed 100 nautical miles, except that up to 3 per cent of the total number of baselines enclosing any archipelago may exceed that length, up to a maximum length of 125 nautical miles.

3. The drawing of such baselines shall not depart to any appreciable extent from the general configuration of the archipelago.

4. Such baselines shall not be drawn to and from low-tide elevations, unless lighthouses or similar installations which are permanently above sea level have been built on them or where a low-tide elevation is situated wholly or partly at a distance not exceeding the breadth of the territorial sea from the nearest island.

5. The system of such baselines shall not be applied by an archipelagic State in such a manner as to cut off from the high seas or the exclusive economic zone the territorial sea of another State.

6. If a part of the archipelagic waters of an archipelagic State lies between two parts of an immediately adjacent neighbouring State, existing rights and all other legitimate interests which the latter State has traditionally exercised in such waters and all rights stipulated by agreement between those States shall continue and be respected.

7. For the purpose of computing the ratio of water to land under paragraph 1, land areas may include waters lying within the fringing reefs of islands and atolls, including that part of a steep-sided oceanic plateau which is enclosed or nearly enclosed by a chain of limestone islands and drying reefs lying on the perimeter of the plateau.

8. The baselines drawn in accordance with this article shall be shown on charts of a scale or scales adequate for ascertaining

their position. Alternatively, lists of geographical co-ordinates of points, specifying the geodetic datum, may be substituted.

9. The archipelagic State shall give due publicity to such charts or lists of geographical co-ordinates and shall deposit a copy of each such chart or list with the Secretary-General of the United Nations.

Article 48
Measurement of the breadth of the territorial sea, the contiguous zone, the exclusive economic zone and the continental shelf

The breadth of the territorial sea, the contiguous zone, the exclusive economic zone and the continental shelf shall be measured from archipelagic baselines drawn in accordance with article 47.

Article 49
Legal status of archipelagic waters, of the air space over archipelagic waters and of their bed and subsoil

1. The sovereignty of an archipelagic State extends to the waters enclosed by the archipelagic baselines drawn in accordance with article 47, described as archipelagic waters, regardless of their depth or distance from the coast.

2. This sovereignty extends to the air space over the archipelagic waters, as well as to their bed and subsoil, and the resources contained therein.

3. This sovereignty is exercised subject to this Part.

4. The régime of archipelagic sea lanes passage established in this Part shall not in other respects affect the status of the archipelagic waters, including the sea lanes, or the exercise by the archipelagic State of its sovereignty over such waters and their air space, bed and subsoil, and the resources contained therein.

Article 50
Delimitation of internal waters

Within its archipelagic waters, the archipelagic State may draw closing lines for the delimitation of internal waters, in accordance with articles 9, 10 and 11.

Article 51
Existing agreements, traditional fishing rights and existing submarine cables

1. Without prejudice to article 49, an archipelagic State shall respect existing agreements with other States and shall recognize traditional fishing rights and other legitimate activities of the immediately adjacent neighbouring States in certain areas falling within archipelagic waters. The terms and conditions for the exercise of such rights and activities, including the nature, the extent and the areas to which they apply, shall, at the request of any of the States concerned, be regulated by bilateral agreements between them. Such rights shall not be transferred to or shared with third States or their nationals.

2. An archipelagic State shall respect existing submarine cables laid by other States and passing through its waters without making a landfall. An archipelagic State shall permit the maintenance and replacement of such cables upon receiving due notice of their location and the intention to repair or replace them.

Article 52
Right of innocent passage

1. Subject to article 53 and without prejudice to article 50, ships of all States enjoy the right of innocent passage through archipelagic waters, in accordance with Part II, section 3.

2. The archipelagic State may, without discrimination in form or in fact among foreign ships, suspend temporarily in specified areas of its archipelagic waters the innocent passage of foreign ships if such suspension is essential for the protection of its security. Such suspension shall take effect only after having been duly published.

Article 53
Right of archipelagic sea lanes passage

1. An archipelagic State may designate sea lanes and air routes thereabove, suitable for the continuous and expeditious passage of foreign ships and aircraft through or over its archipelagic waters and the adjacent territorial sea.

2. All ships and aircraft enjoy the right of archipelagic sea lanes passage in such sea lanes and air routes.

3. Archipelagic sea lanes passage means the exercise in accordance with this Convention of the rights of navigation and overflight in the normal mode solely for the purpose of continuous, expeditious and unobstructed transit between one part of the high seas or an exclusive economic zone and another part of the high seas or an exclusive economic zone.

4. Such sea lanes and air routes shall traverse the archipelagic waters and the adjacent territorial sea and shall include all normal passage routes used as routes for international navigation or overflight through or over archipelagic waters and, within such routes, so far as ships are concerned, all normal navigational channels, provided that duplication of routes of similar convenience between the same entry and exit points shall not be necessary.

5. Such sea lanes and air routes shall be defined by a series of continuous axis lines from the entry points of passage routes to the exit points. Ships and aircraft in archipelagic sea lanes passage shall not deviate more than 25 nautical miles to either side of such axis lines during passage, provided that such ships and aircraft shall not navigate closer to the coasts than 10 per cent of the distance between the nearest points on islands bordering the sea lane.

6. An archipelagic State which designates sea lanes under this article may also prescribe traffic separation schemes for the safe passage of ships through narrow channels in such sea lanes.

7. An archipelagic State may, when circumstances require, after giving due publicity thereto, substitute other sea lanes or traffic separation schemes for any sea lanes or traffic separation schemes previously designated or prescribed by it.

8. Such sea lanes and traffic separation schemes shall conform to generally accepted international regulations.

9. In designating or substituting sea lanes or prescribing or substituting traffic separation schemes, an archipelagic State shall refer proposals to the competent international organization with a view to their adoption. The organization may adopt only such sea lanes and traffic separation schemes as may be agreed with the archipelagic State, after which the archipelagic State may designate, prescribe or substitute them.

10. The archipelagic State shall clearly indicate the axis of the sea lanes and the traffic separation schemes designated or prescribed by it on charts to which due publicity shall be given.

11. Ships in archipelagic sea lanes passage shall respect applicable sea lanes and traffic separation schemes established in accordance with this article.

12. If an archipelagic State does not designate sea lanes or air routes, the right of archipelagic sea lanes passage may be exercised through the routes normally used for international navigation.

Article 54
Duties of ships and aircraft during their passage, research and survey activities, duties of the archipelagic State and laws and regulations of the archipelagic State relating to archipelagic sea lanes passage

Articles 39, 40, 42 and 44 apply *mutatis mutandis* to archipelagic sea lanes passage.

PART V

Exclusive Economic Zone

Article 55
Specific legal régime of the exclusive economic zone

The exclusive economic zone is an area beyond and adjacent to the territorial sea, subject to the specific legal régime established in this Part, under which the rights and jurisdiction of the coastal State and the rights and freedoms of other States are governed by the relevant provisions of this Convention.

Article 56
Rights, jurisdiction and duties of the coastal State in the exclusive economic zone

1. In the exclusive economic zone, the coastal State has:

(a) sovereign rights for the purpose of exploring and exploiting, conserving and managing the natural resources, whether living or non-living, of the waters superjacent to the sea-bed and of the sea-bed and its subsoil, and with regard to other activities for the economic exploitation and exploration of the zone, such as the production of energy from the water, currents and winds;

(b) jurisdiction as provided for in the relevant provisions of this Convention with regard to:

(i) the establishment and use of artificial islands, installations and structures;

(ii) marine scientific research;

(iii) the protection and preservation of the marine environment;

(c) other rights and duties provided for in this Convention.

2. In exercising its rights and performing its duties under this Convention in the exclusive economic zone, the coastal State shall have due regard to the rights and duties of other States and shall act in a manner compatible with the provisions of this Convention.

3. The rights set out in this article with respect to the sea-bed and subsoil shall be exercised in accordance with Part VI.

Article 57
Breadth of the exclusive economic zone

The exclusive economic zone shall not extend beyond 200 nautical miles from the baselines from which the breadth of the territorial sea is measured.

Article 58
Rights and duties of other States in the exclusive economic zone

1. In the exclusive economic zone, all States, whether coastal or land-locked, enjoy, subject to the relevant provisions of this Convention, the freedoms referred to in article 87 of navigation and overflight and of the laying of submarine cables and pipelines, and other internationally lawful uses of the sea related to these freedoms, such as those associated with the operation of ships, aircraft and submarine cables and pipelines, and compatible with the other provisions of this Convention.

2. Articles 88 to 115 and other pertinent rules of international law apply to the exclusive economic zone in so far as they are not incompatible with this Part.

3. In exercising their rights and performing their duties under this Convention in the exclusive economic zone, States shall have due regard to the rights and duties of the coastal State and shall comply with the laws and regulations adopted by the coastal State in accordance with the provisions of this Convention and other rules of international law in so far as they are not incompatible with this Part.

Article 59
Basis for the resolution of conflicts regarding the attribution of rights and jurisdiction in the exclusive economic zone

In cases where this Convention does not attribute rights or jurisdiction to the coastal State or to other States within the exclusive economic zone, and a conflict arises between the interests of the coastal State and any other State or States, the conflict should be resolved on the basis of equity and in the light of all the relevant circumstances, taking into account the respective importance of the interests involved to the parties as well as to the international community as a whole.

Article 60
Artificial islands, installations and structures in the exclusive economic zone

1. In the exclusive economic zone, the coastal State shall have the exclusive right to construct and to authorize and regulate the construction, operation and use of:

(a) artificial islands;

(b) installations and structures for the purposes provided for in article 56 and other economic purposes;

(c) installations and structures which may interfere with the exercise of the rights of the coastal State in the zone.

2. The coastal State shall have exclusive jurisdiction over such artificial islands, installations and structures, including jurisdiction with regard to customs, fiscal, health, safety and immigration laws and regulations.

3. Due notice must be given of the construction of such artificial islands, installations or structures, and permanent means for giving warning of their presence must be maintained. Any installations or structures which are abandoned or disused shall be removed to ensure safety of navigation, taking into account any generally accepted international standards established in this regard by the competent international organization. Such removal shall also have due regard to fishing, the protection of the marine environment and the rights and duties of other States. Appropriate publicity shall be given to the depth, position and dimensions of any installations or structures not entirely removed.

4. The coastal State may, where necessary, establish reasonable safety zones around such artificial islands, installations and structures in which it may take appropriate measures to ensure the safety both of navigation and of the artificial islands, installations and structures.

5. The breadth of the safety zones shall be determined by the coastal State, taking into account applicable international standards. Such zones shall be designed to ensure that they are reasonably related to

the nature and function of the artificial islands, installations or structures, and shall not exceed a distance of 500 metres around them, measured from each point of their outer edge, except as authorized by generally accepted international standards or as recommended by the competent international organization. Due notice shall be given of the extent of safety zones.

6. All ships must respect these safety zones and shall comply with generally accepted international standards regarding navigation in the vicinity of artificial islands, installations, structures and safety zones.

7. Artificial islands, installations and structures and the safety zones around them may not be established where interference may be caused to the use of recognized sea lanes essential to international navigation.

8. Artificial islands, installations and structures do not possess the status of islands. They have no territorial sea of their own, and their presence does not affect the delimitation of the territorial sea, the exclusive economic zone or the continental shelf.

Article 61

Conservation of the living resources

1. The coastal State shall determine the allowable catch of the living resources in its exclusive economic zone.

2. The coastal State, taking into account the best scientific evidence available to it, shall ensure through proper conservation and management measures that the maintenance of the living resources in the exclusive economic zone is not endangered by over-exploitation. As appropriate, the coastal State and competent international organizations, whether subregional, regional or global, shall co-operate to this end.

3. Such measures shall also be designed to maintain or restore populations of harvested species at levels which can produce the maximum sustainable yield, as qualified by relevant environmental and economic factors, including the economic needs of coastal fishing communities and the special requirements of developing States, and taking into account fishing patterns, the interdependence of stocks and any generally recommended international minimum standards, whether subregional, regional or global.

4. In taking such measures the coastal State shall take into consideration the effects on species associated with or dependent upon harvested species with a view to maintaining or restoring populations of such associated or dependent species above levels at which their reproduction may become seriously threatened.

5. Available scientific information, catch and fishing effort statistics, and other data relevant to the conservation of fish stocks shall be contributed and exchanged on a regular basis through competent international organizations, whether subregional, regional or global, where appropriate and with participation by all States concerned, including States whose nationals are allowed to fish in the exclusive economic zone.

Article 62

Utilization of the living resources

1. The coastal State shall promote the objective of optimum utilization of the living resources in the exclusive economic zone without prejudice to article 61.

2. The coastal State shall determine its capacity to harvest the living resources of the exclusive economic zone. Where the coastal State does not have the capacity to harvest the entire allowable catch, it shall, through agreements or other arrangements and pursuant to the terms, conditions, laws and regulations referred to in paragraph 4, give other States access to the surplus of the allowable catch, having particular regard to the provisions of articles 69 and 70, especially in relation to the developing States mentioned therein.

3. In giving access to other States to its exclusive economic zone under this article, the coastal State shall take into account all relevant factors, including, *inter alia*, the significance of the living resources of the area to the economy of the coastal State concerned and its other national interests, the provisions of articles 69 and 70, the requirements of developing States in the subregion or region in harvesting part of the surplus and the need to minimize economic dislocation in States whose nationals have habitually fished in the zone or which have made substantial efforts in research and identification of stocks.

4. Nationals of other States fishing in the exclusive economic zone shall comply with the conservation measures and with the other terms and conditions established in the laws and regulations of the coastal State. These laws and regulations shall be

consistent with this Convention and may relate, *inter alia*, to the following:

(a) licensing of fishermen, fishing vessels and equipment, including payment of fees and other forms of remuneration, which, in the case of developing coastal States, may consist of adequate compensation in the field of financing, equipment and technology relating to the fishing industry;

(b) determining the species which may be caught, and fixing quotas of catch, whether in relation to particular stocks or groups of stocks or catch per vessel over a period of time or to the catch by nationals of any State during a specified period;

(c) regulating seasons and areas of fishing, the types, sizes and amount of gear, and the types, sizes and number of fishing vessels that may be used;

(d) fixing the age and size of fish and other species that may be caught;

(e) specifying information required of fishing vessels, including catch and effort statistics and vessel position reports;

(f) requiring, under the authorization and control of the coastal State, the conduct of specified fisheries research programmes and regulating the conduct of such research, including the sampling of catches, disposition of samples and reporting of associated scientific data;

(g) the placing of observers or trainees on board such vessels by the coastal State;

(h) the landing of all or any part of the catch by such vessels in the ports of the coastal State;

(i) terms and conditions relating to joint ventures or other co-operative arrangements;

(j) requirements for the training of personnel and the transfer of fisheries technology, including enhancement of the coastal State's capability of undertaking fisheries research;

(k) enforcement procedures.

5. Coastal States shall give due notice of conservation and management laws and regulations.

Article 63
Stocks occurring within the exclusive economic zones of two or more coastal States or both within the exclusive economic zone and in an area beyond and adjacent to it

1. Where the same stock or stocks of associated species occur within the exclusive economic zones of two or more coastal States, these States shall seek, either directly or through appropriate subregional or regional organizations, to agree upon the measures necessary to co-ordinate and ensure the conservation and development of such stocks without prejudice to the other provisions of this Part.

2. Where the same stock or stocks of associated species occur both within the exclusive economic zone and in an area beyond and adjacent to the zone, the coastal State and the States fishing for such stocks in the adjacent area shall seek, either directly or through appropriate subregional or regional organizations, to agree upon the measures necessary for the conservation of these stocks in the adjacent area.

Article 64
Highly migratory species

1. The coastal State and other States whose nationals fish in the region for the highly migratory species listed in Annex I shall co-operate directly or through appropriate international organizations with a view to ensuring conservation and promoting the objective of optimum utilization of such species throughout the region, both within and beyond the exclusive economic zone. In regions for which no appropriate international organization exists, the coastal State and other States whose nationals harvest these species in the region shall co-operate to establish such an organization and participate in its work.

2. The provisions of paragraph 1 apply in addition to the other provisions of this Part.

Article 65
Marine mammals

Nothing in this Part restricts the right of a coastal State or the competence of an international organization, as appropriate, to prohibit, limit or regulate the exploitation of marine mammals more strictly than provided for in this Part. States shall co-operate with a view to the conservation of marine mammals and in the case of cetaceans shall in particular work through the appropriate international organizations for their conservation, management and study.

Article 66
Anadromous stocks

1. States in whose rivers anadromous stocks [i.e. stocks ascending rivers to spawn] originate shall have the primary interest in and responsibility for such stocks.

2. The State of origin of anadromous stocks shall ensure their conservation by the establishment of appropriate regulatory measures for fishing in all waters landward of the outer limits of its exclusive economic zone and for fishing provided for in paragraph 3(b). The State of origin may, after consultations with the other States referred to in paragraphs 3 and 4 fishing these stocks, establish total catches for stocks originating in its rivers.

3. (a) Fisheries for anadromous stocks shall be conducted only in waters landward of the outer limits of exclusive economic zones, except in cases where this provision would result in economic dislocation for a State other than the State of origin. With respect to such fishing beyond the outer limits of the exclusive economic zone, States concerned shall maintain consultations with a view to achieving agreement on terms and conditions of such fishing giving due regard to the conservation requirements and the needs of the State of origin in respect of these stocks.

(b) The State of origin shall co-operate in minimizing economic dislocation in such other States fishing these stocks, taking into account the normal catch and the mode of operations of such States, and all the areas in which such fishing has occurred.

(c) States referred to in subparagraph (b), participating by agreement with the State of origin in measures to renew anadromous stocks, particularly by expenditures for that purpose, shall be given special consideration by the State of origin in the harvesting of stocks originating in its rivers.

(d) Enforcement of regulations regarding anadromous stocks beyond the exclusive economic zone shall be by agreement between the State of origin and the other States concerned.

4. In cases where anadromous stocks migrate into or through the waters landward of the outer limits of the exclusive economic zone of a State other than the State of origin, such State shall co-operate with the State of origin with regard to the conservation and management of such stocks.

5. The State of origin of anadromous stocks and other States fishing these stocks shall make arrangements for the implementation of the provisions of this article, where appropriate, through regional organizations.

Article 67
Catadromous species

1. A coastal State in whose waters catadromous species [species descending to or towards the sea to spawn] spend the greater part of their life cycle shall have responsibility for the management of these species and shall ensure the ingress and egress of migrating fish.

2. Harvesting of catadromous species shall be conducted only in waters landward of the outer limits of exclusive economic zones. When conducted in exclusive economic zones, harvesting shall be subject to this article and the other provisions of this Convention concerning fishing in these zones.

3. In these cases where catadromous fish migrate through the exclusive economic zone of another State, whether as junvenile or maturing fish, the management, including harvesting, of such fish shall be regulated by agreement between the State mentioned in paragraph 1 and the other State concerned. Such agreement shall ensure the rational management of the species and take into account the responsibilities of the State mentioned in paragraph 1 for the maintenance of these species.

Article 68
Sedentary species

This Part does not apply to sedentary species as defined in article 77, paragraph 4.

Article 69
Right of land-locked States

1. Land-locked States shall have the right to participate, on an equitable basis, in the exploitation of an appropriate part of the surplus of the living resources of the exclusive economic zones of coastal States of the same subregion or region, taking into account the relevant economic and geographical circumstances of all the States concerned and in conformity with the provisions of this article and of articles 61 and 62.

2. The terms and modalities of such participation shall be established by the

States concerned through bilateral, subregional or regional agreements taking into account, *inter alia*:

(a) the need to avoid effects detrimental to fishing communities or fishing industries of the coastal State;

(b) the extent to which the land-locked State, in accordance with the provisions of this article, is participating or is entitled to participate under existing bilateral, subregional or regional agreements in the exploitation of living resources of the exclusive economic zones of other coastal States;

(c) the extent to which other land-locked States and geographically disadvantaged States are participating in the exploitation of the living resources of the exclusive economic zone of the coastal State and the consequent need to avoid a particular burden for any single coastal State or a part of it;

(d) the nutritional needs of the populations of the respective States.

3. When the harvesting capacity of a coastal State approaches a point which would enable it to harvest the entire allowable catch of the living resources in its exclusive economic zone, the coastal State and other States concerned shall co-operate in the establishment of equitable arrangements on a bilateral, subregional or regional basis to allow for participation of developing land-locked States of the same subregion or region in the exploitation of the living resources of the exclusive economic zones of coastal States of the subregion or region, as may be appropriate in the circumstances and on terms satisfactory to all parties. In the implementation of this provision the factors mentioned in paragraph 2 shall also be taken into account.

4. Developed land-locked States shall, under the provisions of this article, be entitled to participate in the exploitation of living resources only in the exclusive economic zones of developed coastal States of the same subregion or region having regard to the extent to which the coastal State, in giving access to other States to the living resources of its exclusive economic zone, has taken into account the need to minimize detrimental effects on fishing communities and economic dislocation in States whose nationals have habitually fished in the zone.

5. The above provisions are without prejudice to arrangements agreed upon in subregions or regions where the coastal States may grant to land-locked States of the same subregion or region equal or preferential rights for the exploitation of the living resources in the exclusive economic zones.

Article 70
Right of geographically disadvantaged States

1. Geographically disadvantaged States shall have the right to participate, on an equitable basis, in the exploitation of an appropriate part of the surplus of the living resources of the exclusive economic zones of coastal States of the same subregion or region, taking into account the relevant economic and geographical circumstances of all the States concerned and in conformity with the provisions of this article and of articles 61 and 62.

2. For the purposes of this Part, "geographically disadvantaged States" means coastal States, including States bordering enclosed or semi-enclosed seas, whose geographical situation makes them dependent upon the exploitation of the living resources of the exclusive economic zones of other States in the subregion or region for adequate supplies of fish for the nutritional purposes of their populations or parts thereof, and coastal States which can claim no exclusive economic zones of their own.

3. The terms and modalities of such participation shall be established by the States concerned through bilateral, subregional or regional agreements taking into account, *inter alia*:

(a) the need to avoid effects detrimental to fishing communities or fishing industries of the coastal State;

(b) the extent to which the geographically disadvantaged State, in accordance with the provisions of this article, is participating or is entitled to participate under existing bilateral, subregional or regional agreements in the exploitation of living resources of the exclusive economic zones of other coastal States;

(c) the extent to which other geographically disadvantaged States and land-locked States are participating in the exploitation of the living resources of the exclusive economic zone of the coastal State and the consequent need to avoid a particular burden for any single coastal State or a part of it;

(d) the nutritional needs of the populations of the respective States.

4. When the harvesting capacity of a coastal State approaches a point which would enable it to harvest the entire allowable catch of the living resources in its exclusive economic zone, the coastal State and other States concerned shall co-operate in the establishment of equitable arrangements on a bilateral, subregional or regional basis to allow for participation of developing geographically disadvantaged States of the same subregion or region in the exploitation of the living resources of the exclusive economic zones of coastal States of the subregion or region, as may be appropriate in the circumstances and on terms satisfactory to all parties. In the implementation of this provision the factors mentioned in paragraph 3 shall also be taken into account.

5. Developed geographically disadvantaged States shall, under the provisions of this article, be entitled to participate in the exploitation of living resources only in the exclusive economic zones of developed coastal States of the same subregion or region having regard to the extent to which the coastal State, in giving access to other States to the living resources of its exclusive economic zone, has taken into account the need to minimize detrimental effects on fishing communities and economic dislocation in States whose nationals have habitually fished in the zone.

6. The above provisions are without prejudice to arrangements agreed upon in subregions or regions where the coastal States may grant to geographically disadvantaged States of the same subregion or region equal or preferential rights for the exploitation of the living resources in the exclusive economic zones.

Article 71
Non-applicability of articles 69 and 70

The provisions of articles 69 and 70 do not apply in the case of a coastal State whose economy is overwhelmingly dependent on the exploitation of the living resources of its exclusive economic zone.

Article 72
Restrictions on transfer of rights

1. Rights provided under articles 69 and 70 to exploit living resources shall not be directly or indirectly transferred to third States or their nationals by lease or licence, by establishing joint ventures or in any other manner which has the effect of such transfer unless otherwise agreed by the States concerned.

2. The foregoing provision does not preclude the States concerned from obtaining technical or financial assistance from third States or international organizations in order to facilitate the exercise of the rights pursuant to articles 69 and 70, provided that it does not have the effect referred to in paragraph 1.

Article 73
Enforcement of laws and regulations of the coastal State

1. The coastal State may, in the exercise of its sovereign rights to explore, exploit, conserve and manage the living resources in the exclusive economic zone, take such measures, including boarding, inspection, arrest and judicial proceedings, as may be necessary to ensure compliance with the laws and regulations adopted by it in conformity with this Convention.

2. Arrested vessels and their crews shall be promptly released upon the posting of reasonable bond or other security.

3. Coastal State penalties for violations of fisheries laws and regulations in the exclusive economic zone may not include imprisonment, in the absence of agreements to the contrary by the States concerned, or any other form of corporal punishment.

4. In cases of arrest or detention of foreign vessels the coastal State shall promptly notify the flag State, through appropriate channels, of the action taken and of any penalties subsequently imposed.

Article 74
Delimitation of the exclusive economic zone between States with opposite or adjacent coasts

1. The delimitation of the exclusive economic zone between States with opposite or adjacent coasts shall be effected by agreement on the basis of international law, as referred to in Article 38 of the Statute of the International Court of Justice, in order to achieve an equitable solution.

2. If no agreement can be reached within a reasonable period of time, the States concerned shall resort to the procedures provided for in Part XV.

3. Pending agreement as provided for in paragraph 1, the States concerned, in a spirit of understanding and co-operation, shall make every effort to enter into provisional arrangements of a practical nature and, during this transitional period, not to jeopardize or hamper the reaching of the final agreement. Such arrangements shall be without prejudice to the final delimitation.

4. Where there is an agreement in force between the States concerned, questions relating to the delimitation of the exclusive economic zone shall be determined in accordance with the provisions of that agreement.

Article 75
Charts and lists of geographical co-ordinates

1. Subject to this Part, the outer limit lines of the exclusive economic zone and the lines of delimitation drawn in accordance with article 74 shall be shown on charts of a scale or scales adequate for ascertaining their position. Where appropriate, lists of geographical co-ordinates of points, specifying the geodetic datum, may be substituted for such outer limit lines or lines of delimitation.

2. The coastal State shall give due publicity to such charts or lists of geographical co-ordinates and shall deposit a copy of each such chart or list with the Secretary-General of the United Nations.

PART VI

Continental Shelf

Article 76
Definition of the continental shelf

1. The continental shelf of a coastal State comprises the sea-bed and subsoil of the submarine areas that extent beyond its territorial sea throughout the natural prolongation of its land territory to the outer edge of the continental margin, or to a distance of 200 nautical miles from the baselines from which the breadth of the territorial sea is measured where the outer edge of the continental margin does not extend up to that distance.

2. The continental shelf of a coastal State shall not extend beyond the limits provided for in paragraphs 4 to 6.

3. The continental margin comprises the submerged prolongation of the land mass of the coastal State, and consists of the sea-bed and subsoil of the shelf, the slope and the rise. It does not include the deep ocean floor with its oceanic ridges of the subsoil thereof.

4. (a) For the purposes of this Convention, the coastal State shall establish the outer edge of the continental margin wherever the margin extends beyond 200 nautical miles from the baselines from which the breadth of the territorial sea is measured, by either:

(i) a line delineated in accordance with paragraph 7 by reference to the outermost fixed points at each of which the thickness of sedimentary rocks is at least 1 per cent of the shortest distance from such point to the foot of the continental slope; or

(ii) a line delineated in accordance with paragraph 7 by reference to fixed points not more than 60 nautical miles from the foot of the continental slope.

(b) In the absence of evidence to the contrary, the foot of the continental slope shall be determined as the point of maximum change in the gradient at its base.

5. The fixed points comprising the line of the outer limits of the continental shelf on the sea-bed, drawn in accordance with paragraph 4(a)(i) and (ii), either shall not exceed 350 nautical miles from the baselines from which the breadth of the territorial sea is measured or shall not exceed 100 nautical miles from the 2,500 metre isobath, which is a line connecting the depth of 2,500 metres.

6. Notwithstanding the provisions of paragraph 5, on submarine ridges, the outer limit of the continental shelf shall not exceed 350 nautical miles from the baselines from which the breadth of the territorial sea is measured. This paragraph does not apply to submarine elevations that are natural components of the continental margin, such as its plateaux, rises, caps, banks and spurs.

7. The coastal State shall delineate the outer limits of its continental shelf, where that shelf extends beyond 200 nautical miles from the baselines from which the breadth of the territorial sea is measured, by straight lines not exceeding 60 nautical miles in length, connecting fixed points, defined by co-ordinates of latitude and longitude.

8. Information on the limits of the continental shelf beyond 200 nautical miles

from the baselines from which the breadth of the territorial sea is measured shall be submitted by the coastal State to the Commission on the Limits of the Continental Shelf set up under Annex II on the basis of equitable geographical representation. The Commission shall make recommendations to coastal States on matters related to the establishment of the outer limits of their continental shelf. The limits of the shelf established by a coastal State on the basis of these recommendations shall be final and binding.

9. The coastal State shall deposit with the Secretary-General of the United Nations charts and relevant information, including geodetic data, permanently describing the outer limits of its continental shelf. The Secretary-General shall give due publicity thereto.

10. The provisions of this article are without prejudice to the question of delimitation of the continental shelf between States with opposite or adjacent coasts.

Article 77
Rights of the coastal State over the continental shelf

1. The coastal State exercises over the continental shelf sovereign rights for the purpose of exploring it and exploiting its natural resources.

2. The rights referred to in paragraph 1 are exclusive in the sense that, if the coastal State does not explore the continental shelf or exploit its natural resources, no one may undertake these activities without the express consent of the coastal State.

3. The rights of the coastal State over the continental shelf do not depend on occupation, effective or notional, or on any express proclamation.

4. The natural resources referred to in this Part consist of the mineral and other non-living resources of the sea-bed and subsoil together with living organisms belonging to sedentary species, that is to say, organisms which, at the harvestable stage, either are immobile on or under the sea-bed or are unable to move except in constant physical contact with the sea-bed or the subsoil.

Article 78
Legal status of the superjacent waters and air space and the rights and freedoms of other States

1. The rights of the coastal State over the continental shelf do not affect the legal status of the superjacent waters or of the air space above those waters.

2. The exercise of the rights of the coastal State over the continental shelf must not infringe or result in any unjustifiable interference with navigation and other rights and freedoms of other States as provided for in this Convention.

Article 79
Submarine cables and pipelines on the continental shelf

1. All States are entitled to lay submarine cables and pipelines on the continental shelf, in accordance with the provisions of this article.

2. Subject to its right to take reasonable measures for the exploration of the continental shelf, the exploitation of its natural resources and the prevention, reduction and control of pollution from pipelines, the coastal State may not impede the laying or maintenance of such cables or pipelines.

3. The delineation of the course for the laying of such pipelines on the continental shelf is subject to the consent of the coastal State.

4. Nothing in this Part affects the right of the coastal State to establish conditions for cables or pipelines entering its territory or territorial sea, or its jurisdiction over cables and pipelines constructed or used in connection with the exploration of its continental shelf or exploitation of its resources or the operations of artificial islands, installations and structures under its jurisdiction.

5. When laying submarine cables or pipelines, States shall have due regard to cables or pipelines already in position. In particular, possibilities of repairing existing cables or pipelines shall not be prejudiced.

Article 80
Artificial islands, installations and structures on the continental shelf

Article 60 applies *mutatis mutandis* to artificial islands, installations and structures on the continental shelf.

Article 81
Drilling on the continental shelf

The coastal State shall have the exclusive right to authorize and regulate drilling on the continental shelf for all purposes.

Article 82
Payments and contributions with respect to the exploitation of the continental shelf beyond 200 nautical miles

1. The coastal State shall make payments or contributions in kind in respect of the exploitation of the non-living resources of the continental shelf beyond 200 nautical miles from the baselines from which the breadth of the territorial sea is measured.

2. The payments and contributions shall be made annually with respect to all production at a site after the first five years of production at that site. For the sixth year, the rate of payment or contribution shall be 1 per cent of the value or volume of production at the site. The rate shall increase by 1 per cent for each subsequent year until the twelfth year and shall remain at 7 per cent thereafter. Production does not include resources used in connection with exploitation.

3. A developing State which is a net importer of a mineral resource produced from its continental shelf is exempt from making such payments or contributions in respect of that mineral resource.

4. The payments or contributions shall be made through the Authority, which shall distribute them to States Parties to this Convention, on the basis of equitable sharing criteria, taking into account the interests and needs of developing States, particularly the least developed and the land-locked among them.

Article 83
Delimitation of the continental shelf between States with opposite or adjacent coasts

1. The delimitation of the continental shelf between States with opposite or adjacent coasts shall be effected by agreement on the basis of international law, as referred to in Article 38 of the Statute of the International Court of Justice, in order to achieve an equitable solution.

2. If no agreement can be reached within a reasonable period of time, the States concerned shall resort to the procedures provided for in Part XV.

3. Pending agreement as provided for in paragraph 1, the States concerned, in a spirit of understanding and co-operation, shall make every effort to enter into provisional arrangements of a practical nature and, during this transitional period, not to jeopardize or hamper the reaching of the final agreement. Such arrangements shall be without prejudice to the final delimitation.

4. Where there is an agreement in force between the States concerned, questions relating to the delimitation of the continental shelf shall be determined in accordance with the provisions of that agreement.

Article 84
Charts and lists of geographical co-ordinates

1. Subject to this Part, the outer limit lines of the continental shelf and the lines of delimitation drawn in accordance with article 83 shall be shown on charts of a scale or scales adequate for ascertaining their position. Where appropriate, lists of geographical co-ordinates of points, specifying the geodetic datum, may be substituted for such outer limit lines or lines of delimitation.

2. The coastal State shall give due publicity to such charts or lists of geographical co-ordinates and shall deposit a copy of each such chart or list with the Secretary-General of the United Nations and, in the case of those showing the outer limit lines of the continental shelf, with the Secretary-General of the Authority.

Article 85
Tunnelling

This Part does not prejudice the right of the coastal State to exploit the subsoil by means of tunnelling, irrespective of the depth of water above the subsoil.

PART VII

High Seas

Section 1. General Provisions

Article 86
Application of the provisions of this Part

The provisions of this Part apply to all parts of the sea that are not included in the exclusive economic zone, in the territorial sea or in the internal waters of a State, or in the archipelagic waters of an archipelagic State. This article does not entail any abridgement of the freedoms enjoyed by all States in the exclusive economic zone in accordance with article 58.

Article 87
Freedom of the high seas

1. The high seas are open to all States, whether coastal or land-locked. Freedom of the high seas is exercised under the conditions laid down by this Convention and by other rules of international law. It comprises, *inter alia*, both for coastal and land-locked States:

(a) freedom of navigation;

(b) freedom of overflight;

(c) freedom to lay submarine cables and pipelines, subject to Part VI;

(d) freedom to construct artificial islands and other installations permitted under international law, subject to Part VI;

(e) freedom of fishing, subject to the conditions laid down in section 2;

(f) freedom of scientific research, subject to Parts VI and XIII.

2. These freedoms shall be exercised by all States with due regard for the interests of other States in their exercise of the freedom of the high seas, and also with due regard for the rights under this Convention with respect to activities in the area.

Article 88
Reservation of the high seas for peaceful purposes

The high seas shall be reserved for peaceful purposes.

Article 89
Invalidity of claims of sovereignty over the high seas

No State may validly purport to subject any part of the high seas to its sovereignty.

Article 90
Right of navigation

Every State, whether coastal or land-locked, has the right to sail ships flying its flag on the high seas.

Article 91
Nationality of ships

1. Every State shall fix the conditions for the grant of its nationality to ships, for the registration of ships in its territory, and for the right to fly its flag. Ships have the nationality of the State whose flag they are entitled to fly. There must exist a genuine link between the State and the ship.

2. Every State shall issue to ships to which it has granted the right to fly its flag documents to that effect.

Article 92
Status of ships

1. Ships shall sail under the flag of one State only and, save in exceptional cases expressly provided for in international treaties or in this Convention, shall be subject to its exclusive jurisdiction on the high seas. A ship may not change its flag during a voyage or while in a port of call, save in the case of a real transfer of ownership or change of registry.

2. A ship which sails under the flags of two or more States, using them according to convenience, may not claim any of the nationalities in question with respect to any other State, and may be assimilated to a ship without nationality.

Article 93
Ships flying the flag of the United Nations, its specialized agencies and the International Atomic Energy Agency

The preceding articles do not prejudice the question of ships employed on the official service of the United Nations, its specialized agencies or the International Atomic Energy Agency, flying the flag of the organization.

Article 94
Duties of the flag State

1. Every State shall effectively exercise its jurisdiction and control in administrative, technical and social matters over ships flying its flag.

2. In particular every State shall:

(a) maintain a register of ships containing the names and particulars of ships flying its flag, except those which are excluded from generally accepted international regulations on account of their small size; and

(b) assume jurisdiction under its internal law over each ship flying its flag and its master, officers and crew in respect of administrative, technical and social matters concerning the ship.

3. Every State shall take such measures for ships flying its flag as are necessary to ensure safety at sea with regard, *inter alia*, to:

(a) the construction, equipment and seaworthiness of ships;

(b) the manning of ships, labour conditions and the training of crews, taking into account the applicable international instruments;

(c) the use of signals, the maintenance of communications and the prevention of collisions.

4. Such measures shall include those necessary to ensure:

(a) that each ship, before registration and thereafter at appropriate intervals, is surveyed by a qualified surveyor of ships, and has on board such charts, nautical publications and navigational equipment and instruments as are appropriate for the safe navigation of the ship;

(b) that each ship is in the charge of a master and officers who possess appropriate qualifications, in particular in seamanship, navigation, communications and marine engineering, and that the crew is appropriate in qualification and numbers for the type, size, machinery and equipment of the ship;

(c) that the master, officers and, to the extent appropriate, the crew are fully conversant with and required to observe the applicable international regulations concerning the safety of life at sea, the prevention of collisions, the prevention, reduction and control of marine pollution, and the maintenance of communications by radio.

5. In taking the measures called for in paragraphs 3 and 4 each State is required to conform to generally accepted international regulations, procedures and practices and to take any steps which may be necessary to secure their observance.

6. A State which has clear grounds to believe that proper jurisdiction and control with respect to a ship have not been exercised may report the facts to the flag State. Upon receiving such a report, the flag State shall investigate the matter and, if appropriate, take any action necessary to remedy the situation.

7. Each State shall cause an inquiry to be held by or before a suitably qualified person or persons into every marine casualty or incident of navigation on the high seas involving a ship flying its flag and causing loss of life or serious injury to nationals of another State or serious damage to ships or installations of another State or to the marine environment. The flag State and the other State shall co-operate in the conduct of any inquiry held by that other State into any such marine casualty or incident of navigation.

Article 95

Immunity of warships on the high seas

Warships on the high seas have complete immunity from the jurisdiction of any State other than the flag State.

Article 96

Immunity of ships used only on government non-commercial service

Ships owned or operated by a State and used only on government non-commercial service shall, on the high seas, have complete immunity from the jurisdiction of any State other than the flag State.

Article 97

Penal jurisdiction in matters of collision or any other incident of navigation

1. In the event of a collision or any other incident of navigation concerning a ship on the high seas, involving the penal or disciplinary responsibility of the master or of any other person in the service of the ship, no penal or disciplinary proceedings may be instituted against such person except before the judicial or administrative authorities either of the flag State or of the State of which such person is a national.

2. In disciplinary matters, the State which has issued a master's certificate or a certificate of competence or licence shall alone be competent, after due legal process, to pronounce the withdrawal of such certificates, even if the holder is not a national of the State which issued them.

3. No arrest or detention of the ship, even as a measure of investigation, shall be ordered by any authorities other than those of the flag State.

Article 98

Duty to render assistance

1. Every State shall require the master of a ship flying its flag, in so far as he can do so without serious danger to the ship, the crew or the passengers:

(a) to render assistance to any person found at sea in danger of being lost;

(b) to proceed with all possible speed to the rescue of persons in distress, if informed of their need of assistance, in so far as such action may reasonably be expected of him;

(c) after a collision, to render assistance to the other ship, its crew and its passengers and, where possible, to inform the other ship of the name of his own ship, its port of registry and the nearest port at which it will call.

2. Every coastal State shall promote the establishment, operation and maintenance of an adequate and effective search and rescue service regarding safety on and over the sea and, where circumstances so require, by way of mutual regional arrangements co-operate with neighbouring States for this purpose.

Article 99
Prohibition of the transport of slaves

Every State shall take effective measures to prevent and punish the transport of slaves in ships authorized to fly its flag and to prevent the unlawful use of its flag for that purpose. Any slave taking refuge on board any ship, whatever its flag, shall *ipso facto* be free.

Article 100
Duty to co-operate in the repression of piracy

All States shall co-operate to the fullest possible extent in the repression of piracy on the high seas or in any other place outside the jurisdiction of any State.

Article 101
Definition of piracy

Piracy consists of any of the following acts:

(a) any illegal acts of violence or detention, or any act of depredation, committed for private ends by the crew or the passengers of a private ship or a private aircraft, and directed:

(i) on the high seas, against another ship or aircraft, or against persons or property on board such ship or aircraft;

(ii) against a ship, aircraft, persons or property in a place outside the jurisdiction of any State;

(b) any act of voluntary participation in the operation of a ship or of an aircraft with knowledge of facts making it a pirate ship or aircraft;

(c) any act of inciting or of intentionally facilitating an act described in subparagraph (a) or (b).

Article 102
Piracy by a warship, government ship or government aircraft whose crew has mutinied

The acts of piracy, as defined in article 101, committed by a warship, government ship or government aircraft whose crew has mutinied and taken control of the ship or aircraft are assimilated to acts committed by a private ship or aircraft.

Article 103
Definition of a priate ship or aircraft

A ship or aircraft is considered a priate ship or aircraft if it is intended by the persons in dominant control to be used for the purpose of committing one of the acts referred to in article 101. The same applies if the ship or aircraft has been used to commit any such act, so long as it remains under the control of the persons guilty of that act.

Article 104
Retention or loss of the nationality of a pirate ship or aircraft

A ship or aircraft may retain its nationality although it has become a pirate ship or aircraft. The retention or loss of nationality is determined by the law of the State from which such nationality was derived.

Article 105
Seizure of a pirate ship or aircraft

On the high seas, or in any other place outside the jurisdiction of any State, every State may seize a pirate ship or aircraft, or a ship or aircraft taken by piracy and under the control of pirates, and arrest the persons and seize the property on board. The courts of the State which carried out the seizure may decide upon the penalities to be imposed, and may also determine the action to be taken with regard to the ships, aircraft or property, subject to the rights of third parties acting in good faith.

Article 106
Liability for seizure without adequate grounds

Where the seizure of a ship or aircraft on suspicion of piracy has been effected without adequate grounds, the State making the seizure shall be liable to the State the nationality of which is possessed by the ship or aircraft for any loss or damage caused by the seizure.

Article 107
Ships and aircraft which are entitled to seize on account of piracy

A seizure on account of piracy may be carried out only by warships or military aircraft, or other ships or aircraft clearly marked and identifiable as being on government service and authorized to that effect.

Article 108
Illicit traffic in narcotic drugs or psychotropic substances

1. All States shall co-operate in the suppression of illicit traffic in narcotic drugs and psychotropic substances engaged in by ships on the high seas contrary to international conventions.

2. Any State which has reasonable grounds for believing that a ship flying its flag is engaged in illicit traffic in narcotic drugs or psychotropic substances may request the co-operation of other States to suppress such traffic.

Article 109
Unauthorized broadcasting from the high seas

1. All States shall co-operate in the suppression of unauthorized broadcasting from the high seas.

2. For the purposes of this Convention, "unauthorized broadcasting" means the transmission of sound radio or television broadcasts from a ship or installation on the high seas intended for reception by the general public contrary to international regulations, but excluding the transmission of distress calls.

3. Any person engaged in unauthorized broadcasting may be prosecuted before the court of:

(a) the flag State of the ship;

(b) the State of registry of the installation;

(c) the State of which the person is a national;

(d) any State where the transmissions can be received; or

(e) any State where authorized radio communication is suffering interference.

4. On the high seas, a State having jurisdiction in accordance with paragraph 3 may, in conformity with article 110, arrest any person or ship engaged in unauthorized broadcasting and seize the broadcasting apparatus.

Article 110
Right of visit

1. Except where acts of interference derive from powers conferred by treaty, a warship which encounters on the high seas a foreign ship, other than a ship entitled to complete immunity in accordance with articles 95 and 96, is not justified in boarding it unless there is reasonable ground for suspecting that:

(a) the ship is engaged in piracy;

(b) the ship is engaged in the slave trade;

(c) the ship is engaged in unauthorized broadcasting and the flag State of the warship has jurisdiction under article 109;

(d) the ship is without nationality; or

(e) though flying a foreign flag or refusing to show its flag, the ship is, in reality, of the same nationality as the warship.

2. In the cases provided for in paragraph 1, the warship may proceed to verify the ship's right to fly its flag. To this end, it may send a boat under the command of an officer to the suspected ship. If suspicion remains after the documents have been checked, it may proceed to a further examination on board the ship, which must be carried out with all possible consideration.

3. If the suspicions prove to be unfounded, and provided that the ship boarded has not committed any act justifying them, it shall be compensated for any loss or damage that may have been sustained.

4. These provisions apply *mutatis mutandis* to military aircraft.

5. These provisions also apply to any other duly authorized ships or aircraft clearly marked and identifiable as being on government service.

Article 111
Right of hot pursuit

1. The hot pursuit of a foreign ship may be undertaken when the competent authorities of the coastal State have good reason to believe that the ship has violated the laws and regulations of that State. Such pursuit must be commenced when the foreign ship or one of its boats is within the internal waters, the archipelagic waters, the territorial sea or the contiguous zone of the pursuing State, and may only be continued outside the territorial sea or the contiguous zone if the pursuit has not been interrupted. It is not necessary that, at the

time when the foreign ship within the territorial sea or the contiguous zone receives the order to stop, the ship giving the order should likewise be within the territorial sea or the contiguous zone. If the foreign ship is within a contiguous zone, as defined in article 33, the pursuit may only be undertaken if there has been a violation of the rights for the protection of which the zone was established.

2. The right of hot pursuit shall apply *mutatis mutandis* to violations in the exclusive economic zone or on the continental shelf, including safety zones around continental shelf installations, of the laws and regulations of the coastal State applicable in accordance with this Convention to the exclusive economic zone or the continental shelf, including such safety zones.

3. The right of hot pursuit ceases as soon as the ship pursued enters the territorial sea of its own State or of a third State.

4. Hot pursuit is not deemed to have begun unless the pursuing ship has satisfied itself by such practicable means as may be available that the ship pursued or one of its boats or other craft working as a team and using the ship pursued as a mother ship is within the limits of the territorial sea, or, as the case may be, within the contiguous zone or the exclusive economic zone or above the continental shelf. The pursuit may only be commenced after a visual or auditory signal to stop has been given at a distance which enables it to be seen or heard by the foreign ship.

5. The right of hot pursuit may be exercised only by warships or military aircraft, or other ships or aircraft clearly marked and identifiable as being on government service and authorized to that effect.

6. Where hot pursuit is effected by an aircraft:

(a) the provisions of paragraphs 1 to 4 shall apply *mutatis mutandis*;

(b) the aircraft giving the order to stop must itself actively pursue the ship until a ship or another aircraft of the coastal State, summoned by the aircraft, arrives to take over the pursuit, unless the aircraft is itself able to arrest the ship. It does not suffice to justify an arrest outside the territorial sea that the ship was merely sighted by the aircraft as an offender or suspected offender, if it was not both ordered to stop and pursued by the aircraft itself or other aircraft or ships which continue the pursuit without interruption.

7. The release of a ship arrested within the jurisdiction of a State and escorted to a port of that State for the purposes of an inquiry before the competent authorities may not be claimed solely on the ground that the ship, in the course of its voyage, was escorted across a portion of the exclusive economic zone or the high seas, if the circumstances rendered this necessary.

8. Where a ship has been stopped or arrested outside the territorial sea in circumstances which do not justify the exercise of the right of hot pursuit, it shall be compensated for any loss or damage that may have been thereby sustained.

Article 112
Right to lay submarine cables and pipelines

1. All States are entitled to lay submarine cables and pipelines on the bed of the high seas beyond the continental shelf.

2. Article 79, paragraph 5, applies to such cables and pipelines.

Article 113
Breaking or injury of a submarine cable or pipeline

Every State shall adopt the laws and regulations necessary to provide that the breaking or injury by a ship flying its flag or by a person subject to its jurisdiction of a submarine cable beneath the high seas done wilfully or through culpable negligence, in such a manner as to be liable to interrupt or obstruct telegraphic or telephonic communications, and similarly the breaking or injury of a submarine pipeline or high-voltage power cable, shall be a punishable offence. This provision shall apply also to conduct calculated or likely to result in such breaking or injury. However, it shall not apply to any break or injury caused by persons who acted merely with the legitimate object of saving their lives or their ships, after having taken all necessary precautions to avoid such break or injury.

Article 114
Breaking or injury by owners of a submarine cable or pipeline of another submarine cable or pipeline

Every State shall adopt the laws and regulations necessary to provide that, if persons subject to its jurisdiction who are the owners of a submarine cable or pipeline beneath the high seas, in laying or repairing that cable or pipeline, cause a break in or injury to another cable or pipeline, they shall bear the cost of the repairs.

Article 115
Indemnity for loss incurred in avoiding injury to a submarine cable or pipeline

Every State shall adopt the laws and regulations necessary to ensure that the owners of ships who can prove that they have sacrificed an anchor, a net or any other fishing gear, in order to avoid injuring a submarine cable or pipeline, shall be indemnified by the owner of the cable or pipeline, provided that the owner of the ship has taken all reasonable precautionary measures beforehand.

Section 2. Conservation and Management of the Living Resources of the High Seas

Article 116
Right to fish on the high seas

All States have the right for their nationals to engage in fishing on the high seas subject to:

(a) their treaty obligations;

(b) the rights and duties as well as the interests of coastal States provided for, *inter alia*, in article 63, paragraph 2, and articles 64 to 67; and

(c) the provisions of this section.

Article 117
Duty of States to adopt with respect to their nationals measures for the conservation of the living resources of the high seas

All States have the duty to take, or to co-operate with other States in taking, such measures for their respective nationals as may be necessary for the conservation of the living resources of the high seas.

Article 118
Co-operation of States in the conservation and management of living resources

States shall co-operate with each other in the conservation and management of living resources in the areas of the high seas. States whose nationals exploit identical living resources, or different living resources in the same area, shall enter into negotiations with a view to taking the measures necessary for the conservation of the living resources concerned. They shall, as appropriate, co-operate to establish subregional or regional fisheries organizations to this end.

Article 119
Conservation of the living resources of the high seas

1. In determining the allowable catch and establishing other conservation measures for the living resources in the high seas, States shall:

(a) take measures which are designed, on the best scientific evidence available to the States concerned, to maintain or restore populations of harvested species at levels which can produce the maximum sustainable yield, as qualified by relevant environmental and economic factors, including the special requirements of developing States, and taking into account fishing patterns, the interdependence of stocks and any generally recommended international minimum standards, whether subregional, regional or global;

(b) take into consideration the effects on species associated with or dependent upon harvested species with a view to maintaining or restoring populations of such associated or dependent species above levels at which their reproduction may become seriously threatened.

2. Available scientific information, catch and fishing effort statistics, and other data relevant to the conservation of fish stocks shall be contributed and exchanged on a regular basis through competent international organizations, whether subregional, regional or global, where appropriate and with participation by all States concerned.

3. States concerned shall ensure that conservation measures and their implementation do not discriminate in form or in fact against the fishermen of any State.

Article 120
Marine mammals

Article 65 also applies to the conservation and management of marine mammals in the high seas.

PART VIII

Regime of Islands

Article 121
Régime of islands

1. An island is a naturally formed area of land, surrounded by water, which is above water at high tide.

2. Except as provided for in paragraph 3, the territorial sea, the contiguous zone, the exclusive economic zone and the continental shelf of an island are determined in accordance with the provisions of this Convention applicable to other land territory.

3. Rocks which cannot sustain human habitation or economic life of their own shall have no exclusive economic zone or continental shelf.

PART IX

Enclosed or Semi-Enclosed Seas

Article 122
Definition

For the purposes of this Convention, "enclosed or semi-enclosed sea" means a gulf, basin, or sea surrounded by two or more States and connected to another sea or the ocean by a narrow outlet or consisting entirely or primarily of the territorial seas and exclusive economic zones of two or more coastal States.

Article 123
Co-operation of States bordering enclosed or semi-enclosed seas

States bordering an enclosed or semi-enclosed sea should co-operate with each other in the exercise of their rights and in the performance of their duties under this Convention. To this end they shall endeavour, directly or through an appropriate regional organization:

(a) to co-ordinate the management, conservation, exploration and exploitation of the living resources of the sea;

(b) to co-ordinate the implementation of their rights and duties with respect to the protection and preservation of the marine environment;

(c) to co-ordinate their scientific research policies and undertake where appropriate joint programmes of scientific research in the area;

(d) to invite, as appropriate, other interested States or international organizations to co-operate with them in furtherance of the provisions of this article.

PART X

Right of Access of Land-Locked States to and from the Sea and Freedom of Transit

Article 124
Use of terms

1. For the purposes of this Convention:

(a) "land-locked State" means a State which has no sea-coast;

(b) "transit State" means a State, with or without a sea-coast, situated between a land-locked State and the sea, through whose territory traffic in transit passes;

(c) "traffic in transit" means transit of persons, baggage, goods and means of transport across the territory of one or more transit States, when the passage across such territory, with or without transshipment, warehousing, breaking bulk or change in the mode of transport, is only a portion of a complete journey which begins or terminates within the territory of the land-locked State;

(d) "means of transport" means:

(i) railway rolling stock, sea, lake and river craft and road vehicles;

(ii) where local conditions so require, porters and pack animals.

2. Land-locked States and transit States may, by agreement between them, include as means of transport pipelines and gas lines and means of transport other than those included in paragraph 1.

Article 125
Right of access to and from the sea and freedom of transit

1. Land-locked States shall have the right of access to and from the sea for the purpose of exercising the rights provided for in this Convention including those relating to the freedom of the high seas and the common heritage of mankind. To this end, land-locked States shall enjoy freedom of transit through the territory of transit States by all means of transport.

2. The terms and modalities for exercising freedom of transit shall be agreed between the land-locked States and transit States concerned through bilateral, subregional or regional agreements.

3. Transit States, in the exercise of their full sovereignty over their territory, shall have the right to take all measures necessary to ensure that the rights and facilities provided for in this Part for land-locked

States shall in no way infringe their legitimate interests.

Article 126
Exclusion of application of the most-favoured-nation clause

The provisions of this Convention, as well as special agreements relating to the exercise of the right of access to and from the sea, establishing rights and facilities on account of the special geographical position of land-locked States, are excluded from the application of the most-favoured-nation clause.

Article 127
Customs duties, taxes and other charges

1. Traffic in transit shall not be subject to any customs duties, taxes or other charges except charges levied for specific services rendered in connection with such traffic.

2. Means of transport in transit and other facilities provided for and used by land-locked States shall not be subject to taxes or charges higher than those levied for the use of means of transport of the transit State.

Article 128
Free zones and other customs facilities

For the convenience of traffic in transit, free zones or other customs facilities may be provided at the ports of entry and exit in the transit States, by agreement between those States and the land-locked States.

Article 129
Co-operation in the construction and improvement of means of transport

Where there are no means of transport in transit States to give effect to the freedom of transit or where the existing means, including the port installations and equipment, are inadequate in any respect, the transit States and land-locked States concerned may co-operate in constructing or improving them.

Article 130
Measures to avoid or eliminate delays or other difficulties of a technical nature in traffic in transit

1. Transit States shall take all appropriate measures to avoid delays or other difficulties of a technical nature in traffic in transit.

2. Should such delays or difficulties occur, the competent authorities of the transit States and land-locked States concerned shall co-operate towards their expeditious elimination.

Article 131
Equal treatment in maritime ports

Ships flying the flag of land-locked States shall enjoy treatment equal to that accorded to other foreign ships in maritime ports.

Article 132
Grant of greater transit facilities

This Convention does not entail in any way the withdrawal of transit facilities which are greater than those provided for in this Convention and which are agreed between States Parties to this Convention or granted by a State party. This Convention also does not preclude such grant of greater facilities in the future.

PART XI

The Area

Section 1. General Provisions

Article 133
Use of terms

For the purposes of this Part:

(a) "resources" means all solid, liquid or gaseous mineral resources *in situ* in the Area at or beneath the sea-bed, including polymetallic nodules;

(b) resources, when recovered from the Area, are referred to as "minerals".

Article 134
Scope of this Part

1. This Part applies to the Area.

2. Activities in the Area shall be governed by the provisions of this Part.

3. The requirement concerning deposit of, and publicity to be given to, the charts or lists of geographical co-ordinates showing the limits referred to in article 1, paragraph 1, are set forth in Part VI.

4. Nothing in this article affects the establishment of the outer limits of the continental shelf in accordance with Part VI or the validity of agreements relating to delimitation between States with opposite or adjacent coasts.

Article 135
Legal status of the superjacent waters and air space

Neither this Part nor any rights granted or exercised pursuant thereto shall affect the legal status of the waters superjacent to the Area or that of the air space above those waters.

Section 2. Principles Governing the Area

Article 136
Common heritage of mankind

The Area and its resources are the common heritage of mankind.

Article 137
Legal status of the Area and its resources

1. No State shall claim or exercise sovereignty or sovereign rights over any part of the Area or its resources, nor shall any State or natural or juridical person appropriate any part thereof. No such claim or exercise of sovereignty or sovereign rights nor such appropriation shall be recognized.

2. All rights in the resources of the Area are vested in mankind as a whole, on whose behalf the Authority shall act. These resources are not subject to alienation. The minerals recovered from the Area, however, may only be alienated in accordance with this Part and the rules, regulations and procedures of the Authority.

3. No State or natural or juridical person shall claim, acquire or exercise rights with respect to the minerals recovered from the Area except in accordance with this Part. Otherwise, no such claim, acquisition or exercise of such rights shall be recognized.

Article 138
General conduct of States in relation to the Area

The general conduct of States in relation to the Area shall be in accordance with the provisions of this Part, the principles embodied in the Charter of the United Nations and other rules of international law in the interests of maintaining peace and security and promoting international co-operation and mutual understanding.

Article 139
Responsibility to ensure compliance and liability for damage

1. States Parties shall have the responsibility to ensure that activities in the Area, whether carried out by States Parties, or state enterprises or natural or juridical persons which possess the nationality of States Parties or are effectively controlled by them or their nationals, shall be carried out in conformity with this Part. The same responsibility applies to international organizations for activities in the Area carried out by such organizations.

2. Without prejudice to the rules of international law and Annex III, article 22, damage caused by the failure of a State Party or international organization to carry out its responsibilities under this Part shall entail liability; States Parties or international organizations acting together shall bear joint and several liability. A State Party shall not however be liable for damage caused by any failure to comply with this Part by a person whom it has sponsored under article 153, paragraph 2(b), if the State Party has taken all necessary and appropriate measures to secure effective compliance under article 153, paragraph 4, and Annex III, article 4, paragraph 4.

3. States Parties that are members of international organizations shall take appropriate measures to ensure the implementation of this article with respect to such organizations.

Article 140
Benefit of mankind

1. Activities in the Area shall, as specifically provided for in this Part, be carried out for the benefit of mankind as a whole, irrespective of the geographical location of States, whether coastal or land-locked, and taking into particular consideration the interests and needs of developing States and of peoples who have not attained full independence or other self-governing status recognized by the United Nations in accordance with General Assembly resolution 1514 (XV) and other relevant General Assembly resolutions.

2. The Authority shall provide for the equitable sharing of financial and other economic benefits derived from activities in the Area through any appropriate mechanism, on a non-discriminatory basis, in accordance with article 160, paragraph 2(f)(i).

Article 141
Use of the Area exclusively for peaceful purposes

The Area shall be open to use exclusively for peaceful purposes by all States, whether coastal or land-locked, without discrimination and without prejudice to the other provisions of this Part.

Article 142
Rights and legitimate interests of coastal States

1. Activities in the Area, with respect to resource deposits in the Area which lie across limits of national jurisdiction, shall be conducted with due regard to the rights and legitimate interests of any coastal State across whose jurisdiction such deposits lie.

2. Consultations, including a system of prior notification, shall be maintained with the State concerned, with a view to avoiding infringement of such rights and interests. In cases where activities in the Area may result in the exploitation of resources lying within national jurisdiction, the prior consent of the coastal State concerned shall be required.

3. Neither this Part nor any rights granted or exercised pursuant thereto shall affect the rights of coastal States to take such measures consistent with the relevant provisions of Part XII as may be necessary to prevent, mitigate or eliminate grave and imminent danger to their coastline, or related interests from pollution or threat thereof or from other hazardous occurrences resulting from or caused by any activities in the Area.

Article 143
Marine scientific research

1. Marine scientific research in the Area shall be carried out exclusively for peaceful purposes and for the benefit of mankind as a whole, in accordance with Part XIII.

2. The Authority may carry out marine scientific research concerning the Area and its resources, and may enter into contracts for that purpose. The Authority shall promote and encourage the conduct of marine scientific research in the Area, and shall co-ordinate and disseminate the results of such research and analysis when available.

3. States Parties may carry out marine scientific research in the Area. States Parties shall promote international co-operation in marine scientific research in the Area by:

(a) participating in international programmes and encouraging co-operation in marine scientific research by personnel of different countries and of the Authority;

(b) ensuring that programmes are developed through the Authority or other international organizations as appropriate for the benefit of developing States and technologically less developed States with a view to:

(i) strengthening their research capabilities;

(ii) training their personnel and the personnel of the Authority in the techniques and applications of research;

(iii) fostering the employment of their qualified personnel in research in the Area;

(c) effectively disseminating the results of research and analysis when available, through the Authority or other international channels when appropriate.

Article 144
Transfer of technology

1. The Authority shall take measures in accordance with this Convention:

(a) to acquire technology and scientific knowledge relating to activities in the Area; and

(b) to promote and encourage the transfer to developing States of such technology and scientific knowledge so that all States Parties benefit therefrom.

2. To this end the Authority and States Parties shall co-operate in promoting the transfer of technology and scientific knowledge relating to activities in the Area so that the Enterprise and all States Parties may benefit therefrom. In particular they shall initiate and promote:

(a) programmes for the transfer of technology to the Enterprise and to developing States with regard to activities in the Area, including, *inter alia*, facilitating the access of the Enterprise and of developing States to the relevant technology, under fair and reasonable terms and conditions;

(b) measures directed towards the advancement of the technology of the Enterprise and the domestic technology of developing States, particularly by providing opportunities to personnel from the Enterprise and from developing States for training in marine science and technology and for their full participation in activities in the Area.

Article 145
Protection of the marine environment

Necessary measures shall be taken in accordance with this Convention with respect to activities in the Area to ensure effective protection for the marine environment from harmful effects which may arise from such activities. To this end the Authority shall adopt appropriate rules, regulations and procedures for *inter alia*:

(a) the prevention, reduction and control of pollution and other hazards to the marine environment, including the coastline, and of interference with the ecological balance of the marine environment, particular attention being paid to the need for protection from harmful effects of such activities as drilling, dredging, excavation, disposal of waste, construction and operation or maintenance of installations, pipelines and other devices related to such activities;

(b) the protection and conservation of the natural resources of the Area and the prevention of damage to the flora and fauna of the marine environment.

Article 146
Protection of human life

With respect to activities in the Area, necessary measures shall be taken to ensure effective protection of human life. To this end the Authority shall adopt appropriate rules, regulations and procedures to supplement existing international law as embodied in relevant treaties.

Article 147
Accommodation of activities in the Area and in the marine environment

1. Activities in the Area shall be carried out with reasonable regard for other activities in the marine environment.

2. Installations used for carrying out activities in the Area shall be subject to the following conditions:

(a) such installations shall be erected, emplaced and removed solely in accordance with this Part and subject to the rules, regulations and procedures of the Authority. Due notice must be given of the erection, emplacement and removal of such installations, and permanent means for giving warning of their presence must be maintained;

(b) such installations may not be established where interference may be caused to the use of recognized sea lanes essential to international navigation or in areas of intense fishing activity;

(c) safety zones shall be established around such installations with appropriate markings to ensure the safety of both navigation and the installations. The configuration and location of such safety zones shall not be such as to form a belt impeding the lawful access of shipping to particular maritime zones or navigation along international sea lanes;

(d) such installations shall be used exclusively for peaceful purposes;

(e) such installations do not possess the status of islands. They have no territorial sea of their own, and their presence does not affect the delimitation of the territorial sea, the exclusive economic zone or the continental shelf.

3. Other activities in the marine environment shall be conducted with reasonable regard for activities in the Area.

Article 148
Participation of developing States in activities in the Area

The effective participation of developing States in activities in the Area shall be promoted as specifically provided for in this Part, having due regard to their special interests and needs, and in particular to the special need of the land-locked and geographically disadvantaged among them to overcome obstacles arising from their disadvantaged location, including remoteness from the Area and difficulty of access to and from it.

Article 149
Archaeological and historical objects

All objects of an archaeological and historical nature found in the Area shall be preserved or disposed of for the benefit of mankind as a whole, particular regard being paid to the preferential rights of the State or country of origin, or the State of cultural origin, or the State of historical and archaeological origin.

Section 3. Development of Resources of the Area

Article 150
Policies relating to activities in the Area

Activities in the Area shall, as specifically provided for in this Part, be carried out in such a manner as to foster healthy development of the world economy and balanced growth of international trade, and to promote international co-operation for the over-all development of all countries, especially developing States, and with a view to ensuring:

(a) the development of the resources of the Area;

(b) orderly, safe and rational management of the resources of the Area, including the efficient conduct of activities in the Area and, in accordance with sound principles of conservation, the avoidance of unnecessary waste;

(c) the expansion of opportunities for participation in such activities consistent in particular with articles 144 and 148;

(d) participation in revenues by the Authority and the transfer of technology to the Enterprise and developing States as provided for in this Convention;

(e) increased availability of the minerals derived from the Area as needed in conjunction with minerals derived from other sources, to ensure supplies to consumers of such minerals;

(f) the promotion of just and stable prices remunerative to producers and fair to consumers for minerals derived both from the Area and from other sources, and the promotion of long-term equilibrium between supply and demand;

(g) the enhancement of opportunities for all States Parties, irrespective of their social and economic systems or geographical location, to participate in the development of the resources of the Area and the prevention of monopolization of activities in the Area;

(h) the protection of developing countries from adverse effects on their economies or on their export earnings resulting from a reduction in the price of an affected mineral, or in the volume of exports of that mineral, to the extent that such reduction is caused by activities in the Area, as provided in article 151;

(i) the development of the common heritage for the benefit of mankind as a whole; and

(j) conditions of access to markets for the imports of minerals produced from the resources of the Area and for imports of commodities produced from such minerals shall not be more favourable than the most favourable applied to imports from other sources.

Article 151
Production policies

1. (a) Without prejudice to the objectives set forth in article 150 and for the purpose of implementing subparagraph (h) of that article, the Authority, acting through existing forums or such new arrangements or agreements as may be appropriate, in which all interested parties, including both producers and consumers, participate, shall take measures necessary to promote the growth, efficiency and stability of markets for those commodities produced from the minerals derived from the Area, at prices remunerative to producers and fair to consumers. All States Parties shall co-operate to this end.

(b) The Authority shall have the right to participate in any commodity conference dealing with those commodities and in which all interested parties including both producers and consumers participate. The Authority shall have the right to become a party to any arrangement or agreement resulting from such conferences. Participation of the Authority in any organs established under those arrangements or agreements shall be in respect of production in the Area and in accordance with the relevant rules of those organs.

(c) The Authority shall carry out its obligations under the arrangements or agreements referred to in this paragraph in a manner which assures a uniform and non-discriminatory implementation in respect of all production in the Area of the minerals concerned. In doing so, the Authority shall act in a manner consistent with the terms of existing contracts and approved plans of work of the Enterprise.

2. (a) During the interim period specified in paragraph 3, commercial production shall not be undertaken pursuant to an approved plan of work until the operator has applied for and has been issued a production authorization by the Authority. Such production authorizations may not be applied for or issued more than five years prior to the planned commencement of commercial production under the plan of work unless, having regard to the nature and timing of project development, the rules, regulations and procedures of the Authority prescribe another period.

(b) In the application for the production authorization, the operator shall specify the annual quantity of nickel expected to be recovered under the approved plan of work. The application shall include a schedule of expenditures to be made by the operator after he has received the authorization which are reasonably calculated to allow him to begin commercial production on the date planned.

(c) For the purposes of subparagraphs (a) and (b), the Authority shall establish appropriate performance requirements in accordance with Annex III, article 17.

(d) The Authority shall issue a production authorization for the level of production applied for unless the sum of that level and the levels already authorized exceeds the nickel production ceiling, as calculated pursuant to paragraph 4 in the year of issuance of the authorization, during any year of planned production falling within the interim period.

(e) When issued, the production authorization and approved application shall become a part of the approved plan of work.

(f) If the operator's application for a production authorization is denied pursuant to subparagraph (d), the operator may apply again to the Authority at any time.

3. The interim period shall begin five years prior to 1 January of the year in which the earliest commercial production is planned to commence under an approved plan of work. If the earliest commercial production is delayed beyond the year originally planned, the beginning of the interim period and the production ceiling originally calculated shall be adjusted accordingly. The interim period shall last 25 years or until the end of the Review Conference referred to in article 155 or until the day when such new arrangements or agreements as are referred to in paragraph 1 enter into force, whichever is earliest. The Authority shall resume the power provided in this article for the remainder of the interim period if the said arrangements or agreements should lapse or become ineffective for any reason whatsoever.

4. (a) The production ceiling for any year of the interim period shall be the sum of:

(i) the difference between the trend line values for nickel consumption, as calculated pursuant to subparagraph (b), for the year immediately prior to the year of the earliest commercial production and the year immediately prior to the commencement of the interim period; and

(ii) sixty per cent of the difference between the trend line values for nickel consumption, as calculated pursuant to subparagraph (b), for the year for which the production authorization is being applied for and the year immediately prior to the year of the earliest commercial production.

(b) For the purposes of subparagraph (a):

(i) trend line values used for computing the nickel production ceiling shall be those annual nickel consumption values on a trend line computed during the year in which a production authorization is issued. The trend line shall be derived from a linear regression of the logarithms of actual nickel consumption for the most recent 15-year period for which such data are available, time being the independent variable. This trend line shall be referred to as the original trend line;

(ii) if the annual rate of increase of the original trend line is less than 3 per cent, then the trend line used to determine the quantities referred to in subparagtaph (a) shall instead be one passing through the original trend line at the value for the first year of the relevant 15-year period, and increasing at 3 per cent annually; provided however that the production ceiling established for any year of the interim period may not in any case exceed the difference between the original trend line value for that year and the original trend line value for the year immediately prior to the commencement of the interim period.

5. The Authority shall reserve to the Enterprise for its initial production a quantity of 38,000 metric tonnes of nickel from the available production ceiling calculated pursuant to paragraph 4.

6. (a) An operator may in any year produce less than or up to 8 per cent more than the level of annual production of minerals from polymetallic nodules specified in his production authorization, provided that the over-all amount of production shall not exceed that specified in the authorization. Any excess over 8 per cent and up to 20 per cent in any year, or any excess in the first and subsequent years following two consecutive years in which excesses occur, shall be negotiated with the Authority, which may require the operator to obtain a supplementary production authorization to cover additional production.

(b) Applications for such supplementary production authorizations shall be considered by the Authority only after all pending applications by operators who have not yet received production authorizations have been acted upon and due account has been taken of other likely applicants. The Authority shall be guided by the principle of not exceeding the total production allowed under the production ceiling in any year of the interim period. It shall not authorize the production under any plan of work of a quantity in excess of 46,500 metric tonnes of nickel per year.

7. The levels of production of other metals such as copper, cobalt and manganese extracted from the polymetallic nodules that are recovered pursuant to a production authorization should not be higher than those which would have been produced had the operator produced the maximum level of nickel from those nodules pursuant to this article. The Authority shall establish rules, regulations and procedures pursuant to Annex III, article 17, to implement this paragraph.

8. Rights and obligations relating to unfair economic practices under relevant multilateral trade agreements shall apply to the exploration for and exploitation of minerals from the Area. In the settlement of disputes arising under this provision, States Parties which are Parties to such multilateral trade agreements shall have recourse to the dispute settlement procedures of such agreements.

9. The Authority shall have the power to limit the level of production of minerals from the Area, other than minerals from polymetallic nodules, under such conditions and applying such methods as may be appropriate by adopting regulations in accordance with article 161, paragraph 8.

10. Upon the recommendation of the Council on the basis of advice from the Economic Planning Commission, the Assembly shall establish a system of compensation or take other measures of economic adjustment assistance including co-operation with specialized agencies and other international organizations to assist developing countries which suffer serious adverse effects on their export earnings or economies resulting from a reduction in the price of an affected mineral or in the volume of exports of that mineral, to the extent that such reduction is caused by activities in the Area. The Authority on request shall initiate studies on the problems of those States which are likely to be most seriously affected with a view to minimizing their difficulties and assisting them in their economic adjustment.

Article 152
Exercise of powers and functions by the Authority

1. The Authority shall avoid discrimination in the exercise of its powers and functions, including the granting of opportunities for activities in the Area.

2. Nevertheless, special consideration for developing States, including particular consideration for the land-locked and geographically disadvantaged among them, specifically provided for in this Part shall be permitted.

Article 153
System of exploration and exploitation

1. Activities in the Area shall be organized, carried out and controlled by the Authority on behalf of mankind as a whole in accordance with this article as well as other relevant provisions of this Part and the relevant Annexes, and the rules, regulations and procedures of the Authority.

2. Activities in the Area shall be carried out as prescribed in paragraph 3:

(a) by the Enterprise, and

(b) in association with the Authority by States Parties, or state enterprises or natural or juridical persons which possess the nationality of States Parties or are effectively controlled by them or their nationals, when sponsored by such States, or any group of the foregoing which meets the requirements provided in this Part and in Annex III.

3. Activities in the Area shall be carried out in accordance with a formal written plan of work drawn up in accordance with Annex III and approved by the Council after review by the Legal and Technical Commission. In the case of activities in the Area carried out as authorized by the Authority by the entities specified in paragraph 2(b), the plan of work shall, in accordance with Annex III, article 3, be in the form of a contract. Such contracts may provide for joint arrangements in accordance with Annex III, article 11.

4. The Authority shall exercise such control over activities in the Area as is

necessary for the purpose of securing compliance with the relevant provisions of this Part and the Annexes relating thereto, and the rules, regulations and procedures of the Authority, and the plans of work approved in accordance with paragraph 3. States Parties shall assist the Authority by taking all measures necessary to ensure such compliance in accordance with article 139.

5. The Authority shall have the right to take at any time any measures provided for under this Part to ensure compliance with its provisions and the exercise of the functions of control and regulation assigned to it thereunder or under any contract. The Authority shall have the right to inspect all installations in the Area used in connection with activities in the Area.

6. A contract under paragraph 3 shall provide for security of tenure. Accordingly, the contract shall not be revised, suspended or terminated except in accordance with Annex III, articles 18 and 19.

Article 154
Periodic review

Every five years from the entry into force of this convention, the Assembly shall undertake a general and systematic review of the manner in which the international régime of the Area established in this convention has operated in practice. In the light of this review the Assembly may take, or recommend that other organs take, measures in accordance with the provisions and procedures of this Part and the Annexes relating thereto which will lead to the improvement of the operation of the régime.

Article 155
The Review Conference

1. Fifteen years from 1 January of the year in which the earliest commercial production commences under an approved plan of work, the Assembly shall convene a conference for the review of those provisions of this Part and the relevant Annexes which govern the system of exploration and exploitation of the resources of the Area. The Review Conference shall consider in detail, in the light of the experience acquired during that period:

(a) whether the provisions of this Part which govern the system of exploration and exploitation of the resources of the Area have achieved their aims in all respects, including whether they have benefited mankind as a whole;

(b) whether, during the 15-year period, reserved areas have been exploited in an effective and balanced manner in comparison with non-reserved areas;

(c) whether the development and use of the Area and its resources have been undertaken in such a manner as to foster healthy development of the world economy and balanced growth of international trade;

(d) whether monopolization of activities in the Area has been prevented;

(e) whether the policies set forth in articles 150 and 151 have been fulfilled; and

(f) whether the system has resulted in the equitable sharing of benefits derived from activities in the Area, taking into particular consideration the interests and needs of the developing States.

2. The Review Conference shall ensure the maintenance of the principle of the common heritage of mankind, the international régime designed to ensure equitable exploitation of the resources of the Area for the benefit of all countries, especially the developing States, and an Authority to organize, conduct and control activities in the Area. It shall also ensure the maintenance of the principles laid down in this Part with regard to the exclusion of claims or exercise of sovereignty over any part of the Area, the rights of States and their general conduct in relation to the Area, and their participation in activities in the Area in conformity with this convention, the prevention of monopolization of activities in the Area, the use of the Area exclusively for peaceful purposes, economic aspects of activities in the Area, marine scientific research, transfer of technology, protection of the marine environment, protection of human life, rights of coastal States, the legal status of the waters superjacent to the Area and that of the air space above those waters and accommodation between activities in the Area and other activities in the marine environment.

3. The decision-making procedure applicable at the Review Conference shall be the same as that applicable at the Third United Nations Conference on the Law of the Sea. The Conference shall make every effort to reach agreement on any amendments by way of consensus and there

should be no voting on such matters until all efforts at achieving consensus have been exhausted.

4. If, five years after its commencement, the Review Conference has not reached agreement on the system of exploration and exploitation of the resources of the Area, it may decide during the ensuing 12 months, by a three-fourths majority of the States Parties, to adopt and submit to the States Parties for ratification or accession such amendments changing or modifying the system as it determines necessary and appropriate. Such amendments shall enter into force for all States Parties 12 months after the deposit of instruments of ratification or accession by three-fourths of the States Parties.

5. Amendments adopted by the Review Conference pursuant to this article shall not affect rights acquired under existing contracts.

Section 4. The Authority

Subsection A. General Provisions

Article 156
Establishment of the Authority

1. There is hereby established the International Sea-Bed Authority, which shall function in accordance with this Part.

2. All States Parties are *ipso facto* members of the Authority.

3. Observers at the Third United Nations Conference on the Law of the Sea who have signed the Final Act and who are not referred to in article 305, paragraph 1(c), (d), (e) or (f), shall have the right to participate in the Authority as observers, in accordance with its rules, regulations and procedures.

4. The seat of the Authority shall be in Jamaica.

5. The Authority may establish such regional centres or offices as it deems necessary for the exercise of its functions.

Article 157
Nature and fundamental principles of the Authority

1. The Authority is the organization through which States Parties shall, in accordance with this Part, organize and control activities in the Area, particularly with a view to administering the resources of the Area.

2. The powers and functions of the Authority shall be those expressly conferred upon it by this Convention. The Authority shall have such incidental powers, consistent with this Convention, as are implicit in and necessary for the exercise of those powers and functions with respect to activities in the Area.

3. The Authority is based on the principle of the sovereign equality of all its members.

4. All members of the Authority shall fulfil in good faith the obligations assumed by them in accordance with this Part in order to ensure to all of them the rights and benefits resulting from membership.

Article 158
Organs of the Authority

1. There are hereby established, as the principal organs of the Authority, an Assembly, a Council and a Secretariat.

2. There is hereby established the Enterprise, the organ through which the Authority shall carry out the functions referred to in article 170, paragraph 1.

3. Such subsidiary organs as may be found necessary may be established in accordance with this Part.

4. Each principal organ of the Authority and the Enterprise shall be responsible for exercising those powers and functions which are conferred upon it. In exercising such powers and functions each organ shall avoid taking any action which may derogate from or impede the exercise of specific powers and functions conferred upon another organ.

Subsection B. The Assembly

Article 159
Composition, procedure and voting

1. The Assembly shall consist of all the members of the Authority. Each member shall have one representative in the Assembly, who may be accompanied by alternates and advisers.

2. The Assembly shall meet in regular annual sessions and in such special sessions as may be decided by the Assembly, or convened by the Secretary-General at the request of the Council or of a majority of the members of the Authority.

3. Sessions shall take place at the seat of the Authority unless otherwise decided by the Assembly.

4. The Assembly shall adopt its rules of procedure. At the beginning of each regular session, it shall elect its President and such other officers as may be required. They shall hold office until a new President and other officers are elected at the next regular session.

5. A majority of the members of the Assembly shall constitute a quorum.

6. Each member of the Assembly shall have one vote.

7. Decisions on questions of procedure, including decisions to convene special sessions of the Assembly, shall be taken by a majority of the members present and voting.

8. Decisions on questions of substance shall be taken by a two-thirds majority of the members present and voting, provided that such majority includes a majority of the members participating in the session. When the issue arises as to whether a question is one of substance or not, that question shall be treated as one of substance unless otherwise decided by the Assembly by the majority required for decisions on questions of substance.

9. When a question of substance comes up for voting for the first time, the President may, and shall, if requested by at least one-fifth of the members of the Assembly, defer the issue of taking a vote on that question for a period not exceeding five calendar days. This rule may be applied only once to any question, and shall not be applied so as to defer the question beyond the end of the session.

10. Upon a written request addressed to the President and sponsored by at least one-fourth of the members of the Authority for an advisory opinion on the conformity with this Convention of a proposal before the Assembly on any matter, the Assembly shall request the Sea-Bed Disputes Chamber of the International Tribunal for the Law of the Sea to give an advisory opinion thereon and shall defer voting on that proposal pending receipt of the advisory opinion by the Chamber. If the advisory opinion is not received before the final week of the session in which it is requested, the Assembly shall decide when it will meet to vote upon the deferred proposal.

Article 160
Powers and functions

1. The Assembly, as the sole organ of the Authority consisting of all the members, shall be considered the supreme organ of the Authority to which the other principal organs shall be accountable as specifically provided for in this Convention. The Assembly shall have the power to establish general policies in conformity with the relevant provisions of this Convention on any question or matter within the competence of the Authority.

2. In addition, the powers and functions of the Assembly shall be:

(a) to elect the members of the Council in accordance with article 161;

(b) to elect the Secretary-General from among the candidates proposed by the Council;

(c) to elect, upon the recommendation of the Council, the members of the Governing Board of the Enterprise and the Director-General of the Enterprise;

(d) to establish such subsidiary organs as it finds necessary for the exercise of its functions in accordance with this Part. In the composition of these subsidiary organs due account shall be taken of the principle of equitable geographical distribution and of special interests and the need for members qualified and competent in the relevant technical questions dealt with by such organs;

(e) to assess the contributions of members to the administrative budget of the Authority in accordance with an agreed scale of assessment based upon the scale used for the regular budget of the United Nations until the Authority shall have sufficient income from other sources to meet its administrative expenses;

(f) (i) to consider and approve, upon the recommendation of the Council, the rules, regulations and procedures on the equitable sharing of financial and other economic benefits derived from activities in the Area and the payments and contributions made pursuant to article 82, taking into particular consideration the interests and needs of developing States and peoples who have not attained full independence or other self-governing status. If the Assembly does not approve the recommendations of the Council, the Assembly shall return them to the Council for reconsideration in the light of the views expressed by the Assembly;

(ii) to consider and approve the rules, regulations and procedures of the Authority, and any amendments thereto, provisionally adopted by the Council pursuant to article

162, paragraph 2 (o)(ii). These rules, regulations and procedures shall relate to prospecting, exploration and exploitation in the Area, the financial management and internal administration of the Authority, and, upon the recommendation of the Governing Board of the Enterprise, to the transfer of funds from the Enterprise to the Authority;

(g) to decide upon the equitable sharing of financial and other economic benefits derived from activities in the Area, consistent with this Convention and the rules, regulations and procedures of the Authority;

(h) to consider and approve the proposed annual budget of the Authority submitted by the Council;

(i) to examine periodic reports from the Council and from the Enterprise and special reports requested from the Council or any other organ of the Authority;

(j) to initiate studies and make recommendations for the purpose of promoting international co-operation concerning activities in the Area and encouraging the progressive development of international law relating thereto and its codification;

(k) to consider problems of a general nature in connection with activities in the Area arising in particular for developing States, as well as those problems for States in connection with activities in the Area that are due to their geographical location, particularly for land-locked and geographically disadvantaged States;

(l) to establish, upon the recommendation of the Council, on the basis of advice from the Economic Planning Commission, a system of compensation or other measures of economic adjustment assistance as provided in article 151, paragraph 10;

(m) to suspend the exercise of rights and privileges of membership pursuant to article 185;

(n) to discuss any question or matter within the competence of the Authority and to decide as to which organ of the Authority shall deal with any such question or matter not specifically entrusted to a particular organ, consistent with the distribution of powers and functions among the organs of the Authority.

Subsection C. The Council

Article 161
Composition, procedure and voting

1. The Council shall consist of 36 members of the Authority elected by the Assembly in the following order:

(a) four members from among those States Parties which, during the last five years for which statistics are available, have either consumed more than 2 per cent of total world consumption or have had net imports of more than 2 per cent of total world imports of the commodities produced from the categories of minerals to be derived from the Area, and in any case one State from the Eastern European (Socialist) region, as well as the largest consumer;

(b) four members from among the eight States Parties which have the largest investments in preparation for and in the conduct of activities in the Area, either directly or through their nationals, including at least one State from the Eastern European (Socialist) region;

(c) four members from among States Parties which on the basis of production in areas under their jurisdiction are major net exporters of the categories of minerals to be derived from the Area, including at least two developing States whose exports of such minerals have a substantial bearing upon their economies;

(d) six members from among developing States Parties, representing special interests. The special interests to be represented shall include those of States with large populations, States which are land-locked or geographically disadvantaged, States which are major importers of the categories of minerals to be derived from the Area, States which are potential producers of such minerals, and least developed States;

(e) eighteen members elected according to the principle of ensuring an equitable geographical distribution of seats in the Council as a whole, provided that each geographical region shall have at least one member elected under this subparagraph. For this purpose, the geographical regions shall be Africa, Asia, Eastern European (Socialist), Latin America and Western European and Others.

2. In electing the members of the Council in accordance with paragraph 1, the Assembly shall ensure that:

(a) land-locked and geographically disadvantaged States are represented to a degree which is reasonably proportionate to their representation in the Assembly;

(b) coastal States, especially developing States, which do not qualify under paragraph 1(a), (b), (c) or (d) are represented to a degree which is reasonably proportionate to their representation in the Assembly;

(c) each group of States Parties to be represented on the Council is represented by those members, if any, which are nominated by that group.

3. Elections shall take place at regular sessions of the Assembly. Each member of the Council shall be elected for four years. At the first election, however, the term of one half of the members of each group referred to in paragraph 1 shall be two years.

4. Members of the Council shall be eligible for re-election, but due regard should be paid to the desirability of rotation of membership.

5. The Council shall function at the seat of the Authority, and shall meet as often as the business of the Authority may require, but not less than three times a year.

6. A majority of the members of the Council shall constitute a quorum.

7. Each member of the Council shall have one vote.

8. (a) Decisions on questions of procedure shall be taken by a majority of the members present and voting.

(b) Decisions on questions of substance arising under the following provisions shall be taken by a two-thirds majority of the members present and voting, provided that such majority includes a majority of the members of the Council: article 162, paragraph 2, subparagraphs (f); (g); (h); (i); (n); (p); (v); article 191.

(c) Decisions on questions of substance arising under the following provisions shall be taken by a three-fourths majority of the members present and voting, provided that such majority includes a majority of the members of the Council: article 162, paragraph 1; article 162, paragraph 2, subparagraphs (a); (b); (c); (d); (e); (l); (q); (r); (s); (t); (u) in cases of non-compliance by a contractor or a sponsor; (w) provided that orders issued thereunder may be binding for not more than 30 days unless confirmed by a decision taken in accordance with subparagraph (d); article 162, paragraph 2, subparagraphs (x); (y); (z); article 163, paragraph 2; article 174, paragraph 3; Annex IV, article 11.

(d) Decisions on questions of substance arising under the following provisions shall be taken by consensus: article 162, paragraph 2(m) and (o); adoption of amendments to Part XI.

(e) For the purposes of subparagraphs (d), (f) and (g), "consensus" means the absence of any formal objection. Within 14 days of the submission of a proposal to the Council, the President of the Council shall determine whether there would be a formal objection to the adoption of the proposal. If the President determines that there would be such an objection, the President shall establish and convene, within three days following such determination, a conciliation committee consisting of not more than nine members of the Council, with the President as chairman, for the purpose of reconciling the differences and producing a proposal which can be adopted by consensus. The committee shall work expeditiously and report to the Council within 14 days following its establishment. If the committee is unable to recommend a proposal which can be adopted by consensus, it shall set out in its report the grounds on which the proposal is being opposed.

(f) Decisions on questions not listed above which the Council is authorized to take by the rules, regulations and procedures of the Authority or otherwise shall be taken pursuant to the subparagraphs of this paragraph specified in the rules, regulations and procedures or, if not specified therein, then pursuant to the subparagraph determined by the Council if possible in advance, by consensus.

(g) When the issue arises as to whether a question is within subparagraph (a), (b), (c) or (d), the question shall be treated as being within the subparagraph requiring the higher or highest majority or consensus as the case may be, unless otherwise decided by the Council by the said majority or by consensus.

9. The Council shall establish a procedure whereby a member of the Authority not represented on the Council may send a representative to attend a meeting of the Council when a request is made by such member, or a matter particularly affecting it is under consideration. Such a representative shall be entitled to participate in the deliberations but not to vote.

Article 162
Powers and functions

1. The Council is the executive organ of the Authority. The Council shall have the

power to establish, in conformity with this Convention and the general policies established by the Assembly, the specific policies to be pursued by the Authority on any question or matter within the competence of the Authority.

2. In addition, the Council shall:

(a) supervise and co-ordinate the implementation of the provisions of this Part on all questions and matters within the competence of the Authority and invite the attention of the Assembly to cases of non-compliance;

(b) propose to the Assembly a list of candidates for the election of the Secretary-General;

(c) recommend to the Assembly candidates for the election of the members of the Governing Board of the Enterprise and the Director-General of the Enterprise;

(d) establish, as appropriate, and with due regard to economy and efficiency, such subsidiary organs as it finds necessary for the exercise of its functions in accordance with this Part. In the composition of subsidiary organs, emphasis shall be placed on the need for members qualified and competent in relevant technical matters dealt with by those organs provided that due account shall be taken of the principle of equitable geographical distribution and of special interests;

(e) adopt its rules of procedure including the method of selecting its president;

(f) enter into agreements with the United Nations or other international organizations on behalf of the Authority and within its competence, subject to approval by the Assembly;

(g) consider the reports of the Enterprise and transmit them to the Assembly with its recommendations;

(h) present to the Assembly annual reports and such special reports as the Assembly may request;

(i) issue directives to the Enterprise in accordance with article 170;

(j) approve plans of work in accordance with Annex III, article 6. The Council shall act upon each plan of work within 60 days of its submission by the Legal and Technical Commission at a session of the Council in accordance with the following procedures:

(i) if the Commission recommends the approval of a plan of work, it shall be deemed to have been approved by the Council if no member of the Council submits in writing to the President within 14 days a specific objection alleging non-compliance with the requirements of Annex III, article 6. If there is an objection, the conciliation procedure set forth in article 161, paragraph 8(e), shall apply. If, at the end of the conciliation procedure, the objection is still maintained, the plan of work shall be deemed to have been approved by the Council unless the Council disapproves it by consensus among its members excluding any State or States making the application or sponsoring the applicant;

(ii) if the Commission recommends the disapproval of a plan of work or does not make a recommendation, the Council may approve the plan of work by a three-fourths majority of the members present and voting, provided that such majority includes a majority of the members participating in the session;

(k) approve plans of work submitted by the Enterprise in accordance with Annex IV, article 12, applying, *mutatis mutandis*, the procedures set forth in subparagraph (j);

(l) exercise control over activities in the Area in accordance with article 153, paragraph 4, and the rules, regulations and procedures of the Authority;

(m) take, upon the recommendation of the Economic Planning Commission, necessary and appropriate measures in accordance with article 150, subparagraph (h), to provide protection from the adverse economic effects specified therein;

(n) make recommendations to the Assembly, on the basis of advice from the Economic Planning Commission, for a system of compensation or other measures of economic adjustment assistance as provided in article 151, paragraph 10;

(o) (i) recommend to the Assembly rules, regulations and procedures on the equitable sharing of financial and other economic benefits derived from activities in the Area and the payments and contributions made pursuant to article 82, taking into particular consideration the interests and needs of the developing States and peoples who have not attained full independence or other self-governing status;

(ii) adopt and apply provisionally, pending approval by the Assembly, the rules, regulations and procedures of the Authority, and any amendments thereto, taking into account the recommendations of the Legal and Technical Commission or other subordinate organ concerned. These rules, regulations and procedures shall relate to prospecting, exploration and exploitation in the Area and the financial management and internal administration of the Authority. Priority shall be given to the adoption of rules, regulations and procedures for the exploration for and exploitation of polymetallic nodules. Rules, regulations and procedures for the exploration for and exploitation of any resource other than polymetallic nodules shall be adopted within three years from the date of a request to the Authority by any of its members to adopt such rules, regulations and procedures in respect of such resources. All rules, regulations and procedures shall remain in effect on a provisional basis until approved by the Assembly or until amended by the Council in the light of any views expressed by the Assembly;

(p) review the collection of all payments to be made by or to the Authority in connection with operations pursuant to this Part;

(q) make the selection from among applicants for production authorizations pursuant to Annex III, article 7, where such selection is required by that provision;

(r) submit the proposed annual budget of the Authority to the Assembly for its approval;

(s) make recommendations to the Assembly concerning policies on any question or matter within the competence of the Authority;

(t) make recommendations to the Assembly concerning suspension of the exercise of the rights and privileges of membership pursuant to article 185;

(u) institute proceedings on behalf of the Authority before the Sea-Bed Disputes Chamber in cases of non-compliance;

(v) notify the Assembly upon a decision by the Sea-Bed Disputes Chamber in proceedings instituted under subparagraph (u), and make any recommendations which it may find appropriate with respect to measures to be taken;

(w) issue emergency orders, which may include orders for the suspension or adjustment of operations, to prevent serious harm to the marine environment arising out of activities in the Area;

(x) disapprove areas for exploitation by contractors or the Enterprise in cases where substantial evidence indicates the risk of serious harm to the marine environment;

(y) establish a subsidiary organ for the elaboration of draft financial rules, regulations and procedures relating to:

(i) financial management in accordance with articles 171 to 175; and

(ii) financial arrangements in accordance with Annex III, article 13 and article 17, paragraph 1(c);

(z) establish appropriate mechanisms for directing and supervising a staff of inspectors who shall inspect activities in the Area to determine whether this Part, the rules, regulations and procedures of the Authority, and the terms and conditions of any contract with the Authority are being complied with.

Article 163
Organs of the Council

1. There are hereby established the following organs of the Council:

(a) an Economic Planning Commission;

(b) a Legal and Technical Commission.

2. Each Commission shall be composed of 15 members, elected by the Council from among the candidates nominated by the States Parties. However, if necessary, the Council may decide to increase the size of either Commission having due regard to economy and efficiency.

3. Members of a Commission shall have appropriate qualifications in the area of competence of that Commission. States Parties shall nominate candidates of the highest standards of competence and integrity with qualifications in relevant fields so as to ensure the effective exercise of the functions of the Commissions.

4. In the election of members of the Commissions, due account shall be taken of the need for equitable geographical distribution and the representation of special interests.

5. No State Party may nominate more than one candidate for the same Commission. No person shall be elected to serve on more than one Commission.

6. Members of the Commissions shall hold office for a term of five years. They shall be eligible for re-election for a further term.

7. In the event of the death, incapacity or resignation of a member of a Commission prior to the expiration of the term of office,

the Council shall elect, for the remainder of the term, a member from the same geographical region or area of interest.

8. Members of Commissions shall have no financial interest in any activity relating to exploration and exploitation in the Area. Subject to their responsibilities to the Commissions upon which they serve, they shall not disclose, even after the termination of their functions, any industrial secret, proprietary data which are transferred to the Authority in accordance with Annex III, article 14, or any other confidential information coming to their knowledge by reason of their duties for the Authority.

9. Each Commission shall exercise its functions in accordance with such guidelines and directives as the Council may adopt.

10. Each Commission shall formulate and submit to the Council for approval such rules and regulations as may be necessary for the efficient conduct of the Commission's functions.

11. The decision-making procedures of the Commissions shall be established by the rules, regulations and procedures of the Authority. Recommendations to the Council shall, where necessary, be accompanied by a summary on the divergencies of opinion in the Commission.

12. Each Commission shall normally function at the seat of the Authority and shall meet as often as is required for the efficient exercise of its functions.

13. In the exercise of its functions, each Commission may, where appropriate, consult another commission, any competent organ of the United Nations or of its specialized agencies or any international organizations with competence in the subject-matter of such consultation.

Article 164
The Economic Planning Commission

1. Members of the Economic Planning Commission shall have appropriate qualifications such as those relevant to mining, management of mineral resource activities, international trade or international economics. The Council shall endeavour to ensure that the membership of the Commission reflects all appropriate qualifications. The Commission shall include at least two members from developing States whose exports of the categories of minerals to be derived from the Area have a substantial bearing upon their economies.

2. The Commission shall:

(a) propose, upon the request of the Council, measures to implement decisions relating to activities in thc Area taken in accordance with this convention;

(b) review the trends of and the factors affecting supply, demand and prices of materials which may be derived from the Area, bearing in mind the interests of both importing and exporting countries, and in particular of the developing States among them;

(c) examine any situation likely to lead to the adverse effects referred to in article 150, subparagraph (h), brought to its attention by the State Party or States Parties concerned, and make appropriate recommendations to the Council;

(d) propose to the Council for submission to the Assembly, as provided in article 151, paragraph 10, a system of compensation or other measures of economic adjustment assistance for developing States which suffer adverse effects caused by activities in the Area. The Commission shall make the recommendations to the Council that are necessary for the application of the system or other measures adopted by the Assembly in specific cases.

Article 165
The Legal and Technical Commission

1. Members of the Legal and Technical Commission shall have appropriate qualifications such as those relevant to exploration for and exploitation and processing of mineral resources, oceanology, protection of the marine environment, or economic or legal matters relating to ocean mining and related fields of expertise. The Council shall endeavour to ensure that the membership of the Commission reflects all appropriate qualifications.

2. The Commission shall:

(a) make recommendations with regard to the exercise of the Authority's functions upon the request of the Council;

(b) review formal written plans of work for activities in the Area in accordance with article 153, paragraph 3, and submit appropriate recommendations to the Council. The Commission shall base its recommendations solely on the grounds stated in Annex III and shall report fully thereon to the Council;

(c) supervise, upon the request of the Council, activities in the Area, where appropriate, in consultation and collaboration with any entity carrying out such activities or State or States concerned and report to the Council;

(d) prepare assessments of the environmental implications of activities in the Area;

(e) make recommendations to the Council on the protection of the marine environment, taking into account the views of recognized experts in that field;

(f) formulate and submit to the Council the rules, regulations and procedures referred to in article 162, paragraph 2(o), taking into account all relevant factors including assessments of the environmental implications of activities in the Area;

(g) keep such rules, regulations and procedures under review and recommend to the Council from time to time such amendments thereto as it may deem necessary or desirable;

(h) make recommendations to the Council regarding the establishment of a monitoring programme to observe, measure, evaluate and analyse, by recognized scientific methods, on a regular basis, the risks or effects of pollution of the marine environment resulting from activities in the Area, ensure that existing regulations are adequate and are complied with and co-ordinate the implementation of the monitoring programme approved by the Council;

(i) recommend to the Council that proceedings be instituted on behalf of the Authority before the Sea-Bed Disputes Chamber, in accordance with this Part and the relevant Annexes taking into account particularly article 187;

(j) make recommendations to the Council with respect to measures to be taken, upon a decision by the Sea-Bed Disputes Chamber in proceedings instituted in accordance with subparagraph (i);

(k) make recommendations to the Council to issue emergency orders, which may include orders for the suspension or adjustment of operations, to prevent serious harm to the marine environment arising out of activities in the Area. Such recommendations shall be taken up by the Council on a priority basis;

(l) make recommendations to the Council to disapprove areas for exploitation by contractors or the Enterprise in cases where substantial evidence indicates the risk of serious harm to the marine environment;

(m) make recommendations to the Council regarding the direction and supervision of a staff of inspectors who shall inspect activities in the Area to determine whether the provisions of this Part, the rules, regulations and procedures of the Authority, and the terms and conditions of any contract with the Authority are being complied with;

(n) calculate the production ceiling and issue production authorizations on behalf of the Authority pursuant to article 151, paragraphs 2 to 7, following any necessary selection among applicants for production authorizations by the Council in accordance with Annex III, article 7.

3. The members of the Commission shall, upon request by any State Party or other party concerned, be accompanied by a representative of such State or other party concerned when carrying out their function of supervision and inspection.

Subsection D. The Secretariat

Article 166
The Secretariat

1. The Secretariat of the Authority shall comprise a Secretary-General and such staff as the Authority may require.

2. The Secretary-General shall be elected for four years by the Assembly from among the candidates proposed by the Council and may be re-elected.

3. The Secretary-General shall be the chief administrative officer of the Authority, and shall act in that capacity in all meetings of the Assembly, of the Council and of any subsidiary organ, and shall perform such other administrative functions as are entrusted to the Secretary-General by these organs.

4. The Secretary-General shall make an annual report to the Assembly on the work of the Authority.

Article 167
The staff of the Authority

1. The staff of the Authority shall consist of such qualified scientific and technical and other personnel as may be required to fulfil the administrative functions of the Authority.

2. The paramount consideration in the recruitment and employment of the staff and in the determination of their conditions

of service shall be the necessity of securing the highest standards of efficiency, competence and integrity. Subject to this consideration, due regard shall be paid to the importance of recruiting the staff on as wide a geographical basis as possible.

3. The staff shall be appointed by the Secretary-General. The terms and conditions on which they shall be appointed, remunerated and dismissed shall be in accordance with the rules, regulations and procedures of the Authority.

Article 168
International character of the Secretariat

1. In the performance of their duties the Secretary-General and the staff shall not seek or receive instructions from any government or from any other source external to the Authority. They shall refrain from any action which might reflect on their position as international officials responsible only to the Authority. Each State Party undertakes to respect the exclusively international character of the responsibilities of the Secretary-General and the staff and not to seek to influence them in the discharge of their responsibilities. Any violation of responsibilities by a staff member shall be submitted to the appropriate administrative tribunal as provided in the rules, regulations and procedures of the Authority.

2. The Secretary-General and the staff shall have no financial interest in any activity relating to exploration and exploitation in the Area. Subject to their responsibilities to the Authority, they shall not disclose, even after the termination of their functions, any industrial secret, proprietary data which are transferred to the Authority in accordance with Annex III, article 14, or any other confidential information coming to their knowledge by reason of their employment with the Authority.

3. Violations of the obligations of a staff member of the Authority set forth in paragraph 2 shall, on the request of a State Party affected by such violation, or a natural or juridical person, sponsored by a State Party as provided in article 153, paragraph 2(b), and affected by such violation, be submitted by the Authority against the staff member concerned to a tribunal designated by the rules, regulations and procedures of the Authority. The Party affected shall have the right to take part in the proceedings. If the tribunal so recommends, the Secretary-General shall dismiss the staff member concerned.

4. The rules, regulations and procedures of the Authority shall contain such provisions as are necessary to implement this article.

Article 169
Consultation and co-operation with international and non-governmental organizations

1. The Secretary-General shall, on matters within the competence of the Authority, make suitable arrangements, with the approval of the Council, for consultation and co-operation with international and non-governmental organizations recognized by the Economic and Social Council of the United Nations.

2. Any organization with which the Secretary-General has entered into an arrangement under paragraph 1 may designate representatives to attend meetings of the organs of the Authority as observers in accordance with the rules of procedure of these organs. Procedures shall be established for obtaining the views of such organizations in appropriate cases.

3. The Secretary-General may distribute to States Parties written reports submitted by the non-governmental organizations referred to in paragraph 1 on subjects in which they have special competence and which are related to the work of the Authority.

Subsection E. The Enterprise

Article 170
The Enterprise

1. The Enterprise shall be the organ of the Authority which shall carry out activities in the Area directly, pursuant to article 153, paragraph 2(a), as well as the transporting, processing and marketing of minerals recovered from the Area.

2. The Enterprise shall, within the framework of the international legal personality of the Authority, have such legal capacity as is provided for in the Statute set forth in Annex IV. The Enterprise shall act in accordance with this Convention and the rules, regulations and procedures of the Authority, as well as the general policies established by the Assembly, and shall be

subject to the directives and control of the Council.

3. The Enterprise shall have its principal place of business at the seat of the Authority.

4. The Enterprise shall, in accordance with article 173, paragraph 2, and Annex IV, article 11, be provided with such funds as it may require to carry out its functions, and shall receive technology as provided in article 144 and other relevant provisions of this Convention.

Subsection F. Financial Arrangements of the Authority

Article 171
Funds of the Authority

The funds of the Authority shall include:

(a) assessed contributions made by members of the Authority in accordance with article 160, paragraph 2(e);

(b) funds received by the Authority pursuant to Annex III, article 13, in connection with activities in the Area;

(c) funds transferred from the Enterprise in accordance with Annex IV, article 10;

(d) funds borrowed pursuant to article 174;

(e) voluntary contributions made by members or other entities; and

(f) payments to a compensation fund, in accordance with article 151, paragraph 10, whose sources are to be recommended by the Economic Planning Commission.

Article 172
Annual budget of the Authority

The Secretary-General shall draft the proposed annual budget of the Authority and submit it to the Council. The Council shall consider the proposed annual budget and submit it to the Assembly, together with any recommendations thereon. The Assembly shall consider and approve the proposed annual budget in accordance with article 160, paragraph 2(h).

Article 173
Expenses of the Authority

1. The contributions referred to in article 171, subparagraph (a), shall be paid into a special account to meet the administrative expenses of the Authority until the Authority has sufficient funds from other sources to meet those expenses.

2. The administrative expenses of the Authority shall be a first call upon the funds of the Authority. Except for the assessed contributions referred to in article 171, subparagraph (a), the funds which remain after payment of administrative expenses may, *inter alia*:

(a) be shared in accordance with article 140 and article 160, paragraph 2(g);

(b) be used to provide the Enterprise with funds in accordance with article 170, paragraph 4;

(c) be used to compensate developing States in accordance with article 151, paragraph 10, and article 160, paragraph 2(l).

Article 174
Borrowing power of the Authority

1. The Authority shall have the power to borrow funds.

2. The Assembly shall prescribe the limits on the borrowing power of the Authority in the financial regulations adopted pursuant to article 160, paragraph 2(f).

3. The Council shall exercise the borrowing power of the Authority.

4. States Parties shall not be liable for the debts of the Authority.

Article 175
Annual audit

The records, books and accounts of the Authority, including its annual financial statements, shall be audited annually by an independent auditor appointed by the Assembly.

Subsection G. Legal Status, Privileges and Immunities

Article 176
Legal status

The Authority shall have international legal personality and such legal capacity as may be necessary for the exercise of its functions and the fulfilment of its purposes.

Article 177
Privileges and immunities

To enable the Authority to exercise its functions, it shall enjoy in the territory of each State Party the privileges and immunities set forth in this subsection. The privileges and immunities relating to the Enterprise shall be those set forth in Annex IV, article 13.

Article 178
Immunity from legal process

The Authority, its property and assets, shall enjoy immunity from legal process except to the extent that the Authority expressly waives this immunity in a particular case.

Article 179
Immunity from search and any form of seizure

The property and assets of the Authority, wherever located and by whomsoever held, shall be immune from search, requisition, confiscation, expropriation or any other form of seizure by executive or legislative action.

Article 180
Exemption from restrictions, regulations, controls and moratoria

The property and assets of the Authority shall be exempt from restrictions, regulations, controls and moratoria of any nature.

Article 181
Archives and official communications of the Authority

1. The archives of the Authority, wherever located, shall be inviolable.
2. Proprietary data, industrial secrets or similar information and personnel records shall not be placed in archives which are open to public inspection.
3. With regard to its official communications, the Authority shall be accorded by each State Party treatment no less favourable than that accorded by that State to other international organizations.

Article 182
Privileges and immunities of certain persons connected with the Authority

Representatives of States Parties attending meetings of the Assembly, the Council or organs of the Assembly or the Council, and the Secretary-General and staff of the Authority, shall enjoy in the territory of each State Party:

(a) immunity from legal process with respect to acts performed by them in the exercise of their functions, except to the extent that the State which they represent or the Authority, as appropriate, expressly waives this immunity in a particular case;

(b) if they are not nationals of that State Party, the same exemptions from immigration restrictions, alien registration requirements and national service obligations, the same facilities as regards exchange restrictions and the same treatment in respect of travelling facilities as are accorded by that State to the representatives, officials and employees of comparable rank of other States Parties.

Article 183
Exemption from taxes and customs duties

1. Within the scope of its official activities, the Authority, its assets and property, its income, and its operations and transactions, authorized by this Convention, shall be exempt from all direct taxation and goods imported or exported for its official use shall be exempt from all customs duties. The Authority shall not claim exemption from taxes which are no more than charges for services rendered.
2. When purchases of goods or services of substantial value necessary for the official activities of the Authority are made by or on behalf of the Authority, and when the price of such goods or services includes taxes or duties, appropriate measures shall, to the extent practicable, be taken by States Parties to grant exemption from such taxes or duties or provide for their reimbursement. Goods imported or purchased under an exemption provided for in this article shall not be sold or otherwise disposed of in the territory of the State Party which granted the exemption, except under conditions agreed with that State Party.
3. No tax shall be levied by States Parties on or in respect of salaries and emoluments paid or any other form of payment made by the Authority to the Secretary-General and staff of the Authority, as well as experts performing missions for the Authority, who are not their nationals.

Subsection H. Suspension of the Exercise of Rights and Privileges of Members

Article 184
Suspension of the exercise of voting rights

A State Party which is in arrears in the payment of its financial contributions to the Authority shall have no vote if the amount of its arrears equals or exceeds the amount of the contributions due from it for the preceding two full years. The Assembly may, nevertheless, permit such a member to vote if it is satisfied that the failure to pay is due to conditions beyond the control of the member.

Article 185
Suspension of exercise of rights and privileges of membership

1. A State Party which has grossly and persistently violated the provisions of this Part may be suspended from the exercise of the rights and privileges of membership by the Assembly upon the recommendation of the Council.

2. No action may be taken under paragraph 1 until the Sea-Bed Disputes Chamber has found that a State Party has grossly and persistently violated the provisions of this Part.

Section 5. Settlement of Disputes and Advisory Opinions

Article 186
Sea-Bed Disputes Chamber of the International Tribunal for the Law of the Sea

The establishment of the Sea-Bed Disputes Chamber and the manner in which it shall exercise its jurisdiction shall be governed by the provisions of this section, of Part XV and of Annex VI.

Article 187
Jurisdiction of the Sea-Bed Disputes Chamber

The Sea-Bed Disputes Chamber shall have jurisdiction under this Part and the Annexes relating thereto in disputes with respect to activities in the Area falling within the following categories:

(a) disputes between States Parties concerning the interpretation or application of this Part and the Annexes relating thereto;

(b) disputes between a State Party and the Authority concerning:

(i) acts or omissions of the Authority or of a State Party alleged to be in violation of this Part or the Annexes relating thereto or of rules, regulations and procedures of the Authority adopted in accordance therewith; or

(ii) acts of the Authority alleged to be in excess of jurisdiction or a misuse of power;

(c) disputes between parties to a contract, being States Parties, the Authority or the Enterprise, state enterprises and natural or juridicial persons referred to in article 153, paragraph 2(b), concerning:

(i) the interpretation or application of a relevant contract or a plan of work; or

(ii) acts or omissions of a party to the contract relating to activities in the Area and directed to the other party or directly affecting its legitimate interests;

(d) disputes between the Authority and a prospective contractor who has been sponsored by a State as provided in article 153, paragraph 2(b), and has duly fulfilled the conditions referred to in Annex III, article 4, paragraph 6, and article 13, paragraph 2, concerning the refusal of a contract or a legal issue arising in the negotiation of the contract;

(e) disputes between the Authority and a State Party, a state enterprise or a natural or juridical person sponsored by a State Party as provided for in article 153, paragraph 2(b), where it is alleged that the Authority has incurred liability as provided in Annex III, article 22;

(f) any other disputes for which the jurisdiction of the Chamber is specifically provided in this Convention.

Article 188
Submission of disputes to a special chamber of the International Tribunal for the Law of the Sea or an ad hoc chamber of the Sea-Bed Disputes Chamber or to binding commercial arbitration

1. Disputes between States Parties referred to in article 187, subparagraph (a), may be submitted:

(a) at the request of the parties to the dispute, to a special chamber of the International Tribunal for the Law of the Sea to be formed in accordance with Annex VI, articles 15 and 17; or

(b) at the request of any party to the dispute, to an *ad hoc* chamber of the Sea-Bed Disputes Chamber to be formed in accordance with Annex VI, article 36.

2.(a) Disputes concerning the interpretation or application of a contract referred to in article 187, subparagraph (c)(i), shall be submitted, at the request of any party to the dispute, to binding commercial arbitration, unless the parties otherwise agree. A commercial arbitral tribunal to which the dispute is submitted shall have no jurisdiction to decide any question of interpretation of this Convention. When the dispute also involves a question of the interpretation of Part XI and the Annexes relating thereto, with respect to activities in the Area, that question shall be referred to the Sea-Bed Disputes Chamber for a ruling.

(b) If, at the commencement of or in the course of such arbitration, the arbitral tribunal determines, either at the request of any party to the dispute or *proprio motu*, that its decision depends upon a ruling of the Sea-Bed Disputes Chamber, the arbitral tribunal shall refer such question to the Sea-Bed Disputes Chamber for such ruling. The arbitral tribunal shall then proceed to render its award in conformity with the ruling of the Sea-Bed Disputes Chamber.

(c) In the absence of a provision in the contract on the arbitration procedure to be applied in the dispute, the arbitration shall be conducted in accordance with the UNCITRAL Arbitration Rules or such other arbitration rules as may be prescribed in the rules, regulations and procedures of the Authority, unless the parties to the dispute otherwise agree.

Article 189
Limitation on jurisdiction with regard to decisions of the Authority

The Sea-Bed Disputes Chamber shall have no jurisdiction with regard to the exercise by the Authority of its discretionary powers in accordance with this Part; in no case shall it substitute its discretion for that of the Authority. Without prejudice to article 191, in exercising its jurisdiction pursuant to article 187, the Sea-Bed Disputes Chamber shall not pronounce itself on the question of whether any rules, regulations and procedures of the Authority are in conformity with this Convention, nor declare invalid any such rules, regulations and procedures. Its jurisdiction in this regard shall be confined to decinding claims that the application of any rules, regulations and procedures of the Authority in individual cases would be in conflict with the contractual obligations of the parties to the dispute or their obligations under this Convention, claims concerning excess of jurisdiction or misuse of power, and to claims for damages to be paid or other remedy to be given to the party concerned for the failure of the other party to comply with its contractual obligations or its obligations under this Convention.

Article 190
Participation and appearance of sponsoring States Parties in proceedings

1. If a natural or juridical person is a party to a dispute referred to in article 187, the sponsoring State shall be given notice thereof and shall have the right to participate in the proceedings by submitting written or oral statements.

2. If an action is brought against a State Party by a natural or juridical person sponsored by another State Party in a dispute referred to in article 187, subparagraph (c), the respondent State may request the State sponsoring that person to appear in the proceedings on behalf of that person. Failing such appearance, the respondent State may arrange to be represented by a juridical person of its nationality.

Article 191
Advisory opinions

The Sea-Bed Disputes Chamber shall give advisory opinions at the request of the Assembly or the Council on legal questions arising within the scope of their activities. Such opinions shall be given as a matter of urgency.

PART XII

Protection and Preservation of the Marine Environment

Section 1. General Provisions

Article 192
General obligation

States have the obligation to protect and preserve the marine environment.

Article 193
Sovereign right of States to exploit their natural resources

States have the sovereign right to exploit their natural resources pursuant to their environmental policies and in accordance with their duty to protect and preserve the marine environment.

Article 194
Measures to prevent, reduce and control pollution of the marine environment

1. States shall take, individually or jointly as appropriate, all measures consistent with

this Convention that are necessary to prevent, reduce and control pollution of the marine environment from any source, using for this purpose the best practicable means at their disposal and in accordance with their capabilities, and they shall endeavour to harmonize their policies in this connection.

2. States shall take all measures necessary to ensure that activities under thieir jurisdiction or control are so conducted as not to cause damage by pollution to other States and their environment, and that pollution arising from incidents or activities under their jurisdiction or control does not spread beyond the areas where they exercise sovereign rights in accordance with this Convention.

3. The measures taken pursuant to this Part shall deal with all sources of pollution of the marine environment. These measures shall include, *inter alia*, those designed to minimize to the fullest possible extent:

(a) the release of toxic, harmful or noxious substances, especially those which are persistent, from land-based sources, from or through the atmosphere or by dumping;

(b) pollution from vessels, in particular measures for preventing accidents and dealing with emergencies, ensuring the safety of operations at sea, preventing intentional and unintentional discharges, and regulating the design, construction, equipment, operation and manning of vessels;

(c) pollution from installations and devices used in exploration or exploitation of the natural resources of the sea-bed and subsoil, in particular measures for preventing accidents and dealing with emergencies, ensuring the safety of operations at sea, and regulating the design, construction, equipment, operation and manning of such installations or devices;

(d) pollution from other installations and devices operating in the marine environment, in particular measures for preventing accidents and dealing with emergencies, ensuring the safety of operations at sea, and regulating the design, construction, equipment, operation and manning of such installations or devices.

4. In taking measures to prevent, reduce or control pollution of the marine environment, States shall refrain from unjustifiable interference with activities carried out by other States in the exercise of their rights and in pursuance of their duties in conformity with this Convention.

5. The measures taken in accordance with this Part shall include those necessary to protect and preserve rare or fragile ecosystems as well as the habitat of depleted, threatened or endangered species and other forms of marine life.

Article 195

Duty not to transfer damage or hazards or transform one type of pollution into another

In taking measures to prevent, reduce and control pollution of the marine environment, States shall act so as not to transfer, directly or indirectly, damage or hazards from one area to another or transform one type of pollution into another.

Article 196

Use of technologies or introduction of alien or new species

1. States shall take all measures necessary to prevent, reduce and control pollution of the marine environment resulting from the use of technologies under their jurisdiction or control, or the intentional or accidental introduction of species, alien or new, to a particular part of the marine environment, which may cause significant and harmful changes thereto.

2. This article does not affect the application of this Convention regarding the prevention, reduction and control of pollution of the marine environment.

Section 2. Global and Regional Co-operation

Article 197

Co-operation on a global or regional basis

States shall co-operate on a global basis and, as appropriate, on a regional basis, directly or through competent international organizations, in formulating and elaborating international rules, standards and recommended practices and procedures consistent with this Convention, for the protection and preservation of the marine environment, taking into account characteristic regional features.

Article 198

Notification of imminent or actual damage

When a State becomes aware of cases in which the marine environment is in imminent danger of being damaged or has been damaged by pollution, it shall immediately notify other States it deems likely to be affected by such damage, as well as the competent international organizations.

Article 199
Contingency plans against pollution

In the cases referred to in article 198, States in the area affected, in accordance with their capabilities, and the competent international organizations shall co-operate, to the extent possible, in eliminating the effects of pollution and preventing or minimizing the damage. To this end, States shall jointly develop and promote contingency plans for responding to pollution incidents in the marine environment.

Article 200
Studies, research programmes and exchange of information and data

States shall co-operate, directly or through competent international organizations, for the purpose of promoting studies, undertaking programmes of scientific research and encouraging the exchange of information and data acquired about pollution of the marine environment. They shall endeavour to participate actively in regional and global programmes to acquire knowledge for the assessment of the nature and extent of pollution, exposure to it, and its pathways, risks and remedies.

Article 201
Scientific criteria for regulations

In the light of the information and data acquired pursuant to article 200, States shall co-operate, directly or through competent international organizations, in establishing appropriate scientific criteria for the formulation and elaboration of rules, standards and recommended practices and procedures for the prevention, reduction and control of pollution of the marine environment.

Section 3. Technical Assistance

Article 202
Scientific and technical assistance to developing States

States shall, directly or through competent international organizations:

(a) promote programmes of scientific, educational, technical and other assistance to developing States for the protection and preservation of the marine environment and the prevention, reduction and control of marine pollution. Such assistance shall include, *inter alia*:

(i) training of their scientific and technical personnel;

(ii) facilitating their participation in relevant international programmes;

(iii) supplying them with necessary equipment and facilities;

(iv) enhancing their capacity to manufacture such equipment;

(v) advice on and developing facilities for research, monitoring, educational and other programmes;

(b) provide appropriate assistance, especially to developing States, for the minimization of the effects of major incidents which may cause serious pollution of the marine environment;

(c) provide appropriate assistance, especially to developing States, concerning the preparation of environmental assessments.

Article 203
Preferential treatment for developing States

Developing States shall, for the purpose of prevention, reduction and control of pollution of the marine environment or minimization of its effects, be granted preference by international organizations in:

(a) the allocation of appropriate funds and technical assistance; and

(b) the utilization of their specialized services.

Section 4. Monitoring and Environmental Assessment

Article 204
Monitoring of the risks or effects of pollution

1. States shall, consistent with the rights of other States, endeavour, as far as practicable, directly or through the competent international organizations, to observe, measure, evaluate and analyse, by recognized scientific methods, the risks or effects of pollution of the marine environment.

2. In particular, States shall keep under surveillance the effects of any activities which they permit or in which they engage in order to determine whether these activities are likely to pollute the marine environment.

Article 205
Publication of reports

States shall publish reports of the results obtained pursuant to article 204 or provide such reports at appropriate intervals to the competent international organizations, which should make them available to all States.

Article 206
Assessment of potential effects of activities

When States have reasonable grounds for believing that planned activities under their jurisdiction or control may cause substantial pollution of or significant and harmful changes to the marine environment, they shall, as far as practicable, assess the potential effects of such activities on the marine environment and shall communicate reports of the results of such assessments in the manner provided in article 205.

Section 5. International Rules and National Legislation to Prevent, Reduce and Control Pollution of the Marine Environment

Article 207
Pollution from land-based sources

1. States shall adopt laws and regulations to prevent, reduce and control pollution of the marine environment from land-based sources, including rivers, estuaries, pipelines and outfall structures, taking into account internationally agreed rules, standards and recommended practices and procedures.
2. States shall take other measures as may be necessary to prevent, reduce and control such pollution.
3. States shall endeavour to harmonize their policies in this connection at the appropriate regional level.
4. States, acting especially through competent international organizations or diplomatic conference, shall endeavour to establish global and regional rules, standards and recommended practices and procedures to prevent, reduce and control pollution of the marine environment from land-based sources, taking into account characteristic regional features, the economic capacity of developing States and their need for economic development. Such rules, standards and recommended practices and procedures shall be re-examined from time to time as necessary.
5. Laws, regulations, measures, rules, standards and recommended practices and procedures referred to in paragraphs 1, 2 and 4 shall include those designed to minimize, to the fullest extent possible, the release of toxic, harmful or noxious substances, especially those which are persistent, into the marine environment.

Article 208
Pollution from sea-bed activities subject to national jurisdiction

1. Coastal States shall adopt laws and regulations to prevent, reduce and control pollution of the marine environment arising from or in connection with sea-bed activities subject to their jurisdiction and from artificial islands, installations and structures under their jurisdiction, pursuant to articles 60 and 80.
2. States shall take other measures as may be necesssary to prevent, reduce and control such pollution.
3. Such laws, regulations and measures shall be no less effective than international rules, standards and recommended practices and procedures.
4. States shall endeavour to harmonize their policies in this connection at the appropriate regional level.
5. States, acting especially through competent international organizations or diplomatic conferences, shall establish global and regional rules, standards and recommended practices and procedures to prevent, reduce and control pollution of the marine environment referred to in paragraph 1. Such rules, standards and recommended practices and procedures shall be re-examined from time to time as necessary.

Article 209
Pollution from activities in the Area

1. International rules, regulations and procedures shall be established in accordance with Part XI to prevent, reduce and control pollution of the marine environment from activities in the Area. Such rules, regulations and procedures shall be re-examined from time to time as necessary.
2. Subject to the relevant provisions of this section, States shall adopt laws and regulations to prevent, reduce and control pollution of the marine environment from activities in the Area undertaken by vessels, installations, structures and other devices flying their flag or of their registry or

operating under their authority, as the case may be. The requirements of such laws and regulations shall be no less effective than the international rules, regulations and procedures referred to in paragraph 1.

Article 210
Pollution by dumping

1. States shall adopt laws and regulations to prevent, reduce and control pollution of the marine environment by dumping.

2. States shall take other measures as may be necessary to prevent, reduce and control such pollution.

3. Such laws, regulations and measures shall ensure that dumping is not carried out without the permission of the competent authorities of States.

4. States, acting especially through competent international organizations or diplomatic conference, shall endeavour to establish global and regional rules, standards and recommended practices and procedures to prevent, reduce and control such pollution. Such rules, standards and recommended practices and procedures shall be re-examined from time to time as necessary.

5. Dumping within the territorial sea and the exclusive economic zone or onto the continental shelf shall not be carried out without the express prior approval of the coastal State, which has the right to permit, regulate and control such dumping after due consideration of the matter with other States which by reason of their geographical situation may be adversely affected thereby.

6. National laws, regulations and measures shall be no less effective in preventing, reducing and controlling such pollution than the global rules and standards.

Article 211
Pollution from vessels

1. States, acting through the competent international organization or general diplomatic conference, shall establish international rules and standards to prevent, reduce and control pollution of the marine environment from vessels and promote the adoption, in the same manner, wherever appropriate, of routeing systems designed to minimize the threat of accidents which might cause pollution of the marine environment, including the coastline, and pollution damage to the related interests of coastal States. Such rules and standards shall, in the same manner, be re-examined from time to time as necessary.

2. States shall adopt laws and regulations for the prevention, reduction and control of pollution of the marine environment from vessels flying their flag or of their registry. Such laws and regulations shall at least have the same effect as that of generally accepted international rules and standards established through the competent international organization or general diplomatic conference.

3. States which establish particular requirements for the prevention, reduction and control of pollution of the marine environment as a condition for the entry of foreign vessels into their ports or internal waters or for a call at their off-shore terminals shall give due publicity to such requirements and shall communicate them to the competent international organization. Whenever such requirements are established in identical form by two or more coastal States in an endeavour to harmonize policy, the communication shall indicate which States are participating in such co-operative arrangements. Every State shall require the master of a vessel flying its flag or of its registry, when navigating within the territorial sea of a State participating in such co-operative arrangements, to furnish, upon the request of that State, information as to whether it is proceeding to a State of the same region participating in such co-operative arrangements and, if so, to indicate whether it complies with the port entry requirements of that State. This article is without prejudice to the continued exercise by a vessel of its right of innocent passage or to the application of article 25, paragraph 2.

4. Coastal States may, in the exercise of their sovereignty within their territorial sea, adopt laws and regulations for the prevention, reduction and control of marine pollution from foreign vessels, including vessels exercising the right of innocent passage. Such laws and regulations shall, in accordance with Part II, section 3, not hamper innocent passage of foreign vessels.

5. Coastal States, for the purpose of enforcement as provided for in section 6, may in respect of their exclusive economic zones adopt laws and regulations for the prevention, reduction and control of pollution from vessels conforming to and

giving effect to generally accepted international rules and standards established through the competent international organization or general diplomatic conference.

6.(a) Where the international rules and standards referred to in paragraph 1 are inadequate to meet special circumstances and coastal States have reasonable grounds for believing that a particular, clearly defined area of their respective exclusive economic zones is an area where the adoption of special mandatory measures for the prevention of pollution from vessels is required for recognized technical reasons in relation to its oceanographical and ecological conditions, as well as its utilization or the protection of its resources and the particular character of its traffic, the coastal States, after appropriate consultations through the competent international organization with any other States concerned, may, for that area, direct a communication to that organization, submitting scientific and technical evidence in support and information on necessary reception facilities. Within 12 months after receiving such a communication, the organization shall determine whether the conditions in that area correspond to the requirements set out above. If the organization so determines, the coastal States may, for that area, adopt laws and regulations for the prevention, reduction and control of pollution from vessels implementing such international rules and standards or navigational practices as are made applicable, through the organization, for special areas. These laws and regulations shall not become applicable to foreign vessels until 15 months after the submission of the communication to the organization.

(b) The coastal States shall publish the limits of any such particular, clearly defined area.

(c) If the coastal States intend to adopt additional laws and regulations for the same area for the prevention, reduction and control of pollution from vessels, they shall, when submitting the aforesaid communication, at the same time notify the organization thereof. Such additional laws and regulations may relate to discharges or navigational practices but shall not require foreign vessels to observe design, construction, manning or equipment standards other than generally accepted international rules and standards; they shall become applicable to foreign vessels 15 months after the submission of the communication to the organization, provided that the organization agrees within 12 months after the submission of the communication.

7. The international rules and standards referred to in this article should include *inter alia* those relating to prompt notification to coastal States, whose coastline or related interests may be affected by incidents, including maritime casualties, which involve discharges or probability of discharges.

Article 212
Pollution from or through the atmosphere

1. States shall adopt laws and regulations to prevent, reduce and control pollution of the marine environment from or through the atmosphere, applicable to the air space under their sovereignty and to vessels flying their flag or vessels or aircraft of their registry, taking into account internationally agreed rules, standards and recommended practices and procedures and the safety of air navigation.

2. States shall take other measures as may be necessary to prevent, reduce and control such pollution.

3. States, acting especially through competent international organizations or diplomatic conference, shall endeavour to establish global and regional rules, standards and recommended practices and procedures to prevent, reduce and control such pollution.

Section 6. Enforcement

Article 213
Enforcement with respect to pollution from land-based sources

States shall enforce their laws and regulations adopted in accordance with article 207 and shall adopt laws and regulations and take other measures necessary to implement applicable international rules and standards established through competent international organizations or diplomatic conference to prevent, reduce and control pollution of the marine environment from land-based sources.

Article 214
Enforcement with respect to pollution from sea-bed activities

States shall enforce their laws and regulations adopted in accordance with article 208 and shall adopt laws and regulations and take other measures necessary to implement applicable international rules and standards established through competent international organizations or diplomatic conference to prevent, reduce and control pollution of the marine environment arising from or in connection with sea-bed activities subject to their jurisdiction and from artificial islands, installations and structures under their jurisdiction, pursuant to articles 60 and 80.

Article 215
Enforcement with respect to pollution from activities in the Area

Enforcement of international rules, regulations and procedures established in accordance with Part XI to prevent, reduce and control pollution of the marine environment from activities in the Area shall be governed by that Part.

Article 216
Enforcement with respect to pollution by dumping

1. Laws and regulations adopted in accordance with this Convention and applicable international rules and standards established through competent international organizations or diplomatic conference for the prevention, reduction and control of pollution of the marine environment by dumping shall be enforced:

(a) by the coastal State with regard to dumping within its territorial sea or its exclusive economic zone or onto its continental shelf;

(b) by the flag State with regard to vessels flying its flag or vessels or aircraft of its registry;

(c) by any State with regard to acts of loading of wastes or other matter occurring within its territory or at its off-shore terminals.

2. No State shall be obliged by virtue of this article to institute proceedings when another State has already instituted proceedings in accordance with this article.

Article 217
Enforcement by flag States

1. States shall ensure compliance by vessels flying their flag or of their registry with applicable international rules and standards, established through the competent international organization or general diplomatic conference, and with their laws and regulations adopted in accordance with this Convention for the prevention, reduction and control of pollution of the marine environment from vessels and shall accordingly adopt laws and regulations and take other measures necessary for their implementation. Flag States shall provide for the effective enforcement of such rules, standards, laws and regulations, irrespective of where a violation occurs.

2. States shall, in particular, take appropriate measures in order to ensure that vessels flying their flag or of their registr[y] are prohibited from sailing, until they ca[n] proceed to sea in compliance with th[e] requirements of the international rules a[nd] standards referred to in paragraph [1,] including requirements in respect of des[ign,] construction, equipment and mannin[g of] vessels.

3. States shall ensure that vessels [flying] their flag or of their registry carry on boa[rd] certificates required by and issued pursuant to international rules and standards referred to in paragraph 1. States shall ensure that vessels flying their flag are periodically inspected in order to verify that such certificates are in conformity with the actual condition of the vessels. These certificates shall be accepted by other States as evidence of the condition of the vessels and shall be regarded as having the same force as certificates issued by them, unless there are clear ground for believing that the condition of the vessel does not correspond substantially with the particulars of the certificates.

4. If a vessel commits a violation of rules and standards established through the competent international organization or general diplomatic conference, the flag State, without prejudice to articles 218, 220 and 228, shall provide for immediate investigation and where appropriate institute proceedings in respect of the alleged violation irrespective of where the violation occurred or where the pollution caused by such violation has occurred or has been spotted.

5. Flag States conducting an investigation of the violation may request the assistance of any other State whose co-operation could be useful in clarifying the circumstances of the case. States shall endeavour to meet appropriate requests of flag States.

6. States shall, at the written request of any State, investigate any violation alleged

to have been committed by vessels flying their flag. If satisfied that sufficient evidence is available to enable proceedings to be brought in respect of the alleged violation, flag States shall without delay institute such proceedings in accordance with their laws.

7. Flag States shall promptly inform the requesting State and the competent international organization of the action taken and its outcome. Such information shall be available to all States.

8. Penalities provided for by the laws and regulations of States for vessels flying their flag shall be adequate in severity to discourage violations wherever they occur.

Article 218
Enforcement by port States

1. When a vessel is voluntarily within a port or at an off-shore terminal of a State, that State may undertake investigations and, where the evidence so warrants, institute proceedings in respect of any discharge from that vessel outside the internal waters, territorial sea or exclusive economic zone of that State in violation of applicable international rules and standards established through the competent international organization or general diplomatic conference.

2. No proceedings pursuant to paragraph 1 shall be instituted in respect of a discharge violation in the internal waters, territorial sea or exclusive economic zone of another State unless requested by that State, the flag State, or a State damaged or threatened by the discharge violation, or unless the violation has caused or is likely to cause pollution in the internal waters, territorial sea or exclusive economic zone of the State instituting the proceedings.

3. When a vessel is voluntarily within a port or at an off-shore terminal of a State, that State shall, as far as practicable, comply with requests from any State for investigation of a discharge violation referred to in paragraph 1, believed to have occurred in, caused, or threatened damage to the internal waters, territorial sea or exclusive economic zone of the requesting State. It shall likewise, as far as practicable, comply with requests from the flag State for investigation of such a violation, irrespective of where the violation occurred.

4. The records of the investigation carried out by a port State pursuant to this article shall be transmitted upon request to the flag State or to the coastal State. Any proceedings instituted by the port State on the basis of such an investigation may, subject to section 7, be suspended at the request of the coastal State when the violation has occurred within its internal waters, territorial sea or exclusive economic zone. The evidence and records of the case, together with any bond or other financial security posted with the authorities of the port State, shall in that event be transmitted to the coastal State. Such transmittal shall preclude the continuation of proceedings in the port State.

Article 219
Measures relating to seaworthiness of vessels to avoid pollution

Subject to section 7, States which, upon request or on their own initiative, have ascertained that a vessel within one of their ports or at one of their off-shore terminals is in violation of applicable international rules and standards relating to seaworthiness of vessels and thereby threatens damage to the marine environment shall, as far as practicable, take administrative measures to prevent the vessel from sailing. Such States may permit the vessel to proceed only to the nearest appropriate repair yard and, upon removal of the causes of the violation, shall permit the vessel to continue immediately.

Article 220
Enforcement by coastal States

1. When a vessel is voluntarily within a port or at an off-shore terminal of a State, that State may, subject to section 7, institute proceedings in respect of any violation of its laws and regulations adopted in accordance with this Convention or applicable international rules and standards for the prevention, reduction and control of pollution from vessels when the violation has occurred within the territorial sea or the exclusive economic zone of that State.

2. Where there are clear grounds for believing that a vessel navigating in the territorial sea of a State has, during its passage therein, violated laws and regulations of that State adopted in accordance with this Convention or applicable international rules and standards for the prevention, reduction and control of pollution from vessels, that State, without

prejudice to the application of the relevant provisions of Part II, section 3, may undertake physical inspection of the vessel relating to the violation and may, where the evidence so warrants, institute proceedings, including detention of the vessel, in accordance with its laws, subject to the provisions of section 7.

3. Where there are clear grounds for believing that a vessel navigating in the exclusive economic zone or the territorial sea of a State has, in the exclusive economic zone, committed a violation of applicable international rules and standards for the prevention, reduction and control of pollution from vessels or laws and regulations of that State conforming and giving effect to such rules and standards, that State may require the vessel to give information regarding its identity and port of registry, its last and its next port of call and other relevant information required to establish whether a violation has occurred.

4. States shall adopt laws and regulations and take other measures so that vessels flying their flag comply with requests for information pursuant to paragraph 3.

5. Where there are clear grounds for believing that a vessel navigating in the exclusive economic zone or the territorial sea of a State has, in the exclusive economic zone, committed a violation referred to in paragraph 3 resulting in a substantial discharge causing or threatening significant pollution of the marine environment, that State may undertake physical inspection of the vessel for matters relating to the violation if the vessel has refused to give information or if the information supplied by the vessel is manifestly at variance with the evident factual situation and if the circumstances of the case justify such inspection.

6. Where there is clear objective evidence that a vessel navigating in the exclusive economic zone or the territorial sea of a State has, in the exclusive economic zone, committed a violation referred to in paragraph 3 resulting in a discharge causing major damage or threat of major damage to the coastline or related interests of the coastal State, or to any resources of its territorial sea or exclusive economic zone, that State may, subject to section 7, provided that the evidence so warrants, institute proceedings, including detention of the vessel, in accordance with its laws.

7. Notwithstanding the provisions of paragraph 6, whenever appropriate procedures have been established, either through the competent international organization or as otherwise agreed, whereby compliance with requirements for bonding or other appropriate financial security has been assured, the coastal State if bound by such procedures shall allow the vessel to proceed.

8. The provisions of paragraphs 3, 4, 5, 6 and 7 also apply in respect of national laws and regulations adopted pursuant to article 211, paragraph 6.

Article 221
Measures to avoid pollution arising from maritime casualties

1. Nothing in this Part shall prejudice the right of States, pursuant to international law, both customary and conventional, to take and enforce measures beyond the territorial sea proportionate to the actual or threatened damage to protect their coastline or related interests, including fishing, from pollution or threat of pollution following upon a maritime casualty or acts relating to such a casualty, which may reasonably be expected to result in major harmful consequences.

2. For the purposes of this article, "maritime casualty" means a collision of vessels, stranding or other incident of navigation, or other occurrence on board a vessel or external to it resulting in material damage or imminent threat of material damage to a vessel or cargo.

Article 222
Enforcement with respect to pollution from or through the atmosphere

States shall enforce, within the air space under their sovereignty or with regard to vessels flying their flag or vessels or aircraft of their registry, their laws and regulations adopted in accordance with article 212, paragraph 1, and with other provisions of this Convention and shall adopt laws and regulations and take other measures necessary to implement applicable international rules and standards established through competent international organizations or diplomatic conference to prevent, reduce and control pollution of the marine environment from or through the atmosphere, in conformity with all relevant international rules and standards concerning the safety of air navigation.

Section 7. Safeguards

Article 223
Measures to facilitate proceedings

In proceedings instituted pursuant to this Part, States shall take measures to facilitate the hearing of witnesses and the admission of evidence submitted by authorities of another State, or by the competent international organization, and shall facilitate the attendance at such proceedings of official representatives of the competent international organization, the flag State and any State affected by pollution arising out of any violation. The official representatives attending such proceedings shall have such rights and duties as may be provided under national laws and regulations or international law.

Article 224
Exercise of powers of enforcement

The powers of enforcement against foreign vessels under this Part may only be exercised by officials or by warships, military aircraft, or other ships or aircraft clearly marked and identifiable as being on government service and authorized to that effect.

Article 225
Duty to avoid adverse consequences in the exercise of the powers of enforcement

In the exercise under this Convention of their powers of enforcement against foreign vessels, States shall not endanger the safety of navigation or otherwise create any hazard to a vessel, or bring it to an unsafe port or anchorage, or expose the marine environment to an unreasonable risk.

Article 226
Investigation of foreign vessels

1.(a) States shall not delay a foreign vessel longer than is essential for purposes of the investigations provided for in articles 216, 218 and 220. Any physical inspection of a foreign vessel shall be limited to an examination of such certificates, records or other documents as the vessel is required to carry by generally accepted international rules and standards or of any similar documents which it is carrying; further physical inspection of the vessel may be undertaken only after such an examination and only when:

(i) there are clear grounds for believing that the condition of the vessel or its equipment does not correspond substantially with the particulars of those documents;

(ii) the contents of such documents are not sufficient to confirm or verify a suspected violation; or

(iii) the vessel is not carrying valid certificates and records.

(b) If the investigation indicates a violation of applicable laws and regulations or international rules and standards for the protection and preservation of the marine environment, release shall be made promptly subject to reasonable procedures such as bonding or other appropriate financial security.

(c) Without prejudice to applicable international rules and standards relating to the seaworthiness of vessels, the release of a vessel may, whenever it would present an unreasonable threat of damage to the marine environment, be refused or made conditional upon proceeding to the nearest appropriate repair yard. Where release has been refused or made conditional, the flag State of the vessel must be promptly notified, and may seek release of the vessel in accordance with Part XV.

2. States shall co-operate to develop procedures for the avoidance of unnecessary physical inspection of vessels at sea.

Article 227
Non-discrimination with respect to foreign vessels

In exercising their rights and performing their duties under this Part, States shall not discriminate in form or in fact against vessels of any other State.

Article 228
Suspension and restrictions on institution of proceedings

1. Proceedings to impose penalties in respect of any violation of applicable laws and regulations or international rules and standards relating to the prevention, reduction and control of pollution from vessels committed by a foreign vessel beyond the territorial sea of the State instituting proceedings shall be suspended upon the taking of proceedings to impose penalties in respect of corresponding charges by the flag State within six months of the date on which proceedings were first instituted, unless those proceedings relate

to a case of major damage to the coastal State or the flag State in question has repeatedly disregarded its obligations to enforce effectively the applicable international rules and standards in respect of violations committed by its vessels. The flag State shall in due course make available to the State previously instituting proceedings a full dossier of the case and the records of the proceedings, whenever the flag State has requested the suspension of proceedings in accordance with this article. When proceedings instituted by the flag State have been brought to a conclusion, the suspended proceedings shall be terminated. Upon payment of costs incurred in respect of such proceedings, any bond posted or other financial security provided in connection with the suspended proceedings shall be released by the coastal State.

2. Proceedings to impose penalties on foreign vessels shall not be instituted after the expiry of three years from the date on which the violation was committed, and shall not be taken by any State in the event of proceedings having been instituted by another State subject to the provisions set out in paragraph 1.

3. The provisions of this article are without prejudice to the right of the flag State to take any measures, including proceedings to impose penalties, according to its laws irrespective of prior proceedings by another State.

Article 229
Institution of civil proceedings

Nothing in this Convention affects the institution of civil proceedings in respect of any claim for loss or damage resulting from pollution of the marine environment.

Article 230
Monetary penalties and the observance of recognized rights of the accused

1. Monetary penalties only may be imposed with respect to violations of national laws and regulations or applicable international rules and standards for the prevention, reduction and control of pollution of the marine environment, committed by foreign vessels beyond the territorial sea.

2. Monetary penalties only may be imposed with respect to violations of national laws and regulations or applicable international rules and standards for the prevention, reduction and control of pollution of the marine environment, committed by foreign vessels in the territorial sea, except in the case of a wilful and serious act of pollution in the territorial sea.

3. In the conduct of proceedings in respect of such violations committed by a foreign vessel which may result in the imposition of penalties, recognized rights of the accused shall be observed.

Article 231
Notification to the flag State and other States concerned

States shall promptly notify the flag State and any other State concerned of any measures taken pursuant to section 6 against foreign vessels, and shall submit to the flag State all official reports concerning such measures. However, with respect to violations committed in the territorial sea, the foregoing obligations of the coastal State apply only to such measures as are taken in proceedings. The diplomatic agents or consular officers, and where possible the maritime authority of the flag State, shall be immediately informed of any such measures taken pursuant to section 6 against foreign vessels.

Article 232
Liability of States arising from enforcement measures

States shall be liable for damage or loss attributable to them arising from measures taken pursuant to section 6 when such measures are unlawful or exceed those reasonably required in the light of available information. States shall provide for recourse in their courts for actions in respect of such damage or loss.

Article 233
Safeguards with respect to straits used for international navigation

Nothing in sections 5, 6 and 7 affects the legal régime of straits used for international navigation. However, if a foreign ship other than those referred to in section 10 has committed a violation of the laws and regulations referred to in article 42, paragraph 1(a) and (b), causing or threatening major damage to the marine environment of the straits, the States bordering the straits may take appropriate enforcement measures and if so shall respect *mutatis mutandis* the provisions of this section.

Section 8. Ice-Covered Areas

Article 234
Ice-covered areas

Coastal States have the right to adopt and enforce non-discriminatory laws and regulations for the prevention, reduction and control of marine pollution from vessels in ice-covered areas within the limits of the exclusive economic zone, where particularly severe climatic conditions and the presence of ice covering such areas for most of the year create obstructions or exceptional hazards to navigation, and pollution of the marine environment could cause major harm to or irreversible disturbance of the ecological balance. Such laws and regulations shall have due regard to navigation and the protection and preservation of the marine environment based on the best available scientific evidence.

Section 9. Responsibility and Liability

Article 235
Responsibility and liability

1. States are responsible for the fulfilment of their international obligations concerning the protection and preservation of the marine environment. They shall be liable in accordance with international law.

2. States shall ensure that recourse is available in accordance with their legal systems for prompt and adequate compensation or other relief in respect of damage caused by pollution of the marine environment by natural or juridical persons under their jurisdiction.

3. With the objective of assuring prompt and adequate compensation in respect of all damage caused by pollution of the marine environment, States shall co-operate in the implementation of existing international law and the further development of international law relating to responsibility and liability for the assessment of and compensation for damage and the settlement of related disputes, as well as, where appropriate, development of criteria and procedures for payment of adequate compensation, such as compulsory insurance or compensation funds.

Section 10. Sovereign Immunity

Article 236
Sovereign immunity

The provisions of this Convention regarding the protection and preservation of the marine environment do not apply to any warship, naval auxiliary, other vessels or aircraft owned or operated by a State and used, for the time being, only on government non-commercial service. However, each State shall ensure, by the adoption of appropriate measures not impairing operations or operational capabilities of such vessels or aircraft owned or operated by it, that such vessels or aircraft act in a manner consistent, so far as is reasonable and practicable, with this Convention.

Section 11. Obligations under Other Conventions on the Protection and Preservation of the Marine Environment

Article 237
Obligations under other Conventions on the protection and preservation of the marine environment

1. The provisions of this Part are without prejudice to the specific obligations assumed by States under special Conventions and agreements concluded previously which relate to the protection and preservation of the marine environment and to agreements which may be concluded in furtherance of the general principles set forth in this Convention.

2. Specific obligations assumed by States under special Conventions, with respect to the protection and preservation of the marine environment, should be carried out in a manner consistent with the general principles and objectives of this Convention.

PART XIII

Marine Scientific Research

Section 1. General Provisions

Article 238
Right to conduct marine scientific research

All States, irrespective of their geographical location, and competent international organizations have the right to conduct marine scientific research subject to the rights and duties of other States as provided for in this Convention.

Article 239
Promotion of marine scientific research

States and competent international organizations shall promote and facilitate the development and conduct of marine scientific research in accordance with this Convention.

Article 240
General principles for the conduct of marine scientific research

In the conduct of marine scientific research the following principles shall apply:

(a) marine scientific research shall be conducted exclusively for peaceful purposes;

(b) marine scientific research shall be conducted with appropriate scientific methods and means compatible with this Convention;

(c) marine scientific research shall not unjustifiably interfere with other legitimate uses of the sea compatible with this Convention and shall be duly respected in the course of such uses;

(d) marine scientific research shall be conducted in compliance with all relevant regulations adopted in conformity with this Convention including those for the protection and preservation of the marine environment.

Article 241
Non-recognition of marine scientific research activities as the legal basis for claims

Marine scientific research activities shall not constitute the legal basis for any claim to any part of the marine environment or its resources.

Section 2. International Co-operation

Article 242
Promotion of international co-operation

1. States and competent international organizations shall, in accordance with the principle of respect for sovereignty and jurisdiction and on the basis of mutual benefit, promote international co-operation in marine scientific research for peaceful purposes.

2. In this context, without prejudice to the rights and duties of States under this Convention, a State, in the application of this Part, shall provide, as appropriate, other States with a reasonable opportunity to obtain from it, or with its co-operation, information necessary to prevent and control damage to the health and safety of persons and to the marine environment.

Article 243
Creation of favourable conditions

States and competent international organizations shall co-operate, through the conclusion of bilateral and multilateral agreements, to create favourable conditions for the conduct of marine scientific research in the marine environment and to integrate the efforts of scientists in studying the essence of phenomena and processes occurring in the marine environment and the interrelations between them.

Article 244
Publication and dissemination of information and knowledge

1. States and competent international organizations shall, in accordance with this Convention, make available by publication and dissemination through appropriate channels information on proposed major programmes and their objectives as well as knowledge resulting from marine scientific research.

2. For this purpose, States, both individually and in co-operation with other States and with competent international organizations, shall actively promote the flow of scientific data and information and the transfer of knowledge resulting from marine scientific research, especially to developing States, as well as the strengthening of the autonomous marine scientific research capabilities of developing States through, *inter alia*, programmes to provide adequate education and training of their technical and scientific personnel.

Section 3. Conduct and Promotion of Marine Scientific Research

Article 245
Marine scientific research in the territorial sea

Coastal States, in the exercise of their sovereignty, have the exclusive right to regulate, authorize and conduct marine scientific research in their territorial sea. Marine scientific research therein shall be conducted only with the express consent of and under the conditions set forth by the coastal State.

Article 246
Marine scientific research in the exclusive economic zone and on the continental shelf

1. Coastal States, in the exercise of their jurisdiction, have the right to regulate,

authorize and conduct marine scientific research in their exclusive economic zone and on their continental shelf in accordance with the relevant provisions of this Convention.

2. Marine scientific research in the exclusive economic zone and on the continental shelf shall be conducted with the consent of the coastal State.

3. Coastal States shall, in normal circumstances, grant their consent for marine scientific research projects by other States or competent international organizations in their exclusive economic zone or on their continental shelf to be carried out in accordance with this Convention exclusively for peaceful purposes and in order to increase scientific knowledge of the marine environment for the benefit of all mankind. To this end, coastal States shall establish rules and procedures ensuring that such consent will not be delayed or denied unreasonably.

4. For the purposes of applying paragraph 3, normal circumstances may exist in spite of the absence of diplomatic relations between the coastal State and the researching State.

5. Coastal States may however in their discretion withhold their consent to the conduct of a marine scientific research project of another State or competent international organization in the exclusive economic zone or on the continental shelf of the coastal State if that project:

(a) is of direct significance for the exploration and exploitation of natural resources, whether living or non-living;

(b) involves drilling into the continental shelf, the use of explosives or the introduction of harmful substances into the marine environment;

(c) involves the construction, operation or use of artificial islands, installations and structures referred to in articles 60 and 80;

(d) contains information communicated pursuant to article 248 regarding the nature and objectives of the project which is inaccurate or if the researching State or competent international organization has outstanding obligations to the coastal State from a prior research project.

6. Notwithstanding the provisions of paragraph 5, coastal States may not exercise their discretion to withhold consent under subparagraph (a) of that paragraph in respect of marine scientific research projects to be undertaken in accordance with the provisions of this Part on the continental shelf, beyond 200 nautical miles from the baselines from which the breadth of the territorial sea is measured, outside those specific areas which coastal States may at any time publicly designate as areas in which exploitation or detailed exploratory operations focused on those areas are occurring or will occur within a reasonable period of time. Coastal States shall give reasonable notice of the designation of such areas, as well as any modifications thereto, but shall not be obliged to give details of the operations therein.

7. The provisions of paragraph 6 are without prejudice to the rights of coastal States over the continental shelf as established in article 77.

8. Marine scientific research activities referred to in this article shall not unjustifiably interfere with activites undertaken by coastal States in the exercise of their sovereign rights and jurisdiction provided for in this Convention.

Article 247
Marine scientific research projects undertaken by or under the auspices of international organizations

A coastal State which is a member of or has a bilateral agreement with an international organization, and in whose exclusive economic zone or on whose continental shelf that organization wants to carry out a marine scientific research project, directly or under its auspices, shall be deemed to have authorized the project to be carried out in conformity with the agreed specifications if that State approved the detailed project when the decision was made by the organization for the undertaking of the project, or is willing to participate in it, and has not expressed any objection within four months of notification of the project by the organization to the coastal State.

Article 248
Duty to provide information to the coastal State

States and competent international organizations which intend to undertake marine scientific research in the exclusive economic zone or on the continental shelf of a coastal State shall, not less than six months in advance of the expected starting date of the marine scientific research project, provide that State with a full description of:

(a) the nature and objectives of the project;

(b) the method and means to be used, including name, tonnage, type and class of vessels and a description of scientific equipment;

(c) the precise geographical areas in which the project is to be conducted;

(d) the expected date of first appearance and final departure of the research vessels, or deployment of the equipment and its removal, as appropriate;

(e) the name of the sponsoring institution, its director, and the person in charge of the project; and

(f) the extent to which it is considered that the coastal State should be able to participate or to be represented in the project.

Article 249
Duty to comply with certain conditions

1. States and competent international organizations when undertaking marine scientific research in the exclusive economic zone or on the continental shelf of a coastal State shall comply with the following conditions:

(a) ensure the right of the coastal State, if it so desires, to participate or be represented in the marine scientific research project, especially on board research vessels and other craft or scientific research installations, when practicable, without payment of any remuneration to the scientists of the coastal State and without obligation to contribute towards the costs of the project;

(b) provide the coastal State, at its request, with preliminary reports, as soon as practicable, and with the final results and conclusions after the completion of the research;

(c) undertake to provide access for the coastal State, at its request, to all data and samples derived from the marine scientific research project and likewise to furnish it with data which may be copied and samples which may be divided without detriment to their scientific value;

(d) if requested, provide the coastal State with an assessment of such data, samples and research results or provide assistance in their assessment or interpretation;

(e) ensure, subject to paragraph 2, that the research results are made internationally available through appropriate national or international channels, as soon as practicable;

(f) inform the coastal State immediately of any major change in the research programme;

(g) unless otherwise agreed, remove the scientific research installations or equipment once the research is completed.

2. This article is without prejudice to the conditions established by the laws and regulations of the coastal State for the exercise of its discretion to grant or withhold consent pursuant to article 246, paragraph 5, including requiring prior agreement for making internationally available the research results of a project of direct significance for the exploration and exploitation of natural resources.

Article 250
Communications concerning marine scientific research projects

Communications concerning the marine scientific research projects shall be made through appropriate official channels, unless otherwise agreed.

Article 251
General criteria and guidelines

States shall seek to promote through competent international organizations the establishment of general criteria and guidelines to assist States in ascertaining the nature and implications of marine scientific research.

Article 252
Implied consent

States or competent international organizations may proceed with a marine scientific research project six months after the date upon which the information required pursuant to article 248 was provided to the coastal State unless within four months of the receipt of the communication containing such information the coastal State has informed the State or organization conducting the research that:

(a) it has withheld its consent under the provisions of article 246; or

(b) the information given by that State or competent international organization regarding the nature or objectives of the project does not conform to the manifestly evident facts; or

(c) it requires supplementary information relevant to conditions and the information provided for under articles 248 and 249; or

(d) outstanding obligations exist with respect to a previous marine scientific research project carried out by that State or organization, with regard to conditions established in article 249.

Article 253
Suspension or cessation of marine scientific research activities

1. A coastal State shall have the right to require the suspension of any marine scneitific research activities in progress within its exclusive economic zone or on its continental shelf if:

(a) the research activities are not being conducted in accordance with the information communicated as provided under article 248 upon which the consent of the coastal State was based; or

(b) the State or competent international organization conducting the research activities fails to comply with the provisions of article 249 concerning the rights of the coastal State with respect to the marine scientific research project.

2. A coastal State shall have the right to require the cessation of any marine scientific research activities in case of any non-compliance with the provisions of article 248 which amounts to a major change in the research project or the research activities.

3. A coastal State may also require cessation of marine scientific research activities if any of the situations contemplated in paragraph 1 are not rectified within a reasonable period of time.

4. Following notification by the coastal State of its decision to order suspension or cessation, States or competent international organizations authorized to conduct marine scientific research activities shall terminate the research activities that are the subject of such a notification.

5. An order of suspension under paragraph 1 shall be lifted by the coastal State and the marine scientific research activities allowed to continue once the researching State or competent international organization has complied with the conditions required under articles 248 and 249.

Article 254
Rights of neighbouring land-locked and geographically disadvantaged States

1. States and competent international organizations which have submitted to a coastal State a project to undertake marine scientific research referred to in article 246, paragraph 3, shall give notice to the neighbouring land-locked and geographically disadvantaged States of the proposed research project, and shall notify the coastal State thereof.

2. After the consent has been given for the proposed marine scientific research project by the coastal State concerned, in accordance with article 246 and other relevant provisions of this Convention, States and competent international organizations undertaking such a project shall provide to the neighbouring land-locked and geographically disadvantaged States, at their request and when appropriate, relevant information as specified in article 248 and article 249, paragraph 1(f).

3. The neighbouring land-locked and geographically disadvantaged States referred to above shall, at their request, be given the opportunity to participate, whenever feasible, in the proposed marine scientific research project through qualified experts appointed by them and not objected to by the coastal State, in accordance with the conditions agreed for the project, in conformity with the provisions of this Convention, between the coastal State concerned and the State or competent international organizations conducting the marine scientific research.

4. States and competent international organizations referred to in paragraph 1 shall provide to the above-mentioned land-locked and geographically disadvantaged States, at their request, the information and assistance specified in article 249, paragraph 1(d), subject to the provisions of article 249, paragraph 2.

Article 255
Measures to facilitate marine scientific research and assist research vessels

States shall endeavour to adopt reasonable rules, regulations and procedures to promote and facilitate marine scientific research conducted in accordance with this Convention beyond their territorial sea and, as appropriate, to facilitate, subject to the provisions of their laws and regulations, access to their harbours and promote assistance for marine scientific research vessels which comply with the relevant provisions of this Part.

Article 256
Marine scientific research in the Area

All States, irrespective of their geographical location, and competent international organizations have the right, in conformity with the provisions of Part XI, to conduct marine scientific research in the Area.

Article 257
Marine scientific research in the water column beyond the exclusive economic zone

All States, irrespective of their geographical location, and competent international organizations have the right, in conformity with this Convention, to conduct marine scientific research in the water column beyond the limits of the exclusive economic zone.

Section 4. Scientific Research Installations or Equipment in the Marine Environment

Article 258
Deployment and use

The deployment and use of any type of scientific research installations or equipment in any area of the marine environment shall be subject to the same conditions as are prescribed in this Convention for the conduct of marine scientific research in any such area.

Article 259
Legal status

The installations or equipment referred to in this section do not possess the status of islands. They have no territorial sea of their own, and their presence does not affect the delimitation of the territorial sea, the exclusive economic zone or the continental shelf.

Article 260
Safety zones

Safety zones of a reasonable breadth not exceeding a distance of 500 metres may be created around scientific research installations in accordance with the relevant provisions of this Convention. All States shall ensure that such safety zones are respected by their vessels.

Article 261
Non-interference with shipping routes

The deployment and use of any type of scientific research installations or equipment shall not constitute an obstacle to established international shipping routes.

Article 262
Identification markings and warning signals

Installations or equipment referred to in this section shall bear identification markings indicating the State of registry or the international organization to which they belong and shall have adequate internationally agreed warning signals to ensure safety at sea and the safety of air navigation, taking into account rules and standards established by competent international organizations.

Section 5. Reponsibility and Liability

Article 263
Responsibility and liability

1. States and competent international organizations shall be responsible for ensuring that marine scientific research, whether undertaken by them or on their behalf, is conducted in accordance with this Convention.

2. States and competent international organizations shall be responsible and liable for the measures they take in contravention of this Convention in respect of marine scientific research conducted by other States, their natural or juridical persons or by competent international organizations, and shall provide compensation for damage resulting from such measures.

3. States and competent international organizations shall be responsible and liable pursuant to article 235 for damage caused by pollution of the marine environment arising out of marine scientific research undertaken by them or on their behalf.

Section 6. Settlement of Disputes and Interim Measures

Article 264
Settlement of disputes

Disputes concerning the interpretation or application of the provisions of this Convention with regard to marine scientific research shall be settled in accordance with Part XV, sections 2 and 3.

Article 265
Interim measures

Pending settlement of a dispute in accordance with Part XV, sections 2 and 3, the State or competent international organization authorized to conduct a marine scientific research project shall not allow research activities to commence or continue without the express consent of the coastal State concerned.

PART XIV

Development and Transfer of Marine Technology

Section 1. General Provisions

Article 266
Promotion of the development and transfer of marine technology

1. States, directly or through competent international organizations, shall co-operate in accordance with their capabilities to promote actively the development and transfer of marine science and marine technology on fair and reasonable terms and conditions.

2. States shall promote the development of the marine scientific and technological capacity of States which may need and request technical assistance in this field, particularly developing States, including land-locked and geographically disadvantaged States, with regard to the exploration, exploitation, conservation and management of marine resources, the protection and preservation of the marine environment, marine scientific research and other activities in the marine environment compatible with this Convention, with a view to accelerating the social and economic development of the developing states.

3. States shall endeavour to foster favourable economic and legal conditions for the transfer of marine technology for the benefit of all parties concerned on an equitable basis.

Article 267
Protection of legitimate interests

States, in promoting co-operation pursuant to article 266, shall have due regard for all legitimate interests including, *inter alia*, the rights and duties of holders, suppliers and recipients of marine technology.

Article 268
Basic objectives

States, directly or through competent international organizations, shall promote:

(a) the acquisition, evaluation and dissemination of marine technological knowledge and facilitate access to such information and data;

(b) the development of appropriate marine technology;

(c) the development of the necessary technological infrastructure to facilitate the transfer of marine technology;

(d) the development of human resources through training and education of nationals of developing States and countries and especially the nationals of the least developed among them;

(e) international co-operation at all levels, particularly at the regional, subregional and bilateral levels.

Article 269
Measures to achieve the basic objectives

In order to achieve the objectives referred to in article 268, States, directly or through competent international organizations, shall endeavour, *inter alia*, to:

(a) establish programmes of technical co-operation for the effective transfer of all kinds of marine technology to States which may need and request technical assistance in this field, particularly the developing land-locked and geographically disadvantaged States, as well as other developing States which have not been able either to establish or develop their own technological capacity in marine science and in the exploration and exploitation of marine resources or to develop the infrastructure of such technology;

(b) promote favourable conditions for the conclusion of agreements, contracts and other similar arrangements, under equitable and reasonable conditions;

(c) hold conferences, seminars and symposia on scientific and technological subjects, in particular on policies and methods for the transfer of marine technology;

(d) promote the exchange of scientists and of technological and other experts;

(e) undertake projects and promote joint ventures and other forms of bilateral and multilateral co-operation.

Section 2. International Co-operation

Article 270
Ways and means of international co-operation

International co-operation for the development and transfer of marine technology shall be carried out, where feasible and appropriate, through existing bilateral, regional or multilateral programmes, and also through expanded and new programmes in order to facilitate marine scientific research, the transfer of marine technology, particularly in new fields, and appropriate international funding for ocean research and development.

Article 271
Guidelines, criteria and standards

States, directly or through competent international organizations, shall promote the establishment of generally accepted guidelines, criteria and standards for the transfer of marine technology on a bilateral basis or within the framework of international organizations and other fora, taking into account, in particular, the interests and needs of developing States.

Article 272
Co-ordination of international programmes

In the field of transfer of marine technology, States shall endeavour to ensure that competent international organizations co-ordinate their activities, including any regional or global programmes, taking into account the interests and needs of developing States, particularly land-locked and geographically disadvantaged States.

Article 273
Co-operation with international organizations and the Authority

States shall co-operate actively with competent international organizations and the Authority to encourage and facilitate the transfer to developing States, their nationals and the Enterprise of skills and marine technology with regard to activities in the Area.

Article 274
Objectives of the Authority

Subject to all legitimate interests including, *inter alia*, the rights and duties of holders, suppliers and recipients of technology, the Authority, with regard to activities in the Area, shall ensure that:

(a) on the basis of the principle of equitable geographical distribution, nationals of developing States, whether coastal, land-locked or geographically disadvantaged, shall be taken on for the purposes of training as members of the managerial, research and technical staff constituted for its undertakings;

(b) the technical documentation on the relevant equipment, machinery, devices and processes is made available to all States, in particular developing States which may need and request technical assistance in this field;

(c) adequate provision is made by the Authority to facilitate the acquisition of technical assistance in the field of marine technology by States which may need and request it, in particular developing States, and the acquisition by their nationals of the necessary skills and know-how, including professional training;

(d) States which may need and request technical assistance in this field, in particular developing States, are assisted in the acquisition of necessary equipment, processes, plant and other technical know-how through any financial arrangements provided for in this Convention.

Section 3. National and Regional Marine Scientific and Technological Centres

Article 275
Establishment of national centres

1. States, directly or through competent international organizations and the Authority, shall promote the establishment, particularly in developing coastal States, of national marine scientific and technological research centres and the strengthening of existing national centres, in order to stimulate and advance the conduct of marine scientific research by developing coastal States and to enhance their national capabilities to utilize and preserve their marine resources for their economic benefit.

2. States, through competent international organizations and the Authority, shall give adequate support to facilitate the establishment and strengthening of such national centres so as to provide for advanced training facilities and necessary equipment, skills and know-how as well as technical experts to such States which may need and request such assistance.

Article 276

Establishment of regional centres

1. States, in co-ordination with the competent international organizations, the Authority and national marine scientific and technological research institutions, shall promote the establishment of regional marine scientific and technological research centres, particularly in developing States, in order to stimulate and advance the conduct of marine scientific research by developing States and foster the transfer of marine technology.

2. All States of a region shall co-operate with the regional centres therein to ensure the more effective achievement of their objectives.

Article 277

Functions of regional centres

The functions of such regional centres shall include, *inter alia*:

(a) training and educational programmes at all levels on various aspects of marine scientific and technological research, particularly marine biology, including conservation and management of living resources, oceanography, hydrography, engineering, geological exploration of the sea-bed, mining and desalination technologies;

(b) management studies;

(c) study programmes related to the protection and preservation of the marine environment and the prevention, reduction and control of pollution;

(d) organization of regional conferences, seminars and symposia;

(e) acquisition and processing of marine scientific and technological data and information;

(f) prompt dissemination of results of marine scientific and technological research in readily available publications;

(g) publicizing national policies with regard to the transfer of marine technology and systematic comparative study of those policies;

(h) compilation and systematization of information on the marketing of technology and on contracts and other arrangements concerning patents;

(i) technical co-operation with other States of the region.

Section 4. Co-operation Among International Organizations

Article 278

Co-operation among international organizations

The competent international organizations referred to in this Part and in Part XIII shall take all appropriate measures to ensure, either directly or in close co-operation among themselves, the effective discharge of their functions and responsibilities under this Part.

PART XV

Settlement of Disputes

Section 1. General Provisions

Article 279

Obligation to settle disputes by peaceful means

States Parties shall settle any dispute between them concerning the interpretation or application of this Convention by peaceful means in accordance with Article 2, paragraph 3, of the Charter of the United Nations and, to this end, shall seek a solution by the means indicated in Article 33, paragraph 1, of the Charter.

Article 280

Settlement of disputes by any peaceful means chosen by the parties

Nothing in this Part impairs the rights of any States Parties to agree at any time to settle a dispute between them concerning the interpretation or application of this Convention by any peaceful means of their own choice.

Article 281

Procedure where no settlement has been reached by the parties

1. If the States Parties which are parties to a dispute concerning the interpretation or application of this Convention have agreed to seek settlement of the dispute by a peaceful means of their own choice, the procedures provided for in this Part apply only where no settlement has been reached by recourse to such means and the agreement between the parties does not exclude any further procedure.

2. If the parties have also agreed on a time-limit, paragraph 1 applies only upon the expiration of that time-limit.

Article 282

Obligations under general, regional or bilateral agreements

If the States Parties which are parties to a dispute concerning the interpretation or application of this Convention have agreed, through a general, regional or bilateral agreement or otherwise, that such dispute shall, at the request of any party to the dispute, be submitted to a procedure that entails a binding decision, that procedure shall apply in lieu of the procedures provided for in this Part, unless the parties to the dispute otherwise agree.

Article 283
Obligation to exchange views

1. When a dispute arises between States Parties concerning the interpretation or application of this Convention, the parties to the dispute shall proceed expeditiously to an exchange of views regarding its settlement by negotiation or other peaceful means.

2. The parties shall also proceed expeditiously to an exchange of views where a procedure for the settlement of such a dispute has been terminated without a settlement or where a settlement has been reached and the circumstances require consultation regarding the manner of implementing the settlement.

Article 284
Conciliation

1. A State Party which is a party to a dispute concerning the interpretation or application of this Convention may invite the other party or parties to submit the dispute to conciliation in accordance with the procedure under Annex V, section 1, or another conciliation procedure.

2. If the invitation is accepted and if the parties agree upon the conciliation procedure to be applied, any party may submit the dispute to that procedure.

3. If the invitation is not accepted or the parties do not agree upon the procedure, the conciliation proceedings shall be deemed to be terminated.

4. Unless the parties otherwise agree, when a dispute has been submitted to conciliation, the proceedings may be terminated only in accordance with the agreed conciliation procedure.

Article 285
Application of this section to disputes submitted pursuant to Part XI

This section applies to any dispute which pursuant to Part XI, section 5, is to be settled in accordance with procedures provided for in this Part. If an entity other than a State Party is a party to such a dispute, this section applies *mutatis mutandis*.

Section 2. Compulsory Procedures Entailing Binding Decisions

Article 286
Application of procedures under this section

Subject to section 3, any dispute concerning the interpretation or application of this Convention shall, where no settlement has been reached by recourse to section 1, be submitted at the request of any party to the dispute to the court or tribunal having jurisdiction under this section.

Article 287
Choice of procedure

1. When signing, ratifying or acceding to this Convention or at any time thereafter, a State shall be free to choose, by means of a written declaration, one or more of the following means for the settlement of disputes concerning the interpretation or application of this Convention:

(a) the International Tribunal for the Law of the Sea established in accordance with Annex VI;

(b) the International Court of Justice;

(c) an arbitral tribunal constituted in accordance with Annex VII;

(d) a special arbitral tribunal constituted in accordance with Annex VIII for one or more of the categories of disputes specified therein.

2. A declaration made under paragraph 1 shall not affect or be affected by the obligation of a State Party to accept the jurisdiction of the Sea-Bed Disputes Chamber of the International Tribunal for the Law of the Sea to the extent and in the manner provided for in Part XI, section 5.

3. A State Party, which is a party to a dispute not covered by a declaration in force, shall be deemed to have accepted arbitration in accordance with Annex VII.

4. If the parties to a dispute have accepted the same procedure for the settlement of the dispute, it may be submitted only to that procedure, unless the parties otherwise agree.

5. If the parties to a dispute have not accepted the same procedure for the settlement of the dispute, it may be submitted only to arbitration in accordance

with Annex VII, unless the parties otherwise agree.

6. A declaration made under paragraph 1 shall remain in force until three months after notice of revocation has been deposited with the Secretary-General of the United Nations.

7. A new declaration, a notice of revocation or the expiry of a declaration does not in any way affect proceedings pending before a court or tribunal having jurisdiction under this article, unless the parties otherwise agree.

8. Declarations and notices referred to in this article shall be deposited with the Secretary-General of the United Nations, who shall transmit copies thereof to the States Parties.

Article 288
Jurisdiction

1. A court or tribunal referred to in article 287 shall have jurisdiction over any dispute concerning the interpretation or application of this Convention which is submitted to it in accordance with this Part.

2. A court or tribunal referred to in article 287 shall also have jurisdiction over any dispute concerning the interpretation or application of an international agreement related to the purposes of this Convention, which is submitted to it in accordance with the agreement.

3. The Sea-Bed Disputes Chamber of the International Tribunal for the Law of the Sea established in accordance with Annex VI, and any other chamber or arbitral tribunal referred to in Part XI, section 5, shall have jurisdiction in any matter which is submitted to it in accordance therewith.

4. In the event of a dispute as to whether a court or tribunal has jurisdiction, the matter shall be settled by decision of that court or tribunal.

Article 289
Experts

In any dispute involving scientific or technical matters, a court or tribunal exercising jurisdiction under this section may, at the request of a party or *proprio motu*, select in consultation with the parties no fewer than two scientific or technical experts chosen preferably from the relevant list prepared in accordance with Annex VIII, article 2, to sit with the court or tribunal but without the right to vote.

Article 290
Provisional measures

1. If a dispute has been duly submitted to a court or tribunal which considers that *prima facie* it has jurisdiction under this Part or Part XI, section 5, the court or tribunal may prescribe any provisional measures which it considers appropriate under the circumstances to preserve the respective rights of the parties to the dispute or to prevent serious harm to the marine environment, pending the final decision.

2. Provisional measures may be modified or revoked as soon as the circumstances justifying them have changed or ceased to exist.

3. Provisional measures may be prescribed, modified or revoked under this article only at the request of a party to the dispute and after the parties have been given an opportunity to be heard.

4. The court or tribunal shall forthwith give notice to the parties to the dispute, and to such other States Parties as it considers appropriate, of the prescription, modification or revocation of provisional measures.

5. Pending the constitution of an arbitral tribunal to which a dispute is being submitted under this section, any court or tribunal agreed upon by the parties or, failing such agreement within two weeks from the date of the request for provisional measures, the International Tribunal for the Law of the Sea or, with respect to activities in the Area, the Sea-Bed Disputes Chamber, may prescribe, modify or revoke provisional measures in accordance with this article if it considers that *prima facie* the tribunal which is to be constituted would have jurisdiction and that the urgency of the situation so requires. Once constituted, the tribunal to which the dispute has been submitted may modify, revoke or affirm those provisional measures, acting in conformity with paragraphs 1 to 4.

6. The parties to the dispute shall comply promptly with any provisional measures prescribed under this article.

Article 291
Access

1. All the dispute settlement procedures specified in this Part shall be open to States Parties.

2. The dispute settlement procedures specified in this Part shall be open to entities other than States Parties only as specifically provided for in this Convention.

Article 292
Prompt release of vessels and crews

1. Where the authorities of a State Party have detained a vessel flying the flag of another State Party and it is alleged that the detaining State has not complied with the provisions of this Convention for the prompt release of the vessel or its crew upon the posting of a reasonable bond or other financial security, the question of release from detention may be submitted to any court or tribunal agreed upon by the parties or, failing such agreement within 10 days from the time of detention, to a court or tribunal accepted by the detaining State under article 287 or to the International Tribunal for the Law of the Sea, unless the parties otherwise agree.

2. The application for release may be made only by or on behalf of the flag State of the vessel.

3. The court or tribunal shall deal without delay with the application for release and shall deal only with the question of release, without prejudice to the merits of any case before the appropriate domestic forum against the vessel, its owner or its crew. The authorities of the detaining State remain competent to release the vessel or its crew at any time.

4. Upon the posting of the bond or other financial security determined by the court or tribunal, the authorities of the detaining State shall comply promptly with the decision of the court or tribunal concerning the release of the vessel or its crew.

Article 293
Applicable law

1. A court or tribunal having jurisdiction under this section shall apply this Convention and other rules of international law not incompatible with this Convention.

2. Paragraph 1 does not prejudice the power of the court or tribunal having jurisdiction under this section to decide a case *ex aequo et bono*, if the parties so agree.

Article 294
Preliminary proceedings

1. A court or tribunal provided for in article 287 to which an application is made in respect of a dispute referred to in article 297 shall determine at the request of a party, or may determine *proprio motu*, whether the claim constitutes an abuse of legal process or whether *prima facie* it is well founded. If the court or tribunal determines that the claim constitutes an abuse of legal process or is *prima facie* unfounded, it shall take no further action in the case.

2. Upon receipt of the application, the court or tribunal shall immediately notify the other party or parties of the application, and shall fix a reasonable time-limit within which they may request it to make a determination in accordance with paragraph 1.

3. Nothing in this article affects the right of any party to a dispute to make preliminary objections in accordance with the applicable rules of procedure.

Article 295
Exhaustion of local remedies

Any dispute between States Parties concerning the interpretation or application of this Convention may be submitted to the procedures provided for in this section only after local remedies have been exhausted where this is required by international law.

Article 296
Finality and binding force of decisions

1. Any decision rendered by a court or tribunal having jurisdiction under this section shall be final and shall be complied with by all the parties to the dispute.

2. Any such decision shall have no binding force except between the parties and in respect of that particular dispute.

Section 3. Limitations and Exceptions to Applicability of Section 2

Article 297
Limitations on applicability of section 2

1. Disputes concerning the interpretation or application of this Convention with regard to the exercise by a coastal State of its sovereign rights or jurisdiction provided for in this Convention shall be subject to the procedures provided for in section 2 in the following cases:

(a) when it is alleged that a coastal State has acted in contravention of the provisions of this Convention in regard to the freedoms and rights of navigation, overflight or the laying of submarine cables and pipelines, or in regard to other internationally lawful uses of the sea specified in article 58;

(b) when it is alleged that a State in exercising the aforementioned freedoms, rights or uses has acted in contravention of this Convention or of laws or regulations adopted by the coastal State in conformity with this Convention and other rules of international law not incompatible with this Convention; or

(c) when it is alleged that a coastal State has acted in contravention of specified international rules and standards for the protection and preservation of the marine environment which are applicable to the coastal State and which have been established by this Convention or through a competent international organization or diplomatic conference in accordance with this Convention.

2.(a) Disputes concerning the interpretation or application of the provisions of this Convention with regard to marine scientific research shall be settled in accordance with section 2, except that the coastal State shall not be obliged to accept the submission to such settlement of any dispute arising out of:

(i) the exercise by the coastal State of a right or discretion in accordance with article 246; or

(ii) a decision by the coastal State to order suspension or cessation of a research project in accordance with article 253.

(b) A dispute arising from an allegation by the researching State that with respect to a specific project the coastal State is not exercising its rights under articles 246 and 253 in a manner compatible with this Convention shall be submitted, at the request of either party, to conciliation under Annex V, section 2, provided that the conciliation commission shall not call in question the exercise by the coastal State of its discretion to designate specific areas as referred to in article 246, paragraph 6, or of its discretion to withhold consent in accordance with article 246, paragraph 5.

3.(a) Disputes concerning the interpretation or application of the provisions of this Convention with regard to fisheries shall be settled in accordance with section 2, except that the coastal State shall not be obliged to accept the submission to such settlement of any dispute relating to its sovereign rights with respect to the living resources in the exclusive economic zone or their exercise, including its discretionary powers for determining the allowable catch, its harvesting capacity, the allocation of surpluses to other States and the terms and conditions established in its conservation and management laws and regulations.

(b) Where no settlement has been reached by recourse to section 1 of this Part, a dispute shall be submitted to conciliation under Annex V, section 2, at the request of any party to the dispute, when it is alleged that:

(i) a coastal State has manifestly failed to comply with its obligations to ensure through proper conservation and management measures that the maintenance of the living resources in the exclusive economic zone is not seriously endangered;

(ii) a coastal State has arbitrarily refused to determine, at the request of another State, the allowable catch and its capacity to harvest living resources with respect to stocks which that other State is interested in fishing; or

(iii) a coastal State has arbitrarily refused to allocate to any State, under articles 62, 69 and 70 and under the terms and conditions established by the coastal State consistent with this Convention, the whole or part of the surplus it has declared to exist.

(c) In no case shall the conciliation commission substitute its discretion for that of the coastal State.

(d) The report of the conciliation commission shall be communicated to the appropriate international organizations.

(e) In negotiating agreements pursuant to articles 69 and 70, States Parties, unless they otherwise agree, shall include a clause on measures which they shall take in order to minimize the possibility of a disagreement concerning the interpretation or application of the agreement, and on how they should proceed if a disagreement nevertheless arises.

Article 298
Optional exceptions to applicability of section 2

1. When signing, ratifying or acceding to this Convention or at any time thereafter, a State may, without prejudice to the obligations arising under section 1, declare in writing that it does not accept any one

or more of the procedures provided for in section 2 with respect to one or more of the following categories of disputes:

(a)(i) disputes concerning the interpretation or application of articles 15, 74 and 83 relating to sea boundary delimitations, or those involving historic bays or titles, provided that a State having made such a declaration shall, when such a dispute arises subsequent to the entry into force of this Convention and where no agreement within a reasonable period of time is reached in negotiations between the parties, at the request of any party to the dispute, accept submission of the matter to conciliation under Annex V, section 2; and provided further that any dispute that necessarily involves the concurrent consideration of any unsettled dispute concerning sovereignty or other rights over continental or insular land territory shall be excluded from such submission;

(ii) after the conciliation commission has presented its report, which shall state the reasons on which it is based, the parties shall negotiate an agreement on the basis of that report; if these negotiations do not result in an agreement, the parties shall, by mutual consent, submit the question to one of the procedures provided for in section 2, unless the parties otherwise agree;

(iii) this subparagraph does not apply to any sea boundary dispute finally settled by an arrangement between the parties, or to any such dispute which is to be settled in accordance with a bilateral or multilateral agreement binding upon those parties;

(b) disputes concerning military activities, including military activities by government vessels and aircraft engaged in non-commercial service, and disputes concerning law enforcement activities in regard to the exercise of sovereign rights or jurisdiction excluded from the jurisdiction of a court or tribunal under article 297, paragraph 2 or 3;

(c) disputes in respect of which the Security Council of the United Nations is exercising the functions assigned to it by the Charter of the United Nations, unless the Security Council decides to remove the matter from its agenda or calls upon the parties to settle it by the means provided for in this Convention.

2. A State Party which has made a declaration under paragraph 1 may at any time withdraw it, or agree to submit a dispute excluded by such declaration to any procedure specified in this Convention.

3. A State Party which has made a declaration under paragraph 1 shall not be entitled to submit any dispute falling within the excepted category of disputes to any procedure in this Convention as against another State Party, without the consent of that party.

4. If one of the States Parties has made a declaration under paragraph 1(a), any other State Party may submit any dispute falling within an excepted category against the declarant party to the procedure specified in such declaration.

5. A new declaration, or the withdrawal of a declaration, does not in any way affect proceedings pending before a court or tribunal in accordance with this article, unless the parties otherwise agree.

6. Declarations and notices of withdrawal of declarations under this article shall be deposited with the Secretary-General of the United Nations, who shall transmit copies thereof to the States Parties.

Article 299
Right of the parties to agree upon a procedure

1. A dispute excluded under article 297 or excepted by a declaration made under article 298 from the dispute settlement procedures provided for in section 2 may be submitted to such procedures only by agreement of the parties to the dispute.

2. Nothing in this section impairs the right of the parties to the dispute to agree to some other procedure for the settlement of such dispute or to reach an amicable settlement.

PART XVI

General Provisions

Article 300
Good faith and abuse of rights

States Parties shall fulfil in good faith the obligations assumed under this Convention and shall exercise the rights, jurisdiction and freedoms recognized in this Convention in a manner which would not constitute an abuse of right.

Article 301
Peaceful uses of the seas

In exercising their rights and performing their duties under this Convention, States

Parties shall refrain from any threat or use of force against the territorial integrity or political independence of any State, or in any other manner inconsistent with the principles of international law embodied in the Charter of the United Nations.

Article 302
Disclosure of information

Without prejudice to the right of a State Party to resort to the procedures for the settlement of disputes provided for in this Convention, nothing in this Convention shall be deemed to require a State party, in the fulfilment of its obligations under this Convention, to supply information the disclosure of which is contrary to the essential interests of its security.

Article 303
Archaeological and historical objects found at sea

1. States have the duty to protect objects of an archaeological and historical nature found at sea and shall co-operate for this purpose.

2. In order to control traffic in such objects, the coastal State may, in applying article 33, presume that their removal from the sea-bed in the zone referred to in that article without its approval would result in an infringement within its territory or territorial sea of the laws and regulations referred to in that article.

3. Nothing in this article affects the rights of identifiable owners, the law of salvage or other rules of admiralty, or laws and practices with respect to cultural exchanges.

4. This article is without prejudice to other international agreements and rules of international law regarding the protection of objects of an archaeological and historical nature.

Article 304
Responsibility and liability for damage

The provisons of this Convention regarding responsibility and liability for damage are without prejudice to the application of existing rules and the development of further rules regarding responsibility and liability under international law.

PART XVII

Final Provisions

Article 305
Signature

1. This Convention shall be open for signature by:

(a) all States;

(b) Namibia, represented by the United Nations Council for Namibia;

(c) all self-governing associated States which have chosen that status in an act of self-determination supervised and approved by the United Nations in accordance with General Assembly resolution 1514 (XV) and which have competence over the matters governed by this Convention, including the competence to enter into treaties in respect of those matters;

(d) all self-governing associated States which, in accordance with their respective instruments of association, have competence over the matters governed by this Convention, including the competence to enter into treaties in respect of those matters;

(e) all territories which enjoy full internal self-government, recognized as such by the United Nations, but have not attained full independence in accordance with General Assembly resolution 1514 (XV) and which have competence over the matters governed by this Convention, including the competence to enter into treaties in respect of those matters;

(f) international organizations, in accordance with Annex IX.

2. This Convention shall remain open for signature until 9 December 1984 at the Ministry of Foreign Affairs of Jamaica and also, from 1 July 1983 until 9 December 1984, at United Nations Headquarters in New York.

Article 306
Ratification and formal confirmation

This Convention is subject to ratification by States and the other entities referred to in article 305, paragraph 1(b), (c), (d) and (e), and to formal confirmation, in accordance with Annex IX, by the entities referred to in article 305, paragraph 1(f). The instruments of ratification and of formal confirmation shall be deposited with the Secretary-General of the United Nations.

Article 307
Accession

This Convention shall remain open for accession by States and the other entities referred to in article 305. Accession by the entities referred to in article 305, paragraph 1(f), shall be in accordance with Annex IX. The instruments of accession shall be deposited with the Secretary-General of the United Nations.

Article 308
Entry into force

1. This Convention shall enter into force 12 months after the date of deposit of the sixtieth instrument of ratification or accession.

2. For each State ratifying or acceding to this Convention after the deposit of the sixtieth instrument of ratification or accession, the Convention shall enter into force on the thirtieth day following the deposit of its instrument of ratification or accession, subject to paragraph 1.

3. The Assembly of the Authority shall meet on the date of entry into force of this Convention and shall elect the Council of the Authority. The first Council shall be constituted in a manner consistent with the purpose of article 161 if the provisions of that article cannot be strictly applied.

4. The Rules, regulations and procedures drafted by the Preparatory Commission shall apply provisionally pending their formal adoption by the Authority in accordance with Part XI.

5. The Authority and its organs shall act in accordance with resolution II of the Third United Nations Conference on the Law of the Sea relating to preparatory investment and with decisions of the Preparatory Commission taken pursuant to that resolution.

Article 309
Reservations and exceptions

No reservations or exceptions may be made to this Convention unless expressly permitted by other articles of this Convention.

Article 310
Declarations and statements

Article 309 does not preclude a State, when signing, ratifying or acceding to this Convention, from making declarations or statements, however phrased or named, with a view, *inter alia*, to the harmonization of its laws and regulations with the provisions of this Convention, provided that such declarations or statements do not purport to exclude or to modify the legal effect of the provisions of this Convention in their application to that State.

Article 311
Relation to other Conventions and international agreements

1. This Convention shall prevail, as between States Parties, over the Geneva Conventions on the Law of the Sea of 29 April 1958.

2. This Convention shall not alter the rights and obligations of State Parties which arise from other agreements compatible with this Convention and which do not affect the enjoyment by other States Parties of their rights or the performance of their obligations under this Convention.

3. Two or more States Parties may conclude agreements modifying or suspending the operation of provisions of this Convention, applicable solely to the relations between them, provided that such agreements do not relate to a provision derogation from which is incompatible with the effective execution of the object and purpose of this Convention, and provided further that such agreements shall not affect the application of the basic principles embodied herein, and that the provisions of such agreements do not affect the enjoyment by other States Parties of their rights or the performance of their obligations under this Convention.

4. States Parties intending to conclude an agreement referred to in paragraph 3 shall notify the other States Parties through the depositary of this Convention of their intention to conclude the agreement and of the modification or suspension for which it provides.

5. This article does not affect international agreements expressly permitted or preserved by other articles of this Convention.

6. States Parties agree that there shall be no amendments to the basic principle relating to the common heritage of mankind set forth in article 136 and that they shall not be party to any agreement in derogation thereof.

Article 312
Amendment

1. After the expiry of a period of 10 years from the date of entry into force of this Convention, a State Party may, by written communication addressed to the Secretary-General of the United Nations, propose specific amendments to this Convention, other than those relating to activities in the Area, and request the

convening of a conference to consider such proposed amendments. The Secretary-General shall circulate such communication to all States Parties. If, within 12 months from the date of the circulation of the communication, not less than one half of the States Parties reply favourably to the request, the Secretary-General shall convene the conference.

2. The decision-making procedure applicable at the amendment conference shall be the same as that applicable at the Third United Nations Conference on the Law of the Sea unless otherwise decided by the conference. The conference should make every effort to reach agreement on any amendments by way of consensus and there should be no voting on them until all efforts at consensus have been exhausted.

Article 313
Amendment by simplified procedure

1. A State Party may, by written communication addressed to the Secretary-General of the United Nations, propose an amendment to this Convention, other than an amendment relating to activities in the Area, to be adopted by the simplified procedure set forth in this article without convening a conference. The Secretary-General shall circulate the communication to all States Parties.

2. If, within a period of 12 months from the date of the circulation of the communication, a State Party objects to the proposed amendment or to the proposal for its adoption by the simplified procedure, the amendment shall be considered rejected. The Secretary-General shall immediately notify all States Parties accordingly.

3. If, 12 months from the date of the circulation of the communication, no State Party has objected to the proposed amendment or to the proposal for its adoption by the simplified procedure, the proposed amendment shall be considered adopted. The Secretary-General shall notify all States Parties that the proposed amendment has been adopted.

Article 314
Amendments to the provisions of this Convention relating exclusively to activities in the Area

1. A State Party may, by written communication addressed to the Secretary-General of the Authority, propose an amendment to the provisions of this Convention relating exclusively to activities in the Area, including Annex VI, section 4. The Secretary-General shall circulate such communication to all States Parties. The proposed amendment shall be subject to approval by the Assembly following its approval by the Council. Representatives of States Parties in those organs shall have full powers to consider and approve the proposed amendment. The proposed amendment as approved by the Council and the Assembly shall be considered adopted.

2. Before approving any amendment under paragraph 1, the Council and the Assembly shall ensure that it does not prejudice the system of exploration for and exploitation of the resources of the Area, pending the Review Conference in accordance with article 155.

Article 315
Signature, ratification of, accession to and authentic texts of amendments

1. Once adopted, amendments to this Convention shall be open for signature by States Parties for 12 months from the date of adoption, at United National Headquarters in New York, unless otherwise provided in the amendment itself.

2. Articles 306, 307 and 320 apply to all amendments to this Convention.

Article 316
Entry into force of amendments

1. Amendments to this Convention, other than those referred to in paragraph 5, shall enter into force for the States parties ratifying or acceding to them on the thirtieth day following the deposit of instruments of ratification or accession by two thirds of the States Parties or by 60 States Parties, whichever is greater. Such amendments shall not affect the enjoyment by other States Parties of their rights or the performance of their obligations under this Convention.

2. An amendment may provide that a large number of ratifications or accessions shall be required for its entry into force than are required by this article.

3. For each State Party ratifying or acceding to an amendment referred to in paragraph 1 after the deposit of the required number of instruments of ratification or accession, the amendment shall enter into

force on the thirtieth day following the deposit of its instrument of ratification or accession.

4. A State which becomes a Party to this Convention after the entry into force of an amendment in accordance with paragraph 1 shall, failing an expression of a different intention by that State:

(a) be considered as a Party to this Convention as so amended; and

(b) be considered as a Party to the unamended Convention in relation to any State Party not bound by the amendment.

5. Any amendment relating exclusively to activities in the Area and any amendment to Annex VI shall enter into force for all States Parties one year following the deposit of instruments of ratification or accession by three-fourths of the States Parties.

6. A State which becomes a Party to this Convention after the entry into force of amendments in accordance with paragraph 5 shall be considered as a Party to this Convention as so amended.

Article 317
Denunciation

1. A State Party may, by written notification addressed to the Secretary-General of the United Nations, denounce this Convention and may indicate its reasons. Failure to indicate reasons shall not affect the validity of the denunciation. The denunciation shall take effect one year after the date of receipt of the notification, unless the notification specifies a later date.

2. A State shall not be discharged by reason of the denunciation from the financial and contractual obligations which accrued while it was a Party to this Convention, nor shall the denunciation affect any right, obligation or legal situation of that State created through the execution of this Convention prior to its termination for that State.

3. The denunciation shall not in any way affect the duty of any State Party to fulfil any obligation embodied in this Convention to which it would be subject under international law independently of this Convention.

Article 318
Status of Annexes

The Annexes form an integral part of this Convention and, unless expressly provided otherwise, a reference to this Convention or to one of its Parts includes a reference to the Annexes relating thereto.

Article 319
Depositary

1. The Secretary-General of the United Nations shall be the depositary of this Convention and amendments thereto.

2. In addition to his functions as depositary, the Secretary-General shall:

(a) report to all States Parties, the Authority and competent international organizations on issues of a general nature that have arisen with respect to this Convention;

(b) notify the Authority of ratifications and formal confirmations of and accessions to this Convention and amendments thereto, as well as of denunciations of this Convention;

(c) notify States Parties of agreements in accordance with article 311, paragraph 4;

(d) circulate amendments adopted in accordance with this Convention to States Parties for ratification or accession;

(e) convene necessary meetings of States Parties in accordance with this Convention.

3.(a) The Secretary-General shall also transmit to the observers referred to in article 156:

(i) reports referred to in paragraph 2(a);

(ii) notifications referred to in paragraph 2(b) and (c); and

(iii) texts of amendments referred to in paragraph 2(d), for their information.

(b) The Secretary-General shall also invite those observers to participate as observers at meetings of States Parties referred to in paragraph 2(e).

Article 320
Authentic texts

The original of this Convention, of which the Arabic, Chinese, English, French, Russian and Spanish texts are equally authentic, shall, subject to article 305, paragraph 2, be deposited with the Secretary-General of the United Nations.

IN WITNESS WHEREOF, the undersigned Plenipotentiaries, being duly authorized thereto, have signed this Convention.

DONE AT MONTEGO BAY, this tenth day of December, one thousand nine hundred and eighty-two.

ANNEX I

Highly Migratory Species

1. Albacore tuna: *Thunnus alalunga*.
2. Bluefin tuna: *Thunnus thynnus*.
3. Bigeye tuna: *Thunnus obesus*.
4. Skipjack tuna: *Katsuwonus pelamis*.
5. Yellowfin tuna: *Thunnus albacares*.
6. Blackfin tuna: *Thunnus atlanticus*.
7. Little tuna: *Euthynnus alletteratus*; *Euthynnus affinis*.
8. Southern bluefin tuna: *Thunnus maccoyii*.
9. Frigate mackerel: *Auxis thazard*; *Auxis rochei*.
10. Pomfrets: Family *Bramidae*.
11. Marlins: *Tetrapturus angustirostris*; *Tetrapturus belone*; *Tetrapturus pfluegeri*; *Tetrapturus albidus*; *Tetrapturus audax*; *Tetrapturus georgei*; *Makaira mazara*; *Makaira indica*; *Makaira nigricans*.
12. Sail-fishes: *Istiophorus platypterus*; *Istiophorus albicans*.
13. Swordfish: *Xiphias gladius*.
14. Sauries: *Scomberesox saurus*; *Cololabis saira*; *Cololabis adocetus*; *Scomberesox saurus scombroides*.
15. Dolphin: *Coryphaena hippurus*; *Coryphaena equiselis*.
16. Oceanic sharks: *Hexanchus griseus*; *Cetorhinus maximus*; Family *Alopiidae*; *Rhincodon typus*; Family *Carcharhinidae*; Family *Sphyrnidae*; Family *Isurida*.
17. Cetaceans: Family *Physeteridae*; Family *Balaenopteridae*; Family *Balaenidae*; Family *Eschrichtiidae*; Family *Monodontidae*; Family *Ziphiidae*; Family *Delphinidae*.

ANNEX II

Commission on the Limits of the Continental Shelf

Article 1

In accordance with the provisions of article 76, a Commission on the Limits of the Continental Shelf beyond 200 nautical miles shall be established in conformity with the following articles.

Article 2

1. The Commission shall consist of 21 members who shall be experts in the field of geology, geophysics or hydrography, elected by States Parties to this Convention from among their nationals, having due regard to the need to ensure equitable geographical representation, who shall serve in their personal capacities.

2. The initial election shall be held as soon as possible but in any case within 18 months after the date of entry into force of this Convention. At least three months before the date of each election, the Secretary-General of the United Nations shall address a letter to the States Parties, inviting the submission of nominations, after appropriate regional consultations, within three months. The Secretary-General shall prepare a list in alphabetical order of all persons thus nominated and shall submit it to all the States Parties.

3. Elections of the members of the Commission shall be held at a meeting of States Parties convened by the Secretary-General at United Nations Headquarters. At that meeting, for which two thirds of the States Parties shall constitute a quorum, the persons elected to the Commission shall be those nominees who obtain a two-thirds majority of the votes of the representatives of States Parties present and voting. Not less than three members shall be elected from each geographical region.

4. The members of the Commission shall be elected for a term of five years. They shall be eligible for re-election.

5. The State Party which submitted the nomination of a member of the Commission shall defray the expenses of that member while in performance of Commission duties. The coastal State concerned shall defray the expenses incurred in respect of the advice referred to in article 3, paragraph 1(b), of this Annex. The secretariat of the Commission shall be provided by the Secretary-General of the United Nations.

Article 3

1. The functions of the Commission shall be:

(a) to consider the data and other material submitted by coastal States concerning the outer limits of the continental shelf in areas where those limits extend beyond 200 nautical miles, and to make recommendations in accordance with article 76 and the Statement of Understanding adopted on 29 August 1980 by the Third United Nations Conference on the Law of the Sea;

(b) to provide scientific and technical advice, if requested by the coastal State concerned during the preparation of the data referred to in subparagraph (a).

2. The Commission may co-operate, to the extent considered necessary and useful, with the Intergovernmental Oceanographic Commission of UNESCO, the International Hydrographic Organization and other competent international organizations with a view to exchanging scientific and technical information which might be of assistance in discharging the Commission's responsibilities.

Article 4

Where a coastal State intends to establish, in accordance with article 76, the outer limits of its continental shelf beyond 200 nautical miles, it shall submit particulars of such limits to the Commission along with supporting scientific and technical data as soon as possible but in any case within 10 years of the entry into force of this Convention for that State. The coastal State shall at the same time give the names of any Commission members who have provided it with scientific and technical advice.

Article 5

Unless the Commission decides otherwise, the Commission shall function by way of sub-commissions composed of seven members, appointed in a balanced manner taking into account the specific elements of each submission by a coastal State. Nationals of the coastal State making the submission who are members of the Commission and any Commission member who has assisted a coastal State by providing scientific and technical advice with respect to the delineation shall not be a member of the sub-commission dealing with that submission but has the right to participate as a member in the proceedings of the Commission concerning the said submission. The coastal State which has made a submission to the Commission may send its representatives to participate in the relevant proceedings without the right to vote.

Article 6

1. The sub-commission shall submit its recommendations to the Commission.

2. Approval by the Commission of the recommendations of the sub-commission shall be by a majority of two-thirds of Commission members present and voting.

3. The recommendations of the Commission shall be submitted in writing to the coastal State which made the submission and to the Secretary-General of the United Nations.

Article 7

Coastal States shall establish the outer limits of the continental shelf in conformity with the provisions of article 76, paragraph 8, and in accordance with the appropriate national procedures.

Article 8

In the case of disagreement by the coastal State with the recommendations of the Commission, the coastal State shall, within a reasonable time, make a revised or new submission to the Commission.

Article 9

The actions of the Commission shall not prejudice matters relating to delimitation of boundaries between States with opposite or adjacent coasts.

ANNEX III

Basic Conditions of Prospecting, Exploration and Exploitation

Article 1
Title to minerals

Title to minerals shall pass upon recovery in accordance with this Convention.

Article 2
Prospecting

1.(a) The Authority shall encourage prospecting in the Area.

(b) Prospecting shall be conducted only after the Authority has received a satisfactory written undertaking that the proposed prospector will comply with this Convention and the relevant rules, regulations and procedures of the Authority concerning co-operation in the training programmes referred to in articles 143 and 144 and the protection of the marine environment, and will accept verification by the Authority of compliance therewith. The proposed prospector shall, at the same time, notify the Authority of the approximate area or areas in which prospecting is to be conducted.

(c) Prospecting may be conducted simultaneously by more than one prospector in the same area or areas.

2. Prospecting shall not confer on the prospector any rights with respect to resources. A prospector may, however, recover a reasonable quantity of minerals to be used for testing.

Article 3
Exploration and exploitation

1. The Enterprise, States Parties, and the other entities referred to in article 153, paragraph 2(b), may apply to the Authority for approval of plans of work for activities in the Area.

2. The Enterprise may apply with respect to any part of the Area, but applications by others with respect to reserved areas are subject to the additional requirements of article 9 of this Annex.

3. Exploration and exploitation shall be carried out only in areas specified in plans of work referred to in article 153, paragraph 3, and approved by the Authority in accordance with this Convention and the relevant rules, regulations and procedures of the Authority.

4. Every approved plan of work shall:

(a) be in conformity with this Convention and the rules, regulations and procedures of the Authority;

(b) provide for control by the Authority of activities in the Area in accordance with article 153, paragraph 4;

(c) confer on the operator, in accordance with the rules, regulations and procedures of the Authority, the exclusive right to explore for and exploit the specified categories of resources in the area covered by the plan of work. If, however, the applicant presents for approval a plan of work covering only the stage of exploration or the stage of exploitation, the approved plan of work shall confer such exclusive right with respect to that stage only.

5. Upon its approval by the Authority, every plan of work, except those presented by the Enterprise, shall be in the form of a contract concluded between the Authority and the applicant or applicants.

Article 4
Qualifications of applicants

1. Applicants, other than the Enterprise, shall be qualified if they have the nationality or control and sponsorship required by article 153, paragraph 2(b), and if they follow the procedures and meet the qualification standards set forth in the rules, regulations and procedures of the Authority.

2. Except as provided in paragraph 6, such qualification standards shall relate to the financial and technical capabilities of the applicant and his performance under any previous contracts with the Authority.

3. Each applicant shall be sponsored by the State Party of which it is a national unless the applicant has more than one nationality, as in the case of a partnership or consortium of entities from several States, in which event all States Parties involved shall sponsor the application, or unless the applicant is effectively controlled by another State Party or its nationals, in which event both States Parties shall sponsor the application. The criteria and procedures for implementation of the sponsorship requirements shall be set forth in the rules, regulations and procedures of the Authority.

4. The sponsoring State or States shall, pursuant to article 139, have the responsibility to ensure, within their legal systems, that a contractor so sponsored shall carry out activities in the Area in conformity with the terms of its contract and its obligations under this Convention. A sponsoring State shall not, however, be liable for damage caused by any failure of a contractor sponsored by it to comply with its obligations if that State Party has adopted laws and regulations and taken administrative measures which are, within the framework of its legal system, reasonably appropriate for securing compliance by persons under its jurisdiction.

5. The procedures for assessing the qualifications of States Parties which are applicants shall take into account their character as States.

6. The qualification standards shall require that every applicant, without exception, shall as part of his application undertake:

(a) to accept as enforceable and comply with the applicable obligations created by the provisions of Part XI, the rules, regulations and procedures of the Authority, the decisions of the organs of the Authority and terms of his contracts with the Authority;

(b) to accept control by the Authority of activities in the Area, as authorized by this Convention;

(c) to provide the Authority with a written assurance that his obligations under the contract will be fulfilled in good faith;

(d) to comply with the provisions on the transfer of technology set forth in article 5 of this Annex.

Article 5
Transfer of technology

1. When submitting a plan of work, every applicant shall make available to the Authority a general description of the equipment and methods to be used in carrying out activities in the Area, and other relevant non-proprietary information about the characteristics of such technology and information as to where such technology is available.

2. Every operator shall inform the Authority of revisions in the description and information made available pursuant to paragraph 1 whenever a substantial technological change or innovation is introduced.

3. Every contract for carrying out activities in the Area shall contain the following undertakings by the contractor:

(a) to make available to the Enterprise on fair and reasonable commercial terms and conditions, whenever the Authority so requests, the technology which he uses in carrying out activities in the Area under the contract, which the contractor is legally entitled to transfer. This shall be done by means of licences or other appropriate arrangements which the contractor shall negotiate with the Enterprise and which shall be set forth in a specific agreement supplementary to the contract. This undertaking may be invoked only if the Enterprise finds that it is unable to obtain the same or equally efficient and useful technology on the open market on fair and reasonable commercial terms and conditions;

(b) to obtain a written assurance from the owner of any technology used in carrying out activities in the Area under the contract, which is not generally available on the open market and which is not covered by subparagraph (a), that the owner will, whenever the Authority so requests, make that technology available to the Enterprise under licence or other appropriate arrangements and on fair and reasonable commercial terms and conditions, to the same extent as made available to the contractor. If this assurance is not obtained, the technology in question shall not be used by the contractor in carrying out activities in the Area;

(c) to acquire from the owner by means of an enforceable contract, upon the request of the Enterprise and if it is possible to do so without substantial cost to the contractor, the legal right to transfer to the Enterprise any technology used by the contractor, in carrying out activities in the Area under the contract, which the contractor is otherwise not legally entitled to transfer and which is not generally available on the open market. In cases where there is a substantial corporate relationship between the contractor and the owner of the technology, the closeness of this relationship and the degree of control or influence shall be relevant to the determination whether all feasible measures have been taken to acquire such a right. In cases where the contractor exercises effective control over the owner, failure to acquire from the owner the legal right shall be considered relevant to the contractor's qualification for any subsequent application for approval of a plan of work;

(d) to facilitate, upon the request of the Enterprise, the acquisition by the Enterprise of any technology covered by subparagraph (b), under licence or other appropriate arrangements and on fair and reasonable commercial terms and conditions, if the Enterprise decides to negotiate directly with the owner of the technology;

(e) to take the same measures as are prescribed in subparagraphs (a), (b), (c) and (d) for the benefit of a developing State or group of developing States which has applied for a contract under article 9 of this Annex, provided that these measures shall be limited to the exploitation of the part of the area proposed by the contractor which has been reserved pursuant to article 8 of this Annex and provided that activities under the contract sought by the developing State or group of developing States would not involve transfer of technology to a third State or the nationals of a third State. The obligation under this provision shall only apply with respect to any given contractor where technology has not been requested by the Enterprise or transferred by that contractor to the Enterprise.

4. Disputes concerning undertakings required by paragraph 3, like other provisions of the contracts, shall be subject to compulsory settlement in accordance with Part XI and, in cases of violation of these undertakings, suspension or termination of the contract or monetary penalties may be ordered in accordance with article 18 of this Annex. Disputes as to whether offers made by the contractor are within the range of fair and reasonable commercial terms and conditions may be submitted by either party to binding commercial arbitration in accordance with the UNCITRAL Arbitration Rules or such other arbitration rules as may be prescribed in the rules, regulations and procedures of the Authority. If the finding is that the offer made by the contractor is not within the range of fair and reasonable commercial terms and conditions, the contractor shall be given 45 days to revise his offer to bring it within that range before the Authority takes any action in accordance with article 18 of this Annex.

5. If the Enterprise is unable to obtain on fair and reasonable commercial terms and conditions appropriate technology to enable it to commence in a timely manner the recovery and processing of minerals from the Area, either the Council or the Assembly may convene a group of States Parties composed of those which are engaged in activities in the Area, those which have sponsored entities which are engaged in activities in the Area and other States Parties having access to such technology. This group shall consult together and shall take effective measures to ensure that such technology is made available to the Enterprise on fair and reasonable commercial terms and conditions. Each such State Party shall take all feasible measures to this end within its own legal system.

6. In the case of joint ventures with the Enterprise, transfer of technology will be in accordance with the terms of the joint venture agreement.

7. The undertakings required by paragraph 3 shall be included in each contract for the carrying out of activities in the Area until 10 years after the commencement of commercial production by the Enterprise, and may be invoked during that period.

8. For the purposes of this article, "technology" means the specialized equipment and technical know-how, including manuals, designs, operating instructions, training and technical advice and assistance, necessary to assemble, maintain and operate a viable system and the legal right to use these items for that purpose on a non-exclusive basis.

Article 6
Approval of plans of work

1. Six months after the entry into force of this Convention, and thereafter each fourth month, the Authority shall take up for consideration proposed plans of work.

2. When considering an application for approval of a plan of work in the form of a contract, the Authority shall first ascertain whether:

(a) the applicant has complied with the procedures established for applications in accordance with article 4 of this Annex and has given the Authority the undertakings and assurances required by that article. In cases of non-compliance with these procedures or in the absence of any of these undertakings and assurances, the applicant shall be given 45 days to remedy these defects;

(b) the applicant possesses the requisite qualifications provided for in article 4 of this Annex.

3. All proposed plans of work shall be taken up in the order in which they are received. The proposed plans of work shall comply with and be governed by the relevant provisions of this Convention and the rules, regulations and procedures of the Authority, including those on operational requirements, financial contributions and the undertakings concerning the transfer of technology. If the proposed plans of work conform to these requirements, the Authority shall approve them provided that they are in accordance with the uniform and non-discriminatory requirements set forth in the rules, regulations and procedures of the Authority, unless:

(a) part or all of the area covered by the proposed plan of work is included in an approved plan of work or a previously submitted proposed plan of work which has not yet been finally acted on by the Authority;

(b) part or all of the area covered by the proposed plan of work is disapproved by the Authority pursuant to article 162, paragraph 2(x); or

(c) the proposed plan of work has been submitted or sponsored by a State Party which already holds:

(i) plans of work for exploration and exploitation of polymetallic nodules in non-reserved areas that, together with either part of the area covered by the application for a plan of work, exceed in size 30 per cent of a circular area of 400,000 square kilometres surrounding the centre of either part of the area covered by the proposed plan of work;

(ii) plans of work for the exploration and exploitation of polymetallic nodules in non-reserved areas which, taken together, constitute 2 per cent of the total sea-bed area which is not reserved or disapproved for exploitation pursuant to article 162, paragraph 2(x).

4. For the purpose of the standard set forth in paragraph 3(c), a plan of work submitted by a partnership or consortium shall be counted on a *pro rata* basis among the sponsoring States Parties involved in accordance with article 4, paragraph 3, of this Annex. The Authority may approve plans of work covered by paragraph 3(c) if it determines that such approval would not permit a State Party or entities sponsored by it to monopolize the conduct of activities in the Area or to preclude other States Parties from activities in the Area.

5. Notwithstanding paragraph 3(a), after the end of the interim period specified in article 151, paragraph 3, the Authority may adopt by means of rules, regulations and procedures other procedures and criteria consistent with this Convention for deciding which applicants shall have plans of work approved in cases of selection among applicants for a proposed area. These procedures and criteria shall ensure approval of plans of work on an equitable and non-discriminatory basis.

Article 7

Selection among applicants for production authorizations

1. Six months after the entry into force of this Convention, and thereafter each fourth month, the Authority shall take up for consideration applications for production authorizations submitted during the immediately preceding period. The Authority shall issue the authorizations applied for if all such applications can be approved without exceeding the production limitation or contravening the obligations of the Authority under a commodity agreement or arrangement to which it has become a party, as provided in article 151.

2. When a selection must be made among applicants for production authorizations because of the production limitation set forth in article 151, paragraphs 2 to 7, or because of the obligations of the Authority under a commodity agreement or arrangement to which it has become a party, as provided for in article 151, paragraph 1, the Authority shall make the selection on the basis of objective and non-discriminatory standards set forth in its rules, regulations and procedures.

3. In the application of paragraph 2, the Authority shall give priority to those applicants which:

(a) give better assurance of performance, taking into account their financial and technical qualifications and their performance, if any, under previously approved plans of work;

(b) provide earlier prospective financial benefits to the Authority, taking into account when commercial production is scheduled to begin;

(c) have already invested the most resources and effort in prospecting or exploration.

4. Applicants which are not selected in any period shall have priority in subsequent periods until they receive a production authorization.

5. Selection shall be made taking into account the need to enhance opportunities for all States Parties, irrespective of their social and economic systems or geographical locations so as to avoid discrimination against any State or system, to participate in activities in the Area and to prevent monopolization of those activities.

6. Whenever fewer reserved areas than non-reserved areas are under exploitation, applications for production authorizations with respect to reserved areas shall have priority.

7. The decisions referred to in this article shall be taken as soon as possible after the close of each period.

Article 8

Reservation of areas

Each application, other than those submitted by the Enterprise or by any other entities for reserved areas, shall cover a total area, which need not be a single continuous area, sufficiently large and of sufficient estimated commercial value to allow two mining operations. The applicant shall indicate the co-ordinates dividing the area into two parts of equal estimated commercial value and submit all the data obtained by him with respect to both parts. Without prejudice to the powers of the Authority pursuant to article 17 of this Annex, the data to be submitted concerning polymetallic nodules shall relate to mapping, sampling, the abundance of nodules, and their metal content. Within 45 days of receiving such data, the Authority shall designate which part is to be reserved solely for the conduct of activities by the Authority through the Enterprise or in association with developing States. This designation may be deferred for a further period of 45 days if the Authority requests an independent expert to assess whether all data required by this article have been submitted. The area designated shall become a reserved area as soon as the plan of work for the non-reserved area is approved and the contract is signed.

Article 9
Activities in reserved areas

1. The Enterprise shall be given an opportunity to decide whether it intends to carry out activities in each reserved area. This decision may be taken at any time, unless a notification pursuant to paragraph 4 is received by the Authority, in which event the Enterprise shall take its decision within a reasonable time. The Enterprise may decide to exploit such areas in joint ventures with the interested State or entity.

2. The Enterprise may conclude contracts for the execution of part of its activities in accordance with Annex IV, article 12. It may also enter into joint ventures for the conduct of such activities with any entities which are eligible to carry out activities in the Area pursuant to article 153, paragraph 2(b). When considering such joint ventures, the Enterprise shall offer to States Parties which are developing States and their nationals the opportunity of effective participation.

3. The Authority may prescribe, in its rules, regulations and procedures, substantive and procedural requirements and conditions with respect to such contracts and joint ventures.

4. Any State Party which is a developing State or any natural or juridical person sponsored by it and effectively controlled by it or by other developing State which is a qualified applicant, or any group of the foregoing, may notify the Authority that it wishes to submit a plan of work pursuant to article 6 of this Annex with respect to a reserved area. The plan of work shall be considered if the Enterprise decides, pursuant to paragraph 1, that it does not intend to carry out activities in that area.

Article 10
Preference and priority among applicants

An operator who has an approved plan of work for exploration only, as provided in article 3, paragraph 4(c), of this Annex shall have a preference and a priority among applicants for a plan of work covering exploitation of the same area and resources. However, such preference or priority may be withdrawn if the operator's performance has not been satisfactory.

Article 11
Joint arrangements

1. Contracts may provide for joint arrangements between the contractor and the Authority through the Enterprise, in the form of joint ventures or production sharing, as well as any other form of joint arrangement, which shall have the same protection against revision, suspension or termination as contracts with the Authority.

2. Contractors entering into such joint arrangements with the Enterprise may receive financial incentives as provided for in article 13 of this Annex.

3. Partners in joint ventures with the Enterprise shall be liable for the payments required by article 13 of this Annex to the extent of their share in the joint ventures, subject to financial incentives as provided for in that article.

Article 12
Activities carried out by the Enterprise

1. Activities in the Area carried out by the Enterprise pursuant to article 153, paragraph 2(a), shall be governed by Part XI, the rules, regulations and procedures of the Authority and its relevant decisions.

2. Any plan of work submitted by the Enterprise shall be accompanied by

evidence supporting its financial and technical capabilities.

Article 13
Financial terms of contracts

1. In adopting rules, regulations and procedures concerning the financial terms of a contract between the Authority and the entities referred to in article 153, paragraph 2(b), and in negotiating those financial terms in accordance with Part XI and those rules, regulations and procedures, the Authority shall be guided by the following objectives:

(a) to ensure optimum revenues for the Authority from the proceeds of commercial production;

(b) to attract investments and technology to the exploration and exploitation of the Area;

(c) to ensure equality of financial treatment and comparable financial obligations for contractors;

(d) to provide incentives on a uniform and non-discriminatory basis for contractors to undertake joint arrangements with the Enterprise and developing States or their nationals, to stimulate the transfer of technology thereto, and to train the personnel of the Authority and of developing States;

(e) to enable the Enterprise to engage in sea-bed mining effectively at the same time as the entities referred to in article 153, paragraph 2(b); and

(f) to ensure that, as a result of the financial incentives provided to contractors under paragraph 14, under the terms of contracts reviewed in accordance with article 19 of this Annex or under the provisions of article 11 of this Annex with respect to joint ventures, contractors are not subsidized so as to be given an artificial competitive advantage with respect to land-based miners.

2. A fee shall be levied for the administrative cost of processing an application for approval of a plan of work in the form of a contract and shall be fixed at an amount of $US 500,000 per application. The amount of the fee shall be reviewed from time to time by the Council in order to ensure that it covers the administrative cost incurred. If such administrative cost incurred by the Authority in processing an application is less than the fixed amount, the Authority shall refund the difference to the applicant.

3. A contractor shall pay an annual fixed fee of $US 1 million from the date of entry into force of the contract. If the approved date of commencement of commercial production is postponed because of a delay in issuing the production authorization, in accordance with article 151, the annual fixed fee shall be waived for the period of postponement. From the date of commencement of commercial production, the contractor shall pay either the production charge or the annual fixed fee, whichever is greater.

4. Within a year of the date of commencement of commercial production, in conformity with paragraph 3, a contractor shall choose to make his financial contribution to the Authority by either:

(a) paying a production charge only; or

(b) paying a combination of a production charge and a share of net proceeds.

5.(a) If a contractor chooses to make his financial contribution to the Authority by paying a production charge only, it shall be fixed at a percentage of the market value of the processed metals produced from the polymetallic nodules recovered from the area covered by the contract. This percentage shall be fixed as follows:

(i) years 1–10 of commercial production 5 per cent

(ii) years 11 to the end of commercial production 12 per cent.

(b) The said market value shall be the product of the quantity of the processed metals produced from the polymetallic nodules extracted from the area covered by the contract and the average price for those metals during the relevant accounting year, as defined in paragraphs 7 and 8.

6. If a contractor chooses to make his financial contribution to the Authority by paying a combination of a production charge and a share of net proceeds, such payments shall be determined as follows:

(a) The production charge shall be fixed at a percentage of the market value, determined in accordance with subparagraph (b), of the processed metals produced from the polymetallic nodules recovered from the area covered by the contract. This percentage shall be fixed as follows:

(i) first period of commercial production 2 per cent

(ii) second period of commercial production 4 per cent.

If, in the second period of commercial production, as defined in subparagraph (d), the return on investment in any accounting year as defined in subparagraph (m) falls below 15 per cent as a result of the payment of the production charge at 4 per cent, the production charge shall be 2 per cent instead of 4 per cent in that accounting year.

(b) The said market value shall be the product of the quantity of the processed metals produced from the polymetallic nodules recovered from the area covered by the contract and the average price for those metals during the relevant accounting year as defined in paragraphs 7 and 8.

(c)(i) The Authority's share of net proceeds shall be taken out of that portion of the contractor's net proceeds which is attributable to the mining of the resources of the area covered by the contract, referred to hereinafter as attributable net proceeds.

(ii) The Authority's share of attributable net proceeds shall be determined in accordance with the following incremental schedule:

	Share of the Authority	
Portion of attributable net proceeds	*First period of commercial production*	*Second period of commercial production*
That portion representing a return on investment which is greater than 0 per cent, but less than 10 per cent	35 per cent	40 per cent
That portion representing a return on investment which is 10 per cent or greater, but less than 20 per cent	42.5 per cent	50 per cent
That portion representing a return on investment which is 20 per cent or greater	50 per cent	70 per cent

(d)(i) The first period of commercial production referred to in subparagraphs (a) and (c) shall commence in the first accounting year of commercial production and terminate in the accounting year in which the contractor's development costs with interest on the unrecovered portion thereof are fully recovered by his cash surplus, as follows: In the first accounting year during which development costs are incurred, unrecovered development costs shall equal the development costs less cash surplus in that year. In each subsequent accounting year, unrecovered development costs shall equal the unrecovered development costs at the end of the preceding accounting year, plus interest thereon at the rate of 10 per cent per annum, plus development costs incurred in the current accounting year and less contractor's cash surplus in the current accounting year. The accounting year in which unrecovered development costs become zero for the first time shall be the accounting year in which the contractor's development costs with interest on the unrecovered portion thereof are fully recovered by his cash surplus. The contractor's cash surplus in any accounting year shall be his gross proceeds less his operating costs and less his payments to the Authority under subparagraph (c).

(ii) The second period of commercial production shall commence in the accounting year following the termination of the first period of commercial production and shall continue until the end of the contract.

(e) "Attributable net proceeds" means the product of the contractor's net proceeds and the ratio of the development costs in the mining sector to the contractor's development costs. If the contractor engages in mining, transporting polymetallic nodules and production primarily of three processed metals, namely, cobalt, copper and nickel, the amount of attributable net proceeds shall not be less than 25 per cent of the contractor's net proceeds. Subject to subparagraph (n), in all other cases, including those where the contractor engages in mining, transporting polymetallic nodules, and production primarily of four processed metals, namely, cobalt, copper, manganese and nickel, the Authority may, in its rules, regulations and procedures, prescribe appropriate floors which shall bear the same relationship to each case as the 25 per cent floor does to the three-metal case.

(f) "Contractor's net proceeds" means the contractor's gross proceeds less his operating costs and less the recovery of his development costs as set out in subparagraph (j).

(g)(i) If the contractor engages in mining, transporting polymetallic nodules and production of processed metals, "contractor's gross proceeds" means the gross revenues from the sale of the processed metals and any other monies deemed reasonably attributable to operations under the contract in accordance with the financial rules, regulations and procedures of the Authority.

(ii) In all cases other than those specified in subparagraphs (g)(i) and (n)(iii), "contractor's gross proceeds" means the gross revenues from the sale of the semi-processed metals from the polymetallic nodules recovered from the area covered by the contract, and any other monies deemed reasonably attributable to operations under the contract in accordance with the financial rules, regulations and procedures of the Authority.

(h) "Contractor's development costs" means:

(i) all expenditures incurred prior to the commencement of commercial production which are directly related to the development of the productive capacity of the area covered by the contract and the activities related thereto for operations under the contract in all cases other than that specified in subparagraph (n), in conformity with generally recognized accounting principles, including, *inter alia*, costs of machinery, equipment, ships, processing plant, construction, buildings, land, roads, prospecting and exploration of the area covered by the contract, research and development interest, required leases, licences and fees; and

(ii) expenditures similar to those set forth in (i) above incurred subsequent to the commencement of commercial production and necessary to carry out the plan of work, except those chargeable to operating costs.

(i) The proceeds from the disposal of capital assets and the market value of those capital assets which are no longer required for operations under the contract and which are not sold shall be deducted from the contractor's development costs during the relevant accounting year. When these deductions exceed the contractor's development costs the excess shall be added to the contractor's gross proceeds.

(j) The contractor's development costs incurred prior to the commencement of commercial production referred to in subparagraphs (h)(i) and (n)(iv) shall be recovered in 10 equal annual instalments from the date of commencement of commercial production. The contractor's development costs incurred subsequent to the commencement of commercial production referred to in subparagraphs (h)(ii) and (n)(iv) shall be recovered in 10 or fewer equal annual instalments so as to ensure their complete recovery by the end of the contract.

(k) "Contractor's operating costs" means all expenditures incurred after the commencement of commercial production in the operation of the productive capacity of the area covered by the contract and the activities related thereto for operations under the contract, in conformity with generally recognized accounting principles, including, *inter alia*, the annual fixed fee or the production charge, whichever is greater, expenditures for wages, salaries, employee benefits, materials, services, transporting, processing and marketing costs, interest, utilities, preservation of the marine environment, overhead and administrative costs specifically related to operations under the contract, and any net operating losses carried forward or backward as specified herein. Net operating losses may be carried forward for two consecutive years except in the last two years of the contract in which case they may be carried backward to the two preceding years.

(l) If the contractor engages in mining, transporting of polymetallic nodules, and production of processed and semi-processed metals, "development costs of the mining sector" means the portion of the contractor's development costs which is directly related to the mining of the resources of the area covered by the contract, in conformity with generally recognized accounting principles, and the financial rules, regulations and procedures of the Authority, including, *inter alia*, application fee, annual fixed fee and, where applicable, costs of prospecting and exploration of the area covered by the contract, and a portion of research and development costs.

(m) "Return on investment" in any accounting year means the ratio of attributable net proceeds in that year to the development costs of the mining sector. For the purpose of computing this ratio the development costs of the mining sector shall include expenditures on new or replacement equipment in the mining sector less the original costs of the equipment replaced.

(n) If the contractor engages in mining only:

(i) "attributable net proceeds" means the whole of the contractor's net proceeds;

(ii) "contractor's net proceeds" shall be as defined in subparagraph (f);

(iii) "contractor's gross proceeds" means the gross revenues from the sale of the polymetallic nodules, and any other monies deemed reasonably attributable to operations under the contract in accordance with the financial rules, regulations and procedures of the Authority;

(iv) "contractor's development costs" means all expenditures incurred prior to the commencement of commercial production as set forth in subparagraph (h)(i), and all expenditures incurred subsequent to the commencement of commercial production as set forth in subparagraph (h)(ii), which are directly related to the mining of the resources of the area covered by the contract, in conformity with generally recognized accounting principles;

(v) "contractor's operating costs" means the contractor's operating costs as in subparagraph (k) which are directly related to the mining of the resources of the area covered by the contract in conformity with generally recognized accounting principles;

(vi) "return on investment" in any accounting year means the ratio of the contractor's net proceeds in that year to the contractor's development costs. For the purpose of computing this ratio, the contractor's development costs shall include expenditures on new or replacement equipment less the original cost of the equipment replaced.

(o) The costs referred to in subparagraphs (h), (k), (l) and (n) in respect of interest paid by the contractor shall be allowed to the extent that, in all the circumstances, the Authority approves, pursuant to article 4, paragraph 1, of this Annex, the debt-equity ratio and the rates of interest as reasonable, having regard to existing commercial practice.

(p) The costs referred to in this paragraph shall not be interpreted as including payments of corporate income taxes or similar charges levied by States in respect of the operations of the contractor.

7.(a) "Processed metals", referred to in paragraphs 5 and 6, means the metals in the most basic form in which they are customarily traded on international terminal markets. For this purpose, the Authority shall specify, in its financial rules, regulations and procedures, the relevant international terminal market. For the metals which are not traded on such markets, "processed metals" means the metals in the most basic form in which they are customarily traded in representative arm's length transactions.

(b) If the Authority cannot otherwise determine the quantity of the processed metals produced from the polymetallic nodules recovered from the area covered by the contract referred to in paragraphs 5(b) and 6(b), the quantity shall be determined on the basis of the metal content of the nodules, processing recovery efficiency and other relevant factors, in accordance with the rules, regulations and procedures of the Authority and in conformity with generally recognised accounting principles.

8. If an international terminal market provides a representative pricing mechanism for processed metals, polymetallic nodules and semi-processed metals from the nodules, the average price on that market shall be used. In all other cases, the Authority shall, after consulting the contractor, determine a fair price for the said products in accordance with paragraph 9.

9.(a) All costs, expenditures, proceeds and revenues and all determinations of price and value referred to in this article shall be the result of free market or arm's length transactions. In the absence thereof, they shall be determined by the Authority, after consulting the contractor, as though they were the result of free market or arm's length transactions, taking into account relevant transactions in other markets.

(b) In order to ensure compliance with and enforcement of the provisions of this paragraph, the Authority shall be guided by the principles adopted for, and the interpretation given to, arm's length transactions by the Commission on Transnational Corporations of the United Nations, the Group of Experts on Tax Treaties between Developing and Developed Countries and other international organizations, and shall, in its rules, regulations and procedures, specify uniform and internationally acceptable accounting rules and procedures, and the means of selection by the contractor of certified independent accountants acceptable to the Authority for the purpose of carrying out auditing in compliance with those rules, regulations and procedures.

10. The contractor shall make available to the accountants, in accordance with the financial rules, regulations and procedures of the Authority, such financial data as are required to determine compliance with this article.

11. All costs, expenditures, proceeds and revenues, and all prices and values referred to in this article, shall be determined in accordance with generally recognized accounting principles and the financial rules, regulations and procedures of the Authority.

12. Payments to the Authority under paragraphs 5 and 6 shall be made in freely usable currencies or currencies which are freely available and effectively usable on the major foreign exchange markets or, at the contractor's option, in the equivalents of processed metals at market value. The market value shall be determined in accordance with paragraph 5(b). The freely usable currencies and currencies which are freely available and effectively usable on the major foreign exchange markets shall be defined in the rules, regulations and procedures of the Authority in accordance with prevailing international monetary practice.

13. All financial obligations of the contractor to the Authority, as well as all his fees, costs, expenditures, proceeds and revenues referred to in this article, shall be adjusted by expressing them in constant terms relative to a base year.

14. The Authority may, taking into account any recommendations of the Economic Planning Commission and the Legal and Technical Commission, adopt rules, regulations and procedures that provide for incentives, on a uniform and non-discriminatory basis, to contractors to further the objectives set out in paragraph 1.

15. In the event of a dispute between the Authority and a contractor over the interpretation or application of the financial terms of a contract, either party may submit the dispute to binding commercial arbitration, unless both parties agree to settle the dispute by other means, in accordance with article 188, paragraph 2.

Article 14
Transfer of data

1. The operator shall transfer to the Authority, in accordance with its rules, regulations and procedures and the terms and conditions of the plan of work, at time intervals determined by the Authority all data which are both necessary for and relevant to the effective exercise of the powers and functions of the principal organs of the Authority in respect of the area covered by the plan of work.

2. Transferred data in respect of the area covered by the plan of work, deemed proprietary, may only be used for the purposes set forth in this article. Data necessary for the formulation by the Authority of rules, regulations and procedures concerning protection of the marine environment and safety, other than equipment design data, shall not be deemed proprietary.

3. Data transferred to the Authority by prospectors, applicants for contracts or contractors, deemed proprietary, shall not be disclosed by the Authority to the Enterprise or to anyone external to the Authority, but data on the reserved areas may be disclosed to the Enterprise. Such data transferred by such persons to the Enterprise shall not be disclosed by the Enterprise to the Authority or to anyone external to the Authority.

Article 15
Training programmes

The contractor shall draw up practical programmes for the training of personnel of the Authority and developing States, including the participation of such personnel in all activities in the Area which are covered by the contract, in accordance with article 144, paragraph 2.

Article 16
Exclusive right to explore and exploit

The Authority shall, pursuant to Part XI and its rules, regulations and procedures, accord the operator the exclusive right to explore and exploit the area covered by the plan of work in respect of a specified category of resources and shall ensure that no other entity operates in the same area for a different category of resources in a manner which might interfere with the operations of the operator. The operator shall have security of tenure in accordance with article 153, paragraph 6.

Article 17
Rules, regulations and procedures of the Authority

1. The Authority shall adopt and uniformly apply rules, regulations and procedures in accordance with article 160, paragraph 2(f)(ii), and article 162, paragraph 2(o)(ii), for the exercise of its functions as set forth in Part XI on, *inter alia*, the following matters:

(a) administrative procedures relating to prospecting, exploration and exploitation in the Area;

(b) operations:

(i) size of area;

(ii) duration of operations;

(iii) performance requirements including assurances pursuant to article 4, paragraph 6(c), of this Annex;

(iv) categories of resources;

(v) renunciation of areas;

(vi) progress reports;

(vii) submission of data;

(viii) inspection and supervision of operations;

(ix) prevention of interference with other activities in the marine environment;

(x) transfer of rights and obligations by a contractor;

(xi) procedures for transfer of technology to developing States in accordance with article 144 and for their direct participation;

(xii) mining standards and practices, including those relating to operational safety, conservation of the resources and the protection of the marine environment;

(xiii) definition of commercial production;

(xiv) qualification standards for applicants;

(c) financial matters:

(i) establishment of uniform and non-discriminatory costing and accounting rules and the method of selection of auditors;

(ii) apportionment of proceeds of operations;

(iii) the incentives referred to in article 13 of this Annex;

(d) implementation of decisions taken pursuant to article 151, paragraph 10, and article 164, paragraph 2(d).

2. Rules, regulations and procedures on the following items shall fully reflect the objective criteria set out below:

(a) Size of areas:

The Authority shall determine the appropriate size of areas for exploration which may be up to twice as large as those for exploitation in order to permit intensive exploration operations. The size of area shall be calculated to satisfy the requirements of article 8 of this Annex on reservation of areas as well as stated production requirements consistent with article 151 in accordance with the terms of the contract taking into account the state of the art of technology then available for sea-bed mining and the relevant physical characteristics of the areas. Areas shall be neither smaller nor larger than are necessary to satisfy this objective.

(b) Duration of operations:

(i) Prospecting shall be without time-limit;

(ii) Exploration should be of sufficient duration to permit a thorough survey of the specific area, the design and construction of mining equipment for the area and the design and construction of small and medium-size processing plants for the purpose of testing mining and processing systems;

(iii) The duration of exploitation should be related to the economic life of the mining project, taking into consideration such factors as the depletion of the ore, the useful life of mining equipment and processing facilities and commercial viability. Exploitation should be of sufficient duration to permit commercial extraction of minerals of the area and should include a reasonable time period for construction of commercial-scale mining and processing systems, during which period commercial production should not be required. The total duration of exploitation, however, should also be short enough to give the Authority an opportunity to amend the terms and conditions of the plan of work at the time it considers renewal in accordance with rules, regulations and procedures which it has adopted subsequent to approving the plan of work.

(c) Performance requirements:

The Authority shall require that during the exploration stage periodic expenditures be made by the operator which are reasonably related to the size of the area covered by the plan of work and the expenditures which would be expected of a *bona fide* operator who intended to bring the area into commercial production within the time-limits established by the Authority. The required expenditures should not be established at a level which would discourage prospective operators with less costly technology than is prevalently in use. The Authority shall establish a maximum time interval, after the exploration stage is completed and the exploitation stage begins, to achieve commercial production. To determine this interval, the Authority should take into consideration that construction of large-scale mining and processing systems cannot be initiated until after the termination of the exploration stage and the commencement of the exploitation stage. Accordingly, the interval to bring an area into commercial production should take into account the time necessary for this construction after the completion of the exploration stage and reasonable allowance should be made for unavoidable delays in the construction schedule. Once commercial production is achieved, the Authority shall within reasonable limits and taking into consideration all relevant factors require the operator to maintain commercial production throughout the period of the plan of work.

(d) Categories of resources:

In determining the category of resources in respect of which a plan of work may be approved, the Authority shall give emphasis *inter alia* to the following characteristics:

(i) that certain resources require the use of similar mining methods; and

(ii) that some resources can be developed simultaneously without undue interference between operators developing different resources in the same area.

Nothing in this subparagraph shall preclude the Authority from approving a plan of work with respect to more than one category of resources in the same area to the same applicant.

(e) Renunciation of areas:

The operator shall have the right at any time to renounce without penalty the whole or part of his rights in the area covered by a plan of work.

(f) Protection of the marine environment:

Rules, regulations and procedures shall be drawn up in order to secure effective protection of the marine environment from harmful effects directly resulting from activities in the Area or from shipboard processing immediately above a mine site of minerals derived from that mine site, taking into account the extent to which such harmful effects may directly result from drilling, dredging, coring and excavation and from disposal, dumping and discharge into the marine environment of sediment, wastes or other effluents.

(g) Commercial production:

Commercial production shall be deemed to have begun if an operator engages in sustained large-scale recovery operations which yield a quantity of materials sufficient to indicate clearly that the principal purpose is large-scale production rather than production intended for information gathering, analysis or the testing of equipment or plant.

Article 18
Penalties

1. A contractor's rights under the contract may be suspended or terminated only in the following cases:

(a) if, in spite of warnings by the Authority, the contractor has conducted his activities in such a way as to result in serious, persistent and wilful violations of the fundamental terms of the contract, Part XI and the rules, regulations and procedures of the Authority; or

(b) if the contractor has failed to comply with a final binding decision of the dispute settlement body applicable to him.

2. In the case of any violation of the contract not covered by paragraph 1(a), or in lieu of suspension or termination under paragraph 1(a), the Authority may impose upon the contractor monetary penalties proportionate to the seriousness of the violation.

3. Except for emergency orders under article 162, paragraph 2(w), the Authority may not execute a decision involving monetary penalties, suspension or termination until the contractor has been accorded a reasonable opportunity to exhaust the judicial remedies available to him pursuant to Part XI, section 5.

Article 19
Revision of contract

1. When circumstances have arisen or are likely to arise which, in the opinion of either party, would render the contract inequitable or make it impracticable or impossible to achieve the objectives set out in the contract or in Part XI, the parties shall enter into negotiations to revise it accordingly.

2. Any contract entered into in accordance with article 153, paragraph 3, may be revised only with the consent of the parties.

Article 20
Transfer of rights and obligations

The rights and obligations arising under a contract may be transferred only with the consent of the Authority, and in accordance with its rules, regulations and procedures. The Authority shall not unreasonably withhold consent to the transfer if the proposed transferee is in all respects a qualified applicant and assumes all of the obligations of the transferor and if the transfer does not confer to the transferee a plan of work, the approval of which would be forbidden by article 6, paragraph 3(c), of this Annex.

Article 21
Applicable law

1. The contract shall be governed by the terms of the contract, the rules, regulations and procedures of the Authority, Part XI and other rules of international law not incompatible with this Convention.

2. Any final decision rendered by a court or tribunal having jurisdiction under this Convention relating to the rights and obligations of the Authority and of the contractor shall be enforceable in the territory of each State Party.

3. No State Party may impose conditions on a contractor that are inconsistent with Part XI. However, the application by a State Party to contractors sponsored by it, or to ships flying its flag, of environment or other laws and regulations more stringent than those in the rules, regulations and procedures of the Authority adopted pursuant to article 17, paragraph 2(f), of this Annex shall not be deemed inconsistent with Part XI.

Article 22
Responsibility

The contractor shall have responsibility or liability for any damage arising out of wrongful acts in the conduct of its operations, account being taken of contributory acts or omissions by the Authority. Similarly, the Authority shall have responsibility or liability for any damage arising out of wrongful acts in the exercise of its powers and functions, including violations under article 168, paragraph 2, account being taken of contributory acts or omissions by the contractor. Liability in every case shall be for the actual amount of damage.

ANNEX IV

Statute of the Enterprise

Article 1
Purposes

1. The Enterprise is the organ of the Authority which shall carry out activities in the Area directly, pursuant to article 153, paragraph 2(a), as well as the transporting, processing and marketing of minerals recovered from the Area.

2. In carrying out its purposes and in the exercise of its functions, the Enterprise shall act in accordance with this Convention and the rules, regulations and procedures of the Authority.

3. In developing the resources of the Area pursuant to paragraph 1, the Enterprise shall, subject to this Convention, operate in accordance with sound commercial principles.

Article 2
Relationship to the Authority

1. Pursuant to article 170, the Enterprise shall act in accordance with the general policies of the Assembly and the directives of the Council.

2. Subject to paragraph 1, the Enterprise shall enjoy autonomy in the conduct of its operations.

3. Nothing in this Convention shall make the Enterprise liable for the acts or obligations of the Authority, or make the Authority liable for the acts or obligations of the Enterprise.

Article 3
Limitation of liability

Without prejudice to article 11, paragraph 3, of this Annex, no member of the

Authority shall be liable by reason only of its membership for the acts or obligations of the Enterprise.

Article 4
Structure

The Enterprise shall have a Governing Board, a Director-General and the staff necessary for the exercise of its functions.

Article 5
Governing Board

1. The Governing Board shall be composed of 15 members elected by the Assembly in accordance with article 160, paragraph 2(c). In the election of the members of the Board, due regard shall be paid to the principle of equitable geographical distribution. In submitting nominations of candidates for election to the Board, members of the Authority shall bear in mind the need to nominate candidates of the highest standard of competence, with qualifications in relevant fields, so as to ensure the viability and success of the Enterprise.

2. Members of the Board shall be elected for four years and may be re-elected; and due regard shall be paid to the principle of rotation of membership.

3. Members of the Board shall continue in office until their successors are elected. If the office of a member of the Board becomes vacant, the Assembly shall, in accordance with article 160, paragraph 2(c), elect a new member for the remainder of his predecessor's term.

4. Members of the Board shall act in their personal capacity. In the performance of their duties they shall not seek or receive instructions from any government or from any other sources. Each member of the Authority shall respect the independent character of the members of the Board and shall refrain from all attempts to influence any of them in the discharge of their duties.

5. Each member of the Board shall receive remuneration to be paid out of the funds of the Enterprise. The amount of remuneration shall be fixed by the Assembly, upon the recommendation of the Council.

6. The Board shall normally function at the principal office of the Enterprise and shall meet as often as the business of the Enterprise may require.

7. Two-thirds of the members of the Board shall constitute a quorum.

8. Each member of the Board shall have one vote. All matters before the Board shall be decided by a majority of its members. If a member has a conflict of interest on a matter before the Board he shall refrain from voting on that matter.

9. Any member of the Authority may ask the Board for information in respect of its operations which particularly affect that member. The Board shall endeavour to provide such information.

Article 6
Powers and functions of the Governing Board

The Governing Board shall direct the operations of the Enterprise. Subject to this Convention, the Governing Board shall exercise the powers necessary to fulfil the purposes of the Enterprise, including powers:

(a) to elect a Chairman from among its members;

(b) to adopt its rules of procedure;

(c) to draw up and submit formal written plans of work to the Council in accordance with article 153, paragraph 3, and article 162, paragraph 2(j);

(d) to develop plans of work and programmes for carrying out the activities specified in article 170;

(e) to prepare and submit to the Council applications for production authorizations in accordance with article 151, paragraphs 2 to 7;

(f) to authorize negotiations concerning the acquisition of technology, including those provided for in Annex III, article 5, paragraph 3(a), (c) and (d), and to approve the results of those negotiations;

(g) to establish terms and conditions, and to authorize negotiations, concerning joint ventures and other forms of joint arrangements referred to in Annex III, articles 9 and 11, and to approve the results of such negotiations;

(h) to recommend to the Assembly what portion of the net income of the Enterprise should be retained as its reserves in accordance with article 160, paragraph 2(f), and article 10 of this Annex;

(i) to approve the annual budget of the Enterprise;

(j) to authorize the procurement of goods and services in accordance with article 12, paragraph 3, of this Annex;

(k) to submit an annual report to the Council in accordance with article 9 of this Annex;

(l) to submit to the Council for the approval of the Assembly draft rules in respect of the organization, management, appointment and dismissal of the staff of the Enterprise and to adopt regulations to give effect to such rules;

(m) to borrow funds and to furnish such collateral or other security as it may determine in accordance with article 11, paragraph 2, of this Annex;

(n) to enter into any legal proceedings, agreements and transactions and to take any other actions in accordance with article 13 of this Annex;

(o) to delegate, subject to the approval of the Council, any non-discretionary powers to the Director-General and to its committees.

Article 7
Director-General and staff of the Enterprise

1. The Assembly shall, upon the recommendation of the Council and the nomination of the Governing Board, elect the Director-General of the Enterprise who shall not be a member of the Board. The Director-General shall hold office for a fixed term, not exceeding five years, and may be re-elected for further terms.

2. The Director-General shall be the legal representative and chief executive of the Enterprise and shall be directly responsible to the Board for the conduct of the operations of the Enterprise. He shall be responsible for the organization, management, appointment and dismissal of the staff of the Enterprise in accordance with the rules and regulations referred to in article 6, subparagraph (l), of this Annex. He shall participate, without the right to vote, in the meetings of the Board and may participate, without the right to vote, in the meetings of the Assembly and the Council when these organs are dealing with matters concerning the Enterprise.

3. The paramount consideration in the recruitment and employment of the staff and in the determination of their conditions of service shall be the necessity of securing the highest standards of efficiency and of technical competence. Subject to this consideration, due regard shall be paid to the importance of recruiting the staff on an equitable geographical basis.

4. In the performance of their duties the Director-General and the staff shall not seek or receive instructions from any government or from any other source external to the Enterprise. They shall refrain from any action which might reflect on their position as international officials of the Enterprise responsible only to the Enterprise. Each State Party undertakes to respect the exclusively international character of the responsibilities of the Director-General and the staff and not to seek to influence them in the discharge of their responsibilities.

5. The responsibilities set forth in article 168, paragraph 2, are equally applicable to the staff of the Enterprise.

Article 8
Location

The Enterprise shall have its principal office at the seat of the Authority. The Enterprise may establish other offices and facilities in the territory of any State Party with the consent of that State Party.

Article 9
Reports and financial statements

1. The Enterprise shall, not later than three months after the end of each financial year, submit to the Council for its consideration an annual report containing an audited statement of its accounts and shall transmit to the Council at appropriate intervals a summary statement of its financial position and a profit and loss statement showing the results of its operations.

2. The Enterprise shall publish its annual report and such other reports as it finds appropriate.

3. All reports and financial statements referred to in this article shall be distributed to the members of the Authority.

Article 10
Allocation of net income

1. Subject to paragraph 3, the Enterprise shall make payments to the Authority under Annex III, article 13, or their equivalent.

2. The Assembly shall, upon the recommendation of the Governing Board, determine what portion of the net income of the Enterprise shall be retained as reserves of the Enterprise. The remainder shall be transferred to the Authority.

3. During an initial period required for the Enterprise to become self-supporting, which shall not exceed 10 years from the commencement of commercial production by it, the Assembly shall exempt the Enterprise from the payments referred to in paragraph 1, and shall leave all of the net income of the Enterprise in its reserves.

Article 11
Finances

1. The funds of the Enterprise shall include:

(a) amounts received from the Authority in accordance with article 173, paragraph 2(b);

(b) voluntary contributions made by States Parties for the purpose of financing activities of the Enterprise;

(c) amounts borrowed by the Enterprise in accordance with paragraphs 2 and 3;

(d) income of the Enterprise from its operations;

(e) other funds made available to the Enterprise to enable it to commence operations as soon as possible and to carry out its functions.

2.(a) The Enterprise shall have the power to borrow funds and to furnish such collateral or other security as it may determine. Before making a public sale of its obligations in the financial markets or currency of a State Party, the Enterprise shall obtain the approval of that State Party. The total amount of borrowings shall be approved by the Council upon the recommendation of the Governing Board.

(b) States Parties shall make every reasonable effort to support applications by the Enterprise for loans on capital markets and from international financial institutions.

3.(a) The Enterprise shall be provided with the funds necessary to explore and exploit one mine site, and to transport, process and market the minerals recovered therefrom and the nickel, copper, cobalt and manganese obtained, and to meet its initial administrative expenses. The amount of the said funds, and the criteria and factors for its adjustment, shall be included by the Preparatory Commission in the draft rules, regulations and procedures of the Authority.

(b) All States Parties shall make available to the Enterprise an amount equivalent to one half of the funds referred to in subparagraph (a) by way of long-term interest-free loans in accordance with the scale of assessments for the United Nations regular budget in force at the time when the assessments are made, adjusted to take into account the States which are not members of the United Nations. Debts incurred by the Enterprise in raising the other half of the funds shall be guaranteed by all States Parties in accordance with the same scale.

(c) If the sum of the financial contributions of States Parties is less than the funds to be provided to the Enterprise under subparagraph (a), the Assembly shall, at its first session, consider the extent of the shortfall and adopt by consensus measures for dealing with this shortfall, taking into account the obligation of States Parties under subparagraphs (a) and (b) and any recommendations of the Preparatory Commission.

(d)(i) Each State Party shall, within 60 days after the entry into force of this Convention, or within 30 days after the deposit of its instrument of ratification or accession, whichever is later, deposit with the Enterprise irrevocable, non-negotiable, non-interest-bearing promissory notes in the amount of the share of such State party of interest-free loans pursuant to subparagraph (b).

(ii) The Board shall prepare, at the earliest practicable date after this Convention enters into force, and thereafter at annual or other appropriate intervals, a schedule of the magnitude and timing of its requirements for the funding of its administrative expenses and for activities carried out by the Enterprise in accordance with article 170 and article 12 of this Annex.

(iii) The States Parties shall, thereupon, be notified by the Enterprise, through the Authority, of their respective shares of the funds in accordance with paragraph 3(b), required for such expenses. The Enterprise shall encash such amounts of the promissory notes as may be required to meet the expenditure referred to in the schedule with respect to interest-free loans.

(iv) States Parties shall, upon receipt of the notification, make available their respective shares of debt guarantees for the Enterprise in accordance with subparagraph (b).

(e)(i) If the Enterprise so requests, State Parties may provide debt guarantees in addition to those provided in accordance with the scale referred to in subparagraph (b).

(ii) In lieu of debt guarantees, a State Party may make a voluntary contribution to the Enterprise in an amount equivalent to that portion of the debts which it would otherwise be liable to guarantee.

(f) Repayment of the interest-bearing loans shall have priority over the repayment of the interest-free loans. Repayment of interest-free loans shall be in accordance with a schedule adopted by the Assembly, upon the recommendation of the Council and the advice of the Board. In the exercise of this function the Board shall be guided by the relevant provisions of the rules, regulations and procedures of the Authority, which shall take into account the paramount importance of ensuring the effective functions of the Enterprise and, in particular, ensuring its financial independence.

(g) Funds made available to the Enterprise shall be in freely usable currencies or currencies which are freely available and effectively usable in the major foreign exchange markets. These currencies shall be defined in the rules, regulations and procedures of the Authority in accordance with prevailing international monetary practice. Except as provided in paragraph 2, no State Party shall maintain or impose restrictions on the holding, use or exchange by the Enterprise of these funds.

(h) "Debt guarantee" means a promise of a State party to creditors of the Enterprise to pay, *pro rata* in accordance with the appropriate scale, the financial obligations of the Enterprise covered by the guarantee following notice by the creditors to the State party of a default by the Enterprise. Procedures for the payment of those obligations shall be in conformity with the rules, regulations and procedures of the Authority.

4. The funds, assets and expenses of the Enterprise shall be kept separate from those of the Authority. This article shall not prevent the Enterprise from making arrangements with the Authority regarding facilities, personnel and services and arrangements for reimbursement of administrative expenses paid by either on behalf of the other.

5. The records, books and accounts of the Enterprise, including its annual financial statements, shall be audited annually by an independent auditor appointed by the Council.

Article 12
Operations

1. The Enterprise shall propose to the Council projects for carrying out activities in accordance with article 170. Such proposals shall include a formal written plan of work for activities in the Area in accordance with article 153, paragraph 3, and all such other information and data as may be required from time to time for its appraisal by the Legal and Technical Commission and approval by the Council.

2. Upon approval by the Council, the Enterprise shall execute the project on the basis of the formal written plan of work referred to in paragraph 1.

3.(a) If the Enterprise does not possess the goods and services required for its operations it may procure them. For that purpose, it shall issue invitations to tender and award contracts to bidders offering the best combination of quality, price and delivery time.

(b) If there is more than one bid offering such a combination, the contract shall be awarded in accordance with:

(i) the principle of non-discrimination on the basis of political or other considerations not relevant to the carrying out of operations with due diligence and efficiency; and

(ii) guidelines approved by the Council with regard to the preferences to be accorded to goods and services originating in developing States, including the land-locked and geographically disadvantaged among them.

(c) The Governing Board may adopt rules determining the special circumstances in which the requirement of invitations to bid may, in the best interests of the Enterprise, be dispensed with.

4. The Enterprise shall have title to all minerals and processed substances produced by it.

5. The Enterprise shall sell its products on a non-discriminatory basis. It shall not give non-commercial discounts.

6. Without prejudice to any general or special power conferred on the Enterprise under any other provision of this Convention, the Enterprise shall exercise such powers incidental to its business as shall be necessary.

7. The Enterprise shall not interfere in the political affairs of any State Party; nor shall it be influenced in its decisions by the political character of the State Party concerned. Only commercial considerations shall be relevant to its decisions, and these considerations shall be weighed impartially in order to carry out the purposes specified in article 1 of this Annex.

Article 13
Legal status, privileges and immunities

1. To enable the Enterprise to exercise its functions, the status, privileges and immunities set forth in this article shall be accorded to the Enterprise in the territories of States Parties. To give effect to this principle the Enterprise and States Parties may, where necessary, enter into special agreements.

2. The Enterprise shall have such legal capacity as is necessary for the exercise of its functions and the fulfilment of its purposes and, in particular, the capacity:

(a) to enter into contracts, joint arrangements or other arrangements, including agreements with States and international organizations;

(b) to acquire, lease, hold and dispose of immovable and movable property;

(c) to be a party to legal proceedings.

3.(a) Actions may be brought about the Enterprise only in a court of competent jurisdiction in the territory of a State Party in which the Enterprise:

(i) has an office or facility;

(ii) has appointed an agent for the purpose of accepting service or notice of process;

(iii) has entered into a contract for goods or services;

(iv) has issued securities; or

(v) is otherwise engaged in commercial activity.

(b) The property and assets of the Enterprise, wherever located and by whomsoever held, shall be immune from all forms of seizure, attachment or execution before the delivery of final judgment against the Enterprise.

4.(a) The property and assets of the Enterprise, wherever located and by whomsoever held, shall be immune from requisition, confiscation, expropriation or any other form of seizure by executive or legislative action.

(b) The property and assets of the Enterprise, wherever located and by whomsoever held, shall be free from discriminatory restrictions, regulations, controls and moratoria of any nature.

(c) The Enterprise and its employees shall respect local laws and regulations in any State or territory in which the Enterprise or its employees may do business or otherwise act.

(d) States Parties shall ensure that the Enterprise enjoys all rights, privileges and immunities accorded by them to entities conducting commercial activities in their territories. These rights, privileges and immunities shall be accorded to the Enterprise on no less favourable a basis than that on which they are accorded to entities engaged in similar commercial activities. If special privileges are provided by States Parties for developing States or their commercial entities, the Enterprise shall enjoy those privileges on a similarly preferential basis.

(e) States Parties may provide special incentives, rights, privileges and immunities to the Enterprise without the obligation to provide such incentives, rights, privileges and immunities to other commercial entities.

5. The Enterprise shall negotiate with the host countries in which its offices and facilities are located for exemption from direct and indirect taxation.

6. Each State Party shall take such action as is necessary for giving effect in terms of its own law to the principles set forth in this Annex and shall inform the Enterprise of the specific action which it has taken.

7. The Enterprise may waive any of the privileges and immunities conferred under this article or in the special agreements referred to in paragraph 1 to such extent and upon such conditions as it may determine.

ANNEX V

Conciliation

Section 1. Conciliation Procedure Pursuant to Section 1 of Part XV

Article 1
Institution of proceedings

If the parties to a dispute have agreed, in accordance with article 284, to submit it to conciliation under this section, any such party may institute the proceedings by written notification addressed to the other party or parties to the dispute.

Article 2
List of conciliators

A list of conciliators shall be drawn up and maintained by the Secretary-General of the United Nations. Every State Party shall be entitled to nominate four conciliators, each of whom shall be a person enjoying the highest reputation for fairness, competence and integrity. The names of the persons so nominated shall constitute the list. If at any time the conciliators nominated by a State Party in the list so constituted shall be fewer than four, that State Party shall be entitled to make further nominations as necessary. The name of a conciliator shall remain on the list until withdrawn by the State Party which made the nomination, provided that such conciliator shall continue to serve on any conciliation commission to which that conciliator has been appointed until the completion of the proceedings before that commission.

Article 3
Constitution of conciliation commission

The conciliation commission shall, unless the parties otherwise agree, be constituted as follows:

(a) Subject to subparagraph (g), the conciliation commission shall consist of five members.

(b) The party instituting the proceedings shall appoint two conciliators to be chosen preferably from the list referred to in article 2 of this Annex, one of whom may be its national, unless the parties otherwise agree. Such appointments shall be included in the notification referred to in article 1 of this Annex.

(c) The other party to the dispute shall appoint two conciliators in the manner set forth in subparagraph (b) within 21 days of receipt of the notification referred to in article 1 of this Annex. If the appointments are not made within that period, the party instituting the proceedings may, within one week of the expiration of that period, either terminate the proceedings by notification addressed to the other party to request the Secretary-General of the United Nations to make the appointments in accordance with subparagraph (e).

(d) Within 30 days after all four conciliators have been appointed, they shall appoint a fifth conciliator chosen from the list referred to in article 2 of this Annex, who shall be chairman. If the appointment is not made within that period, either party may, within one week of the expiration of that period, request the Secretary-General of the United Nations to make the appointment in accordance with subparagraph (e).

(e) Within 30 days of the receipt of a request under subparagraph (c) or (d), the Secretary-General of the United Nations shall make the necessary appointments from the list referred to in article 2 of this Annex in consultation with the parties to the dispute.

(f) Any vacancy shall be filled in the manner prescribed for the initial appointment.

(g) Two or more parties which determine by agreement that they are in the same interest shall appoint two conciliators jointly. Where two or more parties have separate interests or there is a disagreement as to whether they are of the same interest, they shall appoint conciliators separately.

(h) In disputes involving more than two parties having separate interests, or where there is disagreement as to whether they are of the same interest, the parties shall apply subparagraphs (a) to (f) in so far as possible.

Article 4
Procedure

The conciliation commission shall, unless the parties otherwise agree, determine its own procedure. The commission may, with the consent of the parties to the dispute, invite any State Party to submit to it its views orally or in writing. Decisions of the commission regarding procedural matters, the report and recommendations shall be made by a majority vote of its members.

Article 5
Amicable settlement

The commission may draw the attention of the parties to any measures which might facilitate an amicable settlement of the dispute.

Article 6
Functions of the commission

The commission shall hear the parties, examine their claims and objections, and make proposals to the parties with a view to reaching an amicable settlement.

Article 7
Report

1. The commission shall report within 12 months of its constitution. Its report shall record any agreements reached and, failing agreement, its conclusions on all questions of fact or law relevant to the matter in dispute and such recommendations as the commission may deem appropriate for an amicable settlement. The report shall be deposited with the Secretary-General of the United Nations and shall immediately be transmitted by him to the parties to the dispute.

2. The report of the commission, including its conclusions or recommendations, shall not be binding upon the parties.

Article 8
Termination

The conciliation proceedings are terminated when a settlement has been reached, when the parties have accepted or one party has rejected the recommendations of the report by written notification addressed to the Secretary-General of the United Nations, or when a period of three months has expired from the date of transmission of the report to the parties.

Article 9
Fees and expenses

The fees and expenses of the commission shall be borne by the parties to the dispute.

Article 10
Right of parties to modify procedure

The parties to the dispute may by agreement applicable solely to that dispute modify any provision of this Annex.

Section 2. Compulsory Submission to Conciliation Procedure Pursuant to Section 3 of Part XV

Article 11
Institution of proceedings

1. Any party to a dispute which, in accordance with Part XV, section 3, may be submitted to conciliation under this section, may institute the proceedings by written notification addressed to the other party or parties to the dispute.

2. Any party to the dispute, notified under paragraph 1, shall be obliged to submit to such proceedings.

Article 12
Failure to reply or to submit to conciliation

The failure of a party or parties to the dispute to reply to notification of institution of proceedings or to submit to such proceedings shall not constitute a bar to the proceedings.

Article 13
Competence

A disagreement as to whether a conciliation commission acting under this section has competence shall be decided by the commission.

Article 14
Application of section 1

Articles 2 to 10 of section 1 of this Annex apply subject to this section.

ANNEX VI

Statute of the International Tribunal for the Law of the Sea

Article 1
General provisions

1. The International Tribunal for the Law of the Sea is constituted and shall function in accordance with the provisions of this Convention and this Statute.

2. The seat of the Tribunal shall be in the Free and Hanseatic City of Hamburg in the Federal Republic of Germany.

3. The Tribunal may sit and exercise its functions elsewhere whenever it considers this desirable.

4. A reference of a dispute to the Tribunal shall be governed by the provisions of Parts XI and XV.

Section 1. Organization of the Tribunal

Article 2
Composition

1. The Tribunal shall be composed of a body of 21 independent members, elected from among persons enjoying the highest reputation for fairness and integrity and of recognized competence in the field of the law of the sea.

2. In the Tribunal as a whole the representation of the principal legal systems of the world and equitable geographical distribution shall be assured.

Article 3
Membership

1. No two members of the Tribunal may be nationals of the same State. A person who for the purposes of membership in the Tribunal could be regarded as a national of more than one State shall be deemed to be a national of the one in which he ordinarily exercises civil and political rights.

2. There shall be no fewer than three members from each geographical group as established by the General Assembly of the United Nations.

Article 4
Nominations and elections

1. Each State Party may nominate not more than two persons having the qualifications prescribed in article 2 of this Annex. The members of the Tribunal shall be elected from the list of persons thus nominated.

2. At least three months before the date of the election, the Secretary-General of the United Nations in the case of the first election and the Registrar of the Tribunal in the case of subsequent elections shall address a written invitation to the States Parties to submit their nominations for members of the Tribunal within two months. He shall prepare a list in alphabetical order of all the persons thus nominated, with an indication of the States Parties which have nominated them, and shall submit it to the States Parties before the seventh day of the last month before the date of each election.

3. The first election shall be held within six months of the date of entry into force of this Convention.

4. The members of the Tribunal shall be elected by secret ballot. Elections shall be held at a meeting of the States Parties convened by the Secretary-General of the United Nations in the case of the first election and by a procedure agreed to by the States Parties in the case of subsequent elections. Two-thirds of the States Parties shall constitute a quorum at that meeting. The persons elected to the Tribunal shall be those nominees who obtain the largest number of votes and a two-thirds majority of the States Parties present and voting, provided that such majority includes a majority of the States Parties.

Article 5
Term of office

1. The members of the Tribunal shall be elected for nine years and may be re-elected; provided, however, that of the members elected at the first election, the terms of seven members shall expire at the end of three years and the terms of seven more members shall expire at the end of six years.

2. The members of the Tribunal whose terms are to expire at the end of the above-mentioned initial periods of three and six years shall be chosen by lot to be drawn by the Secretary-General of the United Nations immediately after the first election.

3. The members of the Tribunal shall continue to discharge their duties until their places have been filled. Though replaced, they shall finish any proceedings which they may have begun before the date of their replacement.

4. In the case of the resignation of a member of the Tribunal, the letter of resignation shall be addressed to the President of the Tribunal. The place becomes vacant on the receipt of that letter.

Article 6
Vacancies

1. Vacancies shall be filled by the same method as that laid down for the first election, subject to the following provision: the Registrar shall, within one month of the occurrence of the vacancy, proceed to issue the invitations provided for in article 4 of this Annex, and the date of the election shall be fixed by the President of the Tribunal after consultation with the States Parties.

2. A member of the Tribunal elected to replace a member whose terms of office has not expired shall hold office for the remainder of his predecessor's term.

Article 7
Incompatible activities

1. No member of the Tribunal may exercise any political or administrative function, or associate actively with or be financially interested in any of the operations of any enterprise concerned with the exploration for or exploitation of the

resources of the sea or the sea-bed or other commercial use of the sea or the sea-bed.

2. No member of the Tribunal may act as agent, counsel or advocate in any case.

3. Any doubt on these points shall be resolved by decision of the majority of the other members of the Tribunal present.

Article 8
Conditions relating to participation of members in a particular case

1. No member of the Tribunal may participate in the decision of any case in which he has previously taken part as agent, counsel or advocate for one of the parties, or as a member of a national or international court or tribunal, or in any other capacity.

2. If, for some special reason, a member of the Tribunal considers that he should not take part in the decision of a particular case, he shall so inform the President of the Tribunal.

3. If the President considers that for some special reason one of the members of the Tribunal should not sit in a particular case, he shall give him notice accordingly.

4. Any doubt on these points shall be resolved by decision of the majority of the other members of the Tribunal present.

Article 9
Consequence of ceasing to fulfil required conditions

If, in the unanimous opinion of the other members of the Tribunal, a member has ceased to fulfil the required conditions, the President of the Tribunal shall declare the seat vacant.

Article 10
Privileges and immunities

The members of the Tribunal, when engaged on the business of the Tribunal, shall enjoy diplomatic privileges and immunities.

Article 11
Solemn declaration by members

Every member of the Tribunal shall, before taking up his duties, make a solemn declaration in open session that he will exercise his powers impartially and conscientiously.

Article 12
President, Vice-President and Registrar

1. The Tribunal shall elect its President and Vice-President for three years; they may be re-elected.

2. The Tribunal shall appoint its Registrar and may provide for the appointment of such other officers as may be necessary.

3. The President and the Registrar shall reside at the seat of the Tribunal.

Article 13
Quorum

1. All available members of the Tribunal shall sit; a quorum of 11 elected members shall be required to constitute the Tribunal.

2. Subject to article 17 of this Annex, the Tribunal shall determine which members are available to constitute the Tribunal for the consideration of a particular dispute, having regard to the effective functioning of the chambers as provided for in articles 14 and 15 of this Annex.

3. All disputes and applications submitted to the Tribunal shall be heard and determined by the Tribunal, unless article 14 of this Annex applies, or the parties request that it shall be dealt with in accordance with article 15 of this Annex.

Article 14
Sea-Bed Disputes Chamber

A Sea-Bed Disputes Chamber shall be established in accordance with the provisions of section 4 of this Annex. Its jurisdiction, powers and functions shall be as provided for in Part XI, section 5.

Article 15
Special chambers

1. The Tribunal may form such chambers, composed of three or more of its elected members, as it considers necessary for dealing with particular categories of disputes.

2. The Tribunal shall form a chamber for dealing with a particular dispute submitted to it if the parties so request. The composition of such a chamber shall be determined by the Tribunal with the approval of the parties.

3. With a view to the speedy dispatch of business, the Tribunal shall form annually a chamber composed of five of its elected members which may hear and determine disputes by summary procedure. Two alternative members shall be selected for

the purpose of replacing members who are unable to participate in a particular proceeding.

4. Disputes shall be heard and determined by the chambers provided for in this article if the parties so request.

5. A judgment given by any of the chambers provided for in this article and in article 14 of this Annex shall be considered as rendered by the Tribunal.

Article 16
Rules of the Tribunal

The Tribunal shall frame rules for carrying out its functions. In particular it shall lay down rules of procedure.

Article 17
Nationality of members

1. Members of the Tribunal of the nationality of any of the parties to a dispute shall retain their right to participate as members of the Tribunal.

2. If the Tribunal, when hearing a dispute, includes upon the bench a member of the nationality of one of the parties, any other party may choose a person to participate as a member of the Tribunal.

3. If the Tribunal, when hearing a dispute, does not include upon the bench a member of the nationality of the parties, each of those parties may choose a person to participate as a member of the Tribunal.

4. This article applies to the chambers referred to in articles 14 and 15 of this Annex. In such cases, the President, in consultation with the parties, shall request specified members of the Tribunal forming the chamber, as many as necessary, to give place to the members of the Tribunal of the nationality of the parties concerned, and, failing such, or if they are unable to be present, to the members specially chosen by the parties.

5. Should there be several parties in the same interest, they shall, for the purpose of the preceding provisions, be considered as one party only. Any doubt on this point shall be settled by the decision of the Tribunal.

6. Members chosen in accordance with paragraphs 2, 3 and 4 shall fulfil the conditions required by articles 2, 8 and 11 of this Annex. They shall participate in the decision on terms of complete equality with their colleagues.

Article 18
Remuneration of members

1. Each elected member of the Tribunal shall receive an annual allowance and, for each day on which he exercises his functions, a special allowance, provided that in any year the total sum payable to any member as special allowance shall not exceed the amount of the annual allowance.

2. The President shall receive a special annual allowance.

3. The Vice-President shall receive a special allowance for each day on which he acts as President.

4. The members chosen under article 17 of this Annex, other than elected members of the Tribunal, shall receive compensation for each day on which they exercise their functions.

5. The salaries, allowances and compensation shall be determined from time to time at meetings of the States Parties, taking into account the work load of the Tribunal. They may not be decreased during the term of office.

6. The salary of the Registrar shall be determined at meetings of the States Parties, on the proposal of the Tribunal.

7. Regulations adopted at meetings of the States Parties shall determine the conditions under which retirement pensions may be given to members of the Tribunal and to the Registrar, and the conditions under which members of the Tribunal and Registrar shall have their travelling expenses refunded.

8. The salaries, allowances, and compensation shall be free of all taxation.

Article 19
Expenses of the Tribunal

1. The expenses of the Tribunal shall be borne by the States Parties and by the Authority on such terms and in such a manner as shall be decided at meetings of the States Parties.

2. When an entity other than a State Party or the Authority is a party to a case submitted to it, the Tribunal shall fix the amount which that party is to contribute towards the expenses of the Tribunal.

Section 2. Competence

Article 20
Access to the Tribunal

1. The Tribunal shall be open to States Parties.

2. The Tribunal shall be open to entities other than States Parties in any case expressly provided for in Part XI or in any case submitted pursuant to any other agreement conferring jurisdiction on the Tribunal which is accepted by all the parties to that case.

Article 21
Jurisdiction

The jurisdiction of the Tribunal comprises all disputes and all applications submitted to it in accordance with this Convention and all matters specifically provided for in any other agreements which confers jurisdiction on the Tribunal.

Article 22
Reference of disputes subject to other agreements

If all the parties to a treaty or convention already in force and concerning the subject-matter covered by this Convention so agree, any disputes concerning the interpretation or application of such treaty or convention may, in accordance with such agreement, be submitted to the Tribunal.

Article 23
Applicable law

The Tribunal shall decide all disputes and applications in accordance with article 293.

Section 3. Procedure

Article 24
Institution of proceedings

1. Disputes are submitted to the Tribunal, as the case may be, either by notification of a special agreement or by written application, addressed to the Registrar. In either case, the subject of the dispute and the parties shall be indicated.

2. The Registrar shall forthwith notify the special agreement or the application to all concerned.

3. The Registrar shall also notify all States Parties.

Article 25
Provisional measures

1. In accordance with article 290, the Tribunal and its Sea-Bed Disputes Chamber shall have the power to prescribe provisional measures.

2. If the Tribunal is not in session or a sufficient number of members is not available to constitute a quorum, the provisional measures shall be prescribed by the chamber of summary procedure formed under article 15, paragraph 3, of this Annex. Notwithstanding article 15, paragraph 4, of this Annex, such provisional measures may be adopted at the request of any party to the dispute. They shall be subject to review and revision by the Tribunal.

Article 26
Hearing

1. The hearing shall be under the control of the President or, if he is unable to preside, of the Vice-President. If neither is able to preside, the senior judge present of the Tribunal shall preside.

2. The hearing shall be public, unless the Tribunal decides otherwise or unless the parties demand that the public be not admitted.

Article 27
Conduct of case

The Tribunal shall make orders for the conduct of the case, decide the form and time in which each party must conclude its arguments, and make all arrangements connected with the taking of evidence.

Article 28
Default

When one of the parties does not appear before the Tribunal or fails to defend its case, the other party may request the Tribunal to continue the proceedings and make its decision. Absence of a party or failure of a party to defend its case shall not constitute a bar to the proceedings. Before making its decision, the Tribunal must satisfy itself not only that it has jurisdiction over the dispute, but also that the claim is well founded in fact and law.

Article 29
Majority for decision

1. All questions shall be decided by a majority of the members of the Tribunal who are present.

2. In the event of an equality of votes, the President or the member of the Tribunal who acts in his place shall have a casting vote.

Article 30
Judgment

1. The judgment shall state the reasons on which it is based.
2. It shall contain the names of the members of the Tribunal who have taken part in the decision.
3. If the judgment does not represent in whole or in part the unanimous opinion of the members of the Tribunal, any member shall be entitled to deliver a separate opinion.
4. The judgment shall be signed by the President and by the Registrar. It shall be read in open court, due notice having been given to the parties to the dispute.

Article 31
Request to intervene

1. Should a State Party consider that it has an interest of a legal nature which may be affected by the decision in any dispute, it may submit a request to the Tribunal to be permitted to intervene.
2. It shall be for the Tribunal to decide upon this request.
3. If a request to intervene is granted, the decision of the Tribunal in respect of the dispute shall be binding upon the intervening State Party in so far as it relates to matters in respect of which that State Party intervened.

Article 32
Right to intervene in cases of interpretation or application

1. Whenever the interpretation or application of this Convention is in question, the Registrar shall notify all States Parties forthwith.
2. Whenever pursuant to article 21 or 22 of this Annex the interpretation or application of an international agreement is in question, the Registrar shall notify all the parties to the agreement.
3. Every party referred to in paragraphs 1 and 2 has the right to intervene in the proceedings; if it uses this right, the interpretation given by the judgment will be equally binding upon it.

Article 33
Finality and binding force of decisions

1. The decision of the Tribunal is final and shall be complied with by all the parties to the dispute.
2. The decision shall have no binding force except between the parties in respect of that particular dispute.
3. In the event of dispute as to the meaning or scope of the decision, the Tribunal shall construe it upon the request of any party.

Article 34
Costs

Unless otherwise decided by the Tribunal, each party shall bear its own costs.

Section 4. Sea-Bed Disputes Chamber

Article 35
Composition

1. The Sea-Bed Disputes Chamber referred to in article 14 of this Annex shall be composed of 11 members, selected by a majority of the elected members of the Tribunal from among them.
2. In the selection of the members of the Chamber, the representation of the principal legal systems of the world and equitable geographical distribution shall be assured. The Assembly of the Authority may adopt recommendations of a general nature relating to such representation and distribution.
3. The members of the Chamber shall be selected every three years and may be selected for a second term.
4. The Chamber shall elect its President from among its members, who shall serve for the term for which the Chamber has been selected.
5. If any proceedings are still pending at the end of any three-year period for which the Chamber has been selected, the Chamber shall complete the proceedings in its original composition.
6. If a vacancy occurs in the Chamber, the Tribunal shall select a successor from among its elected members, who shall hold office for the remainder of his predecessor's term.
7. A quorum of seven of the members selected by the Tribunal shall be required to constitute the Chamber.

Article 36
Ad Hoc Chambers

1. The Sea-Bed Disputes Chamber shall form an *ad hoc* chamber, composed of three of its members, for dealing with a particular dispute submitted to it in

accordance with article 188, paragraph 1(b). The composition of such a chamber shall be determined by the Sea-Bed Disputes Chamber with the approval of the parties.

2. If the parties do not agree on the composition of an *ad hoc* chamber, each party to the dispute shall appoint one member, and the third member shall be appointed by them in agreement. If they disagree, or if any party fails to make an appointment, the President of the Sea-Bed Disputes Chamber shall promptly make the appointment or appointments from among its members, after consultation with the parties.

3. Members of the *ad hoc* chamber must not be in the service of, or nationals of, any of the parties to the dispute.

Article 37
Access

The Chamber shall be open to the States Parties, the Authority and the other entities referred to in Part XI, section 5.

Article 38
Applicable law

In addition to the provisions of article 293, the Chamber shall apply;

(a) the rules, regulations and procedures of the Authority adopted in accordance with this Convention; and

(b) the terms of contracts concerning activities in the Area in matters relating to those contracts.

Article 39
Enforcement of decisions of the Chamber

The decisions of the Chamber shall be enforceable in the territories of the States Parties in the same manner as judgments or orders of the highest court of the State Party in whose territory the enforcement is sought.

Article 40
Applicability of other sections of this Annex

1. The other sections of this Annex which are not incompatible with this section apply to the Chamber.

2. In the exercise of its functions relating to advisory opinions, the Chamber shall be guided by the provisions of this Annex relating to procedure before the Tribunal to the extent to which it recognizes them to be applicable.

Section 5. Amendments

Article 41
Amendments

1. Amendments to this Annex, other than amendments to section 4, may be adopted only in accordance with article 313 or by consensus at a conference convened in accordance with this Convention.

2. Amendments to section 4 may be adopted only in accordance with article 314.

3. The Tribunal may propose such amendments to this Statute as it may consider necessary, by written communications to the States Parties for their consideration in conformity with paragraphs 1 and 2.

ANNEX VII

Arbitration

Article 1
Institution of proceedings

Subject to the provisions of Part XV, any party to a dispute may submit the dispute to the arbitral procedure provided for in this Annex by written notification addressed to the other party or parties to the dispute. The notification shall be accompanied by a statement of the claim and the grounds on which it is based.

Article 2
List of arbitrators

1. A list of arbitrators shall be drawn up and maintained by the Secretary-General of the United Nations. Every State Party shall be entitled to nominate four arbitrators, each of whom shall be a person experienced in maritime affairs and enjoying the highest reputation for fairness, competence and integrity. The names of the persons so nominated shall constitute the list.

2. If at any time the arbitrators nominated by a State Party in the list so constituted shall be fewer than four, that State Party shall be entitled to make further nominations as necessary.

3. The name of an arbitrator shall remain on the list until withdrawn by the State Party which made the nomination, provided that such arbitrator shall continue to serve on any arbitral tribunal to which that

arbitrator has been appointed until the completion of the proceedings before that arbitral tribunal.

Article 3
Constitution of arbitral tribunal

For the purpose of proceedings under this Annex, the arbitral tribunal shall, unless the parties otherwise agree, be constituted as follows:

(a) Subject to subparagraph (g), the arbitral tribunal shall consist of five members.

(b) The party instituting the proceedings shall appoint one member to be chosen preferably from the list referred to in article 2 of this Annex, who may be its national. The appointment shall be included in the notification referred to in article 1 of this Annex.

(c) The other party to the dispute shall, within 30 days of receipt of the notification referred to in article 1 of this Annex, appoint one member to be chosen preferably from the list, who may be its national. If the appointment is not made within that period, the party instituting the proceedings may, within two weeks of the expiration of that period, request that the appointment be made in accordance with subparagraph (e).

(d) The other three members shall be appointed by agreement between the parties. They shall be chosen preferably from the list and shall be nationals of third States unless the parties otherwise agree. The parties to the dispute shall appoint the President of the arbitral tribunal from among those three members. If, within 60 days of receipt of the notification referred to in article 1 of this Annex, the parties are unable to reach agreement on the appointment of one or more of the members of the tribunal to be appointed by agreement, or on the appointment of the President, the remaining appointment or appointments shall be made in accordance with subparagraph (e), at the request of a party to the dispute. Such request shall be made within two weeks of the expiration of the aforementioned 60-day period.

(e) Unless the parties agree that any appointment under subparagraphs (c) and (d) be made by a person or a third State chosen by the parties, the President of the International Tribunal for the Law of the Sea shall make the necessary appointments. If the President is unable to act under this subparagraph or is a national of one of the parties to the dispute, the appointment shall be made by the next senior member of the International Tribunal for the Law of the Sea who is available and is not a national of one of the parties. The appointments referred to in this subparagraph shall be made from the list referred to in article 2 of this Annex within a period of 30 days of the receipt of the request and in consultation with the parties. The members so appointed shall be of different nationalities and may not be in the service of, ordinarily resident in the territory of, or nationals of, any of the parties to the dispute.

(f) Any vacancy shall be filled in the manner prescribed for the initial appointment.

(g) Parties in the same interest shall appoint one member of the tribunal jointly by agreement. Where there are several parties having separate interests of where there is disagreement as to whether they are of the same interest, each of them shall appoint one member of the tribunal. The number of members of the tribunal appointed separately by the parties shall always be smaller by one than the number of members of the tribunal to be appointed jointly by the parties.

(h) In disputes involving more than two parties, the provisions of subparagraphs (a) to (f) shall apply to the maximum extent possible.

Article 4
Functions of arbitral tribunal

An arbitral tribunal constituted under article 3 of this Annex shall function in accordance with this Annex and the other provisions of this Convention.

Article 5
Procedure

Unless the parties to the dispute otherwise agree, the arbitral tribunal shall determine its own procedure, assuring to each party a full opportunity to be heard and to present its case.

Article 6
Duties of parties to a dispute

The parties to the dispute shall facilitate the work of the arbitral tribunal and, in particular, in accordance with their law and using all means at their disposal, shall:

(a) provide it with all relevant documents, facilities and information; and

(b) enable it when necessary to call witnesses or experts and receive their evidence and to visit the localities to which the case relates.

Article 7
Expenses

Unless the arbitralt tribunal decides otherwise because of the particular circumstances of the case, the expenses of the tribunal, including the remuneration of its members, shall be borne by the parties to the dispute in equal shares.

Article 8
Required majority for decisions

Decisions of the arbitral tribunal shall be taken by a majority vote of its members. The absence or abstention of less than half of the members shall not constitute a bar to the tribunal reaching a decision. In the event of an equality of votes, the President shall have a casting vote.

Article 9
Default of appearance

If one of the parties to the dispute does not appear before the arbitral tribunal or fails to defend its case, the other party may request the tribunal to continue the proceedings and to make its award. Absence of a party or failure of a party to defend its case shall not constitute a bar to the proceedings. Before making its award, the arbitral tribunal must satisfy itself not only that it has jurisdiction over the dispute but also that the claim is well founded in fact and law.

Article 10
Award

The award of the arbitral tribunal shall be confined to the subject-matter of the dispute and state the reasons on which it is based. It shall contain the names of the members who have participated and the date of the award. Any member of the tribunal may attach a separate or dissenting opinion to the award.

Article 11
Finality of award

The award shall be final and without appeal, unless the parties to the dispute have agreed in advance to an appellate procedure. It shall be complied with by the parties to the dispute.

Article 12
Interpretation or implementation of award

1. Any controversy which may arise between the parties to the dispute as regards the interpretation or manner of implementation of the award may be submitted by either party for decision to the arbitral tribunal which made the award. For this purpose, any vacancy in the tribunal shall be filled in the manner provided for in the original appointments of the members of the tribunal.

2. Any such controversy may be submitted to another court or tribunal under article 287 by agreement of all the parties to the dispute.

Article 13
Application to entities other than States Parties

The provisions of this Annex shall apply *mutatis mutandis* to any dispute involving entities other than States Parties.

ANNEX VIII

Special Arbitration

Article 1
Institution of proceedings

Subject to Part XV, any party to a dispute concerning the interpretation or application of the articles of this Convention relating to (1) fisheries, (2) protection and preservation of the marine environment, (3) marine scientific research, or (4) navigation, including pollution from vessels and by dumping, may submit the dispute to the special arbitral procedure provided for in this Annex by written notification addressed to the other party or parties to the dispute. The notification shall be accompanied by a statement of the claim and the grounds on which it is based.

Article 2
Lists of experts

1. A list of experts shall be established and maintained in respect of each of the fields of (1) fisheries, (2) protection and preservation of the marine environment, (3) marine scientific research, and (4)

navigation, including pollution from vessels and by dumping.

2. The lists of experts shall be drawn up and maintained, in the field of fisheries by the Food and Agriculture Organization of the United Nations, in the field of protection and preservation of the marine environment by the United Nations Environment Programme, in the field of marine scientific research by the Inter-Governmental Oceanographic Commission, in the field of navigation, including pollution from vessels and by dumping, by the International Maritime Organization, or in each case by the appropriate subsidiary body concerned to which such organization, programme or commission has delegated this function.

3. Every State Party shall be entitled to nominate two experts in each field whose competence in the legal, scientific or technical aspects of such field is established and generally recognized and who enjoy the highest reputation for fairness and integrity. The names of the persons so nominated in each field shall constitute the appropriate list.

4. If at any time the experts nominated by a State Party in the list so constituted shall be fewer than two, that State Party shall be entitled to make further nominations as necessary.

5. The name of an expert shall remain on the list until withdrawn by the State Party which made the nomination, provided that such expert shall continue to serve on any special arbitral tribunal to which that expert has been appointed until the completion of the proceedings before that special arbitral tribunal.

Article 3
Constitution of special arbitral tribunal

For the purpose of proceedings under this Annex, the special arbitral tribunal shall, unless the parties otherwise agree, be constituted as follows:

(a) Subject to subparagraph (g), the special arbitral tribunal shall consist of five members.

(b) The party instituting the proceedings shall appoint two members to be chosen preferably from the appropriate list or lists referred to in article 2 of this Annex relating to the matters in dispute, one of whom may be its national. The appointments shall be included in the notification referred to in article 1 of this Annex.

(c) The other party to the dispute shall, within 30 days of receipt of the notification referred to in article 1 of this Annex, appoint two members to be chosen preferably from the appropriate list or lists relating to the matters in dispute, one of whom may be its national. If the appointments are not made within that period, the party instituting the proceedings may, within two weeks of the expiration of that period, request that the appointments be made in accordance with subparagraph (e).

(d) The parties to the dispute shall by agreement appoint the President of the special arbitral tribunal, chosen preferably from the appropriate list, who shall be a national of a third State, unless the parties otherwise agree. If, within 30 days of receipt of the notification referred to in article 1 of this Annex, the parties are unable to reach agreement on the appointment of the President, the appointment shall be made in accordance with subparagraph (e), at the request of a party to the dispute. Such request shall be made within two weeks of the expiration of the aforementioned 30-day period.

(e) Unless the parties agree that the appointment be made by a person or a third State chosen by the parties, the Secretary-General of the United Nations shall make the necessary appointments within 30 days of receipt of a request under subparagraphs (c) and (d). The appointments referred to in this subparagraph shall be made from the appropriate list or lists of experts referred to in article 2 of this Annex and in consultation with the parties to the dispute and the appropriate international organization. The members so appointed shall be of different nationalities and may not be in the service of, ordinarily resident in the territory of, or nationals of, any of the parties to the dispute.

(f) Any vacancy shall be filled in the manner prescribed for the initial appointment.

(g) Parties in the same interest shall appoint two members of the tribunal jointly by agreement. Where there are several parties having separate interest or where there is disagreement as to whether they are of the same interest, each of them shall appoint one member of the tribunal.

(h) In disputes involving more than two parties, the provisions of subparagraphs (a) to (f) shall apply to the maximum extent possible.

Article 4
General provisions

Annex VII, articles 4 to 13, apply *mutatis mutandis* to the special arbitration proceedings in accordance with this Annex.

Article 5
Fact finding

1. The parties to a dispute concerning the interpretation or application of the provisions of this Convention relating to (1) fisheries, (2) protection and preservation of the marine environment, (3) marine scientific research, or (4) navigation, including pollution from vessels and by dumping, may at any time agree to request a special arbitral tribunal constituted in accordance with article 3 of this Annex to carry out an inquiry and establish the facts giving rise to the dispute.

2. Unless the parties otherwise agree, the findings of fact of the special arbitral tribunal acting in accordance with paragraph 1, shall be considered as conclusive as between the parties.

3. If all the parties to the dispute so request, the special arbitral tribunal may formulate recommendations which, without having the force of a decision, shall only constitute the basis for a review by the parties of the questions giving rise to the dispute.

4. Subject to paragraph 2, the special arbitral tribunal shall act in accordance with the provisions of this Annex, unless the parties otherwise agree.

ANNEX IX

Participation by International Organizations

Article 1
Use of terms

For the purposes of article 305 and of this Annex, "international organization" means an intergovernmental organization constituted by States to which its member States have transferred competence over matters governed by this Convention, including the competence to enter into treaties in respect of those matters.

Article 2
Signature

An international organization may sign this Convention if a majority of its member States are signatories of this Convention. At the time of signature an international organization shall make a declaration specifying the matters governed by this Convention in respect of which competence has been transferred to that organization by its member States which are signatories, and the nature and extent of that competence.

Article 3
Formal confirmation and accession

1. An international organization may deposit its instrument of formal confirmation or of accession if a majority of its member States deposit or have deposited their instruments of ratification or accession.

2. The instruments deposited by the international organization shall contain the undertakings and declarations required by articles 4 and 5 of this Annex.

Article 4
Extent of participation and rights and obligations

1. The instrument of formal confirmation or of accession of an international organization shall contain an undertaking to accept the rights and obligations of States under this Convention in respect of matters relating to which competence has been transferred to it by its member States which are Parties to this Convention.

2. An international organization shall be a Party to this Convention to the extent that it has competence in accordance with the declarations, communications of information or notifications referred to in article 5 of this Annex.

3. Such an international organization shall exercise the rights and perform the obligations which its member States which are Parties would otherwise have under this Convention, on matters relating to which competence has been transferred to it by those member States. The member States of that international organization shall not exercise competence which they have transferred to it.

4. Participation of such an international organization shall in no case entail an increase of the representation to which its member States which are States Parties

would otherwise be entitled, including rights in decision-making.

5. Participation of such an international organization shall in no case confer any rights under this Convention on member States of the organization which are not States Parties to this Convention.

6. In the event of a conflict between the obligations of an international organization under this Convention and its obligations under the agreement establishing the organization or any acts relating to it, the obligations under this Convention shall prevail.

Article 5
Declarations, notifications and communications

1. The instrument of formal confirmation or of accession of an international organization shall contain a declaration specifying the matters governed by this Convention in respect of which competence has been transferred to the organization by its member States which are Parties to this Convention.

2. A member State of an international organization shall, at the time it ratifies or accedes to this Convention or at the time when the organization deposits its instrument of formal confirmation or of accession, whichever is later, make a declaration specifying the matters governed by this Convention in respect of which it has transferred competence to the organization.

3. States Parties which are member States of an international organization which is a Party to this Convention shall be presumed to have competence over all matters governed by this Convention in respect of which transfers of competence to the organization have not been specifically declared, notified or communicated by those States under this article.

4. The international organization and its member States which are States Parties shall promptly notify the depositary of this Convention of any changes to the distribution of competence, including new transfers of competence, specified in the declaration under paragraphs 1 and 2.

5. Any State Party may request an international organization and its member States which are States Parties to provide information as to which, as between the organization and its member States, has competence in respect of any specific question which has arisen. The organization and the member States concerned shall provide this information within a reasonable time. The international organization and the member States may also, on their own initiative, provide this information.

6. Declarations, notifications and communications of information under this article shall specify the nature and extent of the competence transferred.

Article 6
Responsibility and liability

1. Parties which have competence under article 5 of this Annex shall have responsibility for failure to comply with obligations or for any other violation of this Convention.

2. Any State Party may request an international organization or its member States which are State Parties for information as to who has responsibility in respect of any specific matter. The organization and the member States concerned shall provide this information. Failure to provide this information within a reasonable time or the provision of contradictory information shall result in joint and several liability.

Article 7
Settlement of disputes

1. At the time of deposit of its instrument of formal confirmation or of accession, or at any time thereafter, an international organization shall be free to choose, by means of a written declaration, one or more of the means for the settlement of disputes concerning the interpretation or application of this Convention, referred to in article 287, paragraph 1(a), (c) or (d).

2. Part XV applies *mutatis mutandis* to any dispute between Parties to this Convention, one or more of which are international organizations.

3. When an international organization and one or more of its member States are joint parties to a dispute, or parties in the same interest, the organization shall be deemed to have accepted the same procedures for the settlement of disputes as the member States; when, however, a member State has chosen only the International Court of Justice under article 287, the organization and the member State concerned shall be deemed to have accepted

arbitration in accordance with Annex VII, unless the parties to the dispute otherwise agree.

Article 8

Applicability of Part XVII

Part XVII applies *mutatis mutandis* to an international organization, except in respect of the following:

(a) the instrument of formal confirmation or of accession of an international organization shall not be taken into account in the application of article 308, paragraph 1;

(b)(i) an international organization shall have exclusive capacity with respect to the application of articles 312 and 315, to the extent that it has competence under article 5 of this Annex over the entire subject-matter of the amendment;

(ii) the instrument of formal confirmation or of accession of an international organization to an amendment, the entire subject-matter over which the international organization has competence under article 5 of this Annex, shall be considered to be the instrument of ratification or accession of each of the member States which are States Parties, for the purposes of applying article 316, paragraphs 1, 2 and 3;

(iii) the instrument of formal confirmation or of accession of the international organization shall not be taken into account in the application of article 316, paragraphs 1 and 2, with regard to all other amendments;

(c)(i) an international organization may not denounce this Convention in accordance with article 317 if any of its member States is a State Party and if it continues to fulfil the qualifications specified in article 1 of this Annex;

(ii) an international organization shall denounce this Convention when none of its member States is a State Party or if the international organization no longer fulfils the qualifications specified in article 1 of this Annex. Such denunciation shall take effect immediately.

Appendix 2

Maritime Journals (including Annuals)

Listed in this appendix are current newspapers, journals and annuals dealing with various aspects of maritime affairs, grouped according to subject-matter and classified as international or by country under each subject-matter heading.

Abbreviations used in the following pages are as follows:

a. = annual
d. = daily
f. = fortnightly
irr. = irregular
m. = monthly
qu. = quarterly
w. = weekly

Maritime Law

Diritto Marittimo (in Italian, English & French) (qu.)
Francesco Berlingeri, via Roma 10/2, Genoa, Italy

Le Droit Maritime Français (m.)
190 blvd. Haussmann, 75008 Paris, France

Journal of Shipping, Customs and Transport Law (m.)
Milan Law Publishers, Box 4591, 15–2 Navjivan, Bombay 400008, India

Lega Navale (m.)
Lega Navale Italiana, via 24 Maggio 11. 00187 Rome, Italy

Lloyd's Maritime and Commercial Law Quarterly
Lloyd's of London Press, Sheepen Place, Colchester, Essex CO3 3LP, UK

Marine Policy (qu.)
Butterworth Scientific Ltd., Box 63, Westbury House, Bury St., Guildford, Surrey GU2 5BH, England

Maritime Lawyer (semi-a.)
Tulane Univ. School of Law, New Orleans, LA 70118, USA

Proceedings of the Law of the Sea Institute
University of Hawaii, 2444 Dole St., Honolulu, Hawaii 96822, USA

Recht der Schiffahrt (Maritime Law Review) (bi-m.)
Otto Meissners Verlag, Schlossstr. 10, Postfach 106, 2122 Bleckede, Fed. Rep. of Germany

Ships, Shipping, Shipbuilding and Ports

INTERNATIONAL

AISM/IALA Bulletin (qu.)
International Association of Lighthouse Authorities, 13 rue Yvon Villarceau, 75116 Paris, France

Alamar Informativo (w.)
Asociación Latinoamericana de Armadores, Casilla de Correo 767, Montevideo, Uruguay

Al-Mersa Newsletter; Annual Review; ASRY News (bi-m.)
Arab Shipbuilding & Repair Yard Co., P.O. Box 5110, Manama, Bahrain

Annual Report
Comité des Associations d'Armateurs des Communautés Européennes, rue Joseph II, 5, B-1040 Brussels, Belgium

Annual Report; Traffic Report (a.)
St Lawrence Seaway Authority, Tower A, Place de Ville, 320 Queen St., Ottawa K1R 5A3, Canada

Annual Report
West Indies Shipping Corporation, P.O. Box 448, POS Trinidad, West Indies

Arab Shipping (a.)
Seatrade, Fairfax House, Colchester, Essex CO1 1RJ, England

Bohman Ocean Shipping News Summary (m.)
335 E Broadway, Gardner, MA 01440, USA

Brandon's Shipper and Forwarder (w.)
One World Trade Center, Suite 3169, New York, NY 10048, USA

The Bulk Carrier Register (a.)
H. Clarkson & Co. Ltd., 12 Camomile St., London EC3A 7BP, England

Bulk Systems International (m.)
C. S. Publications Ltd., 54 Cheam Common Rd., Worcester Park, Surrey KT4 8RJ, England

CMI Newsletter (qu.)
Comité Maritime International, 17 Borzestraat, B-2000 Antwerp, Belgium

Comecon Merchant Ships Annual (bi-a.)
Kenneth Mason Publications Ltd., The Old Harbourmaster's, 8 North St., Emsworth, Hants PO10 7DD, England

Containerisation International (m.)
National Magazine Co. Ltd., 72 Broadwick St., London W1V 2BP, England

Croner's World Directory of Freight Conferences (m.)
Croner Publications Ltd., 173 Kingston Rd., New Malden, Surrey KT3 3SS, England

Directory of Shipowners, Shipbuilders & Marine Engineers (a.)
Industrial Press, Business Press International, Sutton, Surrey SM2 5AS, England

European Rig & Supply Ship Owners (including *Offshore Bases*) (a.)
Selvig Publishing, P.O. Box 9070, Vaterland, Oslo 1, Norway (& K. J. Hendry, West House, West St., Faversham, Kent ME13 7JB, England)

Fairplay International Shipping Weekly; Fairplay World Shipping Year Book
Fairplay Publications Ltd., 52–54 Southwark St., London SE1, England

Far East Shipping (a.)
Seatrade Publications Ltd., Fairfax House, Colchester, Essex CO1 1RJ, England

Ford's Freighter Travel Guide (semi-a.); *Ford's International Cruise Guide* (qu.)
Ford's Travel Guides, Box 505, 22151 Clarendon St., Woodland Hills, CA 19365, USA

Freighter Travel News (m.)
Freighter Travel Club of America, Box 12693, Salem, OR 97309, USA

Hellenic Shipping International (bi-m.)
26–27 Conduit St., London W1, England

Holiday Calendar (a.)
BIMCO, 19 Kristianiagade, DK-2100, Copenhagen, Denmark

ICMA Bulletin
International Christian Maritime Association, 81 Orwell Rd., Felixstowe, IP11 7PY, England

ICMM Newsletter (2 a year)
International Congress of Maritime Museums, c/o Mystic Seaport Inc., Mystic, CT 06355, USA

The International Hydrographic Review (2 a year)
B. P. 345, MC 98000 Monaco

International Shipbuilding Progress (m.)
Inpress, 193 Heemraadssingel, 3023 CB Rotterdam, Netherlands

International Shipping and Shipbuilding Directory (a.)
Benn Publications Ltd., Sovereign Way, Tonbridge, Kent TN9 1RW, England

International Transport Journal—Overseas Digest/Internationale Transport-Zeitschrift/Journal pour le Transport International (w.)
Rittmann Ltd., Postfach 4000, Basle 3, Switzerland

Latin American Shipping (a.)
Seatrade, Fairfax House, Colchester, Essex CO1 1RJ, England

Jane's Freight Containers (a.)
Jane's Yearbooks, 238 City Rd., London EC1V 2PU, England

Liquid Gas Carrier Register (a.)
H. Clarkson & Co. Ltd., 12 Camomile St., London EC3A 7BP, England

Lloyd's European Loading List (w.); *Lloyd's List* (d.); *Lloyd's Maritime Directory—International Shipping and Shipbuilding Directory* (a.); *Lloyd's Monthly List of Laid-Up Vessels; Lloyd's Nautical Year Book; Lloyd's Voyage Record* (w.); *Lloyd's Weekly Casualty Reports*

Lloyd's of London Press, Sheepen Place, Colchester CO3 3LP, England

Lloyd's Register Book (a.)
Lloyd's Register Printing House, Manor Royal, Crawley, West Sussex RH10 2QN, England

Marine Directory (a.)
Simmons Boardman Publishing Corp., 345 Hudson St., New York, NY 10014, USA

Marine Propulsion International (m.)
Fuel and Metallurgical Journals Ltd., Queensway House, 2 Queensway, Redhill, Surrey RH1 1QS, England

Marine Stores International (10 a year)
Industrial Newspapers Ltd., Queensway House, Queensway, Redhill, Surrey RH1 1QS, England

Mariner (qu.)
Marconi International Marine Co. Ltd., Elettra House, Westway, Chelmsford, Essex CM1 3BH, England

The Nautical Magazine
Arab Maritime Transport Academy, Sharjah, United Arab Emirates

OAG Worldwide Cruise and Shipline Guide (6 a year)
Official Airlines Guides Inc., 2000 Clearwater Dr., Oak Brook, IL 60521, USA

The Offshore Service Vessel Register (a.)
H. Clarkson & Co. Ltd., 12 Camomile St., London EC3A 7BP, England

Ports and Harbors (10 a year)
International Association of Ports and Harbors, Kotohira Kaikan Bldg., 1-2-8, Toranomon, Minato-ku, Tokyo 105, Japan

Ports of the World (a.)
Benn Publications Ltd., Sovereign Way, Tonbridge, Kent TN9 1RW, England

Reed's Special Ships (m.)
Thomas Reed Publications Ltd., Saracen's Head Bldgs., 36–37 Cock Lane, London EC1A 9BY, England

Safety at Sea International (m.)
Fuel & Metallurgical Journals Ltd., Queensway House, 2 Queensway, Redhill, Surrey RH1 1QS, England

Scandinavian Fishing and Coastal Vessels (a.)
Selvig Publishing, P.O. Box 9070, Vaterland, Oslo 1, Norway (& K. J. Hendry, West House, West St., Faversham, Kent ME13 7JB, England)

Scandinavian Shipping Gazette (m.)
Nyt Skandinavisk Forlag, Bernhard Bangsalle 28, DK-2000 Copenhagen, Denmark

The Sea (bi-m.)
The Missions to Seamen, St. Michael Paternoster Royal, College Hill, London EC4R 2RL, England

Ship & Boat International (10 a year); *Shipbuilding and Marine Engineering International* (10 a year)
Whitehall Press Ltd., Earl House, 27 Earl St., Maidstone, Kent ME14 1DE, England

Shipping Statistics and Economics (m.); *Shipping Studies* (10 a year); *Shipping Surveys* (2–4 times a year)
H. P. Drewry (Shipping Consultants) Ltd., 34 Brock St., London W1Y 2LL, England

Shipping World & Shipbuilder (m.)
Marine Publications International Ltd., 42–43 Lower Marsh, London SE1 7RQ, England

The Tanker Register (a.)
H. Clarkson & Co. Ltd., 12 Camomile St., London EC3 7BP, England

Tug World Newsletter (qu.)
Thomas Reed Publications Ltd., 36–37 Cock Lane, London EC1A 9BY, England

Windjammer (qu.)
Mariners International Club, 58 Woodville Rd., Barnet, Herts. EN5 5NG, England

World Bulk Fleet (semi-a.)
Box 1158, Sentrum, Oslo 1, Norway

World Dredging and Marine Construction (m.)
(Wodcon Association) Symcon Publishing Co., 44 Ocean Bld., Box 31, Long Beach, CA 90802, USA

World Ports (8 a year)
Amundsen Publications Inc., 1612 K St. NW, Washington DC 20006, USA

World Ports and Harbours News (m.)
BHRA Fluid Engineering, Cranfield, Bedford MK43 0AT, England

World Ships on Order (qu.)
Fairplay Publications Ltd., 52–54 Southwark St., London SE1 1UJ, England

World Tanker Fleet Review (bi-a.)
John I. Jacobs plc, 5 Devonshire Square, London EC2M 4YD, England

World Wide Shipping Guide (a.); *WWS/World Ports* (7 a year)
77 Moehring Drive, Blauvelt, NY 10913, USA

Yearbook
International Hydrographic Organization, B.P. 345, MC 98000, Monaco

Yearbook (Annuaire)
Comité Maritime International, 17 Borzestraat, B-2000 Antwerp, Belgium

ARGENTINA

Industria Naval (w.)
Blumenau SACIFIA, Lavalle 1672, Buenos Aires, Argentina

Navitécnica y Comercio Marítimo (m.)
Navitécnica SA, Alsina 1360, Buenos Aires, Argentina

Review of the River Plate (3 a month)
Bulnes 44, 1176, Casilla 294, Buenos Aires 1413, Argentina

AUSTRALIA

Annual Report
Maritime Services Board of NSW, Box 32, GPO Sydney NSW, Australia

Asia Pacific Work and Patrol Boat (m.)
Baird Publications Pty. Ltd., 427 Chapel St., South Yarra 3141, GPO Box 2673 X, Melbourne 3001, Australia

Australian "Seatrader" (qu.)
14 Bent St., Greenwich, Sydney 2065, Australia

Freight and Container Transportation (m.)
Shennen Publishing & Publicity Co., 64 Kippax St., Surry Hills, NSW 2010, Australia

Navigation (a.)
Australian Institute of Navigation, P.O. Box 2250, Sydney, NSW, Australia

Port Statistics Handbook (a.); *Ports of NSW* (journal)
Maritime Services Board of NSW, Box 32, GPO Sydney, NSW, Australia

Slipway (qu.)
Federated Shipwrights and Ship Constructors Association of Australia, 188 George St., Sydney, NSW 2000, Australia

BANGLADESH

Karnaphuli Shipping News (2 a week)
86 Ghatforhadbeg, Kazem Ali Rd., Chittagong, Bangladesh

BELGIUM

Annual Report and Statistics
Belgische Redersvereniging/Union des Armateurs Belges, Lijnwaadmarkt 9, B-2000 Antwerp, Belgium

Courrier Nautique (m.)
8 rue du Sceptre, B-1040 Brussels, Belgium

Hinterland (of port of Antwerp) (qu.)
Publitra PVBA, Brouwersvliet 33, 2000 Antwerp, Belgium

Mededelingen (a.)
Académie de Marine, Steenplein 1, Antwerp, Belgium

Quotidien International des Transports (d.)
5300 Fr. Lloyd Anversois SA, Eiermarkt 23, B-2000 Antwerp, Belgium

BRAZIL

Navigator (semi-a.)
Ministerio da Marinha, Serviço de Documentação Geral da Marinha, Rua Dom Manuel 15, 20010 Rio de Janeiro RJ, Brazil

Portos e Navios (m.)
Revista Técnica e Informativa Ltda., Rua Leandro Martíns 10, CP 2791, ZC 05, Rio de Janeiro, Brazil

Revista Marítima Brasileira (qu.)
SDGM, Rua D. Manuel 15, 30, Centro, Rio de Janeiro CEP 20.010, Brazil

BULGARIA

Korabostroene i Koraboplavane (Shipbuilding and Shipping) (m.)
Ministerstvo na Transporta, Sofia, Bulgaria (distr. by Hemus, 6 Rouski Blvd., 1000 Sofia, Bulgaria)

CAMEROON

Cameroon Inter-Ports (qu.)
Office National des Ports, P.O. Box 4020, Douala, Cameroon

CANADA

Canadian Forwarder (bi-w.)
Trenholme Ave., Montreal H4B 1X9, Canada

Canadian Shipping and Marine Engineering News (m.)
Arthurs Publications Ltd., 5200 Dixie Rd., Suite 204, Mississauga, Ontario, Canada

Harbour and Shipping (m.)
Progress Publishing Co. Ltd., C-310 Marine Bldg., 355 Burrard St., Vancouver, BC V6C 2G6, Canada

Marine Trades (qu.)
Arthurs Publications Ltd., Suite 204, 5200 Dixie Rd., Mississauga, Ont., Canada

Radio Aids to Marine Navigation (qu.)
Transport Canada, Telecommunications & Electronics Branch, Ottawa, Ont., Canada

Seaports and the Shipping World (m.)
Gallery Publications Ltd., 4634 St Catherine St. W, Montreal, Que. H3Z 2W6, Canada

Shipping Register and Shipbuilder (bi-m.)
Anchor Press, 1434 St Catherine St. W, Montreal, Que., Canada

CHILE

Mar (m.)
Liga Marítima de Chile, Box 117-V, Valparaíso, Chile

CHINA

Jian-Chuan Zhishi (Naval and Merchant Ships) (m.)
Guoji Shudian, P.O. Box 339, Beijing, China

Ship Engineering (bi-m.); *Ship Knowledge* (m.); *Shipbuilding of China* (qu.)
The Chinese Society of Naval Architecture and Marine Engineering, P.O. Box 817, Beijing, China

CYPRUS

Annual Report
Cyprus Ports Authority, P.O. Box 2007, Nicosia, Cyprus

DENMARK

Danmarks Skibsfart
Danmarks Skibsførerforening, Havnegade 55, 1058 Copenhagen K, Denmark

Nyt Navigatør (10 a year)
Navigatørnes Hus, Havnegade 55, 1058 Copenhagen K, Denmark

Skibs og Baadebygning (10 a year)
A. og B. Mogensen Ap.S., Hambros Alle 3, 2900 Hellerup, Denmark

Søfart (m.)
Association for the Promotion of the Danish Merchant Marine, Dampfaergevej 3, 2100 Copenhagen OE, Denmark

FINLAND

The Aaland Shipping Gazette (bi-m.); *Annual Report*
Aalands Redarförening r.f., 31 Aalandsvägen, 22100 Mariehamn, Aalands Islands, Finland

Navigator (m.)
Oy Laivastolethi, Annankatu 25 A 52, 00100 Helsinki 10, Finland

FRANCE

Antenne (d.)
17, rue Venture, 13231 Marseille Cédex, France

Avis aux Navigateurs (w.)
EDSHOM, B.P. 426, 29275 Brest Cédex, France

Bateaux (m.)
Socpresse, 14 rue Brunel, 75017, Paris, France (& Fay Redding Associates, 30 Moffat's Close, Sandhurst, Camberley, Surrey, GU17 8EN, England)

Bureau Véritas Bulletin Technique (m. in French, 4 a year in English).
38 bis rue Paul Vaillant-Couturier, 92300 Levaillois-Perret, France

Courrier de la Compagnie Générale Maritime (qu.)
Tour Winterthur, Cédex 18, 92095 Paris, France (& Focal House, 84-90 East St., Barking, Essex, England)

Industries Nautiques (qu.)
Editions de Chabassol, 30 rue de Gramont, 75002 Paris, France

Le Journal de la Marine Marchande (w.)
190 blvd. Haussmann, 75008 Paris, France

Journal de la Navigation (w.)
Société d'Editions Commerciales et Techniques, 29 blvd. Henri IV, 75004 Paris, France

Le Modèle Réduit de Bateau (m.)
Publications M.R.A., 12 rue Mulet, 69001 Lyon, France

Navigation (qu.)
Institut Français de Navigation, 3 av. Octave Gréard, 75007 Paris, France

Navires, Ports et Chantiers (m.)
190 blvd. Haussmann, 75008, Paris, France

Petit Perroquet (bi-m.)
Editions des 4 Seigneurs, 39 rue Marceau, 38000 Grenoble, France

GERMAN DEMOCRATIC REPUBLIC

Annual Report
DDR-Schiffs-Revision und -Klassifikation, DDR-1615 Zeuthen bei Berlin, Eichenallee 12, German Dem. Rep.

Schiffbauforschung (qu.)
VEB Kombinat Schiffbau, Stammbetrieb, Döranerstr. 110/111, 25 Rostock, German Dem. Rep.

Seewirtschaft (m.)
VEB Verlag Technik, Postfach 201, 1020 Berlin, German Dem. Rep.

Wissenschaftliche Beiträge (4 a year)
Ingenieurhochschule für Seefahrt, 2530 Rostock-Warnemünde, Richard-Wagner-Str., German Dem. Rep.

FEDERAL REPUBLIC OF GERMANY

Antrieb (bi-m.)
Verein der Schiffsingenieure in Bremen e.V., Geeren 26/28, 2800 Bremen 1, Fed. Rep. of Germany

Cargoworld (m.); *Die Deutsche Handelsflotte* (a.); *Hamburger Hafen-Nachrichten* (w.)
Seehafen-Verlag Erik Blumenfeld GmbH & Co., Postfach 105 605, 2000 Hamburg, Fed. Rep. of Germany

Hansa Shipping-Shipbuilding-Ports (bi-m.)
Schiffahrts-Verlag Hansa C. Schroedter GmbH & Co. KG, Stubbenhuk 10, 2000 Hamburg 11, Fed. Rep. of Germany
Kehrwieder
Verband Deutscher Reeder, Postfach 305 840, 2000 Hamburg, 36, Fed. Rep. of Germany

Schiffahrt International (m.)
Köhlers Verlagsgesellschaft mbH Postfach 2352, 4900 Herford, Fed. Rep. of Germany

Schiffstechnik (4 a year); *Transport-Dienst* (w.)
Schiffahrts-Verlag Hansa C. Schroedter GmbH & Co., KG, Stubbenhuk 10, 2000 Hamburg 11, Fed. Rep. of Germany

Der Seewart (6 a year)
Kommissions-Verlag Eckardt und Messtorff, Rödingsmarkt 16, 2000 Hamburg 11, Fed. Rep. of Germany

Shipping Statistics (m.)
Institut für Seeverkehrswirtschaft, Börsenhof A, Am Dom 5a, 2800 Bremen 1, Fed. Rep. of Germany

GREECE

Naftika Chronika (in English & Greek) (m.)
Box 76, Piraeus 77, Greece

Naftiki Ellas (m.)
Papangopoulou St., Athens 2, Greece

Naftiliaka Nea (f.)
6 Dragatsaniou St., Athens, Greece

Naftiliaki (m.)
4–6 Efplias St., P.O. Box 162, Piraeus, Greece

Naftiliaka Nea (f.)
6 Dragatsaniou St., Athens, Greece

Naftiliaki (m.)
4–6 Efplias St., P.O. Box 162, Piraeus, Greece

Output (m.)
T. & T. Publishing & Trading Co., 8 Aristotelus St., P.O. Box 19107, Makrygianni, Athens, Greece (& K. Hendry Publishers Consultants Ltd., West Ave., West St., Faversham, Kent, England)

GUYANA

Transport and Harbours Department—Annual Report.
Battery Rd., Kingston, Georgetown, Guyana

HONG KONG

Asian Shipping (m.)
Asia Trade Journals Ltd., Box 20014, Hennessy Rd., Hong Kong

Cargonews Asia (m.)
Trade News Asia Pte. Ltd., Room 1913, Hanglung Centre, 2-20 Paterson St., Causeway Bay, Hong Kong

Marintec China Journal (bi-m.)
Marintec Press (Far East) Ltd., 1108 Swire House, Hong Kong (& Marintec Press (Europe) Ltd., 54 Station Rd. East, Oxted, Surrey, England)

Modern Marine Technology (in Chinese) (a.)
Asia Trade Journals Ltd., P.O. Box 20014, Hennessy Rd., Hong Kong

INDIA

Indian Shipping (m.)
Indian National Shipowners Association, 22 Maker Tower F, Cuffe Parade, Bombay 400 005, India

Indian Shipping and Shipbuilding (m.)
V. S. Chhabra, 5 B Bakhtavar, Nariman Point, Bombay 400 021, India

Journal
Institution of Marine Technology, c/o Ericson & Richards, 32 Nicol Rd., Ballard Estate, Bombay 400 038, India

Oceanite (qu.)
Maritime Union of India, Udyog Bhavan, 4th floor, 29 Walchand Hirachand Marg, Ballard Estate, Bombay 400 038, India

Shipping and Marine Industries Journal (qu.)
V. J. Joseph, 3 Radhe Nivas, 36th Rd., Bandra, Bombay 400 050, India

Shipyard Review (in English & Telugu) (qu.)
Hindustan Shipyard Ltd., Visakhapatnam 5, India

INDONESIA

Dunia Maritim (m.)
Directorate General of Sea Communications, Jl. Merdeka Timur 5, Jakarta, Indonesia

Warta Ekonomi Maritim Review for Entrepreneurs (m.)
Maritime Press Foundation, Jalan Raya Pelabuhan No. 7, Tandjung Priok, Jakarta, Indonesia

ISRAEL

Business Digest Trade Lists (incl. shipping movements) (w.)
37 Harbour St, Haifa, Israel

Sapanut (Shipping)
Israel Shipping and Aviation Research Institute, P.O.B. 1860, Haifa, Israel

The Sea (2 a year)
Israel Maritime League, Hane'emanim 8, Haifa, Israel

ITALY

Cargo Afrique (m.); *Cargo Italia* (f.)
Edizioni Turistampa, Via Confienza 19, 10121 Turin, Italy

CISCO Notiziario/Newsletter (m.)
Centro Italiano Studi Containers, c/o Camera di Commercio, via Garibaldi 4, 16124 Genoa, Italy

Corriere dei Trasporti (w.)
Astral s.a.s., Salita Viale 1-21, 16128 Genoa, Italy

Corriere Mercantile Politico d'Informazioni (w.)
Galleria Umberto I 83, 80132 Naples, Italy

Italia sul Mare (m.)
Via in Arcione 71, Rome, Italy

Marina Italiana (Rassegne delle Industrie del Mare) (m.); *La Marina Mercantile* (m.)
Silvio Basile, Lungo Bisagno Istria, 34, 16141 Genoa, Italy

Nautica (m.)
Via Tevere 44, 00198 Rome, Italy

JAPAN

Electronic Navigation Review/Denpa Koho (in Japanese) (m.)
c/o Kaijo Hoan-cho Todai-bu, 2-1-3, Kasumigaseki, Chiyoda-ku, Tokyo 100, Japan

IHI Engineering Review (qu.)
Ishikawajima-Harima Heavy Industries Co. Ltd. (Ishikawajima Harima Jukogyo K.K.), 2-1. 2-chome, Ohtemachi, Chiyoda-ku, Tokyo 100, Japan

Japan Shipbuilding & Marine Engineering (qu.)
Japan Association for Technical Information, Nihon Gijutsu Koho Kyokai, 4-7-107 Yamazakicho, Machida, Tokyo 194-01, Japan

Journal of the Society of Naval Architects of Japan (2 a year)
Nihon Zosen Gakkai, Sempako-Shinko Bldg., 15-16 Toranomon 1-chome, Minato-ku, Tokyo 105, Japan

Kaiun (Shipping) (m.)
Mitui Rokugo-kan, 2-8 Muromachi, Nihombashi, Chuo-ku, Tokyo, Japan

Mitsui Zosen Giho (Mitsui Zosen Technical Review) (qu.)
Mitsui Zosen K. K. Gijyutsu Kaihatsu Honbu, 6–4, Tsukiji 5-chome, Chuo-ku, Tokyo, Japan

NKK News (incl. shipbuilding in English) (m.)
Nippon Kohan K.K., 1-1-2 Marunouchi, Chiyoda-ku, Tokyo 100, Japan

Report (qu.)
Port and Harbour Research Institute, 1-1, 3-chome Nagase, Yokosuka, Kanagawa, Japan

Report (bi-m.)
Ship Research Institute, 38-1, 6-chome, Shinkawa, Mitaka, Tokyo, Japan

Senapku (m.)
Tennen Sha, 50 Akagi-Shitamachi, Shinjuku-ko, Tokyo 162, Japan

Shipping and Trade News (d.)
Tokyo News Service, Nippon Press Center Bldg, 5th floor, 2-1 Uchisaiwaicho 2-chome, Chiyoda-ku, Tokyo 100, Japan

Shipping Gazette (in English & Japanese) (w.)
Japan Press Ltd., C.P.O. Box 6, Tokyo, Japan

Shipping/Kaiun (in Japanese) (m.)
Japan Shipping Exchange Inc., Mitsui Rokugokan No. 8, Muromachi 2-chome, Nihonbashi, Chuo-ku, Tokyo 103, Japan

Zosen (in English)
Tokyo News Service Ltd., Tokyo Nyusu Tsushinsha, Tsukiji Hamarikyu Bldg., 10th floor, 3-3 Tsukiji 5-chome, Chuo-ku, Tokyo 104, Japan

Zosen kai (6 a year)
1-5-16, Toranomon, Minato-ku, Tokyo 105, Japan

REPUBLIC OF KOREA

Korea Shipping Gazette (w.)
43-1 Tongeni-dong, Jongro-ku, C.P.O. Box 3198, Seoul, Rep. of Korea

KSA Bulletin (w.)
Korea Shipowners' Association, Room 1002, Baejae Bldg., 55-4 Seosomun-dong, Chung-ku, Seoul 100, Rep. of Korea

LIBERIA

Liberian Shipping Bulletin & Trading Review (m.)
Arthur H. Thrower, 44-46 South Ealing Rd., Ealing, London W5, England

MOZAMBIQUE

Portos e Caminhos de Ferro (qu.)
C.P. 276, Maputo, Mozambique

NETHERLANDS

Annual Report
Koninklijke Nederlandse Redersvereniging, Box 16638, 2500 BP, The Hague 2515 BM, Netherlands

De Blauwe Wimpel (m.)
C. de Boer Jr. N.V., Box 507, 1200 AM Hilversum, Netherlands

Elektronaut (3 a year)
Radio-Holland BV, Box 9094, 1069 CC Amsterdam, Netherlands

Holland Shipbuilding (m.)
C. E. Radius en P. Gruppelaar Publishing Co., Box 277, 3300 AG Dordrecht, Netherlands

Holland's Export Magazine (m.)
Van Kouteren's Publishing Co., Box 4115, 3006 AC Rotterdam, Netherlands

Ports Magazine (bi-m.)
Internationale Publiciteits Diensten, Box 317, 4350 Terneuzen, Netherlands

Schip en Werf (f.)
Heemraadssingel 193, 3023 CB, Rotterdam, Netherlands

Terra et Aqua (2 a year)
International Association of Dredging Companies, P.O. Box 80521, 2508 GM The Hague, Netherlands

Tijdschrift voor Zeegeschiedenis (semi-a.)
Kruipbrem 27, 3068 TG Rotterdam, Netherlands

Uit Europoortkringen (m.)
Uitgeversmaatschappij L. A. van Beek B.V., Box 53, 2650 AB Berkel 2H, Netherlands

NEW ZEALAND

Annual Report
New Zealand Ports Authority, P.O. Box 10059, Wellington, New Zealand

New Zealand Shipping Gazette (w.)
Mercantile Gazette of New Zealand Ltd., Box 20-034, Christchurch 5, New Zealand

Report of the Ministry of Transport (a.)
Private Bag, Wellington, New Zealand

Sea Spray (m.)
NZ News, UBD Centre, Dominion Rd., Auckland, New Zealand

NORWAY

Baatbyggeren (bi-m.)
Norwegian Boatbuilders' Association, Boks 137, 1601 Fredrikstad, Norway

Fraktemann (6 a year)
Freighter Owners' Association, Boks 198, Bergen, Norway

Frivakt (11 a year)
Bygdøy. Alle 21, Oslo 2, Norway

Maanesskrift (m.)
Norwegian National Boatbuilders Association, Gaustadalleen 30, Oslo 3, Norway

Norsk Baatindustri (bi-m.)
Norsk Baatinformasjon, Boks 317, 1601 Fredrikstad, Norway

The North Sea Observer (m.)
Teknisk Presse AS, Hovfaret 17, Skoeyen, Oslo 2, Norway

Norwegian Maritime Research (qu.)
Norges Teknisk-Naturvitenskapelige Forskningsraad/Royal Norwegian Council for Scientific and Industrial Research, Selvig Publishing S.A., Box 9070, Vaterland, Oslo 1, Norway

Norwegian Shipping News (16 a year)
Chr. Krohgsgatan 16 A. Oslo 1, Norway

Reports (irr.)
Ship Research Institute of Norway, Boks 4125, N-7001 Trondheim, Norway

Seilas & Batliv (Sailing & Boat Life) (m.)
Boks 5928, Oslo 3, Norway

Shipyards, Boatbuilders and Marine Engines (a.)
Selvig Publishing Co., Boks 9070, Vaterland, Oslo 1, Norway
(& K. J. Hendry, West House, West St., Faversham, Kent ME13 7JB, England)

Skip (maritimt teknisk tidsskrift) (10 a year)
Bjarne H. Reenskaug A-S, Boks 130, 2261 Kirkenaer, Norway

Skipsfartens Innkjøpsbok (a.)
Boks 102, Lilleaker, Oslo 2, Norway

Skipsnytt (m.)
Lunder Presse A-S, Boks 132, 1501 Moss, Norway

Skips-Revyen (6 a year)
Norigon A-S, Boks 693, 5001 Bergen, Norway

PARAGUAY

Revista Navigación y Puertos
Administración Nacional de Navigación y Puertos, Colón y Isabel la Católica, Asunción, Paraguay

POLAND

Budownictwo Okretowe (Naval Architecture) (m.)
Swietokrzyska 14a, Warsaw, Poland

Morze (m.)
00-023 Warsaw, Widok 10, Poland

Prace Instytutu Morskiego
80-958 Gdansk, Dlugi Targ 41/42, Poland

Przeglad Zachodnio-Pomorski (qu.)
Instytut Zachodnio-Pomorski, Ryceska 3, 70-537 Szczecin, Poland

Technika i Gospodarka Morska (Maritime Technology and Management) (m.)
Ministry of Foreign Trade and Shipping, Wydawnictwo Morskie, Szeroka 38/40, 80-835 Gdansk, Poland

Zescyty Naukowe (qu.)
Merchant Navy Academy, Waly Chrobrego 1, 70-500 Szczecin, Poland

PORTUGAL

Boletim (semi-a.)
Direcção-Geral da Marinha do Comercio, Praça Luis de Camões 22-1 Dt, 1200 Lisbon, Portugal

Boletim Informativo do APAMM (m.)
Associação Portuguesa dos Armadores da Marinha Mercante, Rua de São Julio 80-2°, 1100 Lisbon, Portugal

SINGAPORE

Maritime Asia (m.)
Marintec Press Pte. Ltd., 864 World Trade Centre, Singapore

Report (qu.)
National Maritime Board, Singapore

SASAR News (m.); *Singapore Shipbuilding and Repairing Directory* (bi-a.)
Singapore Association of Shipbuilders & Repairers, 1 Maritime Square 09–50, World Trade Centre, Singapore 0409

Singapore Shipping and Air Gazette (semi-m.)
Immedia Pte. Ltd., 2213 International Plaza, 10 Anson Rd., Singapore 3

Singapore Shipping 'N' Shipbuilder (m.)
Cosmic Media, P.O. Box 3163, Singapore

SOUTH AFRICA

Portcullis (qu.)
Charter Registrars (Pty.) Ltd., Box 1568, Port Elizabeth, South Africa

South African Shipping News and Fishing Industry Review (m.)
Thomson Publications S.A. (Pty.) Ltd., Box 8308, Johannesburg 2000, South Africa

Two Oceans Journal
South African Institute of Marine Engineers and Naval Engineers, c/o P.O.B. 61019, Marshalltown 2107, South Africa

SOVIET UNION

Morskoi Flot (journal of USSR merchant marine) (m.)
Izdatel'stvo Transport, Basmannyi Tupik 60, Moscow B-175, USSR

Soviet Merchant Ships Annual (bi-a.)
Kenneth Mason Publications Ltd., The Old Harbourmaster's, 8 North St., Emsworth, Hants PO10 7DD, England

Soviet Shipping (in English) (qu.)
4 Rakhmanovsky, Moscow, GSP-4, 101412, USSR

Sudostroenie (Shipbuilding) (m.)
Izdatel'stvo Sudostroenie, Ul. Gogolya 8, Leningrad D-65, USSR

SPAIN

Bilbao Marítimo (w.)
Antonio Aysa Rodríguez, Ercilla 24-4, Bilbao 11, Spain

Marítimas Información Comercial (d.)
Publicaciones Men-Car, Paseo de Colón 24, Barcelona 2, Spain

Nautilus (revista general del mar)
Príncipe 9, Apdo. de Correos 658, Madrid 12, Spain

Playamar (revista técnica de actualidad náutica) (m.)
Editorial Borrmart SA, Ramón de la Cruz 68, Madrid 1, Spain

Rotación (m.); *Sernaval (Servicio Información Naval)* (m.)
Editorial Pedeca, Maria Auxiliadora 5, Madrid 20, Spain

SUDAN

Annual Report; Annual Statistics Bulletin
Sea Ports Corporation, Port Sudan, Sudan

SWEDEN

Loggen (bi-m.)
Frank Stenvalls Foerlag, Malmgatan 3, S-211 32, Malmö, Sweden

Nautisk Tidskrift (m.)
Skeppsbron 32, S-111 30, Stockholm, Sweden

Svensk Sjöfarts Tidning (w.)
Box 53090, S-40014, Göteborg, Sweden

Transport-Nytt (10 a year)
Box 3044, S-122 03 Enskede, Sweden

SWITZERLAND

Strom und See (7 a year)
Verlag Schiffahrt und Weltverkehr AG, Blumenrain 12, 4001 Basle, Switzerland

UNITED ARAB EMIRATES

The Nautical Magazine (in Arabic)
Arab Maritime Transport Agency, Sharjah, United Arab Emirates

UNITED KINGDOM

ABC Shipping Guide (m.)
ABC Travel Guides Ltd., World Time-Table Centre, Dunstable, Beds. LU5 4HB, England

Annual Report
General Council of British Shipping, 30/32 St. Mary Axe, London EC3A 8ET, England

Annual Report; Annual Statistics of the UK Ports Industry; Annual Trade Statistics
British Ports Association, Commonwealth House, 1-19 New Oxford St., London WC1A 1DZ, England

British Shipper (m.)
National Magazine House, 72 Broadwick St., London W1, England

Chandler & Boat Builder (m.)
IPC Business Press Ltd., Surrey House 1, Throwley Way, Sutton SM1 4QQ, England

Coastguard (qu.)
Room 438, 1 Victoria St., London SW1 OET, England

Dock and Harbour Authority (m.)
Foxlow Publications Ltd., 19 Harcourt St., London W1, England

Dredging and Port Construction (m.)
Fuel and Metallurgical Journals Ltd., Queensway House, 2 Queensway, Redhill, Surrey RH1 1QS, England

Drydock (bi-m.)
Benn Publications Ltd., 25 New Street Square, London EC4A 3JA, England

Freight (m.)
Freight Transport Association Ltd., Hermes House, St. John's Rd., Tunbridge Wells, TN4 9UZ, England

Freight Forwarding UK (m.)
The Institute of Freight Forwarders Ltd., Suffield House, 9 Paradise Rd., Richmond, Surrey TW9 1SA, England

Freight News (f.)
Link House Magazines plc, Link House, Dingwall Ave., Croydon CR9 2TA, England

Freighting World (w.)
Journal of Commerce & Shipping Telegraph Ltd., 63 Shelton St., London WC2H 9HE, England

Handy Shipping Guide (w.)
Wilkinson Bros. Ltd., 230-4 Long Lane, London SE1 4QE, England

High-Speed Surface Craft (bi-m.)
Capstan Publishing Co. Ltd., Lewin House, Dorking Rd., Tadworth, Surrey KT20 5SA, England

Hunting Group Review (3 a year)
Hunting Group Management Ltd., 243 Knightsbridge, London SW7 1DH, England

Intalink (Shipping & Industry) (qu.)
Welbecson Ltd., Strawberry St., Hull, Humberside HU9 1EX, England

Journal (qu.)
Honourable Company of Master Mariners, c/o HQS Wellington, Temple Stairs, Victoria Embankment, London WC25 2PN, England

Journal (10 a year)
The Royal Institution of Naval Architects, 10 Upper Belgrave St., London SW1X 8BQ, England

Journal of Abstracts (m.)
British Ship Research Association, Wallsend Research Station, Wallsend, Tyne and Wear NE28 6UY, England

Journal of Commerce & Freighting World (d.)
Journal of Commerce and Shipping Telegraph Ltd., 213 Tower Bldg., Water St., Liverpool L3 1LN, England

Journal of Navigation (3 a year)
Cambridge University Press, Shaftesbury Rd., Cambridge CB2 2RV, England

The Link (qu.)
Society of Consulting Marine Engineers and Ship Surveyors, 6 Lloyd's Ave., London EC3N 3AX, England

Lloyd's Export Shipping (every 2 months); *Lloyd's Loading List (UK Edition)* (w.); *Lloyd's Ship Manager* (m.); *Lloyd's Shipping Economist* (m.)
Lloyd's of London Press Ltd., Sheepen Place, Colchester, Essex CO3 3LP, England

Marine Engineering Log (m.)
Simmons Boardman Publishing Corporation, Kenneth J. Hendry, West House, West St., Faversham, Kent ME13 7JB, England

Marine Engineers Bulletin (m.); *Marine Engineers Review* (m.)
Marine Management (Holdings) Ltd., 76 Mark Lane, London EC3R 7JN, England

Marine News (m.)
World Ship Society, 28 Natland Rd., Kendal LA9 7LT, England

Marine Observer (qu.)
HMSO Subscriptions, P.O. Box 569, London SE1 9NH, England

Marine Policy (qu.)
Butterworth Scientific Ltd., Journals Div., P.O. Box 63, Westbury House, Bury St., Guildford, Surrey GU2 5BH, England

Mariners' Mirror (qu.)
Society for Nautical Research, Meadow Bank, 26 Lucastes Rd., Haywards Heath, West Sussex, England

Maritime Policy and Management (qu.)
Taylor & Francis Ltd., 4 John St., London WC1N 2ET, England

Maritime Studies Current Awareness (w.)
Faculty of Maritime Studies, Plymouth Polytechnic, Drake Circus, Plymouth PL4 8AA, England

The Motor Ship (m.)
IPC Industrial Press Ltd., Quadrant House, The Quadrant, Sutton, Surrey SM2 5AS, England

Nautical Magazine (m.)
Brown, Son & Ferguson Ltd., 4-10 Darnley St., Glasgow G41 2SD, Scotland

Naval Engineers Journal (every 2 months)
Birch Cottage, Combleland Rd., Alcombe, nr. Minehead, Somerset TA24 6BS, England

Naval Record (every 2 months)
29 Kennedy Rd., Bicester, Oxon OX6 8BE, England

New Construction (shipbuilding) (qu.); *Sea Breezes* (m.)
Jocast Ltd., 202 Cotton Exchange Bldg., Old Hall St., Liverpool L3 9LA, England

The Port (m.)
Port Publishing Co. Ltd., Focal House, 18-19 Sheds, Tilbury Dock, Essex RM18 7ND, England

The Seafarer (qu.)
The Marine Society, 202 Lambeth Rd., London SE1 7LQ, England

Seahorse (bi-m.)
Ocean Publications Ltd., 22-24 Buckingham Palace Rd., London SW1W OQP, England

The Seaman (8 a year)
National Union of Seamen, Maritime House, Old Town, Clapham, London SW4 OJP, England

Seatrade (m.)
Seatrade Publications Ltd., Fairfax House, Colchester, Essex, England

Seaways (m.)
The Nautical Institute, 202 Lambeth Rd., London SE1 7LQ, England

Ship and Boat Builders' National Federation Handbook (a.)
Sell's Publications Ltd., Sell's House, 39 East St., Epsom, Surrey KT17 1BL, England

Ship Care & Management (m.)
Fuel and Metallurgical Journals Ltd., Queensway House, 2 Queensway, Redhill, Surrey RY1 1QS, England

The Shipbroker (m.)
Ryston Publications Ltd., Bank Chambers, Downham Market, Norfolk PF38 9BU (for the Institute of Chartered Shipbrokers, 24 St. Mary Axe, London EC3A 8DE), England

Shipbuilding News (m.)
113-115 The Broadway, Leigh-on-Sea, Essex, England

Ships Monthly
Waterways Productions Ltd., Kottingham House, Dale St., Burton-on-Trent, Staffs. DE14 3TD, England

Small Ships (bi-m.)
IPC Industrial Press Ltd., Quadrant House, The Quadrant, Sutton, Surrey SM2 5AS, England

Telegraph
Merchant Navy and Airline Officers Association, 750/760 High Rd., Leytonstone, London E11 3BB, England

Tide, Time & Distance Tables (a.)
James Munro Co. Ltd., 1 Raith Rd., Fenwick, Kilmarnock KA3 6DQ, Ayrshire, Scotland

Transactions (7 a year)
Institution of Engineers and Shipbuilders in Scotland, 183 Bath St., Glasgow G2 4HT, Scotland

Transactions (4 a year)
North East Coast Institution of Engineers and Shipbuilders, 12 Windsor Terrace, Jesmond, Newcastle upon Tyne NE1 1TB, England

UNITED STATES

American Shipper (m.)
Howard Publications Inc., 33 S. Hogan St., Suite 230, Box 4728, Jacksonville, FL 33201, USA

Award Service (3 a year)
Society of Maritime Arbitrators, 26 Broadway, Suite 1200, New York, NY 10004, USA

Boston Marine Guide
89 Broad St., Boston, MA 02110, USA

Daily Commercial News and Shipping Guide
C.A. Page Publishing Co., 3181 Fernwood Ave, Lynwood, CA 90262, USA

FACS Forum (m.)
Federation of American Controlled Shipping, 50 Broadway, New York, NY 10004, USA

Fleet Owner (m.)
McGraw-Hill Publications Co., 1221 Ave. of the Americas, New York, NY 10026, USA (& McGraw-Hill House, Maidenhead, Berks. SL6 2QL, England)

Handling and Shipping (m.)
Penton/IPC, 1111 Chester Ave., Cleveland, OH 44114, USA

Inbound Traffic Guide (qu.)
Thomas Publishing Co., One Penn Plaza, 259 W. 34th St., New York, NY 10001, USA

Jacksonville Seafarer (m.)
Howard Publications Inc., 33 S. Hogan St., Suite 230, Box 4728, Jacksonville, FL 32201, USA

Journal of Ship Research (qu.)
Society of Naval Architecture and Marine Engineering, One World Trade Center, Suite 1369, New York, NY 10048, USA

Lykes Fleet Flashes (bi-m.)
Lykes Bros. Steamship Co. Inc., Lykes Center, 300 Poydras St., New Orleans, LA 70130, USA

Marine Digest (w.)
Box 3954, 1732 4th South, Seattle, WA 98124, USA

Marine Engineering/Log (m.)
Simmons Boardman Publishing Corporation, 345 Hudson St., New York, NY 10014, USA

Marine Management Letter (10 a year)
Fleet Data Service, 1710 Dairy Ashford, Suite 109, Houston TX 77077, USA

Marine Policy Reports (5 a year)
Center for the Study of Marine Policy, Robinson Hall 301, University of Delaware, Newark, Delaware 19716, USA

Maritime Association of the Port of New York Newsletter (f.)
McDonald Communications, 80 Broad St., 34th Fl., New York, NY 10004, USA

Maritime Newsletter (m.)
AFL-CIO Maritime Trades Department, 815 16th St. NW, Rm. 510, Washington DC 20006, USA

Maritime Reporter and Engineering News (f.)
Maritime Activity Reports, 107 E 31st St., New York, NY 10016, USA

May Day Pictorial News (m.)
Pier 38-40, San Francisco, CA 84107, USA

Nautical Quarterly
373 Park Ave. South, New York, NY 10016, USA

Nautical Research Journal (qu.)
Nautical Research Guild Inc., 6413 Dahlonega Rd., Bethesda, MD 20816, USA

Naval Engineers Journal (bi-m.)
American Society of Naval Engineers Inc., 1452 Duke St., Alexandria, VA 22314, USA

Ocean Industry (m.)
Gulf Publishing Co., P.O. Box 2608, Houston, Texas 77001, USA

Official Intermodal Equipment Register (qu.)
Intermodal Publishing Co. Ltd., 424 West 33 St., New York, NY 10001, USA

On Scene (qu.); *Proceedings* (m.); *Safe Boating* (qu.); *Vessel Safety Review* (m.)
US Coast Guard Search and Rescue Co-ordinator, 2100 Second St. SW, Washington DC 20593, USA

Pacific Shipper (w.)
1050 Sansome St., San Francisco, CA 94111, USA

Pacific Traffic (m.)
2230 Big Ranch Rd., Napa, CA 94558, USA

Proceedings of the Marine Safety Council (m.)
US Coast Guard, 2100 Second St. SW, Washington DC 20593, USA

Quarterly and Annual Reports
Sea Grant Program, Massachusetts Institute of Technology, E 38-366, 77 Mass. Ave., Cambridge, Mass. 02139, USA

Sea (m.)
CBS Consumer Publishing West, 1499 Monrovia Ave., Newport Beach, CA 92663, USA

Sea & Pacific Skipper (m.)
Pennant Publishing Co. Inc., 419 Newport Blvd. N, Newport Beach, CA 92663, USA

Sea Heritage News (qu.)
Sea Heritage Foundation, 254-26, 75 Ave., Glen Oaks, NY 11004, USA

Shipping Digest (m.)
Geyer-McAllister Publications, 51 Madison Ave., New York, NY 10010, USA

Shipyard Bulletin (m.)
Newport News Shipbuilding, Newport News, VA 23607, USA

Shipyard Weekly; Statistical Quarterly
Shipbuilders' Council of America, 1110 Vermont Ave. NW, Washington DC 20005, USA

Vessel Inventory Report (semi-a.)
US Maritime Administration, Office of Trade Studies and Statistics, Nassif Bldg., 400 7th St. SW, Washington DC 20590, USA

Work Boat (m.)
H. L. Peace Publications, Box 2400, Covington, LA 70434, USA

URUGUAY

Servicio de Oceanografía e Hidrografía. Avisos a los Navegantes (m.)
Capurro 980, Casilla de Correo No. 1381, Montevideo, Uruguay

YUGOSLAVIA

Brodogradnja (Shipbuilding) (bi-m.)
Box 68, Miramarska 22-V, 41000 Zagreb, Yugoslavia

Suvremeni promet (Modern Transport) (bi-m.)
Faculty of Maritime and Transportation Studies, Sveuciliste "Vladimir Bakaric" u Rijeci, 5100 Rijeka, Studentska 2, Yugoslavia

Fisheries

INTERNATIONAL

Annual Report
Inter-American Tropical Tuna Commission, c/o Scripps Institution of Oceanography, La Jolla, Calif. 92093, USA

Annual Report
International Center for Living Aquatic Resources Management Inc. (ICLARM), MCC P.O. Box 1501, Makati, Metro Manila, Philippines

Annual Report; Statistical Yearbook
International North Pacific Fisheries Commission, 6640 NW Marine Drive, Vancouver, Canada V6T 1X2

Annual Report
International Pacific Halibut Commission, P.O. Box 95009, Seattle WA 98145-2009, USA

Annual Report
International Pacific Salmon Fisheries Commission, P.O. Box 30, New Westminster, BC V3L 4X9, Canada

Annual Report
International Whaling Commission, 135 Station Road, Histon, Cambridge CB4 4NP, England

Annual Report; Statistical Bulletin (a.)
North-West Atlantic Fisheries Organization (NAFO), P.O. Box 638, Dartmouth, NS B2Y 3Y9, Canada

Annual Report
South Pacific Bureau for Economic Co-operation (SPEC), P.O. Box 856, Suva, Fiji

Biennial Report; Statistical Bulletin (a.)
International Commission for the Conservation of Atlantic Tunas, Príncipe de Vergara 17, 28001 Madrid, Spain

CECAF Statistical Bulletin
Fishery Committee for the Eastern Central Atlantic, c/o UNDP, BP 154, Dakar, Senegal

Fishing News International (m.)
Heighway Publications Ltd., Heighway House, 87 Blackfriars Road, London SE1 8HB, England

International Atlantic Salmon Foundation Newsletter (bi-m.)
P.O. Box 429, St. Andrews, NB E6O 2X0, Canada

Journal du Conseil
International Council for the Exploration of the Sea (ICES), Palaegade 2-4, DK-1261 Copenhagen, Denmark

Journal of Northwest Atlantic Fishery Science (a.)
P.O. Box 638, Dartmouth, NS B2Y 3Y9, Canada

Nordmar (a.)
Nordisk Kollegium for Marinbiologi, P.O. Box 333, Blindern, Oslo 3, Norway

Reports of Annual Meetings
North-East Atlantic Fisheries Commission, Room 339, Great Westminster House, Horseferry Road, London SW1P 2AE, England

SPC Fisheries Newsletter (qu.)
South Pacific Commission, Post Box D5, Nouméa Cédex, New Caledonia

World Fishing (m.)
IPC Industrial Press Ltd., Quadrant House, The Quadrant, Sutton, Surrey SM2 5AS, England

Yearbook of Fisheries Statistics—Catches and Landings
FAO, via delle Terme di Caracalla, 00100 Rome, Italy

Yearbook of Fishery Statistics—Fishery Commodities
FAO, via delle Terme di Caracalla, 00100 Rome, Italy

ARGENTINA

Instituto Nacional de Investigación y Desarrollo Pesquero, Revista (semi-a.)
Casilla de Correo 175, 7600 Mar del Plata, Argentina

AUSTRALIA

Australian Fish Trades Review (bi-m.)
24 Henry Street, Carlton NSW 2218, Australia

Australian Fisheries Magazine (m.)
Dept. of Primary Industry, Fisheries Division, Barton, Canberra, ACT 2600, Australia

FINS (Fishing Industry News Service) (3 a year)
Dept. of Fisheries and Wildlife, 108 Adelaide Tce., Perth WA 6000, Australia

Fintas (qu.)
Tasmanian Fisheries Development Authority, Box 619 F, Hobart, Tas. 7001, Australia

Fisherman's Journal (m.)
Rala Publications (for Union of Fishermen's Co-operatives), GPO Box 2457, Sydney 2001, Australia

Modern Fishing (m.)
Modern Magazines (Holdings) Ltd., Ryrie House, 15 Boundary Street, Rushcutters Bay, NSW 2011, Australia

Professional Fisherman (m.)
Baird Publications Pty. Ltd., 427 Chapel Street, South Yarra, Vic. 3141, Australia

Tasmanian Fisheries Research (semi-a.)
Box 619 F, Hobart, Tas. 7001, Australia

BANGLADESH

Bangladesh Journal of Fisheries (qu.)
Dept. of Fisheries, Biology and Limnology, PO Agricultural University, Mymensingh, Bangladesh

BRAZIL

Boletím de Estudos de Pesca (3 a year)
Superintendência do Desenvolvimento do Nordeste, Edif. Entreposto Federal de Pesca, Cais de Santa Rita, 8 Andar, Recife, Pernambuco, Brazil

Revista Nacional da Pesca (m.)
Divulgação da Pesca Maritima Ltda., Box 716, 04041 São Paulo, Brazil

BULGARIA

Ribno Stopanstvo (8 a year)
Izdatelstvo Profizdat, 82 Dondukov Blvd, Sofia, Bulgaria

CANADA

Annual Report
Canadian Institute of Fisheries Technology, Technical Univ. of Nova Scotia, POB 1000, Halifax, NS B3J 2X4, Canada

Cahiers d'Informations
Centre de Documentation des Pêches Maritimes, 96 Montée Sandy Beach, CP 1070 Gaspé, G0C 1R0, Canada

Canadian Bulletin of Fisheries and Aquatic Sciences
Fisheries and Oceans, Scientific Information and Publication Branch, 240 Sparks Street, Ottawa, Ont. K1A 0E6, Canada

Canadian Fisherman & Ocean Science (m.)
Sentinel Business Publications,
6725 Darlington Ave, Suite 200, Montreal,
Que. H3S 2J7, Canada

Canadian Journal of Fisheries & Aquatic Sciences (m.)
Fisheries and Oceans, Scientific
Information and Publication Branch, 240
Sparks Street, Ottawa, Ont. K1A 0E6,
Canada

Facts on Fish (m.)
Fisheries Association of British Columbia,
Rm. 400, 100 W. Pender Street,
Vancouver, BC V6B 1R8, Canada

Fisheries Council of Canada Bulletin (m.)
Suite 603, 77 Metcalfe Street, Ottawa,
Ont. K1P 5L6, Canada

Fisherman (f.)
Fisherman Publishing Society (for United
Fishermen and Allied Workers Union),
138 E Cordova Street, Vancouver, BC
V6A 1K9, Canada

Pacific Trollers Association Newsletter (m.)
Box 94336, Richmond, BC, Canada

Sou'Wester (bi-m.)
Fundy Group Publications, Box 128,
Yarmouth, NS, Canada

Western Fisheries (m.)
Special Interest Publications, Maclean
Hunter Ltd., Suite 202, 1132 Hamilton
Street, Vancouver, BC V6B 2S2, Canada

CHINA

Journal of Fisheries in China (in Chinese) (qu.)
Guoji Shudian, P.O. Box 339, Beijing,
China

CUBA

Mar y Pesca (m.)
Instituto Nacional de la Pesca de Cuba,
San Ignacio 303, Havana, Cuba

Revista Cubana de Investigaciones Pesqueras (qu.)
Centro de Investigaciones Pesqueras, av.
Primera y 26, Miramar, Playa, Havana,
Cuba

DENMARK

DANA (Journal of Fisheries and Marine Research) (irr.)
Danish Institute for Fishery and Marine
Research, 2920 Charlottenlund, Denmark

Dansk Fiskeritidende (w.)
Dansk Fiskeriforening, Studistraede 3, 2,
1455 Copenhagen K, Denmark

Fisk og Hav (a.)
Danish Institute for Fishery and Marine
Research, 2920 Charlottenlund, Denmark

Tidsskriftet Fisker-Bladet (qu.)
Sct. Laurenti Vej 112, 9990 Skagen,
Denmark

ECUADOR

Revista Cientifica de Ciencias Marinas y Limnología
Instituto Nacional de Pesca, Casilla 5918,
Guayaquil, Ecuador

FAROE ISLANDS

Fiskirannsóknir
Fiskirannsoknarstovan, Devesartrod,
Torshavn, Faroe Islands

FINLAND

Finnish Fisheries Research (irr.)
Finnish Game and Fisheries Research
Institute, Fisheries Division, Box 193,
SF-00131 Helsinki 13, Finland

Fiskeritidskrift foer Finland (bi-m.)
Centralfoerbundet foer
Fiskerihushaallming, Repslagaregatan 7 B
23, 00180 Helsinki 18, Finland

Kalastaja (Fisherman) (5 a year)
Kalatalouden Keskusliitto,
Koydenpunojankatu 7 B 23, 00180
Helsinki, Finland

Suomen Kalastuslehti (8 a year)
Koydenpunojankatu 7 B 23, 00180 Helsinki
18, Finland

FRANCE

France Pêche Internationale (10 a year)
Société Générale d'Editions, BP 95, 56107
Lorient Cédex, France

Institut Scientifique et Technique des Pêches Maritimes: Revue des Travaux (qu.)
BP 1049, 44037 Nantes Cédex, France

La Pêche et les Poissons (m.)
Gerpresse, 14 rue Brunel, 75017 Paris,
France

La Pêche Maritime (m.)
190 blvd. Haussmann, 75008 Paris, France

Science et Pêche (m.)
Institut Scientifique et Technique des
Pêches Maritimes, BP 1049, 44037 Nantes
Cédex, France

FEDERAL REPUBLIC OF GERMANY

Das Fischerblatt (m.)
Landesfischereiverband Schleswig-Holstein, Holstenstr. 108, 2300 Kiel, Fed. Rep. of Germany

Informationen für die Fischwirtschaft (qu.)
Bundesforschunganstalt für Fischerei, Palmaille 9, 2000 Hamburg 50, Fed. Rep. of Germany

Informationen über die Fischwirtschaft des Auslandes (m.)
Bundesministerium für Ernährung, Landwirtschaft und Forsten, 5300 Bonn, Fed. Rep. of Germany

Protokolle zur Fischereitechnik (1-3 a year)
Bundesforschungsanstalt für Fischerei, Institut für Fangtechnik, Palmaille 9, 2000 Hamburg 50, Fed. Rep. of Germany

ICELAND

Aegir (The Sea) (m.)
c/o Fiskifélag Islands, Reykjavik, Iceland

Sjávarfréttir (m.)
Armúli 18, 105 Reykjavik, Iceland

INDIA

Fishery Technology (semi-a.)
Society of Fisheries Technologists (India), c/o Central Institute of Fisheries Technology, Matsyapuri, PO Cochin 682 029, India

Ichthyologica (semi-a.)
International Society of Ichthyology and Hydrobiology, Box 64, Srinagar, Kashmir, India

INDONESIA

Bulletin Perikanan
Faculty of Fisheries, Bogor Agricultural University, Institut Pertanian Bogor, Fl. Raya Pajajaraz, Bogor, Indonesia

ISRAEL

Fisheries and Fishbreeding in Israel (qu.)
P.O. Box 1036, Haifa 31009, Israel

ITALY

Bollettino di Pesca, Piscicoltura e Idrobiologia (semi-a.)
Laboratorio Centrale di Idrobiologia , via Luigi Roncionotto 1, 00154 Rome, Italy

Corriere della Pesca (m.)
Consorzio Nazionale Cooperativa Pescatori ed Affini, via Tirso 90, 00198 Rome, Italy

Gazzettino della Pesca (m.)
Ente Autonomo Fiera di Ancona, Molo Sud, 60100 Ancona, Italy

Rivista di Diritto Economia e Tecnica della Pesca (qu.)
Centro Italiano Studi per la Pesca, via Cassia 6, 00131 Rome, Italy

JAPAN

Fisheries Economic Society Journal (qu.)
Tokyo-Suisan University, 4-5-7 Minato-ku, Tokyo 108, Japan

Fisheries World/Suisan Kai (in Japanese) (m.)
Dainihon Suisankai, 1-9-13 Akasaka, Minato-ku, Tokyo 107, Japan

Hokkaido Fisheries Experiment Station Journal (in Japanese) (m.)
238 Hamanaka-cho, Yoichi-machi Yoichi-gun, Hokkaido 146, Japan

Japanese Regional Fisheries Research Laboratory Bulletin (2 a year)
5939-22 Hamaura, Nishifunami-chu, Nigata 951, Japan

Japanese Society of Scientific Fisheries Bulletin (m.)
4-5-7 Konan, Minato-ku, Tokyo 108, Japan

Tohoku Regional Fisheries Research Laboratory Bulletin (semi-a.)
27-5 Shinhama-cho, Shiogama-shi, Miyagi 985, Japan

Tokai Regional Fisheries Research Laboratory Bulletin (qu.)
5-5-1 Kachidoki, Chuo-ku, Tokyo 104, Japan

Tokyo University of Fisheries Journal
4-5-7- Konan, Minato-ku, Tokyo 108, Japan

REPUBLIC OF KOREA

Korean Fisheries Society Bulletin (qu.)
c/o National Fisheries University of Busan, Namgu 608, Rep. of Korea

MEXICO

Técnica Pesquera (m.)
Ediciones Mundo Marina SA, Illinois 57, Mexico 18, DF, Mexico

NETHERLANDS

Fisheries Research (qu.)
Elsevier Scientific Publishing Co., Box 211, 1000 AE Amsterdam, Netherlands

Visserij (8-9 a year)
Ministerie van Landbouw en Visserij, Bezuidenhoutseweg 73, The Hague, Netherlands

Visserij Nieuws (w.)
Postbus 84055, 2508 AB, The Hague, Netherlands

NEW ZEALAND

Annual Report
Ministry of Agriculture and Fisheries, Media Services, Private Bag, Wellington, New Zealand

New Zealand Marine Sciences Newsletter (a.)
P.O. Box 12346, Wellington, New Zealand

NIGERIA

Nigerian Journal of Fisheries and Hydrobiology
Fisheries Society of Nigeria, PMB 12529, Lagos, Nigeria

NORWAY

Fiskaren (semi-w.)
A-S Fiskaren, Slottsgt. 3, Box 4053, N-5015 Bergen-Dreggen, Norway

Fiskeribladet (semi-w.)
Boks 562, 9401 Harstad, Norway

Fiskerinytt (10 a year)
Veiten 2, 5000 Bergen, Norway

Fiskets Gang (f.)
Fiskeridirektoratet, Box 185, 5001 Bergen, Norway

Me'a (m.)
Box 519, 7001 Trondheim, Norway

Skagerrak (fortn.)
Box 338, Arendal, Norway

PHILIPPINES

ICLARM Newsletter (qu.)
MCC Box 1501, Makati, Metro Manila, Philippines

Philippine Fishing Journal (m.)
Business Masters International, 55 UE Tech. Ave., University Hills, Subdivision Malabon, Rizal, Philippines

UPV Fisheries Journal
College of Fisheries, University of the Philippines in the Visayas, Iliolo City, Philippines

POLAND

Bulletin of the Sea Fisheries Institute
Morski Instytut Rybocki, 81-345 Gdynia, Aleja Zjednoczenia 1, Poland

Gospodarka Rybna (Fishing Industry) (m.)
Al. Jerozolimskie 28, Warsaw, Poland

PORTUGAL

Boletim de Pesca (qu.)
Gabinete de Estudos da Pesca, R. S. Bento 644, Lisbon, Portugal

Revista de Marinha (m.)
Empresa de Jornal do Comercio, Rua Dr Luis de Almeida e Albuquerque, 5, Lisbon 2, Portugal

Revista do Pescador (m.)
Ave. Visconde de Valmor, 52-4 Esq., Lisbon 1, Portugal

SOUTH AFRICA

Annual Report of the Director
Fishing Industry Research Institute, University of Cape Town, P. Bag, Rondebosch 7700, South Africa

South African Journal of Marine Science
Sea Fisheries Research Institute, Private Bag X 2, Rogge Bay 8012, South Africa

SPAIN

Industrias Pesqueras (semi-m.)
Servicios Industriales Pesqueros, S.A., Policarpo Sanz 21-2, Vigo (Pontevedra), Spain

Investigación Pesquera (4 a year)
Instituto de Investigaciones Pesqueras, Paseo Nacional, Barcelona 3, Spain

Sindicato Nacional de la Pesca Boletín de Información (m.)
Paseo del Prado 18-20, Madrid, Spain

SRI LANKA

Dhivara (in Sinhalese) (m.)
Ministry of Fisheries, Galle Face, Colombo 3, Sri Lanka

Journal of the National Aquatic Resources Agency
Crow Island, Mattakkuliya, Colombo-15, Sri Lanka

THAILAND

Thai Fisheries Gazette (qu.)
Ministry of Agriculture, Dept. of Fisheries, Rajadamnern Ave., Bangkok, Thailand

UNITED KINGDOM

Commercial Fishing (m.)
Commercial Fishing Enterprises, 78 North Albert Street, Fleetwood FY7 6HS, England

Co-operative Fishermen's Bulletin (qu.)
International Co-operative Alliance, 11 Upper Grosvenor Street, London W1X 9PA, England

Fisheries Management (qu.)
Blackwell Scientific Publications Ltd. (for the Institute of Fisheries Management), Osney Mead, Oxford OX2 0EL, England

Fishing News (w.)
Heighway Publications Ltd., Heighway House, 87 Blackfriars Road, London SE1 8HB, England

Fishing Prospects (a.)
Directorate of Fisheries Research, Fisheries Laboratory, Lowestoft, Suffolk, England

Interfish (qu.)
Commercial Fishing Enterprises Ltd., Fish Trades Bldg., Wyre Dock, Fleetwood FY7 6HS, England

Journal of Fish Diseases (bi-m.)
Blackwell Scientific Publications Ltd., Osney Mead, Oxford OX2 0EL, England

Offshore Fishing (m.)
Ravenhill Publishing Co. Ltd., Standard House, Bonhill Street, London EC2A 4DA, England

UNITED STATES

Alaska Seas and Coasts (5 a year)
University of Alaska Sea Grant Program, Fairbanks, AK 99701, USA

Alaska Fisherman's Journal (m.)
Waterfront Press Co., 1115 NW 46 St., Seattle, WA 98107, USA

American Fisheries Society Transactions (bi-m.)
5410 Grosvenor Lane, Suite 110, Bethesda, MD 20814, USA

Fish Health News (qu.)
US Fish & Wildlife Service, Dept. of the Interior, Washington DC 20240, USA

Fisheries (bi-m.)
American Fisheries Society, c/o Carl R. Sullivan, Ed., 5410 Grosvenor Lane, Suite 110, Bethesda, MD 20814, USA

Fishermen's News (semi-m.)
Fishermen's News, Inc. Fishermen's Terminal, C-3 Bldg., Rm. 110, Seattle WA 98119, USA

Fishery Bulletin (qu.)
National Marine Fisheries Service, Scientific Publication Office, 7600 Sandpoint Way, NE Bin C57100, Seattle, WA 98115, USA

Fishing Gazette (13 a year)
Fishing Gazette Publishing Corp., 461 Eighth Ave., New York, NY 10001, USA

Marine Fish Management (m.)
Nautilus Press, Inc., 1056 National Press Bldg., Washington DC 20045, USA

Marine Fisheries Review (qu.)
National Marine Fisheries Service, Scientific Publications Office, 7600 Sandpoint Way, NE Bin C57100 Seattle, WA 98115, USA

Marine Resource Bulletin (bi-m.)
Virginia Institute of Marine Science, I & E Office, Gloucester Point, VA 23062, USA

National Fisherman (m.)
Journal Publications (Camden), 21 Elm Street, Camden, ME 04843, USA

North American Journal of Fisheries Management (qu.)
American Fisheries Society, 5410 Grosvenor Lane, Suite 110, Bethesda, MD 20814, USA

Pacific Fishing (m.)
2208 NW Market Street, Seattle WA 98107, USA

Pesca y Marina (bi-m.)
c/o Fernando Flores, Box 38038, Los Angeles, CA 90038, USA

VENEZUELA

Caza y Pesca Náutica (m.)
Apdo. 66-764, Caracas 1060 A, Venezuela

YUGOSLAVIA

Morsko Ribarstvo/Marine Fisheries (qu.)
Poslovno Udruzenje Ribarske Privrede, Park Narodnog Heroja V, Vlahovica 6, Zagreb, Yugoslavia

Ocean Sciences

INTERNATIONAL

IMS Newsletter (qu.)
UNESCO, Div. of Marine Sciences, 7-9 Place de Fontenoy, 75700 Paris, France

Sea Frontiers (2 a year); *Sea Secrets* (2 a year)
International Oceanographic Foundation, 3979 Rickenbacher Causeway, Miami, FL 31149, USA

ALGERIA

Pelagos (semi-a.)
Institut des Sciences de la Mer et de l'Aménagement du Littoral, B.P. 90, Algiers, Algeria

ARGENTINA

Acta Oceanographica Argentina (semi-a.)
International Association for the Physical Sciences of the Ocean, Comité Nacional, Buenos Aires, Argentina

Contribuciones Cientificas
Centro de Investigación de Biología Marina, Hipólito Irigoyen 3780, 1208 Buenos Aires, Argentina

Contribuciones Cientificas IADO
Instituto Argentino de Oceanografía, Avda, Alem 53, 8000 Bahia Blanca, Argentina

AUSTRALIA

Australian Journal of Marine and Freshwater Research (6 a year)
CSIRO, 314 Albert St., East Melbourne, Vic. 3002, Australia

Australian Marine Sciences Association Bulletin (qu.)
c/o CSIRO, Div. of Fisheries and Oceanography, Cronulla, NSW 2230, Australia

CSIRO Marine Laboratories Research Report (bi-a.)
GPO Box 1538, Hobart, Tasmania 7001, Australia

BRAZIL

Arquivos de Ciencias do Mar (semi-a.)
Univ. Federal de Ceara, Laboratorio de Ciencias do Mar, Ave. da Universidade 2853, 60000 Fortaleza, Brazil

Boletím do Instituto de Biologia Marinha da Universidade de Rio Grande do Norte
Departamento de Oceanografia e Limnologia, Praia de Mãe Luiza S/N, Univ. Federal do Rio Grande do Norte, Natal RN-59000, Brazil

Boletím do Instituto Oceanográfico
Univ. de São Paulo, CP 8191, 05508 São Paulo, SP, Brazil

CANADA

Annual Review of Activities
Institute of Ocean Sciences, Box 6000, Sidney, BC V8Z 4B2, Canada

Atmosphere-Ocean (qu.)
Canadian Meteorological and Oceanographic Society, Suite 903, 151 Slater St., Ottawa, Ont. K1P 5H3, Canada

Cahier d'informations
Dept. of Oceanography, Univ. de Québec à Rimouski, 300 ave. des Ursulines, Rimouski, Que. G5L 3A1, Canada

C-CORE News (3 a year)
Centre for Cold Ocean Resources Engineering, Memorial Univ., St John's, Nfld. A1B 3X5, Canada

CHILE

Investigaciones Marinas (semi-a.)
Universidad Católica de Valparaíso, Escuela de Ciencias del Mar, Box 1020, Valparaíso 1, Chile

Revista de Biología Marina (semi-a.)
Instituto de Oceanología, Univ. de Valparaíso, Casilla 13-D, Montemar, Viña del Mar, Chile

CHINA

Acta Oceanologica Sinica/Haiyang Xuebao (in Chinese) (bi-m)
Guoji Shudian, Box 339, Beijing, China

Chinese Journal of Oceanology and Limnology (2 a year)
7 Nanhai Rd, Qingdao, China

Journal of Shandong College of Oceanography
Qingdao, Shandong Prov., China

Ocean Science and Technology
Qingdao Ocean Shipping Marine College, Qingdao, Shandong Prov., China

Oceanologia et Limnologia Sinica (bi-m.)
Chinese Society of Oceanology and Limnology, 7 Nanhai Rd., Qingdao, China

Oceans/Haiyang (m.)
China Oceanic Society, Guoji Shudian, P.O. Box 339, Beijing, China

Studia Marina Sinica (1 or 2 a year)
Institute of Oceanology, 7 Nanhai Rd., Qingdao, China

CUBA

Revista de Investigaciones Marinas
Centro de Investigaciones de Biología Marina, Univ. de Habana, Calle San Lázaro esq. L. Vedado, Havana 4, Cuba

ECUADOR

Acta Oceanográfica del Pacifico (semi-a.)
Instituto Oceanográfico de la Armada, Box 5940, Guayaquil, Ecuador

EGYPT

Bulletin of the Institute of Oceanography & Fisheries
101 Sharia Kasr El-Aini, Cairo, Egypt

FRANCE

Annales (semi-a.)
Institut Océanographique, 195 rue Saint-Jacques, 75005 Paris, France

Cahiers de Biologie Marine (qu.)
Place Georges-Teissier, 29211, Roscoff, France

CMAS Bulletin d'Information/CMAS Newsletter (qu.)
World Underwater Federation, 14 rue du Colisée, Paris 8e, France

Centre de Recherches et d'Etudes Océanographiques: Travaux (qu.)
1 Quai Branly, 75007 Paris, France

Dossiers Histoire de la Mer (bi-m.)
Historama, 58 rue Perronet, 92523 Neuilly Cédex, France

Journal (qu.)
Société des Océanistes, Musée de l'Homme, Palais de Chaillot, 75116 Paris, France

Nouvelle Revue Maritime (m.)
70 rue St Lazare, 75009, Paris, France

Oceanis (8 a year)
Institut Océanographique, 195 rue Saint-Jacques, 75005, Paris, France

Océanographie Tropicale (semi-a.)
Office de la Recherche Scientifique et Technique Outre-Mer, 70-74 Route d'Aulnay, 93140 Bondy, France

Oceanologica Acta (qu.)
Centrale des Revues, Gauthier-Villars, B.P. 119, 93102 Montreuil, France

Rapport Annuel
Centre National pour l'Exploitation des Océans (CNEXO), 66 rue d'Iéna, 75116, Paris, France

Tethys (qu.)
Station Marine d'Endourme, rue de la Batterie des Lions, 13007 Marseille, France

FRENCH POLYNESIA

Bulletin (qu.)
Société d'Etudes Océaniennes, BP 110, Papeete-Tahiti, French Polynesia

FEDERAL REPUBLIC OF GERMANY

Deutsche Hydrographische Zeitschrift (6 a year)
Bernhard-Nocht-Str. 78, 2000 Hamburg 4, Fed. Rep. of Germany

Helgoländer Meeresuntersuchungen (in English and German) (qu.)
Biologische Anstalt Helgoland, Notkestr. 31, 2000 Hamburg 52, Fed. Rep. of Germany

Ozean und Technik (semi-m.)
Handelsblatt GmbH, Postfach 1102, 4000 Düsseldorf, Fed. Rep. of Germany

GREECE

Biologia Gallo-Hellenica (3 or 4 a year)
Zoological Laboratory, Panepistimiopolis (Kouponia), Athens GR-15771, Greece

Thalassographica (a.)
Ethniko Ventro Thalassion Ereunon, Aghios Kosmas, 16604 Athens, Greece

ICELAND

Hafrannsóknir (in Icelandic); *Rit Fiskideildar* (in English)
Hafrannsóknastofnunin, Reykjavik, Iceland

INDIA

Indian Journal of Marine Sciences (qu.)
Council of Scientific and Industrial Research, Hillside Rd., New Delhi 110012, India

Journal (2 a year)
Marine Biological Association, Cochin, Kerala, South India

Mahasagar (qu.)
National Institute of Oceanography, Dona Paula, Goa 403004, India

INDONESIA

Marine Research in Indonesia (irr.); *Oceanographic Cruise Report* (irr.); *Oseana* (every 2 months); *Oseanologi Di Indonesia* (qu.)
Lembaga Oseanologi Nasional, POB 580/DAK, Jakarta Utara, Indonesia

ISRAEL

Biennial Report
Israel Oceanographic and Limnological Research Ltd., POB 8030, Haifa 31080, Israel

ITALY

Memorie di Biologia Marina e di Oceanografia (bi-m.)
Università degli Studi di Messina, Istituto de Zoologia, Stazione di Biologia Marina, Messina, Italy

IVORY COAST

Documents Scientifiques (2 a year)
Centre de Recherches Océanographiques, BP V 18, Abidjan, Ivory Coast

JAPAN

Annual Report
Tokai Daigaku, Kaiyo Kenkyusho, 3-20-1 Orido, Shimizu, Shizuoka-ken, Japan 424

Bulletin (m.)
Japan Maritime Research Institute, Kaiun Bldg. 6-4, 2-chome, Hirakawa-cho, Chiyoda-ku, Tokyo, Japan

Bulletin (irr.)
Ocean Research Institute, 15-1, 1-chome, Minamidai, Nakano-ku, Tokyo, Japan

Bulletin of the College of Science
Dept. of Marine Sciences, Univ. of the Ryukyus, 1 Senbaru, Nishihara-cho, Okinawa 903-01, Japan

Bulletin of the Institute of Oceanic Research and Development
Tokai Daigaku, 3-20-1 Orido, Shimizu, Shizuoka-ken, Japan 424

Bulletin of the Society of Sea Water Science
Nippon Kaisui Gakkai c/o Japan Salt Industry Ass., 7-15-14 Roppongi, Minato-ku, Tokyo, Japan

Galaxea (2 a year)
Sesoko Marine Science Center, Univ. of the Ryukyus, Sesoko, Motobu-cho, Okinawa 903-10, Japan

Japan Meteorological Agency: Oceanographic Magazine (semi-a.)
Japan Weather Association, c/o Japan Meteorological Agency, 1.3-4 Otemachi, Chiyoda-ku, Tokyo 100, Japan

Journal of the Faculty of Marine Science and Technology
Tokai University, Orido, Shimuzu, Shizuoka, Japan 424

Oceanographic Society of Japan. Journal (bi-m.)
c/o Ocean Research Institute, Univ. of Tokyo, 1-15-1 Minamidai, Nakano-ku, Tokyo 164, Japan

Sea and Sky (bi-m.)
Oceanographical and Meteorological Society, 7-chome, Ikutaku, Kobe, Japan

MADAGASCAR

Revue de l'Océan Indien
Madagascar Print & Press Co., rue H. Rabesahala, BP 46, Antsakaviro, Antananarivo, Madagascar

NETHERLANDS

Marine Geology (f.)
Elsevier Scientific Publishing Co., Box 211, 1000 AE Amsterdam, Netherlands

Marine Geophysical Researches (qu.)
D. Reidel Publishing Co., Box 17, 3300 AA Dordrecht, Netherlands

Netherlands Journal of Sea Research (qu.)
Netherlands Institute for Sea Research, P.O. Box 59, 1790 AB Den Burg, Texel, Netherlands

NEW ZEALAND

New Zealand Journal of Marine and Freshwater Research (qu.)
Dept. of Scientific and Industrial Research, Box 9741, Wellington, New Zealand

New Zealand Marine Sciences Newsletter (a.)
Oceanographic Institute, P.O. Box 12346, Wellington, New Zealand

NIGERIA

Newsletter
Nigerian Institute for Oceanography and Marine Research, Victoria Beach, PMB 12 529, Lagos, Nigeria

PAKISTAN

Bulletin (2 a year)
Centre of Excellence in Marine Biology, Univ. of Karachi, Karachi 32, Pakistan

POLAND

Nautologia (qu.)
Ossolineum, Publ. House of the Polish Academy of Science, Rynek 9, Wroclaw, Poland

ROMANIA

Cercetari marine (a.)
Constanta, Bd. Lenin 300, CP 53, Romania

SIERRA LEONE

Annual Bulletin
Institute of Marine Biology and Oceanography, Fourah Bay College, Univ. of Sierra Leone, Freetown, Sierra Leone

SOUTH AFRICA

Annual Year Book
Institute of Oceanography, c/o Univ. of Cape Town, P. Bag Rondebosch 7700, South Africa

SOVIET UNION

Academy of Sciences of the USSR: Oceanology (m.)
American Geophysical Union, 2000 Florida Ave. NW, Washington, DC 20009, USA

Biologia morya (bi-m.)
Institute of Marine Biology, Vladivostok 690022, USSR

Ekologiya Morya (qu.)
Ul. Repina 3, 252 601 Kiev, USSR

Izvestia TINRO (1-3 a year)
Pacific Scientific Research Institute of Fisheries and Oceanography, Vladivostok, Ul. Leninskaya 20, USSR

Okeanologiya (bi-m.)
Akademiya Nauk USSSR, Okeanografichnaya Kommissiya, Leninskii prospekt 14, Moscow V-71, USSR

SPAIN

Hoja del Mar (m.)
Instituto Social de la Marina, Genova 24, Madrid, 4, Spain

TAIWAN

The Journal of the National Taiwan College of Marine Science and Technology (a.)
2 Pei-Nien Road, Keelung, Taiwan

TANZANIA

Annual Report
Institute of Marine Sciences, POB 668, Zanzibar, Tanzania

TUNISIA

Bulletin
Institut National Scientifique et Technique d'Océanographie et de Pêche, Salammbô, Tunisia

UNITED KINGDOM

Annual Report
Institute of Marine Biochemistry, St Fitticks Rd., Aberdeen AB1 3RA, Scotland

Annual Report
Scottish Marine Biological Association, Dunstaffnage Marine Research Laboratory, Oban, Argyll PA34 4AD, Scotland

Annual Report
University Marine Biological Station, Millport, Isle of Cumbrae, Strathclyde, Scotland

Applied Ocean Research (qu.)
CML Publications, Ashurst Lodge, Ashurst, Southampton SO4 2AA, England

Challenger Society: Newsletter (2 a year)
c/o Institute of Oceanographic Sciences, Wormley, Godalming, Surrey, England

Continental Shelf Research (qu.)
Pergamon Press, Headington Hill Hall, Oxford OX3 0BW, England; Pergamon Press Inc., Journals Div., Maxwell House, Fairview Park, Elmsford, NY 10523, USA

Estuarine, Coastal and Shelf Science (2 vols. per year)
Academic Press, 24-28 Oval Rd., London NW1 7DX, England; 111 Fifth Ave., New York, NY 10003, USA

Journal of the Marine Biological Association of the United Kingdom (a.)
The Laboratory, Citadel Hill, Plymouth PL1 2PB, England

Marine and Petroleum Geology (qu.)
Butterworth Scientific Ltd., (Journals Division), P.O. Box 63, Westbury House, Bury St., Guildford, Surrey GU2 5BH, England

Marine Behaviour & Physiology (qu.)
Gordon & Breach Science Publishers Ltd., 42 William IV St., London WC2N 4DE, England

Ocean Engineering (bi-m.)
Pergamon Press, Headington Hill Hall, Oxford OX3 0BW, England; and Maxwell House, Fairview Park, Elmsford, NY 10523, USA

Progress in Oceanography (qu.)
Pergamon Press, Headington Hill Hall, Oxford OX3 0BW, England

Underwater Information Bulletin (m.)
Butterworth Scientific Ltd., Journals Div., Box 63, Westbury House, Bury St., Guildford, Surrey GU2 5BH, England

Underwater Systems Design (6 a year)
USD Publishing, 322 St John St., London EC1V 4QH, England

UNITED STATES

Annual Bulletin; Annual Report
Marine Biological Laboratory, Woods Hole, Falmouth, Mass. 02543, USA

Annual Report
College of Ocean & Fishery Sciences, HA-40, Univ. of Washington, Seattle, WA 98195, USA

Annual Report
Scripps Institution of Oceanography, Univ. of California, San Diego, La Jolla, Calif. 92093, USA

Aquanotes (qu.)
Louisiana State University, Office of Sea Grant Development, Center for Wetland Resources Bldg., Baton Rouge, LA 70803, USA

Biannual Report
School of Oceanography, College of Ocean and Fishery Science, University of Washington, Seattle, WA 98195, USA

Biological Bulletin (2 a year)
Marine Biological Laboratory, Woods Hole, Falmouth, Mass. 02543, USA

Biological Oceanography Journal (qu.)
Crane, Russak & Co. Inc., 3 E 44th St., New York, NY 10017, USA

Bulletin of Marine Science (qu.)
Rosenstiel School of Marine and Atmospheric Science, Univ. of Miami, 4600 Rickenbacher Causeway, Miami, FL 33149, USA

Coastal Research (3 a year)
Florida State University, Geology Dept., Tallahassee, FL 32306, USA

Coastal Zone Management Journal (qu.)
Crane, Russak & Co. Inc., 3 E 44th St., New York, NY 10017, USA

Journal of Limnology and Oceanography
Univ. of Washington, Seattle, Wash. 98195, USA

Journal of Marine Research (qu.)
Sears Foundation for Marine Research, Kline Geology Lab., Box 6666, Newhaven, CT 06511, USA

Journal of Marine Resource Economics (qu.)
Crane, Russak & Co. Inc., 3 E 44th St., New York, NY 10017, USA

Journal of Physical Oceanography (m.)
American Meteorological Society, 45 Beacon St., Boston, MA 02108, USA

Marine Geotechnology (qu.)
Crane, Russak & Co. Inc., 3 E 44th St., New York, NY 10017, USA

Marine Resources Information (bi-m.)
Univ. of Rhode Island, Marine Advisory Service, Sea Grant Program, Narragansett Bay Campus, Narragansett, RI 02882, USA

Marine Technology Society Journal (4 a year)
1730 M St. NW, Washington DC 20036, USA

Maritimes (qu.)
Univ. of Rhode Island, Graduate School of Oceanography, Davis Hall, Kingston, RI 02881, USA

Ocean Development and International Law (qu.)
Crane, Russak & Co. Inc., 3 E 44th St., New York, NY 10017, USA

Ocean Industry (m.)
Gulf Publishing Co., Box 2608, Houston, Texas 77001, USA

Ocean Science and Engineering (4 a year)
Marcel Dekker Journals, 270 Madison Ave., New York, NY 10016, USA

Ocean Science News (w.)
Nautilus Press Inc., 1056 National Press Bldg., Washington DC 20045, USA

Ocean World (bi-m.)
Ocean World Publishing Co. Inc., Box 8819, Washington DC 20003, USA

Ocean Year Book
University of Chicago Press, 5801 South Ellis Ave., Chicago, Ill. 60637, USA (Sponsored by the International Ocean Institute)

Oceanus (qu.)
Woods Hole Oceanographic Institution, Woods Hole, MA 02543, USA

The Underwater Naturalist (qu.)
American Littoral Society, Sandy Hook, Highlands, NY 07732, USA

University of Hawaii—Sea Grant College Program. Makai (m.)
1000 Pope Rd., Rm. 200, Honolulu, HI 96822, USA

University of North Carolina—Sea Grant College Newsletter (m.)
105 1911 Bldg., Raleigh, NC 27650, USA

Washington Letter of Oceanography (f.)
Compass Publications Inc. (Arlington), Suite 1000, 1117 N. 19 St., Arlington, VA 22209, USA

VENEZUELA

Lagena (semi-a.)
Universidad de Oriente, Instituto Oceanográfico, Biblioteca, Cumana, Venezuela

Universidad de Oriente, Instituto Oceanográfico—Boletín (semi-a.)
Cumana, Venezuela

YUGOSLAVIA

Acta Adriatica
Institute of Oceanography and Fisheries, Mose Pijade 63, Split, Yugoslavia

Contributiones Studiis Scientorum Maritimarum
Institute for Maritime Sciences of the Yugoslav Academy of Sciences and Arts, POB 100, Split, Yugoslavia

Pomorski Zbornik (a.)
Yugoslav Society for Research and Promotion of Maritime Sciences, POB 391, Rijeka, Yugoslavia

Offshore Exploitation

Norwegian Offshore Index (a.)
Selvig Publishing, P.O. Box 9070, Vaterland, Oslo 1, Norway

Offshore (13 a year)
George D. Ruppert, 1200 South Post Oak Road, Houston, Texas 77027, USA (Robert Lee, 6th Floor, Alliance House, 12 Caxton St., London SW1H 0QS, England)

Offshore Abstracts (bi-m.)
Offshore Information Literature, 37B New Cavendish St., London W1M 8JR, England

The Offshore Engineer (m.)
Thomas Telford Ltd., Publications Division, 26-34 Old St., London EC1V 9AD, England

Offshore Europe
Scientific Surveys Ltd., P.O. Box 21, Beaconsfield, Bucks, England

Offshore Oil International (w.); *Offshore Oil Weekly*
Morton Offshore Ltd., Suite D, Silkhouse Court, Tithebarn St., Liverpool L2 2LZ, England

Offshore Product Information Service (bi-m.)
28 Perowne St., Cambridge CB1 2AY, England

Offshore Rig Location Report (m.); *Offshore Rig Newsletter* (m.)
Offshore Data Services Inc., Box 19909, Houston, TX 77224, USA

Offshore Services & Technology (m.)
Kingston Publications Ltd., 54 Eden St., Kingston upon Thames, Surrey KT1 1EE, England

Weekly Exploration Service
Petroleum Information Ltd., Green Dragon House, 164 High St., Croydon, Surrey CR0 9XN, England

World Pipelines (a.)
P.O. Box 21, Beaconsfield, Bucks, HO9 1NS, England

Environmental Protection

AMBIO—Journal of the Human Environment Research and Management
Royal Swedish Academy of Sciences/ Universitetsforlaget, Stockholm, Sweden

Annual Report
Institute for Marine Environmental Research, Prospect Place, Plymouth PL1 3DH, England

Annual Report
International Oil Pollution Compensation Fund, 4 Albert Embankment, London SE1 7SR, England

Annual Report
The Oil Companies' European Organisation for Environmental and Health Protection (CONCAWE), Babylon-Kantoren A, Koningin-Julianaplein 30–9, 2595 AA Den Haag, Netherlands

Annual Reports
Oslo Commission/Paris Commission, 48 Carey St., London WC2A 2JE, England

Aquatic Environment Monitoring Report (a.)
Directorate of Fisheries Research, Fisheries Laboratory, Lowestoft, Suffolk, England

Baltic Sea Environment Proceedings (Nos. 2–4, 5 B, 6–14, 1981–83)
Baltic Marine Environment Protection Commission, Helsinki, Finland

Marine Environmental Research (m.)
Applied Sciences Publishers Ltd., Ripple Rd., Barking, Essex, England

Marine Pollution Bulletin (m.)
Pergamon Press Ltd., Headington Hill Hall, Oxford OX3 0BW, England

ROCC INFO (3 a year)
Regional Oil Combating Centre for the Mediterranean, Manoel Island, Malta

Naval Warfare

Almanaque Náutico
Instituto y Observatorio de Marina, San Fernando, Cádiz, Spain

Canadian Defence Quarterly
Baxter Publishing Co. Ltd., 100 Adelaide St., W. Ste. 1300, Toronto, Ont. M5H 1S3, Canada

Combat Craft (bi-m.)
Capstan Publishing Co. Ltd., Lewin House, Dorking Rd., Tadworth, Surrey KT20 5SA, England

La Gaceta Militar Naval (m.)
25 de Mayo 55, Montevideo, Uruguay

Marineforum (m.)
Verlag E. S. Mittler & Sohn GmbH, Steintorwall 17, Postfach 2352, 4900 Herford, Fed. Rep. of Germany

Marine-Rundschau
Bernard und Graefe Verlag, Hubertusstr. 5, 8000 Munich 19, Fed. Rep. of Germany

Maritime Defence (m.)
Eldon Publications Ltd., 30–32 Fleet St., London EC4Y 1AH, England

The Naval Review (qu.)
Warner's Cottage, Corhampton, Hants, SO3 1LL, England

Naval Vessels & Machinery on Order (2 a year)
Naval Record Ltd., 29 Kennedy Rd., Bicester, Oxon OX6 8BE, England

Navy List (a.)
HMSO, P.O. Box 276, London SW8 5DT, England

Navy List of Retired Officers (bi-a.)
HMSO, P.O. Box 276, London SW8 5DT, England

Navy News (m.)
Furnival House, 14–18 High Holborn, London WC1V 6DB, England

Neptunus
Force Navale—Belgische Zeemacht, Postbus 17, Ostende 1, Belgium

Revista de Publicaciones Navales (qu.)
Jefatura de Inteligencia del EMCA, Comando en Jefe de la Armada, Buenos Aires, Argentina

Warship (qu.)
Conway Maritime Press Ltd., 24 Bride Lane, London EC4Y 8DR, England

Warship International (qu.)
International Naval Research Organization, 1729 Lois Ct., Toledo OH 43613, USA

Select Bibliography

Atlases

Couper, Alastair (ed.), *The Times Atlas of the Oceans* (Times Books Ltd., London 1983)—indispensable for the serious student of maritime affairs as it covers all aspects of the subject in considerable depth.

Atlas of the Living Resources of the Sea, 4th ed. (FAO, Rome 1982)

Barkley, Richard A., *Oceanographic Atlas of the Pacific Ocean* (Univ. of Hawaii Press)

Bramwell, M., *Atlas of the Oceans* (Mitchell Beazley, London 1977)

Downing, David, *Atlas of Territorial and Border Disputes* (illus.) (International Publications Service, USA, 1980)

Gorshkov, S., *World Ocean Atlas*, Vols. 1-3 (Pergamon, Oxford 1976–83)

Lee, A., & Ramster, J. W. (eds.), *Atlas of the Seas around the British Isles* (Ministry of Agriculture, Fisheries and Food, Directorate of Fisheries Research, London 1981)

Lloyd, Christopher, *Atlas of Maritime History* (Country Life, Hamlyn, London 1981)

Lloyd's Maritime Atlas, 14th ed. (Lloyd's, London 1985)

Morgan, Joseph R., & Valencia, Mark J. (eds.), *Atlas for Marine Policy in the Southeast Asian Seas* (Univ. of California Press 1983)

Stevenson, M. R., & others, *Marine Atlas of the Pacific Coastal Waters of South America* (Univ. of California Press 1971)

Udintsev, G. B. (ed.), *Geophysical Atlas of the Indian Ocean* (Pergamon, Oxford 1976)

Maritime Law

O'Connell, D. P. (Shearer, I. A., ed.), *The International Law of the Sea*, 2 vols. (Oxford Univ. Press 1983–84)—may be considered the standard work on the development of maritime law; it contains an extensive bibliography.

Anand, R. P., *Origin and Development of the Law of the Sea* (Martinus Nijhoff, Netherlands; Kluwer Academic, USA, 1983)

Barston, R. P., & Birnie, Patricia W., *The Maritime Dimension* (George Allen & Unwin, London, 1980)

Bowett, Derek W., *The Legal Regime of Islands in International Law* (Oceana, USA, 1979)

Buzan, Barry, *Seabed Politics* (Praeger, New York 1976)

Chorley, R. S. T., & Giles, O. C., *Shipping Law* (Pitman, London 1980)

La Conférence des Nations Unies sur le droit de la mer, histoire d'une négotiation singulière. No. 38 of publications by the *Revue générale de droit international public* (A. Pédone, Paris 1983)

Dubner, Barry H., *The Law of Territorial Waters of Midocean Archipelagos and Archipelagic States* (Martinus Nijhoff, Netherlands; Kluwer Academic, USA, 1977)

El-Hakim, Ali A., *The Middle Eastern States and the Law of the Sea* (Syracuse U.P. 1979)

Extavour, Winston C., *The Exclusive Economic Zone: A Study of the Evolution and Progressive Development of the International Law of the Sea* (Thèse 297, Institut Universitaire de Hautes Etudes Internationales, Geneva 1978)

Gandhi, D. S., *Shipowners, Mariners and the New Law of the Sea* (Fairplay, London 1977)

Hill, Christopher, *Maritime Law* (Pitman, London; Oceana, USA, 1981)

Hollick, Ann. L., *US Foreign Policy and the Law of the Sea* (Princeton U.P. 1981)

Jonsson, Hannes, *Friends in Conflict. The Anglo-Icelandic Cod Wars and their Influence on the Law of the Sea* (Shoe String, USA, 1982)

Kheng-Lian Koh, *Straits in International Navigation: Contemporary Issues* (Oceana, USA, 1982)

Laursen, Finn, *Toward a New International Marine Order* (Martinus Nijhoff, Netherlands; Kluwer Academic, USA, 1982)

The Law of the Sea—Official Text of the United Nations Convention on the Law of the Sea with Annexes and Index (United Nations, New York 1983)

The Law of the Sea Treaty: Some Crucial Questions for the United Kingdom (Institute for European Defence and Strategic Studies, London 1982)

Limits in the Seas. No. 36. National Claims to Maritime Jurisdictions. 5th Revision (US Dept. of State, Bureau of Intelligence and Research 1985)

Lowe, A. V., & Churchill, R. R., *The Law of the Sea* (Manchester, USA, 1983)

Lumb, R. D., *The Law of the Sea and Australian Off-Shore Areas*, 2nd. ed. (Univ. of Queensland Press 1978)

Macdonald, Charles G., *Iran, Saudi Arabia and the Law of the Sea. Political Interaction and Legal Development in the Persian Gulf* (Greenwood, USA, 1980)

Mangone, Gerard J. (ed.), *International Straits of the World* (Martinus Nijhoff, Netherlands)—a series of seven volumes as follows:

Butler, W. E., *Northeast Arctic Passage* (1978)

Leifer, M., *Malacca, Singapore and Indonesia* (1978)

Ramazani, R. K., *The Persian Gulf and the Strait of Hormuz* (1979)

Truver, S. C., *The Strait of Gibraltar and the Mediterranean* (1980)

Lapidoth-Eschelbacher, R., *The Red Sea and the Gulf of Aden* (1982)

Alexandersson, G., *The Baltic Straits* (1982)

Pharand, Donat, with Legault, Leonard H., *The Northwest Passage: Arctic Straits* (1984)

National Legislation and Treaties relating to the Law of the Sea (UN Legislative Series No. 18)

Prescott, J. R., *Maritime Jurisdiction in Southeast Asia—A Commentary and Map* (E. W. Center, USA, 1981)

Shaw, Malcolm N., *International Law* (Hodder & Stoughton, London 1977)

Simmonds, Kenneth R., *UN Conventions on the Law of the Sea* (Oceana, USA, 1982)

Symmons, C. R., *The Maritime Zones of Islands in International Law* (Martinus Nijhoff, Netherlands, 1979)

Tangsubkul, Phiphat, *ASEAN and the Law of the Sea* (Gower, USA, 1982)

Shipping and Shipbuilding

Greenman, D. (ed.), *Jane's Merchant Ships 1985–86* (Jane's Publishing Co. Ltd., London)—the standard work on the subject.

Abrahamsson, Dr Bernard J., *International Ocean Shipping: Current Concepts and Principles* (Canadian Marine Transportation Centre, Halifax 1979; Westview Press, USA, 1980)

Alderton, P. M., *Sea Transport* (Thomas Reed, UK, 1980)

Booth, E. C. Talbot (ed.), *Merchant Ships* (Kogan Page, London 1978)

Britain and the Sea: Future Dependence, Future Opportunities. (The Greenwich Forum IX, Scottish Academic Press, Edinburgh 1984)

Budd, Rhonda (ed.), *Sailing Boats of the World—A Guide to Classes* (Bayard Books, London 1974)

Branch, A., *Elements of Shipping* (Chapman & Hall, London 1981)

Cahill, Richard A., *Collisions and their Causes* (Fairplay Publications, London)

Caillou, Michel, & Percier, François, *Utilisation du radar à la mer* (Masson SA, Paris 1985)

Commercial Shipper & Shipping Office Handbook (British Shippers' Council, Tunbridge Wells, Kent TW4 9UZ, England)

Container Services Directory (Journal of Commerce, Liverpool)

De Kerchov, René (ed.), *International Maritime Dictionary* (Van Nostrand Reinhold, USA, 1983)

Directory of Land and Hydrographic Survey Services in the United Kingdom (Royal Institute of Chartered Surveyors 1980)

Directory of World Propulsion and Auxiliary Engines (The Motorship, IPC Industrial Press, UK)

Douglas, R. P. A., *Harbour Law*, 2nd ed. (Lloyd's of London Press 1985)

Durham, Capt. C. F., *Marine Surveys* (Fairplay Publications, London)

Ewart, W. D., *Bunkers* (Fairplay Publications, London)

Fairplay Marine Computing Guide 84/85 (Fairplay Publications, London)

Ffooks, Roger C., *Gas Carriers* (Fairplay Publications, London)

Ffooks, Roger C., *Natural Gas by Sea* (Gentry Books, London 1979)

Galbraith, A. A. (ed.). *Fairplay World Ports Directory 1983–84*, 2 vols. (London)

Geen, G. K., & Douglas, R. P. A., *The Law and Administration of Pilotage*, 2nd ed. (Lloyd's of London Press 1985)

Gold, E., *Maritime Transport: the Evolution of International Marine Policy and Shipping Laws* (Lexington Books, USA, 1981)

Goss, R. O., *Studies in Maritime Economics* (Univ. of Cardiff Press 1982)

IMO Search and Rescue Manual (IMOSAR) (IMO, London 1978)

International Manual of Maritime Safety (Marine Publications International Ltd., UK, 1977)

Karmon, Y., *Ports around the World* (Crown Publishers, USA, 1980)

Kemp, Peter K., *Encyclopedia of Ships and Seafaring* (Stanford Maritime, UK, 1984)

Kemp, Peter K. (Ed.), *The Oxford Companion to Ships and the Sea* (Oxford Univ. Press 1976)

Lloyd's Marine Equipment Guide 1983–84 (Lloyd's of London Press 1985)

MacKenzie, Charles H. C., Power, M. E., & McDorman, Ted L., *Liner Shipping Conferences. An Annotated Bibliography* (Canadian Marine Transportation Centre, Halifax)

McLeavy, Roy (ed.), *Jane's Surface Skimmers 1985* (Jane's Publishing Co., London)

Manksbady, Samir (ed.), *International Maritime Organisation* (Croom Helm, London 1984)

Marx, Daniel, *International Shipping Cartels* (Greenwood Press, London 1953)

Merchant Ship and Rescue Manual (MERSAR) (IMO, London 1976)

Nagorski, B., *Port Problems in Developing Countries* (IAHP 1979)

Noel, John V. (ed.), *Dictionary of Ships and the Sea* (Van Nostrand Reinhold, USA, 1980)

Ports of the World 1984 (Lloyd's of London Press 1985)

Product Tankers and Their Role (Fairplay Publications, London)

Review and Outlook of the Shipping Market (Fairplay Publications, London)

Review on Global Development in World Shipbuilding to 1995 (The Association of West European Shipbuilders, Netherlands)

Rules and Regulations for the Construction and Classification of Ships (Lloyd's Register, Crawley, W. Sussex RH10 2QN, England)

Schonknecht, Rolf, *Ships and Shipping of Tomorrow* (MacGregor Publications, UK, 1983)

Stonebridge, Denis, *Performance of "Open Registry" Bulk Fleets* (H. P. Drewry, London 1980)

Sturt, R. F. B., *The Collision Regulations*, 2nd ed. (Lloyd's of London Press 1985)

Thomas, R. S., *Freeports and Foreign Trade Zones* (Cornell Maritime Press, USA, 1980)

Trillo, R. I. (ed.), *Jane's Ocean Technology 1979–80* (Macdonald & J., UK)

Williams, B., *Ships and Other Sea Craft* (Kingfisher Books, UK, 1983)

Yeats, Alexander J., *Shipping and Development Policy: An Integrated Assessment* (Praeger, New York 1981)

Fisheries

Anderson, Lee G. (ed.), *Economic Analysis for Fisheries Management Plans* (Johns Hopkins Univ. Press 1982)

Anderson, Lee G. (ed.), *Economic Impacts of Extended Fisheries Jurisdiction* (Ann Arbor Science Publications 1977)

Anderson, Lee G., *Economics of Fisheries Management* (Johns Hopkins Univ. Press 1977)

Asada, Yohoji, & others, *Fishery Management in Japan* (FAO Fisheries Technical Paper No. 238, Unipublications 1984)

Barney, G. O., *The Global 2000 Report to the President of the US (Fisheries Section)* (Pergamon Press, 1981)

Bell, Frederick W., *Food from the Sea: The Economics of Ocean Fisheries* (Westview, USA, 1978)

Brandt, A. von, *Fish Catching Methods of the World* (Fishing News Books, UK, 1981)

Brown, E. Evan, *World Fish Farming: Cultivation and Economics* (AVI, UK, 1983)

Campbell, J. S., *Types of Parastatal Bodies Concerned with Fisheries Development and their Financial Responsibilities* (FAO, Unipublications 1978)

Cole, R. C., & Rogers, John Frederick, *Handbook for Junior Fisheries Officers* (Tropical Products Institute, UK, 1982)

Connell, J. J. (ed.), *Advances in Fish Science & Technology* (Fishing News Books, UK, 1980)

Coull, James R., *Fisheries of Europe* (Bell & Hyman, UK, 1978)

Couper, A. D., & Smith, H. D., *Multi-Use and Multi-State Management in the North Sea* (Law of the Sea Institute 16th Annual Conference, Halifax, June 1982)

Cushing, D. H., *Climate & Fisheries* (Academic Press, USA)

Cushing, D. H., *Fisheries Biology: A Study in Population Dynamics* (Univ. of Wisconsin Press 1981)

Cushing D. H. (ed.), *Key Papers on Fish Populations* (IRL Press, Oxford 1983)

Cushing, D. H., *Marine Ecology and Fishing* (Cambridge Univ. Press 1975)

Directory of Fishing Technology, Institutions and Services (FAO, Unipublications 1980)

Eddie, G. C., *Engineering Economics and Fisheries Management* (Fishing News Books, UK, 1984)

Eddie, G. C., *The Harvesting of Krill* (Southern Oceans Survey Programmes) (FAO, Unipublications 1977)

Elles, James, & Farnell, John, *In Search of a Common Fisheries Policy* (Gower Pub. Co., UK, 1984)

Everhart, Watson Harry, & Youngs, William D., *Principles of Fishery Science* (Cornell Univ. Press 1981)

Experience in the Management of National Fishing Zones (OECD, Paris, 1984)

Fisheries Catches by Region, 1968–80 (European Communities, HMSO 1982)

Friedheim, L., *Managing Ocean Resources* (Westview Press, USA, 1979)

Fyson, J. F. (ed.), *Food and Agriculture Organization Investigates Ferro-cement Fishing Craft* (Fishing New Books, UK, 1974)

Glantz, M. H., & Thompson, J. D., *Resource Management and Environmental Uncertainty: Lessons from Coastal Upwelling Fisheries* (Wiley, New York 1980)

Gopalakrishnan, Chennat, *The Emerging Marine Economy of the Pacific* (Butterworth, UK, 1984)
Gulland, J. A., *Fish Stock Assessment: A Manual of Basic Methods* (Wiley, New York 1983)
Hannesson, Rognvaldur, *Fisheries Economics* (Universitetsforlaget, Oslo; Columbia Univ. Press, 1979)
Heikoff, Joseph M., *Coastal Resources Management: Institutions and Programs* (Arbor Science Publications, USA, 1977)
Heikoff, Joseph M., *Marine and Shoreland Resources Management* (Arbor Science Publications, USA, 1980)
Hermansson, Birgir, *Training Fishermen at Sea* (Fishing News Books, UK, 1978)
International Directory of Fish Technology Institutes (Fisheries Technical Papers No. 152, Rev. 1, FAO, Unipublications 1980)
Iversen, R. S., *Farming the Edge of the Sea* (Fishing News Books, UK, 1977)
Kerr, N. M., & Kingwell, S. J., *Progress in Farming Marine Fish* (Whitefish Authority, Edinburgh, 1977)
Knight, Gary (ed.), *Marine Fisheries Management Reporter*, 4 vols., loose-leaf (Jonathan, USA, 1984)
Koers, A. W., *The International Regulation of Marine Fisheries* (Fishing News Books, UK, 1976)
Lackey, Robert T., & Nielsen, Larry A. (eds.), *Fisheries Management* (Halsted Press, USA, 1980; Blackwell Scientific, UK, 1981)
Laevastu, Toivo, & Hayes, Murray, *Fisheries Oceanography and Ecology* (Fishing News Books, UK, 1981)
Laevastu, Toivo, & Larkins, Herbert A., *The Marine Fisheries Ecosystem: Its Quantitative Evaluation and Management* (Unipublications, USA, 1981)
Lewis, Mary J., *Directory of North American Fisheries Scientists* (American Fisheries Society 1984)
Liu Sien, Chia, & MacAndrews, *South East Asian Seas: Frontiers for Development* (McGraw-Hill, USA, 1981)
Marr, James, *The Natural History and Geography of the Antarctic Krill* (Euphasia Superba Dana, 1962)
Mason, C. M. (ed.), *The Effective Management of Resources: The International Politics of the North Sea* (Frances Pinter, London 1979)
Matthews I. W., *The Natural History of the Whale* (Weidenfeld & Nicolson, London 1980)
Mitson, R. B., *Fisheries Sonar* (Fishing News Books, UK, 1983)
Modern Fishing Gears of the World, 3 vols. (Fishing News Books, UK, 1979)
Nadelec, C. (ed.), *Food and Agriculture Organization Catalogue of Small Scale Fishing Gear* (Fishing News Books, UK, 1975)
Neuhaus, O. W., & Halver, John (eds.), *Fish in Research* (Academic Press, USA, 1970)
Occupational Safety of Fishermen: Working Group Report (Dept. of Trade, HMSO 1979)
An Overview of Fisheries in the Commonwealth (Commonwealth Secretariat, London)
Perry, W. H. (ed.), *Fishermen's Handbook* (Fishing News Books, UK, 1980)
Pitcher, T., & Hart, P., *Fisheries Ecology* (Croom Helm, UK, 1982)
Recommended Code of Safety for Fishermen (Dept. of Trade, HMSO 1979)
Resource Prospects for Canada's Atlantic Fisheries, 1981–87 (Communications Branch, Dept. of Fisheries and Oceans, Ottawa)
Review of Fisheries in OECD Member Countries (OECD, HMSO 1983)
Rothchild, B. J., *Global Fisheries: Perspectives for the 1980s* (Springer-Verlag, London & New York 1983)
Scharfe, Joachim (ed.), *Food and Agriculture Organization Catalogue of Fishing Gear Designs* (Fishing News Books, UK, 1979)
Scott, Ian, *The Importance of the Fishery Resources of the North Sea* (Whitefish Authority, Edinburgh 1979)
Shults, Eric, *Fisherman's Guide to Sea Fishing* (Marshall Cavendish, UK, 1979)
Steele, J. M. (ed.), *Fisheries Mathematics* (Academic Press, USA, 1977)
Tønnessen, J. N., & Johnsen, A. O., *The History of Modern Whaling* (Hurst/ANU Press, London & Canberra 1982)
Underdal, A., *The Politics of Fisheries Management: the Case of the North-East Atlantic* (Oslo Univ. Press 1980)
Vander Zwaag, D. L., *Fish Feud: The United States and Canadian Boundary Dispute* (Lexington Books, USA, 1983)
Went, A. E. J., *The Atlantic Salmon: Its Future* (Fishing News Books, UK, 1980)

Offshore Resources Exploitation

Tiratsoo, E. N., *Oilfields of the World*, 3rd ed. (Scientific Press, UK, 1984)—a standard work with annual statistics up to 1982.

Baram, M. S., Rice, D., & Lee, W., *Marine Mining of the Continental Shelf* (Ballinger Publishing Co. 1978)
Brown, E. D., *Seabed Energy and Mineral Resources and the Law of the Sea. Vol. 1: The Area within National Jurisdiction* (Graham & Trotman, London)

Directory of Current United Kingdom Research and Development relating to Offshore Structures and Pipelines (Construction Industr. Research & Information Association 1979)

Directory of Current United Kingdom Research and Development relevant to Offshore Instrumentation and Measurement (Do. 1979)

Directory of Current United Kingdom Research and Development relevant to Underwater Inspection and Repair (Do. 1979)

Earney, F. C. F., *Petroleum and Hard Minerals from the Sea* (Edward Arnold, London 1980)

Faulkner, D., Cowling, M. J., & Frieze, P. A., *Integrity of Offshore Structures* (Applied Science Publications, UK, 1981)

Haux, G. F. K., *Subsea Manned Engineering*, 3rd ed. (Baillière, UK, 1982)

Jones, Michael E. W., *Deepwater Oil Production and Manned Underwater Structures* (Graham & Trotman, London 1981)

Kash, D. E. & others, *Energy under the Oceans: A Technology Assessment of Outer Continental Shelf Oil and Gas Operations* (Univ. of Oklahoma Press 1973)

Nelson, J. G. N., & Jessine, S., *The Scottish and Alaskan Offshore Oil and Gas Experience and the Canadian Beaufort Sea* (Univ. of Waterloo, Ontario, 1981)

Odell, P. R., & Rosing, K. E., *The North Sea Oil Province: An Attempt to Simulate its Exploration and Development 1969–2029.* (Kogan Page, London 1975)

Oo Jin Bee, *The Petroleum Resources of Indonesia* (Oxford Univ. Press 1981)

Siddayao, C. M., *The Offshore Petroleum Resources of South East Asia* (Oxford Univ. Press 1981)

The UN Sea Bed Mineral Series. Vol. 1: *Assessment of Manganese Nodule Resources* (1982); Vol. 2: *Analysis of Exploration and Mining Technology for Manganese Nodules* (1984); Vol. 3: *Analysis of Processing Technology for Manganese Nodules* (1984) (Graham & Trotman, London)

Valencia, Mark J., *The South China Sea: Hydrocarbon Potential and Possibilities of Joint Development*. (Pergamon, Oxford 1981)

Wildavesky, A., & Tenenbaum, E., *The Politics of Mistrust. Estimating American Oil and Gas Resources* (Sage Publications, USA, 1981)

Underwater Activities

Bass, George F., & Winslow, R. K., *A History of Seafaring Based on Underwater Archaeology* (Walker, New York 1972)

Cousteau, Jacques-Yves, & Dugan, James, *The Living Sea* (Harper & Row, New York 1963)

Cousteau, Jacques-Yves, & Dumas, Frédéric, *The Silent World* (Harper & Row, New York; Hamish Hamilton, London 1953)

Diolé, Philippe, *Four Thousand Years under the Sea* (Simon & Schuster, New York 1954)

Dugan, James, *Man under the Sea* (Harper & Brothers, New York 1956)

Faulkner, Douglas, *The Hidden Sea* (Viking Press, New York 1970)

Hass, Hans, *Conquest of the Underwater World* (David & Charles, Newton Abbot 1975)

Idyll, C. P., *Exploring the Ocean World* (Crowell, New York 1972)

Latil, P. de, & Rivoire, J., *Man and the Underwater World* (G. P. Putnam & Sons, New York 1956)

Muckelroy, K. (ed.), *Archaeology under Water: an Atlas of the World's Submerged Sites* (McGraw-Hill, USA, 1980)

Piccard, Jacques, & Dietz, Robert S., *Seven Miles Down: The Story of the Bathyscaphe Trieste* (G. P. Putnam & Sons, New York 1961)

Ocean Sciences

Alexander, Dr Lewis, *Regional Cooperation in Marine Sciences* (Intergovernmental Oceanographic Commission, Paris 1980)

Behrman, D., *Assault on the Largest Unknown* (The International Indian Ocean Expedition) (UNESCO, Paris 1981)

Beriashev, K. A., & Serebriakov, V. V., *International Marine Organizations: Essays on Structure and Activities* (Martinus Nijhoff, Netherlands, 1981)

Brin, A., *Energy and the Oceans* (Westbury House, Guildford, 1981)

Carson, Rachel, *The Sea Around Us*, rev. ed. (Oxford Univ. Press 1961)

Cousteau, Jacques-Yves, *Man Re-enters the Sea* (Abrams, New York 1974)

Cousteau, Jacques-Yves, *The Ocean World* (Abrams, New York 1979)

Davies, Eryl, *Ocean Frontiers* (Viking, New York 1980)

Davis, R. A., *Principles of Oceanography* (Addison-Wesley Publishing Co., Reading, Mass. 1972)

Groves, Donald G., & Hunt, Lee M., *The Ocean World Encyclopedia* (McGraw-Hill, USA, 1980)

International Directory of Marine Scientists, 3rd ed. (UNESCO, Paris; FAO, Rome 1983)

Kent, George, & Valencia, Mark J. (eds.), *Marine Policy in Southeast Asian Seas* (Univ. of California Press 1984)

McConnell, A., *No Sea too Deep. The History of Oceanographic Instruments* (Adam Hilger, Bristol 1982)

Marchuk, G., & Kagan, B., *Ocean Tides* (Pergamon, Oxford 1983)

Perry, H. A., & Walker, J. M., *The Ocean Atmosphere System* (Longman, Harlow 1977)

Voipio, A., *The Baltic Sea* (Oceanography Series No. 30) (Elsevier, Amsterdam, Oxford & New York 1981)

Environmental Protection

Abecassis, David, *Oil Pollution from Ships* (Butterworth, London 1978)

Baker, Jennifer M. (ed.), *Marine Ecology and Oil Pollution* (Applied Science Publications, USA, 1976)

Gilbert, John T. E. (ed.), *Environmental Planning Guidelines for Offshore Oil and Gas Development* (Univ. Press of Honolulu, Hawaii)

International Safety Guide for Oil Tankers and Terminals (Witherby & Co., London 1984)

Johnston, D. M., *The Environmental Law of the Sea* (International Union for the Conservation of Nature and Natural Resources, Gland, Switzerland, 1981)

Patin, S. A., *Pollution and the Biological Resources of the Oceans* (Butterworth, London 1982)

Promotion of the Establishment of Marine Parks and Reserves in the Northern Indian Ocean including the Red Sea and Persian Gulf (International Union for the Conservation of Nature and Natural Resources, Gland, Switzerland, 1976)

Tait, R. B., *Elements of Marine Ecology*, 3rd ed. (Butterworth Scientific, UK, 1981)

Van Hoorn, H., & others (eds.), *The North Sea: Environment and Problems* (Werkgroep Noordzee, Amsterdam 1980)

Naval Warfare

Barston, R. P., & Birnie, Patricia, *The Maritime Dimension* (George Allen & Unwin, London 1980)

Moore, Capt. John, RN, *Jane's Fighting Ships 1984–85* (Jane's Publishing Co., London)

Pemsel, Helmut, *Atlas of Naval Warfare* (Arms & Armour Press, UK, 1977)

Index

The references in *italics* (in parentheses) indicate the articles and paragraphs of the 1982 United Nations Convention on the Law of the Sea as given in Appendix 1.

B

E

G

N

O